A Publication of The National Underwriter Company

2002 Field Guide

To Estate Planning, Business Planning, & Employee Benefits

Donald F. Cady,
J.D., LL.M., CLU

The
NATIONAL
UNDERWRITER
Company
PROFESSIONAL PUBLISHING GROUP

P.O. Box 14367 • Cincinnati, Ohio 45250-0367
1-800-543-0874 • www.nationalunderwriter.com

Page Layout design: Donald R. Heyl

This publication is designed to provide accurate and authoritative information in regard to the subject matter covered. It is sold with the understanding that the publisher is not engaged in rendering legal, accounting or other professional service. If legal advice or other expert assistance is required, the services of a competent professional should be sought. – **From a Declaration of Principles jointly adopted by a Committee of the American Bar Association and a Committee of Publishers and Associations.**

ISBN: 0-87218-609-1
ISSN: 1053-4407

Printed in U. S. A.

ACKNOWLEDGMENTS

I am most grateful to the many individuals – financial services professionals, clients, students, and allied professionals – who over the years have both knowingly and unknowingly contributed to this book. It is the product of their many insights, tough questions, sales and planning ideas.

I also wish to express my sincere appreciation to the staff of The National Underwriter Company, particularly April K. Caudill, J.D., CLU, ChFC, Sonya E. King, J.D., LL.M., Deborah A. Miner, J.D., CLU, ChFC, Deborah Price Rambo, J.D., Joseph F. Stenken, J.D., CLU, ChFC, and William J. Wagner, J.D., LL.M., CLU, for their shared tax expertise, to Susan Massmann for her research contributions, to Connie L. Jump and Mary P. O'Leary for their able and cheerful assistance in preparing the manuscript, and to Kimberly T. Plunkett, Kelly D. Meadows, and Lorrie L. Royse for their work in the setup and production of this book.

And finally, a special word of thanks to my wife, Joan, for her love and understanding in providing me the time and environment for writing.

D.F.C. 2002
Fort Myers Beach, Florida

ABOUT THE AUTHOR

Donald F. Cady is an attorney and a Chartered Life Underwriter. He is a graduate of St. Lawrence University with a B.A. in Economics, where he received the Wall Street Journal Award for excellence in that subject. He received his J.D. degree from Columbia University School of Law, holds the degree of LL.M. (Taxation) from Emory University School of Law, and is a member of the New York Bar.

Don is an independent consultant working with The National Underwriter Company in providing support materials and services to the financial planning industry. In addition to this publication, he is the author of *Field Guide Online[1]*, the web version of this book updated monthly throughout the year. Currently he is also engaged in writing *Field Guide To Financial Planning*, scheduled for publication later this year.

For twenty years Don was with the Aetna Life Insurance & Annuity Company in various advanced underwriting positions. Prior to this, Don was a member of the U.S. Army Judge Advocate Generals Corps, with tours of duty in both Vietnam and Europe. He and his wife live in Fort Myers Beach, Florida.

Don is a frequent speaker on the subjects of estate planning, business planning, and employee benefits, before business and professional organizations, estate planning associations, life underwriter's meetings and various civic groups. Through these appearances, together with his work with agents, their clients and advisers, Don has shared the frustrations of trying to effectively explain and communicate planning concepts and techniques to both student and laymen. This edition of *Field Guide* represents his response to that challenge.

Don can be reached by e-mail at cady@efieldguide.com or by leaving a voice message at 1-800-544-0620 (extension 4115).

---

[1] *Field Guide Online* is a trademark of The National Underwriter Company.

TABLE OF CONTENTS

Page

Page

EMPLOYEE BENEFITS

Page

APPENDIX

Page

Page

Page

INTRODUCTION

The Purpose Of This Book

This book is intended to provide you with a ready means of identifying and understanding the concepts and techniques used in estate, business, and employee benefit planning. Recognizing that we live in a world of visual communication, numerous drawings and charts have been included to assist you in identifying and understanding many of the concepts which are most frequently encountered when working with clients and other professionals. It can serve as a desktop reference source, a classroom training aid, or, carried in your briefcase, as a resource to be shared with your client or his advisors. However, it is not intended to be a replacement for competent legal or tax counsel; only qualified professionals can provide such advice.

Organization

The *Field Guide* has been organized into three sections, dealing with the subjects of estate planning, business planning, and employee benefits. Each section is in turn divided into units typically consisting of a chart and accompanying text. Following most of the charts you will find a section entitled "Information Required For Analysis & Proposal." This is the minimum information you must obtain in order to prepare an analysis and proposal for your client. Also included are cross references to *Tax Facts 1*, and the footnotes. Following the charts you will find references that support the subjects of estate planning, business planning, and employee benefits. Terms & Concepts contains expanded discussions of the materials previously referred to in the text and footnotes.

In using this book first refer to the chart and read the accompanying text. Also, be sure to read the footnotes; they will provide you with a better understanding of the subject matter and references to additional materials.

Cross References To Tax Facts 1

No attempt is made to provide either an exhaustive technical analysis or extensive citations to legal authority (Internal Revenue Code sections, regulations, case law, revenue rulings and private letter rulings). For these purposes, you are encouraged to refer to the appropriate questions in the 2002 edition of *Tax Facts 1*, published by The National Underwriter Company. The cross references contain the question number followed by a brief description of the material covered (e.g., "**Q 513**. Valuation of closely held business interest for federal estate tax purposes"). The Guidex contained in *Tax Facts 1* should also be consulted for additional materials and analysis.

Where appropriate, there are also cross references to the *Advanced Sales Reference Service (ASRS)*, edited and published monthly by The National Underwriter Company. The National Underwriter's *TAXLINE*, provided monthly to ASRS subscribers, or by separate subscription, keeps the reader informed on current developments, major changes and ongoing revisions to our tax laws.

TABLE OF CONTENTS

POINTERS

Planning In The Aftermath Of EGTRRA 2001.

By its very nature, estate planning is intended to provide some degree of predictability over the long-term. However, the phase-in and sunset provisions of EGTRRA 2001 have created uncertainty and confusion (page 88). Given such an ever-changing tax environment, your clients will require a continuous monitoring of their estate plans.

Estate taxes. The increased credits provided by EGTRRA 2001 effectively shield the "smaller" estate from federal transfer taxes, provided the estate has been properly planned (page 29). Under current law, estate taxes are not going to disappear; they are merely going to take a one-year sabbatical in the year 2010 (i.e., a "suspension," *not* a "repeal"). Between now and 2010, there will be no less than four congressional and two presidential elections (page 88). Obviously, this will create opportunities for more changes and less clarity. As in the past, there continues to be many compelling nontax reasons for your clients to plan their estates (page 7).

State death taxes. The phase-out of the state death tax credit, and its replacement with a deduction, will result in a substantial loss of revenue in many states (pages 92-93). Individual states are not likely to long suffer this revenue loss at the hands of Congress. No matter what happens to the federal estate tax, many of your client's estates will continue to be subject to state death taxes that are independent of the federal estate tax.

Unexpected allocations. Tax driven formulas in the typical exemption trust will place an amount equal to the exemption equivalent in the "B" trust (page 29). Assuming an estate of sufficient size, these formulas will pass increasing amounts to the "B" trust – $1,000,000 in 2002, then increasing in stages to $3,500,000 in 2009, and possibly the *entire* estate in 2010 (pages 88-89). Such allocations may be substantially more than was intended when your client's will was originally executed.

Flexibility. In order to adjust to future changes in the uncertain world of estate taxes, increased flexibility should be built into your client's estate plan. Disclaimers offer a surviving spouse the opportunity to adjust to changing circumstances by controlling the amount of property going into the nonmarital trust after your client's death (page 29).

Trusts. Effective estate planning often requires the use of trusts. For most of your clients, the irrevocable life insurance trust will continue to be a viable estate planning tool – but with an important new feature. New trusts might include an "escape clause" allowing termination of the trust if the federal estate tax is repealed. Alternatively, an individual might be given a special power of appointment to reconfigure the trust (page 434). The QTIP trust, combined with a disclaimer, will be more frequently used (page 35). For the larger estate, the intentionally defective trust is a very flexible wealth-transferring device (page 69).

Carryover basis. Prior to EGTRRA 2001, the income tax burden on property left to heirs was limited to IRD (page 402). Should the modified carryover basis rules become a reality, the loss of the step-up in basis at death means that heirs may also pay income taxes if estate assets are sold (page 473). It is not too soon to begin discussing with your clients the need to protect their assets from shrinkage caused by this potential *income tax* liability. In addition, many clients should immediately begin the onerous record keeping necessary to track the income tax basis of the estate assets.

Life insurance. Delaying the purchase of currently needed life insurance could be disastrous, particularly if your client becomes uninsurable while waiting for Congress to clarify the future status of the federal estate tax (pages 88-89). Where appropriate, convertible term insurance should be used. Some companies are now offering permanent policies that give the policyowner the option of surrendering the policy without penalty if the federal estate tax is repealed. If the carryover basis rules are implemented, cash value life insurance will become increasingly attractive – since the cash values will merge into income tax-free death benefit that is not subject to carryover basis, and is not taxed as IRD.

Gifts. Each and every year, your clients should consider taking full advantage of "present interest" gifts and the increased unified credits (pages 49, 53 and 88). However, most authorities agree that they should avoid making large gifts that would require payment of gift taxes (page 395).

The Tax Line.

The tax line will help you better understand and explain the basic concepts underlying those estate planning techniques that are designed to minimize or avoid gift and estate taxes. Within the family unit, we can think of the tax line as existing between generations – although technically it exists between individuals who are

not married to each other. Think of it as a horizontal dotted line. Above the line are husband and wife. Below the line are the children. We know that by taking advantage of the marital deduction, husband and wife can pass unlimited amounts of property between themselves – by gift during lifetime, or by will at death. But husband and wife are limited as to the amount of property they can pass to their children, free of gift and estate taxes. As long as the property remains above the tax line, it will continue to appreciate. Effective estate tax planning must be designed to: (1) use "present interest" gifts and the unified credit to pass property down through the line; (2) avoid unnecessary future appreciation above the line; and (3) use life insurance and the life insurance trust to create untaxed property below the line. The charts on pages 29, 35, 39, 53, 57, and 69 demonstrate techniques your clients can use in dealing with the tax line.

Coordination With Business Plans And Employee Benefits.

It is often difficult, if not impossible, to design an effective estate plan without considering your client's business disposition plans and employee benefit programs. Effective planning cannot be achieved unless there is an awareness of the interplay between the various strategies and techniques of estate planning, business planning and employee benefits. For example, the liquidity needs of a business owner's estate plan are directly influenced by whether the business is to be sold, continued, or liquidated (see chart, page 120). If the business is to be *sold*, then a funded purchase agreement may well provide all of the dollars needed for estate liquidity and family income. If the business is to be *continued*, then an employee benefit, such as split-dollar, could provide the necessary funds. However, the death proceeds of an improperly installed split-dollar plan will be taxed in your client's estate (i.e., death proceeds designed to pay estate taxes end up generating more estate taxes).

Estate Planning Is More Than Tax Planning.

Looking at the subject matter of the charts in this chapter . . . over half of them relate to gift, estate, and generation-skipping taxes . . . you might incorrectly conclude that estate planning is mostly about taxes. On the contrary, estate planning is about people and their desire to provide for their loved ones! Most of your clients will devote the time and energy that is necessary to develop and adopt an effective estate plan providing for the support of their surviving family and the orderly distribution of their estate. For other individuals, the motivation to plan may be found in their desire to assure the survival of a business, to provide for their church or a charity, or to avoid being best remembered for their generosity to the federal government. Absent one or more of these motivations, your best planning recommendations are not likely to be implemented.

The Nontax Reasons For Estate Planning.

Estate creation, income replacement, and the orderly transfer of property from one generation to the next continue to be the primary objectives of most estate plans – unaffected by the tax uncertainty and confusion of EGTRRA 2001. Your clients will need to provide care for minor children, support for disabled children and elderly parents, and protection of loved ones from creditors. Most importantly, are there enough life insurance proceeds, liquid assets, and other sources of income to maintain the current living standards of your client's surviving family?

ESTATE PLANNING MATRIX

In the traditional sense, estate planning means preparing for the orderly and efficient transfer of assets at *death*. Within this definition, the basic objectives of estate planning are set forth in the discussion of the Estate Funnel on page 10.

However, estate planning has also come to involve planning for the accumulation and distribution of an estate during *lifetime* as well as at death. It must also be recognized that comprehensive estate planning will often involve the concepts and techniques contained in the business planning and employee benefits chapters of this guide. For example, although additional estate liquidity would be provided from the sale of a business interest, estate taxes will be increased through inclusion of the proceeds of the sale in the taxable estate. Likewise, an effective estate plan should maximize employee benefits, while at the same time taking into consideration their impact upon the estate.

The following matrix should provide a better understanding of how the concepts and techniques, represented in the charts, can be used to solve estate planning problems.

PROBLEM	SOLUTION(S)	PAGE
Loss of Estate Value Through Estate Tax	EXEMPTION TRUST WILL provides the opportunity to reduce estate taxes (the COMPARISON OF WILLS chart on page 33 illustrates the substantial savings).	28
	QTIP TRUST provides opportunity to reduce taxes while controlling disposition of estate.	34
	GIFTS & SPLIT-GIFTS remove property from the estate.	48
	GIVING - THE TAX ADVANTAGES demonstrates the benefits of using the unified credit to make larger gifts and contrasts the gift of life insurance with gifts of other property.	52
	LIFE INSURANCE AS PROPERTY shows how life insurance can be excluded from the gross estate for federal tax purposes.	72
	LIFE INSURANCE TRUST can remove life insurance death proceeds from the estate.	96
	CHARITABLE REMAINDER TRUST can remove from estate taxable property that can be replaced by life insurance in a Wealth Replacement Trust.	60

PROBLEM	SOLUTION(S)	PAGE
Loss of Estate Value Through Estate Tax (continued)	GENERATION-SKIPPING TRANSFERS shows use of exemption in 2002 to transfer $1,100,000 to grandchildren.	38
Estimating the Estate Tax	FEDERAL ESTATE TAX explains the calculations.	18
Payment of Estate Costs	LIFE INSURANCE PRODUCTS can be used to provide funds to pay these costs. Chart compares alternative plans and explains their basic characteristics and essential differences.	76
Distribution of Estate	SIMPLE WILL can provide for the distribution of estate assets, including specific bequests.	26
	EXEMPTION TRUST WILL offers added tax savings and the post death management of assets.	28
Replacement of Income: Upon Death	LIFE INSURANCE PRODUCTS can provide funds to replace lost income in case of death (one approach to determining the necessary funds is contained in the discussion of HUMAN LIFE VALUE on page 14).	76
Upon Disability	DIABILITY – THE LIVING DEATH demonstrates the need for proper planning before disability occurs.	246
Upon Retirement	DEFERRED ANNUITY can be used to accumulate retirement funds on a tax-favored basis.	182
Insufficient Income or Assets for Custodial Care In Retirement	LONG-TERM planning provides an understanding of the risk and cost of long-term care and how the risk can be managed.	258
Orderly Payment of Income to Spouse and Children	LIFE INSURANCE TRUST provides for ongoing payments.	56
	EXEMPTION TRUST WILL with provisions for payment of continuing income to beneficiaries.	28
Guardianship of Children	SIMPLE WILL with provisions for appointment of guardian (EXEMPTION TRUST WILL can also contain these same provisions).	26
Client Motivation	TAXFLATION is not a technique of estate planning, but rather brings a sense of urgency to the estate planning process.	22

THE ESTATE FUNNEL

The estate funnel helps to explain the types of property found in most estates, the problems often encountered in settling an estate, and the objectives of estate planning.

All property is created in one of two ways, either people at work or capital at work. Wages are the product of **people at work**, while interest, dividends, and capital appreciation are the products of **capital at work**.

The property found in most estates generally falls into one of five categories:

Personal property, such as furniture, cars, jewelry, cash, bonds, savings, and other personal effects.

Real estate, such as a home, a vacation house, land, and rental property such as apartments or office buildings.[1]

Business interests, in the form of closely held corporations, partnerships, or sole proprietorships.

Life insurance, either group insurance or individual policies.

Government benefits, such as social security, disability, retirement and survivor income benefits.

Unfortunately, at death there is often a great deal of **CONFLICT**. This occurs due to the differing and conflicting ways in which many of these assets pass to the family or other heirs. For example, personal property can pass by will, by state law if there is no will, by title, or by trust.[2] Real estate and business interests may also pass by all of these means, as well as by agreement. Generally life insurance passes by beneficiary designation, and government benefits by federal statute.

These conflicts, together with the generally slow probate process, can easily result in a **DELAY** of *1 to 2 years or more*.[3]

Considerable **EXPENSE** may also be incurred during the estate settlement process. For example, existing debts must be paid. There are also medical expenses, funeral expenses, attorney fees, income taxes and estate taxes. The final result is often a *shrinkage of 30% or more* by the time an estate is passed to the surviving family.[4]

The basic objectives of estate planning are to provide for the orderly and efficient accumulation, conservation and distribution of an estate, while **avoiding conflict**, **shortening delays** and **reducing expenses**.[5]

Footnotes on page 13

PEOPLE AT WORK - CAPITAL AT WORK

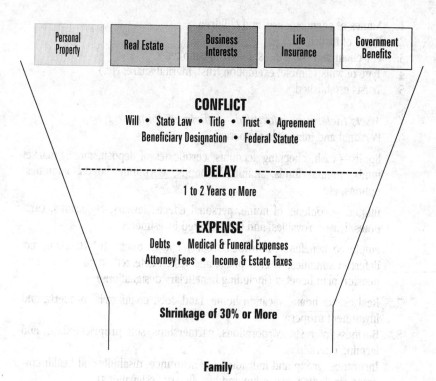

| Personal Property | Real Estate | Business Interests | Life Insurance | Government Benefits |

CONFLICT
Will • State Law • Title • Trust • Agreement
Beneficiary Designation • Federal Statute

---------------------- **DELAY** ----------------------
1 to 2 Years or More

EXPENSE
Debts • Medical & Funeral Expenses
Attorney Fees • Income & Estate Taxes

Shrinkage of 30% or More

Family

OBJECTIVES OF ESTATE PLANNING

Avoid Conflict • Shorten Delays • Reduce Expenses

INFORMATION REQUIRED FOR ANALYSIS & PROPOSAL

1. Names of client, spouse, and children.
2. Dates of birth.
3. For client and spouse – smoker/nonsmoker.
4. Type of wills (simple, exemption trust, marital share, etc.).
5. Trusts established.

Assets (determine how titled – individual, joint, etc.)
6. Personal and intangible property:

   liquid – cash, checking accounts, certificates of deposit, money market funds, mutual funds, municipal bonds, corporate bonds, annuities, options, etc.

   illiquid – contents of home, personal effects, jewelry, collections, cars, notes, leases, royalties, and tax sheltered investments.

   employee benefits – individual retirement accounts, HR-10 plans, tax deferred annuities, 401(k) plans, and vested deferred compensation and pension plan benefits (including beneficiary designations).
7. Real estate: home, vacation home, land, lots, commercial property, and investment property.
8. Business interests: corporations, partnerships, sole proprietorships, and farming operations.
9. Insurance: group and individual life insurance, disability and health coverage (including ownership and beneficiary designations).
10. Government benefits: social security disability payments, survivor benefits and retirement payments.

Liabilities
11. Short-term debt: bills payable, loans, notes, consumer debt.
12. Long-term debt: home mortgage and home equity loans.

Obligations and Objectives
13. Debt to be paid at death (including final expenses).
14. Charitable bequests.
15. Monthly income required by surviving family.
16. Monthly income required by spouse after children are grown.
17. Cost for children's education (per year).
18. Monthly income in case of long-term disability or retirement.

Special Circumstances
19. Support for ex-spouse or children from prior marriage.
20. Support for other dependents.

Footnotes

[1] Where more than one person owns real estate or certain types of personal property, the **form** of ownership determines how the property is passed upon death. The form of ownership also determines the extent to which the property is includable in the gross estate for federal estate tax purposes:

   a. Where the property is owned in a **tenancy in common**, each tenant – or co-owner – has a fractional, divisible interest in the property. Upon the death of a co-owner, his fractional interest is probate property and passes by will or by state intestacy laws. Each surviving co-tenant retains his proportionate interest in the property. The fair market value of the decedent's fractional interest is includable in the federal gross estate.

   b. Where the property is owned in **joint tenancy with right of survivorship**, each joint tenant has an undivided interest in the entire property. The survivorship right is the key characteristic: upon the death of a joint tenant, the decedent's interest passes by operation of law to the surviving tenant or tenants. The decedent's interest is not a probate asset and therefore cannot be disposed of by will or intestacy law. For federal estate tax purposes, joint tenancy with right of survivorship does not necessarily prevent all or any of the property from inclusion in the federal gross estate upon the death of a joint owner. However, a joint-and-survivorship property interest created *between spouses* after 1976 is considered to be a "qualified joint interest." As such, only *one-half* of the value is included in the gross estate for federal tax purposes. All other joint-and-survivorship property is *fully* includable in the gross estate of the first owner to die, except to the extent that the decedent's estate can demonstrate that the survivor contributed to the purchase price. However, jointly owned property obtained through gift or inheritance is included in proportion to the decedent's ownership interest.

   c. Some states recognize a **tenancy by the entirety**. Generally, this form of ownership parallels joint-and-survivorship property except that it may be created by husband and wife only.

   d. In **community property** states each spouse is considered to own an undivided one-half interest in such property during the marriage, and each spouse is free to dispose of his or her share of community property upon death. One-half of the fair market value of community property is includable in the decedent spouse's estate. See the expanded discussion of community property on pages 359-360.

[2] The unlimited marital deduction allows jointly owned property to pass to a surviving spouse free of the federal estate tax. However, having virtually all property in joint title with right of survivorship can defeat the potential estate tax advantages of the Exemption Trust Will (chart, page 29). When property is jointly owned, it passes by law directly to the surviving spouse and therefore cannot pass into the non-marital, or "B" trust. Such overqualification of the unlimited marital deduction means that the property may be subject to taxation upon the subsequent death of the surviving spouse. Furthermore, there may be certain *income tax* disadvantages to having property jointly owned if and when the surviving spouse sells the property. See page 473 for an expanded discussion of stepped-up basis.

[3] For specific examples of the time delays that can occur when the valuation of closely held stock is left to chance, refer to the materials on pages 193-198. See also page 438 for a discussion of the probate process.

[4] Typical estate debts, costs and taxes for various size estates are set forth on page 90. See also page 345 for a discussion of asset protection techniques.

[5] During the fact finding phase of estate planning it is important to obtain for review numerous client documents. A checklist of these documents is set forth on page 84. However, a nonattorney should not provide specific advice regarding the modification or drafting of legal documents, since this activity could be construed as the unauthorized practice of law.

HUMAN LIFE VALUE

In determining how much life insurance should be carried for family income purposes, two basic methods are used. The **needs approach** involves a determination of the family's actual income requirements. The **human life value approach** involves a capitalization of that part of the breadearner's income devoted to the support of his family.[1]

Calculating an individual's human life value involves first determining the amount of his income allocated to family support. This is done by deducting income taxes, personal life and health insurance premiums, and the cost of self-maintenance from the breadearner's annual income from personal efforts. Assume that the result is $10,000 per year.[2]

The next step involves determining the number of working years to retirement. Our example assumes the figure of 5 years.[3] A reasonable discount rate is then applied to arrive at the present value of these anticipated future earnings. For example, 5 percent might be used as representing a conservative after-tax rate of return for the surviving family.

NO GROWTH. The present value of future earnings after the first year can then be calculated by multiplying them by the appropriate discount factors (e.g., multiplying the $10,000 expected to be earned for the family in the second year by a factor of .9524, we find that its present value is $9,524). When this amount is added to the present values of anticipated earnings in the other years, we determine a human life value of $45,459 (for the limited five-year period).[4]

8% GROWTH. However, it is important to anticipate that in future years the income devoted to the breadearner's family will likely *increase*. If we assume an annual increase of 8 percent, earnings are projected to be $10,800 in the second year. The present value of these earnings is $10,286 ($10,800 x .9524). Adding this amount to the present values of the anticipated earnings in the other years, we determine a human life value of $52,941, *16 percent more* than if "no growth" had been projected.

The more years to retirement, the greater the contrast between "no growth" and "growth." An accurate estimate of human life values requires not only projections of anticipated growth but periodic reviews and updates of insurance needs as well.[5]

———————————

Footnotes on page 17

NO GROWTH

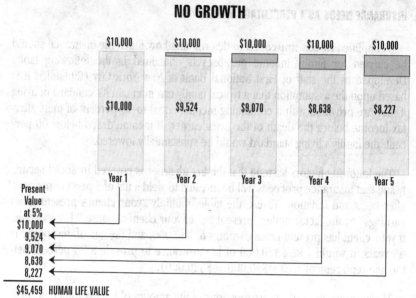

8% GROWTH

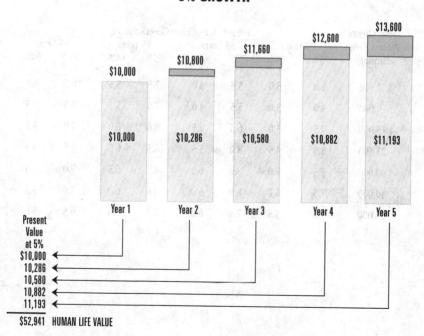

INSURANCE NEEDS AS A PERCENTAGE OF EARNINGS

A simplified **needs approach** to determining how much life insurance should be carried for family income purposes is contained in the following table. Developed by the staff of First National Bank of New York City (Citibank), it is based upon the assumption that a typical family can maintain its standard of living if they are provided with a continuing income equal to 75 percent of their after-tax income before the death of the breadearner. If income drops below 60 percent, the family's living standard would be substantially lowered.

The following factors assume that the breadearner is covered by social security and that insurance proceeds will be invested to yield a net of 5 percent per year, after taxes and inflation. To use the table, multiply "your client's present gross earnings" by the factor under "present age of your client's spouse." For example, if your client has present gross earnings of $40,000, and the age of the spouse is 45 years, it would take $320,000 of life insurance to provide a 75 percent net-income replacement (8.0 x $40,000 = $320,000).

These results are only approximations of the amount of life insurance needed. It is generally a good practice to confirm the results with a more detailed needs analysis comparing specific family income objectives to available resources.

Your Client's Present Gross Earnings	Present Age of Your Client's Spouse							
	25 Years		35 Years		45 Years		55 Years	
	75%	60%	75%	60%	75%	60%	75%	60%
$ 7,500	4.0	3.0	5.5	4.0	7.5	5.5	6.5	4.5
9,000	4.0	3.0	5.5	4.0	7.5	5.5	6.5	4.5
15,000	4.5	3.0	6.5	4.5	8.0	6.0	7.0	5.5
23,500	6.5	4.5	8.0	5.5	8.5	6.5	7.5	5.5
30,000	7.5	5.0	8.0	6.0	8.5	6.5	7.0	5.5
40,000	7.5	5.0	8.0	6.0	8.0	6.0	7.0	5.5
65,000	7.5	5.5	7.5	6.0	7.5	6.0	6.5	5.0

Footnotes

[1] In the discussion of the Estate Funnel on page 10, it was recognized that there are essentially two ways to earn money. One is by "capital at work," that is, income from savings, stocks, bonds and real estate holdings. The other is by "people at work," that is, income from individual work and effort. Human life value is a measure of "people at work." The concept is of particular importance to the client who has little in the way of capital, or relatively high earnings as compared to capital assets. Many highly compensated professionals, such as physicians, attorneys, and accountants have estates that are relatively modest in comparison to their incomes. Because of this, their families become highly dependent upon "people at work," with little "capital at work" in reserve.

[2] The figure of $10,000 has been chosen for illustration because it is an easy number from which to make further determinations of human life value. If the actual amount were $20,000, the human life value figures would be twice those illustrated; and if the actual amount were $50,000, the human life value figures would be five times those illustrated.

[3] Although five years have been selected for purposes of demonstrating the concept of human life value, most individuals who are concerned about family income requirements have far more than five working years until retirement (e.g., a 35-year old breadearner anticipating retirement at age 65 would have thirty years to retirement).

[4] A table of human life values at varying growth rates appears on page 100. Factors for calculating human life value can be obtained from the Compound Interest Table, on page 499, and the Compound Discount Table, on page 502. The following is an example of how to use this table to calculate the human life value assuming: (1) a 41-year old breadearner; (2) age 65 retirement; (3) earnings of $55,000 per year, of which $45,000 is devoted to family maintenance; and (4) a projected 4 percent rate of earnings growth.

Working Years to Retirement:	24
Projected Growth in Earnings:	4%
Factor From Table (page 100)	215,465
Number of $10,000s	x 4.5
	$969,593

Note that in calculating human life value the first year earnings are not discounted in the chart on page 15 and in the table on page 100. This recognizes that the surviving family needs funds immediately upon the breadearner's death, not one year after his death.

[5] Life insurance offers a replacement for human life value by providing "capital at work" to replace "people at work." But what type of life insurance should be used? Obviously, insurance providing a *decreasing* death benefit appears inappropriate for the client whose human life value may increase in the future (e.g., upon periodic review the growth rate is found to be greater than initially projected). At the very least, insurance providing a *level* death benefit is necessary. It might even be advisable for the younger client to "take an option on tomorrow," by purchasing coverage which will provide *additional* insurance in later years through increasing term riders, paid-up additions, guaranteed purchase options, or an increasing death benefit equal to the annual increase of universal life cash values (sometimes referred to as either Option 2 or Option B). With two wage-earner families the use of a first-to die life insurance product may be appropriate (page 393). When applying for insurance to cover an increasing human life value it is important to be familiar with any financial underwriting requirements (see expanded discussion on page 392).

FEDERAL ESTATE TAX

One of the potential expenses of settling an estate is the federal estate tax. It is a continuous lien on your client's property, but its foreclosure date is yet to be determined.[1] Proper planning involves anticipating and reducing the estate tax liability wherever possible as well as providing for payment of the tax. Unlike other expenses of settling an estate, it can be particularly burdensome in that it is generally due and payable *in cash* 9 months after death.[2]

The estate tax computation is not difficult, and in many ways resembles the calculations involved in determining income tax. When we file our *income* tax return each year, the calculations involve terms such as gross income, taxable income, deductions, and credits.

When an *estate* tax return is filed, we are likewise dealing with terms such as gross estate, adjusted gross estate, taxable estate, deductions, and credits.[3]

Generally, the **gross estate** includes *all* property of any description and wherever located, to the extent the decedent had any interest in the property at the time of death.[4] It may even include property previously given away or over which the decedent had no control at the time of his death.

To illustrate, assume that in 2002 we have an estate totalling $2,700,000. In determining the adjusted gross estate, we can subtract the decedent's debts, such as loans, notes, and mortgages, plus the debts of the estate, such as funeral and administrative expenses. If these debts totalled $200,000, then the **adjusted gross estate** would be $2,500,000. For this discussion, assume that the taxable estate is also $2,500,000.[5] With a taxable estate of $2,500,000 the **tentative tax** would be $1,025,800.

However, in 2002 there is a **unified credit** available which can offset up to $345,800 of the tentative tax.[6] Generally, the unified credit allows an individual to pass $1,000,000 of property free of federal gift and estate taxes during lifetime or at death.[7]

After taking advantage of the credit, the estate will still owe a tax of $680,000, which means that the amount of the original estate remaining for the children or other heirs has been reduced to $1,820,000.

Footnotes on page 21

GROSS ESTATE
$2,700,000

D
E $200,000
B
T

ADJUSTED GROSS ESTATE
(Taxable Estate)

$2,500,000

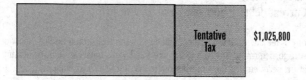

Tentative
Tax $1,025,800

BENEFIT OF UNIFIED CREDIT
($345,800)

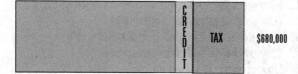

C
R
E   TAX $680,000
D
I
T

REMAINING

$1,820,000

INFORMATION REQUIRED FOR ANALYSIS & PROPOSAL

Current listing and values of all property to include:

1. Cash.
2. Liquid assets (stocks, bonds).
3. Real estate (home, land, rental property).
4. Personal property (household goods, collections, jewelry).
5. Business interests (closely held stock, partnership interests, sole proprietorships).
6. Life insurance owned or insurance payable to estate (group insurance and individual policies).
7. Employee benefits (IRA, HR-10, 403(b) annuity, pension/profit sharing, 401(k) plan).
8. Current debts (short-term and long-term).

Note: A copy of the client's latest personal financial statement should disclose most of this information. Be sure to determine how the assets are titled (i.e., separate, joint ownership with spouse, community property, etc.). A copy of wills and trusts should also be obtained. See also pages 12 and 84.

CROSS REFERENCES TO TAX FACTS 1 (2002)

Q 726. Taxation of income in respect of a decedent.
Q 751. Who must file a return and when tax is payable.
Q 752. How federal estate tax is computed.
Q 753. What items are included in gross estate.
Q 754. Property held jointly between spouses.
Q 762. How property is valued for estate tax purposes.
Q 763. Deductions which are allowed.
Q 764. Description of estate tax marital deduction.
Q 765. Deduction allowed for qualified family owned business interest.
Q 766. Credits that may be taken against the estate tax.
Q 767. Description of unified credit.

Footnotes

[1] This lien is not as "continuous" as it once was. See pages 88-89, Phase-In and Sunset Provisions of EGTRRA 2001.

[2] If certain strict conditions are met, payment of the *federal* estate tax can be deferred (see pages 369-370). However, this does not mean that payment of applicable state inheritance and estate taxes can be similarly postponed (see page 93). A federal estate tax return (Form 706), if required, must be filed, and the tax paid, by the executor within nine months after death. The *penalty* for failure to file a timely return is 5 percent of the tax for each month the return is past due, up to a maximum of 25 percent. A detailed listing of these penalties is on page 430.

[3] The instructions to the United States Estate Tax Return (Form 706) are 28 pages in length. The actual estate tax return (Form 706) is 44 pages in length. The first pages of the estate tax return and instructions for filing Form 706 are reproduced on pages 488-489.

[4] The gross estate also includes "income in respect of a decedent" (IRD), which refers to those amounts to which a decedent was entitled as gross income, but which were not includable in his taxable income for the year of death. IRD is subject to income taxation in the hands of the person who receives it. For an expanded discussion see page 402.

[5] For purposes of illustration, this chart assumes there is no surviving spouse and that the adjusted gross estate is equal to the taxable estate. In the usual calculation sequence, debts (including funeral expenses), administrative expenses, and losses during administration are subtracted from the gross estate (as reduced by exclusions) to arrive at the adjusted gross estate. Charitable and marital deductions are then subtracted from the adjusted gross estate to determine the taxable estate. The principal deduction in this latter step has always been the marital deduction. Since it has been assumed that there is no surviving spouse, there can be no marital deduction, and therefore the adjusted gross estate is equal to the taxable estate. In community property states, the assumption of "no surviving spouse" means that all property is assumed to be separately owned.

[6] Under EGTRRA 2001, the unified credit is scheduled to increase during the years 2004 to 2009. These increases are: $555,800 in 2004 and 2005, $780,800 in 2006 thru 2008, and $1,455,800 in 2009. The corresponding unified credit equivalents, also called "applicable exclusions" or "applicable exclusion amounts," are: $1,500,000 in 2004 and 2005, $2,000,000 in 2006 thru 2008, and $3,500,000 in 2009. The "unified credit equivalent" was previously called the "exemption equivalent."

[7] Because of the "unified" gift and estate tax rates, prior taxable gifts made during his lifetime would, in effect, reduce the amount of credit available at death. Upon death all adjusted taxable gifts made since 1976 are added to the estate when calculating the estate tax. However, this is not as bad as it might first appear, since the estate is, in effect, given a credit for prior gift taxes actually paid, or payable. The impact of this system is to push later transfers made during lifetime or at death into higher and higher tax brackets (due to the progressive estate and gift tax rates).

TAXFLATION

Estate planning has traditionally dealt with facts as established at a single point in time. Thus, it has been common for the estate planner to assume that the client has just died and now has the opportunity of looking over his executor's shoulder as the estate is settled. While this approach is still appropriate as a starting point, it does not go far enough, as inflation and progressive taxation make it essential to deal with projections of estate growth.[1] While not necessarily resulting in an immediate solution to tomorrow's problems, such an approach will at least bring a sense of urgency to the estate planning process.[2]

Taxflation is the product of our *increased living standards*, *inflation*, and *progressive taxation*. It can cause the liquidity in an estate to be eroded by an ever-increasing estate tax burden. To put it simply, "the bigger the pie, the bigger Uncle Sam's slice of that pie."

TODAY. For purposes of illustration, assume that in 2002 we have an unmarried individual with an estate valued at $1,500,000. Upon death, this estate will be subject to $210,000 of federal estate taxes.[3] This represents a **shrinkage of 14%**.

5 YEARS. Now let's assume that this individual lives for another 5 years, during which time the estate grows at a rate of 8 percent per year. The estate will have grown to $2,203,992, but estate taxes will have decreased to $91,796.[4] This represents a **shrinkage of 4%**.[5]

10 YEARS. Should this individual have the good fortune to live 10 years, the estate will have increased in value to $3,238,387. Likewise, the federal estate taxes will have increased, this time to $1,076,113.[6] This represents a **shrinkage of 33%**.

Most individuals are pleased by the prospect that their estates are likely to double in value in just 10 years.[7] But there is a cost, and that cost is the fact that their **federal estate taxes will increase over 5 times**. This phenomenon is referred to as "taxflation" or "bracket creep." But whatever it is called, the impact is the same: a smaller and smaller percentage of the estate will be available for the children and other heirs.[8]

Footnotes on page 25

ESTATE TAXES AND INFLATION

Growth of Estate: 8% per year

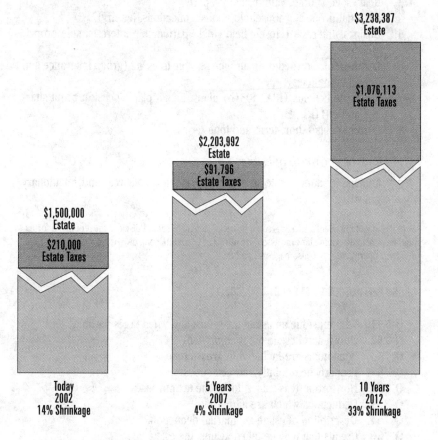

$3,238,387
Estate

$1,076,113
Estate Taxes

$2,203,992
Estate

$91,796
Estate Taxes

$1,500,000
Estate

$210,000
Estate Taxes

Today
2002
14% Shrinkage

5 Years
2007
4% Shrinkage

10 Years
2012
33% Shrinkage

INFORMATION REQUIRED FOR ANALYSIS & PROPOSAL

To Calculate Current Estate Tax

1. Cash.
2. Liquid assets (stocks, bonds).
3. Real estate (home, land, rental property).
4. Personal property (household goods, collections, jewelry).
5. Business interests (closely held stock, partnership interests, sole proprietorships).
6. Life insurance owned or insurance payable to estate (group insurance and individual policies).
7. Employee benefits (IRA, 403(b) plans, Keogh plans, pension/profit sharing, and 401(k) plans).
8. Current debts (short-term and long-term).

To Project Growth of Estate

9. Anticipated annual rate of growth, to include both real and inflationary growth.

Note: A copy of the client's latest personal financial statement should disclose most of this information. Be sure to determine how the assets are titled (i.e., separate, joint ownership with spouse, community property, etc.). See also pages 12 and 84.

CROSS REFERENCES TO TAX FACTS 1 (2002)

Q 751. Who must file an estate tax return and when tax is payable.
Q 752. How federal estate tax is computed.
Q 753. What items are included in gross estate.
Q 754. Property held jointly between spouses.
Q 762. How property is valued for estate tax purposes.
Q 763. Deductions which are allowed.
Q 764. Description of estate tax marital deduction.
Q 766. Credits that may be taken against the estate tax.
Q 767. Description of unified credit.

Footnotes

[1] In spite of the federal estate tax reductions under EGTRRA 2001, larger estates will continue to be impacted by taxflation. See pages 86-87, Impact Of Appreciation On Estate Tax.

[2] The problem of increasing estate values is likely to be worse than shown, since estate values are affected by both *real* growth and *inflationary* growth. For a listing of the various planning techniques that have been adopted in order to minimize this growth, refer to the Transferring Appreciation chart on page 43. When applying for life insurance intended to pay anticipated future estate taxes, it is important to be familiar with any financial underwriting requirements (see expanded discussion on page 392).

[3] The estate in this chart is equivalent to the adjusted gross estate/taxable estate used in the Federal Estate Tax chart on page 19. The taxes demonstrated are those which also would have been paid at the death of both spouses and the passage of the estate to children or other heirs (assuming that the first spouse dies with a simple will leaving the entire estate to the surviving spouse).

[4] This reduction of estate taxes, from $210,000 in 2002 to $91,796 in 2007, is caused by both a reduction in the tax rates and an increase in the unified credit under EGTRRA 2001. Estate taxes for the years not illustrated are: $264,000 in 2003; $112,320 in 2004; $175,306 in 2005; $18,737 in 2006; $171,140 in 2008; $0 in 2009 and 2010; and $944,209 in 2011. With larger estates and higher rates of growth, EGTRRA 2001 generally results in less benefit to the taxpayer. See pages 86-87, Impact Of Appreciation On Estate Tax.

[5] Estate growth can be calculated by using the Compound Interest Table on page 498. For example, for 8 percent growth over 5 years the table provides a factor of 1.469. Multiplying this factor by the estate's current value projects an estate value of $2,203,500 in 5 years (1.469 x 1,500,000 = 2,203,500). However, because the factors on page 499 are provided to only three places, this estate value is not exactly the same as shown in the chart on page 23 (i.e., the chart provides a more precise estate value of $2,203,992).

[6] The estate taxes in this chart reflect the increased credits provided by EGTRRA 2001. These increases are $555,800 in 2004 and 2005, $780,800 in 2006 thru 2008, $1,455,800 in 2009, and $345,800 in 2011 and thereafter. The Impact Of Appreciation On Estate Tax, on pages 86-87, suggests that –for many estates – these increases may offer only temporary relief from burdensome estate taxes. In fact, with some larger estates, the conversion of the state death tax credit into a deduction may actually *increase* taxes, depending upon the state of domicile. See table on page 495, state death tax credit.

[7] A handy method of determining the impact of inflation upon the value of various assets is the "rule of 72." If you take any rate of inflation and divide it into the number 72, you will get the number of years it takes for that asset to double in value at the particular rate of inflation. Thus, at 8 percent inflation, an estate of $1,500,000 will be worth $3,000,000 in only 9 years (72 ÷ 8 = 9). At 4 percent inflation, an estate of $1,000,000 will be worth $2,000,000 in 18 years (72 ÷ 4 = 18). With the "rule of 72" in mind, it is easier to understand why the federal estate tax will, sooner rather than later, affect estates not currently threatened by estate taxes.

[8] The Consumer Price Index table on page 307 will provide a better appreciation of the impact of inflation on the costs of the goods and services. The Inflation Adjuster table on page 95 shows the amount of additional life insurance required to maintain the purchasing power of existing life insurance. The Declining Value Of A Dollar table, on page 308, provides a comparison of the costs of various consumer goods over a period of 60 years.

SIMPLE WILL

A will is the single most basic and necessary tool in estate planning. By having a will, we can be sure that property goes to *whom* we want, and in the *amounts* we want, rather than as provided under a state's intestacy laws.

Although there are various types of wills, the most common is often called the *simple* will.[1] The majority of simple wills provide for: (1) payment of just debts and expenses; (2) appointment of an executor or executrix; (3) specific bequests; (4) transfer of the entire estate to the surviving spouse; (5) if there is no surviving spouse, then transfer of the estate to children or other heirs; and (6) appointment of a guardian or guardians for minor children and their property.

Our example assumes that in 2002 we an estate of $2,500,000.[2]

UPON THE FIRST DEATH, the simple will generally passes *all* property to the surviving spouse. Note that **no taxes** will be paid on this transfer. This is possible because of the unlimited marital deduction.

UPON THE SECOND DEATH, the estate will be heavily taxed in the amount of $680,000, and this tax must generally be paid before the balance of the estate can be passed to the children.

After payment of these taxes the estate remaining to be passed to the children is $1,820,000. This estate has now been *reduced* to only 73 percent of its original size.

For the individual who has a relatively small estate, the simple will is usually adequate. However, as an estate grows, this most basic of wills does not take advantage of the unified credit that is available at the first death. This failure to provide any tax savings means that federal estate taxes will consume 27 percent of the estate in our example.[3]

---

[1] Some commentators have suggested that, because it passes all property to the surviving spouse, the simple will should be called the "I love you" will. Without a will, property passes according to state law (see Degrees Of Kindred, page 103, Intestate's Will, page 104, and State Laws On Intestate Succession, pages 105-111).

[2] In order to simplify the explanation, the estate of $2,500,000 is the same as the adjusted gross estate in the Federal Estate Tax chart on page 19, and it is assumed that the surviving spouse had no separate property. Had there been separate property, the taxes at the second death would be greater than shown. It is also assumed that death occurs in 2002, there has been no prior use of the unified credit through lifetime gifts, and the surviving spouse is a U.S. citizen (see pages 426 and 442). Under EGTRRA 2001, a taxable estate of $2,500,000 will no longer be subject to estate taxes in the years 2009 and 2010. See Impact Of Appreciation On Estate Tax, page 86-87, and Phase-In and Sunset Provisions of EGTRRA 2001, pages 88-89.

[3] Note that the simple will has resulted in unnecessarily high taxes which are payable upon the surviving spouse's subsequent death. Although the simple will *defers taxes* by taking maximum advantage of the unlimited marital deduction, it fails to use the unified tax credit available at the first death.

ESTATE

$2,500,000

UPON THE FIRST DEATH

All Property To Spouse

↓

No Taxes $2,500,000

UPON THE SECOND DEATH

To Children

↓

$680,000   TAX $1,820,000

EXEMPTION TRUST WILL

A will creating an exemption trust can result in substantial savings by taking full advantage of the unified credit, which allows an individual in 2002 to pass $1,000,000 of property free of federal gift and estate taxes during lifetime or at death. The trust can also provide for the continued management of part or all of an estate.

As in the Simple Will chart on page 27, our example in 2002 uses an estate of $2,500,000.[1]

UPON THE FIRST DEATH, with the typical exemption trust will, the estate is divided into *two* parts, with one part equal to $1,000,000 placed in a family or nonmarital trust ("B" trust in the chart).[2] No taxes are paid on this amount since the trust takes full advantage of the $345,800 unified credit available in 2002 (i.e., the amount that each individual can pass tax-free to the next generation).[3]

Unless there is a disclaimer, the remaining $1,500,000 of the estate is passed to the surviving spouse.[4] This qualifies for the unlimited marital deduction and can be passed free of federal estate taxes.[5] Although it is sometimes given outright, this portion of the estate is often placed in trust, which is referred to as either the "A" trust or the "marital deduction" trust.[6] If the property is placed in trust, the spouse should be given a life estate with a power of appointment or a QTIP interest.[7]

The surviving spouse can also be given a right to *all income* from the "B" trust, as well as the right to demand, each year, either $5,000 or 5 percent of the trust corpus, whichever amount is larger. Property subject to a $5,000 or 5 percent demand right held at death is subject to taxation in the surviving spouse's estate only to the extent of the demand right.

UPON THE SECOND DEATH, the estate subject to taxation will generally be limited to $1,500,000. After paying taxes of $210,000, there remains $1,290,000 to be passed to the children, or other heirs, along with the $1,000,000 from the "B" trust (assuming that the surviving spouse had no separate property).[8] The amount previously placed in the "B" trust passes tax-free to the children under the terms previously established in that trust. Since the surviving spouse has no power to control the disposition of property placed in this trust, it is not subject to taxation in her estate.

Footnotes on page 31

ESTATE

$2,500,000

UPON THE FIRST DEATH

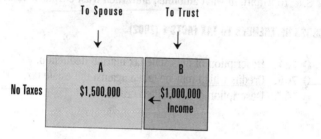

To Spouse   To Trust

	A	B
No Taxes	$1,500,000	$1,000,000 ← Income

UPON THE SECOND DEATH

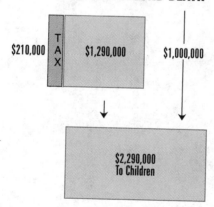

$210,000 TAX $1,290,000 $1,000,000

$2,290,000
To Children

INFORMATION REQUIRED FOR ANALYSIS & PROPOSAL

Attorney Drafting Will Must Know

1. Spouse's name.
2. Children's names.
3. Name of executor/executrix.
4. Ages of minor children.
5. Names and ages of other beneficiaries.
6. Trustee after testator's death.
7. To whom, in what amounts, and when trust income is to be paid.
8. To whom, in what amounts, and when trust corpus is to be paid.

CROSS REFERENCES TO TAX FACTS 1 (2002)

Q 764. Description of the estate tax marital deduction.
Q 766. Credits which may be taken against the estate tax.
Q 767. Description of the unified credit.

Footnotes

[1] As with the Simple Will chart, the $2,500,000 estate is equivalent to the adjusted gross estate as shown in the Federal Estate Tax chart on page 19. It is also assumed there were no prior lifetime taxable gifts which required use of the unified credit.

[2] This is often referred to as a *limited* trust will, in that the amount placed in the "B" trust is limited to the unified credit equivalent, $1,000,000 in 2002 – if no lifetime taxable gifts were made (see footnote 6, page 21). This trust is also referred to as a bypass, unified credit, credit shelter, credit amount, or credit equivalent bypass trust. If most property is held by a husband and wife in joint title with right of survivorship, the "A" trust could be *overqualified* and there may not be $1,000,000 of other property available to place in the "B" trust. In contrast, when a tax-driven formula is used to determine the amount going to the "B" trust, it may become overfunded (e.g., when a will directs that the amount to the "B" trust shall be the maximum amount that can be passed without paying an estate tax). Under such formulas, the substantial increases in the unified credit equivalent under EGTRRA 2001 could place unanticipated large amounts in the "B" trust, leaving little or nothing to go to the "A" trust. See Phase-In and Sunset Provisions of EGTRRA 2001, pages 88-89. In contrast to the Exemption Trust Will, see Marital Plan Will, page 461.

[3] The $1,100,000 generation skipping transfer tax (GSTT) exemption can be used when there is a desire to pass property to grandchildren while avoiding estate or gift taxation at the children's generation (see chart, page 39). The reverse QTIP election can be used when there is a desire to take full advantage of the $1,100,000 GSTT exemption, while avoiding estate taxes at the first death (see page 454).

[4] There may be occasions when it is desired to give the surviving spouse the opportunity to take more, or less, property than would be received under the typical exemption trust will. This can be accomplished with the use of disclaimers, which are more fully explained on page 374.

[5] There may be circumstances in which the testator will *not* wish to take advantage of the unlimited marital deduction. For example, by taking full advantage of the marital deduction, the business asset will continue to appreciate in the estate of the surviving spouse. This potential appreciation would be eliminated by passing the business to the children or other heirs upon the first death. However, the cost to do this is the early payment of estate taxes on business values in excess of $1,000,000. Of course, considerations other than financial ones may influence the ultimate decision (e.g., adult children working in the family business have a strong desire to take over operation and full ownership of the business, rather than to receive the business upon the ultimate death of the surviving parent). Generally, the marital deduction is unavailable when the surviving spouse is not a United States citizen unless the transfer is to a qualified domestic trust (see expanded discussions, pages 426 and 442). For an expanded discussion of the marital deduction, see page 419.

[6] One type of marital deduction trust is also referred to as a "power of appointment" trust, in that the surviving spouse is given a general power of appointment over the trust during lifetime or at death. For a discussion of the power of appointment trust, see page 419.

[7] Refer to page 35 for a chart illustrating the use of a qualified terminable interest trust. Also, see page 434 for a discussion of powers of appointment.

[8] To simplify the example, the tax is calculated assuming there are no debts, expenses, deductions, or prior taxable gifts. This means the computation base is equal to the gross estate (see calculation steps set forth on page 85). The tentative tax of $555,800 is calculated from the tax table on page 493. Subtracting the unified credit of $345,800 produces a tax of $210,000 ($555,800 - $345,800 = $210,000). Survivorship life insurance is often used when all estate taxes are deferred until the deaths of *both* husband and wife. The premium outlay for a survivorship policy insuring both husand and wife is typically less than that required for a policy insuring either the husband or the wife (see discussion, page 475).

COMPARISON OF WILLS

With the **SIMPLE WILL** leaving all property outright to the surviving spouse in 2002, the children would receive $1,820,000 (see chart, page 27).

On the other hand, with the **EXEMPTION TRUST WILL**, they would receive $2,290,000 (see chart, page 29). By using this estate planning tool, it is possible for a husband and wife to take full advantage of the unified credit remaining at each of their deaths.[1]

Another way of viewing this is to compare the amount of money being left to the federal government in the form of federal estate taxes. With the simple will the government receives $680,000, whereas with the exemption trust will the government gets only $210,000.

That is a *saving* of $470,000!

The choice is simple. Either the children or other heirs get the difference of $470,000, or the federal government does. Most people would prefer to leave this $470,000 to someone other than the federal government.[2]

---

[1] The savings that can be realized increase as the estate grows. For example, with a $4,000,000 estate the savings are $500,000 (assuming utilization at both deaths of the $345,800 unified credit available in 2002).

[2] The fact that these savings inure to the benefit of children or other heirs, rather than your client or his spouse, can sometimes give rise to statements such as: "I only wish I had been able to start out with what my kids stand to get under our existing wills." Such a reaction may be difficult to handle, until it is realized that the dollars lost by not having a trust will go directly to the federal government.

SIMPLE WILL   EXEMPTION TRUST WILL

$1,820,000
To Children

$2,290,000
To Children

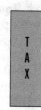

$680,000
To Government

27% Shinkage

$210,000
To Government

8% Shrinkage

A SAVINGS OF $470,000

QTIP TRUST

The QTIP trust provides a way to defer estate taxes by taking advantage of the marital deduction, yet "control from the grave" by directing who will eventually receive the property upon the death of the surviving spouse.[1]

Under such a trust all income must be paid at least annually to the surviving spouse.[2] The trust can be invaded only for the benefit of the surviving spouse, and no conditions can be placed upon the surviving spouse's right to the income (e.g., it is not permitted to terminate payments of income should the spouse remarry). However, in order to qualify the executor must make an irrevocable election to have the marital deduction apply to property placed in the trust.[3] This requirement not only gives the executor the power to determine how much, if any, of the estate will be taxed at the first death, it also provides great flexibility for post death planning based upon changing circumstances.[4]

Our example assumes that in 2002 we have an estate of $3,000,000.[5]

UPON THE FIRST DEATH, the estate is divided into *two* parts, with one part equal to $1,000,000 placed in a family or nonmarital trust ("B" trust in the chart).[6] No taxes are paid on this amount since the trust takes full advantage of the $345,800 unified credit (i.e., the amount of credit in 2002 that allows each individual to pass $1,000,000 tax-free to the next generation). The remaining $2,000,000 is placed in the QTIP trust.[7]

The executor may elect to have all, some or none of this property treated as marital deduction property. Assume that in order to equalize the estates and save overall estate taxes the executor decides to make a partial election of $1,500,000 (i.e., of the $2,000,000 placed in the QTIP trust only $1,500,000 will be sheltered from estate taxes at the first death).[8] This means that $500,000, the "nonelected" property, will be taxed at the first death. Although $210,000 of estate taxes must be paid, the remaining $290,000 will now be excluded from the taxable estate of the surviving spouse (any appreciation of this property after the first death will also be excluded).[9] If authorized under the trust document or by state law, the executor can sever the QTIP trust into separate trusts.[10]

UPON THE SECOND DEATH, the estate subject to taxation is limited to $1,500,000 (the amount remaining in the trust for which estate taxes were deferred). After paying taxes of $210,000, there remains $1,290,000.[11] This amount, together with the $290,000 from the severed trust and the $1,000,000 from the "B" trust, are passed to the beneficiaries under the terms previously established in these trusts.[12]

Footnotes on page 37

ESTATE

$3,000,000

UPON THE FIRST DEATH

To QTIP Trust   To "B" Trust

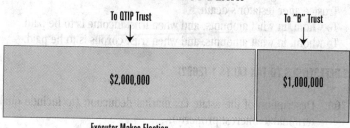

$2,000,000 $1,000,000

Executor Makes Election
(all, some or none)

Partial Election $210,000

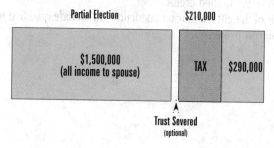

$1,500,000
(all income to spouse)   TAX $290,000

Trust Severed
(optional)

UPON THE SECOND DEATH

$210,000

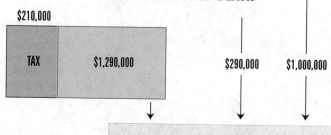

TAX $1,290,000 $290,000 $1,000,000

$2,580,000
To Beneficiaries As Specified In Trusts

INFORMATION REQUIRED FOR ANALYSIS & PROPOSAL

Attorney Drafting Will And Trust Must Know

1. Spouse's name.
2. Children's names.
3. Name of executor/executrix.
4. Ages of minor children.
5. Information regarding children of prior marriages.
6. Names and ages of other beneficiaries.
7. Trustee after testator's death.
8. To whom, in what amounts, and when trust income is to be paid.
9. To whom, in what amounts, and when trust corpus is to be paid.

CROSS REFERENCES TO TAX FACTS 1 (2002)

Q 764. Description of the estate tax marital deduction (to include qualified terminable interest property).

Q 766. Credits which may be taken against the estate tax.

Q 767. Description of the unified credit.

Q 820. Description of the gift tax marital deduction (to include qualified terminable interest property).

Footnotes

[1] QTIP stands for "qualified terminable interest property." Assets placed in a QTIP trust are referred to as qualified terminable interest property. Under the exemption trust will, to take advantage of the unlimited marital deduction the traditional "A" trust (marital trust) must give the surviving spouse the power to appoint, during lifetime or at death, all property placed in this trust in favor of the surviving spouse or the surviving spouse's estate (see chart, page 29). However, this arrangement is objectionable to some individuals, since control is lost over the eventual disposition of the property (e.g., a surviving widow could pass the property to her new husband or to her children by a prior marriage).

[2] Property placed in a QTIP trust must be income producing and the surviving spouse is typically given the power to force the trustee to make trust property productive. The spouse's *income* interest may be contingent upon the executor's election. Also, limited powers given to the spouse to invade the *corpus* of the QTIP trust may be contingent (e.g., upon the executor's election or upon the spouse not remarrying).

[3] This election by the executor *cannot* be mandated by the deceased prior to his death. It must be done on the estate tax return and cannot be revoked after the date for filing the return.

[4] For a discussion of the nontax reasons why a testator may *not* wish to take advantage of the marital deduction, see footnote 5, page 31.

[5] The $3,000,000 estate is equivalent to the adjusted gross estate (see chart, page 19). To simplify the example, the taxes are calculated assuming no debts, expenses, deductions, or prior taxable gifts, and no prior use of the unified credit.

[6] Funding of the "B" trust is limited to the unified credit equivalent, $1,000,000 in 2002 (see footnote 6, page 21, and footnote 2, page 31). QTIP trusts combined with disclaimers are likely to be increasingly used after EGTRRA 2001. For example, rather than using a tax-driven formula to allocate property to the "B" trust, a single QTIP type trust might be established. This would allow the surviving spouse to disclaim assets that would then pass into either the marital trust or the "B" trust. Also, the QTIP trust could be used to secure the $3,000,000 spousal step-up in basis, while maintaining control over the disposition of the property upon the surviving spouse's death (in 2010, assuming carryover basis becomes a reality under EGTRRA 2001).

[7] This example shows the QTIP trust being used only with the "B" trust (family trust). When the "A" trust (marital trust) is also used, it provides the executor even greater flexibility in allocating assets between the QTIP trust and "A" trust (see chart, page 29).

[8] Potential tax savings in this example come from two sources. The appreciation of assets removed from the surviving spouses estate will not be taxed in her estate. Also, in large estates, equalizing the estate between spouses can move assets from higher to lower tax rates. With a $6,000,000 estate in 2002 the potential estate tax savings are $70,000 ($1,930,000 of taxes upon second death versus $930,000 upon each death; $1,930,000 - ($930,000 + $930,000) = $70,000).

[9] Liquidity for paying estate taxes at the first death might come from the tax-free death proceeds paid to an irrevocable Life Insurance Trust (see chart, page 57).

[10] The division of the QTIP trust must be done on a fractional or percentage basis to reflect the partial election. It is not necessary that each asset be divided pro rata between the severed trusts; so long as it is based upon the fair market value of all trust assets at the time of the division.

[11] The estate has a right of recovery for any taxes paid, unless waived by the deceased spouse (if there is no waiver, then the failure to recover is subject to gift taxes).

[12] A "reverse" QTIP election is used when there is a desire to take full advantage of the $1,100,000 GSTT exemption, while avoiding estate taxes at the first death (see page 454). Lifetime QTIP trusts are used as an alternative to outright gifts.

GENERATION-SKIPPING TRANSFERS

The basic intent of the federal estate tax system is to tax property as it is passed from one generation to the next. The generation-skipping transfer tax (GSTT) is intended to prevent wealthy families from reducing estate taxes by skipping one or more generations (e.g., grandparents pass their estate to grandchildren in order to reduce or avoid estate taxes in their children's estates).

The GSTT is *in addition* to the normal estate or gift tax and is applied to the transfer of property to a person two or more generations younger than the transferor (e.g., from grandparent to grandchild).[1] The *maximum* estate tax rate, 50 percent in 2002, is used in calculating the GSTT.[2] However, there is an exemption which allows aggregate transfers of $1,100,000, as indexed in 2002 for inflation, during lifetime or at death to be exempt from the tax ($2,200,000 total for both husband and wife).[3]

To illustrate, assume that Grandparents have an estate totalling $3,000,000. Assume also that their Children have substantial estates in their own right and the Grandparents desire to fully use their GSTT exemptions.

UPON THE FIRST GRANDPARENT'S DEATH. In order to take maximum advantage of the GSTT exemption in 2002, $1,100,000 must be passed to the Grandchildren. This $1,100,000 could be placed in a family or nonmarital trust (the "B" trust) that would provide income to the surviving Grandparent.[4] To pass the full $1,100,000 to the "B" trust requires payment of $69,492 in federal estate taxes.[5]

UPON THE SECOND GRANDPARENT'S DEATH. Again, in order to take maximum advantage of the GSTT exemption, an additional $1,100,000 must now be passed to the Grandchildren. After payment of $358,729 in federal estate taxes on a taxable estate of $1,830,508, $1,100,000 is passed to the Grandchildren. In order to avoid any GST taxes, the remaining $371,779 is passed to the Children.[6] The $1,100,000 originally placed in the "B" trust is also distributed to the Grandchildren. Of the original $3,000,000 estate, estate taxes totalling $428,221 have been paid ($69,492 at the first death and $358,729 at the second death). Full use of the Grandparent's GSTT exemptions has the potential of producing estate tax savings of $1,100,000 at the Children's generation.[7]

Application of the GSTT can be quite complicated and its impact is substantial in larger estates. Careful analysis by qualified counsel is essential if unexpected tax consequences are to be avoided.[8]

Footnotes on page 41

GRANDPARENT'S ESTATE

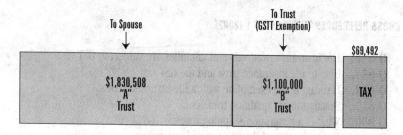

$3,000,000

UPON THE FIRST GRANDPARENT'S DEATH

To Spouse

To Trust
(GSTT Exemption)

$69,492

$1,830,508
"A"
Trust

$1,100,000
"B"
Trust

TAX

UPON THE SECOND GRANDPARENT'S DEATH

$1,830,508 Estate

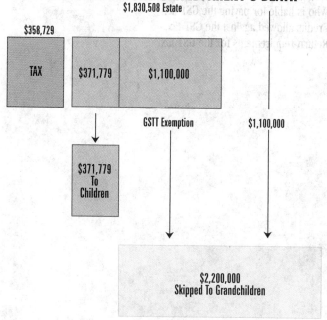

$358,729

TAX

$371,779

$1,100,000

GSTT Exemption

$1,100,000

$371,779
To
Children

$2,200,000
Skipped To Grandchildren

INFORMATION REQUIRED FOR ANALYSIS & PROPOSAL

1. Size of grandparent's estate.
2. Nature of prior gifts, if any, made by grandparents.
3. Numbers and ages of children and grandchildren.
4. Size of children's estates and ability of children to support themselves without inherited assets.

See also information required for exemption trust wills on page 30.

CROSS REFERENCES TO TAX FACTS 1 (2002)

Q 650. Life insurance proceeds and annuities are subject to GST tax.

Q 651. Gifts to life insurance trust and the GST tax.

Q 652. Leveraging the exemption with a life insurance trust.

Q 817. Discussion of "qualified transfers."

Q 850. What is a generation-skipping transfer (GST).

Q 851. Determination of the GST tax and exemption.

Q 852. How individuals are assigned to generations.

Q 853. Split gifts can be made for purposes of the GST tax.

Q 854. Who is liable for paying the GST tax.

Q 855. Credits allowed against the GST tax.

Q 856. Return requirements for the GST tax.

Footnotes

[1] Because grandchildren are two or more generations below the grandparent (transferor), they are known as *skip persons*, whereas children are known as *nonskip persons* (the transferor's spouse is also a nonskip person, since she is of the same generation as the transferor). When the transfer is directly from one generation to a person two or more generations younger than the transferor it is referred to as a "direct skip" (e.g., in his will grandfather leaves property to grandchild). In the case of a direct skip, the GSTT is payable at the time of the transfer, not upon the death of the person in the skipped generation (e.g., the GSTT is payable upon the grandfather's death, not when the child dies). Any transfer is generally not subject to the GSTT if the person in the intervening generation (the child) is not alive at the time of the transfer to the skip person (the grandchild).

[2] The amount of tax is calculated by multiplying the "taxable amount" by the "applicable rate." In fact, the applicable rate is itself a product of the maximum federal estate tax rate times the "inclusion ratio." The inclusion ratio, in turn, depends on allocations of the "GST exemption." For example, assume G transfers irrevocably in trust for his grandchildren $4,000,000 in 2002 and allocates all his $1,100,000 GST exemption to the transfer. The applicable fraction is 1,100,000 ÷ 4,000,000, or .275. The inclusion ratio is 1 minus .275, or .725. The maximum estate tax rate, 50 percent, is applied against the inclusion ratio, .725. The resulting percentage, 36.3 percent, is applied against the value of the property transferred, $4,000,000, to produce a GSTT of $1,452,000.

[3] In 2002 and 2003, the generation-skipping exemption is $1,100,000 (subject to indexing for inflation). From 2004 to 2009, the generation-skipping exemption is the same as the federal estate tax unified credit equivalent. As with the federal estate tax, in 2010 the generation-skipping transfer tax is repealed for one year. In 2011, the generation-skipping exemption reverts back to $1,100,000 (subject to indexing for inflation). See table, Phase-In and Sunset Provisions of EGTRRA 2001, pages 88-89. This exemption can be elected on the gift tax return of the transferor, or on the estate tax return if claimed on a bequest. There is no GSTT imposed on direct skip gifts that come within the annual gift tax exclusion (see chart on page 49) or that are "qualified transfers." In general, qualified transfers are payments for the education or medical care of a skip person. Special rules apply to transfers in trusts such as the irrevocable life insurance trust (see footnote 8 below).

[4] Since it also applies to taxable distributions and terminations, it is not possible to use a trust to avoid application of the GSTT. A taxable *distribution* may occur with a distribution from a trust to the grandchild of the grantor. A taxable *termination* occurs upon the death of the child where a trust provides for a life income to the child with remainder to the grandchild. But, in this example, allocation of the full $1,100,000 GSTT exemption eliminates the GSTT because the inclusion ratio is zero (1 - (1,100,000 ÷ 1,100,000) = 0). For further discussion, see footnote 2 above.

[5] Because the tax paid is subject to estate taxes in the Grandparent's estate, the taxable estate is "grossed up" (e.g., using the estate tax table on page 493 the tentative tax on a $1,169,492 estate is calculated as $345,800 + (.41 x $169,492), or $415,292; the tax due is $415,292 - $345,800, or $69,492; therefore the net amount that is passed to the "B" trust is $1,169,492 - $69,492, or $1,100,000. However, with the "reverse QTIP election," all estate taxes could be deferred until the second death (see expanded discussion on page 454).

[6] Upon the second death the entire estate could be passed to the Grandchildren, but that would require payment of a GSTT in addition to the federal estate tax.

[7] This assumes that the Child's estate, often referred to as the "intervening generation's estate," would be subject to a maximum federal estate tax rate of 50 percent in 2002 (.50 x $2,200,000 = $1,100,000).

[8] Although a life insurance trust can be very effective in leveraging the GSTT exemption, application of the GSTT can be complicated. The GSTT generally applies to an irrevocable life insurance trust whenever grandchildren are trust beneficiaries. It is essential to maintain a zero inclusion ratio (see footnotes 3 and 5 above). To shelter such a trust from the GSTT, the exemption must be allocated by filing a timely gift tax return *after each gift* to the trust.

TRANSFERRING APPRECIATION

Estate planning techniques have traditionally focused on preparing for the *eventual disposition* of estate assets upon death, disability, or retirement. However, with the impact of inflation and the rapid growth of many estate assets, particularly business interests, effective planning should also include consideration of a *lifetime transfer* of these interests to children or other heirs.[1]

When adopting one or more of these estate freezing techniques, the objective is to create a freeze line beyond which *future* appreciation is transferred to another. By this means substantial value can sometimes be transferred to the next generation without being subject to estate taxes.[2]

The most popular of these techniques includes: **installment sales** where an asset is sold today in return for an income stream payable over a specified number of years; **private annuities** where property is sold in return for a promise to pay a periodic income for life; **gifts** of appreciating assets; **intentionally defective trusts** followed by gifts and installment sales; **family partnerships** which allow children to share in the partnership's growth and profits; **recapitalizations** followed by a gift of common stock; **family holding companies** which are similar to partnerships; **grantor retained income, annuity** and **unitrusts**, where a grantor places property in trust but retains rights to payments; and **remainder interest transactions** which involve the current sale of a future interest in property.

However, to take advantage of any of these techniques the transfers must take place *prior* to the appreciation. This often means that it is up to the client's advisors to motivate him to take actions that will not produce tax savings until many years in the future.

---

[1] When an estate freezing technique culminates in the *sale* of a business interest, or other estate asset, the value represented by that interest is replaced in the estate by either the proceeds of the sale, or the obligation of the purchaser, both of which are estate assets subject to taxation. Likewise, if there is a *giving* of a substantial interest, use of the available unified credit means that it effectively cannot again be used at death. In either case, the sale or giving of an asset generally shifts only *future* appreciation out of an estate. However, exceptions to this general rule are valuation discounts, private annuities and "present interest" gifts. See the chart on page 49, entitled Gifts & Split-Gifts.

[2] The impact of the special valuation provisions of Chapter 14 should be carefully evaluated when considering the transferring of estate assets. In this regard, see the discussion of estate freezes on pages 386-387. Also, see pages 86-87 for the impact of appreciation on estate taxes and page 101 for the value of making annual gifts.

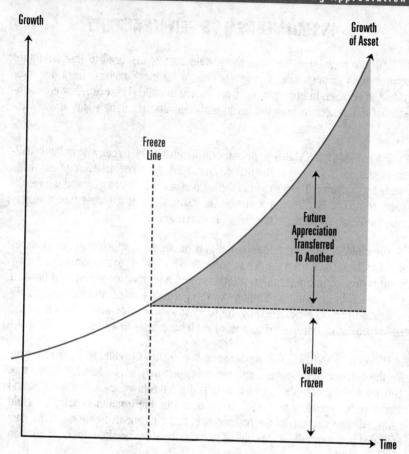

TECHNIQUES EMPLOYED TO
TRANSFER FUTURE APPRECIATION

INSTALLMENT SALE & PRIVATE ANNUITY

Both the installment sale and the private annuity are used to transfer future appreciation through sale of property (e.g., a business interest) from one individual to another, in our example, from parent to child. There are, however, substantial differences in both the tax implications and resulting rights and obligations.[1]

INSTALLMENT SALE. The primary distinguishing characteristic of the installment sale, as compared to the private annuity, is the *fixed schedule* of payments made by the buyer. The parent (as seller) can spread a large gain and the resulting income tax liability over a number of years, while at the same time transferring future appreciation to the child (as purchaser).

The child's obligation to the parent may be *secured*, which also distinguishes the installment sale from the private annuity. With respect to the parent, each payment is divided into gain, interest income, and a nontaxable recovery of basis. If the parent dies, payments continue to the parent's estate.[2] Although the child's obligation could be cancelled by the parent's executor, or passed by will to the child, previously unreported gain would still be taxable to the estate.[3]

PRIVATE ANNUITY. The private annuity obligates the child to make payments for the *lifetime* of the parent, and the obligation may not be secured in any way. Like the installment sale, each payment is divided into gain, interest income, and a nontaxable recovery of basis.[4] However, unlike the installment sale, the child cannot deduct any part of the payments. Because payments terminate at the parent's death, the annuity is considered to have no value and should escape taxation in the parent's estate.

In considering a private annuity, both parties must recognize that if the parent lives for many years, the child could end up paying more for the asset then would have been paid with an installment sale. The parent must also recognize that the expected income could be in jeopardy if the child were to die. However, providing for insurance on the child's life sufficient to meet the annuity obligation can usually eliminate this risk.

Footnotes on page 47

INSTALLMENT SALE

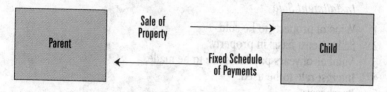

- May be secured

- Each payment is divided into gain, interest income, and a nontaxable recovery of basis

- Child deducts interest portion

- If parent dies, payments continue until obligation satisfied

PRIVATE ANNUITY

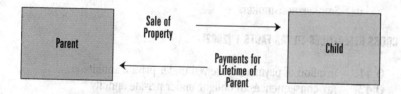

- May not be secured

- Each payment is divided into gain, interest income, and a nontaxable recovery of basis

- Child cannot deduct any part of payments

- When parent dies, payments terminate

INFORMATION REQUIRED FOR ANALYSIS & PROPOSAL

Installment Sale

1. Value of property to be sold.
2. Seller's cost basis in property.
3. Number of years payments are to be made.
4. Interest rate to be used.
5. Purchaser:
    a. Sex.
    b. Date of birth.
    c. Smoker/nonsmoker.

Private Annuity

1. Value of property.
2. Seller's cost basis in property.
3. Seller's date of birth.
4. Purchaser:
    a. Sex.
    b. Date of birth.
    c. Smoker/nonsmoker.

CROSS REFERENCES TO TAX FACTS 1 (2002)

Q 41. Taxation of payments received under private annuity.

Q 42. Tax consequences to obligor under private annuity.

Q 508. Usual private annuity results in nothing to be included in estate of annuitant (unless benefits payable to survivor).

Q 706. Nature and taxation of installment sale.

Q 813. Chapter 14 valuation rules should not negatively affect installment sales and private annuities.

Footnotes

[1] The selection of either the installment sale or the private annuity depends upon a consideration of many factors, which include: the relative income and anticipated marginal tax brackets of the parties; the age of the seller; the need for flexibility in determining payments and tax consequences; the degree of trust between the parties; and the relationship between the parties (i.e., family members or disinterested third persons).

The tax implications can be compared by summarizing the breakdown of payments and tax allocations. The following calculations assume that real estate valued at $250,000 is transferred, with a cost basis to the seller of $100,000. The installment sale calculation assumes payments are made over a period of years approximating the seller's life expectancy and uses 5.46 percent interest (the January 2002 long-term applicable federal rate). The private annuity calculation uses 5.4 percent interest (the January 2002 Section 7520 applicable federal rate). See *ASRS*, Sec. 57, ¶150.

	18-Year Installment Sale	*Private Annuity To Male, Age 60*
Annual Payment	$22,162	$21,860
Taxation To Seller:		
Gain	8,333	6,198
Interest Income	8,273	11,508
Nontaxable Recovery Of Basis	5,556	4,153
Taxation To Purchaser:		
Interest Expense	8,273	-0-
Nondeductible Capital Expenditure	13,889	21,860

Note that such comparisons are heavily influenced by the assumed interest rate and the duration of the installment sale, as well as the age of the seller, who is also the annuitant in the private annuity arrangement.

[2] Use of an installment sale to purchase part or all of a business, or other property interest, after the owner's death offers little or no tax advantage to the estate. Because of the stepped-up basis, the estate will usually have no taxable gain, and thus no tax reason to spread gain over a period of years. In fact, reliance on the installment sale could be to the detriment of the estate and the heirs if the purchaser fails to make the agreed payments. Provided the business owner is insurable, funding a buyout agreement with life insurance is generally far better than an installment sale. If an installment sale is used, life insurance on the purchaser's life will assure that, if the purchaser dies, funds are available to make the required payments.

[3] The cancellation of an obligation between "related" parties (i.e., parent and child) will result in the seller, or his estate, having to recognize gain in an amount equal to the difference between the fair market value of the obligation on the date of cancellation and the seller's basis in the obligation. Passing a note by will to the purchaser is treated as a cancellation. There is no stepped-up basis, since this is "income in respect a decedent," or IRD (see footnote 6 on page 21, and page 402). See the expanded discussion of Self-Cancelling Installment Notes (SCINs) on page 465.

[4] Any gain to the parent will be a capital gain if the asset qualifies for capital gain treatment. In this regard, see the discussion of the Capital Gains on page 350. Recovery of basis and gain is spread equally over a period of years measured by the parent's life expectancy. After this period, each annuity payment will be entirely interest income.

GIFTS & SPLIT-GIFTS

Making gifts on a regular basis is an estate planning tool which can reduce estate taxes while avoiding gift tax liability.[1]

INDIVIDUAL GIFTS. To illustrate, assume that a donor has money that is not needed for his own support. Under the federal gift tax provisions, an individual may give – under most circumstances – up to $11,000 per person, as indexed in 2002 for inflation, annually free of gift tax.[2] Thus, with three children the donor could give each of them $11,000 per year.[3] This per-donee exclusion is allowed each and every year, but it is *not cumulative* (i.e., an exclusion unused in any year may not be "carried over" to the following year).

In order for the gift to be one that qualifies for the annual exclusion, it must be a *present interest gift*: the donee must be entitled to its immediate use and enjoyment.[4] If within the year the donor makes only present-interest gifts, and gifts do not exceed a total of $11,000 per donee, the donor will *not* be required to file a gift tax return for that year and – under most circumstances – have no further income, gift or estate tax consequences from the gift.[5] Likewise, the gift is not included in the donee's taxable income.

SPLIT-GIFTS. With split-gifts the spouse joins in making the gift, and this allows a married couple to increase their gifts to $22,000 per year to each donee. This can be done without tax consequences, provided it is a present interest gift. The funds could still be entirely either the husband's or the wife's, but by having a spouse join in making each gift, they are able to double the amount of their tax-free gifts. However, in order to claim the benefits of these provisions of the law, they must file a gift tax return.[6] Gift taxes, if any, are normally paid by the donor.[7]

Present interest gifts that qualify for the annual exclusion are particularly attractive in reducing the donor's estate, since they will: (1) avoid the gift tax; and (2) likely be excluded from his estate for federal estate tax purposes no matter how soon death occurs after making the gift (e.g., the day after or even the moment after the gift is made).[8]

Footnotes on page 51

INDIVIDUAL GIFTS

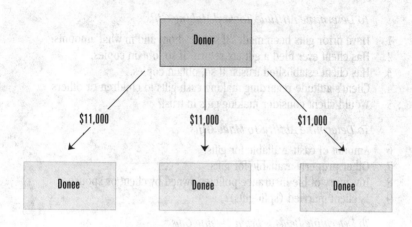

SPLIT-GIFTS

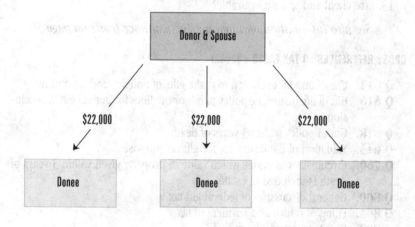

INFORMATION REQUIRED FOR ANALYSIS & PROPOSAL

To Determine Attitude Toward Making Gifts

1. Have prior gifts been made? If so, to whom and in what amounts?
2. Has client ever filed a gift tax return? If so, obtain copies.
3. Has client established trusts? If so, obtain copies.
4. Client's attitude regarding making cash gifts to children or others.
5. Would client consider making gifts in trust?

To Determine Ability To Make Gifts

6. Amount of cash available for gifts.
7. Other property available for gifts.
8. Inventory of life insurance policies owned by client or spouse.
9. Is client married (split-gifts)?

To Determine Benefits From Making Gifts

10. Numbers and ages of children and grandchildren.
11. Size of estate (i.e., to determine if currently subject to estate taxes).
12. Anticipated rate of estate growth (see Taxflation chart, page 23).
13. Are client and spouse insurable?

See also information required for life insurance trusts on page 58.

CROSS REFERENCES TO TAX FACTS 1 (2002)

Q 612. Use of annual exclusion to make gifts of policies and premiums.

Q 616. Gift of life insurance policy to minor qualifies for annual gift tax exclusion.

Q 618. Gift of policy within 3 years of death.

Q 643. Valuation of life insurance for gift tax purposes.

Q 760. Circumstances under which value of property given within 3 years of death is included in estate.

Q 800. General discussion of federal gift tax.

Q 801. Filing of return and payment of tax.

Q 802. Computation of gift tax.

Q 803. Types of gifts subject to gift tax.

Q 807. "Split-gift" provisions.

Q 809. Valuation of property for gift tax purposes.

Q 811. Valuation of net gifts (donee pays tax).

Q 817. Gift tax exclusions.

Q 818. Gifts of "future interests" which do not qualify for annual gift tax exclusion.

Q 819. Gift to minor generally qualifies for annual exclusion.

Q 820. Gift tax marital deduction.

Q 822. Unified credit and how it is applied against gift tax.

Footnotes

[1] The chart on page 53 shows that there is a potential tax savings of $94,655, assuming gifts of $11,000 per year over 10 years, an estate of $1,500,000 and an estate growth of 8 percent (see also Annual Gifts - Value of Making, on page 101). EGTRRA 2001 did not impact present interest gifts. They continue to be a highly effective estate planning tool.

[2] The annual exclusion for gifts is indexed for inflation after 1998, and was increased from $10,000 to $11,000 in 2002. This cost-of-living adjustment is the percentage, if any, by which the Consumer Price Index (CPI) for the preceding calendar year exceeds the CPI for the current calendar year (for these purposes a CPI calendar year ends August 31). However, any increases are rounded down to the next lowest multiple of $1,000.

[3] While gifts are generally discussed in a family setting, anyone can make gifts under these rules, whether the donor is a father, mother, child, distant relative, or even a benevolent stranger. In most states a gift to a minor under either the Uniform Transfers to Minors Act or the Uniform Gift to Minors Act will qualify as a present interest gift, even though the minor does not have legal capacity to make demands upon the custodian (see Minors And Life Insurance on page 425). The irrevocable life insurance trust offers an excellent means of taking advantage of the yearly opportunity to make present interest gifts through annual gifts to the trust for premium payments (see chart, page 57).

[4] When a gift is made late in the year in the form of a check it should be deposited in time to clear the donor's bank by the end of the year, otherwise the gift might not be considered complete until the following year. Payments made directly for medical or educational bills are not considered gifts for gift tax purposes, and therefore are not subject to gift taxes (the funds should be paid to the provider of medical services or the educational institution, not to the donee). Gifts to a charity can qualify for the gift tax charitable deduction (see discussion regarding charitable gifts of life insurance, page 352, and charitable remainder trust chart, page 61).

[5] Although the donee is not liable for income taxes upon receiving the gift, if the property is subsequently sold the donee would be liable for reporting and paying taxes on any gain realized from the sale. For the purpose of calculating gain the donee's income tax basis is generally the same as the donor's basis in the property, often referred to as a "substituted" basis.

[6] The gift tax return, Form 709, must be filed by the donor on or before April 15 following the close of the calendar year in which the donor makes the gift, except that an extension of time granted for filing the income tax return serves also as an extension of time for filing the gift tax return (see first pages of the gift tax return and instructions for filing the gift tax return, pages 490-491). In order to avoid having to file a gift tax return, one spouse could transfer funds to the other spouse, and thereafter each spouse could then make separate gifts to the trust. Only a husband and wife can take advantage of split-gifts; unmarried individuals may not.

[7] Although the donor is the party having primary liability for payment of the gift tax, a gift can be made subject to a condition that the gift tax is paid by the donee (or by the trustee if the gift is in trust). The value of the gift is reduced by the amount of the tax. In effect, the amount of the gift tax paid by the donee reduces the value of the gift and the gift tax liability. This net gift technique can be useful when the donor desires to transfer large amounts of property, but does not have cash to pay the gift tax. However, the donor ends up in the same position whether he transfers $1,500,000 to a donee and the donee pays $500,000 in gift tax, or he transfers $1,000,000 to a donee and pays the $500,000 gift tax himself. If the donor gives property, the donor will have to recognize income to the extent any gift tax paid by the donee exceeds the donor's basis in the property.

[8] One important exception is that proceeds of a life insurance policy *transferred* from the insured within three years of the insured's death are brought back into the insured's estate. See footnote 1, page 55 concerning certain gifts made within three years of death.

GIVING – THE TAX ADVANTAGES

A systematic gift program can result in substantial tax savings. Not only are there no gift taxes on gifts of up to $11,000 per year, as indexed for inflation, to any one individual, but the value of the gift and all subsequent appreciation on the gift are removed from the donor's taxable estate.[1]

NO GIFT PROGRAM. To illustrate, assume that in 2002 we have an unmarried person with an estate currently valued at $1,500,000. If the estate grows at 8 percent over the next 10 years it will increase in value to $3,238,387.[2]

The effect of the gift and estate tax laws is to place an imaginary "Tax Line" between generations.[3] Whenever property is passed through this tax line it is generally exposed to either gift or estate taxation.[4] Assuming death in the 10th year, this $3,238,387 estate will be subject to $1,076,113 of estate taxes, leaving only $2,162,274 for the heirs.

ANNUAL GIFT PROGRAM. Under the federal gift tax provisions, an individual may give up to $11,000 per person free of gift tax, provided the gifts are given outright with no strings attached. Such gifts will qualify for the gift tax annual exclusion, meaning that they pass through the tax line free of gift taxes. Now assume this same individual establishes a gift program under which he gives $11,000 each year to a child.[5]

If the estate grows at 8 percent over the next 10 years it will increase in value to $3,066,287. This is less than with "no gift program" because *both* the amount of the annual gifts and the appreciation on these gifts has been removed from the estate (a total of $172,100). Assuming death occurs in the 10th year the estate is subject to $981,458 of estate taxes, leaving $2,084,829 for the heirs. A total of $2,256,929 has been passed through the tax line (the $110,000 of annual gifts, the $62,100 of growth on these gifts and the $2,084,829 passed to the heirs at death).

When compared to "no gift program," the potential estate tax savings are $94,655 ($2,256,929 - $2,162,274 = $94,655). However, these savings can only be realized when there has been a systematic annual gift program. If a gift is not made during the calendar year it cannot be "carried over" to the next year (i.e., the donor cannot double-up and give $22,000 the next year).[6]

In order to "leverage" these $11,000 gifts, the donor should consider establishing an irrevocable life insurance trust. Tax-free gifts can be made to the trust for the purpose of purchasing life insurance that will provide estate tax-free death benefits.[7]

Footnotes on page 55

NO GIFT PROGRAM

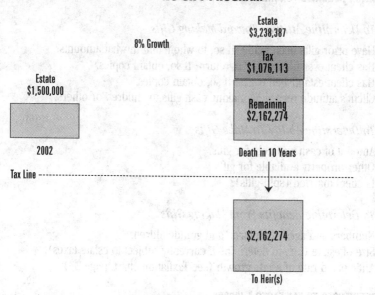

Estate
$3,238,387

8% Growth

Tax
$1,076,113

Estate
$1,500,000

Remaining
$2,162,274

2002

Death in 10 Years

Tax Line -

$2,162,274

To Heir(s)

ANNUAL GIFT PROGRAM

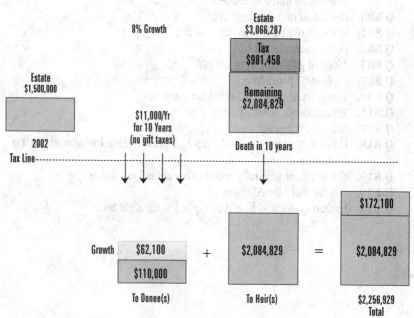

Potential Tax Savings: $94,655

Estate
$3,066,287

8% Growth

Tax
$981,458

Estate
$1,500,000

Remaining
$2,084,829

$11,000/Yr
for 10 Years
(no gift taxes)

2002

Death in 10 years

Tax Line -

$172,100

Growth $62,100   + $2,084,829   = $2,084,829

$110,000

To Donee(s)   To Heir(s) $2,256,929
                                                 Total

INFORMATION REQUIRED FOR ANALYSIS & PROPOSAL

To Determine Attitude Toward Making Gifts

1. Have prior gifts been made? If so, to whom and in what amounts?
2. Has client ever filed a gift tax return? If so, obtain copies.
3. Has client established trusts? If so, obtain copies.
4. Client's attitude regarding making cash gifts to children or others.

To Determine Ability To Make Gifts

5. Amount of cash available for gifts.
6. Other property available for gifts.
7. Is client married (split-gifts)?

To Determine Benefits From Making Gifts

8. Numbers and ages of children and grandchildren.
9. Size of estate (i.e., to determine if currently subject to estate taxes).
10. Anticipated rate of estate growth (see Taxflation chart, page 23).

CROSS REFERENCES TO TAX FACTS 1 (2002)

Q 760. Circumstances under which value of property given within 3 years of death is included in estate.

Q 800. Definition of federal gift tax.

Q 801. Filing of return and payment of tax.

Q 802. Computation of gift tax.

Q 803. Types of gifts subject to gift tax.

Q 807. "Split-gift" provisions.

Q 809. Valuation of property for gift tax purposes.

Q 811. Valuation of net gifts (donee pays tax).

Q 817. Gift tax exclusions.

Q 818. Gifts of "future interests" which do not qualify for annual gift tax exclusion.

Q 819. Gift to minor generally qualifies for annual exclusion.

Q 820. Gift tax marital deduction.

Q 822. Unified credit and how it is applied against gift tax.

Footnotes

[1] Under some limited circumstances the full *date-of-death value* of a gift will be included in the estate of the donor who dies within three years of making a gift. Included are: (a) transfers with retained life interests; (b) transfers taking effect at death with reversionary interests retained; (c) transfers with powers retained to revoke or amend; (d) relinquishment of retained interests within three years of death; and (e) transfers of life insurance on the donor's life. The date-of-death value of gifts within three years of death is also used for the purpose of determining the estate's qualification for a Section 303 stock redemption, current use valuation, and property subject to estate tax liens.

[2] In 2012, this estate will be taxed at a 55 percent federal estate tax rate. Under EGTRRA 2001, the maximum rate will be 50 percent in 2002, 49 percent in 2003, 48 percent in 2004, 47 percent in 2005, 46 percent in 2006, 45 percent in 2007-2009, suspended in 2010, and 55 percent in 2011 and thereafter. To better understand the impact that appreciation can have, refer to the Taxflation chart, on page 23.

[3] In fact, except as between husband and wife, this imaginary tax line generally limits the amount of property that can be passed during lifetime or at death between any two persons. The marital deduction allows unlimited amounts of property to be passed between husband and wife during lifetime or at death (see page 419). However, the marital deduction is limited if the surviving spouse is a noncitizen (see pages 426 and 442).

[4] This exposure has been altered as a result of EGTRRA 2001. For example, rather than increasing in steps from $700,000 to $1,000,000 during the period 2002 to 2006, for estate tax purposes the unified credit equivalent will increase in steps from $1,000,000 to $3,500,000 during the period 2002 to 2009. For gift tax purposes, the unified credit equivalent (footnote 6, page 21) will increase to $1,000,000 in 2002, and remain level thereafter. In 2010, the estate tax is repealed for one year, only to resume again in 2011, with a unified credit equivalent of $1,000,000. See also the table, Phase-In and Sunset Provisions of EGTRRA 2001, pages 88-89.

[5] This chart demonstrates only annual present interest gifts (see chart, Gifts & Split-Gifts, on page 49). The taxes saved will depend upon the size of the estate (see table, at page 101, setting forth the value of making annual gifts). However, with the unified credit, $1,000,000 of property can be given away in 2002 without paying a gift tax. Unfortunately, the substantive and sunset provisions of EGTRRA 2001 complicate any analysis and decision to make even larger gifts that may trigger payment of a gift tax. These provisions of EGTRRA 2001 include changes in the rates of tax, as well as future increases in the unified credit available to estates, but not available for gifts prior to death (e.g., in 2003 only $1,000,000 can be given tax-free, whereas in 2004 $1,500,000 can be passed at death free of estate taxes). Any decision must also be made in light of the provisions that provide for repeal of the estate tax in 2010, followed by a reversion in 2011 to the law as it generally existed prior to EGTRRA 2001. See pages 88-89, Phase-In and Sunset Provisions of EGTRRA 2001. Despite these uncertainties, under some circumstances and assumptions, giving more than $1,000,000 of property and paying a gift tax could be advantageous for taxpayers who have larger estates, *provided* the donor lives for more than three years after having made the gift. See page 395 for an example of the savings opportunities.

[6] Giving also offers *income tax* advantages if income-producing property is given to a donee in a lower income tax bracket than the donor. The resulting increase in after-tax income can be put to many uses, including the purchase of needed life insurance on the life of the donor.

[7] The amount of the prior annual exclusion gifts to the trust will not be included in the estate, even if death should occur within 3 years of making the gift. If other than annual exclusion gifts are made to the trust, the estate could be pushed into higher estate tax brackets. Insurance purchased by another individual is not include in the insured's estate even when death occurs within three years (e.g., the trustee obtains insurance as applicant, owner and beneficiary). See chart, page 57, and pages 388-389 for an expanded discussion.

LIFE INSURANCE TRUST

The trust is one of the most basic tools of estate planning. When made *irrevocable* and funded with life insurance, it accomplishes multiple objectives. For example, it can:

- Provide Income for a Family
- Provide Funds for Estate Settlement Costs
- Avoid Increasing Estate Taxes
- Avoid Probate Costs
- Provide for Management of Assets
- Maintain Confidentiality
- Take Advantage of Gift Tax Laws
- Help Create a Minimal Drain on Present Funds

DURING LIFETIME, it is possible for a grantor to establish a trust that will eventually accomplish all of these objectives. The beneficiaries of such a trust are normally members of the grantor's family and likely to be estate beneficiaries.[1]

Once the trust is created, policies on the life of the grantor can be given to the trust. If no such policies are available, then the trustee would obtain the needed life insurance.[2] In either case, funds are given to the trust, which, in turn, pays the premiums to the insurance company.

In order to take full advantage of the gift tax laws, the beneficiaries must have a limited right to demand the value of any gifts made to the trust each year.[3] However, in order not to defeat the purpose of the trust, the beneficiaries should not exercise this right to demand. In this way, each year up to $10,000 per beneficiary, as indexed for inflation, can be given tax-free to the trust.[4]

UPON DEATH, the grantor's property passes to his estate. At the same time, the insurance company also pays a death benefit to the trust. If the policies have been purchased by the trustee, or if the grantor has lived for over 3 years after having given the insurance to the trust, the death benefit will be received free of federal estate taxes.[5]

There are basically two ways the trustee can make these funds available for payment of estate settlement costs. The trust either **makes loans** to the estate, or the estate **sells assets** to the trust. In any event, guided by specific will and trust provisions the beneficiaries can receive distributions of **income** and **property**.[6]

Footnotes on page 59

DURING LIFETIME

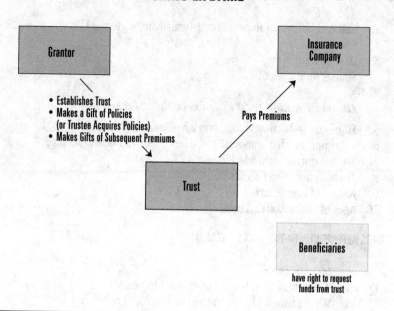

Grantor

- Establishes Trust
- Makes a Gift of Policies
  (or Trustee Acquires Policies)
- Makes Gifts of Subsequent Premiums

Insurance
Company

Pays Premiums

Trust

Beneficiaries

have right to request
funds from trust

UPON DEATH

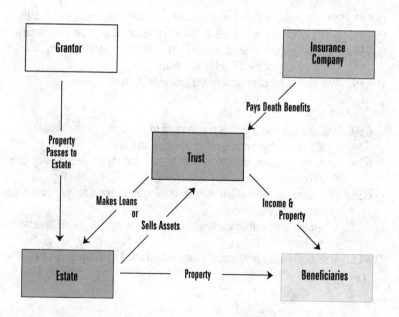

Grantor

Insurance
Company

Pays Death Benefits

Property
Passes to
Estate

Trust

Makes Loans
or
Sells Assets

Income &
Property

Estate

Property

Beneficiaries

INFORMATION REQUIRED FOR ANALYSIS & PROPOSAL

1. Name of individual to be insured (usually trust grantor).
2. Sex.
3. Date of birth.
4. Smoker/nonsmoker.

Attorney Drafting Trust Instrument Must Also Know

5. To whom, in what amounts, and when trust income is to be paid.
6. To whom, in what amounts, and when trust corpus is to be paid.
7. Trustee during insured's lifetime.
8. Trustee after insured's death.
9. Names of beneficiaries.
10. Ages of minor beneficiaries.

CROSS REFERENCES TO TAX FACTS 1 (2002)

Income Tax

Q 261. When income of funded trust taxed to grantor.
Q 264. When income taxable to trust or to trust beneficiaries.
Q 266. Death proceeds received by trust free of income taxes.

Estate Tax

Q 551. When proceeds either included or excluded from insured's estate.
Q 553. When value of trust assets included in estate of income beneficiary.
Q 554. Insurance proceeds included in insured's estate when trustee required to pay estate debts and taxes.
Q 555. Transfer of income-producing property to trust.

Gift Tax

Q 619. Value of gift when policy transferred to trust.
Q 624. Qualification for annual gift tax exclusion.
Q 625. Annual exclusion and irrevocable trust for minor beneficiary (Sec. 2503(c)).
Q 626. Qualification for annual exclusion of gifts to trust to pay premiums (Crummey rules).
Q 627. When lapse of withdrawal right can result in gift from one beneficiary to another beneficiary.
Q 814. Irrevocable life insurance trusts not affected by Chapter 14 valuation rules.

Footnotes

[1] Just as the surviving spouse is often made a beneficiary of the family trust under the exemption trust will ("B" trust on page 29), the surviving spouse can also be made a beneficiary and given "present interest" demand powers under the irrevocable life insurance trust (see footnote 4 below).

[2] During the insured's lifetime the trustee is typically an individual other than the grantor who: (1) takes possession of the life insurance policies; (2) applies for a taxpayer identification number using IRS form SS-4, Application for Employer Identification Number; (3) opens a checking account; (4) receives funds placed in the trust; (5) notifies beneficiaries of their right to make demands of these funds; and (6) pays premiums as they come due. It is usually advisable for a corporate trustee to be named at the insured's death. The new trustee then administers the life insurance proceeds according to the trust provisions.

[3] With respect to a demand power, the IRS has taken the position that the annual exclusion is available only when the powerholder is a *primary* trust beneficiary who has a substantial economic interest in the trust (e.g., child of the insured who stands to receive distributions from the trust). However, a Tax Court case has held that a powerholder who is a beneficiary with only a *contingent remainder interest* would also qualify for the annual exclusion (e.g., grandchild would only take under the trust if his parent, who is the primary beneficiary, were deceased).

[4] The *right* to demand qualifies gifts for the annual exclusion as "present interest" gifts. Where there is more than one trust beneficiary this power is often limited to the greater of $5,000 or 5 percent of the trust corpus (often referred to as a "5-or-5" power). This right is considered a general power of appointment. When the beneficiary fails to exercise a general power of appointment, the "lapse" is deemed a non present interest gift from that beneficiary to the other trust beneficiaries to the extent that the property with respect to which the power lapsed exceeds the greater of $5,000 or 5 percent of the trust corpus. Such "gifts" *between beneficiaries* will result in an unnecessary utilization by the beneficiaries of their unified credit, or even payment of gift taxes. When premiums exceed $5,000 times the number of trust beneficiaries, one means of avoiding a lapse of the beneficiary's power of withdrawal is to use a *"hanging" Crummey power*. With this provision the beneficiary's entire power of withdrawal does not terminate within a specified period of time, but rather the beneficiary retains and accumulates his rights to demand gifts to the trust in excess of the "5-or-5" limit ($5,000, or 5 percent of the trust corpus, whichever is greater). Such accumulations of future rights of withdrawal (i.e., the hanging powers) give beneficiaries the right to demand distribution of prior gifts which exceeded the "5-or-5" limits. If in a future year the grantor makes no gifts to the trust, these accumulated powers lapse within the limits of the "5-or-5" power. The building up of substantial cash values would accelerate the lapse of these accumulated powers, since each beneficiary would have the right to demand the *greater of* $5,000, or 5 percent of the trust corpus (e.g., 5 percent of $150,000 in cash values is $7,500, and this is substantially more than $5,000). The *testamentary power of appointment* provides another means of avoiding the lapse of amounts in excess of $5,000 or 5 percent. Under such an arrangement, amounts exceeding $5,000 or 5 percent "partially lapse" to a limited testamentary power of appointment in favor of a designated class of beneficiaries (typically, the power holder's heirs). If the power is not exercised in the holder's will, then the amounts subject to the power vest in the trust. However, the amounts subject to this power are likely to be included in the holder's estate. The *cumulative power of appointment* is another technique used to avoid this problem (see page 367 for an additional discussion of present interest gifts).

[5] Provided the policy is purchased by another person, including a trustee, it now appears certain that, provided the proceeds are payable outside the estate, the death benefits of a life insurance contract will be excluded from the insured's estate no matter when death occurs (see the discussion on pages 388-389).

[6] There may also be provisions in both the trust and the grantor's will which provide for a merging of the trust and estate assets, with subsequent management of the combined assets for the beneficiaries. These are often referred to as "pourover" provisions.

CHARITABLE REMAINDER TRUST

The charitable remainder trust enables an individual to make a substantial deferred gift to a favored charity while retaining a right to payments from the trust. Under the right circumstances use of such a trust offers multiple tax and nontax advantages, particularly to the individual who owns substantially appreciated property. These advantages include a charitable deduction resulting in reduced taxes, an increase in current cash flow, avoidance of capital gains upon a sale of the appreciated property, the eventual reduction or elimination of estate taxes, and the satisfaction of knowing that property placed in the trust will eventually pass to charity. When combined with a wealth replacement trust the full value of the estate can still be preserved for heirs.

DURING LIFETIME the grantor, after establishing a charitable remainder trust, gives property to the trust while retaining a right to payments from the trust.[1] A **unitrust** would provide for the grantor to receive annually a fixed *percentage* of the trust value (valued annually), whereas an **annuity trust** would provide for the grantor to receive annually a fixed *amount*.[2] Either type of trust could require that payments be made for the joint lives of the grantor and another person, such as the grantor's spouse.

At the time the property is given to the trust, the grantor can claim a current income tax deduction equal to the present value of the charity's remainder interest.[3] Upon receipt of the gift, the trustee will often sell the appreciated property and reinvest the proceeds in order to better provide the cash flow required to make the payments to the grantor. This sale by the trust is usually free of any capital gains tax.[4]

The tax savings and increased cash flow offered by the use of a charitable remainder trust will often enable the grantor to use some or all of these savings to fund a **wealth replacement trust** for the benefit of his heirs, thereby providing for the tax effective replacement of property which had been transferred to the charitable remainder trust. If the wealth replacement trust is established as an irrevocable life insurance trust it is often possible to gain gift tax advantages during the grantor's lifetime, while at death entirely avoiding inclusion of the life insurance proceeds in the estates of the grantor and his spouse.[5]

UPON DEATH the property placed in the charitable remainder trust passes to the designated charity. At the same time a tax-free death benefit is paid to the wealth replacement trust, which funds can then be paid as income or corpus to the grantor's heirs pursuant to the terms of this trust.

Footnotes on page 63

DURING LIFETIME

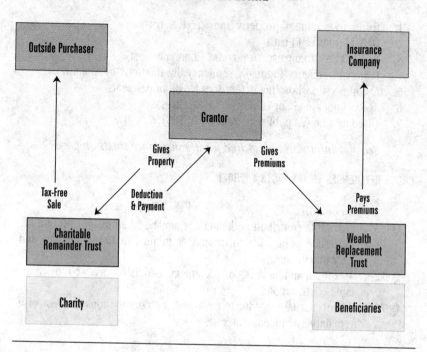

UPON DEATH

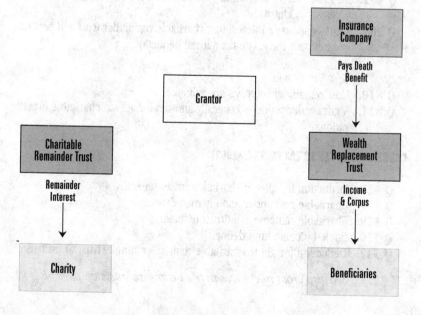

INFORMATION REQUIRED FOR ANALYSIS & PROPOSAL

1. Fair market value of property transferred to trust.
2. Date of transfer to trust.
3. Payout rate (if unitrust) or amount (if annuity trust).
4. Payment frequency (annually, semiannually, quarterly, or monthly).
5. Age of person whose life determines length of payments.
6. Age of joint annuitant (if payout for two lives).
7. Discount rate (as published monthly by IRS).

See also information required for life insurance trusts on page 58.

CROSS REFERENCES TO TAX FACTS 1 (2002)

Income Tax

Q 107. Charitable contribution deductions may be taken for the gift of a life insurance policy, life insurance premiums, maturing annuity, and endowment contract.

Q 723. Maximum annual limits on income tax deductions allowed for charitable contributions.

Q 724. When charitable deduction allowed for contributions in trust of a remainder or income interest.

Estate Tax

Q 763. An estate tax deduction is generally allowed for the full amount of bequests to charity.

Q 764. Value of spouse's interest in a charitable remainder trust will generally qualify for the estate tax marital deduction.

Gift Tax

Q 810. How remainder interests are valued.

Q 821. A gift tax deduction is generally allowed for gifts to charitable organizations.

CROSS REFERENCES TO TAX FACTS 2 (2002)

Q 327. Deduction for gifts to charitable trusts generally.
Q 328. Charitable remainder annuity trust defined.
Q 329. Charitable remainder unitrust defined.
Q 330. Pooled income fund defined.
Q 332. Deduction for gift to charitable remainder annuity trust or unitrust.

See also cross references to life insurance trusts on page 58.

Footnotes

[1] The term "grantor" is used to describe a person who establishes a trust, whereas the term "donor" is used to describe a person who makes a gift. For simplicity, only the term "grantor" has been used in describing the charitable remainder trust.

[2] Characteristics common to both unitrusts and annuity trusts are: (1) payments must be made at least annually and may not be less than 5 percent, nor more than 50 percent, of the net fair market value of the trust assets (determined when trust is created with an annuity; determined annually with a unitrust); (2) value of charity's remainder must be at least 10 percent of trust assets; (3) the trustee cannot be required to invest in specific assets (e.g., stock in a corporation or life insurance); and (4) payments may be for a term not greater than 20 years, or for the life or lives of the beneficiary(ies). Any individual beneficiary must be living when the trust is created.

[3] Selection of a payout rate can have a substantial impact upon the current income tax deduction (i.e., the present value of the charitable remainder interest). If the deduction is to be meaningful, the payout rate is usually limited to 7 percent or less. For example, assuming a $100,000 gift to a charitable remainder unitrust to be paid for the beneficiary's life, the following table illustrates the interrelationship of the beneficiary's age and the selected payment percentage:

Age of Beneficiary	Payout	Deduction
50	5%	27,229
	10%	10,344
60	5%	39,034
	10%	18,852
70	5%	52,843
	10%	31,362

[4] With gifts of long-term capital gain property the full present value of the remainder interest is deductible if the property is intangibles or real estate. Tangible personal property is not appropriate.

Whether the deduction can be taken in a particular year depends upon the application of three percentage limitations that relate to the taxpayer's "contribution base" (i.e., adjusted gross income computed without regard to net operating loss carryback). These limits depend upon whether the gift is to a public charity or a private foundation (see page 436); and whether the gift is one of either cash or ordinary income property, or a gift of long-term capital gain property. The deduction cannot usually exceed the following percentages of the taxpayer's contribution base:

	Cash or Ordinary Income Property	Long-Term Capital Gain Property
Public Charities	50%	30%
Private Foundations	30%	20%

If the gift is made to a public charity there is a five-year carryover of any unused deduction.

A charitable remainder trust (CRT) that has unrelated business income (UBI) is subject to income taxation on all of its income. Generally, UBI is the net income from the conduct of a trade or business that is not substantially related to the exempt purpose of the CRT. Income from property that is debt-financed and not related to the exempt function of the CRT is generally considered UBI. However, debt-financed income is excluded from UBI for the first ten years following transfer to the CRT if the debt had been placed on the property more than five years prior to the transfer.

[5] The "wealth replacement trust" is another name for an irrevocable life insurance trust (see chart on page 57). For an expanded discussion of the gift and estate tax ramifications of an irrevocable life insurance trust, see the discussion on page 56. Funding with survivorship life insurance can be particularly attractive (see page 475).

PRIVATE SPLIT-DOLLAR

Whereas a traditional split-dollar plan involves an employer and an employee, a private split-dollar plan is an agreement between individuals, or between an individual and a trust.[1] A private split-dollar plan enables an insured to *both* have the policy cash values available for emergency and retirement purposes and exclude life insurance proceeds from his estate. For example, assume that a married couple wishes to establish a private split-dollar plan.[2]

DURING LIFETIME. The individual who will become the insured establishes an irrevocable life insurance trust with his spouse and children as trust beneficiaries.[3] The trustee then applies for a life insurance policy on his life and enters into a collateral assignment split-dollar agreement with the spouse.[4] This agreement provides for the sharing of both premiums and death benefits between the spouse and the trust. However, the spouse owns all cash values and retains the sole right to borrow against or withdraw policy cash valves. By this means the insured has indirect access to the cash values.[5]

The trust's share of the premium is equal to the "economic benefit" of the death benefit payable to the trust.[6] To fund the trust's portion of the premium, the insured makes annual gifts to the trust. These will qualify as "present interest" gifts provided the trust beneficiaries have Crummey withdrawal powers.[7]

The spouse pays the balance of the premium. These funds either come from the spouse's separate property or are given by the insured to his spouse free of any gift tax liability (i.e., the marital deduction enables married persons to pass unlimited amounts of property to each other during lifetime or upon death free of gift or estate taxes).[8]

Prior to or during retirement the spouse can access policy cash values free of income taxes through withdrawals or loans against the policy.[9]

UPON DEATH. The death benefit payable to the spouse is the greater of the total premiums paid by the spouse or the policy cash values (less any outstanding loans). The trust receives the balance of the death benefit. Since the insured had no incidents of ownership in the policy, none of the death benefit is included in his estate.[10] Guided by the specific provisions of the trust, these estate tax-free proceeds are used to pay trust income and principal to the trust beneficiaries.

Footnotes on page 67

DURING LIFETIME

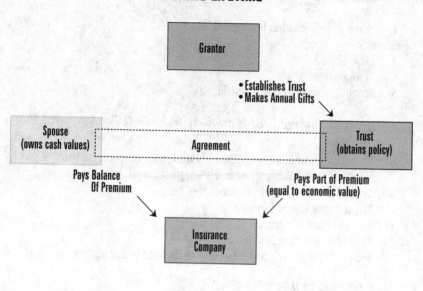

UPON DEATH

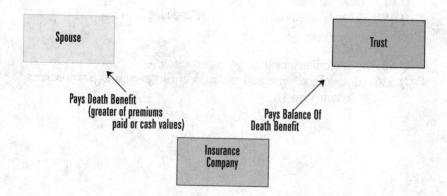

INFORMATION REQUIRED FOR ANALYSIS & PROPOSAL

1. Name of individual to be insured.
2. Sex.
3. Date of birth.
4. Smoker/nonsmoker.
5. Amount of desired death benefit.

   Attorney Drafting Trust Instrument And Split-Dollar Agreement Must Also Know

6. To whom, in what amounts, and when trust income is to be paid.
7. To whom, in what amounts, and when trust corpus is to be paid.
8. Trustee during insured's lifetime.
9. Trustee after insured's death.
10. Names of beneficiaries.
11. Ages of minor beneficiaries.
12. Name of spouse who will be a party to the split-dollar agreement.

CROSS REFERENCES TO TAX FACTS 1 (2002)

Split-Dollar
Q 266. Death proceeds received by trust free of income taxes.
Q 425. Description of split-dollar.
Q 427. Income tax consequences of transfer or "rollout" of split-dollar policy.
Q 429. Description of private split-dollar and how it is taxed.

Estate Tax
Q 515. Estate taxation of split-dollar.
Q 551. When proceeds either included or excluded from insured's estate.

Gift Tax
Q 624. Qualification for annual gift tax exclusion.
Q 626. Qualification for annual exclusion of gifts to trust to pay premiums (Crummey rules).

Footnotes

[1] Authority for traditional split-dollar plans in an employer and employer relationship is derived from numerous revenue rulings dating back to the 1960's. In contrast, it was not until 1996 that private letter rulings, which only apply to the taxpayer requesting the ruling, began to provide positive guidance on how to structure a private split-dollar plan. Under these circumstances, it would be wise to seek the advice of qualified tax counsel when adopting a private split-dollar plan. In regard to the weight to be given revenue rulings and private letter rulings, see page 477.

[2] When involving family members, such an arrangement is also referred to as "family split-dollar" (and incorrectly referred to as private "reverse" split-dollar).

[3] This trust would be similar to that shown in the chart on page 57. Private split-dollar involving both an irrevocable life insurance trust and a split-dollar plan requires a great deal of planning, implementation and ongoing administration. If estate tax-free death benefits are important but access to cash values is unimportant, then third party ownership or an irrevocable life insurance trust should be considered (see chart, page 57). On the other hand, if access to cash values is important but estate tax-free death benefits are unimportant, then the insured might better own the policy (see the discussion of life insurance as property on page 72).

[4] Alternatively, the spouse and trustee could obtain the insurance through joint application and ownership, resulting in a form of endorsement split-dollar. An expanded discussion of collateral assignment and endorsement split-dollar is contained in footnote 2, page 167.

[5] A stable marriage and confidence in the noninsured spouse is essential. Other less attractive alternatives involve having the cash values owned by a QTIP trust, adult child, S corporation or a limited partnership.

[6] In the past, this "economic benefit" was measured by using either the insurer's one-year term rates or the P.S. 58 rates (see page 496). Under IRS Notice 2002-8, it appears that the P.S. 58 rates can continue to be used for private split-dollar plans established prior to January 28, 2002. Plans established on or after that date should use the Table 2001 rates as first set forth in IRS Notice 2001-10. See note on page 496.

[7] For an expanded discussion of Crummey withdrawal powers see page 367. As the insured gets older the trust's portion of the premium will increase substantially, particularly if the insured lives past age 80. If the spouse is also a trust beneficiary, failure of the trust to pay its portion of the premium could be considered a gift by the spouse to the trust with a retained life interest. This would cause a portion of death proceeds to be included in the *spouse's* estate (see discussion of retained life estate on page 389). To avoid imputed gifts from the spouse to the trust, the trust must continue paying for any death benefits it receives (even if premiums are not currently being paid). If the trust's portion of the premium exceeds the amount that can be qualified as a present interest gift to the trust, then a portion of the gift becomes taxable and the insured must either use some of his unified credit or pay gift taxes. Attempts to avoid these problems have involved: (1) establishing a trust-owned premium prepayment account; and (2) reducing in later years the death benefit paid to the trust.

[8] The marital deduction is more fully discussed on page 419.

[9] To avoid income taxation, withdrawals are made up to the spouse's income tax basis in the policy. Thereafter, loans could be taken against the policy (see page 424).

[10] If the spouse dies *before* the insured and the spouse's interests in the policy cash values pass in any way that cause the insured to have an incident of ownership in the policy, upon his subsequent death the death proceeds will be included in his estate. This means that the insured cannot be a trustee of a trust holding the policy, nor can he act as executor of the deceased spouse's estate if the policy is part of the estate. See discussion of incidents ownership on page 388.

INTENTIONALLY DEFECTIVE TRUST

The intentionally defective trust is a wealth-transferring device used by larger estates. It is an irrevocable trust that has been carefully drafted to cause the grantor to be taxed on trust income, yet have trust assets excluded from the grantor's estate.[1] Once established, it can offer multiple planning opportunities and benefits, particularly when combined with both gifts and installment sales.[2]

TRUST ESTABLISHED. When establishing the trust, the grantor will typically retain a right to substitute assets of equivalent value. Retention of this right in a nonfiduciary capacity violates one of the grantor trust rules.[3] The grantor is then considered the "owner" of the trust for income tax purposes, but not for estate, gift, and generation-skipping tax purposes. As to income taxes, the grantor and the trust are considered one and the same; trust income, deductions, and credits are passed through to the grantor.

Once established, the grantor then makes a gift of cash or other liquid assets to the trust, equal in value to 10 percent or more of the value of the property that will be sold to the trust in the subsequent installment sale.[4]

INSTALLMENT SALE. Thereafter, the grantor and the trustee enter into a sales agreement providing for the purchase of additional assets from the grantor at fair market value. Under this agreement the trustee gives the grantor an installment note providing for payment of interest only for a number of years, followed by a balloon payment of principal at the end of the term.[5] The assets sold will typically consist of property subject to a valuation discount (e.g., a non-controlling interest in a limited partnership, a limited liability company, or an S corporation).[6] The amount of this valuation discount is immediately removed from the grantor's estate.[7]

SUBSEQUENT ADVANTAGES. Payment of taxes by the grantor upon the trust income enables the trust to grow income tax-free, and is a tax-free gift from the grantor to the trust beneficiaries. The interest and principal payments by the trust are "tax neutral," meaning that they have no income tax consequences for either the grantor or the trust. Any growth of invested trust assets is excluded from the grantor's estate.[8]

If appropriate, the trustee could also use cash flow in excess of required interest payments to purchase life insurance on the grantor. Since the grantor/insured is not the "owner" of the trust for estate tax purposes, the death proceeds would be excluded from the grantor's estate.

Footnotes on page 71

TRUST ESTABLISHED

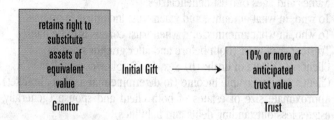

INSTALLMENT SALE

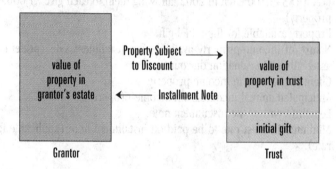

SUBSEQUENT ADVANTAGES

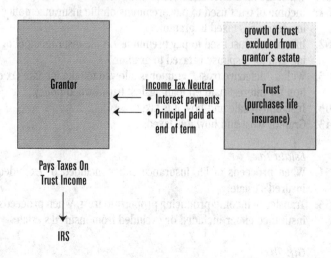

INFORMATION REQUIRED FOR ANALYSIS & PROPOSAL

1. Names and ages of trust beneficiaries.
2. To who, in what amounts, and when trust income is to be paid?
3. To who, in what amounts, and when trust corpus is to be paid?
4. Trustee(s) of trust (both before and after grantor's death).
5. Client's: (a) Date of birth; (b) Sex; (c) Smoker/nonsmoker.
6. Client's annual taxable income (to determine marginal tax bracket).
7. Approximate size of estates of both client and spouse (generally, gross estates less outstanding debts and liabilities).
8. Extent to which client and spouse have used their annual gift exclusion ($11,000 each in 2002).
9. Extent to which client and spouse have each used their available unified credit ($345,800 each in 2002, allowing them to each give $1,000,000 of property).
10. Property available for the initial gift.
11. Nature of income-property available for installment sale (preferably, an asset subject to valuation discount).
12. Client's cost basis in income-property.
13. Anticipated annual income from income-property.
14. Length (term) of the installment note.
15. Minimum interest rate to be paid on installment note (applicable federal rate).

CROSS REFERENCES TO TAX FACTS 1 (2002)

Income Tax

Q 260. When life insurance trust will provide income tax savings for grantor.

Q 261. Income of trust used to pay premiums on life insurance policy insuring grantor is taxed to grantor.

Q 262. Income of trust used to pay premiums on life insurance policy insuring grantor's spouse is taxed to grantor.

Q 265. With a "defective trust," grantor is allowed to take income tax deduction for interest paid on loan against trust-owned policy.

Q 706. Installment sale and how it is taxed.

Q 743. Grantor trust and how it is taxed.

Estate Tax

Q 551. When proceeds of life insurance either included or excluded from insured's estate.

Q 555. Transfer of income-producing property to trust. When proceeds of life insurance either included or excluded from insured's estate.

Gift Tax

Q 822. Unified credit and the gift tax.

Footnotes

[1] This trust is also referred to as a "grantor trust," or an "intentionally defective irrevocable trust (IDIT)." Historically, the inadvertent inclusion of these powers in a trust resulted in the grantor being taxed on the trust income. Since the grantor was usually in a *higher* tax bracket than the trust, the results were undesirable, and the trust was considered defective. Today, the grantor will likely be in a *lower* tax bracket than the trust (compare the federal income tax tables on page 492).

[2] The intentionally defective trust is most often merely funded with a large gift of income-producing property. The additional installment sale funding is typically used when the grantor has no available gift tax exemption, or when the needs of the trust are very large (e.g., to pay premiums on a very large life insurance policy).

[3] See page 397 for a more complete explanation of the grantor trust rules, and other applications of the defective trust.

[4] In order to keep the trust free of any generation-skipping transfer taxes (GSTT), the grantor should file a gift tax return allocating GST exemption to the trust in the amount of the gift. However, provided it falls within the grantor's available annual exclusion and/or gift tax exemption, the gift can be made without paying gift taxes (see chart, Gifts & Split-Gifts, page 49, and Gift Tax vs. Estate Tax, page 395). The primary reason for making this initial gift is to establish that the trust has a degree of independence from the grantor. The concern here is that the IRS might challenge the installment sale as a sham, by arguing that it is unlikely a valuable asset would be sold to someone who has no ability to pay. Funding of the trust prior to the installment sale will also help defend against a challenge by the IRS that the asset should be brought back into the grantor's estate; under the Section 2036(a)(1) theory that the sale was actually a transfer with a retained interest. See also, the discussion on page 389.

[5] Unlike the assets sold, the note will not appreciate in the grantor's estate. However, upon the grantor's death the assets will not receive a stepped-up basis. Although the term of the note could be 20 years or more, to avoid any suggestion that the transaction creates an income interest for the grantor's lifetime, the term should be less than the grantor's life expectancy. The federal mid-term rate is used for installment notes of more than three years, and not more than nine years; whereas, the higher federal long-term rate is used for notes more than nine years. Choice of a shorter deferral period takes advantage of lower interest rates, reduces the amount paid to the grantor, and improves the chances that the loan will be paid off prior to the grantor's death. See footnote 7, below.

[6] Such discounts can range from 35 percent to as much as 65 percent. Rather than selling assets directly to the trust, the grantor will often place the assets in a family limited partnership, which is then sold at a discount to the trust.

[7] If the grantor dies prior to final payment the estate includes the promissory note. There is disagreement among commentators, as to whether gain on the outstanding note must be recognized upon the grantor's death (i.e., at death the defective trust becomes non-defective, and the estate becomes a separate tax-paying entity).

[8] The installment sale to a defective grantor trust resembles a grantor retained income trust (GRAT). Both are intended to remove an asset from the grantor's estate and affect a tax-free transfer of assets to heirs. Although many features of the defective grantor trust are superior to a GRAT, unlike the GRAT there is no specific statutory authority for a defective trust (the IRS will not issue a ruling on them). The defective trust is a sophisticated estate planning technique that should only be undertaken with the advice of competent tax counsel.

LIFE INSURANCE AS PROPERTY

Life insurance differs from most other kinds of contracts because life insurance can potentially place specific rights in three types of persons: the *insured*, the *owner*, and the *beneficiary*. These characteristics make life insurance unique when compared to other types of property. In fact, their arrangement will determine whether or not the death benefit will be subject to estate or even gift taxes.[1]

   A   Death proceeds *Will* **be included in the gross estate** if the insured possesses any incidents of ownership in the contract at the time of his death, or within three years of his death, no matter who might be the beneficiary.[2]

   B   Likewise, when the insured's estate is named beneficiary, the death proceeds will be included in the gross estate, even though the insured may have possessed no incidents of ownership.

   C   Death proceeds *Will Not* **be included in the gross estate** of the insured if he possesses no incidents of ownership in the policy at death or within three years before death and proceeds are not payable to his estate. However, there may be gift tax problems where the insured, the owner, and the beneficiary are all different persons. This arises, for example, where one spouse is the insured, the other spouse the owner (with a right to change beneficiaries), and a child the beneficiary. When the insured dies, the surviving spouse will be considered as having made a gift of the death proceeds to the child. For purposes of the gift tax, property owned by one person (the surviving spouse) is transferred upon the insured's death to another (the child). This deemed transfer from owner to beneficiary is a gift and could result in the surviving spouse having to pay a *gift tax*, or in having to use up some or all of the available unified credit.[3]

   D   To avoid these estate and gift tax problems, all incidents of ownership should be held by the beneficiary from the issuance of the policy.[4] For example, one individual would be the insured and the policy would be owned by and payable to either his spouse, a child, or an irrevocable life insurance trust.[5] This arrangement will assure that the proceeds from the life insurance contract are received untouched, untaxed and on time: **untouched** in that they would be payable directly to the heirs; **untaxed** in that they would be free of income and estate taxes; and **on time** in that they would be paid when needed at death, whether death occurs immediately or at some indefinite time in the future.[6]

Footnotes on page 75

Death Proceeds WILL Be Included In Estate

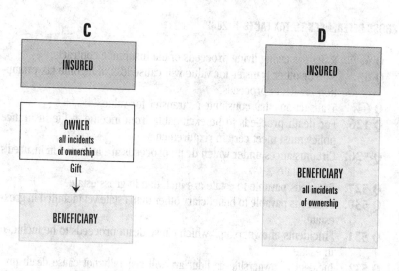

Death Proceeds WILL NOT Be Included In Estate

INFORMATION REQUIRED FOR ANALYSIS & PROPOSAL

1. Obtain copies of all insurance policies.
2. Determine original applicant, owner and beneficiary from photostat copy of application contained in policy.
3. Review endorsements that may reveal a subsequent change of owner or beneficiary.
4. Ascertain premium payor.

TRANSFER FOR VALUE

The following transfers of ownership will *not* violate the transfer for value rules:

1. A bona fide gift (as to another family member) – is not considered to be a transfer for value.
2. Transfers for value to:
   a. the insured.
   b. a partner of the insured.
   c. a partnership in which the insured is a partner.
   d. a corporation in which the insured is a stockholder or an officer.
   e. a corporation from another corporation in a tax-free reorganization.

Note: An expanded discussion of these rules is contained on pages 479-480.

CROSS REFERENCES TO TAX FACTS 1 (2002)

Q 6. Rules for taxing living proceeds of life insurance contracts.
Q 63. Sale or other transfer for value will cause loss of income tax exemption for death proceeds.
Q 64. Transactions that constitute a "transfer for value."
Q 126. For death proceeds to be excludable from income, a life insurance policy must meet certain requirements.
Q 526. Circumstances under which death proceeds are included in insured's gross estate.
Q 527. Proceeds payable to estate are included in gross estate.
Q 530. Proceeds payable to beneficiary other than estate yet included in gross estate.
Q 531. "Incidents of ownership" which cause death proceeds to be included in estate.
Q 532. Incident of ownership as fiduciary will generally not cause death proceeds to be included in gross estate (but see Fifth Circuit position in text).
Q 542. Estate taxation of life insurance policy given away within 3 years of death.
Q 635. Policy owned by someone other than insured can result in gift if beneficiary is not also owner.

Footnotes

[1] As property, the cash values of a life insurance policy are potentially subject to income taxes when there is a *withdrawal* from or *surrender* of the policy. However, when received, the cash values are taxed under the "cost recovery rules," meaning that such amounts are included in gross income only to the extent they exceed the investment in the policy (e.g., cash surrender values of $21,000 and total premiums of $15,000 would result in a $6,000 taxable gain, assuming no dividends and no prior distributions from the policy). A *loan* is not includable in income provided the policy is not a modified endowment contract. Distributions and loans from a modified endowment contract are taxed under different rules (see expanded discussion on pages 413-414).

[2] Thus, if the insured owns a contract of insurance on his own life and then makes a gift of the policy to another, he would have to live *more than* 3 years before the proceeds would be excluded from his estate. An incident of ownership includes the right to:

    a. change the beneficiary.
    b. surrender or cancel the policy.
    c. assign the policy.
    d. revoke an assignment.
    e. pledge the policy for a loan.
    f. obtain a policy loan.

[3] As shown in Diagram "C" of the chart, *gift* tax consequences may result when owner and beneficiary are not the same (i.e., "non-parallel" owner and beneficiary). However, when the deemed transfer of death proceeds occurs in a corporate setting, it can cause serious *income* tax problems when a contract owned by a corporation pays a death benefit to the widow of a stockholder. Payment of the death benefit will likely be non-deductible to the corporation and taxable as a *dividend* to the widow – despite the fact that under a different arrangement the payment could have qualified as a tax-free receipt of death proceeds. At best, the corporation could deduct the payment as a salary continuation expense, but the payment would be includable in the gross income of the estate or beneficiary as "income in respect of a decedent." See discussion on page 402.

[4] After numerous losses, including the *Leder*, *Headrick* and *Perry* cases, the Internal Revenue Service issued an action on decision announcing it would no longer litigate the issue of whether life insurance proceeds are includable in the insured's estate, where the life insurance policy is procured by a third party at the instance of the insured, the insured pays the insurance premiums, and the insured dies within three years of procurement of the policy by the third person (i.e., the "beamed transfer" theory). For an expanded discussion, see Estate Taxation of Life Insurance, pages 388-389. Also see ownership and beneficiary arrangements on page 96.

[5] With the unlimited marital deduction the decedent spouse's estate may well be free of federal estate taxes, but substantial taxes may be levied at the surviving spouse's death. For this reason, if it is desired to reduce exposure to estate taxes, the spouse of the insured should *not* be owner and beneficiary of the policy. Where the spouse is both owner and beneficiary, the arrangement is often referred to as a "cross-owned policy" and the death benefit received upon the insured's death will *increase* the surviving spouse's estate. In order to shift these death benefits from one generation to another free of estate taxes, it may be advisable to have the policy owned by an adult child, or placed in a Life Insurance Trust, as described in the chart on page 57. See also the discussion of minors and life insurance on page 425.

[6] The underlying principles discussed in this chart are as applicable to the analysis of existing policies as they are to proposed new insurance coverage. With many new clients, some of the easiest, yet most effective, estate planning recommendations will come from a policy audit involving an analysis and restructuring of the ownership and beneficiary provisions of existing insurance. As to new insurance, it is important to be familiar with the requirement that an applicant have an insurable interest in the life to be insured (see expanded discussion, page 405). Life insurance proceeds payable to a C corporation are not necessarily free of income taxes. For an expanded discussion, see Alternative Minimum Tax, pages 342-344.

LIFE INSURANCE PRODUCTS

TERM INSURANCE. If an estate plan is to be built on a solid foundation, life insurance protection is essential. Term insurance provides protection for a *limited* period of time for a younger person whose insurance needs must be met on a modest budget. However, the premium for this protection will usually increase each and every year, until it becomes prohibitively expensive for most people to maintain. While term insurance can provide a lot of protection for a lesser cost, it builds no cash values and has no permanent values. In this sense it has been described as "rented" but not "owned."[1]

PERMANENT INSURANCE, in contrast to term insurance, provides for a tax-deferred build-up of cash values over the life of the contract.[2] This cash value element, combined with level or limited premium increases, means that the death benefit will be available for an *unlimited* period. While the outlay for permanent insurance is usually greater than term insurance in the early years, most plans provide for payment of a level premium. Even if the plan requires an increasing premium, these increases are usually limited in both amount and duration. Typically, both the cash values and the death benefits are guaranteed, unless they are dependent upon payment of projected dividends.[3]

UNIVERSAL LIFE INSURANCE offers flexible premium payments, an adjustable death benefit, and cash values that are sensitive to current interest rates.[4] Most contracts pay a *current interest rate* which is highly competitive with that available in the money market. However, these rates are subject to change and are not guaranteed over the life of the contract. The *guaranteed interest rate* is usually very modest and will likely result in a lapse of the policy if additional premiums are not paid. Likewise, most universal life policies offer lower *current (nonguaranteed) mortality* charges, but provided for higher *guaranteed mortality* charges. Taken together, the lower guaranteed interest rate and higher guaranteed mortality charges represent the "down-side risk" of a universal life contract. The policyholder is asked to accept this risk in return for the opportunity to receive the benefits of higher current interest rates and lower charges for the amount-at-risk element in the contract.[5]

VARIABLE LIFE INSURANCE is similar to universal life insurance, except that the underlying cash values can be invested in an equity portfolio, typically a mutual fund or bonds.[6] The policyowner is usually given the opportunity to redirect his investment to another portfolio although some limitations and restrictions may be imposed.[7]

Footnotes on page 79

TERM LIFE INSURANCE
(increasing premium)

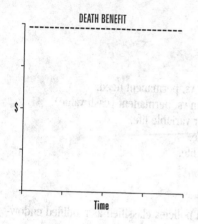

PERMANENT INSURANCE
(fixed premium)

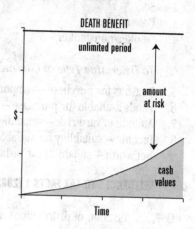

UNIVERSAL LIFE INSURANCE
(flexible premium)

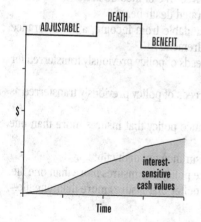

VARIABLE LIFE INSURANCE
(flexible premium)

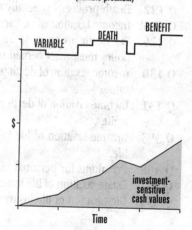

INFORMATION REQUIRED FOR ANALYSIS & PROPOSAL

1. Name of individual to be insured.
2. Sex.
3. Date of birth.
4. Smoker/nonsmoker.

To Determine Type of Contract

5. Reasons for purchase – temporary vs. permanent need.
6. Funds available for purchase – term vs. permanent (cash value).
7. Attitude toward risk – suitability for variable life.
8. Income – suitability for variable life.
9. Net worth – suitability for variable life.

CROSS REFERENCES TO TAX FACTS 1 (2002)

Q 7. Taxation of distributions from policies classified as modified endowment contracts.

Q 29. Income tax results when contract surrendered for cash values.

Q 105. Annual cash value increases generally not taxable income to policyholder.

Q 122. Death proceeds generally received free of income taxes.

Q 123. Income taxation of an "accelerated death benefit."

Q 126. For death proceeds to be excludable from income, a life insurance policy must meet certain requirements.

Q 130. Income taxation of death proceeds of policy previously transferred for value.

Q 131. Income taxation of death proceeds of policy previously transferred as a gift.

Q 393. Income taxation of life insurance policy that insures more than one life.

Q 408. Premiums for personal life insurance not deductible.

Q 571. Estate taxation of life insurance policy that insures more than one life.

Q 632. Gift taxation of life insurance policy that insures more than one life.

Footnotes

1 Term insurance is available in many forms, the most common being annual renewable, five-year renewable (and/or convertible), 10-year renewable and convertible (R&C), 15-year R&C, 20-year R&C, and term to a specific age, such as age 65. A specialized form of term insurance, decreasing term, is also available, and usually purchased to cover a decreasing loan or mortgage obligation. Term insurance can be tailored to fit almost any temporary insurance need – level, decreasing, or even increasing.

2 Permanent life insurance is often called "whole life." This is because, so long as the policy remains in force, it provides protection for the "whole of life." The whole of life is assumed to be to age 100 under many mortality tables, although in recent years lesser ages have been used (i.e., age 90 or 95). If the insured lives to age 100, the policy endows with the cash values equaling the face amount of the policy.

3 Both term and permanent insurance are available as *participating* policies, which offer the opportunity for dividends that may be used to: reduce the premium outlay; purchase paid-up additions (which accrue their own cash values); enhance the amount of available death benefit through a combination of one-year term insurance and paid-up additions (the fifth dividend option); or augment the cash values by being left to accumulate at interest.

4 Universal life insurance has many unique features not found in traditional whole life policies. Most importantly, your *client controls* many aspects of the contract because of the built-in flexibility of the universal life policy. Specific features of universal life include:

   a. An adjustable death benefit that may be increased or decreased to suit the obligations and needs of the insured (often subject to insurability if the death benefit is increased).
   b. Tax-deferred current interest earnings on cash values.
   c. Flexible premiums that allow changes in payments to suit individual needs (but see the discussion regarding life insurance premium limitations, pages 413-414).

5 Interest-sensitive whole life is a hybrid between permanent (whole life) insurance and universal life insurance. It is also known as excess-interest whole life, current assumption whole life, irreplaceable life, pseudo universal life, fixed premium universal life, and adjustable cash value whole life. The product typically requires a fixed premium, and in return provides a *guaranteed* death benefit and minimum interest rates, and current higher nonguaranteed interest rates. Premiums are usually fixed, although additional funds can be "dumped" into the policy in order to vanish, or short pay, premiums. As with universal life, a surrender charge is often assessed when the contract is surrendered in the early years, although some contracts allow withdrawals of "excess" earnings. A "bailout feature" may be offered, which enables the policyholder to withdraw funds without penalty if the credited interest rate drops below a certain level.

6 Variable life insurance is considered a fourth type of insurance, in that the death benefit and cash values reflect the performance of an underlying portfolio of equity investments, such as stocks and bonds. While these investments can provide a hedge against inflation, and the possibility for growth in both cash reserves and death benefits, there is also the risk that investment performance will be poor and that the cash reserves will decrease or be lost. Since variable life insurance is a security, the agent must hold a valid federal securities license (and state license where required) in order to sell the product. In addition, *a prospectus must be delivered* with or preceding a specific proposal to a prospect or client.

7 In recent years joint life insurance policies insuring multiple-lives have become popular for funding a variety of insurance needs (see First-To-Die Insurance, page 393, and Survivorship Life Insurance, page 475). Corporate owned life insurance (COLI) is used to fund a number of nonqualified benefits (page 364). A table of comparative Insurance Company Ratings is set forth on page 506.

DISCOUNTED DOLLARS

The death benefits of a life insurance contract are often referred to as "discounted," in the sense that payment of a relatively small yearly premium, from 1 to 5 percent of the death benefit, depending upon age and rating category, will guarantee that the full face amount will be available when needed.

In this sense, the purchase of life insurance is analogous to the *leverage* obtained by the individual who invests in property with a small down payment and a large mortgage. The investor expects to benefit from the future appreciation of an asset worth many times his cash investment, whereas payment of modest insurance premiums enables the insured to provide a substantial death benefit as security for his family.

WITH INSURANCE, assume that a 35-year old insured purchases $100,000 of level death protection for his family requiring an annual premium of $1,000 per year.[1] This purchase guarantees $100,000 of discounted dollars payable upon death at any time. The *discount* is represented by the difference between the death benefit and *cumulative premiums* paid.[2] After 20 years the discount would amount to $80,000 ($100,000 - $20,000). If our insured lives for 40 years and pays premiums totalling $40,000 there is still a discount of $60,000.[3]

WITHOUT INSURANCE, a surviving family might be forced to borrow in order to pay estate settlement costs. Repaying a 6 percent loan of $100,000 in 10 equal annual installments requires total payments of $135,870.[4] If the family were able to obtain a 40-year loan under the same terms, its total payments would be $265,880. However, it is unlikely that a surviving family would be able to borrow money at only 6 percent interest. A more realistic rate would probably be 12 percent, in which case the family's total repayments are more likely to be $176,990 over 10 years, or $485,240 over 40 years.

Paying estate settlement costs with the discounted dollars of life insurance is far better than putting a surviving family in the position of having to borrow large sums of money at high rates of interest. Most families would find it far easier to pay premiums totaling $40,000 over a 40-year period than to make loan repayments of $485,240 over a similar period of time.[5] Properly arranged, the discounted dollars provided from a life insurance contract will be received untouched, untaxed and on time: **untouched** in that they are paid directly to the beneficiary; **untaxed** in that they are free of income and estate taxes; and **on time** in that they are paid when needed, whenever death occurs.[6]

Footnotes on page 83

WITH LIFE INSURANCE

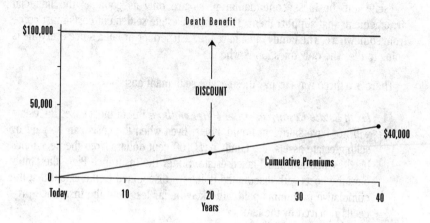

WITHOUT LIFE INSURANCE

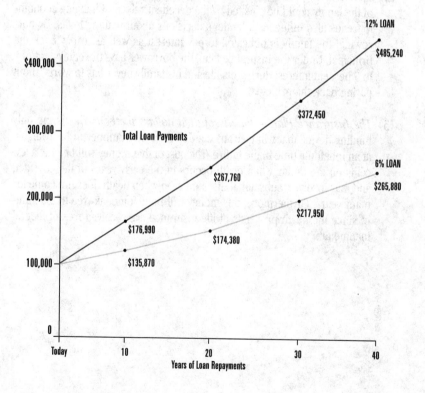

WHY LIFE INSURANCE?

Estate and business continuation plans are only as good as the financial arrangements that support them. The cash for estate settlement costs must come from somewhere. The family must have the cash sooner or later, since everyone is going to die. The only question is when.

There are three ways to pay these estate settlement costs:

(1) *From Estate Resources – the 100% method.* But in most cases the estate will not have sufficient liquid assets. Even when the costs can be paid by selling estate assets, the family pays 100-cent dollars from the decedent's hard-earned and hard-taxed estate. Under the Insurance Plan, the family pays the costs with discounted dollars – discounted to the extent that the cumulative premiums paid will likely be far less than the insurance proceeds received by the family.

(2) *By Borrowing the Money – the 100%+ method.* But the credit standing of the family could be affected by the decedent's death. Changing economic trends also influence a lender's decisions about making loans. By borrowing, the family is obligated to pay interest as well as to pay back the principal. Under the Insurance Plan, the borrower pays the equivalent of 1 to 5 percent interest during his life and his family never has to worry about paying back the principal.

(3) *The Insurance Plan – the discounted dollars method.* This is the only funding device that will guarantee a definite sum of money to be available at an indefinite time in the future. The cost of that money will be only a few cents on the dollar when death occurs in the early years of the contract, and may involve a substantial discount even when death does not come for many years. Furthermore, this money will be income tax-free to the family, since the death proceeds of life insurance are received free of federal income tax.

Footnotes

[1] This example assumes the purchase of a non-participating permanent contract. If participating insurance were illustrated, the premium might be higher, but dividends would likely be available. If the dividends were used to *reduce* premiums, the "cumulative premiums" would increase at a decreasing, or slower, rate. If the dividends were used to buy *paid-up additions* (the fifth dividend option), the "death benefit" would not be level, but would increase from year to year. If the dividends were used to purchase *term insurance*, then the "death benefit" would also increase, but at a much faster rate, until the age at which the term coverage was no longer available. At this point, the coverage in excess of the basic amount initially issued would terminate.

[2] The *cash values* of the contract have intentionally not been mentioned. The concept of discounted dollars involves only the *cumulative* premium payments relative to the death benefit payable. However, under many circumstances, cumulative cash values will exceed total payments in the later years of the contract, depending upon the product, the age of the insured at the time of issue, and the rating. The term "discounted dollars" should *not* be used in discussing the cost of a life insurance policy. In this regard, see the discussion of the interest adjusted net cost method on page 406.

[3] The actual life expectancy for a 35-year old male is 38.61 years. For other average future life spans, see the Commissioners 1980 Standard Ordinary Mortality Table (page 498).

[4] From the Amortization Table on page 505, it can be seen that a loan of $1,000 for 10 years at 6 percent interest requires annual payments of $135.87. Therefore, annual payments for a $100,000 loan would be $13,587 (100 x $135.87).

[5] This chart also demonstrates the benefits of *insuring existing liquidity* in an estate. For example, if $100,000 of estate liquidity were preserved for the surviving family, and amortized over 10 years at only 6 percent, they would receive $35,870 of interest income over that period. If they were able to amortize this same $100,000 over 10 years at 12 percent, they would receive $76,990 of interest income. Amortizing the $100,000 at 12 percent for longer periods of 20 and 30 years would yield total interest income of $167,760 and $272,450. Actually, these figures would be higher if the family reinvests the original $100,000 as it is repaid to them. The purchase of discounted dollars will assure that this existing liquidity is preserved. Over 20 years your client would pay cumulative premiums of $20,000. On the other hand, if your client died, the preserved liquidity would provide at least $167,760 of interest income for the family, if amortized at 12 percent over the same 20-year period.

[6] Life insurance proceeds payable to a C corporation are not necessarily free of income taxes. For an expanded discussion, see Alternative Minimum Tax, pages 342-344. With a living benefits rider it has become possible for the death benefit to be paid prior to death if the insured has a terminal illness that is expected to result in death within twelve months (see page 338).

CHECKLIST OF DOCUMENTS

Check As
Obtained

1. Wills   – client   ❑
           – spouse   ❑

2. Trust Agreements   ❑

3. Life Insurance Policies   – client   ❑
                             – spouse   ❑

4. Medical Insurance Policies   ❑

5. Disability Income Policies   ❑

6. Personal Balance Sheet (or similar listing ❑
    of cash, securities, real estate, personal
    effects, mortgages and other liabilities)

7. Business Balance Sheets   ❑

8. Business Profit and Loss Statements   ❑

9. Business Disposition Agreements (buy/sell ❑
    agreements, partnership agreements, etc.)

10. Employee Benefits (retirement plans, stock ❑
     options, deferred compensation, etc.)

11. Income Tax Return (most recent)   ❑

12. Gift Tax returns   ❑

13. Dates of Birth (of family members)   ❑

14. Other: _____

        _____

        _____

        _____

        _____

Date of Meeting:_____
Time: _____
Place:_____

GIFT TAX CALCULATION STEPS

Gross Value of Current Gift(s)	$ _____
Less: 50% of Gift if Split-Gift(s)	(_____)
Annual Exclusion[1]	(_____)
Marital Deduction[2]	(_____)
Charitable Deduction[2]	(_____)
Current Taxable Gift(s)	$ _____
Plus: Sum of All Prior Taxable Gifts	
Total Cumulative Taxable Gifts	$ _____
Tax on Total Cumulative Taxable Gifts[3]	$ _____
Less: Taxes Paid on Prior Taxable Gifts	(_____)
Tentative Tax	$ _____
Less: Unified Credit	(_____)
Gift Tax Payable[4]	$ _____

ESTATE TAX CALCULATION STEPS

Gross Estate	$ _____
Less: Debts of Decedent	(_____)
Administration Expenses	(_____)
Losses during Administration	(_____)
Adjusted Gross Estate	$ _____
Less: Marital Deduction[2]	(_____)
Charitable Deduction[2]	(_____)
Taxable Estate	$ _____
Plus: Adjusted Taxable Gifts	
Computation Base	$ _____
Tentative Tax[3]	$ _____
Less: Post-1976 Gift Taxes Payable	(_____)
Unified Credit	(_____)
State Death Tax Credit	(_____)
Pre-1977 Gift Tax Credit	(_____)
Foreign Death Tax Credit	(_____)
Credit for Tax on Prior Transfers	(_____)
Estate Tax Payable[5]	$ _____

---

[1] See page 48 for details regarding annual gift tax exclusion.

[2] Full value of property passed to spouse or charity may be taken as a deduction.

[3] See pages 493-494 for estate and gift tax rates.

[4] Transfer taxes payable during life may also include the generation-skipping transfer tax.

[5] Transfer taxes payable at death may also include the generation-skipping transfer tax (see chart, page 39).

IMPACT OF APPRECIATION ON ESTATE TAX

Under EGTRRA 2001

Growth Rate		Year					
		2002	2003	2004	2005	2006	2007
8%	Estate	1,000,000	1,080,000	1,166,400	1,259,712	1,360,489	1,469,328
	Tax	0	32,800	0	0	0	0
	Shrinkage	0	3.0	0	0	0	0
10%	Estate		1,100,000	1,210,000	1,331,000	1,464,100	1,610,510
	Tax		41,000	0	0	0	0
	Shrinkage		3.7	0	0	0	0
12%	Estate		1,120,000	1,254,400	1,404,928	1,573,519	1,762,342
	Tax		49,200	0	0	0	0
	Shrinkage		4.4	0	0	0	0
8%	Estate	1,750,000	1,890,000	2,041,200	2,204,496	2,380,856	2,571,324
	Tax	322,500	385,500	244,776	321,113	175,194	257,096
	Shrinkage	18.4	20.4	12.0	14.6	7.4	10.0
10%	Estate		1,925,000	2,117,500	2,329,250	2,562,175	2,818,393
	Tax		401,250	281,400	379,748	258,601	368,277
	Shrinkage		20.8	13.3	16.3	10.1	13.1
12%	Estate		1,960,000	2,195,200	2,458,624	2,753,659	3,084,098
	Tax		417,000	318,696	440,553	346,683	487,844
	Shrinkage		21.3	14.5	17.9	12.6	15.8
8%	Estate	2,500,000	2,700,000	2,916,000	3,149,280	3,401,222	3,673,320
	Tax	680,000	778,000	664,680	765,162	644,562	752,994
	Shrinkage	27.2	28.8	22.8	24.3	19.0	20.5
10%	Estate		2,750,000	3,025,000	3,327,500	3,660,250	4,026,275
	Tax		802,500	717,000	848,925	763,715	911,824
	Shrinkage		29.2	23.7	25.5	20.9	22.6
12%	Estate		2,800,000	3,136,000	3,512,320	3,933,798	4,405,854
	Tax		827,000	770,280	935,790	889,547	1,082,634
	Shrinkage		29.5	24.6	26.6	22.6	24.6
8%	Estate	10,000,000	10,800,000	11,664,000	12,597,120	13,604,890	14,693,281
	Tax	4,430,000	4,747,000	4,863,720	5,205,647	5,338,250	5,711,977
	Shrinkage	44.3	44.0	41.7	41.3	39.2	38.9
10%	Estate		11,000,000	12,100,000	13,310,000	14,641,000	16,105,100
	Tax		4,845,000	5,073,000	5,540,700	5,814,860	6,347,295
	Shrinkage		44.0	41.9	41.6	39.7	39.4
12%	Estate		11,200,000	12,544,000	14,049,280	15,735,194	17,623,417
	Tax		4,943,000	5,286,120	5,888,162	6,318,189	7,030,537
	Shrinkage		44.1	42.1	41.9	40.2	39.9
Exemption Equivalent		1,000,000	1,000,000	1,500,000	1,500,000	2,000,000	2,000,000

Explanation of Table. The federal estate taxes in this table reflect the increased credits provided by EGTRRA 2001. These increases are: $345,800 in 2002 and 2003, $555,800 in 2004 and 2005, $780,800 in 2006 thru 2008, and $1,455,800 in 2009. In 2010 the estate tax is repealed. However, under the sunset provisions of EGTRRA 2001, the estate tax reappears in 2011, as it existed prior to EGTRRA 2001. Estate shrinkage caused by the estate tax is given as a percentage (e.g., 322,500 ÷ 1,750,000 = 18.4%).

(continued on next page)

IMPACT OF APPRECIATION ON ESTATE TAX (continued)

Under EGTRRA 2001

Growth Rate		2002	2008	2009	2010	2011	2012
8%	Estate	1,000,000	1,586,874	1,713,824	1,850,930	1,999,005	2,158,925
	Tax	0	0	0	0	434,552	512,873
	Shrinkage	0	0	0	0	21.7	23.8
10%	Estate		1,771,561	1,948,717	2,143,589	2,357,948	2,593,742
	Tax		0	0	0	610,395	729,683
	Shrinkage		0	0	0	25.9	28.1
12%	Estate		1,973,823	2,210,681	2,475,963	2,773,079	3,105,848
	Tax		0	0	0	824,732	1,003,216
	Shrinkage		0	0	0	29.7	32.3
8%	Estate	1,750,000	2,777,030	2,999,192	3,239,128	3,498,258	3,778,119
	Tax	322,500	349,664	0	0	1,219,042	1,372,966
	Shrinkage	18.4	12.6	0	0	34.8	36.3
10%	Estate		3,100,232	3,410,255	3,751,280	4,126,408	4,539,049
	Tax		495,104	0	0	1,564,524	1,791,477
	Shrinkage		16.0	0	0	37.9	39.5
12%	Estate		3,454,190	3,868,692	4,332,936	4,852,888	5,435,234
	Tax		654,386	165,911	0	1,964,089	2,284,379
	Shrinkage		18.9	4.3	0	40.5	42.0
8%	Estate	2,500,000	3,967,186	4,284,561	4,627,326	4,997,512	5,397,312
	Tax	680,000	885,234	353,053	0	2,043,632	2,263,522
	Shrinkage	27.2	22.3	8.2	0	40.9	41.9
10%	Estate		4,428,903	4,871,793	5,358,972	5,894,869	6,484,356
	Tax		1,093,006	617,307	0	2,537,178	2,861,396
	Shrinkage		24.7	12.7	0	43.0	44.1
12%	Estate		4,934,557	5,526,704	6,189,908	6,932,697	7,764,621
	Tax		1,320,551	912,017	0	3,107,983	3,565,542
	Shrinkage		26.8	16.5	0	44.8	45.9
8%	Estate	10,000,000	15,868,743	17,138,243	18,509,302	19,990,046	21,589,250
	Tax	4,430,000	6,240,935	6,137,210	0	10,648,725	11,528,288
	Shrinkage	44.3	39.3	35.8	0	53.3	53.4
10%	Estate		17,715,610	19,487,171	21,435,888	23,579,477	25,937,425
	Tax		7,072,025	7,194,227	0	12,622,912	13,919,783
	Shrinkage		39.9	36.9	0	53.5	53.7
12%	Estate		19,738,227	22,106,814	24,759,632	27,730,788	31,058,482
	Tax		7,982,203	8,373,066	0	14,906,133	16,736,366
	Shrinkage		40.4	37.9	0	53.8	53.9
Exemption Equivalent		1,000,000	2,000,000	3,500,000	repealed	1,000,000	1,000,000

Explanation of Table. The federal estate taxes in this table reflect the increased credits provided by EGTRRA 2001. These increases are: $345,800 in 2002 and 2003, $555,800 in 2004 and 2005, $780,800 in 2006 thru 2008, and $1,455,800 in 2009. In 2010 the estate tax is repealed. However, under the sunset provisions of EGTRRA 2001, the estate tax reappears in 2011, as it existed prior to EGTRRA 2001. Estate shrinkage caused by the estate tax is given as a percentage (e.g., 322,500 ÷ 1,750,000 = 18.4%).

PHASE-IN AND SUNSET PROVISIONS OF EGTRRA 2001[1]

Estate, Gift, and Generation-Skipping

	Years					
	2001	2002	2003	2004	2005	2006
Estate Tax						
Unified Credit Equivalent[2]	675,000	1,000,000	1,000,000	1,500,000	1,500,000	2,000,000
Estate Tax Unified Credit	220,550	345,800	345,800	555,800	555,800	780,800
Maximum Rate	55%	50%	49%	48%	47%	46%
Minimum Effective Rate	37%	41%	41%	45%	45%	46%
Surtax[3]	5%	repealed	repealed	repealed	repealed	repealed
Gift Tax						
Unified Credit Equivalent[2]	675,000	1,000,000	1,000,000	1,000,000	1,000,000	1,000,000
Gift Tax Unified Credit	220,550	345,800	345,800	345,800	345,800	345,800
Maximum Rate	55%	50%	49%	48%	47%	46%
Generation-Skipping Tax						
GST Exemption	1,060,000	1,100,000	1,100,000[4]	1,500,000	1,500,000	2,000,000
Rate	55%	50%	49%	48%	47%	46%
Cost Basis At Death	stepped-up	stepped-up	stepped-up	stepped-up	stepped-up	stepped-up
State Death Tax Credit	graduated rate up to 16%	reduced by 25%[5]	reduced by 50%[5]	reduced by 75%[5]	Repealed and replaced by a deduction for death taxes actually paid.	
Estate Tax Deferral - Closely Held Business 2% Interest Rate Limitation	441,000	484,000	484,000[6]	513,000[6]	507,000[6]	506,000[6]
Qualified Family-Owned Business Deduction	675,000	675,000	675,000	repealed	repealed	repealed
Qualified Conservation Easement Exclusion	400,000	500,000	500,000	500,000	500,000	500,000
Presidential Election	no	no	no	yes	no	no
Congressional Election	no	yes	no	yes	no	yes

[1] Officially known as the Economic Growth and Tax Relief Reconciliation Act of 2001, but also called H.R. 1836. Under the sunset provision, in 2011, all tax law changes revert to year 2001 levels, unless Congress re-enacts the 2010 repeal changes into law. The act has been described as "wreckless" by columnist Jane Bryant Quinn, see page 324.

[2] Also variously referred to as "unified credit exemption equivalent," "exclusion amount," "exclusion equivalent," "applicable exclusion," and "applicable exclusion amount." With the advent of EGTRRA 2001, and the unraveling of the unified estate and gift tax system, we now encounter "estate tax exemption," "estate tax exemption equivalent," "gift tax exemption," and "gift tax exemption equivalent." The Code continues to refer to the term "unified credit," despite the fact that EGTRRA 2001 clearly makes the gift and estate tax systems anything but unified.

[3] This surtax of 5 percent on transfers in excess of $10,000,000 (but not exceeding $17,184,000) was designed to take away the benefit of the lower graduated rates.

[4] Subject to indexing for inflation.

[5] From 2001 amounts.

[6] As indexed for 2002. Increases in the estate tax unified credit and reduction of the estate tax rates indirectly change the maximum amount of estate tax that can be deferred at 2% interest.

(continued on next page)

PHASE-IN AND SUNSET PROVISIONS OF EGTRRA 2001 (continued)

Estate, Gift, and Generation-Skipping

	Years				
	2007	2008	2009	2010	2011
Estate Tax					
Unified Credit Equivalent[1]	2,000,000	2,000,000	3,500,000	repealed[3]	1,000,000
Estate Tax Unified Credit	780,800	780,800	1,455,800	repealed[3]	345,800
Maximum Rate	45%	45%	45%	repealed[3]	55%
Minimum Effective Rate	45%	45%	45%	repealed[3]	37%
Surtax[2]	repealed	repealed	repealed	repealed	5%
Gift Tax					
Unified Credit Equivalent[1]	1,000,000	1,000,000	1,000,000	1,000,000	1,000,000
Gift Tax Unified Credit	345,800	345,800	345,800	330,800	345,800
Maximum Rate	45%	45%	45%	35%	55%
Generation-Skipping Tax					
GST Exemption	2,000,000	2,000,000	3,500,000	repealed[3]	1,100,000[4]
Rate	45%	45%	45%	repealed[3]	55%
Cost Basis At Death	stepped-up	stepped-up	stepped-up	modified carryover[5]	stepped-up
State Death Tax Credit	Repealed and replaced by a deduction for death taxes actually paid.				same as 2001
Estate Tax Deferral - Closely Held Business 2% Interest Rate Limitation	495,000[6]	495,000[6]	495,000[6]	n/a	484,000[6]
Qualified Family-Owned Business Deduction	repealed	repealed	repealed	n/a	675,000
Qualified Conservation Easement Exclusion	500,000	500,000	500,000	n/a	500,000
Presidential Election	no	yes	no	no	no
Congressional Election	no	yes	no	yes	no

[1] Also variously referred to as "unified credit exemption equivalent," "exclusion amount," "exclusion equivalent," "applicable exclusion," and "applicable exclusion amount." With the advent of EGTRRA 2001, and the unraveling of the unified estate and gift tax system, we now encounter "estate tax exemption," "estate tax exemption equivalent," "gift tax exemption," and "gift tax exemption equivalent." The Code continues to refer to the term "unified credit," despite the fact that EGTRRA 2001 clearly makes the gift and estate tax systems anything but unified.

[2] This surtax of 5 percent on transfers in excess of $10,000,000 (but not exceeding $17,184,000) was designed to take away the benefit of the lower graduated rates.

[3] Although the law uses the word "repealed," the word "suspended" would more accurately describes a repeal that under the sunset provision only lasts for one year.

[4] Subject to indexing for inflation.

[5] Basis is equal to the lower of fair market value at date of death, or adjusted basis. However, the following limited basis increases will be available: (1) $1,300,000 aggregate; (2) $3,000,000 for "qualified spousal property" (i.e., not a terminable interest); and (3) unused losses. The $1.3 million and $3 million amounts are indexed for inflation after 2010, assuming EGTRRA 2001 does not sunset at the end of 2010.

[6] As indexed for 2002. Increases in the estate tax unified credit and reduction of the estate tax rates indirectly change the maximum amount of estate tax that can be deferred at 2% interest.

TYPICAL ESTATE DEBTS, COSTS AND TAXES

GROSS ESTATE	DEBTS AND LIABILITIES	+	PROBATE COSTS	+	STATE TAX	+	FEDERAL TAX	=	TOTAL EXPENSES
100,000	5,600		5,000		1,700		0		12,300
200,000	10,600		9,900		4,400		0		24,900
300,000	15,600		14,700		6,000		0		36,300
400,000	20,400		19,600		11,000		0		51,000
500,000	25,000		22,500		16,600		0		64,100
600,000	29,400		26,880		21,400		0		77,680
700,000	33,600		31,220		26,700		0		91,520
800,000	37,600		35,520		32,600		0		105,720
900,000	41,400		39,780		38,900		0		120,080
1,000,000	45,000		44,000		45,800		0		134,800
1,500,000	62,250		65,250		71,800		112,995		312,295
2,000,000	84,000		86,000		100,000		292,980		562,980
3,000,000	120,000		126,000		180,000		686,736		1,112,736
4,000,000	154,000		164,000		260,000		1,085,504		1,663,504
5,000,000	185,000		200,000		350,000		1,476,140		2,211,140

Explanation of Table. Debts and Liabilities are calculated on a descending scale from 5.6 to 3.7 percent and Probate Costs on a descending scale from 5.0 to 4.0 percent. Both reflect actual government studies involving estates of various sizes. The State and Federal Taxes assume that death has occurred in 2002. The Federal Tax is net after the credit for State Death Taxes paid, and does not take into account the possible availability of the unlimited marital deduction. Specific debts, costs, and taxes will differ from those illustrated. The Federal Estate Tax accounts for changes made by EGTRRA 2001.

ESTATE TAXES ASSUMING NO PLANNING

TAXABLE ESTATE	AMOUNT	MAXIMUM TAX RATE
up to 1,000,000	0	0%
1,250,000	102,500	41
1,500,000	210,000	43
2,000,000	435,000	45
2,500,000	680,000	49
3,000,000	930,000	50
4,000,000	1,430,000	50
5,000,000	1,930,000	50
10,000,000	4,430,000	50

Explanation of Table. Note that once an estate becomes subject to estate taxes the minimum rate is 41 percent. The Maximum Tax Rate is the marginal rate paid on the last dollars in the estate (e.g., with a taxable estate of $1,500,000, the last $250,000 is taxed at 43 percent). All figures are for 2002 and have been obtained from the Federal Estate and Gift Tax table on page 493.

HISTORY OF THE FEDERAL ESTATE TAX[1]

In view of the following tortured history, it is hard to imagine what will happen to the federal estate tax post EGTRRA 2001. Intelligent planning does not rely on a permanent repeal of the tax.

1797 – The first federal "estate" tax was passed to help fund a naval buildup. This was actually a *stamp* duty on legacies and intestate shares of personalty, and was not effective until 1798. The tax was 25¢ on a share over $50 and under $100, 75¢ on a share between $100 and $500, plus $1 per additional $500 share, or portion thereof.

1802 – The stamp tax was repealed.

1862 – To help fund the Civil War, Congress imposed a *legacy* tax on personalty if personal estate exceeded $1,000 (share of spouse was *exempt*) and a *stamp* tax on probates of wills and letters of administration (from 50¢ to $20 for estates up to $150,000, with $10 more for each additional $50,000, or fraction thereof).

1864 – The legacy tax was increased and a succession tax on realty was added, ranging from 1% to 6% on the basis of relationship to the deceased.

1870 – The legacy succession tax was repealed.

1872 – The stamp tax was repealed.

1894 – At the beginning of the Spanish-American War, a 2% "income" tax was imposed upon "money and value of all personal property acquired by gift or inheritance."

1898 – The rates were changed, and ranged from .75% to 2.25%, but estates under $10,000 were exempt (as well as legacies to surviving spouses).

1902 – The "income" tax was repealed.

1916-21 – The modern estate tax was enacted, followed by a succession of changes. Initially, there was an exemption of $50,000, and the rates ranged from 1% on the first $50,000, to 10% on estates over $5 million. Thereafter, the 1% rate increased to 1.5%, then to 2%; and the 10% rate increased to 15%, then to 25% (on estates over $10 million).

1924 – The gift tax was imposed, a state credit was allowed, and the estate tax was increased on all taxable estates over $100,000 (estates over $10 million were taxed at 40%).

1926 – The gift tax was repealed, the exemption was raised from $50,000 to $100,000, and the 1924 rates were retroactively removed. As a result, $250 million was refunded to just seven estates, while other estates received lesser refunds.

1931 – The exemption was reduced from $100,000 to $50,000, and rates were more than doubled.

1932 – For estates over $1 million, the maximum rate was increased from 19% to 45%.

1934 – For estates over $10 million, the maximum rate was increased to 60%.

1935 – The exemption was further reduced to $40,000, and the rates were increased to 2% on the first $10,000 bracket, and increased to 70% on amounts over $50 million.

1940 – To help finance World War II, a "temporary" defense tax increased estate taxes 10%.

1941 – The progressive rates were increased, and the "temporary" defense tax became permanent. The rates were increased to 3% on the first $5,000 bracket, and increased to 77% on amounts over $10 million.

1981-99 – During this 19-year period, no less than 126 new estate tax laws were enacted (an average of seven per year).[2]

---

[1] This history has been compiled from an exhaustive work by Louis Eisenstein, contained in "The Rise and Decline of the Estate Tax," *Tax Law Review*, 1956, pages 223-259.

[2] See, Hal Graff, "Estate Tax Law Changes: More Sales Opportunities for Financial Advisors," *Journal of Financial Service Professionals*, July 2001, page 87.

FEDERAL CREDIT STATES[1]

The following states do not have a separate state inheritance or estate tax, but claim only the maximum federal credit.[2]

Alabama	Kansas	North Dakota
Alaska	Maine	Oregon
Arizona	Massachusetts	Rhode Island
Arkansas	Michigan	South Carolina
California	Minnesota	Texas
Colorado	Mississippi	Utah
Delaware	Missouri	Vermont
District of Columbia	Montana	Virginia
Florida	Nevada	Washington
Georgia	New Mexico	West Virginia
Hawaii	New York	Wisconsin
Idaho	North Carolina	Wyoming
Illinois		

Although the following states are not credit states, they do exempt from taxation all transfers to a decedent's spouse (by either an unlimited marital deduction or an exemption).

Connecticut	Maryland	Oklahoma
Indiana	Nebraska	Pennsylvania
Iowa	New Hampshire	South Dakota
Kentucky	New Jersey	Tennessee
Louisiana	Ohio	

Although the following states are not credit states, they do exempt from taxation all transfers to a child.

Connecticut	Kentucky	New Hampshire
Iowa	Maryland	New Jersey

COMMUNITY PROPERTY STATES[3]

In the following states community property laws govern the ownership of property between husband and wife.

Alaska[4]	Louisiana	Texas
Arizona	Nevada	Washington
California	New Mexico	Wisconsin
Idaho		

---

[1] Last researched: November 2001.
[2] Under EGTRRA 2001, the credit for federal estate taxes is being reduced and then replaced with a deduction.
[3] Community property is discussed on pages 359-360.
[4] In Alaska a married couple must opt into the community property system.

STATE INHERITANCE & ESTATE TAXES

VALUE OF TOTAL ESTATE PASSING TO ADULT CHILD

	100,000	250,000	500,000	1,000,000	2,000,000
Indiana	0	3,750	14,250	45,250	132,250
Louisiana	1,230	3,930	8,450	17,450	35,450
Nebraska	900	2,400	4,900	9,900	19,900
Ohio	0	0	9,700	44,700	114,700
Oklahoma	0	0	0	9,600	82,850
Pennsylvania	4,500	11,250	22,500	45,000	90,000
South Dakota	3,000	14,250	33,000	70,500	145,500
Tennessee	0	0	0	19,700	111,900
Maximum Federal Credit	0	0	0	0	74,700

The above calculations are based upon research conducted in November 2001. It is assumed that the "Value of Total Estate" is equal to the Adjusted Gross Estate in common-law states and deceased's taxable half of the community property in Louisiana. Exemptions for specific types of property have not been considered. An inheritance tax is levied on the share of each heir at rates which vary according to the heir's relationship with the deceased. An estate tax is levied on the value of the entire estate, normally in a manner similar to the federal estate tax.

Where the amount of regular state inheritance or estate tax is less than the maximum federal credit amount, the state will collect an amount equal to the maximum federal credit. Under EGTRRA 2001, the credits allowed are being reduced by 25 percent in 2002, 50 percent in 2003, and 75 percent in 2004 (e.g., for a $2,000,000 estate passing to an adult child the maximum credit of $99,600 in 2001 will be reduced to $74,700 in 2002, $49,800 in 2003, and $24,900 in 2004; for a $1,000,000 estate the maximum credit is $0 for 2002-2004). From 2005 to 2009 the credit is replaced with a deduction. In states maintaining an independent state death tax system, a deduction is likely to be of less benefit to the taxpayer than a credit. These changes will not increase or decrease overall estate taxes paid by an estate if a state imposes only a death tax equal to the federal credit (i.e., a "pick-up" state). However, the reduction and repeal of the state death tax credit will result in significant revenue losses in many states, and will likely lead to enactment of new state death tax laws designed to recoup the lost revenue (e.g., a state law imposing a state death tax, "equal to the federal credit as it existed prior to EGTRRA 2001").

STATE EXEMPTIONS FOR LIFE INSURANCE

The following states, unless otherwise noted, completely exempt from taxation insurance proceeds payable to a named beneficiary, provided the named beneficiary is not the insured's estate. Because of the many variations among state laws, it is recommended that the specific statute be reviewed when developing an individual's estate plan.

Connecticut[1]   Maryland
Indiana   Nebraska
Iowa   New Jersey
Kentucky   Ohio
Louisiana   Pennsylvania[2]

---

[1] Also exempt is insurance payable to the insured's estate.

[2] All proceeds are exempt, including those paid to estate.

INFLATION ADJUSTER

Additional Life Insurance Required In 2002
To Keep Up With Inflation

Year Policy Purchased	Death Benefit Of Original Life Insurance Policy				
	50,000	100,000	250,000	500,000	1,000,000
2001	1,400	2,800	7,000	14,000	28,000
2000	3,148	6,295	15,738	31,476	62,952
1999	4,317	8,634	21,584	43,168	86,337
1998	5,186	10,372	25,930	51,859	103,718
1997	6,455	12,910	32,276	64,552	129,104
1996	8,149	16,298	40,744	81,488	162,977
1995	9,777	19,554	48,885	97,770	195,540
1994	11,331	22,662	56,656	113,312	226,624
1993	13,171	26,342	65,856	131,712	263,423
1992	15,066	30,133	75,331	150,663	301,326
1991	17,799	35,598	88,995	177,991	355,981
1990	21,460	42,920	107,301	214,602	429,204
1989	24,890	49,781	124,452	248,903	497,806
1988	27,961	55,922	139,804	279,608	559,216
1987	30,767	61,535	153,837	307,674	615,348
1986	32,302	64,604	161,510	323,020	646,040
1985	35,265	70,530	176,324	352,649	705,297
1984	38,931	77,862	194,656	389,312	778,625
1983	41,777	83,554	208,885	417,770	835,541
1982	47,467	94,934	237,336	474,672	949,345

Explanation: This table shows the amount of additional insurance required to maintain a given purchasing power. For example, if $100,000 of insurance had been purchased in 1993, then an additional $26,342 of insurance would have to be available to provide the same purchasing power in 2002 (i.e., what $100,000 would have purchased in 1993 will require $126,342 in 2002). All calulations are based upon the CPI figures set forth on page 307.

OWNERSHIP AND BENEFICIARY ARRANGEMENTS

	Advantages	Disadvantages
POLICY OWNER		
Insured	Insured retains control of policy and owns cash values. See page 72.	Proceeds subject to estate tax. Policy transferred within 3 years also included in estate.
Spouse of Insured	Simple to arrange. Insured retains indirect control of policy (provided marriage stable). See footnote 5, page 75.	If spouse predeceases insured policy ownership could return to insured (by will, intestacy laws or policy provisions). Proceeds not given away or consumed included in spouse's estate.
Children of Insured	Simple to arrange. Not taxed in estate. No costs to establish. See page 425.	Insured loses control of policy (or never had control if children were applicants). If children minors, must have legal guardian appointed before proceeds paid (time consuming and costly).
Irrevocable Trust	Proceeds not subject to estate tax. Continued maintenance of policy if insured becomes incompetent. See page 56.	Insured does not control policy and cannot change or revoke trust. Costs to establish and trustee fees after death.
POLICY BENEFICIARY		
Individual - paid as lump sum	Simple to arrange. No costs to establish or collect proceeds. No delay in payment of death benefit.	Control of proceeds by beneficiary may lead to loss of funds or refusal to make proceeds available to pay settlement costs and taxes. With minor beneficiary guardian must be appointed.
Individual – paid under settlement option	Simple to arrange. No costs to establish or collect proceeds. Funds remaining with carrier are secure.	Not flexible, insurance company must pay under original option despite beneficiaries changing circumstances. Proceeds not available to pay estate settlement costs and taxes.
Estate of Insured	Simple to arrange. No costs to establish or collect proceeds. Provides liquidity to estate.	Proceeds subject to estate tax and claims of creditors, as well as increasing probate costs.
Irrevocable Trust	Flexible, trust can give trustee broad authority to pay or withhold benefits, provide for successor beneficiaries, and make proceeds available for settlement costs. Provides professional management and investment advice. Not subject to claims of creditors.	Time consuming to establish. Initial costs for drafting of trust and trustee fees after funded by death benefit. Must coordinate with remainder of estate plan.

FACTS ABOUT . . .

Facts About Fathers

Father's Age When Child Is Born	Fathers Who Will Die Before Child	
	Enters College	Graduates
25	1 in 26	1 in 18
30	1 in 19	1 in 13
35	1 in 13	1 in 9
40	1 in 9	1 in 6

Facts About Mothers

Mother's Age When Child Is Born	Mothers Who Will Die Before Child	
	Enters College	Graduates
25	1 in 33	1 in 23
30	1 in 24	1 in 17
35	1 in 17	1 in 12
40	1 in 12	1 in 9

Facts About Children

The Cost Of Raising A Child To Age 18		The Annual Costs Of A College Education	
Family Income	Costs	Year	Amount
less than $38,000	$121,230	2002	$21,611
$38,000 - $64,000	165,630	2007	27,582
more than $64,000	241,770	2012	35,202
		2017	44,928

Source of facts about fathers and mothers: Calculations based upon the Commissioners 1980 Standard Ordinary Mortality Table, and assume that the child enters a 4-year college at age 18.

Source of costs of raising a child to age 18: Calculations based upon annual expenditures in 2000, as contained in Statistical Abstract of the United States, 2001, Table 656 on page 429. These costs do not include increases in consumer prices beyond the year 2000.

Source of the annual costs of a college education: Author research of college internet sites during the month of February, 2002, supplemented by direct inquiry when required. College costs are for the 2001-2002 year, and are based upon a representative sampling of 42 state and private colleges in 39 states (see page 99). Projections are based upon cost increases of 5 percent per year. In recent years actual college costs have increased more than 5 percent.

FACTS ABOUT . . . (continued)

Facts About The Value Of An Education

Having an education will often determine the economic opportunities available over a lifetime. Persons with a bachelor's degree or more on the average earn over 3½ times more than those who have completed less than 9th grade, and over 2 times more than those who have completed only high school.

Median Annual Income

	Less than 9th grade	High school graduate	Bachelor's degree or more
Men	$18,743	$30,414	$66,810
Women	12,392	18,092	36,755

Facts About Funerals

According to a 2001 survey conducted by the National Funeral Directors Association the average adult funeral costs $6,130. However, the ultimate costs will depend upon the specific items and services.

Item/Service	Cost
Professional service charges	$1,213
Embalming	420
Other preparations (Cosmetology, hair, etc.)	150
Visitation/Viewing	275
Funeral at Funeral Home	350
Transfer of remains to funeral home	154
Hearse (local)	185
Service Car/Van	85
Acknowledgement cards	18
Casket	2,330
Vault	950
Total	$6,130

Source of Facts About The Value Of An Education: Statistical Abstract of the United States, 2001, Table 677 on page 441.

Source of Facts About Funerals: See www.nfda.org/resources/2001gpl. These costs do not include cemetery charges, such as a grave space, opening and closing grave, crypts and mausoleum, monument or marker.

COLLEGE COSTS PROJECTED

Yearly Tuition, Fees, Supplies, Room & Board

NAME OF INSTITUTION	LOCATION	Assuming Increases of 5% Per Year			
		2002	2007	2012	2017
Auburn University	Auburn, Ala.	9,600	12,252	15,637	19,958
Bowdoin College	Brunswick, Maine	34,280	43,751	55,839	71,266
Brigham Young University	Provo, Utah	7,840	10,006	12,771	16,299
Bucknell University	Lewisburg, Pa.	33,583	42,861	54,703	69,817
The Citadel	Charleston, S.C.	13,806	17,620	22,489	28,702
Colorado State University	Ft. Collins, Colo.	12,152	15,509	19,794	25,263
Columbia College	New York, N.Y.	35,188	44,910	57,318	73,153
Dartmouth College	Hanover, N.H.	34,458	43,978	56,128	71,636
De Paul University	Chicago, Ill.	22,695	28,965	36,968	47,181
Drake University	Des Moines, Iowa	22,830	29,138	37,188	47,462
Duke University	Durham, N.C.	34,458	43,978	56,128	71,636
Emory University	Atlanta, Ga.	33,792	43,128	55,044	70,251
Florida State University	Tallahassee, Fla.	8,535	10,893	13,903	17,744
George Washington Univ.	Washington, D.C.	35,013	44,686	57,032	72,790
Hamline University	St. Paul, Minn.	23,255	29,680	37,880	48,345
Harvard College	Cambridge, Mass.	37,750	48,180	61,491	78,480
Jackson State University	Jackson, Miss.	7,458	9,519	12,148	15,505
Kansas State University	Manhattan, Kans.	6,832	8,720	11,129	14,203
Loyola College in Md.	Baltimore, Md.	30,340	38,722	49,421	63,075
Marquette University	Milwaukee, Wis.	26,646	34,008	43,404	55,395
Michigan State University	E. Lansing, Mich.	10,386	13,255	16,918	21,592
Middlebury College	Middlebury, Vt.	34,500	44,032	56,197	71,723
Ohio State University	Columbus, Ohio	10,819	13,808	17,623	22,492
Oral Roberts University	Tulsa, Okla.	18,550	23,675	30,216	38,564
Purdue University	W. Lafayette, Ind.	12,334	15,742	20,091	25,642
Rutgers College	New Brunswick, N.J.	13,098	16,717	21,335	27,230
St. Lawrence University	Canton, N.Y.	32,605	41,613	53,110	67,783
Salem International Univ.	Salem, W.Va.	18,072	23,065	29,437	37,570
Seattle University	Seattle, Washington	24,563	31,349	40,011	51,065
Southern Methodist Univ.	Dallas, Tex.	28,349	36,181	46,178	58,936
Stanford University	Stanford, Calif.	34,221	43,676	55,742	71,143
Texas A & M University	College Sta., Tex.	11,797	15,056	19,216	24,525
Tulane University	New Orleans, La.	33,698	43,008	54,890	70,056
University of Arkansas	Fayetteville, Ark.	9,678	12,352	15,764	20,120
University of California	Berkley, Calif.	13,161	16,797	21,438	27,361
University of Louisville	Louisville, Ky.	7,392	9,434	12,041	15,367
University of New Mexico	Albuquerque, N.Mex.	8,356	10,665	13,611	17,372
University of Rhode Island	Kingston, R.I.	12,712	16,224	20,707	26,427
University of Virginia	Charlottesville, Va.	9,370	11,959	15,263	19,480
Vanderbilt University	Nashville, Tenn.	34,483	44,010	56,169	71,688
Yale University	New Haven, Conn.	34,030	43,432	55,431	70,746
Yeshiva University	New York, N.Y.	24,980	31,882	40,690	51,932
Average Cost		21,611	27,582	35,202	44,928

Explanation of Table. Costs for public schools assume the student is a resident of the state. Costs (i.e., tuition) for out-of-state students are generally substantially more then shown. Costs for supplies are included when available. Since over the past decade college costs have more than kept pace with the rate of inflation, it seems highly likely that costs will continue to escalate in the years to come. In this regard, see the Consumer Price Index on page 307. Source of 2001-2002 college education costs: Author research of college internet sites during the month of February, 2002, supplemented by direct inquiry when required.

HUMAN LIFE VALUE

The value of $10,000 in annual earnings, discounted by 5 percent, according to the number of "working years to retirement" and rates of projected growth.

Working Years To Retirement	Projected Growth In Earnings				
	4%	5%	6%	7%	8%
1	10,000	10,000	10,000	10,000	10,000
2	19,905	20,000	20,095	20,191	20,286
3	29,719	30,000	30,290	30,576	30,862
4	39,436	40,000	40,578	41,157	41,745
5	49,062	50,000	50,960	51,943	52,935
6	58,597	60,000	61,444	62,935	64,444
7	68,037	70,000	72,032	74,136	76,286
8	77,389	80,000	82,721	85,550	88,467
9	86,655	90,000	93,509	97,177	100,995
10	95,828	100,000	104,397	109,025	113,880
11	104,913	110,000	115,392	121,100	127,135
12	113,912	120,000	126,489	133,408	140,770
13	122,826	130,000	137,692	145,947	154,790
14	131,656	140,000	149,003	158,728	169,214
15	140,404	150,000	160,424	171,754	184,049
16	149,067	160,000	171,953	185,025	199,306
17	157,647	170,000	183,589	198,548	215,001
18	166,146	180,000	195,339	212,331	231,144
19	174,564	190,000	207,197	226,375	247,747
20	182,902	200,000	219,171	240,687	264,826
21	191,159	210,000	231,258	255,273	282,393
22	199,339	220,000	243,461	270,135	300,460
23	207,449	230,000	255,779	285,277	319,044
24	215,465	240,000	268,217	300,714	338,160
25	223,413	250,000	280,773	316,442	357,823
26	231,286	260,000	293,447	332,468	378,045
27	239,081	270,000	306,239	348,797	398,843
28	246,802	280,000	319,152	365,438	420,235
29	254,452	290,000	332,193	382,400	442,242
30	262,028	300,000	345,353	399,680	464,873
31	269,532	310,000	358,643	417,294	488,159
32	276,966	320,000	372,061	435,246	512,112
33	284,330	330,000	385,605	453,538	536,748
34	291,622	340,000	399,281	472,179	562,087
35	298,846	350,000	413,086	491,177	588,153
36	306,000	360,000	427,021	510,535	614,958
37	313,088	370,000	441,091	530,264	642,535
38	320,104	380,000	455,289	550,360	670,887
39	327,056	390,000	469,624	570,842	700,054
40	333,938	400,000	484,092	591,708	730,046

Explanation of Table. Footnote 4 on page 17 contains an explanation of how to use this table to calculate human life value.

ANNUAL GIFTS - VALUE OF MAKING

Gifts Of $11,000 Per Year and 8% Appreciation

Current Estate	At The End Of 10 Years		At The End Of 20 Years	
	Estate Value	Taxes Saved	Estate Value	Taxes Saved
500,000	907,363	32,580	1,786,828	257,863
600,000	1,123,255	71,468	2,252,925	278,253
700,000	1,339,148	74,228	2,719,020	293,390
800,000	1,555,040	77,445	3,185,116	299,010
900,000	1,770,933	77,445	3,651,212	299,010
1,000,000	1,986,825	83,803	4,117,308	299,010
1,500,000	3,066,288	94,655	6,447,789	299,011
2,000,000	4,145,751	94,656	8,778,269	299,012
3,000,000	6,304,677	94,657	13,439,230	326,196
4,000,000	8,463,603	94,656	18,100,191	299,015
5,000,000	10,622,529	103,262	22,761,152	299,016
10,000,000	21,417,158	94,659	46,065,956	299,025

Gifts Of $22,000 Per Year and 8% Appreciation

Current Estate	At The End Of 10 Years		At The End Of 20 Years	
	Estate Value	Taxes Saved	Estate Value	Taxes Saved
500,000	735,262	32,580	1,243,176	497,234
600,000	951,155	122,003	1,709,272	533,014
700,000	1,167,047	146,573	2,175,368	568,541
800,000	1,382,940	152,550	2,641,464	590,848
900,000	1,598,832	154,890	3,107,560	598,019
1,000,000	1,814,725	161,248	3,573,656	598,019
1,500,000	2,894,188	187,194	5,904,136	598,020
2,000,000	3,973,651	189,311	8,234,617	598,021
3,000,000	6,132,577	189,312	12,895,578	652,386
4,000,000	8,291,503	189,312	17,556,539	598,024
5,000,000	10,450,428	206,522	22,217,499	598,025
10,000,000	21,245,058	189,314	45,522,304	598,034

Explanation of Table. The annual gifts of $11,000 and $22,000 are assumed to qualify as "present interest gifts" (see chart on page 49, and discussion in footnote 4, page 59). The column entitled "Estate Value" represents the value of the appreciated estate, assuming 8 percent appreciation and reductions for the annual gifts. For example, assume an individual with a $1,000,000 estate made gifts of $11,000 per year. At the end of 10 years, the estate would have appreciated to $1,986,825, despite having made $110,000 of gifts ($11,000 per year for 10 years). The estate tax savings are $83,803. At the end of 20 years, the estate would have appreciated to $4,117,308, despite having made $220,000 of gifts ($11,000 per year for 20 years). The estate tax savings are $299,010.

TRUSTS AND THEIR USES

TYPE	CHARACTERISTICS	TAX IMPLICATIONS		
		Income	Gift	Estate
Revocable	Created during grantor's life. If unfunded, acts as a will substitute. If funded, can manage property for benefit of grantor, spouse and other beneficiaries.	Trust income taxable to grantor.	No gifts, since grantor retains control of property.	No estate tax advantages, but payment of insurance proceeds to trust can provide greater flexibility than settlement options.
Irrevocable	Created during grantor's life. Grantor gives up all control over assets in order to gain estate tax advantages (chart, page 57). Also see Dynasty Trust, page 378.	Trust pays tax if income accumulated in trust. Beneficiaries pay taxes if income distributed. Income taxed to grantor if certain strings retained.	When property placed in trust there is a gift. With "Crummey powers," gifts are considered present interest gifts which qualify for the annual exclusion (chart, page 49).	Generally not included in estate, except proceeds of life insurance given to trust within 3 years of death (pages 388-389), or if grantor retains interest in trust.
Testamentary	Created upon death pursuant to a will (chart, page 29, and page 419).	None, trust created at death.	None, trust created at death.	Taxable in testator's estate.
Minor's Trust (Section 2503(c))	Created during grantor's life. Trust's accumulated income and principal must be paid to beneficiary upon attaining age 21 (further discussion, page 481).	Trust pays taxes if income accumulated in trust. Beneficiaries pay taxes if income distributed.	When property placed in trust there is a gift which qualifies for the annual exclusion.	Not included in grantor's estate, except life insurance given within 3 years of death.
Income Trust (Section 2503(b))	Created during grantor's life. Trust must distribute income annually, but principal need not be paid to beneficiary (further discussion, page 481).	Beneficiaries pay taxes when income is distributed.	When property placed in trust there is a gift which qualifies for the annual exclusion.	Not included in grantor's estate, except life insurance given within 3 years of death

DEGREES OF KINDRED

Solid lines indicate the paths of direct descendancy. Full cousins are to the right of the principal. Cousins above the principal are "cousins in the ascendancy." Cousins below the principal are "cousins in descendancy." Numbers in lower right corners indicate the degree of kindred to principal (e.g., uncle and nephew are both in the 3rd degree of kindred and therefore would likely inherit in equal amounts, if the principal died intestate without any heirs in the 1st or 2nd degree, and no other heirs in the 3rd degree).

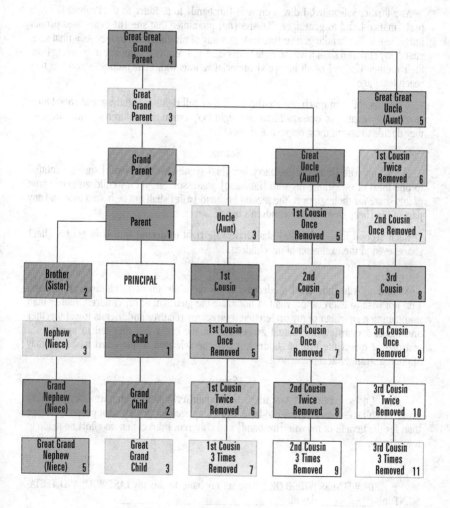

INTESTATE'S WILL

Being of sound mind and memory, I _____, do hereby publish this as my Last Will and Testament:

First

I give my wife [husband] only one-third of my possessions, and I give my children the remaining two-thirds.

I appoint my wife [husband] as guardian of my children, but as a safeguard I require that she [he] report to the Probate Court each year and render an accounting of how, why and where she [he] spent the money necessary for the proper care of my children.

As a further safeguard, I direct my wife [husband] to produce to the Probate Court, a performance bond to guarantee that she [he] guarantee that she [he] exercises proper judgement in the handling, investing and spending of my children's money. As a final safeguard, my children shall have the right to demand and receive a complete accounting from their mother [father] of all her [his] financial actions with their money as soon as they reach legal age.

When my children reach age 18, they shall have full rights to withdraw and spend their share of my estate. No one shall have any right to question my children's actions on how they decide to spend their respective shares.

Second

Should my wife [husband] remarry, her [his] second husband [wife] shall be entitled to one-third of everything my wife [husband] possesses. Should my children need some of this share for their support, the second husband [wife] shall not be bound to spend any part of his [her] share on my children's behalf.

Such second husband [wife] shall have sole right to decide who is to get his [her] share, even to the exclusion of my children.

Third

Should my wife [husband] predecease me or die while any of my children are minors, I do not wish to exercise my right to nominate the guardian of my children. Rather than nominating a guardian of my preference, I direct my relatives and friends to get together and select a guardian by mutual agreement. In the event that they fail to agree on a guardian, I direct the Probate Court to make the selection. If the court wishes, it may appoint a stranger acceptable to it.

Fourth

Under existing tax law, there are certain legitimate techniques open to me to lower death taxes. Since I prefer to have my money used for government purposes rather than for the benefit of my wife [husband] and children, I direct that no effort be made to lower taxes.

IN WITNESS WHEREOF, I have set my hand to this my LAST WILL AND TESTA-MENT this _____ day of _____, 20_____.

_____

STATE LAWS ON INTESTATE SUCCESSION

When someone dies without a will, state law effectively provides a "one-size-fits-all" will through intestate succession statutes. It is important to remember, though, that just as a will may not control all of a decedent's property, state intestate succession statutes may not determine how all of a decedent's property is distributed at his death. Determining how the law will divide the property of a decedent who dies without a will can be complex. Property may pass by title (e.g., joint ownership with rights of survivorship), by contract (e.g., a life insurance beneficiary designation), or by some state statute other than the intestate succession statute.

These "other" statutes include dower and curtesy statutes, homestead statutes, right of election statutes, family allowance and support statutes, and statutes in common law states preserving the community property nature of property previously acquired by a married couple in a community property state. These statutes can be significant in determining the ultimate disposition of an intestate decedent's property.

Nonetheless, the statutes of intestate succession are quite important. The following briefly summarizes the shares into which the various states' intestate succession statutes divide the intestate estate when a decedent dies without a will and *leaves a surviving spouse and child(ren) but no other issue* (i.e., no grandchildren, no great grandchildren, etc.). Special rules may determine whether certain individuals–such as adopted, step or illegitimate children of the decedent–will qualify as "children" of the decedent for purposes of intestate succession.

Unless separately stated, community property includes "quasi-community property" (generally defined as property acquired in another state that would have been considered community property had it been acquired within the community property state). See discussion of community property on pages 359-360. Unless otherwise noted, property passing to the decedent's children is divided equally among them.

One final note of caution! Because state laws can change, the reader should consult local counsel for current law.

Alabama
If all children are issue of the surviving spouse also: spouse gets first $50,000, plus ½ of balance; remainder to child(ren).
If any child is not issue of surviving spouse: ½ to spouse; ½ to child(ren).

Alaska
If all children are issue of the surviving spouse and the decedent leaves no other surviving descendants or parents: all to spouse.
If any child is not issue of the surviving spouse: spouse gets first $100,000 plus ½ of balance; remainder to child(ren).

Arizona

If all children are issue of the surviving spouse also, spouse gets entire estate.

If any child is not issue of surviving spouse: spouse gets ½ of decedent's *separate* property, and none of decedent's share of *community* property; remainder to child(ren).

Arkansas

All property to child(ren).

California

Community property: all to spouse.

Separate property: if one child, then ½ to spouse and ½ to child; if more than one child, then ⅓ to spouse and ⅔ to children.

Colorado

If all children are issue of the surviving spouse also and there are no other issue of the surviving spouse: all to the spouse.

If all of the children are issue of the surviving spouse also but the surviving spouse has one or more surviving issue who are not also issue of the decedent: first $150,000 plus ½ of any balance to the spouse; the rest to the decedent's child(ren).

If one or more of the children is not also issue of the surviving spouse, and all such children are adults: the first $100,000 plus ½ of any balance to the spouse; the rest to the decedent's child(ren).

If one or more of the children is not also issue of the surviving spouse, and if any of such children is a minor: ½ to the surviving spouse; the rest to the decedent's child(ren).

Connecticut

If all children are issue of the surviving spouse also: spouse gets first $100,000, plus ½ of balance; remainder to child(ren).

If any child is not issue of surviving spouse: ½ to spouse; ½ to child(ren).

Delaware

If all children are issue of the surviving spouse also: spouse gets first $50,000 of the *personal* estate, plus ½ of balance of the personal estate, plus a life estate in the *real* estate; rest to child(ren).

If any child is not issue of surviving spouse: spouse gets ½ of *personal* estate, plus a life estate in the *real* estate; rest to child(ren).

District of Columbia

⅓ to spouse; ⅔ to child(ren).

Florida

If all children are issue of the surviving spouse also: spouse gets first $60,000 plus ½ of balance; remainder to child(ren).

If any child is not issue of surviving spouse: ½ to spouse; ½ to child(ren).

Georgia
Spouse shares equally with child(ren); but spouse entitled to at least ⅓.

Hawaii
If all children are issue of the surviving spouse also and there are no other issue of the surviving spouse: all to spouse.

If all children are issue of the surviving spouse also but the surviving spouse has one or more surviving issue who are not the issue of the decedent: first $150,000 plus ½ of balance to spouse; the rest to the decedent's child(ren).

If one or more of the children is not also issue of the surviving spouse: the first $100,000 plus ½ of balance to surviving spouse; the remainder to the decedent's child(ren).

Idaho
Community property: all to spouse.

Separate property: spouse gets ½ of estate and ½ goes to child(ren).

Illinois
½ to spouse; ½ to child(ren).

Indiana
½ to spouse; ½ to child(ren). If no child is a child of the surviving spouse, such spouse takes ½ of personal property, remainder of personal property to child(ren); but the real property goes to the child(ren) subject to spouse's life estate in ⅓.

Iowa
If all children are issue of the surviving spouse also: spouse gets all of *real* property, plus all *personal* property that was exempt from execution in hands of decedent as head of family at death, plus all of remainder not necessary for payment of debts and charges.

If any child is not issue of surviving spouse: spouse gets ½ of *real* property, plus all *personal* property that was exempt from execution in hands of decedent as head of family at death, plus ½ of remaining *personal* property not necessary for payment of debts and charges; remainder to child(ren) (but spouse entitled to minimum of $50,000 in value from entire net estate).

Kansas
½ to spouse; ½ to child(ren).

Kentucky
All to child(ren).

Louisiana
Community property: decedent's share to children, but subject to usufruct in favor of surviving spouse (beneficial use until remarriage, unless decedent spouse specifies such use shall be for life or a shorter period).

Separate property: all to children.

Maine

If all children are issue of the surviving spouse also: spouse gets first $50,000, plus ½ of balance; remainder to child(ren).

If any child is not issue of surviving spouse: ½ to spouse; ½ to child(ren).

Maryland

If a surviving minor child: ½ to spouse; ½ to child(ren).

If no surviving minor child: spouse gets first $15,000, plus ½ of balance; remainder to child(ren).

Massachusetts

½ to spouse; ½ to child(ren).

Michigan

If all children are issue of the surviving spouse also: spouse gets first $150,000 plus ½ of balance; remainder to children.

If any child is not issue of surviving spouse: $100,000 plus ½ of balance to spouse; remainder to children.

Minnesota

If all children are issue of the surviving spouse also and the surviving spouse has no other surviving issue: all to spouse.

If all children are issue of the surviving spouse also but the surviving spouse has one or more surviving issue who are not issue of the decedent, or if any child is not issue of the surviving spouse also: the first $150,000 plus ½ of any balance to the spouse; the rest to the decedent's child(ren).

Mississippi

Spouse shares equally with child(ren).

Missouri

If all children are issue of the surviving spouse also: spouse gets first $20,000, plus ½ of balance; remainder to child(ren).

If any child is not issue of surviving spouse: ½ to spouse; ½ to child(ren).

Montana

If all children are issue of the surviving spouse also and the surviving spouse has no other surviving issue: all to spouse.

If all children are issue of the surviving spouse but the surviving spouse has any surviving issue who is not also issue of the decedent: the spouse gets first $150,000, plus ½ of any balance; the rest to decedent's child(ren).

If any child is not also issue of the surviving spouse: spouse gets first $100,000, plus ½ of balance; the rest to the decedent's child(ren).

Nebraska

If all children are issue of the surviving spouse also: spouse gets first $50,000, plus ½ of balance; remainder to child(ren).

If any child is not issue of surviving spouse: ½ to spouse; ½ to child(ren).

Nevada

Community property: all to spouse.

Separate property: if one child, then ½ to spouse and ½ to child; if more than one child, then ⅓ to spouse and ⅔ to children.

New Hampshire

If all children are issue of the surviving spouse also: spouse gets first $50,000, plus ½ of balance; remainder to child(ren).

If any child is not issue of surviving spouse: ½ to spouse; ½ to child(ren).

New Jersey

If all children are issue of the surviving spouse also: spouse gets first $50,000, plus ½ of balance; remainder to child(ren).

If any child is not issue of surviving spouse: ½ to spouse; ½ to child(ren).

New Mexico

Community property: all to spouse.

Separate property: ¼ to spouse; ¾ to child(ren).

New York

$50,000 plus ½ of the balance to spouse; the rest to child(ren).

North Carolina

If only one child: *real* property goes ⅓ to spouse and ⅔ to child; with respect to *personal* property, spouse gets first $30,000 plus ½ of balance, and remainder to child.

If two or more children: *real* property goes ⅓ to spouse and ⅔ to children; with respect to *personal* property, spouse gets first $30,000 plus ⅓ of balance, and remainder to children.

North Dakota

If all children are issue of the surviving spouse also and the surviving spouse has no other surviving issue: all to spouse.

If all children are issue of the surviving spouse also but the surviving spouse has one or more surviving issue who are not issue of the decedent: the first $150,000 plus ½ of any balance to the spouse; the rest to the decedent's child(ren).

If any child is not issue of the surviving spouse also: the first $100,000 plus ½ of any balance to the spouse; the rest to the decedent's child(ren).

Ohio

If only one child: spouse gets all if spouse is natural or adoptive parent of child, or first $20,000 if spouse is not natural or adoptive parent of child, plus ½ of balance; remainder to child.

If two or more children: spouse gets first $60,000 if spouse is natural or adoptive parent of one of the children, but not all, or first $20,000 if spouse is parent of none of children, plus ⅓ of balance; remainder to children.

Oklahoma

If all children are issue of the surviving spouse also: an undivided ½ interest in the property of the estate to spouse; the balance in undivided equal shares to child(ren).

If any child is not issue of surviving spouse: an undivided ½ interest in property acquired by joint industry of husband and wife during marriage to spouse; the spouse and the child(ren) take equal undivided shares in the property of the decedent not acquired by the joint industry of the husband and wife during marriage; the remainder of estate in undivided equal shares to the child(ren).

Oregon

If all children are issue of the surviving spouse also, spouse gets entire estate.

If any child is not issue of surviving spouse: ½ to spouse; ½ to child(ren).

Pennsylvania

If all children are issue of the surviving spouse also: spouse gets first $30,000, plus ½ of balance; remainder to child(ren).

If any child is not issue of surviving spouse: ½ to spouse; ½ to child(ren).

Rhode Island

Real property: all to child(ren).

Personal property: ½ to spouse; ½ to child(ren).

South Carolina

½ to spouse; ½ to child(ren).

South Dakota

If all children are issue of the surviving spouse also, spouse gets entire estate.

If any child is not issue of the surviving spouse: spouse gets first $100,000 plus ½ of any balance remainder to child(ren).

Tennessee

Spouse shares equally with child(ren); but spouse entitled to at least ⅓.

Texas

Community property: If all children are also issue of the surviving spouse, then all to the surviving spouse; if any child is not issue of the surviving spouse, then ½ of the community estate is retained by the surviving spouse and ½ passes to child(ren).

Separate property: with respect to *personal* property, ⅓ to spouse and ⅔ to child(ren); with respect to *real* property, spouse takes life estate in ⅓, remainder to child(ren) [Presumably by "remainder" the statute means the remainder interest in the spouse's life estate *and* the fee interest in the remaining ⅔ of the real estate].

Utah

If all children are issue of the surviving spouse also, spouse gets entire estate.

If any child is not issue of surviving spouse: ½ to spouse; ½ to child(ren).

Vermont

At least ⅓ of personal estate to spouse, other property to child(ren).

Virginia

If all children are issue of the surviving spouse also, spouse gets entire estate.

If any child is not issue of surviving spouse: ⅓ to spouse; ⅔ to child(ren).

Washington

Community property: all to spouse.

Separate property: ½ to spouse; ½ to child(ren).

West Virginia

If all children are issue of the surviving spouse also and the surviving spouse has no other surviving issue, spouse gets entire estate.

If all children are issue of the surviving spouse also but the surviving spouse has any surviving issue who is not also issue of the decedent: ⅗ to spouse; ⅖ to decedent's child(ren).

If any child is not issue of the surviving spouse: ½ to spouse; ½ to decedent's child(ren).

Wisconsin

If all children are issue of the surviving spouse also, spouse gets entire net intestate estate.

If any child is not issue of surviving spouse: spouse gets ½ of net intestate estate consisting of decedent's property other than marital property (i.e., property acquired during marriage); remainder to child(ren).

Wyoming

½ to spouse; ½ to child(ren).

TABLE OF CONTENTS

POINTERS

Value And Control.

It is essential for any successful business continuation or disposition plan to consider the factors of value and control. Complete control of a business with no value is worthless; and value in a business you do not control is tenuous. With most successful operating businesses, value and control are typically fixed and determined. In the small closely-held business it is generally accepted that the

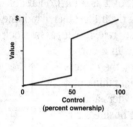

same individual, or group of individuals, both control the business and own the value. But what happens to control and value upon the death of the business owner? This is the essential question you must address in developing an effective business succession plan. By charting the interrelationship of these two factors you can better appreciate how control dictates value. Greater control means greater value – less control means less value. But the relationship is not linear! Having a controlling interest (i.e., more than 50 percent) in a closely-held corporation produces a "control premium," as can be seen from the sharp increase in value in the chart. The flip side of the control premium is the discount allowed for a minority interest (page 390).

Continued – Sold – Liquidated.

There is no better place to begin a discussion of business succession planning than by asking the questions set forth on page 121. But before you begin the discussion, visit the chart on page 119. Where would you place your client on this chart? Just as importantly, where would your client place himself on this chart? This insight should enable you to more effectively work with your client in developing and implementing a business disposition plan.

Know The Entity.

Before proceeding, it is essential to identify the type, or format, of the business: corporation, S corporation, partnership, limited liability company, or sole proprietorship. The form of organization is an important consideration in selecting an agreement to be used if it is intended that the business will be sold (e.g., a stock redemption agreement does not work very well with a sole proprietorship). In this regard, you may wish to consult the materials on pages 182-184, 200-201, 415, 427-429, 432, 419, and 458-460. Knowing the type of business is also important when considering employee benefits (pages 286-292).

Retain Control . . . Shift Value.

If your client's business is to be continued by a family member, there are many techniques that can be used to reduce estate taxes – while at the same time maintaining control (page 43). Implementation of a specific arrangement will often depend not only upon your client's willingness to proceed, but also upon the ability of your client's professional advisors to work as a team.

Compare The Charts.

The cross purchase agreement involves an agreement between the owners to buy and sell their respective interests. You might think of it as a horizontal obligation running from business owner to business owner. On the other hand, the entity purchase agreement, also referred to as a stock

←——Cross Purchase——→ redemption agreement if used with a corporation, involves an agreement by the owners to sell their respective interests to the business. You might think of it as a vertical obligation running between the business owners and the business. However, because of changing individual and business circumstances, choosing between a cross purchase agreement and an entity purchase agreement can be difficult. To keep their options open, your clients may prefer to use the highly flexible "wait and see" buy/sell agreement. With this arrangement, the decision as to who will make the purchase is delayed until after the death of an owner. All of these agreements provide for the complete sale of a business interest, and can be used with either a corporation or a partnership, but not with a sole proprietorship. To gain a better understanding of these plans, compare the charts on pages 129, 133 and 141.

Entity Purchase

"Wait And See"

Business Valuation Is Art . . . Not Science.

With the business owner the subject of business valuation is a wonderful "ice breaker." However, do not promise more than you can deliver. Business valuation is art, it is not science. The chart on page 125 provides a good place to begin, but a capitalization of earnings approach is not relevant in valuing many businesses (e.g., a medical practice or professional corporation). If appropriate, do not hesitate to advise your client to retain an accredited expert to perform a comprehensive business valuation.

Risk Management.

You should discuss "risk management" with the business owner. As stated by Judge Staley, "The business that insures its buildings and machinery and automobiles from every possible hazard can hardly be expected to exercise less care in protecting itself from the loss of its most vital assets – managerial skill and experience" (see quotable quotes, page 334). The statistics on pages 185 and 186 will help you quantify this risk for your business owner clients.

Sales Between Surviving Family Members.

When a business represents a large percentage of an estate, it has been an accepted practice to arrange for active family members to purchase the business interest from inactive family members (e.g., daughter active in business prior to father's death purchases inactive son's inherited 25 percent interest). If carryover basis becomes a reality, the loss of a step-up in basis will cause this purchase to be subject to income taxation (page 6). If "estate equalization" is your client's objective, then income taxation could be avoided by providing life insurance for the inactive son – either as direct owner and beneficiary of a contract insuring your client, or as beneficiary of an irrevocable life insurance trust (page 57).

Understand The Attribution Rules.

These rules have been aptly described as "infamous and insidious." While at first they may appear esoteric and difficult, they are important to understand. In family held corporations, if stock owned by one family member is to be sold to the corporation it is extremely important to consider the effect of the attribution rules (pages 176-181). Violation of these rules means that the sale will be treated and taxed as a stock dividend.

Reality Checks . . . They Are Important!

Often your business owner client will want to retain the business for the benefit of a son or daughter. Good planning will usually help this happen, but not if the child is a 2-year old. Then there is the sole proprietor, who is convinced that his key man will take over the business and run it for the benefit of his survivors. This sounds just fine, until you discover that the "keyman" is a stock clerk hired just a year ago – but he is a "bright" young man. And then there is the physician, who is practicing as a sole proprietor, and who is convinced that his practice is easily worth five or six times annual billings, plus the book value of all the equipment he purchased a few years back. These clients will be well served if you help them perform a "reality check-up."

DEVELOPMENT CYCLE OF A BUSINESS

This chart will help us to better understand the typical life cycle of the owner-managed business. Such businesses are usually owned by rugged individualists who were drafted into business in a variety of ways. Although the growth curve is different for each business, it can generally be separated into four distinct phases, with the first two involving a lot of hard work.

The first stage is best described as the **Wonder Stage**, because sooner or later he will wonder, "How in the world did I get into this mess?" A seven-day work-week is the norm, for which he gets *freedom, power*, and the *last word* on how the job is to be done. Undercapitalized and overextended, he expends maximum energy just to keep creditors at bay, avoid taxes, and end up with a profit to finance future growth. The large majority of new businesses don't survive this stage.

It is during the **Blunder Stage** that the last of the failures quit, while the survivors experience substantial growth, work 18-hour days, learn to trust no one, and become *highly secretive*. This leads to a reluctance to teach the business to others.

By the time the **Thunder Stage** is reached, the business owner has become a respected and substantial member of his community. He enjoys his success! Secrecy and a *total lack of review* of his decisions have become hallmarks of his management style. The creation of myths at this stage is commonplace. These include the notion that the business is too unique for anyone else to run; that his experience is all that counts, and business practices should stay the same; that the business is his, to do what he wants with; that HE is *truly immortal*.

It is now that he draws the collective attention of the community's life underwriters and financial advisers. He desperately needs their services, but proves to be distrustful of advice. This dilemma could have been avoided had a relationship of trust and service been established *before* the thunder stage.

During the **Plunder Stage** the owner may tend to lose his appetite for risk, preferring instead just to keep what he has. He must learn to teach and share, not destroy on the way down what he built on the way up. Such teaching and sharing will allow for a renaissance of wonder, the opportunity for a successor's hard work and continued business growth. All too often the alternative is liquidation!

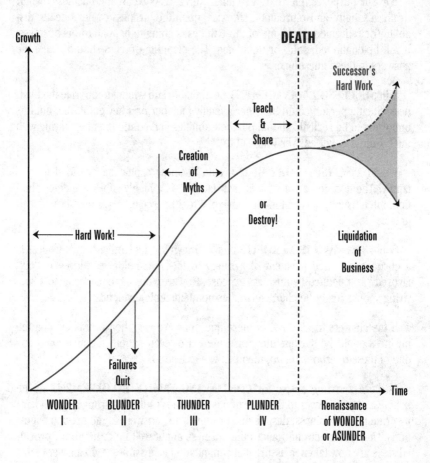

This chart and the accompanying text have been taken from Chapter Three of *Beyond Survival*, by Léon A. Danco, Ph.D., and are reprinted by permission of the publisher. This book has proven to be an invaluable guide to the advisor who desires to understand and effectively communicate with the owner of the closely held business. In addition, Dr. Danco has written *Inside The Family Business*, and *Outside Directors In The Family Owned Business*. Dr. Danco's books may be obtained by writing The Center for Family Business, P.O. Box 24268, Cleveland, Ohio 44124.

DISPOSITION OF A BUSINESS INTEREST

For our purposes, there are essentially three risks facing the business owner: death, disability, and retirement. Likewise, upon the business owner's death, disability, or retirement, only one of three things is going to happen to his business: it will be continued, sold, or liquidated. The planning process should reveal the answers to these questions:

Will **SUCCESSOR MANAGEMENT** be available and willing to operate the business? Such a person could be either a family member or a key employee, but it is important to be realistic about both their abilities and commitment to staying with the business. A *yes* answer will lead to . . .

Would a **SATISFACTORY RETURN** on business capital be provided for the family? The decision as to what is "satisfactory" is a highly subjective determination, but it usually falls within the range of 6 to 20 percent.[1] A *yes* answer will lead to . . .

Could **TAX-FAVORED PROFITS** be withdrawn for the family? If the business is a corporation, then payment of a salary to the stockholder-employee is "tax-favored" as a deductible business expense. However, the same payments to a surviving spouse might be characterized as nondeductible dividends.[2]

If the answers to all three of these questions are *yes*, then it is likely that the business could be successfully **continued**. However, should the answer to any one of these questions be *no*, then this would lead to . . .

Is there a *strong* desire for **CONTINUING FAMILY INVOLVEMENT** in the business? A *yes* answer to this question is often the result of a strong sense of family pride in the business, despite one or more "no" answers to the previous questions. Under such circumstances the business might well be **continued**, provided steps are now taken to assure that continuation is possible.[3] A *no* answer to this question will lead to . . .

Would a **BUYER** be readily available? If the answer is *yes*, then the business should be **sold**, with a binding agreement and adequate funding in order to assure that the sale takes place. A *no* answer to this question means that the business is likely to be **liquidated** and its assets sold for pennies on the dollar.

Footnotes on page 123

UPON DEATH, DISABILITY OR RETIREMENT

THE ANSWERS TO THESE QUESTIONS

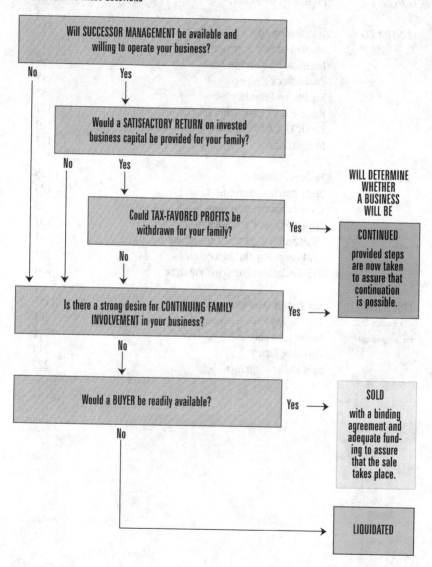

Will SUCCESSOR MANAGEMENT be available and willing to operate your business?

No / Yes

Would a SATISFACTORY RETURN on invested business capital be provided for your family?

No / Yes

Could TAX-FAVORED PROFITS be withdrawn for your family?

Yes →

No

Is there a strong desire for CONTINUING FAMILY INVOLVEMENT in your business?

Yes →

No

Would a BUYER be readily available?

Yes →

No

WILL DETERMINE WHETHER A BUSINESS WILL BE

CONTINUED

provided steps are now taken to assure that continuation is possible.

SOLD

with a binding agreement and adequate funding to assure that the sale takes place.

LIQUIDATED

PLANNING MATRIX

Footnotes

[1] A determination of business value would be a starting point for deciding what would be a "satisfactory" return on business capital. For example, $10,000 of annual income from a business worth $500,000 would probably not be satisfactory. If the business could be sold for $400,000, and the funds invested at 8 percent, the resulting before-tax income would be $32,000 per year, over three times that provided if the business were retained.

[2] There are numerous cases that have held that payments to stockholder-heirs are not deductible to the corporation. In the case of *The Barbourville Brick Company v. Commissioner*, 37 T.C. 7 (1961), the United States Tax Court held that payments to the surviving widow were dividends. Judge Brown, concurring in the denial of any income tax deduction to the corporation, considered the payments nondeductible as not a "reasonable business expense." In his written opinion, Judge Brown observed that:

> "[A]pparently there were no employees, stockholders, or members of [the decedent's] family, qualified to take over the management of petitioner's business. There is neither claim nor evidence that the widow performed any services for [the business]. Finally there is neither claim nor showing that the payments in question were in the nature of extra compensation for past services rendered by petitioner's deceased president . . . income tax deductions are a matter of legislative grace . . . and are to be justified as ordinary and necessary expenses of carrying on a trade or business."

[3] The "steps" relate to preparing for the eventual transfer of a healthy business to other family members or key employees. In this regard, the business planning charts on the following pages demonstrate techniques that will assist in providing the plans and funds for such a smooth transfer of the business. A comparison of life insurance and other sources of estate settlement costs is set forth on page 82.

BUSINESS VALUATION

There are many reasons why the owner of a closely held business must have some idea of the value of his business:

- When *obtaining loans* a higher, yet realistic, value could result in increased credit.
- If the *reasonableness of compensation* to an employee-stockholder is challenged by the IRS, knowing the value of the business will be helpful.[1]
- In *determining a price* for the business when it is sold upon death, disability, or retirement.[2]
- For *estate planning* purposes, the higher the value, the greater the potential estate tax.[3]

Valuation is an art; it is not a science.[4] With the closely held business, the concept of valuation is often elusive. Pat answers rarely exist. However, with many businesses, "capitalizing" expected earnings can be a useful starting point for determining fair market value.

For example, we know that assets, plus the talents of good management, are expected to produce earnings. Assume that a business had assets of $1,400,000 and liabilities of $400,000. By subtracting liabilities from assets, we can determine that book value is $1,000,000.[5] This is the net worth of the business, which is often referred to as stockholder's equity. Also assume that the business has earnings of $220,000.

The first step in capitalizing expected earnings is to determine what rate of return an outside purchaser would expect on his investment. Assume that, after a careful consideration of the risks inherent in this particular business, the *expected* rate of return is determined to be 12 percent.[6] If the sales price were set at book value, or only $1,000,000, expected earnings would then be $120,000. This means that there are *excess* earnings of $100,000, which should be reflected in the sales price as goodwill.

Goodwill is determined by deciding how much a purchaser should pay for these excess earnings, which are the product of such intangibles as reputation and market position. A careful consideration of both the age of the business and the likelihood of continuing excess earnings might reveal that the purchaser should pay for five years of excess earnings, or $500,000. By adding this $500,000 of good will to the $1,000,000 of book value, we get a fair market value for the business of $1,500,000.[7]

Footnotes on page 127

CAPITALIZING EXPECTED EARNINGS

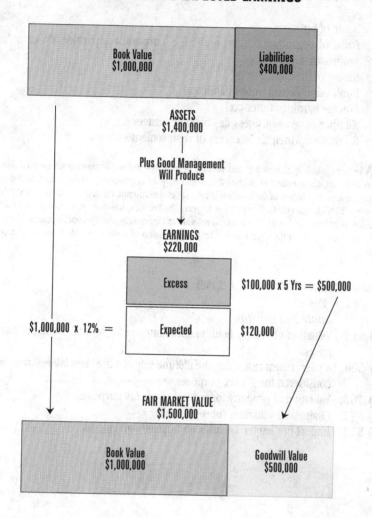

INFORMATION REQUIRED FOR ANALYSIS & PROPOSAL

1. Name of business.
2. Form of organization (corporation, S corporation, partnership or sole proprietorship).
3. Nature of business.
4. Book value (assets minus liabilities).
5. Average earnings (after-tax).
6. Number of years business has been in existence.
7. Salaries of principals in excess of replacement salaries.

Note: Whenever possible, at least a 3-year average of earnings and book value should be used. The salaries of principals in excess of salaries that would be paid to replacements is typically added to average earnings. The nature of the business is relevant to determining the appropriate expected rate of return ("12%" in the chart). The number of years the business has been in existence, and thus its stability, reputation and market position, is relevant to determining the appropriate capitalization of earnings factor ("5" in the chart). For a further discussion of these rates, see footnote 6, page 127.

CROSS REFERENCES TO TAX FACTS 1 (2002)

Estate and Gift Tax

Q 513. Valuation of closely held business interest for federal estate tax purposes.

Q 606. An agreement restricting the lifetime sale of a business interest may be considered for gift tax purposes.

Q 762. Valuation of property for federal estate tax purposes.

Q 812. Chapter 14 valuation rules generally.

Q 815. Impact of Chapter 14 rules on buy/sell agreements.

Footnotes

[1] Knowing the value of the business will help defend the reasonableness of salary and other fringe benefits. In this regard, see the expanded discussion of Unreasonable Compensation on page 483.

[2] Common means of selling businesses are set forth in the Entity Purchase Agreement chart on page 129 and the Cross Purchase Agreement chart on page 133.

[3] Under the Chapter 14 special valuation provisions, the value of property for gift and estate tax purposes is determined without regard to any agreement to acquire the property at less than fair market value. However, this rule does not apply if the agreement is: (1) a *bona fide* business arrangement; (2) not a *device* to transfer the property to members of the decedent's family for less than full and adequate consideration; and (3) in its terms, *comparable* to similar arrangements entered into by persons in an arm's length transaction. All three of these tests are presumed to be met if the agreement is between unrelated individuals (i.e., an agreement exclusively among persons who are not the natural objects of each others' bounty).

In agreements between related individuals maintenance of family ownership and control could be a *bona fide* reason for using a particular business value, thereby satisfying the first test. But the stipulated value will not be controlling for estate tax purposes unless the agreement also meets the *device* and *comparable* tests. In order to satisfy all three of these requirements in family held businesses there is likely to be an increased utilization of both *appraisal* and generally accepted *formula* methods of business valuation (see pages 386-387).

For estate tax purposes, the executor of an estate may elect special methods for valuing *real property* used in a farm, trade, or business. A discussion of the strict qualifications and restrictions imposed appears on pages 448-449.

[4] When valuation is left to chance, it opens the door to litigation with the Internal Revenue Service. The table of Contested Business Valuations (pages 193-198) contains a listing of specific types of businesses which ended up being the subjects of extensive litigation when the owners failed to properly plan for their estate tax valuation. The state of the art is at best uncertain for those who fail to "peg" properly the value of their business interests. It is also important to recognize that valuation may mean different things to different people, depending upon the purpose of the valuation. However, as far as the Internal Revenue Service is concerned, it is based upon a consideration of *all relevant facts*, and in particular those eight factors set forth in the expanded discussion of Fair Market Value on page 390. Financial ratio analysis provides another means of determining business value (see page 192).

[5] In using this approach to business valuation, care must be taken to assure that Book Value accurately reflects the true value of business assets (see page 347).

[6] Selection of appropriate *expected rate of return* and *capitalization of earning* factors is very subjective. Nevertheless, the following may provide some idea of the ranges used:

Expected rate of return		Capitalization of earnings	
8-11%	safe business	1-3	volatile earnings
12-17%	average business	4-6	average, variable earnings
18-22%	speculative business	7-9	stable earnings

[7] This chart demonstrates an application of what has come to be known as the "ARM 34" formula. It is most appropriately used with manufacturing firms involving substantial investments of both plant and equipment. The letters "ARM" stand for "Committee on Appeals and Review Memorandum." This committee no longer exists under the present judicial system. Another, more direct, method of capitalizing earnings is sometimes referred to as the "straight capitalization method" and is best demonstrated by the following question: "If a buyer expects to make 12 percent on his investment, and the business is producing earnings of $220,000 per year, what would the buyer be willing to pay for the business?" The calculation required to answer this question produces a substantially higher valuation than the ARM 34 formula shown in the chart:

Value x .12 = $220,000 *or* Value = $220,000 ÷ .12 = $1,833,333

ENTITY PURCHASE AGREEMENT

The entity purchase agreement is another means of providing for the complete disposition of a business interest. Under such an arrangement the contract is with the business rather than with the other owners.[1]

DURING LIFETIME. To illustrate how it works, assume that we have a corporation that is owned equally by A and B.[2] They would each enter into an agreement with the business for the purchase and sale of their respective interests. Typically, this agreement is *binding*, in that it obligates both A and B, and their estates, to sell, and the business to buy, upon the death, disability or retirement of either one of them.[3]

Rather than relying on its ability to accumulate or borrow sufficient funds to meet its obligations to purchase these interests, the business obtains separate life insurance contracts insuring A and B. The business pays the premiums and is owner and beneficiary of the contracts. In this manner, the business pre-funds its obligations with life insurance. With the use of life insurance to fund an entity purchase agreement the business is in effect *amortizing* the cost of the purchase over the lifetime of the insured.[4]

UPON DEATH. Should A die first, his stock interest passes to his family or estate. At the same time, the insurance company pays a potentially tax-free death benefit to the business as beneficiary of the contract insuring A's life.[5]

Pursuant to the agreement, in return for cash, A's family, or estate, will then transfer A's *entire interest* to the business.[6] In this way a fully funded agreement *guarantees* that the surviving family will receive a fair price for A's interest.[7] If A's estate is subject to estate taxes, the agreement can also serve to help "peg," or establish, the value of the stock for estate tax purposes, thereby avoiding the extensive negotiations and potential litigation with the Internal Revenue Service that may occur when valuation is left to chance.[8]

Footnotes on page 131

DURING LIFETIME

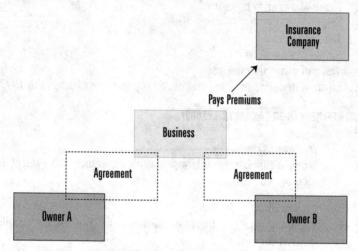

The Business Obtains Life Insurance On Each Owner

UPON DEATH

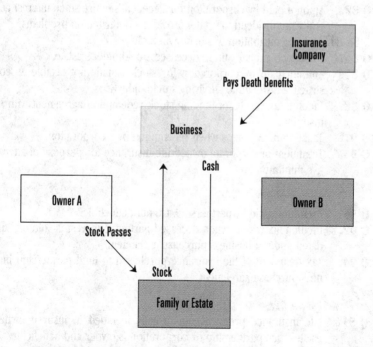

INFORMATION REQUIRED FOR ANALYSIS & PROPOSAL

1. Name of owner to be insured.
2. Sex.
3. Date of birth.
4. Smoker/nonsmoker.
5. Value of ownership interest.
6. Form of organization (corporation, S corporation or partnership).

CROSS REFERENCES TO TAX FACTS 1 (2002)

Income Tax

Q 62. When death benefits of business life insurance are exempt from income tax.

Corporation

Q 46. Premiums paid on business life insurance not usually taxable to insured employee.

Q 47. Premiums paid by corporation on policies insuring the life of a stock-holder or employee usually not deductible.

Q 49. Premiums paid by corporation to fund stock redemption not taxable to insured stockholder.

Q 82. Amount paid by corporation for decedent's entire stock interest generally not dividend to estate, provided no attribution problems.

Q 83-84. Avoiding attribution of stock ownership.

Q 86. Usually no capital gain to deceased stockholder's estate.

Q 87. Amount paid by corporation for stock usually not taxable as constructive dividend to surviving stockholder(s).

Q 88. Income tax results of funding stock redemption agreement with life insurance.

Q 91. Taxation of payments when redemption by S corporation.

Q 95. Treatment of corporate owned life insurance for purpose of alternative minimum tax.

Partnership

Q 56. Premiums paid by partnership are not deductible.

Q 92. Income tax results when deceased partner's interest is sold or liquidated under a business purchase agreement.

Q 94. Tax treatment of life insurance purchased to fund partnership business purchase agreement.

Estate Tax

Q 512. Life insurance proceeds not directly included in insured owner's estate when partnership or corporation is owner and beneficiary.

Q 815. Impact of Chapter 14 valuation rules on buy/sell agreements.

Footnotes

[1] Note that in contrast to the cross purchase agreement, the entity agreement requires that the *business* purchase the interest, not the other owners (compare entity purchase agreement with cross purchase agreement using the materials on page 200). The entity agreement can be used by either a partnership or a corporation with more than one stockholder. It is often the preferred method with *multiple* stockholders or partners, since only one policy on the life of each owner is required (but see, First-to-Die Insurance, page 393, which can be used to fund multiple-owner cross purchase agreements). An entity purchase agreement cannot be used by a corporation with only one stockholder or a sole proprietorship, since the corporation cannot own itself and the sole proprietorship is not a separate entity that can make the purchase. When used to fund the purchase of corporate stock, it is usually referred to as a "stock redemption" or "section 302(b)(3) stock redemption" agreement (see footnote 7, page 151). In this sense, the terms "entity purchase" and "stock redemption" are interchangeable.

[2] It is also assumed that A and B are *not* related to each other. If they were, and the business was a corporation, then the attribution rules would have to be considered (attribution is more fully explained on pages 176-181).

[3] If the agreement is binding upon disability as well as death, consideration should also be given to funding the agreement with disability buy-out insurance (see expanded discussion on page 371). The tax treatment of various disability income arrangements is set forth on page 317.

[4] By having the corporation purchase and pay the insurance premiums, it is often possible to utilize after-tax "enhanced dollars." A full discussion of Enhanced Dollars is found on page 380. Even if the corporation is not in a lower tax bracket than its stockholders, the entity purchase may still be the preferred method, since the corporate check is usually far easier to obtain for premium payments than a client's personal check. The likelihood that life insurance will be used can be estimated by referring to the Odds of Death tables on pages 185 and 186. Corporate borrowing as an alternative to life insurance funding is usually unattractive, as can be seen from the Cost of Borrowed Dollars table on page 189.

[5] Under some circumstances a portion of annual cash value increases and death proceeds could be subject to the Alternative Minimum Tax, as discussed on pages 342-344.

[6] Note that B is now the sole owner of the business. However, B's cost basis for purposes of income taxes has not been increased, because the business, not B, purchased A's interest. If the business were subsequently sold by B, he would have substantially more gain than would have been the case had B previously purchased A's interest under a cross purchase agreement at A's death. With regard to a corporation, once an entity purchase agreement has been funded with life insurance, it *is generally not* possible to use the same policies when changing to a cross purchase agreement. This is because of the Transfer For Value rule, as more fully explained on pages 479-480.

[7] Various means can be used in the agreement to determine the purchase price. A *fixed price* could be established, with a further provision providing for periodic review and redetermination between the business and the owners. Alternatively, a *formula method* could be used, under which specific factors would be employed to calculate a value. For an example of a *capitalization formula*, see the Business Valuation chart on page 125. Another approach to determining a price is to provide for an *appraisal* at the time of sale (i.e., after the first owner's death, or earlier if a lifetime sale is contemplated).

[8] To help "peg" the value of the business for estate tax purposes, the parties must be required to sell during lifetime for the same price as provided for a sale at death. Also, the agreement must specifically *bind* A's estate or family and further comply with the Chapter 14 requirements (see footnote 3, page 127). The listing of Contested Business Valuations on pages 193-198 provides specific examples of what can happen when there is a failure to properly "peg" the value of stock in a closely held corporation. The cases on page 199 demonstrate that a buy/sell agreement really ly does help fix the value.

CROSS PURCHASE AGREEMENT

The cross purchase agreement is one means of providing for the complete disposition of a business interest.[1] Under this arrangement the owners agree, among themselves, to buy and sell their respective interests.[2]

DURING LIFETIME. To illustrate how this works, assume that we have a corporation equally owned by two individuals, A and B. They enter into an agreement providing for the purchase and sale of their respective interests. Typically, this agreement is *binding* and obligates both parties, or their representatives, to either buy or sell upon the death, disability, or retirement of either one of them.[3]

Rather than trying to accumulate or borrow sufficient funds to buy B's interest, A obtains a life insurance contract insuring B. A applies for this coverage, pays the premiums, and is both owner and beneficiary of the contract. Likewise, B applies for a life insurance contract insuring A, pays the premiums, and is both owner and beneficiary. By this means, A and B can use life insurance to *fully* fund their mutual obligations to each other.[4]

UPON DEATH. Assuming that A dies first, his stock interest would then pass to his family or estate. At the same time, the insurance company pays a death benefit to B, as beneficiary of the contract insuring A's life. B receives these funds free of all income taxes, since they are received as the death benefit of a life insurance contract.[5]

Pursuant to the agreement, A's family, or estate, transfers A's entire stock interest in the corporation to B, in return for which B pays the cash received from the insurance company.

The fully funded agreement will *assure* that A's surviving family receives a fair price for his interest in the business. But such an agreement can also serve another very important function. If the estate had been subject to estate taxes, it is possible that extensive negotiations and even litigation could result if the estate tax value of the business had been left to chance. These problems of delay and litigation can be avoided by having a cross purchase agreement which helps establish, or "peg," the value of the stock.[6]

Footnotes on page 135

DURING LIFETIME

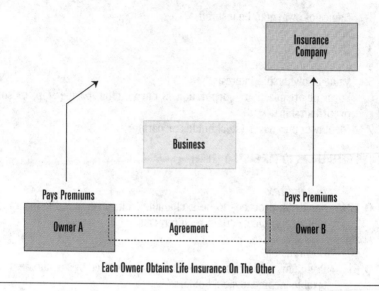

Each Owner Obtains Life Insurance On The Other

UPON DEATH

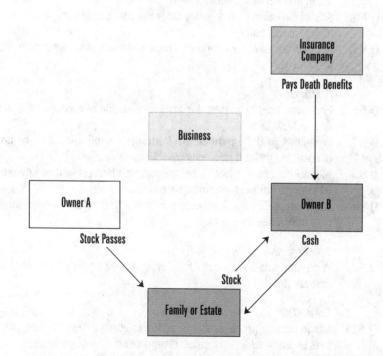

INFORMATION REQUIRED FOR ANALYSIS & PROPOSAL

1. Names of owners to be insured.
2. Sex.
3. Dates of birth.
4. Smoker/nonsmoker.
5. Value of ownership interests.
6. Form of organization (corporation, S corporation, partnership, or sole proprietorship).
7. Identity of purchaser (stockholder or partner).

CROSS REFERENCES TO TAX FACTS 1 (2002)

Income Tax

Q 126. For death proceeds to be excludable from income, a life insurance policy must meet certain requirements.

Corporation

Q 52. Premiums paid by corporation on policies owned by stockholders are taxable income to stockholders.

Q 54. Stockholder cannot deduct premiums paid on policy purchased on life of another stockholder.

Q 80. Sale of deceased's stock will usually not result in income tax liability to deceased's estate.

Q 81. Income tax effects of funding stock purchase agreement with life insurance.

Partnership

Q 56. Premiums paid by partner for insurance on life of copartner are not deductible.

Q 57. Premiums paid by partner for insurance on his own life are not deductible by him if proceeds payable to copartner.

Q 92. Income tax results when deceased partner's interest sold or liquidated under a business purchase agreement.

Q 94. Tax treatment of life insurance purchased to fund partnership business purchase agreement.

Sole Proprietorship

Q 59. Premiums paid by key employee for insurance on life of sole proprietor are not deductible.

Estate Tax

Q 511. Life insurance proceeds not included in insured's estate when partners or stockholders purchase insurance on lives of each other.

Q 815. Impact of Chapter 14 valuation rules on buy/sell agreements.

Footnotes

[1] Compare the cross purchase agreement with the entity purchase agreement using the materials on page 200. The cross purchase agreement can be used with either a corporation or a partnership. With a sole proprietorship, a similar arrangement could be established between the sole proprietor and a key employee (chart, page 145). However, since the key employee has no ownership interest, there are no reciprocal obligations to buy and sell. The sole proprietor would merely be obligated to sell and the key employee obligated to buy. Life insurance funding involves the key employee purchasing a contract on the life of the sole proprietor in order to fund his obligation to purchase. This purchase could be assisted by the split-dollar technique (chart, page 231).

[2] Various means can be used in the agreement to determine a purchase price. A *fixed price* could be established, with a further provision providing for periodic review and redetermination by mutual agreement among the owners. Alternatively, a *formula method* could be employed, under which specific factors would be used to calculate a value. For an example of a *capitalization* formula, refer to the valuation chart on page 125. Another approach to determining a price is to provide for an *appraisal* at the time of sale (i.e., after the first owner's death, or earlier if a lifetime sale is contemplated). Under the right circumstances the price received could be supplemented by a "Springing" Trust, as more fully explained on page 471.

[3] A cross purchase agreement will avoid the attribution problems that can occur in a family held corporation (attribution is more fully explained on pages 176-181). However, a cross purchase agreement with *multiple* stockholders can be cumbersome when the agreement is to be funded with life insurance. For example, with three stockholders, six policies would be required because each stockholder would have to be the owner and beneficiary of a policy on each of the other stockholders. If there were four stockholders, twelve policies would be required. To avoid the problem of multiple policies, preference is often given to using an entity purchase agreement (chart, page 129). A trusteed cross purchase agreement might also be considered (chart, page 137 and comparison page 201). However, the death of one owner could create a transfer for value problem with respect to remaining policies insuring the surviving owners (pages 479-480). Funding with first-to-die insurance should avoid these problems (page 393).

[4] When the obligation is not fully funded, borrowing as an alternative to life insurance is usually unattractive, as can be appreciated by referring to the Cost of Borrowed Dollars table (page 190). The real risk of a death among multiple owners of a business can be estimated by using the Odds Of Death figures on pages 185 and 186. Although the premiums paid for this coverage are not tax-deductible, a split-dollar plan could be used to assist both A and B in purchasing the life insurance (chart, page 231). As an alternative, consider Executive Equity (chart, page 219).

[5] Receipt of the death proceeds allows B to purchase A's business interest *and* obtain an income tax cost basis equal to the purchase price. To illustrate, assume that both A and B originally paid $100,000 for each of their 50 percent stock interests which are now each worth $750,000 (for a total corporate value of $1,500,000). If A dies and the corporation buys A's stock for $750,000, B is then left as the sole stockholder of a corporation valued at $1,500,000. If B then subsequently sells the corporation, his gain on the sale would be $1,400,000 (the $1,500,000 sales price less the $100,000 he originally paid for his stock). However, if upon A's death B had purchased A's stock under a cross purchase agreement, B's basis in his corporate stock would be increased by $750,000. Under these circumstances, B's gain on a later sale of the corporation would be only $650,000 (the $1,500,000 sales price less his basis of $850,000, which includes the $100,000 he paid for his original stock plus the $750,000 he paid for A's shares).

[6] To help "peg" the value, the parties must be required to sell during lifetime for the same price as provided for a sale at death. In addition, the agreement must specifically *bind* A's estate or family and further comply with the Chapter 14 requirements (see footnote 3, page 127 and pages 386-387). The table of Contested Business Valuations on pages 193-198 provides specific examples of what happens when there is a failure to properly "peg" the value of stock in a closely held corporation. The cases on page 199 demonstrate that buy/sell agreements really do help fix the value.

TRUSTEED CROSS PURCHASE AGREEMENT

The trusteed cross purchase agreement is one means of providing for the complete disposition of a business interest.[1] Under this arrangement the owners use a third party to carry out their cross purchase agreement.[2] Although sometimes referred to as a "trustee," this individual is not acting as a trustee in a formal trust sense. Rather, the trusteed cross purchase agreement more closely resembles an escrow arrangement, under which an escrow agent acts as agent for the owners in carrying out their mutual obligations to each other.

DURING LIFETIME. To illustrate how this works, assume that we have a corporation owned by four stockholders, A, B, C and D. They enter into an agreement providing for the purchase and sale of their respective interests.[3] Typically, this agreement is *binding* and obligates all stockholders, or their representatives, to either buy or sell upon their death, disability, or retirement.

To implement the agreement the stockholders transfer their stock certificates to the escrow agent, and further have the escrow agent purchase life insurance on each stockholder. The escrow agent is both owner and beneficiary of these contracts and pays any required premiums.[4] By this means the stockholders can use life insurance to *fully* fund their agreement, while having the assurance that their mutual obligations to each other will be carried out by the escrow agent.[5] Use of an escrow agent can substantially reduce the number of policies required to fund the agreement.[6]

UPON DEATH. Assuming that A dies first, the insurance company pays a death benefit to the escrow agent, as beneficiary of the contract insuring A's life. The escrow agent receives these funds free of all income taxes, since they are received as the death benefit of a life insurance contract. Pursuant to the agreement, the escrow agent then transfers A's entire stock interest in the corporation to the surviving stockholders, in return for which the escrow agent pays the cash received from the insurance company to A's family.[7]

The fully funded agreement will *assure* that A's surviving family receives a fair price for his interest in the business. But such an agreement can also serve another very important function. If the estate had been subject to estate taxes, it is possible that extensive negotiations and even litigation could result if the estate tax value of the business had been left to chance. These problems of delay and litigation can be avoided by having a trusteed cross purchase agreement which helps establish, or "peg," the value of the stock.[8]

Footnotes on page 139

DURING LIFETIME

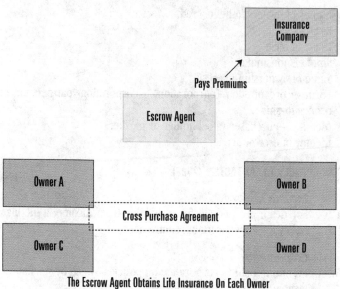

The Escrow Agent Obtains Life Insurance On Each Owner

UPON DEATH

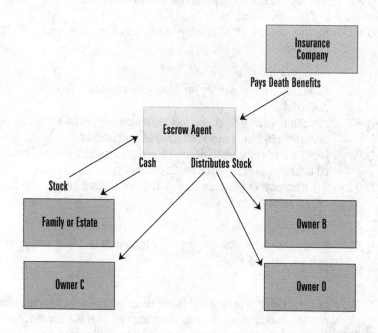

INFORMATION REQUIRED FOR ANALYSIS & PROPOSAL

1. Names of owners to be insured.
2. Sex.
3. Dates of birth.
4. Smoker/nonsmoker.
5. Value of ownership interests.
6. Form of organization (corporation, S corporation, partnership, or sole proprietorship).
7. Identity of purchaser (stockholder or partner).
8. Identity of escrow agent.

CROSS REFERENCES TO TAX FACTS 1 (2002)

Income Tax

Q 126. For death proceeds to be excludable from income, a life insurance policy must meet certain requirements.

Corporation

Q 52. Premiums paid by corporation on policies owned by stockholders are taxable income to stockholders.

Q 54. Stockholder cannot deduct premiums paid on policy purchased on life of another stockholder.

Q 80. Sale of deceased's stock will usually not result in income tax liability to deceased's estate.

Q 81. Income tax effects of funding stock purchase agreement with life insurance.

Partnership

Q 56. Premiums paid by partner for insurance on life of copartner are not deductible.

Q 57. Premiums paid by partner for insurance on his own life are not deductible by him if proceeds payable to copartner.

Q 92. Income tax results when deceased partner's interest sold or liquidated under a business purchase agreement.

Q 94. Tax treatment of life insurance purchased to fund partnership business purchase agreement.

Sole Proprietorship

Q 59. Premiums paid by key employee for insurance on life of sole proprietor are not deductible.

Estate Tax

Q 511. Life insurance proceeds not included in insured's estate when partners or stockholders purchase insurance on lives of each other.

Q 815. Impact of Chapter 14 valuation rules on buy/sell agreements.

Footnotes

[1] Trusteed cross purchase agreements are also known as "custodian" or "escrowed" agreements. The provisions for an escrow agent can be part of the cross purchase agreement, or provided for in a separate agreement. The trusteed cross purchase agreement can be used with either a corporation or a partnership. With a sole proprietorship, a similar escrowed arrangement could be established between the sole proprietor and a key employee (chart, page 145). However, since the key employee has no ownership interest, there are no reciprocal obligations to buy and sell. The sole proprietor would merely be obligated to sell and the key employee obligated to buy.

[2] In recent years there has been a substantial increase in the use of cross purchase agreements (as opposed to entity purchase agreements). The factors contributing to this include: (1) the introduction of the corporate alternative minimum tax that may claim up to 15 percent of the death proceeds paid to a C corporation (see pages 342-344); (2) the avoidance of the attribution rules with a family-held corporation (see pages 176-181); (3) the increase of cost basis for the surviving stockholders, (see footnote 5, page 135); and (4) the ability to convert to a entity purchase agreement using the same policies without running afoul of the transfer for value rules (see page 479-480).

[3] See footnote 2, page 135, for an explanation of the various means that can be used in the agreement to determine a purchase price.

[4] Since the escrow agent pays the premiums on behalf of the owners he obtains the funds from the owners (e.g., B, C and D benefit from and therefore must pay the premiums for the policy insuring A). Although the premiums are not tax-deductible, split-dollar plans could be used to assist the owners in paying for the life insurance (chart, page 231). As an alternative, consider Executive Equity (chart, page 219).

[5] When the obligation is not fully funded, borrowing as an alternative to life insurance is usually unattractive, as can be appreciated by referring to the Cost of Borrowed Dollars table (page 190). The real risk of a death among multiple owners of a business can be estimated by using the Odds Of Death figures on pages 185 and 186.

[6] With multiple stockholders the typical cross purchase agreement has the disadvantage of requiring that each stockholder be the owner and beneficiary of a policy on each of the other stockholders. Example 1, below, requires twelve policies to fund a cross purchase agreement involving just four stockholders (i.e., A must own policies insuring B, C, and D, etc.). Example 2 uses an escrow agent under a *trusteed* cross purchase agreement to reduce the number of policies to the number of insured stockholders.

[7] After the first death there is a potential transfer for value problem upon the transfer of the deceased stockholder's ownership interests in the remaining policies insuring the surviving stockholders (pages 479-480). It has been suggested that this problem could be avoided by using a first-to-die policy (see page 393).

[8] To help "peg" the value, the parties must be required to sell during lifetime for the same price as provided for a sale at death. In addition, the agreement must specifically *bind* A's estate or family and further comply with the Chapter 14 requirements (see footnote 3, page 127 and pages 386-387).

"WAIT AND SEE" BUY/SELL AGREEMENT

Choosing between a cross purchase and entity purchase agreement is often made difficult because of changing individual and business circumstances, as well as the inevitable "reforms" to our tax laws. One answer to this dilemma is the highly flexible "wait and see" buy/sell agreement, under which the owners agree among themselves, and with the business, to buy and sell their respective interests.[1]

DURING LIFETIME. To illustrate how this works, assume that we have a corporation which is owned equally by A and B.[2] As with both cross and entity purchase agreements, the "wait and see" agreement provides for valuation of their interests, sale upon death, disability or retirement, and the specific terms of payment.[3] However, unlike cross and entity purchase agreements, the "wait and see" buy/sell agreement does not specifically identify the purchaser. The purchaser and amounts of purchase are not determined until after the death of either A or B.

Life insurance funding of the agreement can be accomplished in a number of ways.[4] A and B could purchase life insurance contracts on each other (as with cross purchase agreements). Alternatively, the business could purchase life insurance contracts on both A and B (as with entity purchase agreements). A third alternative involves a combination of the first two methods. Our example assumes that A and B purchase life insurance contracts on each other, are the policy owners, premium payors and beneficiaries.[5]

UPON DEATH. Should A die first, his stock passes to his family or estate. At the same time, the insurance company pays a tax-free death benefit to B, as beneficiary of the contract insuring A's life. Pursuant to the agreement the following steps are implemented:

1st - The business has a *first option to purchase* A's stock.[6]

2nd - If the business does not exercise its option, or purchases less than all of A's stock, B has a *second option to purchase* A's stock.[7]

3rd - The business *is required to purchase* any of A's stock not previously purchased by either the business or B.[8]

Under the 1st and 3rd steps the business could obtain funds for purchasing A's stock by borrowing the death proceeds received by B.[9] As with cross and entity purchase agreements, the "wait and see" buy/sell agreement can also serve to help "peg," or establish, the value of the stock for estate tax purposes.[10]

Footnotes on page 143

DURING LIFETIME

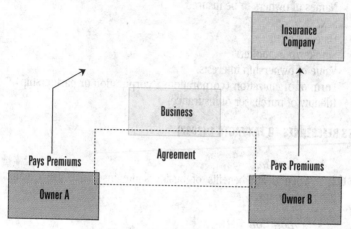

Insurance Company

Business

Pays Premiums

Agreement

Pays Premiums

Owner A

Owner B

Each Owner Obtains Life Insurance On The Other

UPON DEATH

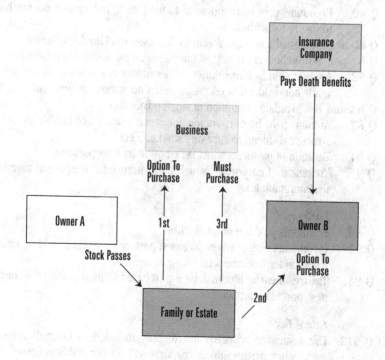

Insurance Company

Pays Death Benefits

Business

Option To Purchase

Must Purchase

Owner A

1st

3rd

Owner B

Stock Passes

Option To Purchase

Family or Estate

2nd

INFORMATION REQUIRED FOR ANALYSIS & PROPOSAL

1. Names of owners to be insured.
2. Sex.
3. Dates of birth.
4. Smoker/nonsmoker.
5. Value of ownership interests.
6. Form of organization (corporation, S corporation or partnership).
7. Identity of purchaser of insurance.

CROSS REFERENCES TO TAX FACTS 1 (2002)

Income Tax

Q 62. When death benefits of business life insurance are exempt from income tax.

Corporation

Q 46. Premiums paid on business life insurance not usually taxable to insured employee.

Q 47. Premiums paid by corporation on policies insuring the life of a stockholder or employee usually not deductible.

Q 49. Premiums paid by corporation to fund stock redemption not taxable to insured stockholder.

Q 80 and 86. Usually no capital gain to deceased stockholder's estate.

Q 81 and 88. Income tax results of funding agreement with life insurance.

Q 82. Amount paid by corporation for decedent's entire stock interest generally not dividend to estate, provided no attribution problems.

Q 83 and 84. Avoiding attribution of stock ownership.

Q 87. Amount paid by corporation for stock usually not taxable as constructive dividend to surviving stockholder(s).

Q 91. Taxation of payments when redemption by S corporation.

Q 95. Treatment of corporate owned life insurance for purpose of alternative minimum tax.

Partnership

Q 56. Premiums paid are not deductible.

Q 92. Income tax results when deceased partner's interest is sold or liquidated under a business purchase agreement.

Q 94. Tax treatment of life insurance purchased to fund partnership business purchase agreement.

Estate Tax

Q 512. Life insurance proceeds not directly included in insured owner's estate when partnership or corporation is owner and beneficiary.

Q 815. Impact of Chapter 14 valuation rules on buy/sell agreements.

Footnotes

[1] The "wait and see" buy/sell agreement is also referred to as the "option" or "flexible" buy/sell. The agreement is not appropriate when a corporation has only one stockholder, or with a sole proprietorship, since the corporation cannot own itself and the sole proprietorship is not a separate entity that can make the purchase.

[2] It is also assumed that A and B are *not* related to each other. If they were, and the business were a corporation, then the attribution rules would have to be considered if there is a purchase of stock by the business under either the 1st or 3rd step (attribution is more fully explained on pages 176-181).

[3] Various means can be used in the agreement to determine the purchase price. A *fixed price* could be established, with a further provision providing for periodic review and redetermination between the business and the owners. Alternatively, a *formula method* could be used, under which specific factors would be employed to calculate a value. For an example of a *capitalization formula*, see the Business Valuation chart on page 125. Another approach to determining a price is to provide for an *appraisal* at the time of sale (i.e., after the first owner's death, or earlier if a lifetime sale is contemplated).

[4] If the agreement is binding upon disability as well as death, consideration should also be given to funding the agreement with disability buy-out insurance. Such coverage will generally provide a lump-sum payment after a stated period of total and permanent disability. The premiums are nondeductible and the benefits are received free of income taxes. An expanded discussion of disability buy-out insurance is on page 371.

[5] Funding of the life insurance owned by A and B could be accomplished with split-dollar (chart, page 231) or executive equity (chart, page 219). Having the stockholders as owners and beneficiaries of the policies avoids any potential alternative minimum tax problem, as discussed on pages 342-344. This also allows the survivor to obtain a stepped-up basis by purchasing some or all of the deceased's stock at the 2nd step (i.e., a cross purchase agreement). The survivor would not have received an increased cost basis if the corporation purchases all of the deceased's stock at the 1st step (i.e., an entity purchase agreement).

[6] Typically the corporation would have from 30 to 90 days to exercise its option at the 1st step. If the corporation purchases all of A's stock the result would be an entity purchase agreement (chart, page 129).

[7] If the corporation does not purchase all of the stock at the 1st step, and B purchases all of A's stock at the 2nd step, the result is a cross purchase agreement (see chart, page 133). Typically B would have from 30 to 90 days to exercise his option. Note that it is important for the surviving stockholder to have an *option*, but not an *obligation*, to purchase stock at the 2nd step. If B had a legal obligation to purchase A's stock, and failed to do so, then the corporation's purchase of stock at the 3rd step would be treated as a dividend to B (i.e., the corporation would be considered as having discharged B's legal obligation).

[8] Note that despite the options involved in the 1st and 2nd steps, the mandatory purchase by the corporation in the 3rd step provides the *binding* agreement that assures A's stock will be sold for the benefit of his family (see footnote 10, below).

[9] Alternatively, the corporation could borrow funds from other sources, or B could make a capital contribution to the corporation, thereby increasing his cost basis in his stock. This also has the advantage of avoiding any problems with the alternative minimum tax, which could occur if the corporation received the death proceeds (see pages 342-344).

[10] To help "peg" the value of the business for estate tax purposes, the parties must be required to sell during lifetime for the same price as provided for a sale at death. In addition, the agreement must specifically *bind* A's estate or family and further comply with the Chapter 14 requirements (see footnote 3, page 127).

KEY PERSON BUY-OUT AGREEMENT

The key person buy-out agreement is one means of providing for the complete disposition of a business interest.[1] Under this arrangement the owner agrees to sell all of his business interest to a key person.[2]

DURING LIFETIME. To illustrate how this works, assume that we have a corporation owned by A. A would enter into an agreement providing for the sale to B, a key person in the business. Typically, this agreement is *binding* and obligates both parties, or their representatives, upon the death, disability, or retirement of A.

Rather than trying to accumulate or borrow sufficient funds to buy A's interest, B obtains a life insurance contract insuring A. B applies for this coverage, pays the premiums, and is both owner and beneficiary of the contract. By this means, B can use life insurance to *fully* fund his obligation to A.[3]

UPON DEATH. Assuming that A dies first, his stock would then pass to his family or estate. At the same time, the insurance company pays a death benefit to B, as beneficiary of the contract insuring A's life. B receives these funds free of all income taxes, since they are received as the death benefit of a life insurance contract.[4]

Pursuant to the agreement, A's family, or estate, transfers A's stock interest in the business to B, in return for which B pays the cash received from the insurance company.

The fully funded agreement will *assure* that A's surviving family receives a fair price for his interest in the business. But such an agreement can also serve another very important function. If the estate had been subject to estate taxes, it is possible that extensive negotiations and even litigation could result if the estate tax value of the business had been left to chance. These problems of delay and litigation can be avoided by having an agreement that helps establish, or "peg," the value of the stock.[5]

Footnotes on page 147

DURING LIFETIME

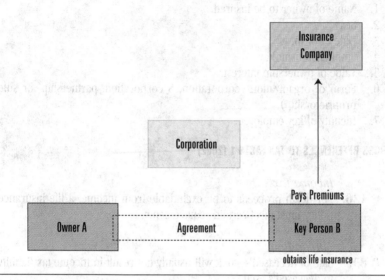

UPON DEATH

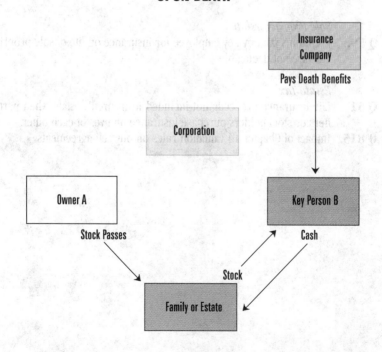

INFORMATION REQUIRED FOR ANALYSIS & PROPOSAL

1. Name of owner to be insured.
2. Sex.
3. Date of birth.
4. Smoker/nonsmoker.
5. Value of ownership interest.
6. Form of organization (corporation, S corporation, partnership, or sole proprietorship).
7. Identity of key employee.

CROSS REFERENCES TO TAX FACTS 1 (2002)

Income Tax

Q 126. For death proceeds to be excludable from income, a life insurance policy must meet certain requirements.

Corporation

Q 80. Sale of deceased's stock will usually not result in income tax liability to deceased's estate.

Q 81. Income tax effects of funding stock purchase agreement with life insurance.

Sole Proprietorship

Q 59. Premiums paid by key employee for insurance on life of sole proprietor are not deductible.

Estate Tax

Q 511. Life insurance proceeds not included in insured's estate when partners or stockholders purchase insurance on lives of each other.

Q 815. Impact of Chapter 14 valuation rules on buy/sell agreements.

Footnotes

[1] Such an agreement can be used with a corporation, a partnership, or a sole proprietorship. Since the key employee has no ownership interest, unlike the cross purchase agreement on page 133, there are no reciprocal obligations to buy and sell. The owner is merely obligated to sell and the key employee obligated to buy. A trusteed key person buy-out agreement might also be considered similar to the trusteed cross purchase agreement (chart, page 137).

[2] Various means can be used in the agreement to determine a purchase price. A *fixed price* could be established, with a further provision providing for periodic review and redetermination by mutual agreement among the owners. Alternatively, a *formula method* could be employed, under which specific factors would be used to calculate a value. For an example of a *capitalization* formula, refer to the valuation chart on page 125. Another approach to determining a price is to provide for an *appraisal* at the time of sale (i.e., after the owner's death, or earlier if a lifetime sale is contemplated).

[3] When the obligation is not fully funded, borrowing as an alternative to life insurance is usually unattractive, as can be appreciated by referring to the Cost of Borrowed Dollars table (page 190). Although the premiums paid for this coverage are not tax-deductible, a split-dollar plan could be used to assist B in purchasing the life insurance (chart, page 231). As an alternative, consider Executive Equity (chart, page 219).

[4] Receipt of the death proceeds allows B to purchase A's business interest *and* obtain an income tax cost basis equal to the purchase price. Assume that A originally paid $100,000 for his stock interest that is now worth $750,000. If A dies and B purchases A's stock under a key person buy-out agreement, B's basis in the stock would be equal to the $750,000 purchase price. B's gain on a later sale of the stock would be equal to the amount by which the sales price exceeds $750,000.

[5] To help "peg" the value, A must be required to sell during lifetime for the same price as provided for a sale at death. In addition, the agreement must specifically *bind* A's estate or family and further comply with the Chapter 14 requirements (see footnote 3, page 127 and pages 386-387). The table of Contested Business Valuations on pages 193-198 provides specific examples of what happens when there is a failure to properly "peg" the value of stock in a closely held corporation. The cases on page 199 demonstrate that buy/sell agreements really do help fix the value.

PARTIAL STOCK REDEMPTION

A partial stock redemption under Section 303 offers a very attractive way of paying estate settlement costs, particularly for a corporation that will be continued by the surviving family.[1]

Under most circumstances, a stockholder who has the corporation redeem less than his entire stock interest will be fully taxed on the proceeds as ordinary income. However, under the special provisions of Section 303, his surviving family can do after death what the stockholder generally cannot do during his lifetime . . . namely, sell only a *portion* of his stock interest to the corporation, and have the sale treated as a capital transaction rather than as a dividend.

DURING LIFETIME. If the stock interest will be *more than* 35 percent of the stockholder's adjusted gross estate, then his stock will qualify under Section 303 for a partial redemption at his death.[2] The *amount* of stock which can be purchased is limited to the sum of all federal and state death taxes, funeral, and administrative expenses. The purchase must also be made from whoever has the obligation to pay these costs, usually the family or estate.[3]

Since few corporations can be expected to accumulate sufficient cash for such a purchase, typically the corporation obtains a life insurance contract insuring the stockholder in his capacity as an employee. The corporation pays the premiums and is both owner and beneficiary of the contract. This is generally a much better solution to the funding problem than attempting to accumulate large cash reserves over a period of time, borrowing at high interest rates, or selling corporate assets.[4]

UPON DEATH, the stock passes to the family or estate. At the same time, the insurance company pays a death benefit to the corporation.[5] This money is usually received free of all income taxes.[6] The corporation can then use the cash to purchase *some* of the stock from the family or estate.

The tax-favored treatment under Section 303 has been made available to the family-owned corporation in order to protect it from being sold or liquidated to pay death taxes and other estate settlement costs. When a corporate interest is the bulk of an estate, it only makes sense to use corporate dollars to provide the necessary cash to pay these costs.[7]

Footnotes on page 151

DURING LIFETIME

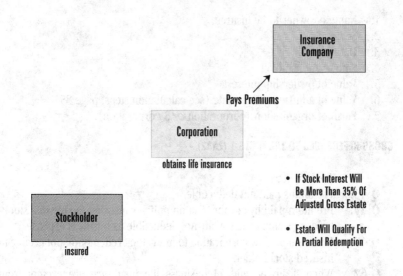

Insurance Company

Pays Premiums

Corporation

obtains life insurance

Stockholder

insured

- If Stock Interest Will Be More Than 35% Of Adjusted Gross Estate

- Estate Will Qualify For A Partial Redemption

UPON DEATH

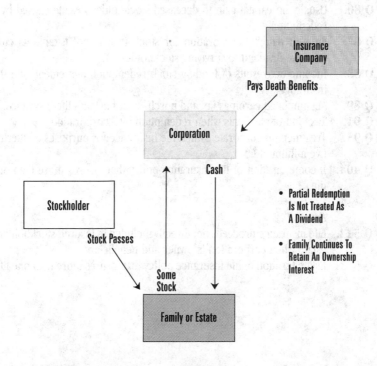

Insurance Company

Pays Death Benefits

Corporation

Cash

Stockholder

Stock Passes

Some Stock

Family or Estate

- Partial Redemption Is Not Treated As A Dividend

- Family Continues To Retain An Ownership Interest

INFORMATION REQUIRED FOR ANALYSIS & PROPOSAL

1. Name of owner to be insured.
2. Sex.
3. Date of birth.
4. Smoker/nonsmoker.
5. Value of ownership interest.
6. Value of adjusted gross estate (see calculation steps, page 85).
7. Form of organization (corporation *or* S corporation).

CROSS REFERENCES TO TAX FACTS 1 (2002)

Income Tax

Q 45. Premiums paid not deductible.

Q 47. Premium paid by corporation on policies insuring the life of a stockholder or employee usually not deductible as business expense.

Q 49. Premium paid by corporation to fund stock redemption not taxable to insured stockholder.

Q 62. When death benefits of business life insurance are exempt from income tax.

Q 85. Requirements for a Section 303 stock redemption.

Q 86. Usually no capital gain to deceased stockholder's estate caused by a redemption.

Q 87. Amount paid by corporation for stock usually not taxable as constructive dividend to surviving stockholder(s).

Q 88. Income tax results of funding stock redemption agreement with life insurance.

Q 89. Accumulated earnings tax and purchase of business life insurance.

Q 91. Taxation of payments when redemption by S corporation.

Q 95. Treatment of corporate owned life insurance for purposes of alternative minimum tax.

Q 404. Income taxation of life insurance policy that insures more than one life.

Estate Tax

Q 512. Life insurance proceeds not directly included in insured stockholder's estate when corporation is owner and beneficiary.

Q 571. Estate taxation of life insurance policy that insures more than one life.

Footnotes

1 Partial stock redemptions are also referred to as "Section 303 Redemptions." Code section 303 authorizes a redemption of less than the entire stock interest of the decedent to be treated as a *sale* of stock, as opposed to a *dividend*. Because of the step-up in basis at death, a sale of stock will generally result in little, if any, taxable gain, since under a capital transaction the seller is not taxed on the basis of the property sold. In contrast, a dividend would be fully taxable as ordinary income (see Stepped-Up Basis, on page 473).

2 The adjusted gross estate is determined by subtracting debts, funeral, and administrative expenses from the gross estate. This requirement provides you with the opportunity to conduct an estate analysis involving a full review of a client's assets. Without this information, it is not possible to determine whether an estate would qualify for a partial stock redemption (see page 12). If a client has more than one corporation, the stock of two or more corporations may be combined to meet the 35 percent test, provided the stockholder owns 20 percent or more of the value of each corporation, and the stock of the corporation is included in his gross estate. Even though an estate may *presently* be expected to qualify for a partial stock redemption, it is important to monitor estate assets to assure that there is not a subsequent disqualification. For example, the corporate stock could become 35 percent or less of the adjusted gross estate if: (1) other estate assets appreciate more than the stock interests; (2) the stock interests decline in value; (3) stock is either sold or given away.

3 The redemption can be made only by that party having liability for the federal and state death taxes, funeral, and administrative expenses. It must usually be made within 3 years and 90 days after the estate tax return is filed (the estate tax return must be filed within 9 months after death). Reduction or potential elimination of the federal estate tax under EGTRRA 2001 will reduce the utility of a partial stock redemption. Also, the effectiveness of a Section 303 redemption is limited when the unlimited marital deduction is used. See discussed on page 461.

4 It is questionable whether many corporations could accumulate sufficiently large cash reserves for effective partial stock redemptions without running afoul of the prohibition against the unreasonable accumulation of earnings (see page 341, Accumulated Earnings Tax). With the purchase of life insurance to fund a partial stock redemption, the corporation is in effect *amortizing* the cost of the redemption over the lifetime of the insured stockholder. The insurance carried is similar to key person insurance as shown in the chart on page 157. If the corporation is in a relatively low tax bracket, the required premium payments can be made with Enhanced Dollars, as explained on page 380. Other variations of insurance ownership and beneficiary designation are shown in the Reverse Section 303 stock redemption chart, on page 153, and the Reverse Split-Dollar chart, on page 165. Funding a partial stock redemption with survivorship life insurance can be particularly attractive when the unlimited marital deduction is used at the first death, since it provides death proceeds at the second death, when the estate taxes can no longer be deferred.

5 This death benefit will *increase* the value of the decedent's stock in his gross estate in proportion to the decedent's interest in the corporation. For example, if the decedent owned 100 percent of the stock, a $100,000 death benefit might increase the value of the stock in the estate by $100,000. However, if the decedent owned only 40 percent of the stock, a $100,000 death benefit might increase the value of the stock in the estate by only $40,000. It could always be argued that there was a loss of corporate value caused by the death of a key employee that offsets some or all of the increase in stock value.

6 Under some circumstances a portion of annual cash value increases and death proceeds could be subject to the Alternative Minimum Tax, as discussed on pages 342-344.

7 In this chart, only *some* stock is redeemed, whereas a redemption of *all* stock is referred to as a "Section 302(b)(3) redemption." Section 302(b)(3) is that section of the Code that enables the redemption, or sale to the corporation, of the *entire* stock interest of a stockholder to be treated as a *sale* of stock, as opposed to a *dividend*. The Entity Purchase Agreement chart, on page 129, explains the Section 302(b)(3) redemption. Unlike the entity purchase agreement, in a family held corporation a partial stock redemption does not cause potential attribution problems (see pages 176-181).

REVERSE SECTION 303

A reverse stock redemption under Section 303 offers a very attractive way of paying estate settlement costs by having an entity other than the corporation purchase insurance to fund the redemption.[1]

DURING LIFETIME. If the stock interest will be *more than* 35 percent of the stockholder's adjusted gross estate, then his stock will qualify under Section 303 for a partial redemption at his death.[2] The *amount* of stock that can be purchased is limited to the sum of all federal and state death taxes, funeral, and administrative expenses.[3] However, the purchase must be made from whoever has the obligation to pay these costs, usually the family or estate.

One way to implement a reverse Section 303 is for the stockholder to establish a life insurance trust that then obtains a life insurance contract insuring the stockholder.[4] The trust pays the premiums and is both owner and beneficiary of the contract.[5]

UPON DEATH. The stock passes to the family or estate. At the same time, the insurance company pays a death benefit to the trust, which is received free of all income taxes.[6] The trust then loans the money to the corporation, which uses it to purchase *some*, but not all, of the stock from the family or estate.

In repaying this loan the corporation can make tax-deductible interest payments to the trust. Although these interest payments would be taxable income to the trust, repayments of the loan principal would be received by the trust free of income taxes. By this means the family can continue to retain ownership and control of the corporation, while at the same time receiving, as trust beneficiaries, the benefits of the untaxed repayment of loan principal.

Of course, it is not necessary for a trust to be established. Anyone who has substantial funds can loan them to the corporation for the purpose of a partial stock redemption. For example, a son or daughter of the stockholder could be owner and beneficiary of life insurance contracts insuring the parent. After receipt of the death benefit, the proceeds could be loaned by the children to the corporation, which would then repay the loan together with interest.[7]

Footnotes on page 155

DURING LIFETIME

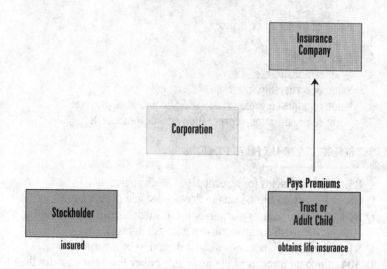

UPON DEATH

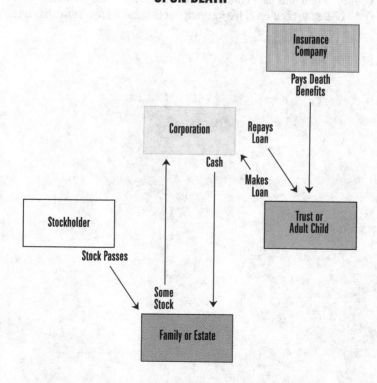

INFORMATION REQUIRED FOR ANALYSIS & PROPOSAL

1. Name of owner to be insured.
2. Sex.
3. Date of birth.
4. Smoker/nonsmoker.
5. Value of ownership interest.
6. Value of adjusted gross estate (see calculation steps, page 85).
7. Form of organization (corporation *or* S corporation).

CROSS REFERENCES TO TAX FACTS 1 (2002)

Q 85.   Requirements for a Section 303 stock redemption.

Q 86.   Usually no capital gain to deceased stockholder's estate.

Q 87.   Amount paid by corporation for stock usually not taxable as constructive dividend to surviving stockholder(s).

Q 91.   Taxation of payments when redemption by S corporation.

Q 404.   Income taxation of life insurance policy that insures more than one life.

Q 408.   Premiums paid on life insurance generally not deductible.

Q 571.   Estate taxation of life insurance policy that insures more than one life.

Footnotes

[1] Section 303 is that section of the Code that authorizes a redemption of less than the entire stock interest of the decedent to be treated as a *sale* of stock, as opposed to a *dividend*. Because of the step-up in basis at death, a sale of stock will generally result in little, if any, taxable gain, since under a capital transaction the seller is not taxed on the basis of the property sold. In contrast, a dividend would be fully taxable as ordinary income (see Stepped-Up Basis, on page 473).

[2] The adjusted gross estate is determined by subtracting debts, funeral, and administrative expenses from the gross estate. This requirement provides you with an opportunity for an estate analysis involving a full review of a client's assets (see page 12). Without this information, it is not possible to determine whether an estate will qualify for a partial stock redemption. If a client has more than one corporation, the stock of two or more corporations may be combined to meet the 35 percent test, provided the stockholder owns 20 percent or more of the value of each corporation, and the stock of the corporation is included in his gross estate. Even though an estate may *presently* be expected to qualify for a Section 303 redemption, it is important to monitor estate assets in order to assure that the estate continues to qualify. For example, the corporate stock could become 35 percent or less of the adjusted gross estate if: (1) other estate assets appreciate more than the stock interests; (2) the stock interests decline in value; (3) some of the stock is either sold or given away.

[3] The reduction or potential elimination of the federal estate tax under EGTRRA 2001 will reduce the utility of a Reverse Section 303.

[4] The details of establishing a life insurance trust are set forth in the chart on page 57. Funding a reverse Section 303 stock redemption with survivorship life insurance can be particularly attractive when the unlimited marital deduction is used at the first death, since it provides death proceeds at the second death, when the estate taxes can no longer be deferred.

[5] Since premiums must come from after-tax dollars, having someone other than the corporation own the insurance contract and pay the premiums could take advantage of a lower tax bracket (see Enhanced Dollars, on page 380).

[6] Use of a reverse Section 303 may be advisable when there is a concern regarding the Alternative Minimum Tax (see pages 342-344). With the usual Section 303 redemption, as shown in the chart on page 149, the payment of the death benefit to the corporation exposes the corporation to the alternative minimum tax. With a reverse Section 303 redemption the death benefit is paid outside the corporation, meaning that there is no increase in adjusted current earnings, and thus no exposure to the alternative minimum tax.

[7] When the insurance is owned by and payable to either children or a trust, the reverse 303 technique avoids the problem of increasing the value of the deceased's taxable estate, as occurs when death proceeds are paid to a corporation under the usual Section 303 arrangement (see the chart on page 149, and footnote 5 on page 151).

KEY PERSON INSURANCE

Multipurpose key person insurance is designed to help protect a business from the financial losses that can occur when a key employee dies. Such a key employee could be the owner of the business, or a non-owner employee whose very specialized abilities are critical to the operation of the business and difficult or costly to replace.[1] Adequate amounts of key person insurance are essential in any risk management program. Since the existence of business debt "signals a need for insurance," key person insurance can function as a form of commercial loan protection, as well as provide needed funds when a business is to be continued, sold, or liquidated.[2]

DURING LIFETIME. This protection is provided by having the business obtain insurance on the life of the key employee. As both owner and beneficiary of the contract, the business pays the premiums directly to the insurance company.[3] The contract's cash values are carried as a business asset, and are available as collateral for securing commercial loans, or for direct borrowing from the insurance company at generally favorable interest rates.[4]

Many guidelines are used in estimating the *dollar value* of a particular key employee. However, the value can be most easily estimated by using a factor of three to ten times the employee's salary. Other guidelines that have been employed involve either a determination of the employee's replacement cost, or an estimation of lost profits or credit.[5]

UPON DEATH of the key employee the insurance company pays the death benefit directly to the business. The funds are treated as an addition to surplus and are received free of any direct income taxes.[6]

The proceeds can then be used for various purposes. Should it be determined that the business will be *continued*, these can be used to obtain a qualified replacement, replace lost profits, protect its credit position, provide a financial cushion, fund a partial stock redemption or make survivor income payments. If the business is to be *sold*, then there is money available to fund a full stock redemption. In case of *liquidation*, the cash will benefit the surviving family by offsetting lost business value.[7]

Footnotes on page 159

DURING LIFETIME

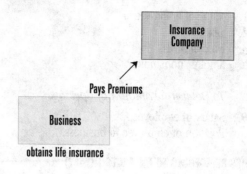

Insurance
Company

Pays Premiums

Business

obtains life insurance

Key Employee

insured

UPON DEATH

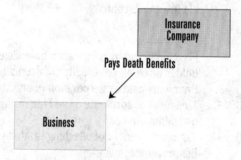

Insurance
Company

Pays Death Benefits

Business

Key Employee

Proceeds Can Be Used To:

- Replace Lost Profits
- Protect Credit Position
- Provide Financial Cushion
- Offset Lost Business Value
- Obtain Qualified Replacement
- Make Survivor Income Payments
- Fund Entity Purchase Agreement (Sec. 302)
- Fund Partial Stock Redemption (Sec. 303)

INFORMATION REQUIRED FOR ANALYSIS & PROPOSAL

1. Name of employee.
2. Sex.
3. Date of birth.
4. Smoker/nonsmoker.

To Determine Amount of Coverage

5. Salary of employee.
6. Position of employee in business.

CROSS REFERENCES TO TAX FACTS 1 (2002)

General Rules

Q 7.   Taxation of distributions from policies classified as modified endowment contracts.

Q 45.   Premiums paid usually not deductible as business expense.

Q 46.   Premiums paid usually not taxable to insured employee.

Q 405.   Taxability of policy loans.

Q 406.   Deduction of interest on policy loans.

Q 407.   Deduction of interest on indebtedness incurred to purchase or carry life insurance contract.

Corporation

Q 47.   Premiums paid by corporation on policies insuring the life of a stockholder or employee usually not deductible as business expense.

Q 48.   Premiums paid by corporation not taxable to insured employee.

Q 95.   Treatment of corporate owned life insurance for purposes of alternative minimum tax.

Q 157.   Tax consequences of attaching disability income rider to key person life insurance policy.

Partnership

Q 56.   Premiums paid by partnership are not deductible.

Q 57.   Premiums paid by partner for insurance on his own life not deductible by him if proceeds payable to partnership.

Estate Tax

Q 509.   Life insurance payable to partnership generally not includible in insured partner's estate (but included as part of partnership interest).

Q 510.   Life insurance payable to corporation generally not includible in insured's estate, provided insured had no "incidents of ownership" in policy (but included in valuing corporate stock).

Footnotes

[1] The loss of a good manager can mean the loss of a good business. The table, Why Businesses Fail, on page 187, indicates that 28.7 percent of all business failures are attributable to inadequate management and finances. It has been said that, "debt signals a need for life insurance" (see Quotable Quotes, page 330). The classic statement regarding the need for key person insurance was made by the U.S. Court of Appeals, 3rd Circuit (1951), in the case of *The Emeloid Co., Inc. v. Commissioner*:

> "What corporate purpose could be more essential then key [person] insurance? The business that insures its buildings and machinery and automobiles from every possible hazard can hardly be expected to exercise less care in protecting itself against the loss of two of its most vital assets – managerial skill and experience."

[2] Key person insurance can also be thought of as a "line of credit." As such, it will assure that money is available when needed, without any repayment of the debt, i.e., a forgiveness of the "loan." Relying on borrowed funds may be ill advised, as can be seen by referring to the table, Cost Of Borrowed Dollars, on page 189.

[3] The "cost" of key person insurance is sometimes measured as the difference between the premium paid and the cash value increase. This view tends to argue in favor of permanent insurance with cash values, as opposed to term insurance with no cash values (but such an approach ignores the time value of money, as discussed in Interest Adjusted Net Cost on page 406). It should also be recognized that the cash values of permanent insurance, carried for a bona fide business purpose, are not subject to the unreasonable accumulation of earnings tax. An expanded discussion of this subject is contained on page 341. If cash values are borrowed, it would be to the business's advantage to be sure it could deduct interest paid on the borrowed funds (see Minimum Deposit Insurance, on page 424). If borrowing of cash values is contemplated, then it is important to avoid having the policy classified as a Modified Endowment Contract (see expanded discussion on pages 413-414).

[4] Under some circumstances a portion of annual cash value increases and death proceeds could be subject to the Alternative Minimum Tax, as discussed on pages 342-344. However, this problem is not present in an S corporation, since it is not subject to the alternative minimum tax adjusted current earnings adjustment. In fact, key person insurance in an S corporation may be particularly attractive in view of the opportunity to make tax-free withdrawals of the death proceeds where the S corporation has no accumulated earnings and profits (see S Corporation, pages 458-460). With a C corporation the alternative minimum tax problem can be avoided by using the Reverse Key Person Insurance technique (see chart, page 161).

[5] See page 188 for various formulas used to value a key person. Another approach to the valuation of a key person is to discount all future salary payments to normal retirement age. For example, referring to the Compound Discount Table on page 503, it can be determined that, using a time value of money assumption of 8 percent, a 45-year old employee earning $50,000 per year, who is expected to retire in 20 years (age 65), has a present value of $490,900 ($50,000 x 9.818 = $490,900). No matter which approach is used, valuation of a key person is much like valuation of a business, the process may be more art than science. However, application of these guidelines will provide a useful starting point for determining a key person's value to a business.

[6] An explanation and illustration of proper accounting entries for policy premiums and values is set forth in Accounting For Business Life Insurance on pages 339-340.

[7] Whether a business is likely to be continued, sold, or liquidated upon the death of a key employee, will depend upon answers to the questions set forth in the Disposition Of A Business Interest chart on page 121.

REVERSE KEY PERSON INSURANCE

Reverse key person insurance offers an alternative means of providing key employee insurance by having someone other than the business purchase insurance on the life of the key employee. It is particularly useful with C corporations, where the alternative minimum tax can reduce by up to 15 percent the death benefit received by the corporation.[1] With reverse key person insurance there is no exposure to the alternative minimum tax, because the death benefit is not paid to the corporation. If the key employee is also a stockholder, payment of the death benefit outside the corporation also avoids increasing the value of the deceased's stock and thereby avoids any increase in estate taxes.[2]

DURING LIFETIME. Such a program can be established by having the trustee of an irrevocable life insurance trust purchase insurance on the key employee.[3] As both owner and beneficiary of the contract, the trustee pays the premiums directly to the insurance company.[4]

Many guidelines are used in estimating the dollar value of a particular key employee. However, the value can be most easily estimated by using a factor of three to ten times the employee's salary. Other guidelines that have been employed involve either a determination of the employee's replacement cost, or an estimation of lost profits or credit.

UPON DEATH of the key employee the insurance company pays the death benefit directly to the trustee of the trust. The proceeds are received free of income taxes as the death benefit of a life insurance contract.

The funds can then be loaned by the trustee to the corporation.[5] In repaying this loan the corporation makes tax-deductible interest payments to the trust.[6] Although these interest payments are taxable income to the trust, repayments of the loan principal are received by the trust free of income taxes.

Of course, it is not necessary for a trust to be established. Anyone who has the funds can loan them to the corporation for the purpose of key person insurance. For example, an adult child could be the owner and beneficiary of a life insurance contract insuring his parent. After receipt of the death benefit, the proceeds could be loaned by the child to the corporation, which would then repay the loan together with interest.[7]

Footnotes on page 163

DURING LIFETIME

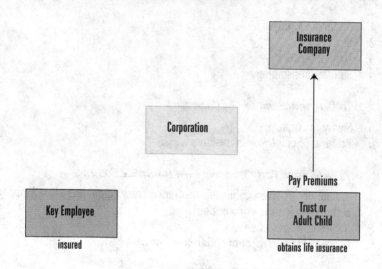

UPON DEATH

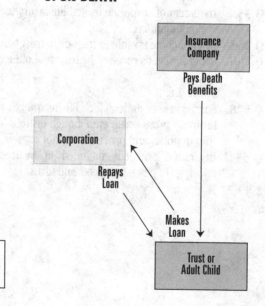

INFORMATION REQUIRED FOR ANALYSIS & PROPOSAL

1. Name of employee.
2. Sex.
3. Date of birth.
4. Smoker/nonsmoker.

To Determine Amount of Coverage

5. Salary of employee.
6. Position of employee in business.

To Determine Party Who Will Own Insurance Contract

7. Availability of irrevocable life insurance trust (including trust language authorizing loan to corporation).
8. Names and ages of children.
9. Degree of involvement of children in business.

CROSS REFERENCES TO TAX FACTS 1 (2002)

Income Tax

Q 95. Treatment of corporate owned life insurance for purposes of alternative minimum tax.

Q 264. When income taxable to trust or to trust beneficiaries.

Q 266. Death proceeds received by trust free of income taxes.

Estate Tax

Q 528. Circumstances under which life insurance proceeds are includable in insured's gross estate even though insured has no incident of ownership in policy and proceeds are not payable to estate.

Q 554. Insurance proceeds included in insured's estate when trustee *required* to pay estate debts and taxes.

Footnotes

[1] This reduction is only likely with a C corporation; there is no exposure with an S corporation or a partnership. With Key Person Insurance, as shown in the chart on page 157, the death benefit paid to a C corporation is included in adjusted current earnings as part of the alternative minimum tax calculations. The larger the death benefit relative to anticipated corporate earnings, the greater the likelihood that the alternative minimum tax will reduce the death benefit. Alternatively, the smaller the death benefit relative to anticipated corporate earnings, the lesser the likelihood of a reduction in death benefits on account of the alternative minimum tax. A more detailed explanation of the Alternative Minimum Tax is contained on pages 342-344. The table on page 344 provides examples of the relationship between the amount of the death benefit and anticipated corporate earnings.

[2] When the insurance is owned by and payable to either a trust or an adult child, the Reverse Key Person Insurance technique also avoids the problem of increasing the value of the deceased's estate, as can occur when death proceeds are paid to a corporation under the typical Key Person Insurance arrangement (see the chart on page 157, and footnote 5 on page 151). In this regard, note the similarity between Reverse Key Person Insurance and Reverse Section 303 (see chart, page 153).

[3] The details of establishing and administering an irrevocable life insurance trust are set forth on pages 56-59.

[4] When considering Reverse Key Person Insurance it is important to determine how the premiums will be paid. With Key Person Insurance the premium is an obligation of the corporation as owner of the insurance contract. In contrast, with *Reverse* Key Person Insurance the contract is owned by a trustee, or an adult child, who has the obligation to make the premium payments. Corporate funds could be used to assist in paying the premiums using either Executive Equity, chart page 219, or Split-Dollar Insurance, chart page 227.

[5] The trustee must have authority to make a loan to the corporation. Although many irrevocable life insurance trusts will give the trustee broad authority to purchase assets and make loans to the estate and others, it would be prudent to give the trustee specific authority to make loans at prevailing interest rates to the corporation. However, the trust language *should not* require the trustee to make such loans, as this would likely cause the death proceeds to be included in the insured's estate. Although the trustee cannot be required to make the loan, preserving the family business for the trust beneficiaries would likely motivate the trustee to make the loan, particularly if the trustee was also responsible for maintaining and preserving the business (see footnote 6, page 59).

[6] Interest payments are deductible by the corporation but taxable to the trust unless distributed and taxed to the trust beneficiaries. Distribution of trust income may be advisable in view of the very high income tax rates applicable to trusts (e.g., the table on page 492 indicates that in 2002 income in excess of $9,200 is subject to a 38.6% tax rate). On the other hand, creation of a debt from the corporation to the trustee, or an adult child, offers the advantage of being able to subsequently withdraw the loan principal from the corporation free of income taxes. This is similar to the same advantage offered by the Reverse Section 303 (see chart, page 153).

[7] Because it is not possible to obligate the adult child to loan the death proceeds to the corporation, it is extremely important to be sure the child will be highly motivated to make such a loan (e.g., the child is the "heir apparent" to the business and would suffer financially should the corporation fail to continue operations).

REVERSE SPLIT-DOLLAR

Reverse split-dollar offers a means by which a business can obtain *key person insurance* to protect itself from the financial losses that occur when a key employee dies. Like traditional split-dollar, the premiums are shared between the business and the employee. However, unlike traditional split-dollar, most of the death benefit is received by the business, and *the employee owns all policy cash values*.[1]

DURING LIFETIME. In order to implement the plan, the employee applies for and purchases a life insurance contract on his life.[2] Thereafter, a formal agreement is adopted stipulating the exact death benefit to be received by the employer, as well as the length of the agreement, which will usually run from 10 to 20 years or longer, depending upon the employee's age and the need for key person insurance. A portion of the death benefit equal to the cash values could also be retained by the employee and made payable to his personal beneficiary.[3]

This agreement will also provide for the business to pay a portion of the premium.[4] The employee is responsible for paying the balance of the premium.[5] As with other split-dollar plans, the employee's share of premiums could be paid with bonuses from the business, provided the employee's total compensation is considered reasonable.

If the employee lives until the agreement terminates, the business will then release all of its interests in the death benefits. As sole owner of the policy the employee has many options; he can withdraw the cash value in a lump sum, purchase a retirement annuity, or retain the policy as paid-up insurance.

UPON DEATH. Should the employee die prior to the end of the agreement, the insurance company would pay to the business most, if not all, of the death benefit.[6] However, a pre-existing survivor income agreement could be established, requiring that these proceeds be paid by the business to the employee's personal beneficiary. Of course, the funds would not then be available as indemnification for the loss of the key employee, and they would be taxable income to the beneficiary.[7]

Footnotes on page 167

DURING LIFETIME

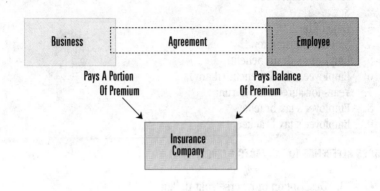

UPON DEATH

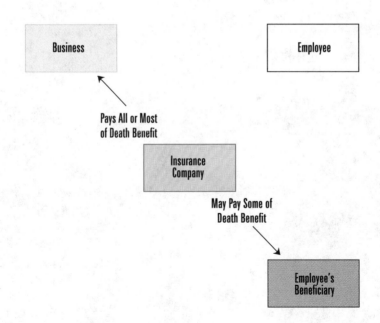

INFORMATION REQUIRED FOR ANALYSIS & PROPOSAL

1. Name of employee.
2. Sex.
3. Date of birth.
4. Smoker/nonsmoker.
5. Employer's death benefit.
6. Employee's death benefit (if any).
7. Years for agreement to run.
8. Employer's tax bracket.
9. Employee's tax bracket.

CROSS REFERENCE TO TAX FACTS 1 (2002)

Q 428. Description of reverse split-dollar.
Q 515. Estate taxation of reverse split-dollar.

Footnotes

[1] See page 202 for a comparison of split-dollar and reverse split-dollar. Do not confuse Reverse Split-Dollar with the highly aggressive technique referred to as Charitable Split-Dollar (see discussion, page 353).

[2] As with all split-dollar arrangements, there are essentially two ways in which the agreement can be established, endorsement *or* collateral assignment. Under the *endorsement* form, the rights and obligations of the parties are set forth in an endorsement contained in the policy, usually at the time of initial issue. Under the *collateral assignment* form, the policy is issued to the individual owner, who executes a limited collateral assignment to the business, which is then filed with the insurance company. Under either arrangement the resulting rights and obligations are the same, and they should always reflect and implement the underlying split-dollar agreement. It must be recognized that there is substantial disagreement regarding the actual tax consequences of reverse split-dollar, since it has not been ruled on by the Internal Revenue Service, and the Service's position is unknown at this writing. IRS Notice 2002-8 did not specifically address reverse split-dollar (see footnote 4, below).

[3] If the employee names a personal beneficiary for a portion of the death benefit, there will likely be imputed income to the employee to the extent that there has been no employee premium payment in that year.

[4] IRS Notice 2002-8 states that split-dollar arrangements, entered into before January 28, 2002, may continue to use the P.S. 58 rates when the "contractual arrangement between an employer and employee provides that the P.S. 58 rates will be used to determine the value of current life insurance protection provided to the employee . . ." However, under reverse split-dollar, the insurance protection being measured is that provided to the *employer*, not to the employee. Despite this, it appears reasonable to: (1) use the P.S. 58 rates for reverse split-dollar arrangements entered into before January 28, 2002 (under the "no inference" language of Notice 2002-8); and (2) use the Table 2001 rates, or insurer's published premium rates, for reverse split-dollar arrangements entered into on and after January 28, 2002 (see table of rates on page 496). Note that the Table 2001 rates are substantially *less* than the P.S. 58 rates (a comparison is set forth in the table on page 496). Use of Table 2001 rates will reduce the attractiveness of reverse split-dollar plans, since a *reduction* in the employer's share of the premium results in an *increase* in the employee's share of the premium. Some relief might be provided to the employee through salary bonuses, paying planned lower premiums with universal life insurance, or using dividends to reduce premiums with participating insurance.

[5] With reverse split-dollar the employee has an *obligation* to maintain the policy for the benefit of the business. When funded by either a participating or universal life policy there is a "downside risk" to the employee, in that additional premium payments may be required if dividends are not sufficient to reduce future premium payments, or interest earnings are not sufficient to maintain the death benefit.

[6] Although little, if any, death benefit will be received by the estate, the employee's *ownership* of policy cash values is an "incident of ownership" which will cause *all* death benefits to be included in his estate. However, the IRS in a private letter ruling allowed the estate an offsetting deduction under Code section 2053, as a claim against property included in the estate, provided the split-dollar agreement is a bona fide arrangement entered into for full and adequate consideration. The split-dollar agreement should also clearly establish the corporation's claim against the estate, separate and apart from the beneficiary designation. This whole problem might also be avoided by having the insured's spouse own the policy; but there is no authority for or against this approach. Further, if the insured is a controlling stockholder, the corporation's incidents of ownership are attributable to such stockholder (see page 363).

[7] The death benefit could also be used to fund a partial stock redemption (chart, page 149) or a death benefit only plan (page 368). Under most circumstances, reverse split-dollar would be inappropriate if the insured is an employee-stockholder in an S corporation (pages 458-460) or personal service corporation (see footnote on page 492).

FAMILY LIMITED PARTNERSHIP

The family limited partnership (FLP) is a valuable planning technique offering numerous advantages to the owners of a closely held business.[1] With this technique, business interests and other assets can be transferred to family members at reduced values while maintaining indirect yet effective control.[2]

ESTABLISHING PARTNERSHIP. The FLP is established by an agreement setting forth the partnership's operating rules and the filing of a certificate of limited partnership with state authorities.[3] The typical FLP agreement places restrictions and limitations on ownership of partnership interests, and cannot be changed or terminated for a specified number of years without the concurrence of all partners.[4]

Once the agreement is drawn, the parents then contribute assets to the FLP, which in turn issues both *general* and *limited* partnership interests.[5] Thereafter, the parents make gifts of the limited partnership interests to their children. These gifts can be structured to fall within the annual gift tax exclusion, or the unified credit can be used to immediately transfer large amounts of limited partnership interests.[6]

ADVANTAGES OF PARTNERSHIP. The principal advantages of the FLP are both *control* and *flexibility*.[7] As general partners, the parents have complete power and authority to manage the partnership.[8] As limited partners, the children have no say in the management of the partnership, no liability for partnership debts, and a priority over the general partners in the event of a liquidation.

With a FLP, gifts can be made of assets that are otherwise not easily divisible (e.g., the family farm). Transferring real estate located in another state to the partnership can avoid ancillary probate. Income can be shifted to children in lower income tax brackets.[9] Periodic gifts of limited partnership interests can reduce the parent's taxable estate.[10] Gifts of limited partnership interests are subject to valuation discounts for both minority interests and lack of marketability. Such valuation discounts, which can often range up to 30 percent and more, offer the opportunity to "leverage" these tax-free gifts.[11]

Because the children cannot transfer their limited partnership interests without the consent of all other partners, partnership assets are protected from claims against the individual partners (including those arising out of a divorce). Although creditors might succeed in obtaining a right to partnership distributions, the general partners have the power to withhold distributions by retaining income within the partnership.[12]

Footnotes on page 171

ESTABLISHING PARTNERSHIP

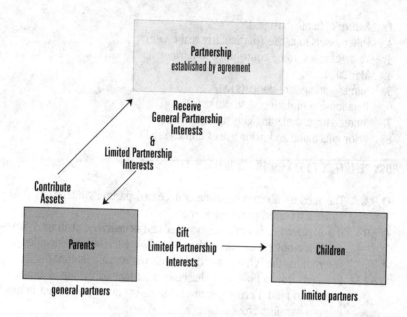

Partnership
established by agreement

Receive
General Partnership
Interests
&
Limited Partnership
Interests

Contribute
Assets

Parents

general partners

Gift
Limited Partnership
Interests

Children

limited partners

ADVANTAGES OF PARTNERSHIP
Control and Flexibility

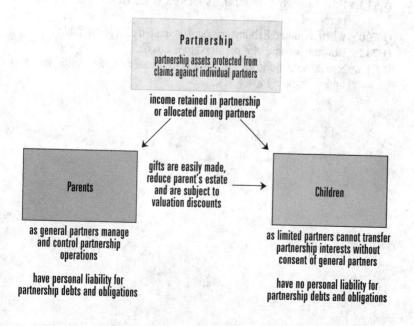

Partnership

partnership assets protected from
claims against individual partners

income retained in partnership
or allocated among partners

Parents

gifts are easily made,
reduce parent's estate
and are subject to
valuation discounts

Children

as general partners manage
and control partnership
operations

have personal liability for
partnership debts and obligations

as limited partners cannot transfer
partnership interests without
consent of general partners

have no personal liability for
partnership debts and obligations

INFORMATION REQUIRED FOR ANALYSIS & PROPOSAL

1. Nature of family business.
2. Other assets in estate (particularly real estate).
3. Value of assets to be contributed to partnership.
4. Marital status.
5. Names and ages of donee(s).
6. Relationship of donee(s) to donor(s).
7. Attitude toward making gifts to family members.
8. Prior gifts made and prior use of unified credit.

CROSS REFERENCE TO TAX FACTS 1 (2002)

Q 92. The income tax results when a deceased partner's interest is sold under a business purchase agreement.

Q 509. If a partnership is both policyowner and beneficiary, insurance proceeds are not includable in the insured's estate (but are included in determining the value of the deceased's partnership interest).

Q 511. Proceeds from a policy purchased by a partner on the life of another partner to fund a cross purchase agreement are not included in the insured partners gross estate.

Q 512. Proceeds from a policy purchased by a partnership on the life of a partner to fund the purchase of the insured partner's interest are not included in the insured's gross estate.

Q 513. How a closely held business interest is valued for federal estate tax purposes.

Q 740. When a limited liability company is treated as a partnership.

Q 741. How the income of a partnership is taxed.

Q 813. Special valuation rules that apply to transfer of partnership interests under Chapter 14.

Footnotes

[1] Partnerships are also used as an alternative to the irrevocable life insurance trust and to avoid transfer for value rules, but the latter use appears very aggressive (see page 429).

[2] Although the family limited partnership is an innovative use of existing laws regarding limited partnerships, it should always be established for legitimate business and estate planning purposes.

[3] The principal *requirements* for a family limited partnership are: (1) capital must be a material income-producing factor, meaning that a personal service business where income consists primarily of fees or commissions would not qualify for operation as a family limited partnership (i.e., lawyer, doctor, photographer, plumber, etc.); (2) if the partnership has been created by gift, the donor (parent) must be given a reasonable salary for services rendered to the partnership before profits can be allocated among the partners (the concept of "gift" also includes intra-family sales); (3) profits of the partnership must be allocated, or divided, in proportion to each partner's capital investment; and (4) all partners must actually own a "capital interest" (i.e., an interest in partnership assets which is distributable to the partner upon his withdrawal from the partnership or upon partnership liquidation).

[4] Generally, the partnership agreement will limit ownership of partnership interests to family members. The agreement is also likely to contain provisions for settling disputes.

[5] Transfer of assets to the partnership is generally done without recognition of either gain or loss. Alternatively, the parents could make a gift of assets to the children who will then contribute these assets to the family limited partnership in return for limited partnership interests.

[6] Often the ultimate goal is for the parents to eventually own only modest partnership interests, with the bulk of the family limited partnership being held by other family members. Although this example assumes that both parents will be general partners, family limited partnerships are often established with only one spouse as the general partner and the other spouse as a limited partner.

[7] Some *disadvantages* of the family limited partnership include: (1) the traditional partnership freeze is subject to the impact of the Chapter 14 valuation rules, see pages 386-387 (however, most of the techniques used to reduce the effect of, or to avoid, these rules with respect to recapitalizations will also work with partnerships); (2) much of the ability to reduce taxes by shifting income from parent to younger children has been curtailed by the "kiddie tax" (see discussion on page 482); (3) there are additional expenses associated with establishing and accounting for a FLP (e.g., an information tax return must be filed); (4) gifts do not receive a step-up in income tax basis; and (5) retained partnership interests continue to appreciate in the parent's estate until they are transferred during lifetime or at death.

[8] The general partners also have liability for all partnership debts and obligations.

[9] Effective income shifting requires that the partnership be one in which capital is a material income-producing factor (see also item (2) in footnote 7, above).

[10] See pages 52 and 395 for discussions regarding the tax advantages of making gifts. Also, see the table on page 101. These gifts could also be made in trust for minor children (see page 481).

[11] Lack of marketability can be established by prohibitions in the partnership agreement against terminating the partnership without the concurrence of all partners (usually limited to 40 years or less). Although valuation discounts of up to 70 percent have been claimed, such overly aggressive discounts are likely to be challenged by the IRS.

[12] The right to partnership distributions is secured by obtaining a charging order. However, because the general partners have the ability to retain profits, the flow-through nature of partnership income taxation gives them the ability to create a tax liability without making cash distributions for tax payments (i.e., an "ugly" asset).

RECAPITALIZATION

A recapitalization through a preferred stock redemption can offer an effective and versatile estate planning technique for corporate stockholders. For example, when combined with a subsequent gifting program, it can:

- Shift substantial future appreciation to children.
- Retain control of the corporation.
- Freeze the value of stock for estate tax purposes.
- Provide an ongoing income stream for retirement.
- Transfer corporate control when, and if, appropriate.
- Motivate younger employees.
- Facilitate distribution of stock at death.

PREFERRED STOCK REDEMPTION. The design of stock to be received in a recapitalization can take many forms. For example, a parent might make a tax-free exchange of *all* his original common stock for a combination of voting cumulative preferred stock and nonvoting common stock.[1] Income would be provided by requiring annual dividends from the preferred stock at a fixed rate.

The voting preferred stock is retained by the parent in order to maintain control of the corporation, and the nonvoting common stock is given to the children, or other donees. As long as the retained preferred stock is entitled to dividends, it will be considered to have a value generally equal to the present value of the right to future payments. Since the value of the common stock is determined by subtracting the value of the preferred stock from the total corporate value, the preferred stock's value has the effect of *decreasing* the value of the common stock, thereby lessening exposure to gift taxes when the common stock is given to the children.[2] However, in order to obtain this increase in value of the retained preferred stock it may be necessary to obligate the corporation to pay substantial cumulative preferred stock dividends.[3]

EFFECT OF SUBSEQUENT APPRECIATION. The prior "freezing" of the value of the preferred stock means that most, if not all, future appreciation is shifted to the common stock owned by the children.[4]

Recapitalizations can be an effective estate planning technique for corporate stockholders who desire to make gifts of stock to children or other heirs.[5] However, they should be undertaken only with the assistance of competent tax counsel.[6]

Footnotes on page 175

PREFERRED STOCK REDEMPTION

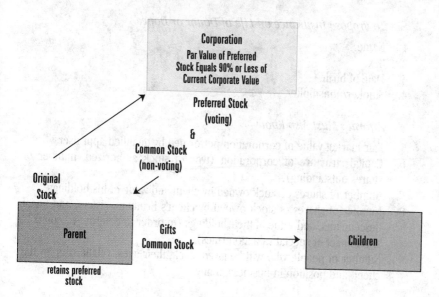

EFFECT OF SUBSEQUENT APPRECIATION

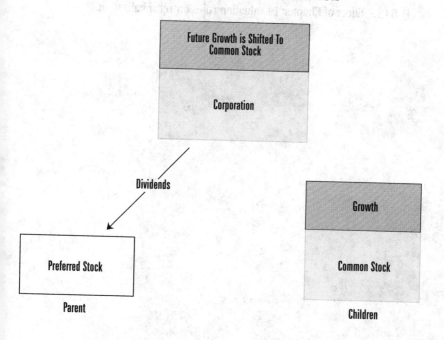

INFORMATION REQUIRED FOR ANALYSIS & PROPOSAL

To Propose Insurance on Life of Donor or Donee

1. Name.
2. Sex.
3. Date of birth.
4. Smoker/nonsmoker.

Attorney Must Also Know

5. Fair market value of corporation performed by qualified appraiser.
6. Capital structure of corporation (type of stock authorized, number of shares outstanding).
7. Number of shares of stock owned by client and value of his holdings.
8. Number of shares of stock owned by client's brothers, sisters, and lineal descendants, and value of their holdings (in order to determine "control" and impact of special valuation rules).
9. Number of people who will be given stock, their ages, relationship to the client, and position in business, if any.

CROSS REFERENCES TO TAX FACTS 1 (2002)

Q 813. Effect of Chapter 14 valuation rules on recapitalization.

Footnotes

[1] This chart does not demonstrate a "true" recapitalization in which there is an exchange of *all* of a stockholder's stock (usually common) for a different class of stock (usually preferred). What is demonstrated is essentially a "preferred stock" distribution, under which the stockholder receives another class of stock (the voting preferred) without actually giving up his common stock that represents the future equity growth of the corporation. Although this receipt of preferred stock is non-taxable, it is essentially equivalent to a stock dividend and will likely be considered "Section 306 stock" (see discussion, page 462). If it were then subsequently sold, the proceeds would be treated as ordinary income, not capital gain (capital gains are discussed on page 350).

[2] Because of the special valuation provisions of Chapter 14 all common stock must be given a value of at least 10 percent of the total value of the corporation (e.g., if the corporation had a value of $1,000,000, the common stock value must be at least $100,000, meaning that the retained preferred stock could, at most, be valued at $900,000). For this purpose the total value of the corporation includes the amount of all corporate indebtedness to the transferor and family members (see discussion on pages 386-387). Obtaining an accurate fair market value of the corporation at the time of recapitalization can also avoid unexpected tax problems. For example, if the value placed on the new preferred stock is *greater than* the original common stock, the stockholder may be considered as having received a dividend from the corporation. On the other hand, when a second stockholder exists at the time of the recapitalization, undervaluing the new preferred can lead to either income or gift tax liabilities. If the value placed on the new preferred is *less than* the original common stock the amount of the undervaluation might be treated as taxable income to the co-stockholder (either salary, or worse yet, a nondeductible corporate dividend). It could be treated as a gift if the co-stockholder were a family member.

[3] Under Chapter 14 these cumulative dividends *must actually be paid*, or there will be exposure to *future* gift or estate taxes. If the retained preferred stock is to have a value greater than zero the stock dividend rights must constitute "qualified payments" (i.e., dividends payable on a periodic basis and at a fixed rate or at a variable rate with a fixed relationship to market value). See the expanded discussion of qualified payments on pages 386-387. In the desire to have the retained preferred stock highly valued in order to reduce the exposure to gift taxes when the common is given to children, care must be taken not to obligate the corporation to unrealistic and onerous preferred stock dividends, which are not deductible to the corporation.

[4] Because *future* appreciation is being shifted out of the estate, a recapitalization will generally not reduce *present* estate settlement costs. The value of the stock retained by the donor will still be included in his gross estate. A partial stock redemption under Section 303 can provide an effective means of paying these costs, particularly when funded with life insurance. Dividends paid on the stock transferred by gift can be used by the donee to pay for insurance on the life of the donor using the reverse section 303 technique described in the chart on page 153. However, because of the grantor trust rules, the donee should be an individual, not a trust. Since there is some possibility that the donee will predecease the donor, the donor may wish to insure the donee in order to purchase stock from the donee's estate.

[5] A recapitalization can also be an effective way to accomplish the non-tax objectives of transferring growth and control to one child while providing income for another child. For example, assume that both nonvoting preferred and voting common were issued pursuant to a recapitalization. If Child A were not involved in the business he could be given the *nonvoting* preferred stock (with an income stream provided by dividends). Child B, who is working in the business, might then be given the voting common stock (with both its control and potential for future appreciation).

[6] These less restrictive anti-freeze provisions in the form of special valuation rules are contained in Chapter 14 of the Code.

ATTRIBUTION

When it is intended that continued ownership would be held within a family, it is extremely important to consider the effect of the attribution rules when planning for the sale of stock to a corporation. Unfortunately, all too often the operation of these rules is poorly understood, and the adverse tax consequences can be disastrous (they have been aptly described as "infamous and insidious").

The basic problem arises under Section 302(b)(3) of the Code, which requires that to qualify as a "capital transaction" the sale of stock to a corporation must result in a *complete* disposition of the stockholder's interest (both actually owned and constructively owned). If there is a redemption of *less* than the stockholder's entire interest, then the transaction is likely to be treated and taxed as a stock dividend. However, merely selling all directly owned stock to the corporation, may not satisfy this requirement if stock owned by others is attributed to the selling stockholder or his estate. There are two types of attribution, family attribution and entity attribution. Whereas family attribution can be waived (charts, pages 180-181), entity attribution cannot be waived (charts, page 179). To summarize the rules of family attribution:

1. An individual is deemed (i.e., considered) to own any stock owned directly or *indirectly* by his:
   a. parents
   b. spouse
   c. children
   d. grandchildren

2. There is *no* family attribution with respect to one's grandparent, brother, sister, uncle, aunt, nephew, cousin, or in-law.

3. There is no "secondary" attribution under the family attribution rules (e.g., stock attributed from daughter-in-law to son cannot then be again attributed from the son to his parents).

Depending upon the particular family relationship, an individual may, or may not, be considered to own the stock of other members of his family. For example, assume we have an extended family composed of a husband, his wife, his grandfather, grandmother, father, mother, and brother; as well as his son, daughter-in-law and grandson. In this family the **husband** is considered as owning the stock of *his* father, mother, wife, son and grandson. On the other hand, his **wife** will be considered as owning the stock of only *her* father, mother, husband, son and grandson.

FAMILY ATTRIBUTION

Husband is considered to own the stock of *his* Father,
Mother, Wife, Son and Grandson.

Wife is considered to own the stock of *her* Father,
Mother, Husband, Son and Grandson.

Moving Up One Generation

Father is considered to own the stock of
Grandfather, Grandmother, Mother, Brother, Husband, and Son
(i.e., of *his* father, mother, wife, sons, and grandson).

FAMILY ATTRIBUTION

Moving Down One Generation

Son is considered to own the stock of
Husband, Wife, Daughter-in-law, and Grandson
(i.e., of *his* father, mother, wife, and son)

Daughter-in-law is considered to own the stock of
Her Parents, Son and Grandson
(i.e., of *her* parents, husband and son)

CROSS REFERENCES TO TAX FACTS 1 (2002)

Q 82. Amount paid by corporation for decedent's entire stock interest generally not dividend to estate, provided no attribution problems.

Q 83. Avoiding attribution of stock ownership among family members.

Q 84. Avoiding attribution of stock ownership from estate beneficiary to estate.

ENTITY ATTRIBUTION

Attribution From An Estate

Stock owned by an Estate is attributed to the Beneficiaries
in proportion to their interests in the estate

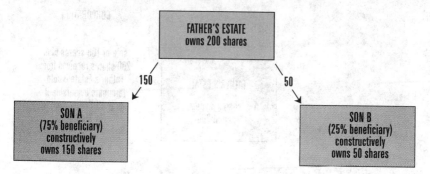

Attribution To An Estate

Stock actually or constructively owned by a beneficiary
is attributed *in full* to the estate, without regard for the
beneficiaries' percentage of interest in the estate
(the attribution of Son A's 100 shares
to the estate cannot be waived)

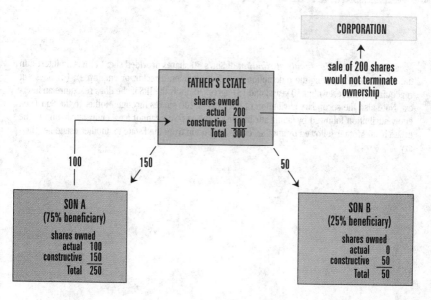

FAMILY & ENTITY ATTRIBUTION

Waiver Of Family Attribution
Sale by Mother

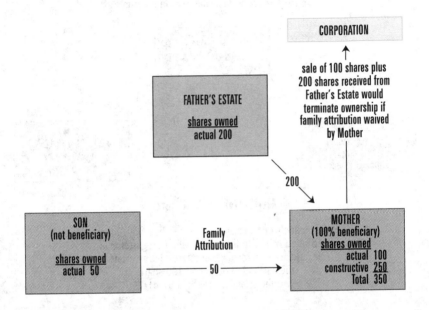

Note: Mother can *waive family attribution* of Son's 50 shares provided she: (1) has no interest in the corporation following the redemption (i.e., as an officer, director, or employee); (2) does not reacquire an interest within 10 years; and (3) agrees to notify the IRS if she does reacquire an interest. Note also the secondary attribution of the Estate's 200 shares through Mother to the Son (i.e., entity attribution followed by family attribution). However, you cannot have entity attribution to the estate from Mother followed by another entity attribution from the Estate to another estate beneficiary.

FAMILY & ENTITY ATTRIBUTION

Waiver Of Family Attribution
Sale by Estate

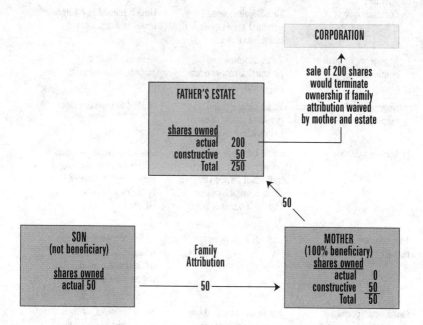

Note: Even though an entity, Father's Estate can *waive* family attribution of Son's 50 shares to Mother. This breaks the chain of secondary attribution from Son to Mother to Father's Estate (i.e., family attribution followed by entity attribution). The waiver by the estate is dependent upon both the entity (i.e., the estate) and those through whom ownership is attributed (i.e., the mother) agreeing to join in the waiver. Both the entity and the beneficiary must hold no interest in the corporation, cannot acquire an interest within 10 years of the redemption, and must agree to notify the Internal Revenue Service should an interest be acquired. If Son predeceased Mother, as an estate beneficiary Son's 50 shares would be attributed in full to the estate (see bottom chart, page 179). There can be no waiver of entity attribution.

BUSINESS COMPARISON

Question	Unincorporated	Incorporated
What is the extent of liability for: Contract?	To all business and personal assets of each individual owner.	Usually limited to business assets in most states.
Negligence of owner-employees?	To all business and personal assets of each individual owner.	Generally limited to business assets except professional liability.
Negligence of employees?	To all business and personal assets of each individual owner.	Limited to business assets.
Business debts?	To all business and personal assets of each individual owner (but see discussion of Limited Liability Company, page 415).	Limited to business assets except where owners have personally guaranteed loan by endorsement or otherwise.
To whom are profits taxed?	Individual owners.	To the corporation if retained as earnings. To owner-employees if paid out as reasonable compensation or dividends (page 483).
Can a small portion of the ownership interest have full control?	Not in any practical way (but see Family Limited Partnership chart, page 169).	Yes – by use of voting preferred and non-voting stock (page 172).
Can the business interest be easily transferred to one or more purchasers or recipients?	No – transfer of individual assets or creation of new entity can result in complications.	Yes – stock may be easily transferred to either the corporation, other stockholders, key persons, or outsiders (pages 128, 132 and 144).
Who pays income taxes on dollars used to pay for life insurance funding a buy/sell agreement?	Individual owners.	Choice of corporation or stockholder-employee.
Can the business purchase a portion of a deceased owner's interest on a tax-favored basis?	No	Yes – under Section 303 the corporation can purchase some stock, while allowing the surviving family to retain an ownership interest (page 148).

Note: "Unincorporated" refers to sole proprietorships and partnerships, but not to limited partners; "incorporated" refers to C corporations, but not to S corporations.

Question	Unincorporated	Incorporated
Does the business entity enjoy any tax-favored investment advantages?	No	Yes – under Section 243 a corporation can deduct from 70% to 100% of the dividends received from domestic corporations.
Can the business have a different fiscal year than the owners?	Not in any practical way.	Yes
What is the annual cost of Social Security for each owner-employee?	In 2002 12.40% OASDI tax on first $84,900 of self-employment income and 2.90% hospital insurance tax without limit, all paid by the individual owner.	In 2002 6.20% OASDI tax on first $84,900 of income and 1.45% hospital insurance tax without limit, paid by the owner-employee. Equal amounts of tax are also paid by the corporation, but deductible as a business expense.
What is the cost of unemployment taxes for each owner-employee?	None	In 2002 both state and federal (FUTA) taxes will be at least $434 per employee, i.e., 6.2% of first $7,000 in wages.
What is the cost of worker's compensation?	None	If set by state law, can often be exempt from coverage. If paid, it is considered a deductible business expense.
Is there any extra cost for franchise fees and bookkeeping?	–	A small annual franchise fee is usually payable. Corporate minutes must be kept on an annual basis. Bookkeeping costs may be somewhat higher.
Is there any extra cost to prepare a corporate tax return?	–	Preparation of corporate return can cost more, but usually not much greater then Schedule C (Profit or Loss From Business or Profession) or Form 1065 (U.S. Partnership Return of Income).
Could there be a problem with unreasonable compensation to owner-employees?	No	Yes – under Section 162 only a reasonable allowance for compensation can be deducted. This is usually not a serious problem, but should be considered (page 483).

Note: "Unincorporated" refers to sole proprietorships and partnerships, but not to limited partners; "incorporated" refers to C corporations, but not to S corporations.

Question	Unincorporated	Incorporated
Is there a potential for double taxation?	No	Yes – if not properly planned there could be a corporate income tax, plus a personal income tax on dividends received.
Could a personal holding company penalty tax of 38.6% be levied?	No	Yes – a penalty tax could be applied if 60% of income is essentially passive, such as dividends, rents and royalties.
Can individual owner-employees have deferred compensation?	No	Yes – Income may be deferred (Deferred Compensation, page 242).
Can the business pay premiums for personal life insurance, and have the premiums paid tax-free for owner-employees?	No	Yes – up to $50,000 of group insurance is available under Section 79 (Group Insurance, page 210).
Are tax-favored personal life insurance programs available to owner-employees?	No	Yes – individual plans can be established (Executive Equity, page 218, and Split-Dollar Insurance, page 226).
Is a qualified retirement program available?	Yes – HR-10 permits sole proprietors and partners to be covered under qualified plan.	Yes – under qualified plan rules (Qualified Retirement Plans, pages 262, 403 and 466).
Are other tax-deductible benefits available to owner-employees, such as:		
Disability income plans?	No	Yes – under Sections 105 and 106 (Disability Income Plan, page 250).
Medical and Dental. expense reimbursement plans?	Not generally, but limited deduction available (footnote 2, page 257).	Yes – under Sections 105 and 106 (Medical Expense Reimbursement Plans, page 254).
Survivor income Plans?	No	Yes – as a form of salary continuation death benefit (Survivor Income, page 238).

Note: "Unincorporated" refers to sole proprietorships and partnerships, but not to limited partners; "incorporated" refers to C corporations, but not to S corporations.

ODDS OF DEATH BEFORE AGE 65

When a business has two or more owners, the odds of at least one death before age 65 increase dramatically. *The risk is not remote*. Proper planning calls for making provisions for the continuation of the business as well as providing support for the surviving family.

One-Owner Business

Ages	Odds of Death Male	Female	Ages	Odds of Death Male	Female
30	23.5%	16.2%	45	20.4%	13.6%
35	22.8	15.6	50	18.3	11.8
40	21.8	14.8	55	14.9	9.2

Two-Owner Business

Ages	Odds Of One Death Male	Female	Ages	Odds Of One Death Male	Female
30-30	41.5%	29.8%	45-45	36.7%	25.3%
30-35	40.9	29.3	45-50	35.0	23.7
30-40	40.2	28.6	45-55	32.3	21.5
35-35	40.4	28.8	50-50	33.2	22.2
35-40	39.6	28.1	50-55	30.4	19.9
35-45	38.5	27.0	50-60	25.9	16.6
40-40	38.9	27.4	55-55	27.6	17.5
40-45	37.8	26.3	55-60	22.8	14.1
40-50	36.1	24.8	60-60	17.8	10.6

Three-Owner Business

Ages	Odds Of One Death Male	Female	Ages	Odds Of One Death Male	Female
30-30-30	55.2%	41.2%	40-45-50	49.2%	35.0%
30-35-40	53.8	39.7	40-50-60	42.1	28.9
30-40-50	51.1	37.0	45-45-45	49.6	35.4
35-35-35	54.0	39.9	45-50-55	44.6	30.7
35-40-45	52.0	37.8	50-50-50	45.4	31.3
35-45-55	47.7	33.7	50-55-60	36.9	24.3
40-40-40	52.3	38.1	55-55-55	38.3	25.1

Using the following percentages, it is possible to calculate the odds of at least one death before age 65 for any particular group of owners. After multiplying the percent for each owner by the percent for each other owner, subtract the results from 1. For example, the calculations for the odds of at least one death for three male owners, ages 40, 45, and 50: 1 - (.7816 x .7958 x .8174) = 1 - .5084 = 49.2%.

Age	Living To Age 65 Male	Female	Age	Living To Age 65 Male	Female	Age	Living To Age 65 Male	Female	Age	Living To Age 65 Male	Female
30	76.51%	83.79%	38	77.74%	84.85%	46	79.94%	86.76%	54	84.30%	90.21%
31	76.64	83.90	39	77.95	85.03	47	80.34	87.09	55	85.11	90.81
32	76.78	84.02	40	78.16	85.21	48	80.77	87.44	56	86.02	91.46
33	76.92	84.14	41	78.40	85.42	49	81.24	87.82	57	87.01	92.16
34	77.07	84.27	42	78.66	85.65	50	81.74	88.23	58	88.11	92.90
35	77.22	84.40	43	78.94	85.89	51	82.30	88.67	59	89.33	93.69
36	77.38	84.54	44	79.25	86.16	52	82.90	89.14	60	90.67	94.54
37	77.56	84.69	45	79.58	86.45	53	83.57	89.65			

Source: Commissioners 1980 Standard Ordinary Mortality Table.

ODDS OF DEATH WITHIN 10 AND 20 YEARS

When a business has two or more owners, the odds of at least one death within any given period of time increase dramatically. *The risk is not remote.* Proper planning calls for making provisions for the continuation of the business.

One-Owner Business – MALE
Odds Of Death Within

Age	10 Years	20 Years
30	2.1%	6.4%
35	3.0	9.3
40	4.4	13.8
45	6.5	20.4
50	9.8	30.0
55	14.9	43.1

One-Owner Business – FEMALE
Odds Of Death Within

Age	10 Years	20 Years
30	1.7%	5.0%
35	2.4	7.1
40	3.4	9.9
45	4.8	13.6
50	6.7	19.2
55	9.2	27.7

Two-Owner Business – MALE
Odds Of One Death Within

Ages	10 Years	20 Years
30-30	4.2%	12.4%
30-35	5.0	15.1
30-40	6.4	19.3
35-35	5.8	17.7
35-40	7.2	21.8
35-45	9.3	27.8
40-40	8.6	25.7
40-45	10.6	31.4
40-50	13.8	39.7
45-45	12.6	36.7
45-50	15.7	44.3
45-55	20.4	54.7
50-50	18.7	51.0
50-55	23.3	60.2
50-60	30.0	71.7
55-55	27.6	67.6
55-60	33.9	77.0
55-65	43.1	86.5

Two-Owner Business – FEMALE
Odds Of One Death Within

Ages	10 Years	20 Years
30-30	3.3%	9.8%
30-35	4.0	11.7
30-40	5.0	14.4
35-35	4.7	13.6
35-40	5.7	16.2
35-45	7.0	19.7
40-40	6.7	18.8
40-45	8.1	22.1
40-50	9.9	27.2
45-45	9.4	25.3
45-50	11.2	30.2
45-55	13.6	37.5
50-50	12.9	34.7
50-55	15.3	41.5
50-60	19.2	52.5
55-55	17.5	47.7
55-60	21.4	57.5
55-65	27.7	71.0

Three-Owner Business – MALE
Odds Of One Death Within

Ages	10 Years	20 Years
30-30-30	6.2%	18.0%
30-35-40	9.2	26.8
30-40-50	15.6	43.5
35-35-35	8.6	25.3
35-40-45	13.3	37.8
35-45-55	22.8	58.9
40-40-40	12.6	35.9
40-45-50	19.4	52.0
40-50-60	33.1	75.6
45-45-45	18.3	49.6
45-50-55	28.3	68.3
50-50-50	26.7	65.7
50-55-60	40.4	83.9
55-55-55	38.3	81.6
50-60-70	63.5	97.1

Three-Owner Business – FEMALE
Odds Of One Death Within

Ages	10 Years	20 Years
30-30-30	4.9%	14.4%
30-35-40	7.3	20.4
30-40-50	11.4	30.8
35-35-35	6.9	19.7
35-40-45	10.2	27.6
35-45-55	15.6	41.9
40-40-40	9.9	26.8
40-45-50	14.2	37.0
40-50-60	22.0	57.2
45-45-45	13.7	35.4
45-50-55	19.3	49.5
50-50-50	18.7	47.3
50-55-60	26.6	65.7
55-55-55	25.1	62.1
50-60-70	45.2	90.5

Source: Commissioners 1980 Standard Ordinary Mortality Table.

WHY BUSINESSES FAIL

Underlying Causes	Construction	Manufacturing	Wholesale	Retail	Finance, Insurance & Real Estate	Services
Lack of Business Knowledge	0.4%	0.4%	0.2%	0.1%	0.2%	0.1%
Lack of Line Experience	0.2	0.8	0.4	0.7	0.0	0.2
Lack of Managerial Experience	0.2	0.6	0.8	0.5	0.0	0.2
Experience Totals	0.8	1.8	1.4	1.3	0.2	0.5
Finance	18.8	25.0	18.4	20.3	25.8	32.9
Strategy	0.9	1.9	2.5	0.2	0.5	0.6
Economic Factors	70.1	57.2	63.3	63.3	57.1	60.3
Neglect, Disaster & Fraud	9.4	14.1	14.4	14.9	16.4	5.7
Number of Failures	12,452	7,120	6,744	19,084	6,260	26,871
Average Liabilities Per Failure	$404,498	$1,181,682	$1,247,823	$489,276	$6,614,265	$459,692

INADEQUATE MANAGEMENT and INADEQUATE FINANCES caused 28.7% of business failures

DEBT averaged $971,653 per failure

THE DEATH OR DISABILITY OF A KEY EMPLOYEE IS A SUBSTANTIAL RISK!

Source: The Dun & Bradstreet Corporation, *Business Failure Record 1992*, pages 2, 6-9, and 18.

KEY PERSON VALUATION FORMULAS

No single formula is accepted for valuing a key person or employee. In fact, valuing a key person is much like valuing a business, it is more art than science. Much depends upon the characteristics of the key person (e.g., a sales manager who has a substantial impact upon sales or a financial officer who has access to credit). However, there is little doubt that key persons can have considerable value; and their death or disability can cause substantial financial losses, or even failure of a business. One or more of the following formulas should provide a useful starting point for determining value.

Contribution To Profits. This method evaluates the key person's contributions to profits and then capitalizes this amount to determine value. For example, assume the business has a book value of $500,000, an expected rate of return on book value for this particular type of business is 8 percent and average profits are $120,000. The excess earnings are $80,000 ($500,000 x .08 = $40,000; $120,000 - $40,000 = $80,000). Assuming the key person's contribution to excess earnings is 50 percent, capitalization of the key person's contribution at 12 percent yields a value of $333,200 (.50 x $80,000 = $40,000; 100 ÷ 12 = 8.33 x $40,000 = $333,200). Note that a similar capitalization approach to valuing a business is discussed on page 124. A variation on the contributions to profits method does not capitalize the contribution, but rather reduces the key person's annual contribution as a replacement is recruited, trained and becomes fully effective. Using this variation, the key person's value would be $120,000, assuming annual contributions to profits of $40,000 and 5 years to complete the replacement. The basic method and the variation are calculated as follows:

			Variation
Average Profits	$120,000		
Book Value At 8%	40,000	Year 1	$40,000
Excess Earnings	$80,000	Year 2	32,000
Percent Of Contribution	50	Year 3	24,000
Key Person's Contribution	$40,000	Year 4	16,000
Capitalization Factor	8.33	Year 5	8,000
Key Person Value	$333,200	Key Person Value	$120,000

Business Life Value. This is a variation of the method commonly used to determine human life value. The business estimates its annual loss of earnings if the key person were to die, multiplies that amount by the number of working years to retirement and then discounts the results by an appropriate interest rate. Assuming annual loss of earnings of $40,000, 15 years to retirement and 12 percent interest, the value would be calculated as follows:

Loss Of Earnings	$40,000	
Discount Factor	6.811	(from table on page 502)
Key Person Value	$272,440	

Multiple Of Salary. This method recognizes that the salaries paid to key persons are an indication of their value. Typically a factor of from 3 to 10 times annual salary is used. Assuming an annual salary of $75,000 and a factor of 5, the value would be calculated as follows:

Annual Salary	$75,000
Factor	5
Key Person Value	$375,000

Discount Of Business. This method simply discounts the value of the business to reflect the loss of the key person. Assuming a business value of $900,000 and a discount of 20 percent, the value would be calculated as follows:

Value Of Business	$900,000
Discount	.20
Key Person Value	$180,000

COST OF BORROWED DOLLARS – CORPORATE

$100,000 Loan to a Corporation

Loan Repaid Over	Interest Rate (%)	Yearly Payment	Total Payments	Income Required By Corporation In Tax Bracket Of		
				15%	25%	34%
5 Years	6	23,740	118,700	136,347	152,033	170,215
	8	25,046	125,230	142,877	158,563	176,745
	10	26,380	131,900	149,547	165,233	183,415
	12	27,741	138,705	156,352	172,038	190,220
	15	29,832	149,160	166,807	182,493	200,675
10 Years	6	13,587	135,870	153,517	169,203	187,385
	8	14,903	149,030	166,677	182,363	200,545
	10	16,275	162,750	180,397	196,083	214,265
	12	17,698	176,980	194,627	210,313	228,495
	15	19,925	199,250	216,897	232,583	250,765
15 Years	6	10,296	154,440	172,087	187,773	205,955
	8	11,683	175,245	192,892	208,578	226,760
	10	13,147	197,205	214,852	230,538	248,720
	12	14,682	220,230	237,877	253,563	271,745
	15	17,102	256,530	274,177	289,863	308,045
20 Years	6	8,718	174,360	192,007	207,693	225,875
	8	10,185	203,700	221,347	237,033	255,215
	10	11,746	234,920	252,567	268,253	286,435
	12	13,388	267,760	285,407	301,093	319,275
	15	15,976	319,520	337,167	352,853	371,035

Explanation of Table. This table is designed to show the income required by a corporation to repay a loan of $100,000 at various rates of interest. For example, assume that to redeem stock under an entity or partial stock redemption plan, the corporation is able to borrow $100,000 to purchase the business interest of a deceased stockholder. If the loan is obtained at 8 percent and is repayable in equal annual payments over 10 years, each yearly payment would be $14,903. Total repayments over the 10-year repayment period would be $149,030. However, if the corporation was in a 25 percent tax bracket, the total *before-tax* income required to repay the loan *principal* is $133,333, which is determined by dividing the loan principal by one minus the borrower's marginal tax bracket ($100,000 ÷ .75 = $133,333). This is because the $100,000 principal must come from after-tax funds. In addition, since the interest payments are deductible, it takes $49,030 of before-tax income to make the interest payments. The total cost to pay the loan is $182,363 ($133,333 + $49,030 = $182,363).

See page 190 for *individual* costs of borrowed dollars.

COST OF BORROWED DOLLARS – INDIVIDUAL

$100,000 Loan To An Individual

Loan Repaid Over	Interest Rate (%)	Yearly Payment	Total Payments	Income Required By Individual In Tax Bracket Of			
				15%	27%	30%	35%
5 Years	6	23,740	118,700	139,647	162,603	169,571	182,615
	8	25,046	125,230	147,329	171,548	178,900	192,662
	10	26,380	131,900	155,176	180,685	188,429	202,923
	12	27,741	138,705	163,182	190,007	198,150	213,392
	15	29,832	149,160	175,482	204,329	213,086	229,477
10 Years	6	13,587	135,870	159,847	186,123	194,100	209,031
	8	14,903	149,030	175,329	204,151	212,900	229,277
	10	16,275	162,750	191,471	222,945	232,500	250,385
	12	17,698	176,980	208,212	242,438	252,829	272,277
	15	19,925	199,250	234,412	272,945	284,643	306,538
15 Years	6	10,296	154,440	181,694	211,562	220,629	237,600
	8	11,683	175,245	206,171	240,062	250,350	269,608
	10	13,147	197,205	232,006	270,144	281,721	303,392
	12	14,682	220,230	259,094	301,685	314,614	338,815
	15	17,102	256,530	301,800	351,411	366,471	394,662
20 Years	6	8,718	174,360	205,129	238,849	249,086	268,246
	8	10,185	203,700	239,647	279,041	291,000	313,385
	10	11,746	234,920	276,376	321,808	335,600	361,415
	12	13,388	267,760	315,012	366,795	382,514	411,938
	15	15,976	319,520	375,906	437,699	456,457	491,569

Explanation of Table. This table is designed to show the income required by an individual to repay a loan of $100,000 at various rates of interest. For example, assume that an executor, or a surviving stockholder, must borrow $100,000 to pay estate settlement costs or purchase a business interest of a deceased co-stockholder. If the loan is obtained at 8 percent and is repayable in equal annual payments over 10 years, each yearly payment would be $14,903. Total repayments over the 10-year repayment period would be $149,030. However, if the borrower was in a 27 percent tax bracket, the total before-tax income required to repay the loan is $204,151, which is determined by dividing the total payments by 1 minus borrower's marginal tax bracket ($149,030 ÷ .73 = $204,151). This assumes that the $100,000 principal must come from after-tax funds, and that interest payments are not deductible (i.e., no deduction is allowed for "personal" interest, and it is assumed there is no "net investment income" available in order to take a deduction for "investment" interest).

See page 189 for corporate costs of borrowed dollars.

INTEREST RATES

	2000	1999	1998	1997	1996	1995
Prime Rate Charged by Banks	9.23	8.00	8.35	8.44	8.27	8.83
U.S. Government Securities						
3-Month Treasury Bills	5.82	4.64	4.78	5.06	5.01	5.49
1-Year Treasury Bills	5.78	4.81	4.80	5.35	5.22	5.60
Mortgage Rates						
Conventional, new-home	-	7.45	7.00	7.76	8.03	8.05
Conventional, 15 yr. fixed	7.76	7.09	6.58	7.16	7.28	7.39
Conventional, 30 yr. fixed	8.08	7.46	6.92	7.57	7.76	7.86
Installment Credit						
New Automobiles	9.34	8.44	8.72	9.02	9.05	9.57
Other Consumer Goods	13.90	13.39	13.74	13.91	13.53	13.94
Credit Card Plans	15.71	15.21	15.71	15.76	15.63	16.02

Source: Statistical Abstract of the United States, 2001, Table 1190 on page 735 and Table 1194 on page 737. Conventional new-home mortgages rates were not available for 2000.

FINANCIAL RATIOS

Current Ratio = $\dfrac{\text{Total Current Assets}}{\text{Total Current Liabilities}}$

Also called the "working capital" ratio. The question addressed by this ratio: "Does the business have enough current assets to meet the payment schedule of its current debts with a margin of safety for possible losses in current assets?" A 2 to 1 ratio is generally acceptable.

Quick Ratio = $\dfrac{\text{Cash + Gov't Securities + Receivables}}{\text{Total Current Liabilities}}$

Also called the "acid-test" ratio and "quick current" test. The question addressed by this ratio: "If all sales revenues disappeared, could the business meet its current obligations with the readily convertible 'quick' funds at hand?" An acid-test of 1 to 1 is typical. Quick funds are current assets minus inventory.

Working Capital = Total Current Assets - Total Current Liabilities

A measure of cash flow. Considered an indication of the ability to withstand financial crises.

Debt/Worth Ratio = $\dfrac{\text{Total Liabilities}}{\text{Net Worth}}$

Indicates the extent to which the business is reliant on debt financing.

Gross Margin Ratio = $\dfrac{\text{Gross Profit}}{\text{Net Sales}}$

Gross profit equals net sales minus cost of goods sold. This ratio measures the percentage of sales dollars remaining to pay overhead expenses.

Net Profit Margin Ratio = $\dfrac{\text{Net Profit Before Tax}}{\text{Net Sales}}$

This ratio measures "return on sales" and can be used to evaluate performance in comparison with similar businesses.

Inventory Turnover = $\dfrac{\text{Net Sales}}{\text{Average Inventory At Cost}}$

Measures how well inventory is managed. The more inventory is turned in a given operating cycle the greater the profit.

Return On Assets Ratio = $\dfrac{\text{Net Profit Before Tax}}{\text{Total Assets}}$

Measures how efficiently profits are being generated from the assets employed in the business when compared with ratios of similar firms. A comparatively low ratio indicates an inefficient use of business assets.

Return On Investment = $\dfrac{\text{Net Profit Before Tax}}{\text{Net Worth}}$

A measure of the percentage of return on funds invested in the business. A very important ratio. If the ROI is less than the rate of return on an alternative, risk-free investment the owner may wish to sell and invest elsewhere.

Note: Current Ratio, Quick Ratio and Working Capital are **liquidity** ratios which indicate the ease of turning assets into cash. Debt/Worth Ratio is a **leverage** ratio which mesures how dependant the business is on debt financing. Gross Margin Ratio and Net Profit Margin Ratio are **profitability** ratios. Inventory Turnover, Return On Assets Ratio and Return On Investment are **management** ratios.

CONTESTED BUSINESS VALUATIONS

The Higher The Value – The Greater The Tax

Type of Business	Name of Case	Estate's Value on Return	Value Per Share IRS Challenge	Court's Decision		Delay from Date of Death to Closing of Case	
advertising agency	Katz, Estate of Sidney L. 27 T.C.M. 825	$ 290.00	$ 600.00	$ 300.00	6 yrs	11 mo	11 days
automobile dealer	Leyman, Estate of Harry S. 40 T.C. 100	536.00	700.00	630.00	8 yrs	11 mo	0 days
bank	Davis, Estate of John F. 78,069 P-H Memo T.C.	36.00	75.00	45.00	5 yrs	11 mo	0 days
brewery	Baltimore National Bank v. U.S. 136 F. Supp. 642	1,542.50	2,500.00	2,300.00	8 yrs	5 mo	19 days
brewery equipment manufacturer	Korslin v. U.S. 31 AFTR 2d 1390	25.67	36.72	66.19	6 yrs	11 mo	9 days
carpet manufacturer	Ewing, Estate of Anna C. 9 T.C.M. 1096	2,400.00	6,530.00	4,750.00	7 yrs	6 mo	24 days
citrus grower	Maxcy, Estate of Gregg 28 T.C.M. 783	10,593.79	12,463.28	10,593.79	8 yrs	11 mo	21 days

Type of Business	Name of Case	Value Per Share			Delay from Date of Death to Closing of Case		
		Estate's Value on Return	IRS Challenge	Court's Decision			
cleaning products manufacturer	Louis v. U.S. 369 F. 2d 263	$ 3.25	$ 20.00	$ 5.34	7 yrs	8 mo	27 days
cold storage	Sundquist et al. v. U.S. 74-2 USTC 13,035	270.00	500.00	270.00	7 yrs	9 mo	18 days
construction & paving	Tully, Estate of Edward A. v. U.S. 78-1 USTC 13,228	100.00	344.00	164.77	13 yrs	10 mo	18 days
crude oil processing	Vandenhoeck, Estate of Paul M. 4 T.C. 125	14.00	85.00	40.00	5 yrs	6 mo	9 days
department store	Holmes, Estate of Sue E. 22 B.T.A. 757	160.00	400.00	245.00	4 yrs	10 mo	17 days
dry goods wholesaler	Fitts' Estate v. Commissioner 237 F. 2d 729	150.00	600.00	375.00	7 yrs	9 mo	23 days
electrical parts supplier	Goodall, Estate of Robert A. 24 T.C.M. 807	7.44	10.30	10.30	11 yrs	7 mo	13 days
electric systems manufacturer	Damon, Estate of Robert H. 46 T.C. 108	3.00	6.00	3.75	7 yrs	10 mo	11 days
elevator manufacturer	Heinold, Estate of Matthew I. 24 T.C.M. 26, aff'd 363 F. 2d 329	3.17	10.00	8.00	7 yrs	9 mo	4 days
embalming fluid manufacturer	Yeazel v. Coyle, Jr. 21 AFTR 2d 1681	304.01	450.00	400.00	8 yrs	11 mo	15 days

Type of Business	Name of Case	Value Per Share			Delay from Date of Death to Closing of Case		
		Estate's Value on Return	IRS Challenge	Court's Decision			
farmer	Wilson, Estate of S.A. Regenold 51,247 P-H Memo T.C.	$ 353.92	$ 753.05	$ 395.00	8 yrs	1 mo	23 days
fertilizer manufacturer	Bradley, Estate of Mrs. Sarah H. 2 T.C.M. 609	200.00	430.00	275.00	6 yrs	7 mo	7 days
flour & grain milling	Gwinn, Estate of D. Byrd 25 T.C. 31	40.00	195.00	60.00	4 yrs	9 mo	3 days
furniture sales	Helmers, Estate of George J. 9 T.C.M. 524	500.00	1,000.00	900.00	5 yrs	4 mo	0 days
games manufacturer	Richter v. U.S. 27 AFTR 2d 1691	424.90	1,000.00	700.00	9 yrs	10 mo	23 days
gas company	McIlhenny, Estate of John D. 22 B.T.A. 1093	46.66	62.50	50.00	5 yrs	4 mo	16 days
glass container manufacturer	Hazelton, Estate of Ben F. Jr. 2 T.C.M. 450	41.25	46.25	43.00	3 yrs	5 mo	11 days
grain feed storage	Bader v. U.S. 172 F. Supp. 833	521.83	1,250.00	642.00	7 yrs	9 mo	24 days
grocery wholesaler	Pendleton, Estate of A. S. 20 B.T.A. 618	150.00	400.00	400.00	5 yrs	4 mo	14 days
hair shampoo manufacturer	Goar, Estate of Joseph E. 9 T.C.M. 854	200.00	447.31	275.00	3 yrs	7 mo	8 days

Type of Business	Name of Case	Value Per Share			Delay from Date of Death to Closing of Case		
		Estate's Value on Return	IRS Challenge	Court's Decision			
hardware store	Anderson, Estate of J. Macfie 72,125 P-H Memo T.C.	$ 2,500.00	$ 3,000.00	$ 3,000.00	5 yrs	9 mo	30 days
holding company	Smith, Estate of Loyd R. 9 T.C.M. 907	3,350.00	7,317.28	5,700.00	5 yrs	9 mo	24 days
hotel	McDermott, Estate of James D. 12 T.C.M. 481	50.00	150.00	50.00	6 yrs	0 mo	8 days
insurance company	Maxwell, Estate of William 3 T.C.M. 1207	49.00	52.75	52.75	5 yrs	3 mo	7 days
intercom systems installer	Sobel, Estate of Ephraim F. 10 T.C.M. 613	55.83	187.35	65.00	5 yrs	0 mo	1 day
kitchen appliance manufacturer	Johnson, Estate of Herbert L. 2 T.C.M. 299	31.00	50.00	36.00	5 yrs	5 mo	1 day
laundry supply company	Hogan, Estate of James 3 T.C.M. 315	1,125.00	2,100.00	1,459.00	3 yrs	10 mo	11 days
loading equipment manufacturer	Houghton v. U.S. 15 AFTR 2d 1359	195.00	450.00	375.00	8 yrs	11 mo	25 days
logging company	Garrett, Estate of Jessie R. 12 T.C.M. 1142	50.39	285.65	285.65	6 yrs	6 mo	15 days
meat packing company	Russell v. U.S. 18 AFTR 2d 6278	1,360.00	2,100.00	2,100.00	6 yrs	6 mo	27 days

Type of Business	Name of Case	Value Per Share			Delay from Date of Death to Closing of Case		
		Estate's Value on Return	IRS Challenge	Court's Decision			
mining equipment manufacturer	Schneider-Pass, Est. of Alfred J. 28 T.C.M. 81	$ 4,761.90	$ 38,500.00	$ 23,809.00	11 yrs	1 mo	19 days
motel & restaurant	Wallace Estate v. U.S. 31 AFTR 2d 1395	64.23	147.00	91.50	8 yrs	7 mo	6 days
mushroom grower & supplier	Thompson, Estate of Barbara F. 18 T.C.M. 801	225.00	535.00	283.50	7 yrs	9 mo	27 days
newspaper	S. Carolina Nat'l Bank v. McLeod 256 F. Supp. 913	700.00	980.00	800.00	5 yrs	7 mo	25 days
oil drilling supply sales	Burda, Estate of L.J. 2 T.C.M. 497	3.00	10.00	5.00	1 yrs	6 mo	7 days
paper products wholesaler	Worthen v. U.S. 7 AFTR 2d 1801	100.00	175.00	104.00	7 yrs	6 mo	4 days
ranching	O'Connell, Estate of J.E. 78,191 P-H Memo T.C.	485.33	1,631.00	1,000.00	5 yrs	7 mo	17 days
real estate development	Hanscom, Estate of Edward E. 24 B.T.A. 173	50.00	100.00	100.00	5 yrs	1 mo	18 days
retail shops	Kessler, Estate of Bernard 78,491 P-H Memo T.C.	.50	4.96	3.67	6 yrs	7 mo	20 days
sawmill & finishing plant	Brooks v. Willcuts 78 F. 2d 270	140.00	175.00	175.00	5 yrs	4 mo	22 days

Type of Business	Name of Case	Value Per Share			Delay from Date of Death to Closing of Case		
		Estate's Value on Return	IRS Challenge	Court's Decision			
shipping firm	Brush, Estate of Marjorie G. 22 T.C.M. 900	$ 3.00	$ 7.37	$ 5.50	5 yrs	3 mo	2 days
shoe store	Patton, Estate of Walter L. 10 T.C.M. 1066	300.00	414.25	365.00	7 yrs	2 mo	16 days
steel fabrication	Huntsman, Estate of John L. 66 T.C. 861	18.40	36.64	29.00	5 yrs	6 mo	12 days
steel mill equipment manufacturer	Harrison, Estate of Florence M. 17 T.C.M. 776	4.00	5.85	5.85	5 yrs	7 mo	3 days
tobacco dealer	Nienhuys, Jan W. 17 T.C. 1149	115.00	285.00	172.68	5 yrs	9 mo	6 days
woolen textile manufacturer	Olney, Estate of Lizzie F. 46,138 P-H Memo T.C.	676.00	1,100.00	855.00	3 yrs	10 mo	17 days

AVERAGES IN THE PREVIOUS 54 CASES

Value Per Share			Delay from Date of Death to Closing of Case		
Estate's Value on Return	IRS Challenge	Court's Decision			
$ 654.28	$ 1,680.82	$ 1,202.32	6 yrs	7 mo	20 days

Even in those cases in which the court agreed with the estate, it took an average of 7 years, 7 months and 5 days to resolve the dispute.

BUY/SELL AGREEMENTS HELP FIX THE VALUE

In Each of These Cases the Court Upheld the Value as Established in the Agreement

Type of Business	Name of Case	Value As Provided In Agreement	Value Per Share IRS Challenge	Court's Decision
advertising agency	Mitchell, Estate of John T. H. 37 B.T.A. 1	$ 123.45	$ 348.63	$ 123.45
coal wholesaler	May et al., v. McGowan 194 F. 2d 396	-0-	100.00	-0-
electrical parts wholesaler	Salt, Albert B. 17 T.C. 92	20.00	60.00	20.00
mental hospital	Slocum v. U.S. 256 F. Supp. 753	100.00	1,108.62	100.00
newspaper	Littick, Orville B. 31 T.C. 181	298.50	384.94	298.50
optical & lens manufacturer	Lomb v. Sugden 82 F.2d 166	69.44	100.00	69.44
real estate development	Fieux s Estate 149 N.E. 857	100.00	200.50	100.00
shoe store	Third National Bank v. U.S. 64 F. Supp. 198	100.00	150.00	100.00
soft drink bottler	Strange, Estate of John Q. 42,247 P-H Memo T.C.	250.00	5,953.16	250.00

COMPARISON
CROSS PURCHASE & ENTITY PURCHASE

	Cross Purchase	**Entity Purchase**
Purchaser	Surviving stockholders (see charts, pages 133, 137 and 141).	Corporation (see charts, pages 129 and 141).
Seller	Deceased stockholder's estate.	Deceased stockholder's estate.
Policy Owner	Individual stockholders (or trustee, see chart page 137).	Corporation.
Number of Policies Required	Multiple policies depending upon number of stockholders (unless trusteed cross purchase, or funded with first-to-die insurance, see chart page 137 and page 393).	One policy on each stock-holder.
Premiums	Paid by individual stock-holders and not deductible (but could use split-dollar, see chart, page 231).	Paid by corporation and not deductible.
Taxation of Life Insurance Death Benefits	Received tax-free by surviving stockholders.	Could be subject to corporate alternative minimum tax (see page 342).
Effect on Surviving Stockholders	Stockholder's basis increases in an amount equal to price paid for deceased's stock.	Value of stock owned by survivors increases if corporation retires stock (but no increase in stockholder's basis).
Impact of Attribution	No effect.	Redemption is subject to attribution rules (see pages 176-181).
Taxation of Deceased Stock-holder's Heirs	Basis is stepped-up at death and no gain recognized (see page 473).	Basis is stepped-up at death and no gain recognized, provided redemption meets either Section 302(b)(3) or Section 303 requirements (see footnote 1, page 151 and page 473).
Legality of Arrangement	No problem, unless professional corporation and state law restricts sale to other professionals.	Must meet state laws regarding corporate purchase of own stock.
Flexibility to Change Plans	Transfer of existing policies to corporation could be an exception to transfer for value rules (see page 479).	Transfer of corporate owned policies to co-stockholder violates transfer for value rules, unless co-stockholder is also a partner of the insured (see page 479).

COMPARISON
CROSS PURCHASE & TRUSTEED CROSS PURCHASE

	Cross Purchase	Trusteed Cross Purchase
Purchaser	Surviving stockholders (see chart, page 133).	Trustee as escrow agent for surviving stockholders (see chart, page 137).
Seller	Deceased stockholder's estate.	Deceased stockholder's estate. Stock certificates held in escrow by trustee are transferred to surviving stockholders.
Policy Owner	Individual stockholders.	Trustee as agent for stockholders.
Policy Beneficiary	Individual stockholders.	Trustee as agent for surviving stockholders. Trustee transfers funds to deceased's estate in return for deceased's stock interest.
Number of Policies Required	Multiple policies depending upon number of stockholders (see footnote 3, page 135).	One policy on each stockholder (see footnote 6, page 139).
Premiums	Paid by individual stockholders.	Paid by trustee from funds obtained from stockholders (see footnote 4, page 139).
Taxation of Life Insurance Death Benefits	Received tax-free by surviving stockholders.	Received tax-free by trustee as agent for surviving stockholders.
Effect on Surviving Stockholders	Surviving stockholder's basis in stock increases in an amount equal to price paid for deceased's interest.	Surviving stockholder's basis in stock increases in an amount equal to price paid for deceased's interest.
Taxation of Deceased Stockholder's Heirs	Basis is stepped-up at death and no gain recognized (see page 473).	Basis is stepped-up at death and no gain recognized (see page 473).
Flexibility to Change Plans	Transfer of existing policies to corporation could be an exception to transfer for value rules (see pages 479-480).	Transfer of existing policies to corporation could be an exception to transfer for value rules. However, there is a potential transfer-for-value problem after the first death (see footnote 7, page 139 and pages 479-480).

Note: A trusteed cross purchase agreement can also be used with a partnership (see footnote 1, page 139).

COMPARISON
SPLIT-DOLLAR & REVERSE SPLIT-DOLLAR

	Split-Dollar	**Reverse Split-Dollar**
Premium Payments	Employee pays amount based upon insurer's one-year term rates or Table 2001 rates, employer pays balance. See table on page 228.	Depending upon date of split-dollar arrangement, employer pays amount based upon P.S. 58 rates, Table 2001 rates, or insurer's one-year term rates, employee pays balance. See footnote 4 on page 167.
Death Benefits	Usually shared between employer and employee, with employer death benefit equal to its cumulative premium payments.	All or most go to employer.
Cash Values	Usually shared between employer and employee, but employer typically owns all cash values in early years.	All owned by employee.
Contract Ownership	*Collateral assignment method*: contract is owned by employee with limited assignment to employer. *Endorsement method*: split ownership between employer and employee (but see table on page 228, and discussions on pages 381 and 470).	*Endorsement method*: split ownership between employer and employee. But change of policy endorsement upon termination of agreement might be considered a taxable "transfer" to the employee. *Collateral assignment method*: contract is owned by employee with limited assignment to employer. However, in view of Notice 2002-8, it is not clear how this will affect determination of premiums to be paid by employer. See footnotes 2 and 4, page 167, and table on page 228.

See charts on pages 165 and 227.

TABLE OF CONTENTS

Page

POINTERS

Will The Plan Fit?

Employers and employees come in many shapes and forms. Before proceeding with recommendations as to a specific employee benefit plan, it is essential to ascertain whether your client is doing business as a C corporation, S corporation, partnership, limited liability company, or sole proprietorship (pages 182-184, 286-293, 391, 415, 427-429, 432, 439 and 458-460). In general, the S corporation, partnership, and sole proprietorship provide limited opportunities for creative employee benefit plans for the owner/employee (pages 182-183).

In contrast, C corporations are taxable entities, separate and apart from their stockholders. They offer attractive opportunities for using tax-advantaged employee benefits for employee/stockholders. For example, a deferred compensation plan can be used in the medium to large sized corporation to reward key executives who are stockholders in the corporation (page 243). However, deferred compensation is not appropriate if your client is a sole proprietor. The threshold question is simple: are your client and his business separate taxable entities? If they are, then your client is able to use a "business check" for funding employee benefits, and can take advantage of any tax leverage provided by the difference between employer and employee income tax brackets (pages 208-209 and 380).

You should refer to the following footnotes for guidance regarding the appropriateness of specific employee benefits: group insurance (footnote 1, page 213); executive equity (footnote 2, page 221); split-dollar insurance (footnote 2, page 229); deferred compensation (footnote 6, page 245); disability income plan (footnote 1, page 253); and medical expense reimbursement plans (footnote 1, page 257).

Who Are You Working With?

It is also important to consider *who* you are working with and what their objectives are. Is your client the owner of a small closely-held business who wants to fund his corporate buy/sell agreement with split-dollar life insurance, or is your client the chief financial officer of a larger corporation charged with the responsibility of assembling a selective supplemental retirement plan for a group of key executives? Is the benefit for a "pure" employee (i.e., a nonowner)? Is the nonowner/employee related to your client? Is it expected that the nonowner/employee will eventually become an owner? Answers to these questions will help you design an employee benefit plan that is responsive to your client's objectives. A relevant and responsive plan improves your credibility with your client, and is far more likely to be accepted and implemented.

Time Can Work For You . . . And Against You.

Dollars can grow, but they need time. Some people have more time, and some people have less time. If you are just starting out, time is your friend; the stock market will go up, maybe not today, tomorrow, next week, next month, or even next year, but it will go up. If you are about to retire, time is *not* your friend, particularly if you did not take advantage of time when it was your friend. By allowing before-tax dollars to grow tax-deferred, qualified retirement plans offer a very effective way of using time to secure your retirement years. The materials on pages 262-265, 309-315, 501 and 504, will help you better understand and explain concepts involving the time value of money.

Employee Benefits And EGTRRA 2001.

The news for employee benefits under EGTRRA 2001 was all good. Your clients now have many more opportunities to set aside funds for education and retirement.

Education funding and taxation. It is hard to imagine a subject that is more likely to be of interest to your clients than providing on a tax-favored basis for the education of their children or grandchildren. Distributions under state-sponsored Section 529 plans can now be excluded from the beneficiary's gross income. The Coverdell Education Savings Account, (formerly known as an "Education IRA") even allows for the funding of kindergarten! Your client can now contribute to both a Coverdell Education Savings Account and a Section 529 plan in the same year and for the same child. But some education incentives are mutually exclusive (e.g., Hope Scholarship and Lifetime Learning Credits under Section 25A are not available if an education expense deduction is taken under Section 222). To help sort out the multiplicity of these education tax incentives and their interrelationships, see pages 287, 303, 356-357, 365 and 463.

Increased contribution limits. Increases in the amounts that can be contributed to IRAs, SIMPLE IRAs, 401(k) plans, 403(b) plans, and 457 plans provide your clients with a wealth of planning opportunities (page 299). In particular, note the introduction of special "catch-up" contributions for clients who have reached age 50.

Minimum Distribution Rules.

With qualified retirement plans there are strict rules regarding when, how much, and for how long money can be put away (pages 266-277, 297-302, 403, 409-410 and 466-467). Recent changes to the minimum distribution rules allow your clients to significantly defer income taxes with post-retirement and post-death distribution planning, particularly with regards to IRAs (pages 409-410 and 495). With the new rollover rules under EGTRRA 2001, your clients may now move their retirement funds between IRAs, 401(k) plans, 403(b) plans and 457 plans. Never before have your clients enjoyed such flexibility to transfer or consolidate their retirement funds.

Split-Dollar And The IRS.

There is little doubt that the split-dollar landscape is changing, and will continue to change. Over the years there appears to have been no limit to the variety and complexity of split-dollar plans. In employer/employee split-dollar arrangements the parties have been able to define their rights and obligations in such a manner as to create substantial employee-owned cash values with generally modest employee cost (e.g., use of low company-provided term rates to determine employee's premium contribution; and limiting employer's interest in cash values to cumulative premium outlay). After "rollout," policy loans could be used to access cash values without triggering income taxation, despite the employee's limited "basis" in the contract. Clearly, in Notice 2002-8 the IRS has set forth its intention to issue regulations that will negatively impact this type of "equity" split-dollar design (footnote 4, page 167, and pages 228, 381, 470, 475, 496 and 497).

Despite Notice 2002-8 and the pending regulations, split-dollar will continue to be a viable and attractive way for your clients to purchase needed life insurance protection. However, it will be particularly important for you to monitor changes and seek guidance as to: (1) the impact of Notice 2002-8 on split-dollar agreements entered into on and after January 28, 2002, and before final regulations are issued; (2) the relative advantages and disadvantages of endorsement split-dollar (employer contribution treated as loan to employee) and collateral assignment split-dollar (employee taxed on economic benefit); (3) the proper valuation of survivorship life insurance; (4) the treatment of private split-dollar; and (5) the impact on reverse split-dollar of the IRS decision to discontinue using the P.S. 58 rates.

Disability Income, Long-Term Care, And IRAs.

As with retirement planning concepts, disability income, long-term care, and IRAs are included in this employee benefits section. However, these important needs may well be provided for outside the context of an employer-employee relationship. For example, some of your clients will establish IRAs that have nothing to do with their employer, while other clients may participate in Simple IRAs established by their employer (pages 403 and 466). Likewise, many clients acquire individual disability income contracts outside of a formal disability income plan; while other clients are covered by plans with varying degrees of employer participation (pages 246-249, 250-253, 317 and 372). Long-term care planning does not comfortably fall within the realm of either estate planning or business planning; but it is an important part of financial and retirement planning. Therefore, long-term care has been included in this employee benefits section together with the subjects of retirement and disability planning.

TAXATION OF EMPLOYEE BENEFITS

Employee benefits, once considered an "addition" to wages, have now become an integral part of virtually all compensation packages. Because the rapid increase in their variety and value has made it difficult to evaluate them, this overview is designed to review some of their tax advantages and disadvantages.[1]

Characterization of a benefit as either bad, better, or best, can be made according to its effect upon the income taxes of the employer and the employee. For example, assume that in 2002 we have an employer in a 34 percent marginal tax bracket and an employee in a 27 percent tax bracket.

BAD. A bad employee benefit is one that is *nondeductible* to the employer yet *taxable* to the employee, such as one that results in unreasonable compensation or is treated as a dividend. Because it is nondeductible, on each $1.00 of income the employer must pay 34 cents in taxes. Since the remaining 66 cents is taxable to the employee, 18 cents of employee taxes will further reduce the original $1.00 to only 48 cents. That's bad!

BETTER. A better employee benefit is one that is *deductible* to the employer, although still *taxable* to the employee. Since there are no employer taxes, the full $1.00 is taxable income to the employee. Now 27 cents goes to pay employee taxes, and the remaining 73 cents actually benefits the employee. That's better!

Better benefits include salary allotment plans, executive equity plans, bonused split-dollar insurance, survivor income plans, disability income plans, and deferred compensation.

BEST. The best employee benefit is one that is *deductible* to the employer and either *nontaxable* or *tax deferred* to the employee. Now the entire $1.00 benefits the employee, without any current reduction for either employer or employee taxes. That's the best!

"Best" benefits include group term insurance, medical expense reimbursement plans, SIMPLE IRAs, and qualified retirement plans, including 401(k) plans.[2]

---

[1] The checklist on pages 286-293 describes many employee benefits and the income tax effect on employees.

[2] Specific benefits may not be available to all employees and employers. Although SIMPLE IRAs, and qualified retirement plans, including 401(k) plans, are listed among the "best," it must be recognized that the employee pays taxes when retirement income is actually received. Tax-free group term insurance is limited to $50,000 of coverage. The term "leveraged benefit" can be used to describe some of the best employee benefits, as discussed further on page 412.

BAD

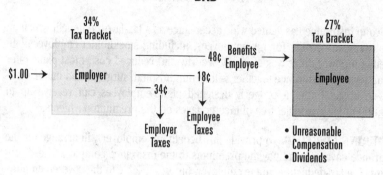

BETTER

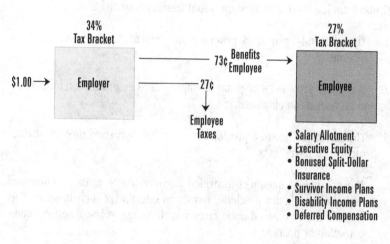

BEST

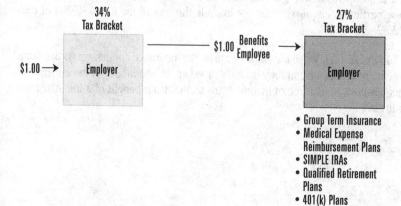

GROUP INSURANCE

Group insurance has gained wide acceptance as a tax-favored benefit which an employer can provide for his employees, including stockholder-employees.[1] In meeting the twin objectives of family security and reduced cost, most plans offer group term life insurance together with group hospital, surgical, and major medical coverage. Under a properly designed plan, employees can receive up to $50,000 of life coverage, free of income taxes on the premium payments.[2]

DURING LIFETIME. To provide this benefit, an employer will arrange for the insurance coverage and pay the premiums to the insurance company. These premiums are tax-deductible to the employer, but *not* taxable to the covered employee.

Group term life insurance must meet four basic requirements:

1. The plan must provide a general death benefit that is excludable from income.

2. It must be provided to a group of employees as compensation for personal services as an employee.

3. The insurance must be provided under a policy carried directly or indirectly by the employer.

4. The amount of insurance provided each employee must be computed under a formula that precludes individual selection of such amounts. This formula must be based upon factors such as age, years of service, compensation or position.[3]

If a group insurance plan *discriminates* in favor of "key employees," then these particular employees may not exclude the cost of the first $50,000 of coverage.[4]

UPON DEATH. When the employee dies, the insurance company pays the death benefit directly to the employee's family or estate, as beneficiary of the insurance.[5] This payment is also free of income taxes as the death benefit of a life insurance contract.[6]

Footnotes on page 213

DURING LIFETIME

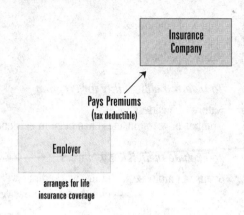

UPON DEATH

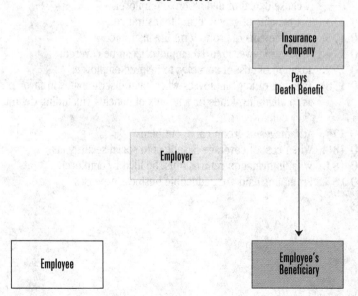

INFORMATION REQUIRED FOR ANALYSIS & PROPOSAL

1. Names of employees.
2. Dates of birth.
3. Salary schedule.

To Determine Eligibility for Program

4. Nature of business.
5. Number of years business has been in existence.

To Exclude Ineligible Employees

6. Status of employees – hours worked per week.
                       – months worked per year.
7. Employment dates.

Note: It is also possible to exclude employees who are: (1) covered by a collective bargaining agreement; and (2) nonresident aliens who received no earned income from the employer from sources within the United States.

CROSS REFERENCES TO TAX FACTS 1 (2002)

Q 81. Use of group term life insurance to fund buy/sell agreement will likely cause denial of deduction to employer.

Q 174. Tax benefits of group term life insurance.

Q 175. Requirements of group term life insurance.

Q 176. Groups of fewer than 10 employees can be covered.

Q 177. Taxation of cost of coverage to insured employee.

Q 178. Taxation of key employees when plan discriminates in favor of them as to eligibility, kinds or amounts of benefits (including definition of "key employee").

Q 179. Advantages of group carve-out plans.

Q 180. When cost of coverage is subject to social security tax.

Q 181. What information returns must be filed by employer.

Q 182. Premiums paid are deductible business expenses.

Footnotes

[1] The tax advantages of group insurance can be made available to the *employees* of a corporation, a partnership, or a sole proprietorship. However, this *does not include* the stockholder-employees of an S corporation who own more than 2 percent of the stock, the partners of a partnership, and the sole proprietor. They are not treated as "employees" for this purpose. Stockholders of a regular corporation, who are also employees, can be covered by the plan as employees. Insurance provided for a non-employee corporate director does not qualify as group insurance.

[2] It is surprising to find how often corporate owners have failed to provide the maximum amount of tax-free coverage for themselves and their key employees. Although federal law allows up to $50,000, state law may set lower limits on the amount of coverage that can be provided by group life insurance. The coverage in excess of $50,000 is taxable income to the employee. To determine the value of this excess coverage, refer to the Table I Rates on page 496. This table is specifically provided by IRS Regulations to measure the value of group term insurance in excess of $50,000. An IRS Notice has indicated that up to $2,000 of coverage on spouse and dependents will also be income tax-free to the employee as a "de minimis" fringe benefit. Although retired employees are generally subject to the same limits as active employees, the $50,000 limit does not apply to disabled retirees.

[3] Generally, there must be at least 10 full-time employees for a plan to qualify as group term life insurance. However, insurance for *fewer than* 10 employees may also qualify as group term life insurance if: (1) it is provided for all full-time employees; and (2) the amount of protection is computed either as a uniform percentage of compensation or on the basis of coverage brackets established by the insurer under which no bracket exceeds 2? times the next lower bracket, and the lowest bracket is at least 10 percent of the highest bracket.

[4] Discrimination as to either *eligibility to participate*, or with respect to the *kind or amount of benefits*, will result in "key employees" having to include in income the higher of actual cost or Table I cost of the entire amount of coverage (see the definition of "key employee" on page 298).

[5] One note of caution regarding group term life insurance – do not attempt to use the death benefits to fund an obligation to purchase the insured's business interest. The adverse tax consequences can be very costly. For example, if there is an attempt to fund an entity purchase agreement (chart, page 129) by making the employer a beneficiary of the policy, the Code specifically prohibits any deduction for the cost of coverage on the life of an employee. In addition, state laws often prohibit the employer from being named beneficiary of group insurance. If there is an attempt to fund a cross purchase agreement (chart, page 133) by naming a co-owner beneficiary of the policy, the arrangement is likely to run afoul of the transfer for value rules (discussion, pages 479-480). Group term insurance is an *employee* fringe benefit, the death benefit of which should be paid to the employee's personal beneficiary. Such a personal beneficiary could properly include the trustee of an irrevocable life insurance trust, to which the insured had assigned ownership of the coverage in order to exclude the death proceeds from his taxable estate. In this regard, refer to the Life Insurance Trust chart on page 57.

[6] Over the years a variety of benefits have been offered as "group" term insurance. Included among these were Retired Lives Reserves (RLR) and "Section 79." RLR was a fund established for continuing group life insurance for retired employees, whereas Section 79 was used to describe the use of individual permanent policies, often by superimposing them on top of existing group coverage, to provide group term life insurance. Neither variation is viable today, as is further discussed under Retired Lives Reserves on page 452.

SALARY ALLOTMENT

The compensation provided to most employees consists of both salary and benefits. Benefits can often equal 30 percent or more of direct payroll costs.[1] With a salary allotment plan, it is possible to contain these expenses, while at the same time offering a valuable benefit with *no direct cost* to the employer.[2]

A salary allotment plan can also be very attractive to employees. By purchasing a base of permanent life insurance during his working years, an employee can avoid the prohibitive costs often associated with converting group life insurance upon retirement. This then guarantees that some life insurance will always be available, whether death occurs before or after retirement.

Under the typical salary allotment plan, employees are given the opportunity to supplement their existing group and other coverages with life insurance, disability income insurance, long-term care insurance, or annuity benefits. This is a purely voluntary program, which each employee can take advantage of through an individual pay allotment to the insurance company.

The advantages of such plans often include:

- Discounted premiums from group billing efficiencies.
- No physical examinations.
- Level premiums that do not increase.
- No lapse of policy upon retirement.
- Convenient payroll deduction of premiums.[3]

To make these benefits available, the insurance carrier will usually require the employer to:

- Provide notice of enrollment opportunity.
- Allow for enrollment at work during business hours.[4]
- Arrange for payroll deductions.

Most employers have found that their employees are grateful for the opportunity to enroll in such plans, since they are often viewed as an extension of existing benefits packages. These plans offer a relatively painless means by which employees pay modest premiums in order to provide substantial life, disability, and annuity benefits for themselves and their families.[5]

Footnotes on page 217

COMPENSATION

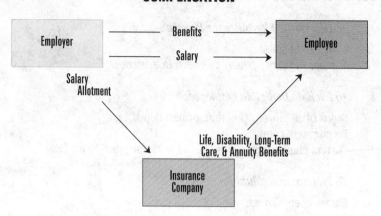

THE ADVANTAGES

- Discounted Premiums
- No Physical Examinations
- Level Premiums
- Permanent Coverage
- Payroll Deduction

INFORMATION REQUIRED FOR ANALYSIS & PROPOSAL

To Determine Eligibility for Program

1. Nature of business.
2. Number of years business has been in existence.

To Exclude Ineligible Employees

3. Status of employees (full time or part time).
4. Employment dates.
5. Current employment status (i.e., at work for prior 30 days).

To Prepare Individual Proposals

6. Names of employees.
7. Dates of birth.
8. Smoker/nonsmoker.
9. Salary schedule (if appropriate).

To Administer Program

10. Payroll dates.
11. Payroll cycle (weekly, biweekly, bifortnightly, or monthly).
12. Payroll clerk's name and telephone number.

CROSS REFERENCES TO TAX FACTS 1 (2002)

Q 47. Life insurance premiums are deductible by corporation as additional compensation provided it has no ownership rights or beneficial interest in policy.

Q 50. Premiums paid by employer on policy owned by employee are taxable income to employee.

Q 191. Disability income benefits received from personally paid policy are tax-free.

Q 275. Within certain limits, benefits received from qualified long-term care policy are tax-free.

Footnotes

[1] The Employee Benefit Statistics, on page 294, indicate that of the companies surveyed in 1998, Total Employee Benefits amounted to 37.2 percent of payroll. Among the best prospects for salary allotment plans are existing group insurance clients. As to the employer, the tax treatment of salary allotment plans is similar to group insurance, in that the amounts paid for insurance are *deductible* (as a compensation expense). However, employee *after-tax* dollars are used to pay for the coverage.

[2] The terms "salary allotment," "salary deduction," and "payroll deduction" are interchangeable. In discussing this market, the terms "voluntary insurance" and "worksite marketing" are also used. If desired, there is no reason why an employer cannot contribute a portion of the premium. Contributions toward *life insurance* coverage are fully included in the employee's income. However, the employee may choose either to include or exclude employer contributions for *disability insurance* (see footnote 5, on page 253, and the table on page 317).

[3] The deduction of premium payments from payroll checks means that the employee will never have to sit down and write a check to the insurance company. A salary allotment plan provides an effective means by which the rank and file employee can set aside for emergencies or retirement some of the earnings projected in the table on page 309.

[4] Favorable enrollment conditions are required in order to obtain high levels of participation. Higher participation enables the insurance carrier to absorb increased losses, which often occur on account of underwriting concessions (i.e., guaranteed standard issue, simplified underwriting, etc.).

[5] Spouse and children riders are frequently available with life insurance offered in salary allotment plans. With disability insurance, the coverage will not necessarily offer level premiums, level benefits, and a guarantee of no policy cancellation. Annuity benefits would likely come from using accumulated life insurance cash values.

EXECUTIVE EQUITY

Executive equity is an employee benefit plan that allows an employer to provide valuable life insurance protection for a *selected* employee on a tax deductible basis to the employer.[1] The employer has total discretion to select the employee, or employees, to be covered by the agreement, and the amounts of insurance to be provided. It can be made available to both the stockholder-employee and the nonstockholder-employee.[2]

DURING LIFETIME. Under the agreement, the employee purchases and owns a permanent life insurance contract on his life.[3] The employer pays premiums to the insurance company, which are fully tax-deductible by the employer as compensation to the employee.[4]

These premiums are considered taxable income to the employee, upon which the employee is responsible for paying taxes to the IRS.[5] However, the *employee owns* the life insurance contract, including all policy cash values, and the annual increase in these values usually more than offsets any taxes paid by the employee. If desired, these taxes could be paid with borrowed or withdrawn policy cash values, or dividends, if funded with a participating policy.[6]

UPON DEATH. At the employee's death, the insurance company pays the total death benefit directly to the employee's beneficiary. Because it is the death benefit of a life insurance contract, this payment is received free of all income taxes.

Executive equity offers something for everyone – tax deductibility to the employer, cash value accumulations for the employee, ease of installation, and premium payments with a business check.[7] If the employee-stockholder's marginal tax bracket is less than his corporation's marginal tax bracket, then executive equity should be attractive to the employee-stockholder who wishes to withdraw profits from the corporation.

Footnotes on page 221

DURING LIFETIME

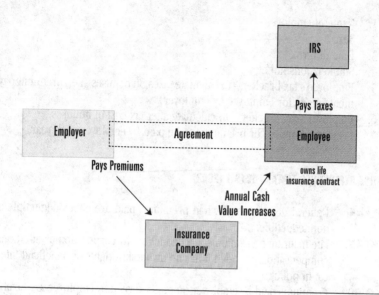

UPON DEATH

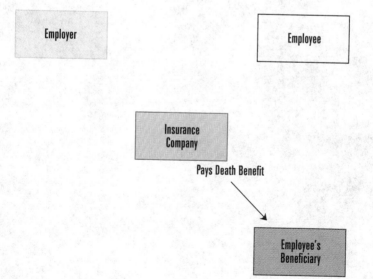

INFORMATION REQUIRED FOR ANALYSIS & PROPOSAL

1. Name of employee.
2. Sex.
3. Date of birth.
4. Smoker/nonsmoker.
5. Employee's tax bracket – to calculate taxes on bonuses (i.e., premium payments made for employee by employer).
6. Employer's tax bracket – to calculate after-tax cost of bonuses.
7. Projected bonuses or premiums to be paid by employer each year.

CROSS REFERENCES TO TAX FACTS 1 (2002)

Q 45. General discussion of when premiums paid are either deductible or nondeductible.

Q 47. Life insurance premiums are deductible by corporation as additional compensation provided it has no ownership rights or beneficial interest in policy.

Q 50. Premiums paid by employer on policy owned by employee are taxable income to employee.

Q 51. Income tax consequences of Section 162 Bonus Plan.

Footnotes

[1] Executive Equity plans are also referred to as "Executive Bonus Plans," "Executive Retirement Bonus Plans," and "Section 162 Bonus Plans" (after Section 162(a)(1) of the Internal Revenue Code, which authorizes a business to deduct a "reasonable allowance" for salaries or other compensation for personal services actually rendered).

[2] If executive equity is to be effective with owner-employees, it must usually be used in a regular corporation (not an S corporation). Neither the sole proprietorship nor the partnership provides the separate taxable entity that is essential for the concept to be an attractive benefit for owner-employees.

[3] Because the contract is entirely owned by the employee, it is not essential that the agreement be in writing, as it is with split-dollar insurance. However, it is good practice to have the terms of any important agreement in writing; and the agreement could help defend against an IRS attempt to characterize the bonuses as nondeductible dividends.

[4] In 2002 married couples filing jointly with less than $171,951 of taxable income, and single taxpayers with less than $141,251 of taxable income, are in a 30 percent or lower tax bracket (see tax rates on page 492). For these individuals, executive equity is an attractive benefit (i.e., "enhanced" individual after-tax dollars are available to pay premiums, whereas a corporation with over $75,000 of taxable income is in a minimum 34 percent tax bracket). For an expanded discussion of Enhanced Dollars, see page 380.

[5] The premiums paid by the employer are reported as "other compensation" on the employee's W-2 form. Likewise, this compensation is subject to both the Social Security Tax (FICA) and the Federal Unemployment Tax (FUTA). Underlying any discussion of employee benefits is the assumption that, if challenged by the Internal Revenue Service, the increased compensation would be considered "reasonable." For an expanded discussion of Unreasonable Compensation, see page 483.

[6] In designing the column arrangements of executive equity illustrations, it is particularly important to emphasize the direct comparison between the yearly *income taxes* paid by the employee and the annual *cash value increases*, all of which are owned by the employee. For example, if the employer pays a premium of $2,500 for $100,000 of insurance protection, this $2,500 will constitute taxable income to the employee. Assuming in 2002 the employee is in a 27 percent tax bracket, he will have to pay $675 of additional income taxes (.27 x $2,500). However, if the cash values *owned* by the employee increased by $1,300 in that year, this more than offsets the taxes paid.

[7] Note that with executive equity, the employer has no interest in either the cash values or the death benefits. This contrasts with a split-dollar arrangement, under which the employer usually owns most, if not all, of the cash values, and receives a portion of the death benefits. To better appreciate these differences, see the Split-Dollar Insurance chart on page 227, and the comparison of Executive Equity and Split-Dollar Insurance on page 295. The Restrictive Bonus Plan discussed in the chart on page 223 provides an interesting alternative to both Executive Equity and Split-Dollar plans.

RESTRICTIVE BONUS PLAN

The restrictive bonus plan is an employee benefit that allows an employer to provide valuable life insurance protection for a *selected* employee on a tax deductible basis to the employer.[1] The employer has total discretion to select the employee, or employees, to be covered by the agreement, and the amounts of insurance to be provided. It is typically made available to the nonstockholder-employee.

DURING LIFETIME. Under the agreement, the employee purchases and owns a permanent life insurance contract on his life. Added to the policy is a restrictive endorsement that requires the employer's consent for the employee to: (1) surrender the policy; (2) assign or pledge the policy for a loan; (3) change ownership of the policy; or (4) borrow the cash values of the policy.[2] The endorsement will typically provide for these restrictions to expire upon the earliest to occur of: (1) the retirement of the employee; (2) attainment of a specific age; (3) release by the employer; or (4) the bankruptcy or dissolution of the employer.

By *separate* written agreement, the employer agrees to provide a bonus to the employee by paying all premiums to the insurance company, which are fully tax-deductible by the employer as compensation to the employee.[3] These premiums are considered taxable income to the employee, upon which the employee is responsible for paying taxes to the IRS.[4]

UPON DEATH. At the employee's death, the insurance company pays the total death benefit directly to the employee's beneficiary. Because it is the death benefit of a life insurance contract, this payment is received free of all income taxes.[5]

The restrictive bonus plan offers something for everyone – tax deductibility to the employer, a simple yet attractive "golden handcuff" for attracting and retaining a key employee, life insurance protection together with cash value accumulations available to the employee upon retirement, ease of installation, and premium payments with a business check.[6]

Footnotes on page 225

DURING LIFETIME

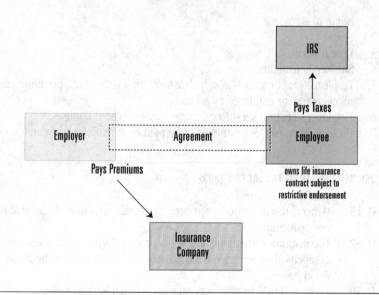

UPON DEATH

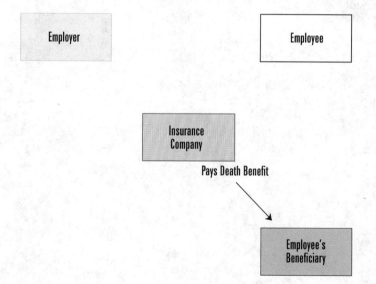

INFORMATION REQUIRED FOR ANALYSIS & PROPOSAL

1. Name of employee.
2. Sex.
3. Date of birth.
4. Smoker/nonsmoker.
5. Employee's tax bracket – to calculate taxes on bonuses (i.e., premium payments made for employee by employer).
6. Employer's tax bracket – to calculate after-tax cost of bonuses.
7. Projected bonuses or premiums to be paid by employer each year.

CROSS REFERENCES TO TAX FACTS 1 (2002)

Q 45. General discussion of when premiums paid are either deductible or nondeductible.

Q 47. Life insurance premiums are deductible by corporation as additional compensation, provided it has no ownership rights or beneficial interest in policy.

Q 50. Premiums paid by employer on policy owned by employee are taxable income to employee.

Footnotes

[1] The restrictive bonus plan is also referred to as a "Restrictive Endorsement Bonus Arrangement (REBA)," a "Golden Executive Bonus Arrangement (GEBA)" and a "Controlled Executive Bonus Plan."

[2] One objection to executive equity plans is that the employee can terminate employment at any time, yet have full access to the cash values of the life insurance contract (see chart, page 219). The restrictive bonus plan is an extension of the executive equity concept that in part answers this objection by giving the employer some measure of control over the employee's use and enjoyment of the policy (i.e., a "golden handcuff").

[3] If desired, a "double bonus" could be given (see similar concept discussed with respect to split-dollar in footnote 5, page 229). The premiums paid by the employer are reported as "other compensation" on the employee's W-2 form. Likewise, this compensation is subject to both the Social Security Tax (FICA) and the Federal Unemployment Tax (FUTA). Underlying any discussion of employee benefits is the assumption that, if challenged by the Internal Revenue Service, the increased compensation would be considered as "reasonable." For an expanded discussion of Unreasonable Compensation, see page 483.

[4] A more aggressive plan design requires the employee to reimburse the employer for some or all of the premiums paid, should the employee terminate employment prior to normal retirement date (or within a certain period of time). While the tax results of this reimbursement are not entirely clear, it seems likely the employee would not be allowed to deduct the repayment and the employer would be required to include the repayment in income. Also, see footnote 6 below regarding the need for the employee's interest to fully vest (i.e., not subject to a substantial risk of forfeiture, thus taxed on bonus).

[5] Note that with both the restrictive bonus plan and executive equity, the employer has no interest in either the cash values or the death benefits. This contrasts with a split-dollar arrangement, under which the employer usually owns most, if not all, of the cash values, and receives a portion of the death benefits.

[6] It is important that the employer have no interest in the life insurance contract, because Code section 264 would disallow the employer's tax deductions for the bonuses if the employer is directly or indirectly a beneficiary under the policy. It is also important to keep the written agreement entirely separate from the policy endorsement, particularly if the employer has a right to be reimbursed for bonuses given the employee. Code section 83 provides, in effect, that the employee is not taxed on property "transferred in connection with the performance of services," if the property: (1) is not transferable by the employee; *and* (2) is subject to a substantial risk of forfeiture. It is clear that the first condition is met since the endorsement prohibits the employee from transferring the policy. Therefore, if the second condition is met, the employee is not taxed and the employer cannot take a current tax deduction. However, most authorities agree that there is no substantial risk of forfeiture provided the employer has no interest in the policy, and employee's agreement to repay bonuses is nothing more than a bare promise set forth in a separate agreement.

SPLIT-DOLLAR INSURANCE

Split-dollar insurance is a highly flexible employee benefit which allows an employer to provide valuable life insurance protection for *selected* employees.[1] It can be made available to one or more employees, and is easy to implement, with few or none of the restrictions which apply to group insurance and other qualified plans.[2] Simply stated, split-dollar is a sharing of premiums, death benefits, and sometimes cash values, between two parties, usually an employer and an employee. It is *not* a particular type of life insurance policy.

DURING LIFETIME. To establish a split-dollar plan, the employer and the employee enter into an agreement under which a permanent life insurance contract on the employee's life is purchased.

The agreement provides for premiums to be shared, or "split" between the employer and the employee. Although there are many types of split-dollar plans, under one of the more popular the employee pays that part of the premium that is equal to the "economic benefit" of the insurance protection received by the employee in that year.[3] The employer then pays the remaining premium.[4]

In order to make the plan more attractive, the employer often pays a bonus to the employee, in an amount equal to the employee's share of the premium. This enables the employer to pay the *entire* premium, yet deduct that part which is considered an employee bonus for tax purposes. This particular variation of split-dollar is often referred to as "single bonus" split-dollar.[5] In addition to being a *partially tax-deductible* employee benefit, under such a plan the employer will own most, if not all, of the cash values accruing in the policy.[6]

Rather than having to come up with expensive after-tax dollars to pay his share of the premium, the employee pays taxes to the IRS on the bonuses received.

UPON DEATH. At the employee's death, the insurance company pays a part of the death benefit to the employer. This usually equals the employer's cumulative contributions to the plan.[7] The remaining death benefit is then paid directly to the employee's beneficiary.[8]

Footnotes on page 229

DURING LIFETIME

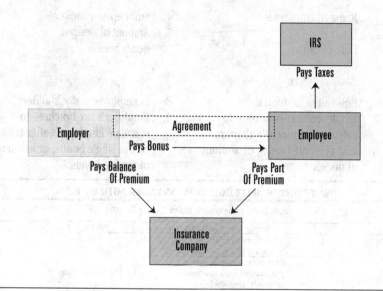

UPON DEATH

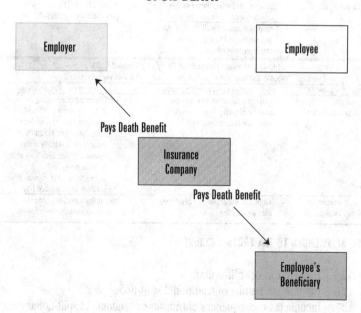

INFORMATION REQUIRED FOR ANALYSIS & PROPOSAL

1. Name of employee.
2. Sex.
3. Date of birth.

4. Smoker/nonsmoker.
5. Amount of desired death benefit.

To Select Plan

6. Position of employee.
7. Employee's tax bracket – to calculate employee's after-tax cost of single bonus, or amount of double bonus.

8. Is employee a stockholder?
9. Employer's tax bracket– to calculate employer's after-tax cost of single bonus, or amount of double bonus.

TREATMENT OF SPLIT DOLLAR PLANS UNDER NOTICE 2002-8		
Split-Dollar Plans Entered *Before* January 28, 2002		
	Taxation Upon Plan Termination	Valuation of Protection
Plan Terminated Before January 1, 2004	Employee *not taxed* on cash value in excess of basis (grandfathered).	1. May use P.S. 58 rates (if specified by split-dollar agreement), or 2. Use insurer's published premium rates, or 3. Use Table 2001 rates as first set forth in Notice 2001-10.
Plan Terminated On Or After January 1, 2004	Employee *not taxed* on equity if plan **converted** to a loan from employer to employee for all periods beginning on or after January 1, 2004 (pre-2004 employer outlays considered beginning loan balance, and subsequent employer premiums added to loan balance). Employee *taxed* on all equity if plan **not converted** to a loan from employer to employee.	
Split-Dollar Plans Entered *On Or After* January 28, 2002 (split-dollar safe harbor provisions – see discussion on page 381)		
Plan Structured As	Taxation Upon Plan Termination	Valuation Of Protection
Endorsement: *employer* owns policy.	Employee *taxed* on all equity upon transfer of policy from employer to employee (i.e., a "rollout").	Until further IRS guidance: 1. Use insurer's published premium rates (for periods after December 31, 2003, insurer must actually make known and sell term insurance at these rates), or 2. Use Table 2001 rates as first set forth in Notice 2001-10.
Collateral assignment: *employee* owns policy.	Employee *not taxed* on equity upon plan termination.	All employer outlays (premium payments) are loans to employee.

CROSS REFERENCES TO TAX FACTS 1 (2002)

Q 425. Description of split-dollar.
Q 426. Income tax results of traditional split-dollar plan.
Q 427. Income tax consequences of transfer or "rollout" of split-dollar policy.
Q 429. Description of private split-dollar and how it is taxed.
Q 515. Estate taxation of split-dollar.

Footnotes

[1] Note that this arrangement involves an employer and employee. In contrast, Private Split-Dollar involves an agreement between individuals, or between an individual and a trust (see chart on page 65).

[2] Split-dollar insurance can be provided for the employees of a corporation, a partnership, or a sole proprietorship. However, in a business setting sole proprietors cannot be covered because there is no separate taxable entity; because of the pass-through nature of taxation of partnerships and S corporations, split-dollar is generally considered not appropriate for partners or employee-stock-holders of S corporations (except to reallocate premiums among owners and when used with a life insurance trust to reduce the value of gifts to the trust, see footnote 4, page 237, and pages 458-460). When the insured is a majority stockholder, the corporation can have no ownership interest in the policy if it is desired to remove the death benefits from the insured's estate (see discussion, page 363).

[3] The "economic benefit" provided by the *death proceeds* is typically measured using either the insurer's published premium rates, or the Table 2001 rates on page 496. See also, the table concerning the Treatment Of Split-Dollar Plans Under Notice 2002-8, on page 228, and the note on page 496 regarding the use of the insurer's published premium rates. Because the rates used to measure the economic benefit to the employee are based upon *standard* risks, one of the best prospects for split-dollar is the employee who must pay a *rated* premium. With survivorship life insurance the economic benefit is often determined by using the extremely low rates calculated under Table 38 (see expanded discussion on page 475, and table on page 497).

[4] In working with a business client, it is important to remember that it is usually far easier to obtain payment of premiums with the *business* check than the *personal* check. Split-dollar enables a client to use his business check to pay for needed life insurance protection. The employer's premium advances are *secured* by either an endorsement to or collateral assignment of the policy (see footnote 2, page 167).

[5] If the bonus is large enough to pay not only the employee's share of the premium, but also the tax on the bonus, the plan is called "double bonus" split-dollar. In either case, the bonus is taxable and reported as "other compensation" on the employee's W-2 form. Underlying any discussion of bonuses is the assumption that, if challenged by the Internal Revenue Service, the increased compensation can be shown to be reasonable. An expanded discussion of Unreasonable Compensation is set forth on page 483. In contrast to single bonus plans, "employer pay all" plans have the employer paying the entire premium. This appears to be a simple, but poor, design since the employee must still include the economic benefit in his income, and it fails to provide the employer with a tax deduction (i.e., the employee bonus).

[6] If the employee owns a portion of the cash surrender values it is referred to as "equity" split-dollar (i.e., the employee has an "equity" interest in the insurance contract). See page 381 for a discussion of the treatment of Equity Split-Dollar. See also the discussion of the Split-Dollar Rollout technique on page 470.

[7] As with the division of cash values, the *death benefit* payable to the employer can vary according to the provisions of the split-dollar agreement. Typically, the employer will receive an amount equal to the cumulative cost of the plan, which is the employer's cumulative *premium* payments, plus, if desired, the cumulative *after-tax cost of bonuses* given the employee. The employee's beneficiary receives the remaining death benefits.

[8] Provided the employer is willing to have no interest in either the cash values or the death benefit, executive equity offers a simpler approach to obtaining needed life insurance protection. It is easier to install, in that there is no required formal agreement between the employer and the employee (see chart, page 219, and comparison, page 295). The Restrictive Bonus Plan in the chart on page 223 provides an interesting alternative to both Split-Dollar and Executive Equity plans.

SPLIT-DOLLAR FUNDING CROSS PURCHASE

Split-dollar insurance is not limited to merely funding the personal insurance needs of an employee. For example, under a split-dollar agreement the employee could chose to insure someone other than himself, such as a spouse or a child. Alternatively, the employee could chose to insure another stockholder whose stock interest he was obligated to purchase.[1]

DURING LIFETIME. Assume that we have a corporation owned by two individuals, Employee A and Employee B. They enter into a cross-purchase agreement providing for the purchase and sale of their respective interests.

In order to fund their mutual obligations to each other, A and B would each obtain a life insurance contract on the life of the other. To help pay for these insurance contracts, they would enter into split-dollar agreements with the corporation providing for a sharing of premiums and death benefits.[2] As with all split-dollar plans, these agreements are intended to provide *employee benefits*, not stockholder benefits. It just happens that the individual being insured is a co-stockholder, rather than the employee entering the split-dollar agreement with the corporation.

Typically, each employee will pay that part of the premium that is equal to the "economic benefit" of the coverage received in that year. However, the life that is used to measure the "economic benefit" is that of the insured co-stockholder, not the employee-stockholder who enters into the split-dollar agreement with the corporation.[3] As it might with any employee, the corporation could provide a yearly "bonus" to assist the employee in paying the premiums. Rather than having to come up with expensive after-tax dollars to pay his share of the premium, the employee pays taxes to the IRS on only the bonuses received.[4]

UPON DEATH. Assuming that A dies first, his stock interest would then pass to his family or estate. At the same time, the insurance company pays a part of the death benefit to the corporation to reimburse it under the terms of the split-dollar agreement.[5] The remainder of the death benefit is paid to B, which is then used by B to purchase A's entire stock interest from A's family or estate.[6]

Footnotes on page 233

DURING LIFETIME

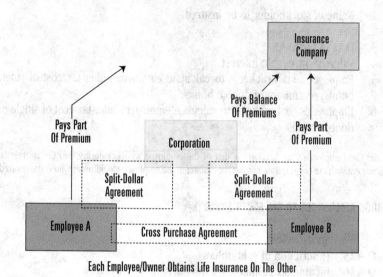

Each Employee/Owner Obtains Life Insurance On The Other

UPON DEATH

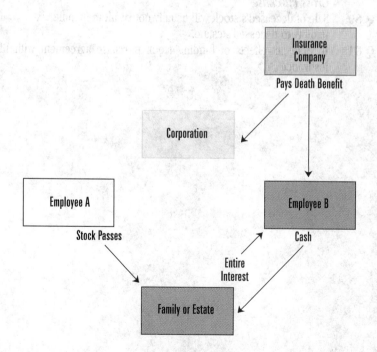

INFORMATION REQUIRED FOR ANALYSIS & PROPOSAL

1. Name of stockholder to be insured.
2. Sex.
3. Date of birth.
4. Value of ownership interest.
5. Employee's tax bracket – to calculate employee's after-tax cost of single bonus, *or* amount of double bonus.
6. Employer's tax bracket – to calculate employer's after-tax cost of single *or* double bonus.

Note: The "employee's tax bracket" is that of the employee who is entering into the split-dollar agreement with the corporation, not the tax bracket of the employee-stockholder who is the insured.

CROSS REFERENCES TO TAX FACTS 1 (2002)

Split-Dollar

Q 425. Description of split-dollar.

Q 426. Income tax results of traditional split-dollar plan.

Q 427. Income tax consequences of transfer or "rollout" of split-dollar policy.

Cross Purchase

Q 80. Sale of deceased's stock will usually not result in income tax liability to deceased's estate.

Q 81. Income tax effects of funding stock purchase agreement with life insurance.

Footnotes

[1] To be viable, split-dollar usually requires that the employer and employee each be a separate taxable entity. Therefore, funding a cross purchase agreement between two owners of a business is generally limited to a regular C corporation, and would *not* be applicable to an S corporation or a partnership. However, it would be feasible to use split-dollar to fund a *key employee* purchase of a stockholder's interest in a corporation, a partnership, or even a sole proprietorship, since in each of these situations the key employee represents a separate taxpayer from his employer.

[2] The employer will usually own all *cash values*, until such time as the cumulative cash values exceed the employer's cumulative "after-tax cost" of the plan. The after-tax cost is usually considered to be the sum of the premium payments made by the employer to the insurance company, plus the after-tax cost of the bonuses paid the employee. If the employee owns a portion of any cash surrender value increase see the discussion of Equity Split-Dollar on page 381. See also the discussion of the Split-Dollar Rollout technique on page 470.

[3] The "economic benefit" provided by the *death proceeds* is typically measured using either the insurer's published premium rates, or the Table 2001 rates on page 496. See also, the table concerning the Treatment Of Split-Dollar Plans Under Notice 2002-8, on page 228, and the note on page 496 regarding the use of the insurer's published premium rates.

[4] In working with a business client it is important to remember that it is usually far easier to obtain payment of premiums with the *corporate* check than the *personal* check. Split-dollar enables employee-stockholders to use a corporate check to pay for life insurance to fund their cross purchase agreement. Where there is a disparity in ages between the insureds, split-dollar can help to de-emphasize the difference because substantial portions of the premiums are paid with corporate dollars.

[5] As with the division of cash values, the *death benefit* payable to the employer can vary according to the provisions of the split-dollar agreement. Typically, the employer will receive an amount equal to the cumulative cost of the plan, which is the employer's cumulative *premium* payments, plus, if desired, the cumulative after-tax cost of *bonuses* given the employee. The surviving employee-stockholder, or key employee, receives the remaining death benefits in order to purchase the business interest.

[6] To fund a cross purchase agreement between employee-stockholders, in some situations Executive Equity may offer a simpler solution, provided there is no requirement that the corporation have any interest in either the cash values or the death benefits (see chart, page 219).

SPLIT-DOLLAR FUNDING
LIFE INSURANCE TRUST

Split-dollar offers a highly effective means of using employer provided dollars to pay premiums for life insurance required for estate taxes and other estate settlement costs. When combined with an irrevocable life insurance trust, it is possible to take advantage of the gift tax laws while at the same time assuring that the proceeds will be received free of estate taxes.

DURING LIFETIME, the employee establishes a trust and the trustee applies for, or obtains, insurance on the employee's life. Thereafter, at the employee's request, the employer and trustee enter into a split-dollar agreement providing for the sharing of premiums and death benefits on the insurance policy owned by the trust.[1] If desired, the agreement can also provide for the sharing of policy cash values.[2]

Although there are many types of split-dollar plans, under one of the more popular the trust agrees to pay that part of the premium equal to the "economic benefit" of the coverage received each year.[3] The balance of the premium is paid by the employer.

In order to provide the trust with funds to pay its portion of the premium the employee makes cash gifts to the trust.[4] These gifts will qualify for the annual gift tax exclusion, provided the trust beneficiaries are given the opportunity to withdraw the funds. Of course, they do not exercise this withdrawal right, since to do so would defeat the purpose of the trust.[5]

Rather than having to come up with expensive after-tax dollars to make these gifts to the trust, the employee will often be given a bonus by his employer, equal in amount to the trust's share of the premium. In turn, the employee makes a gift of this bonus to the trust.[6] Under such a "single bonus" split-dollar plan, the employee's cost is limited to the taxes paid on the bonus received.[7]

UPON DEATH of the employee, the policy proceeds are split between the employer and the trust. The employer typically receives a return of its cumulative contributions to the plan, with the balance of the proceeds paid directly to the trust.[8] The funds are then available to be used or disbursed by the trustee pursuant to the trust provisions, which could include purchase of estate assets, loans to the estate or others, payment of income to beneficiaries, and eventual distribution of trust corpus to beneficiaries.

Footnotes on page 237

DURING LIFETIME

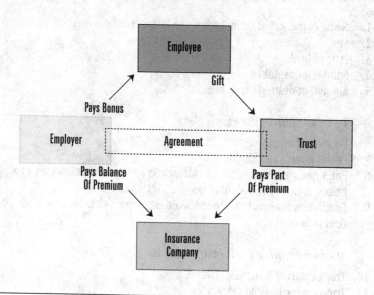

UPON DEATH

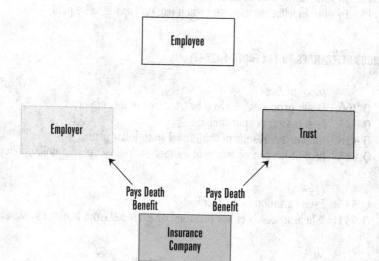

INFORMATION REQUIRED FOR ANALYSIS & PROPOSAL

1. Name of individual or individuals to be insured.
2. Sex.
3. Date of birth.
4. Smoker/nonsmoker.
5. Amount of desired death benefit.

To Select Split-Dollar Plan

6. Position of employee.
7. Is employee a stockholder?
8. Employee's tax bracket – to calculate employee's after-tax cost of single bonus, *or* amount of double bonus.
9. Employer's tax bracket – to calculate employer's after-tax cost of single *or* double bonus.

Attorney Drafting Trust Instrument Must Also Know

10. Trustee during insured's lifetime.
11. Trustee after insured's death.
12. Names of beneficiaries.
13. Ages of minor beneficiaries.
14. To who, in what amount, and when trust *income* is to be paid.
15. To who, in what amount, and when trust *corpus* is to be paid.

CROSS REFERENCES TO TAX FACTS 1 (2002)

Income Tax

Q 266. Death proceeds received by trust free of income taxes.
Q 425. Description of split-dollar.
Q 426. Income tax results of traditional split-dollar plan.
Q 427. Income tax consequences of transfer or "rollout" of split-dollar policy.

Estate Tax

Q 515. Estate taxation of split-dollar.
Q 551. When proceeds either included or excluded from insured's estate.

Gift Tax

Q 624. Qualification for annual gift tax exclusion.
Q 626. Qualification for annual gift tax exclusion when gifts made to trust for premium payments (Crummey rules).

See also cross references to life insurance trusts on page 58.

Footnotes

[1] When the insured is a majority stockholder, the corporation can have no ownership interest in the policy if it is desired to remove the death benefits from his estate (see discussion, page 363).

[2] Typically, under collateral assignment split-dollar the employer will have a security interest in all *cash values*, until such time as the cumulative cash values exceed the employer's cumulative "after-tax cost" of the plan. The after-tax cost is usually considered to be the sum of the premium payments made by the employer to the insurance company, plus, if desired, the after-tax cost of the bonuses paid to the employee. However, if the trustee owns a portion of any cash surrender value, see the discussion of Equity Split-Dollar on page 381. Further, any amount included in the employee's income is considered a gift by the employee to the trust. If the agreement is terminated and the employer releases the trust's assignment under a split-dollar "rollout," all cash values would then be owned by the trust. This release of employer-owned cash values to the trust would be treated as both taxable income to the employee and a gift by the employee to the trust. See also, the table concerning the Treatment Of Split-Dollar Plans Under Notice 2002-8 (page 228), and the discussion of the Split-Dollar Rollout technique (page 470).

[3] The "economic benefit" provided by the *death proceeds* is typically measured using either the insurer's published premium rates, or the Table 2001 rates on page 496. See also, the table concerning the Treatment Of Split-Dollar Plans Under Notice 2002-8 (page 228), and the note on page 496 regarding the use of the insurer's published premium rates. Because the rates used to measure the "economic benefit" to the employee are based upon *standard* risks, one of the best prospects for split-dollar is the employee who must pay a *rated* premium.

[4] When large amounts of insurance are required on older individuals, the premium requirements can often exceed the annual exclusion limits for "present interest" gifts (see footnote 4, page 59, and page 367). With split-dollar funding survivorship life insurance it is possible to substantially reduce the amount of annual gifts to the trust, thereby allowing larger amounts of insurance to be purchased within these "present interest" limits. This reduction had been made possible by using the "Table 38" rates. Because the Table 38 rates measure the probability of *two deaths* in one year, the calculated rates range from only 1 percent to 12 percent of the P.S. 58 rates. However, in Notice 2002-8 the IRS indicated that "taxpayers should make appropriate adjustments to [the Table 2001 rates] if the life insurance covers more than one life." Notice 2002-8 further indicated that P.S. 58 rates would no longer be used for split-dollar plans entered into on and after January 28, 2002 (see Treatment Of Split-Dollar Plans Under Notice 2002-8, on page 228, and note on page 496). It is currently unclear as to how to value life insurance protection under second-to-die policies. However valued, it must be recognized that, after the first death, the lower joint life rates will no longer be applicable, and the value of coverage on the survivor must be measured by higher single life rates (see Survivorship Life Insurance, page 475).

[5] See page 367 for a discussion of these withdrawal rights, which are often referred to as "Crummey" powers.

[6] It is not possible to avoid income to the employee and a gift to the trust by having the employer pay the entire premium. Under such circumstances the "economic benefit" would be treated as both taxable income to the employee and a gift by the employee to the trust (i.e., there would be both imputed income and an imputed gift).

[7] If the bonus is large enough to pay not only the employee's share of the premium, but also the tax on the bonus, the plan is called "double bonus" split-dollar. In either case, the bonus is taxable and reported as "other compensation" on the employee's W-2 form. Underlying any discussion of bonuses is the assumption that, if challenged by the Internal Revenue Service, the increased compensation would be reasonable. An expanded discussion of Unreasonable Compensation is set forth on page 483.

[8] As with the division of cash values, the *death benefit* payable to the employer can vary according to the provisions of the split-dollar agreement. Typically, the employer will receive an amount equal to the cumulative cost of the plan, which is the employer's cumulative *premium* payments, plus, if desired, the cumulative *after-tax cost of bonuses* given the employee. The trustee will receive the balance of the death benefits.

SURVIVOR INCOME

The sudden loss of income at the death of a breadearner can be devastating to a surviving family.[1] A survivor income plan can assure that continuing income will be available and is based upon a written agreement between the employer and the employee.

Benefits under such a plan usually take the form of ongoing and periodic payments for a specified number of years following the employee's death. Typically, such benefits might be set at 50 percent of pay, per year, for 10 years.[2]

DURING LIFETIME, the employer and employee enter into an agreement providing for the employer to make periodic payments to the employee's beneficiary following the employee's death. In order to provide the funds to meet its obligation, the employer purchases a life insurance contract insuring the employee. Neither the employee nor his family has any rights whatsoever in this policy. Because the employer is both owner and beneficiary of this contract, the premium payments are not tax-deductible to the employer. Nor will the premiums be taxable to the employee provided the contract is clearly not tied to the promise to pay the survivor benefit. In this sense, the contract is carried in the same manner as key person insurance, the difference being the *purpose* for which the death benefit will be used.

UPON DEATH, the insurance company pays a death benefit directly to the employer, as beneficiary of the contract insuring the employee.[3] Under the pre-existing agreement, the employer then provides a survivor income benefit to the family. While these payments are fully tax-deductible by the employer, they will be received as taxable income by the family.

Using life insurance to help meet the obligation under a survivor income plan offers tax-leverage to the employer, in that *receipt* of the death benefit by the employer is potentially tax-free, whereas *payments* made to the surviving family are fully tax-deductible. For an employer in a 34 percent marginal tax bracket, payment of $1.00 in benefits will generate a tax savings of 34 cents.[4]

The *insured* survivor income plan provides the security of continuing income to the employee's family, while offering tax-leverage to the employer.[5]

Footnotes on page 241

DURING LIFETIME

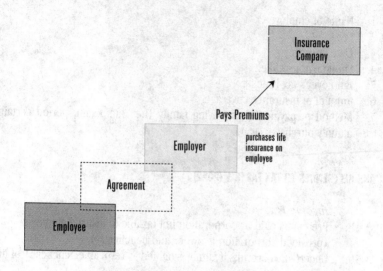

Agreement Provides For Periodic Payments Following Employee's Death

UPON DEATH

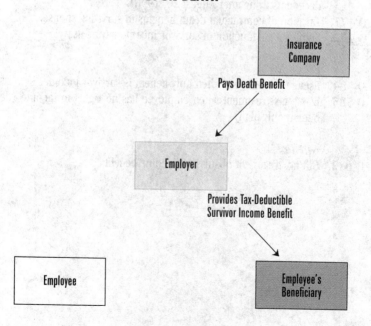

INFORMATION REQUIRED FOR ANALYSIS & PROPOSAL

1. Name of employee.
2. Sex.
3. Date of birth.
4. Smoker/nonsmoker.
5. Employer's tax bracket.
6. Amount of insurance coverage.
7. Method of payment to surviving family (i.e., lump-sum, period certain, annuity purchase, etc.).

CROSS REFERENCES TO TAX FACTS 1 (2002)

Income Tax

Q 48. Premiums paid by corporation not taxable to insured employee (provided corporation is owner and beneficiary).

Q 50. Uncertain tax results if family is named as revocable beneficiary of life insurance contract.

Q 73. Proceeds paid to widow are taxable as compensation for past services of deceased employee.

Q 170. Employee death benefit exclusion of $5,000 (repealed with respect to decedents dying after August 20, 1996).

Q 171. Taxation of contractual death benefits to surviving spouse.

Q 172. Employer's deduction of survivor income payments.

Estate Tax

Q 584. Estate tax treatment when only benefit is survivor income.

Q 585. Estate tax treatment when employee has no rights to income (death benefit only plan).

Gift Tax

Q 642. Gift tax treatment of survivor income benefit.

Footnotes

[1] To better appreciate the total amount of future income lost when a breadearner dies, refer to the table of Projected Earnings on page 309. Human Life Value is also dealt with in the table Life Insurance Needs As a Percentage Of Earnings on page 16. While many surviving families can expect to receive benefits from Social Security, it is probably not advisable for them to rely on the system for the greater part of their financial security. For example, in 2002 the *maximum* survivor's benefits available under Social Security are:

Age of Worker	Surviving Spouse & 1 Child; or 2 Children	Surviving Spouse & 2 Children; or 3 Children	One Child (no parent)	Widow or Age 60	Widower Age 65
25	$2,973	$3,469	$1,486	$1,417	$1,982
30	2,970	3,465	1,485	1,415	1,980
35	2,928	3,416	1,464	1,395	1,952
40	2,907	3,392	1,453	1,385	1,938
45	2,890	3,373	1,445	1,377	1,927
50	2,863	3,341	1,431	1,364	1,909
55	2,793	3,259	1,396	1,331	1,862
60	2,715	3,168	1,357	1,294	1,810

The above table has been extracted from Social Security Table 11, *ASRS*, Sec. 15, ¶90. Note that a surviving family is entitled to payments provided one or more children are under age 18. Once all children are 18 or over, no social security benefits are available until the surviving spouse is age 60. This period between the youngest child's age 18 and spouse's age 60 is often referred to as the Social Security "blackout period."

[2] Although a lump-sum payment could be made, it is usually preferable to provide the family with an income stream more suited to its needs. This will also allow for spreading out of the family's income tax liability and the employer's tax deductions.

[3] Under some circumstances the alternative minimum tax could result in the indirect taxation of life insurance proceeds received by a corporation (see pages 342-344).

[4] For each $1.00 received as a tax-free death benefit by the employer, this employer could afford to pay $1.52 in benefits. The calculations are as follows:

Desired After-Tax Cost	$ 1.00
Reciprocal Of Tax Bracket	÷ .66
Tax-Deductible Payment To Family	$ 1.52
Less Taxes Saved (34% tax bracket)	(.52)
After-Tax Cost	$ 1.00
Less Tax-Free Death Benefit	(1.00)
Cost To Make Payment	$ 0.00

Alternatively, the employer might prefer a return of all premiums, *plus* a tax-free gain to corporate surplus. For example, assume the tax-free death benefit from a $100,000 policy was invested in tax-free 6.6 percent municipal bonds. The employer could then afford to pay a survivor $10,000 per year for life, and eventually receive a return of all premiums and a tax-free gain. The yearly after-tax cost of the $10,000 payment would be covered by the $6,600 of tax-free income ($100,000 x .066). Of course, the above calculations would have to be adjusted downward if the death proceeds were subject to the corporate alternative minimum tax (see page 342-344).

[5] "Death benefit only" plans allow payments from a survivor income plan to be excluded from the employee's federal taxable estate (see Death Benefit Only plan on page 368).

DEFERRED COMPENSATION

In allowing *selected* management or highly compensated employees to defer income until after retirement, deferred compensation offers *multiple tax advantages* to both the employer and the participant.[1]

CORPORATE OBLIGATION. To illustrate, assume we have a key corporate manager who is currently age 45. Under its terms, the plan would provide for retirement payments, at age 65, of $10,000 per year for 10 years.[2] These payments would be *tax-deductible* to the corporation when made, and, although *taxable* to the retired employee, presumably he would pay less in taxes due to a reduced retirement income and resulting lower marginal tax bracket.

Typically, such plans also provide for survivor payments if the employee dies prior to retirement. For example, should the employee die at age 55, a typical plan might pay his surviving family $10,000 per year for 10 years. Since these payments would be tax-deductible to the corporation, each $10,000 payment would cost only $6,600 (assuming a 34 percent corporate marginal tax bracket). However, these payments would be taxable income to the family.[3]

The plan can also be structured to provide disability benefits to the employee. To assure itself of funds to meet its obligation, the employer could purchase a disability income contract, or it could *partially* protect itself by adding a waiver of premium rider to any life insurance contract on the employee's life.[4]

LIFE INSURANCE on the employee can assure the employer that it will have the funds to meet its obligation. Using life insurance for this purpose requires a corporate commitment to spend $4,000 per year during the first 20 years, and $6,600 per year during the 10 years following the employee's retirement (all after taxes).[5] The *cumulative* outlay by the corporation would be $80,000 during the 20 years prior to retirement at age 65, and $146,000 by time the employee reaches age 75.[6]

If life insurance with an increasing death benefit is purchased, it will likely produce a *gain* to corporate surplus when the employee dies, which amount can then be used to make the survivor payments. This gain is the amount by which the death benefit *exceeds* the cumulative outlay by the corporation (i.e., the sum of the premium payments prior to retirement and the after-tax cost of the retirement payments). For example, if the employee died at age 55, payment of a $120,000 death benefit would produce a gain to corporate surplus of $80,000 ($120,000 - $40,000 = $80,000).[7]

Footnotes on page 245

CORPORATE OBLIGATION

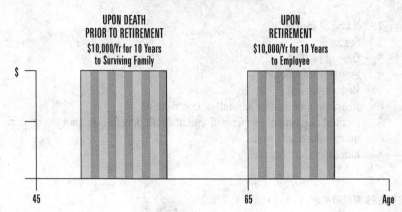

UPON DEATH
PRIOR TO RETIREMENT
$10,000/Yr for 10 Years
to Surviving Family

UPON
RETIREMENT
$10,000/Yr for 10 Years
to Employee

LIFE INSURANCE FUNDING

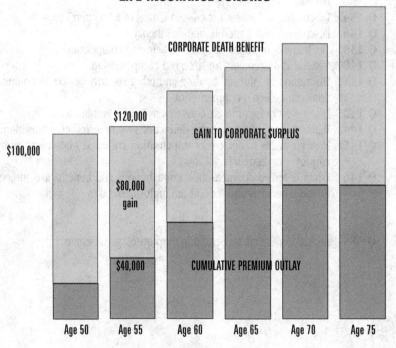

ASSUMPTIONS

Current Age 45 - Premium Outlay $4,000/year for 20 Years
Insurance Contract Provides Increasing Death Benefit
Retirement Outlay $10,000/year for 10 Years Beginning at Age 65
After-Tax Cost of Retirement Outlay is $6,600/year
(34% Tax Bracket)

INFORMATION REQUIRED FOR ANALYSIS & PROPOSAL

1. Name of executive.
2. Sex.
3. Date of birth.
4. Smoker/nonsmoker.
5. Retirement age.
6. Retirement benefit *or* amount of contribution.
7. Method of payment for pre-retirement death benefit (i.e., lump-sum, period certain, annuity purchase, etc.).
8. Employer's tax bracket.

CROSS REFERENCES TO TAX FACTS 1 (2002)

Income Tax

Q 134. Discussion of income tax consequences of a "secular" trust.

Q 136. Discussion of "economic benefit" theory.

Q 139. Tax benefits of informally funded deferred compensation.

Q 140. General requirements for deferred compensation.

Q 141. Discussion of informal funding and other security devices in connection with deferred compensation.

Q 142. Discussion of income tax consequences of a "rabbi" trust.

Q 144. When the employer can take deductions for deferred compensation.

Q 145. How payments of deferred compensation are taxed when received by employee or beneficiary.

Q 146. When deferred compensation contributions and benefits are subject to social security and federal unemployment taxes.

Estate Tax

Q 585. Inclusion of survivor benefit in employee's gross estate.

Footnotes

[1] The corporate owner who is also an employee will find many planning opportunities with deferred compensation that are not subject to the rules of "qualified" retirement plans. For example: (1) deferred reasonable compensation payments to a retired employee-stockholder are deductible to the corporation, whereas inflated payments for stock are not deductible; (2) the cash values of a life insurance contract, carried on the books and intended for deferred compensation, are usually considered to be for the reasonable needs of the business and thus immune from the accumulated earnings tax; (3) the liability for deferred payments to a surviving widow can have the effect of depressing the value of a deceased's stock for estate tax purposes; and (4) corporate owned cash values under a split-dollar arrangement can be used to provide the employer with funds to make deferred compensation payments (see comparison of split-dollar and deferred compensation on page 296).

[2] There are two types of deferred compensation plans: "pure" deferred compensation plans and salary continuation plans. Under a pure deferred compensation plan, the employee agrees to defer receipt of some portion of his present compensation. Under a salary continuation plan, the employer provides a benefit in addition to all other forms of compensation (i.e., there is no reduction in the employee's present compensation). When used with a vesting schedule or a non-competition agreement, a deferred compensation plan provides the "golden handcuffs" to retain a valued employee.

[3] Benefits paid to survivors are generally not subject to FICA and FUTA taxes. However, these taxes can be currently imposed upon participants if the plan provides nonforfeitable benefits. This will not be too great a problem for the executive who's other wages exceed the OASDI wage base.

[4] Backing up the plan with a life insurance contract containing the waiver of premium benefit would relieve the employer of having to make premium payments in case of the employee's disability. Assuming a premium of $4,000, a corporation in a 34 percent tax bracket could pay $6,060 per year to the disabled employee, since the after-tax cost of these payments is equal to the nondeductible premiums being waived ($4,000 divided by one minus the employer's tax bracket, or $4,000 ÷ .66 = $6,060).

[5] During the first 20 years, it is assumed that $4,000 purchases either a universal life insurance contract providing for a death benefit equal to the face plus the cash values (Option 2), or a paid-up at age 65 participating contract (with dividends typically being used to purchase paid-up additions). Once the employee reaches age 65, the chart assumes that the corporation will make retirement payments from *current* cash flow, as opposed to utilizing the contract's cash values. By maintaining the contract, the corporation will eventually receive the death benefit, which may more than offset its cumulative outlay. Assuming a 34 percent tax bracket and no alternative minimum tax, the after-tax cost of making a $10,000 payment is $6,600 (for sample calculations see footnote 4, page 241). Use of computer-prepared illustrations can provide a variety of funding options and schedules. See the discussion of corporate owned life insurance (COLI) on page 364.

[6] Because the corporation is both owner and beneficiary of the life insurance contract, the premium payments that it makes are *not* tax-deductible. In this sense, the contract is carried in the same manner as key person insurance, the difference being the *purpose* for which the death benefit will be used. To avoid any current tax liability to the employee, it is essential that the employee have no vested interest in a fund or any investments intended to secure the deferred compensation payments. The life insurance contract must remain the unrestricted asset of the employer, available to general creditors of the employer, and the employee can have no interest in the contract (see discussion on page 361). Despite this, it is generally recognized that the use of life insurance to back up a deferred compensation agreement provides some psychological security to the employee, in the sense that the employer is preparing to follow through on its commitment. Alternatives such as a Restrictive Bonus Plan, a Rabbi Trust or a Secular Trust might also be considered (see pages 222, 447 and 464).

[7] Under some circumstances, the cash values and death benefits could be subject to the Alternative Minimum Tax, as discussed on pages 342-344.

DISABILITY – THE LIVING DEATH

No estate plan can be considered complete unless there has been an evaluation of the risks of disability. *Planning to live* is as important as *planning to die*, and the risk is greater. For example, for a male age 40, long-term disability is 2.9 times more likely than death.

Before disability, most people are able to acquire savings to the extent income exceeds expenses. However, **after disability** caused by a sickness or injury, income will *fall* and expenses will *rise*.[1]

WITHOUT PLANNING, the expenses of a disability can quickly exhaust the family's savings and create substantial debt. This is true despite the availability of Social Security after six months of continuous and total disability. For most people these payments will rarely fill the gap created between falling income and increasing expenses. When available, Social Security disability payments to a disabled wage earner with children will be substantially more than those to a disabled wage earner without children. The fact that a disabled wage earner is married – and often responsible for the financial needs of a spouse – does not result in an increase in Social Security payments.[2]

Attempting to reduce expenses by selling personal possessions, a car, or even the family home, is unlikely to eliminate the substantial debt which is created by a long-term disability, which is often referred to as "the living death."

WITH PLANNING, the cornerstone of any disability plan is **disability insurance**. Just as life insurance protects a family in case of the insured's death, disability income insurance protects *both* the insured and his family in case of the insured's disability. In addition, before disability strikes, the purchase of a comprehensive **major medical expense plan** offers one of the most effective ways of paying the major expenses of many disabilities. A **waiver of premium rider** on existing or new life insurance policies will provide for payment of premiums after a stated period of disability.[3]

Footnotes on page 249

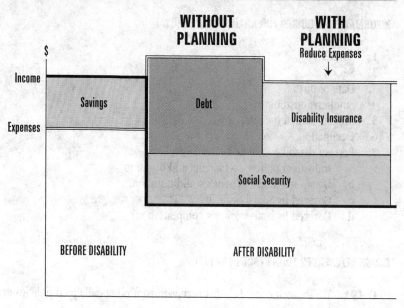

RISK OF LONG-TERM DISABILITY - RISK OF DEATH

(Male)

Age 30 - 4.1 times more likely

Age 40 - 2.9 times more likely

Age 50 - 2.2 times more likely

INFORMATION REQUIRED FOR ANALYSIS & PROPOSAL

1. Name.
2. Sex.
3. Date of birth.
4. Smoker/nonsmoker.
5. Annual earned income.
6. Occupation.
7. Present disability coverage:
    a. Individual policies – benefits and duration.
    b. Group insurance – benefits and duration.
    c. Covered by Social Security?
    d. Covered by state worker's compensation?

CROSS REFERENCES TO TAX FACTS 1 (2002)

Q 191. Disability income benefits received from personally paid policies are tax free.

Q 218. Taxation of benefits when provided for stockholder-employees only.

Q 221. Employer can deduct as a business expense amounts paid for disability income policy for employee.

Q 732. Tax credit for the permanently and totally disabled.

Footnotes

[1] The expenses associated with a long-term disability can be devastating. With death, the funds required are those needed to support a surviving family. With disability, the living death, not only is there a need to provide for the family, but the living and medical expenses of the disabled person must also be provided. The advances of modern medicine and equipment, which have enabled many more people to survive crippling accidents and illnesses, have further added to the expenses of long-term care. See the chart on page 259 regarding the risk and costs of long-term care.

[2] In 2002, after six months of total and continuous disability, the maximum Social Security disability benefit a typical wage earner could expect ranges from $1,793 per month (age 60) to $1,921 per month (age 25). With a spouse and children this maximum benefit ranges from $2,689 to $2,881 per month. The specific amount of payment depends upon age when disabled and previous contributions to the system. A complete description of coverage, benefits, and benefit computations is contained in Social Security Table 12, ASRS, Sec. 15, ¶90.12. All benefits are subject to income taxes, as described on page 468. Qualifying for Social Security disability requires that no less than nine separate tests be met, as set forth on page 373.

[3] In addition to disability income insurance, the owners of a business should consider funding their buy/sell agreements with disability buy-out insurance (see page 371). Also, business overhead expense insurance can provide for payment of specific business expenses during a period of disability (see discussion, page 348).

DISABILITY INCOME PLAN

When a disabled employee is faced with increasing expenses and decreasing income, often many corporations will informally continue his salary for an extended period of time. Such an approach can be unwise when the disabled employee is a stockholder. To illustrate, assume that a corporation's income is $150,000 before paying a $50,000 salary to its employee-stockholder.[1]

NO PLAN. If this employee-stockholder becomes disabled without a pre-existing plan, continued salary payments of $50,000 will likely be treated by the IRS as *nondeductible dividends*, which must come from after-tax profits. Taxable income would then be $150,000, upon which $41,750 of taxes must be paid, with $58,250 remaining after-tax and after payment to the disabled stockholder-employee.

PLAN. A pre-existing disability income plan would enable the corporation to preserve the tax-deductibility of these continued salary payments to the disabled employee-stockholder. This would place the corporation in the same position as existed prior to the employee-stockholder's disability.

To establish a plan, three things are required: (1) a corporate resolution must be adopted; (2) a plan document must be prepared; and (3) notification of the plan's existence must be given to the covered employee.[2] By doing this, the corporation could deduct continued salary payments and retain $77,750 after paying taxes of $22,250. Compared to "no plan," this represents a saving of $19,500 per year. Such plans may be *highly selective*, and a class may consist of just one employee, provided it is a "reasonable" classification. If stockholders are covered, it must be in their capacity as employees.

REDUCED RISK PLAN. Under the reduced risk plan, the corporation shifts a part of its liability to an insurance company.[3] With an individual disability income contract, an insured benefit of $25,000 per year could be paid directly to the disabled employee-stockholder.[4] The corporation would deduct a continued salary payment of $25,000, with $125,000 of taxable income remaining with the corporation. After paying taxes of $32,000, the corporation then retains $93,000. When compared to "no plan," this represents a saving of $34,750 per year.

With a reduced risk plan the premium is deductible by the corporation, yet not taxable to the employee, who is *assured* of receiving disability payments if the corporation should fail.[5]

Footnotes on page 253

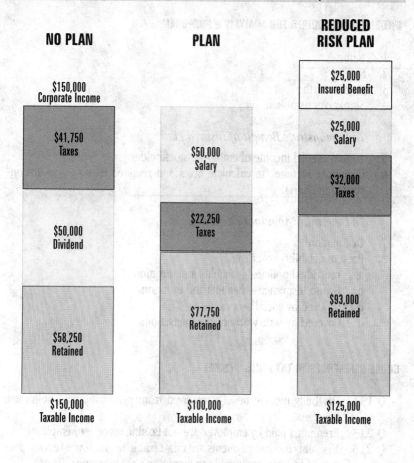

NO PLAN

$150,000
Corporate Income

$41,750
Taxes

$50,000
Dividend

$58,250
Retained

$150,000
Taxable Income

PLAN

$50,000
Salary

$22,250
Taxes

$77,750
Retained

$100,000
Taxable Income

REDUCED RISK PLAN

$25,000
Insured Benefit

$25,000
Salary

$32,000
Taxes

$93,000
Retained

$125,000
Taxable Income

REQUIREMENTS FOR A "PLAN"

- Corporate Resolution
- Plan Document
- Notification to Employee

KEY FEATURES OF THE "REDUCED RISK PLAN"

- Premiums Deductible by Corporation
- Premiums Not Taxable to Employee
- Employee is Assured of Payments

INFORMATION REQUIRED FOR ANALYSIS & PROPOSAL

1. Name.
2. Sex.
3. Date of birth.
4. Smoker/nonsmoker.

To Demonstrate Benefit of Insured Plan

5. Annual earned income of employee-stockholder.
6. Corporate income (to calculate taxes and retained earnings, as demonstrated in chart).

To Determine Amount of Coverage

7. Occupation.
8. Present disability coverage:
   a. Individual policies – benefits and duration.
   b. Group insurance – benefits and duration.
   c. Covered by social security?
   d. Covered by state worker's compensation?

CROSS REFERENCES TO TAX FACTS 1 (2002)

Q 191. Disability income benefits received from personally paid policy are tax-free.

Q 213. Premiums paid by employer are not taxable income to employee.

Q 215. Disability income payments are fully taxable to employee (except portion of income attributable to employee's contributions, if any).

Q 218. Taxation of benefits when provided for employee-stockholders only.

Q 221. Employer can deduct as a business expense amounts paid for disability income policy on employee.

Q 732. Tax credit for the permanently and totally disabled.

Footnotes

[1] Although a corporation has been selected to demonstrate the tax problems that can occur when a employee-stockholder becomes disabled, a disability income plan can be established for the *employees* of a partnership or a sole proprietorship. However, the partners and the sole proprietor are not "employees," and cannot exclude from their incomes premiums paid for disability income insurance. On the positive side, benefits received by a partner or sole proprietor are totally free of income taxes, because premiums are paid with after-tax dollars. For this purpose, the stockholder who owns more than two percent of an S corporation will be treated the same as a partner in a partnership (see pages 458-460).

[2] Notification given by himself as an officer, to himself as an employee, that the board of directors, on which he serves, has established a disability income plan for him, may appear unnecessary, but that is what is required. For appearance sake, it would be preferable to have another officer sign the letter of authorization.

[3] Despite the tax advantages of having a pre-existing plan, it alone *will not guarantee* that salary continuation payments will be made to a disabled employee. This is particularly true if the corporation is liquidated because of the extended absence of the owner during a long-term disability.

[4] The maximum coverage that most insurers will issue for long-term disability is generally limited to 60 percent of pre-disability earned income, reduced to account for other disability insurance and anticipated Social Security or state lump-sum benefits. However, reliance upon Social Security to provide the needed disability benefits may be ill-advised in view of the strict qualification requirements (see Disability Under Social Security, page 373).

[5] Provided they are *reasonable*, corporate premium payments are deductible as a business expense. Although the *premium* is not taxable to the employee, if and when disability *payments* are received by the employee, they will be taxed as salary. In order for the employee to receive tax-free payments, he must have paid the premiums. By including the premiums paid by the employer in his taxable income, the employee will be considered as having paid the premiums with his own after-tax dollars. He can then receive the disability payments tax-free. This is a decision to be made by the employee, and it will not affect the deductibility of the amount equal to the premium paid by the employer. The concept is sometimes referred to as a "Section 162 Bonus Plan," and is similar to that described in the Executive Equity chart on page 219. To determine the various tax ramifications of premium and benefit payments under different arrangements, see the table on page 317.

The calculations of the figures used in this chart:

		No Plan	Plan	Reduced Risk Plan
Corporate Income		$150,000	$150,000	$150,000
Less Salary		0	(50,000)	(25,000)
Taxable Income		$150,000	$100,000	$125,000
Tax on: first	$ 50,000 (15%)	$ 7,500	$ 7,500	$ 7,500
next	25,000 (25%)	6,250	6,250	6,250
next	25,000 (34%)	8,500	8,500	8,500
amount over	100,000 (39%)	19,500	0	9,750
Total Tax		$41,750	$22,250	$32,000

The 5 percent surtax on income between $100,000 and $335,000 is reflected in the 39 percent rate used in this table (see income tax table on page 492).

MEDICAL EXPENSE
REIMBURSEMENT PLANS

Under a medical expense reimbursement plan, it is possible to pay for the medical expenses of an employee and the employee's dependents.[1] These expenses include items such as doctor bills, dentist bills, hospital bills, transportation, medicines, drugs, dentures, nursing services, eyeglasses, and hearing aids. Although reimbursements can be provided by establishing either a self-insured plan or an insured plan, the ideal arrangement has the cost of the benefit tax deductible to the employer and not includable in the employee's income.

SELF-INSURED PLANS will cause highly compensated individuals to be taxed on part or all of any reimbursements, unless the plan is nondiscriminatory as to benefits provided and meets one of three eligibility requirements:[2]

1.   The IRS has found specific eligibility classifications within the plan to be nondiscriminatory;

2.   70 percent or more of employees benefit from the plan; or

3.   70 percent or more of all employees are eligible, and at least 80 percent of the 70 percent actually benefit from the plan.

If a self-insured plan does not meet one of these three requirements, then the highly compensated individuals who will be taxed include:

•   Any stockholder who owns more than 10 percent of the stock.
•   The 5 highest paid officers.
•   Any employee who is among the 25 percent highest paid of all employees.

INSURED PLANS, when established for "employees," are currently considered to be nondiscriminatory, even though they may benefit only a selected class of employees. The tax advantages of such plans are three-fold – the premiums are deductible by the employer, they are not taxable to the employee, and the benefits are excluded from income.[3]

These highly favorable tax benefits could be made available in an insured plan that covers stockholder-employees only, provided that, as a class, they can be rationally segregated from other employees using a criterion other than their being stockholders. A plan covering only active officers, who are being compensated for their services, can qualify for such favorable treatment.[4]

Footnotes on page 257

MEDICAL EXPENSES

Doctor Bills - Dentist Bills - Hospital Bills
Transportation - Medicines - Drugs - Dentures
Nursing Services - Eyeglasses - Hearing Aids

SELF-INSURED PLANS

will cause highly compensated
individuals to be taxed, unless
plan is nondiscriminatory as to benefits
and

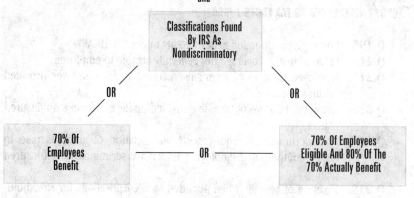

Classifications Found
By IRS As
Nondiscriminatory

OR   OR

70% Of
Employees
Benefit

OR

70% Of Employees
Eligible And 80% Of The
70% Actually Benefit

HIGHLY COMPENSATED INDIVIDUALS INCLUDE

Stockholder Who
Owns More Than
10% Of Stock

5 Highest Paid
Officers

25% Highest Paid
Employees

INSURED PLANS

Established For
"Employees" Are
Nondiscriminatory

INFORMATION REQUIRED FOR ANALYSIS & PROPOSAL

1. Name of employee.
2. Date of birth.
3. Smoker/nonsmoker.
4. Salary.
5. Status of employee (full time or part time).
6. Employment date.
7. Employer's tax bracket.

CROSS REFERENCES TO TAX FACTS 1 (2002)

Q 195. Coverage continuation requirements under "COBRA."

Q 213. Value of health coverage not generally taxable to employee.

Q 215. Employee taxation of payments received under employer provided health insurance.

Q 216. Employee taxation of benefits provided under employer's noninsured plan.

Q 217. Nondiscrimination requirements and taxation of amounts paid to highly compensated employees under a discriminatory self-insured plan.

Q 218. Taxation of benefits when provided by C corporations for stockholder-employees only.

Q 219. Taxation of health insurance coverage for partners, sole proprietors, and S corporation stockholders.

Footnotes

[1] A medical reimbursement plan can be provided for the *employees* of a C corporation, a partnership, or a sole proprietorship. However, the partners of a partnership and the sole proprietor cannot be covered and receive the same tax benefits, as they are not considered "employees." Only the stockholders of a corporation who are also employees of the corporation can be covered and receive the tax benefits. For this purpose, the stockholder-employees of an S corporation who own more than 2 percent of the outstanding stock or voting power, are treated the same as partners (see pages 458-460). In 2002, sole proprietors, partners, and stockholders of S corporations can deduct 70 percent of amounts paid during the taxable year for medical insurance for themselves and their dependents. This is scheduled to increase to 100 percent in 2003 and later years. To take the deduction, the individual must not be eligible to participate in any subsidized health plan maintained by his employer or his spouse's employer. The deduction is allowable in determining adjusted gross income (but is limited to the amount of the individual's income from the business for which the plan was established).

[2] Routine physical examinations, blood tests, and X-rays (that are not for a known illness or symptom) are not subject to the nondiscrimination requirements. In addition, despite having to include in income reimbursements under a discriminatory self-insured plan, a "highly compensated individual" may be able to claim a portion of his reimbursements as an itemized deduction. Medical and dental expenses, prescription drugs, and medical insurance premiums, which in total exceed 7.5 percent of adjusted gross income, may be deducted if the taxpayer itemizes deductions. For example, assume we have two employees, each of whom had $4,000 of medical expenses, which were fully reimbursed under a *discriminatory* medical reimbursement plan:

	Employee A	Employee B
Adjusted Gross Income	$ 25,000	$ 50,000
	x 7.5%	x 7.5%
Amount That Cannot Be Deducted	$ 1,875	$ 3,750
Medical Expenses Reimbursed	$ 4,000	$ 4,000
Less: Amount That *Cannot Be Deducted*	(1,875)	(3,750)
Amount That *Can Be Deducted*	$ 2,125	$ 250

[3] A more expanded statement regarding the tax benefits of insured plans:

    a. The premiums are *deductible* by the employer, if the benefits are payable to the employee or the employee's beneficiary. The coverage can be provided under either a group policy or individual policies.

    b. The premiums are *not taxable* income to the employees. This is true, whether the employer actually pays the premium for the coverage, or reimburses the employee for premiums paid for personally owned insurance.

    c. The benefits are *tax-exempt* to the employee, without limit.

[4] As with other employer provided health insurance, both insured and self-insured plans must comply with COBRA continuation coverage requirements. COBRA stands for Consolidated Omnibus Budget Reconciliation Act. Under its provisions, each qualified beneficiary who would lose coverage under a group health plan as a result of a qualifying event must be permitted to elect, within a given period, continued coverage under the plan (excepted are employers who have fewer than 20 employees). Qualifying events include death, voluntary or involuntary termination, divorce, separation, ceasing to be a dependent of an employee, etc. Continuation coverage must be identical to that provided under the plan. Premiums may be required, but they may not exceed 102 percent of the cost of the coverage (a disabled beneficiary may, under some circumstances, be required to pay as much as 150 percent during an extended period of coverage). Depending upon the circumstances, the coverage will generally extend from 18 to 36 months.

LONG-TERM CARE

Planning for long-term care is an integral part of estate and retirement planning. Long-term care consists of a continuum of services including nursing home care, assisted living, home health and adult day care. The need can arise from an accident, illness, or advanced age.

THE RISK. Statistics make a very good case for long-term care planning when considering retirement. For example, a 65-year-old woman can expect to live another 19.2 years, and a 65-year-old man can expect to live another 15.5 years.[1] During these years it is estimated that the risk of entering a nursing home ranges anywhere from 20 to 49 percent.

THE COST. Nursing care is expensive. Although there is a large variation from one region to another, the average nursing home costs $56,000 or more per year.[2]

MANAGING THE RISK. For an individual with substantial retirement income and assets self-insurance may be a realistic option.[3] However, for those who cannot self-insure reliance upon government programs may be ill advised. For example, after a minimum three-day hospital stay Medicare will only pay for the first 20 days of *skilled nursing* care. From days 21 through 100 the patient must pay the first $101.50 per day, and all costs after 100 days. Medicare does not pay for *custodial* care.[4] Although Medicaid will pay for custodial care, the patient must first "spend down" assets in order to qualify.[5] Private insurance is often considered by those desiring independence and choice of care and benefits.[6] It also provides asset protection from the Medicaid spend down requirements.

PRIVATE INSURANCE provides flexibility by allowing individuals to obtain care in various settings and at different levels (skilled nursing, intermediate and custodial care). Contracts do not require prior hospitalization, are guaranteed renewable and offer level premiums.[7] Daily benefits run from $50 to $300 or more. The benefit periods are typically 2, 3, 4, or 5 years, or lifetime. Benefits are paid when the insured has a cognitive impairment or is unable to perform certain activities called "benefit triggers."[8] A deductible, in the form of an elimination period, will generally last from 0 to 180 days. Provisions for home health care and adult day care will allow the beneficiary to remain in the community. Of particular importance is waiver of premiums to limit premium costs and inflation protection to ensure an adequate daily benefit in the future.[9]

In addition to these basic components, other benefits are often available. These features include spousal discounts, respite care, hospice care, caregiver training, bed reservation, medical equipment, cognitive reinstatement, non-forfeiture benefits, case management and referral services.[10] Choosing from such a range of contract options requires a balancing of benefits and flexibility against premium costs.

Footnotes on page 261

THE RISK

"The estimated risk of a 65-year-old person entering a nursing home at some time in his or her life ranges from 20% to 49%, depending upon the study and methodology used."

THE COST

Nursing home care costs $56,000 or more per year. There is, however, a large variation from one region to another around this national average.

MANAGING THE RISK

Government Programs	Self-Insurance	Private Insurance
• Medicare	• Income	• Independence & Choice
• Medicaid	• Assets	• Protection Of Assets

PRIVATE INSURANCE

- Daily Benefit Amount
- Benefit Period
- When Benefits Paid
- Elimination Period
- Home Health Care
- Adult Day Care
- Waiver Of Premium
- Inflation Protection

- Spousal Discounts
- Respite Care
- Hospice Care
- Caregiver Training
- Bed Reservation

- Medical Equipment
- Cognitive Reinstatement
- Non-Forfeiture Benefits
- Case Management
- Referral Services

INFORMATION REQUIRED FOR ANALYSIS & PROPOSAL

1. Name of individual to be insured.
2. Sex.
3. Date of birth (and spouse's date of birth).
4. Has individual or spouse been hospitalized in the last 5 years?
5. Has individual or spouse had any health problems?
6. What medications is the individual or spouse currently taking (include both dosage and frequency)?
7. What is the current monthly income and what monthly income is anticipated in retirement?
8. What is the net worth of the individual and spouse? (see page 12).

CROSS REFERENCES TO TAX FACTS 1 (2002)

Q 267. Within limitation premiums for a qualified long-term care insurance contract are deductible as medical expenses.

Q 268. Subject to a dollar limitation the self-employed may deduct premiums for a qualified long-term care insurance contract.

Q 269. Premiums paid by an employer for a qualified long-term care insurance contract should be excludable from the employee's gross income.

Q 270. Premiums paid by an employer for a qualified long-term care insurance contract for employees should be deductible by the employer.

Q 271. Description of a "qualified" long-term care insurance contract.

Q 272. Description of a "qualified" long-term care services.

Q 273. Grandfathering of long-term care contracts issued prior to 1997.

Q 274. Taxation of a "nonqualified" long-term care insurance contract.

Q 275. Description of limitations on the amount of benefits received under a qualified long-term care insurance contract that may be excluded from income.

Q 276. Reporting requirements applicable to long-term care benefits.

Footnotes

[1] Life expectancy statistics are from *Aging Into The 21st Century*, National Aging Information Center, prepared in 1996 under contract with the Administration on Aging, U.S. Dept. of Health and Human Services.

[2] Because of the wide range of charges a local cost survey of various levels of care is strongly recommended. The "cost of waiting" to buy long-term care insurance can be considerable. Not only are premiums substantially more at older ages but additional coverage must be purchased to cover inflation (see footnote 9, below).

[3] How much in assets or income does it take to self-insure? *Consumer Reports* in October of 1997 suggested that setting aside "roughly $160,000" at 5 percent compound interest would cover "about four years of care." That is $320,000 for a married couple.

[4] Medicare will pay for medically necessary home health visits that are restorative in nature (i.e., the patient must be improving). However, Medicare will not pay for intermediate care or custodial care (see page 422). It should also be noted that Medigap coverage only pays Medicare deductibles or coinsurance, it does not extend the basic coverage.

[5] Simply put, "spend down" means liquidating assets to pay for long-term care until a level of financial indigence is reached and it is possible to qualify for Medicaid. When does such a "financial meltdown" become significant? The answer depends upon marital status. In most states a single individual cannot have more than $2,000 to $3,000 in assets (and a monthly income of under $100). But the "indigent spouse rules" provide better treatment to a married couple with an at-home spouse. In 2002, most states allowed them to retain up to $89,280, plus the home, automobile, household goods and personal belongings (and a minimum monthly income of $1,452 for the at-home spouse). Amounts over these allowances are referred to as the "Medicaid deductibles."

[6] If an individual needs 24-hour-a-day custodial care, under Medicaid there is little or no provision for "community based care" (i.e., home care, assisted living or adult day care). It is understood that, on average, Medicaid pays about two-thirds as much as the private pay patient. Although a nursing home cannot, by law, treat patients differently depending on who is paying the bills, quality of care remains an issue. The Medicaid patients do not get private rooms. If the quality of care deteriorates, the family of a private pay patient can move him to a different facility.

[7] Premiums can be raised on a class basis. These features are offered either within the base contract or by contract rider. Long-term care insurance is also available on a group basis or as permanent life insurance that advances the death benefit.

[8] Typically, benefit payments are triggered by the loss of two or more activities of daily living (ADLs). These activities include eating, toileting, transferring, bathing, dressing and continence. There has been considerable debate over the quality of benefits under tax qualified versus nontax qualified products (e.g., the nontax qualified products will pay a benefit using the more liberal "medical necessity" standard). See the discussion of Qualified Long-Term Care Insurance on page 444.

[9] In June of 1991 the General Accounting Office projected that long-term care costs would increase at an annual compound rate of 5.8 percent. For younger insureds inflation protection is particularly important (e.g., a 50-year-old will not likely need coverage as soon as a 70-year-old, thus with inflation his care will cost more). Assuming 5 percent inflation per year, care that costs $3,750 a month today will cost $6,108 in 10 years and $9,948 in 20 years (see Compound Interest Table at page 499).

[10] It has been observed that eldercare may soon replace childcare as the number one dependent care issue. Good prospects for long-term care insurance are individuals in the so called "sandwich generation" (i.e., persons in their forties and fifties who still have children living at home, *and* are also providing for their own parents). In taking care of their parents these individuals have come to fully appreciate the problems of long-term care and generally do not want to be a burden on their own children.

QUALIFIED RETIREMENT PLANS

Qualified retirement plans can be established in a variety of ways. Pension plans and profit-sharing plans, including 401(k) plans, can be installed in a corporation, a partnership or a sole proprietorship. With a simplified employee pension plan or a SIMPLE IRA, employer contributions are made to an individual retirement account. Individual retirement arrangements, including both individual retirement *accounts* and individual retirement *annuities*, can also be established by many taxpayers.[1]

To better appreciate the advantages of qualified retirement plans, we can compare the results obtained when after-tax funds are invested outside a qualified plan . . . for example, in certificates of deposit, savings accounts, or treasury bills.[2]

Assume that there are $1,000 of before-tax funds available for investment per year over the next 20 years.[3] If *after-tax* dollars were invested outside of a qualified plan, assuming a 27 percent tax bracket, of the original $1,000 only $730 per year would remain after-taxes for investment.[4] The *earnings* on such a non-qualified investment will also be taxed, which means that although the investment might pay 8 percent interest, it would yield only 5.84 percent after-taxes. The reduced funds available for investment, combined with the reduced after-tax yield, means that in 10 years $10,108 will have accumulated, and in 20 years $27,938.

However, a qualified plan offers the opportunity for *substantially* increased accumulations, because there are no current taxes on contributions, and no current taxes on investment earnings. A tax-deferred growth of 8 percent will accumulate $15,645 in 10 years, and $49,423 in 20 years. This tax leverage offered by the qualified retirement plan means that each year $1,000 will actually be invested, and a full 8 percent rate of interest will actually be credited, neither being subject to current income taxation. Although payments received during retirement will be taxable, after-tax income will usually far exceed that available with a non-qualified investment.[5]

Footnotes on page 265

TAX LEVERAGE OF QUALIFIED PLANS

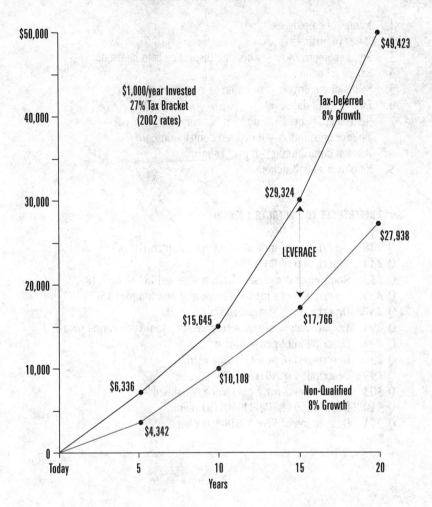

$1,000/year Invested
27% Tax Bracket
(2002 rates)

Tax-Deferred
8% Growth

$49,423

$29,324

LEVERAGE

$17,766

$27,938

$15,645

$10,108

Non-Qualified
8% Growth

$6,336

$4,342

Today   5   10   15   20

Years

NO CURRENT TAXATION ON CONTRIBUTIONS & INVESTMENT EARNINGS

- Pension Plans
- Profit-Sharing Plans
- 401(k) Plans
- Keogh Plans for Self Employed (HR-10)
- Simplified Employee Pension Plans (SEP)
- SIMPLE IRAs
- Individual Retirement Plans (IRAs)

INFORMATION REQUIRED FOR ANALYSIS & PROPOSAL

1. Names of employees.
2. Dates of birth.
3. Smoker/nonsmoker – when life insurance is to be used.
4. Salary schedule.
5. Status of employees – full time *or* part time.
6. Employment dates.
7. Retirement benefit – if defined benefit; *or*
   Dollar contribution – if defined contribution; *or*
   Percent contribution – if profit sharing.
8. Employer's tax bracket.

CROSS REFERENCES TO TAX FACTS 1 (2002)

Q 228. Description of individual retirement plan (IRA).

Q 234. Description of Roth IRA.

Q 235. Rollover or conversion from traditional IRA to Roth IRA.

Q 255. Description of simplified employee pension plan (SEP).

Q 257. Description of SIMPLE IRA plan.

Q 294. Tax advantages of qualified pension and profit sharing plans.

Q 295. Description of pension plan.

Q 296. Description of profit sharing plan.

Q 299. Description of 401(k) plan.

Q 303. Requirements for a plan to be "qualified."

Q 340. Description of SIMPLE 401(k) plan.

Q 351. Description of Keogh (HR-10) plan.

Footnotes

[1] The Qualified Plans Checklist on pages 297-298 provides a brief overview of some of the characteristics of qualified plans. While, strictly speaking, simplified employee pension plans, SIMPLE IRA plans and individual retirement accounts are not qualified plans, they offer many of the same benefits. Although many plans allow contributions of after-tax dollars, the chart on page 263 assumes all contributions are made from pre-tax dollars.

[2] Most individuals are already paying after-tax dollars into the Social Security System. Contributions to this system are substantial, as can be seen from the table on page 305. Individuals covered by Social Security can anticipate receiving some benefits upon retirement. For example, assume a worker had maximum Social Security earnings, in 2002 the projected *maximum* monthly Social Security retirement payments are:

Current Age of Worker	Normal Retirement			Current Age of Worker	Normal Retirement		
	Worker	Spouse	Total		Worker	Spouse	Total
25	$2,011	$1,005	$3,016	45	$1,977	$988	$2,965
30	2,011	1,005	3,016	50	1,960	980	2,940
35	2,006	1,003	3,009	55	1,925	963	2,887
40	1,995	997	2,992	60	1,866	933	2,799

The above table has been extracted from Social Security Table 10, *ASRS*, Sec. 15, ¶90. The retirement age when full benefits are available – previously age 65 – is being increased to age 67 in gradual steps starting in the year 2000. If you were born between 1943 and 1959, your retirement age for full benefits is your 66th birthday plus two months for every year that the year of your birth was after 1954. If you were born in 1960 or after, your retirement age for full benefits is 67. These Social Security benefits are subject to income tax if your income exceeds a "base" amount (see page 468). See also, the table on page 38, Social Security Retirement Benefits – When To Take.

[3] To estimate the total before-tax dollars that a wage earner can expect to receive assuming annual increase in earnings of either 5 percent or 8 percent, refer to the tables of Projected Earnings on page 309. To demonstrate the importance of starting early to save for retirement, refer to the Penalty Of Waiting table on page 310. The table entitled Early Saver vs. Late Saver on page 311 also illustrates the advantage of saving early for retirement. The table entitled How Money Grows on page 313 provides the accumulations for given amounts of monthly savings. How long these savings will last during retirement can be demonstrated using the table How Money Goes on page 314. See also, Facts About Retirement on page 318.

[4] Unlike the traditional IRA, the Roth IRA permits *nondeductible contributions* but *tax-free distributions* (see discussion and analysis on pages 300, 301, 403, 409 and 456).

[5] Assuming a marginal federal tax bracket of 27 percent and a lump-sum distribution of $49,423, payment of $13,344 in taxes would be required, with $36,079 remaining after-taxes. This result is substantially better than the $27,938 available with the non-qualified investment. However, assuming 2002 tax rates, the *worst possible* assumption involves a maximum marginal federal tax bracket of 38.6 percent that would require payment of $19,077 in taxes, with only $30,346 remaining after taxes. The calculations are as follows:

	27% Tax Bracket	30% Tax Bracket	38.6% Tax Bracket
Qualified Plan Accumulation In 20 Years	$49,423	$49,423	$49,423
Less: Tax On Distribution	(13,344)	(14,827)	(19,077)
Qualified Plan Net	36,079	34,596	30,346
Less: Nonqualified Accumulation In 20 Years	(27,938)	(26,051)	(21,103)
Advantage Of Qualified Plan	$ 8,141	$ 8,545	$ 9,243

This table does not reflect income tax rate reductions scheduled under EGTRRA 2001 to take effect after 2002, nor does it reflect the sunset provisions of EGTRRA 2001 (i.e., reversion to 2001 rates in 2011 and thereafter). Lower tax rates would result in a larger amount remaining after taxes.

401(k) PLAN

These plans allow eligible employees to defer compensation or bonuses and contribute the funds to an employer-sponsored profit sharing plan.[1] Known as cash or deferred arrangements (CODAs), they are funded entirely or in part through salary reductions elected by the employees.[2] Because employee participation in 401(k) plans is entirely voluntary, employers will often encourage participation by matching employee contributions. These matching contributions are typically limited to a maximum percentage and/or maximum dollar amount.[3]

One of the better ways of explaining the advantages of participating in a 401(k) plan is to contrast current nonparticipation with the benefits of participation (i.e., a "before and after" presentation).

WITHOUT PARTICIPATION. Assume that a 35-year old married employee with an annual salary of $32,000 currently pays $1,823 in federal income taxes, $960 in state income taxes and $2,448 in Social Security taxes. This leaves $26,770 of "take-home pay," with nothing set aside for retirement.

WITH PARTICIPATION. Now assume that this same employee has the opportunity to participate in a plan with a 50 percent employer match, (i.e., the employer will contribute one dollar for every two dollars of employee elective deferral).[4] If the employee elects to defer 6 percent of salary ($1,920 per year), the employer would then make a matching contribution of $960.[5] The total annual deposits to the employee's account are $2,880, consisting of the employee's elective deferral of $1,920 and his employer's matching contribution of $960. Because his contributions are before tax, the employee's federal income taxes are reduced to $1,535 and his state income taxes are reduced to $902. Social Security taxes are not affected by employee elective deferrals.[6]

Note that a reduction in take-home pay of only $1,574 has produced a deposit of $2,880 into the employee's retirement account. Because he pays $346 less in federal and state income taxes, take-home pay has been reduced by only $1,574, despite having contributed $1,920 to the plan (26,770 - 25,195 = 1,574).

A 35-year old employee can accumulate $242,289 by age 65; assuming level plan contributions and 6 percent interest on plan assets. Over the same 30-year period, total employee contributions amount to only $57,600. Waiting just 5 years to begin participation would reduce age 65 projected accumulations to $167,150, which is $75,139 less than would accumulate assuming immediate participation (242,289 - 167,150 = 75,139).[7]

Footnotes on page 269

WITHOUT PARTICIPATION

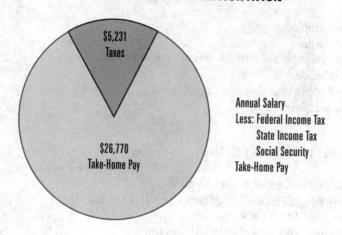

Annual Salary	$32,000
Less: Federal Income Tax	1,823
State Income Tax	960
Social Security	2,448
Take-Home Pay	$26,770

WITH PARTICIPATION

Assuming 6% Deferral and 50% Employer Match

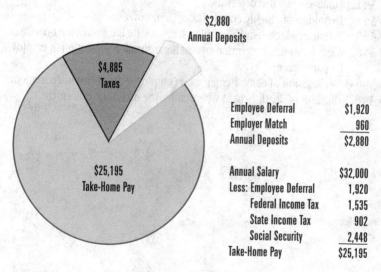

Employee Deferral	$1,920
Employer Match	960
Annual Deposits	$2,880

Annual Salary	$32,000
Less: Employee Deferral	1,920
Federal Income Tax	1,535
State Income Tax	902
Social Security	2,448
Take-Home Pay	$25,195

An annual reduction in Take-Home Pay of
$1,574 produces Annual Deposits of $2,880.

Assuming 6.00% interest and level contribution levels,
an employee age 35 would accumulate $242,289 by age 65.
Total employee contributions would be $57,600.

Waiting 5 years to begin participation would
reduce age 65 projected accumulations to $167,150

INFORMATION REQUIRED FOR ANALYSIS & PROPOSAL

1. Names of employees.
2. Dates of birth.
3. Smoker/nonsmoker – when life insurance is to be used.
4. Salary schedule.
5. Status of employees – full time or part time.
6. Employment dates.

CROSS REFERENCES TO TAX FACTS 1 (2002)

Q 299. General description of 401(k) plan.

Q 337. Special qualification requirements for 401(k) plans.

Q 338-339. The ADP and ACP tests.

Q340. Requirements for a SIMPLE 401(k) plan.

Q 341. Requirements for a 401(k) safe harbor plan.

Q 342. Distributions of excess contributions and excess aggregate contributions.

Q 343. Restrictions that apply to distributions from a 401(k) plan.

Q 344. Limits on elective deferrals.

Q 354. Definition of "highly compensated" employees.

Q 360. Extent to which a qualified plan can provide life insurance benefits.

Q 378. Method used to determine cost of life insurance protection to employee participant.

Q 396-397. Taxation of death benefit when employee dies prior to retirement.

Q 398. Taxation of death benefit when employee dies after retirement.

Footnotes

[1] In addition to meeting the requirements necessary to qualify as a profit sharing or stock bonus plan, 401(k) plans must: (1) limit the forfeitability and distribution of employee elective deferrals; (2) permit participation by the later of age 21 or one year of service; (3) limit elective deferrals to $11,000 in 2002; and (4) meet an annual nondiscrimination requirement (the ADP test), either by comparing ratios of elective deferrals for highly compensated and nonhighly compensated employees, by meeting the requirements for a SIMPLE 401(k) plan, or by meeting the requirements for a 401(k) safe harbor plan. In contrast, see SIMPLE IRA Plans, page 466.

[2] These amounts are referred to as "elective deferrals." It is helpful to remember that 401(k) plans can contain the following:

   a. **Employee elective deferrals** – amounts the employee elects to have the employer contribute instead of receiving cash (the source might be existing salary, salary increases, or bonuses).
   b. **Employer matching contributions** – made by the employer in some ratio to employee elective deferrals (if immediately 100% vested and subject to certain withdrawal restrictions, they are known as "qualified matching contributions").
   c. **Employer nonelective contributions** – made by the employer on behalf of employees and not conditioned upon employee elective deferrals (if immediately 100% vested and subject to certain withdrawal restrictions, they are known as "qualified nonelective contributions").
   d. **Catch-up contributions** – made by employees age 50 or over, beginning in 2002.

[3] In 2002 the employer's tax deduction is increased from 15 percent to 25 percent of total compensation. The typical plan design provides for the employer to match from 25 to 100 percent of employee *contributions* to a maximum of 5 to 10 percent of employee compensation.

[4] The employee elective deferral is limited to $11,000 in 2002. Amounts deferred in excess of this limit are not excludable from income, and, if not timely corrected by distribution, will be taxed a second time when distributed from the plan.

[5] Unless the plan is a SIMPLE 401(k) plan or a safe harbor plan, the amount of elective deferrals must satisfy the ADP test. Matching contributions are often used to improve ADP results. The Actual Deferral Percentage (ADP) test is applied by dividing employees into two groups . . . the *highly* compensated, and the *nonhighly* compensated. The ADP test is met if either: (1) the deferral percentage for eligible highly compensated employees during the year does not exceed the deferral percentage of all other eligible employees in the *preceding* year multiplied by 1.25; *or* (2) the deferral percentage for eligible highly compensated employees during the year is not more than 2 percent higher than, nor more than 2 times, the deferral percentage for all other eligible employees in the *preceding* year (in either case, an election is available to compare current instead of preceding year results). An employee is potentially within the group of "highly compensated employees" if he:

   a. Was a 5 percent owner at any time during the current or preceding year, or
   b. Earned from his employer more than $85,000 for the preceding year (in 2002, as indexed for inflation) and, if the employer elects to apply this clause, was in the top 20 percent in relation to compensation for that year.

[6] Although most states allow an employee to exclude 401(k) contributions from taxable income, it would be advisable to check with individual state authorities.

[7] Provided it is an "incidental benefit," life insurance can be purchased within a 401(k) plan. Up to 49.9 percent of accumulated contributions can be used to purchase whole life insurance (24.9 percent if used to purchase universal life). The participant must include in gross income the "cost" of the insurance coverage (measured by multiplying the difference between the face amount and the cash surrender value by either the P.S. 58 rates or the insurance companies rates for individual 1-year term life insurance). If the employee dies prior to retirement, death proceeds in excess of cash surrender values are received free of income taxes.

403(b) PLANS

403(b) Plans are available to employees of public schools and colleges, and certain non-profit hospitals, charitable, religious, scientific and educational organizations.[1] The employee may supply the funds by agreeing to a salary reduction, or by foregoing a salary increase, or the employer may make contributions as additional compensation to the employee.[2] Contributions are *before taxes*, meaning that a participant is able to exclude the contributions from his current taxable income.[3]

Years Beginning Before 2002

Generally, with a salary reduction plan the lowest of these **three limits** may be excluded from income each year:

• 20 percent of includable compensation (assuming no past service and no contributions to other plans).[4]

• A limit of $10,500 in 2001, which also includes total salary reduction contributions to Section 401(k) Plans, Simplified Employee Pension Plans and SIMPLE IRAs (a "catch up" provision allows certain employees with 15 years of service to increase this amount to as much as $13,500).

• The lesser of $35,000 or 25 percent of compensation, made to all 403(b) plans and, under some circumstances, retirement plans. (Special elections may permit a higher exclusion allowance or overall limit for certain employees.)

Years Beginning After 2001

Generally, with a salary reduction plan the lowest of these **two limits** may be excluded from income each year:

• A limit of $11,000 in 2002, which also includes total salary reduction contributions to Section 401(k) Plans, Simplified Employee Pension Plans and SIMPLE IRAs. "Catch up" provisions allow: (1) employees who have attained age 50 to increase this amount by an additional $1,000 in 2002; and (2) certain employees with 15 years of service to increase this amount by an additional $3,000.

• The lesser of $40,000 or 100 percent of compensation, made to all 403(b) plans and, under some circumstances, retirement plans.

The compounding effect of before tax contributions and tax-deferred growth may result in substantially increased accumulations.[5] Since the annuity is generally portable to another qualified employer, contributions may be continued when changing employment.

Years Beginning Before 2002

Distributions from 403(b) plans are subject to *ordinary income taxes*, unless rolled over into a traditional Individual Retirement Account (IRA) or another 403(b) plan.[6]

Years Beginning After 2001

Distributions from tax deferred annuities are subject to *ordinary income taxes*, unless rolled over into a traditional Individual Retirement Account (IRA), another 403(b) plan, a 401(k) plan, a 457 government plan, or a 401(a) qualified retirement plan.[6]

In addition, withdrawals may be subject to a 10 percent penalty tax. However, penalty-free withdrawals are allowed once the participant has attained age 59½, separated from service after attaining age 55, or under other specific circumstances.[7] With some restrictions, tax-free loans are also available.[8] Required distributions of amounts accruing after 1986 generally must begin by April 1st of the year following the year in which the employee retires or attains age 70½, whichever is later.[9] Payments made under an annuity contract may be for the life of the employee (or lives of the employee and his beneficiary), or a period certain not longer than the life expectancy of the employee (or joint and last survivor life expectancy of the employee and his beneficiary).

Footnotes on page 273

SALARY REDUCTION PLAN
Years Beginning Before 2002

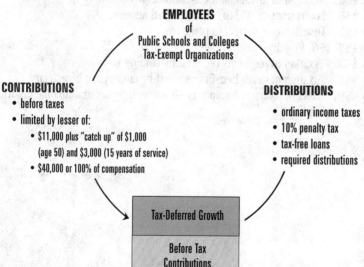

EMPLOYEES
of
Public Schools and Colleges
Tax-Exempt Organizations

CONTRIBUTIONS
- before taxes
- limited by lesser of:
    - 20% of includable compensation
    - $10,500 or $13,500 "catch up"
    - $35,000 or 25% of compensation

DISTRIBUTIONS
- ordinary income taxes
- 10% penalty tax
- tax-free loans
- required distributions

Tax-Deferred Growth

Before Tax
Contributions

SALARY REDUCTION PLAN
Years Beginning After 2001

EMPLOYEES
of
Public Schools and Colleges
Tax-Exempt Organizations

CONTRIBUTIONS
- before taxes
- limited by lesser of:
    - $11,000 plus "catch up" of $1,000
      (age 50) and $3,000 (15 years of service)
    - $40,000 or 100% of compensation

DISTRIBUTIONS
- ordinary income taxes
- 10% penalty tax
- tax-free loans
- required distributions

Tax-Deferred Growth

Before Tax
Contributions

INFORMATION REQUIRED FOR ANALYSIS & PROPOSAL

1. Name of employee.
2. Date of birth.
3. Marital status.
4. Salary (annual, monthly, weekly).
5. Assumed current tax bracket.
6. Employment date.
7. Projected retirement age.
8. Prior participation in tax deferred annuity plan.
9. Current participation in any qualified plan.

CROSS REFERENCES TO TAX FACTS 1 (2002)

Q 417. Rollovers from 403(b) tax sheltered annuities.

Q 430. Tax benefits of 403(b) tax sheltered annuities.

Q 431. Organizations that can make 403(b) tax sheltered annuities available to their employees.

Q 432. Methods of funding 403(b) tax sheltered annuities.

Q 433. Requirements that must be met.

Q 434. Minimum nondiscrimination requirements.

Q 436. Limits on excludable contributions.

Q 437. Calculation of exclusion allowance under pre-2002 law.

Q 438. Section 415 overall limits.

Q 440. Salary reduction limits.

Q 448. Taxation of incidental life insurance protection.

Q 450. Loans under a 403(b) tax sheltered annuity.

Q 452. Distributions subject to penalties.

Q 453-456. Required distributions.

Q 457. Taxation of payments received by employee.

Q 458. Taxation of death benefits received by employee's beneficiary.

Q 459. Effect of salary reduction on social security tax and income tax withholding.

Footnotes

[1] A 403(b) plan is also referrred to as a "tax sheltered annuity," or "TSA." Rather than "tax *sheltered* annuity," the Securities and Exchange Commission prefers the term "tax *deferred* annuity." Many companies now use the terms "tax deferred annuity" and "TDA," particularly when marketing variable annuities (see footnote 3, page 185, regarding licensing and prospectus requirements). 403(b) plans are also referred to as: (1) "qualified" annuity plans; and (2) "501(c)(3) plans" or "501(c)(3) pensions" (Section 501(c)(3) describes certain tax-exempt organizations).

[2] Nondiscrimination rules may apply to both salary reduction and employer contributions.

[3] Where a reduction in salary is taken to provide the premium payments for a 403(b) plan, social security taxes and benefits are based upon the *unreduced* salary (i.e., although income taxes are reduced, there is no reduction in social security taxes).

[4] **Years Beginning Before 2002**: With prior service and contributions the employee's annual exclusion allowance is calculated as follows: (1) take 20 percent of the employee's includable compensation for the current year; (2) multiply this 20 percent of includable compensation by the employee's total number of years of service; and (3) from the result, subtract total excludable contributions made in prior years toward the 403(b) plan and certain other contributions. If the employer pays the premiums for the employee as a *salary increase*, the employee's maximum exclusion allowance is based upon 20 percent of his current basic salary.

Years Beginning After 2001: The 20 percent of includable compensation limit no longer applies.

[5] The chart on page 263 demonstrates the leverage afforded by the typical qualified plan. Investing in a *variable* 403(b) plan provides a particularly attractive opportunity for dollar cost averaging (see graph, page 312).

[6] However, if the employee has an investment in the contract, he is allowed a tax-free recovery of his investment. Examples of an employee's *investment in the contract* include: (1) any premiums that he has paid with nondeductible dollars; (2) any employer contributions that were taxable to him by virtue of having exceeded his exclusion allowance in years before 2002 or the overall limit; (3) the sum of the annual one-year term costs that were taxable to him (where the contract provided life insurance protection); and (4) the amount of any loans included in income as a taxable distribution. When benefits are received in installments, or as a life income, the employee's investment in the contract requires the calculation of an exclusion ratio. The method used to determine the exclusion ratio depends upon the annuity starting date. Distributions are generally subject to mandatory withholding of 20 percent unless the employee elects a direct rollover.

[7] These additional specific circumstances include: (1) death; (2) disability; (3) as a part of substantially equal periodic payments beginning after separation from service; (4) when used for medical expenses exceeding 7.5 percent of adjusted gross income; (5) distribution of excess contributions within the same calendar year; and (6) payments to an alternate payee under a qualified domestic relations order.

[8] The maximum tax-free loan is generally one-half the contract value, or $50,000, whichever is less. However, an exception is available for the first $10,000 of cash value, all of which may be borrowed. Loan repayments must be made at least quarterly and in amounts that allow for amortization over five years, except for loans to purchase a primary residence, which may be repaid over a longer "reasonable" period.

[9] These rules apply to distributions calculated under 1987 proposed regulations as well as to those calculated under 2001 proposed regulations. However, different rules apply when distributions are not made as an annuity. See pages 409-410.

457 PLANS

Section 457 plans are nonqualified deferred compensation plans available to employees of state and local governments and tax-exempt organizations.[1] By deferring income, employees are able to reduce current income taxes while saving more for retirement than they would with the typical after-tax savings plan.[2]

ELIGIBLE PLANS.

Years Beginning Before 2002

Under "eligible" plans, deferrals are limited to the lesser of $8,500, or 33⅓ percent of includable compensation.[3]

Years Beginning After 2001

Under "eligible" plans, deferrals are limited to the lesser of $11,000, or 100 percent of includable compensation.[3]

Benefits usually are not subject to forfeiture. These plans are most often used for the "rank and file" employees of state and local governments, who desire to defer *limited* amounts of compensation on an attractive tax deferred basis. Employees are not taxed until the benefits are actually paid or otherwise made available to them. Tax-exempt organizations can only make these plans available to a select group of management or highly compensated employees.[4] However, these higher paid employees of tax-exempt organizations often prefer "ineligible plans" providing for greater deferrals.[5] The *earliest* plan distributions can be made is at severance of employment, death, an "unforeseeable emergency," or in the calendar year in which the participant reaches age 70½. Plan distributions must generally begin by April 1 of the year following the year in which the employee retires or attains age 70½, whichever is later. Distributions from Section 457 plans are subject to ordinary income taxes. Rollovers are permitted to and from an eligible Section 457 plan of a state or local government, a qualified plan, a Section 403(b) tax sheltered annuity, or an IRA.

INELIGIBLE PLANS. Under "ineligible" plans, employees may make *unlimited* deferrals of compensation, provided the benefits are subject to a "substantial risk of forfeiture."[6] These plans are most often used by tax-exempt organizations to provide substantial deferrals for a *select* group of management or highly compensated employees (the "top hat" group). Use of ineligible plans by state and local governments is generally limited to highly paid employees who can accept a risk of forfeiture, since such a risk is often unacceptable to the "rank and file" employee. Because employees are taxed when there is no longer a substantial risk of forfeiture, vesting provisions must be carefully drafted.[7] Ineligible plans are not required to comply with any specific distribution requirements.

Both eligible and ineligible plans may *not* be formally funded, except for eligible governmental plans. However, it is customary and desirable for employers to "informally" fund their obligations through the purchase of annuities or investment products.[8] Any deferrals, and assets purchased with the deferrals, must remain the property of the employer and are subject to the employer's general creditors.

Footnotes on page 278

EMPLOYEES
of
State and Local Governments
Tax-Exempt Organizations

ELIGIBLE PLANS

- In Years Beginning:

Before 2002	After 2001
deferrals limited to lesser of $8,500 or 33⅓ of compensation	deferrals limited to lesser of $11,000 or 100% of compensation

- Benefits not subject to forfeiture

- Coverage - State and Local Governments have no specific coverage requirements (Tax-Exempt Organizations must limit coverage to "top hat" group)

- Employee taxed when benefits actually paid or otherwise made available

- Distribution requirements:
  - seperation from service
  - unforeseeable emergency
  - age 70 ½

INELIGIBLE PLANS

- Deferrals unlimited

- Benefits subject to a "substantial risk of forfeiture"

- Coverage - Tax-Exempt Organizations must limit coverage to "top hat" group (State and Local Governments have no specific coverage requirements)

- Employee taxed when there is no substantial risk or forfeiture

- No distribution requirements

- May not be formally funded except for eligible governmental plans

- Deferrals subject to employer's creditors except for eligible governmental plans

INFORMATION REQUIRED FOR ANALYSIS & PROPOSAL

1. Name of employee.
2. Date of birth.
3. Marital status.
4. Salary (annual, monthly, weekly).
5. Assumed current tax bracket.
6. Projected retirement age.
7. Prior and current participation in any qualified plans (including state teacher's retirement plans), 403(b) plans, and Section 457 plans.

CROSS REFERENCES TO TAX FACTS 1 (2002)

Q 148. Nonqualified deferred compensation tax benefits that are available to employees of state or local governments and other tax-exempt employers.

Q 149. Requirements that a Section 457 plan must satisfy.

Q 150. Taxation of cost of life insurance protection and death benefits provided under Section 457 plans.

Q 151. Taxation of participants in eligible Section 457 plans, and "ineligible" plans.

Footnotes

[1] "State and local governments" include a state, a political subdivision of a state, or any agency or instrumentality of either of them (e.g., a school district or sewage authority). Tax-exempt organizations include those types of nongovernmental organizations exempt from tax under Code Section 501 (i.e., most nonprofit organizations that serve their members or some public or charitable purpose, but not a church or synagogue). Under "eligible" plans, only individuals may participate, not partnerships or corporations. Partnerships and corporations may participate in "ineligible" plans (see footnote 5, below). Section 457 plans can also be made available to independent contractors, but under somewhat different rules.

[2] The chart on page 263 can be used to demonstrate the leverage afforded by the typical tax deferred plan. Investing in a *variable* tax deferred annuity provides a particularly attractive opportunity for dollar cost averaging (see graph, page 312).

[3] **Years Beginning Before 2002**: Because "includable compensation" does not include amounts excluded under the deferred compensation plan, the employee may defer only 25 percent of compensation before the salary reduction (25 percent before reduction is the same as 33⅓ percent after reduction). "Catch-up" provisions may permit larger deferrals, up to a maximum of $15,000, to be made during the last three years prior to retirement.

Years Beginning After 2001: Both the 33⅓ percent limit and the 25 percent limit under Section 415(c) is repealed. The dollar limit on deferrals to a Section 457 plan is scheduled to be further increased from $11,000 in 2002 to $12,000 in 2003, $13,000 in 2004, $14,000 in 2005, and $15,000 in 2006. Cost-of-living adjustments will be made in $500 increments thereafter. This conforms to the elective deferral limits for 401(k) plans and Section 403(b) plans. "Catch-up" provisions may permit larger deferrals. See the table of Employee Benefit Limits on page 299.

[4] Unlike plans of state and local governments, plans of tax-exempt organizations can be subject to the participation, vesting, and funding requirements of ERISA (see page 384). These ERISA requirements are in conflict with the "no funding" requirements of Section 457 for tax-exempt organizations. This prevents most tax-exempt organizations from having a Section 457 plan unless the plan fits within the ERISA "top hat" exemption (i.e., an unfunded plan for a select group of management or highly compensated employees). This also means that "rank and file" employees of tax-exempt organizations cannot participate in Section 457 plans.

[5] The term "eligible plans" is used to describe the deferred compensation plans of state and local governments and tax-exempt organizations that comply with the provisions of Section 457. Beginning in 2002, when a plan provides for deferrals in *excess* of the lesser of $11,000 or 100 percent of compensation, Section 457(f) states, "compensation shall be included in the gross income of the participant or beneficiary for the 1st taxable year in which there is no substantial risk of forfeiture." Plans falling under Section 457(f) are variously referred to as "ineligible" plans and "Section 457(f)" plans.

[6] A "substantial risk of forfeiture" is said to exist if a participant's right to the compensation is conditioned upon the future performance of substantial services. The risk of forfeiture must be both real and substantial.

[7] For example, payment of compensation might be conditioned upon the continued employment of the participant for a specified period, measured by a pre-established service completion date. At the end of the service completion date, when there are no longer any future service requirements, and therefore no risk of forfeiture, the deferred amount (including earnings accumulated prior to the lapse of the risk) is included in the participant's taxable income. However, the *earnings* credited to the participant's account after the substantial risk of forfeiture ends generally will not be taxable as compensation until actually paid or otherwise made available. It may be desirable to release compensation over a specific period of years in order to reduce the tax burden as the contract conditions are met.

[8] If life insurance is purchased with amounts deferred, the premiums are not taxed to the participant as long as the employer remains the owner and beneficiary of the contract. However, upon the employee's death, payment of the proceeds to the employee's beneficiary would be taxed under the normal annuity rules and would not be treated as tax-free death proceeds.

PENSION MAXIMIZATION

Upon retirement under a qualified pension plan, married workers and their spouses are often faced with making a difficult decision regarding the desired pay-out election.[1] Basically one of two elections may be made: (1) to take a reduced monthly income with a survivor income benefit providing for payments during the lifetimes of both the retiree and his spouse;[2] or (2) to take an increased monthly income for the lifetime of the retiree without provisions for a survivor income benefit. Although plans differ, typically when the survivor income benefit is elected there is a reduction of 25 to 30 percent.[3]

CURRENT PENSION PLAN. For example, assume that the election under the current pension plan involves a choice between a retirement benefit of $1,600 per month to both husband and wife, or $2,100 per month for the retiree only. This difference of $500 per month can be viewed as the "cost" of securing a survivor benefit for the retiree's spouse. The election must be made prior to retirement and under most plans it is irrevocable once retirement begins.[4]

The retiree and his spouse are faced with a dilemma! If the survivor income benefit is elected they will receive only $1,600 per month. And, if his spouse dies first, he will continue to receive only this reduced monthly income. On the other hand, if he elects to receive $2,100 per month and dies before his spouse, no further payments will be made to the surviving spouse.

PURCHASE OF LIFE INSURANCE can provide an alternative means of providing for the surviving spouse.[5] If life insurance is purchased upon retirement, it may be possible, depending upon the particular plan of insurance, for the increased monthly after-tax income to pay for this coverage.[6] However, it is generally better to obtain the insurance some years prior to retirement, when premiums are lower and the worker more likely to be insurable.[7] In either case, the amount of insurance should be sufficient to provide an income in replacement of the survivor benefit which was not elected.[8]

AFTER RETIREMENT the contract insuring the retiree provides great flexibility. If the *retiree* dies first, then the death benefit can be used to pay a lifetime annuity to the surviving spouse. If the *spouse* dies first, then accumulated cash values are available to the retiree.[9] By either terminating the contract, or placing it in a "paid-up" status, the retiree could then stop premium payments and retain his full retirement income of $2,100 per month.[10]

Footnotes on page 281

CURRENT PENSION PLAN

AN ELECTION

With Survivor Income

$1,600 per month

TO BOTH

or

Without Survivor Income

$2,100 per month

RETIREE ONLY

PURCHASE LIFE INSURANCE
Prior To Retirement   or   Upon Retirement

AFTER RETIREMENT

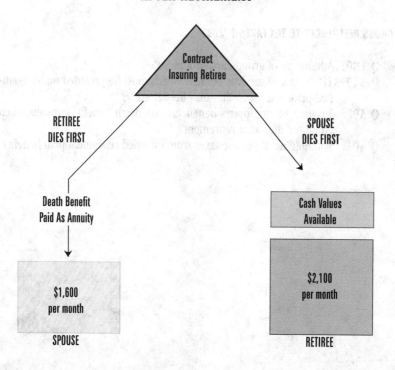

Contract
Insuring Retiree

RETIREE
DIES FIRST

SPOUSE
DIES FIRST

Death Benefit
Paid As Annuity

Cash Values
Available

$1,600
per month

SPOUSE

$2,100
per month

RETIREE

INFORMATION REQUIRED FOR ANALYSIS & PROPOSAL

1. Name.
2. Sex.
3. Date of birth.
4. Smoker/nonsmoker.
5. Anticipated marginal tax bracket during retirement.
6. Spouse's date of birth.
7. Spouse's health.

With Regard to Current Pension Plan

8. What survivor elections are available (joint and full survivor, joint and two-thirds survivor, joint and one-half survivor, etc.)?
9. What is the monthly dollar amount payable under the preferred survivor election?
10. What is the monthly dollar amount payable if no survivor income is elected (i.e., a straight-life annuity is paid to the retiree)?
11. Does the plan provide cost-of-living increases? If so, what annual rate of increase is anticipated?
12. Does the plan require surviving spouse election in order to maintain medical benefits?

CROSS REFERENCES TO TAX FACTS 1 (2002)

Q 180. Advantages of group carve-out plans.

Q 317-318. Forms of survivor benefits which must be provided under qualified plans and when they may be waived.

Q 398. Taxation of employee's beneficiary on death benefit payments when employee dies after retirement.

Q 401. Withholding of income taxes from qualified retirement plan benefits.

Footnotes

[1] "Pension maximization" is also referred to as pension maximizer, pension expander, pension trap, pension predicament and retirement dilemma.

[2] In the chart it is assumed that survivor payments will be in the same amount as those made while both the retiree and spouse are living. This option is known as a "joint and full survivor" annuity. Another option often made available is known as a "joint and two-thirds" annuity (e.g., $2,100 per month to both husband and wife, with $1,400 per month to the survivor). In order to protect surviving spouses, the law requires that qualified pension plans must provide as a minimum a joint and one-half annuity (e.g., $1,800 per month to both husband and wife, with $900 to the survivor). The retiree's *spouse must join* with the retiree in agreeing to waive the minimum joint and survivor annuity in order to obtain the increased benefit for the life of the retiree only.

[3] The reduction will depend upon the survivor option selected. For example, if a straight-life benefit pays $2,100 per month, a joint and full survivor benefit might pay $1,600 per month, whereas a joint and one-half survivor benefit might pay $1,800 per month to both retiree and spouse and $900 per month to the survivor. Typically these options are said to be "actuarially equivalent," in that at retirement they annuitize the value of the retiree's pension benefit according to actuarial tables.

[4] Occasionally a plan may provide for reinstatement of the retiree's full benefits upon the death of his spouse. However, such a "bounce-back" provision will not recapture benefits lost prior to the spouse's death.

[5] Pension maximization may be particularly useful to the retiree who is reluctant to accept a permanently reduced retirement income to assure a survivor income to his terminally ill spouse. However, as with any pension maximization proposal, it is *absolutely essential* to ascertain whether any medical benefits would be lost to the surviving spouse if no survivor option were elected.

[6] Note that the full increase in retirement income will not be available for making premium payments, since these payments must be made with after-tax retirement dollars. On the other hand, if the surviving spouse takes an annuity payout of the tax-free death benefits, less of each payment will be subject to income tax than post-retirement survivor benefits received under a noncontributory pension plan (i.e., less death benefits will be required to provide the surviving spouse a given after-tax income).

[7] When proposed some years prior to retirement, it is appropriate to consider the time value of money, since initial premium payments will come from other than additional after-tax retirement funds. However, the pension maximization concept can be particularly useful in demonstrating the need for ongoing insurance coverage after retirement. In fact, a discussion of the concept may *demonstrate the need for permanent insurance* to a breadwinner who is considering term insurance to meet a family income need (e.g., once children are grown the same insurance can be used to provide protection for a spouse during retirement, thus there is an ongoing but different need for permanent insurance). See also, First-To-Die Insurance, page 393.

[8] When a plan provides cost-of-living adjustments this potential for increasing survivor income would be lost by electing an option providing for no survivor income. However, to some degree this would be offset by the increased annuity payments available to his spouse from a level death benefit (i.e., the longer the retiree lives, the older the surviving spouse; the older the surviving spouse, the larger the annuity payments from a given death benefit). Availability of an *increasing* death benefit might more than make up for such cost-of-living adjustments.

[9] If taken as a lump-sum, cash values in excess of net premiums paid would be subject to income taxation. Alternatively, the retiree might obtain additional income by exercising a settlement option under the contract by receiving existing cash values as an annuity.

[10] Maintaining the policy or taking "paid-up" insurance would preserve the death benefit for children or other heirs.

DEFERRED ANNUITY

It has been said that three things can happen to you. You can die too soon, you can become disabled, or you can live too long. The last of these requires that each of us make advance plans to assure sufficient funds for our retirement years.[1]

Deferred annuities provide an opportunity to accumulate these funds on a tax-favored basis.[2] As a flexible cash accumulation vehicle, these annuities are available with either a *single* payment or *multiple* payments over a number of years (often referred to as a modal annuity). In either case, prior to the annuity starting date, the cash values of the annuity accumulate tax-deferred, with specific contractual guarantees and at generally competitive rates of interest.[3]

LIVE. For the annuitant who lives to retirement, the annuity can provide a guaranteed income for life. The actual amount of each payment will depend upon the values that have accumulated prior to retirement and the desired frequency of payments. When the deferred annuity matures payments can be taken in a variety of ways, to include "full" annuity payments for the life of one person (the annuitant) or "reduced" annuity payments for the lives of the annuitant and another person (e.g., a joint and survivor annuity).

DIE. If the annuitant dies *prior* to the annuity starting date, the then existing values could be used to provide either a lump-sum payment or an ongoing income to one or more beneficiaries. The specific amount and duration of these payments will depend upon the particular settlement option selected.

QUIT. Should the annuitant decide to surrender the contract prior to the annuity starting date, the then existing values, minus any surrender charges, could be taken in a lump-sum cash payment, or applied towards a settlement option providing ongoing income payments. Before making a decision, the tax implications of each of these options should be carefully considered.[4]

Of course, it is possible that the annuitant might die *after* the annuity starting date. To protect a surviving spouse, or other beneficiary, the annuitant can elect a settlement option providing somewhat reduced annuity payments in return for ongoing payments to a survivor. Other options are also available:

- Payments could be elected to begin prior to normal retirement age;
- Payments could be guaranteed for a minimum number of years;
- Payments could be elected for a fixed number of years.[5]

Footnotes on page 285

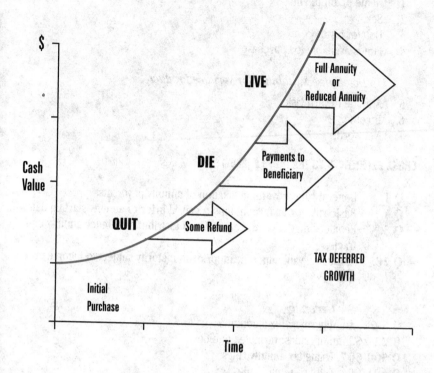

INFORMATION REQUIRED FOR ANALYSIS & PROPOSAL

1. Name of annuitant.
2. Sex.
3. Date of birth.
4. Funds available for purchase.

To Determine Suitability for Variable Product

5. Attitude toward risk.
6. Income.
7. Net worth.

CROSS REFERENCES TO TAX FACTS 1 (2002)

Q 1. General rules governing taxation of annuity payments.

Q 4. Basic rule for taxing amounts received prior to annuity starting date.

Q 5. Penalties that apply to "premature" distributions under annuity contracts.

Q 28. Amount payable upon death prior to maturity subject to income taxation.

See Generally

Q 8-21. Annuity rules: fixed annuities.

Q 22-25. Annuity rules: variable annuities.

Q 500-507. Estate tax annuity rules.

Q 601-604. Gift tax annuity rules.

Footnotes

[1] The Penalty Of Waiting table on page 310 gives the monthly deposit required to save $100,000 by age 65, assuming 6 percent interest. The table also shows the additional savings required if there is a delay of one or 5 years in starting to save for retirement. This same concept is illustrated another way in the table entitled Early Saver vs. Late Saver on page 311.

[2] Annuities are either immediate or deferred. *Immediate* annuities, by definition, are single-premium contracts that begin paying installments immediately. For example, an immediate monthly annuity would begin paying to the annuitant one month after the premium was paid and the contract issued. A *deferred* annuity is one in which payments to the annuitant are delayed to a specified future date more than one payment period in the future.

[3] Deferred annuities are also available as *variable* annuities (see the expanded discussion on page 484). With the variable annuity the cash accumulations reflect the performance of an underlying portfolio of investments such as stocks and bonds. While these investments can provide a hedge against inflation and an increased opportunity for growth, there is also the risk that investment performance will be poor and that an annuity's value will decrease or be lost (in contrast, see the discussion of the equity-indexed annuity on pages 382-383). Since it is a security, in order to sell variable annuities you must hold a valid federal securities license and state license where required. In addition, *a prospectus must be delivered* with or preceding a proposal to a prospect or client. This chart refers to a *nonqualified* annuity, which is purchased with after-tax dollars. A *qualified* annuity is described in the chart entitled 403(b) Plans, on page 271.

[4] An early withdrawal of funds from an annuity can cause serious tax consequences. For example, taxable interest is considered to be distributed first when there is a partial withdrawal from an annuity contract purchased after August 13, 1982. This means that with such a contract a tax-free return of the amount invested in the annuity cannot be received until all accrued interest earnings have been withdrawn. If amounts are invested after August 13, 1982 in a preexisting annuity contract, amounts withdrawn are treated first as return of pre-August 14, 1982 investment, then as income on pre-August 14, 1982 investment, then as income on investment made after August 13, 1982, and finally as return of post-August 13, 1982 investment. In addition, there is a 10 percent penalty tax applied to all taxable withdrawals from the annuity, with certain specific exceptions: such as withdrawals made after age 59½, or on account of disability, or of earnings on investment made before August 14, 1982, or as part of a series of substantially equal payments for life and not modified before age 59½ or within 60 months if modified after age 59½.

[5] These settlement options are similar to those available with most life insurance cash values.

EMPLOYEE BENEFITS CHECKLIST

Benefit	Description	Taxation of Employee
Athletic Facilities	Provided on premises and used by employees, their spouses, and dependent children.	Not included in income.
Automobile	Used for business purpose.	Not included in income.
	Used for personal benefit (including travel from home to office).	Taxable as additional noncash compensation.
Cafeteria Plans	Permit employees to choose between cash and certain tax favored benefits, but not including deferred compensation other than 401(k). The plan must be written, cover only employees or former employees, and may provide benefits for beneficiaries of participants (see page 349).	A participant will not be taxed just because plan offers a choice between cash and non-taxable benefits to extent he selects nontaxable benefits. Plans are subject to special nondiscrimination rules.
Charitable Contributions	Made by employer to organizations designated by key employees.	Not included in income provided contributions made and deducted by employer.
Club Memberships	Used for business purpose or used for both business and personal purposes.	Included in income and not deductible by employee.
Conventions, Meetings, and Business Trips	Attended for a business purpose.	Not included in income.
	When made primarily for a business purpose, but including a nonbusiness side trip.	Meeting and travel expenses to and from meetings are not included in income (if foreign convention, may have to prorate travel expenses).
Deferred Compensation	See chart on page 243.	Not included in income until payments actually or constructively received.
Dependent Care Expenses	Provided to employees to enable them to be gainfully employed. Employee must have at least one dependent under 13 years old or dependent or spouse who cannot care for self. Although plan does not have to be funded, it must be in writing.	Up to $5,000 (not more than employee's earned income, or, if less, the employee's spouse's earned income) excluded from income. Plan must meet non-discrimination and notice requirements for exclusions by highly compensated. No more than 25% of benefits can be Paid to more-than-5% stockholder-employees).

Benefit	Description	Taxation of Employee
Disability Income	See charts on pages 247 and 251.	Refer to table on page 317 and discussion on page 372.
Discounts	Discounts made available to employees, spouses, and children. Discount limited to 20% of the selling price of a service, or the gross profit percentage multiplied by the selling price of merchandise.	Not included in income provided nondiscriminatory.
Eating Facilities	Providing subsidized meals on or near premises.	Not included in income (provided revenue employer receives equals or exceeds direct operating costs).
Educational Expenses	Reimbursed to an employee for maintaining or improving skills required in employment.	Included in income, but deductible.
	Reimbursed to an employee for meeting minimum requirements for employment or qualifying for a new trade or business.	Included in income and not deductible.
	Provided under a nondiscriminatory Educational Assistance Program. Education need not be job related or lead to a degree. Covered expenses include tuition, fees, books, and supplies.	Up to $5,250 not included in income. Amounts over $5,250 are included in income and subject to employment and income tax withholding. Will cover expenses for graduate-level courses beginning after December 31, 2001.
Executive Equity Life Insurance	See chart on page 219.	Taxable as additional compensation.
Financial Counseling & Estate Planning	Provided to key employees for personal investment and estate planning.	Included as additional wages, but deductible to the extent that they are for tax or investment counseling (subject to 2% floor).
401(k) Plans	See chart on page 267.	Employer contributions not included in income. Employee elective deferrals not included in income but limited to $11,000 in 2002.
403(b) Plans	See chart on page 271.	Compensation not currently included in income (employees of public schools and colleges, and certain non-profit organizations), but generally limited to $11,000 in 2002.

Benefit	Description	Taxation of Employee
457 Plans	See chart on page 275.	Compensation not currently included in income (employees of state and local governments and tax-exempt organizations), but limited, in "eligible" plans to $11,000 for 2002.
Gifts	Gifts to employees (but not managers, administrators, and other professional employees if for safety acheivement).	Not included in income provided given in recognition of length of service or safety achievement. Value of award generally limited to $400.
Group Permanent Life Insurance (Section 79)	Superimposed on an existing group term plan, providing whole life insurance for employees (also referred to as "Group Ordinary Life Insurance").	Premium attributable to permanent insurance and term coverage over $50,000 are both taxable as additional compensation.
Group Term Life Insurance	See chart on page 211.	First $50,000 of coverage not included in income and amounts over $50,000 are taxable at the Table I Rates (rates, page 496). Up to $2,000 on spouse and children can be provided tax-free.
Holidays	Granting time off from work on specific dates during the year. Most holidays are set, but employees may be given a number of discretionary paid holiday days.	Wages paid during holidays are included in income.
Interest-Free Loans	Provided to key employees in amounts of $10,000 or less.	Not taxable and no deemed interest provided tax avoidance is not a principal purpose. If loan exceeds $10,000, employee is deemed to have income in an amount equal to foregone interest (page 408). There may be no deduction for the deemed interest payment (page 407).
IRA Contributions	Contributions to the Individual Retirement Accounts of selected key employees.	Taxation depends upon whether employee is covered by certain other plans (see pages 298 and 403).
Keogh Plans (HR-10)	These are qualified retirement plans for the self-employed. Although such individuals (sole proprietors or partners operating a trade, business, or profession) are not employees in the commonly accepted sense of the term, they are treated as	Virtually no distinction is made between pension, profit sharing, and other retirement plans established by the self-employed and those established by corporations.

Benefit	Description	Taxation of Employee
Keogh Plans (HR-10) (continued)	"employees" for the purpose of allowing them to participate in qualified plans ("employees" include any individuals who have net earnings from self-employment in a trade or business).	
Legal Expense Benefit	Providing legal services to employees for a variety of legal matters. Most plans offer scheduled benefits provided by a specified group of lawyers.	Benefits should be received tax-free. If employer pays "premiums" on employee's behalf, employee must include that amount in income. See discussion on page 411.
Meals and Lodging	Provided *on* the employer's premises and "for the convenience of the employer." There must also be a "substantial noncompensatory business reason." Acceptance of lodging must be a condition of employment.	Not included in income.
	Provided *off* the employer's premises while the employee is traveling to and attending a business convention or meeting, or on a business trip.	Not included in income.
Medical Benefits	Providing hospitalization, surgical and major medical expenses for employees and their dependents.	Not included in income. Nondiscrimination requirements apply to self-insured plans.
	Providing reimbursement for medical, dental, and drug expenses (usually those expenses not covered under a group plan). See chart on page 255.	Not included in income. Nondiscrimination requirements apply to self-insured plans.
Medical or Physical Examinations	Made available on a periodic basis to executives and key employees, including blood tests and x-rays.	Not included in income. In discriminatory self-insured plan, included in income if for specific illness or symptom.
Moving Expenses to New Principal Place of Work	Reimbursed to an employee for *direct* expenses, including moving household goods, cars, and family, as well as *indirect* expenses such as pre-move house hunting trips, temporary living expenses while waiting to move into a new home, and certain expenses of selling, purchasing, and leasing an old home or new home.	*Direct* expenses are included in income but deductible from gross income, provided requirements as to length of service and distance from former home are met. *Indirect* expenses are included in income and are not deductible by employee.

Benefit	Description	Taxation of Employee
Parking	Provided to an employee on or near the business premises or on or near a location from which the employee commutes to work by mass transit, in a commuter highway vehicle, or by carpool.	May exclude from gross income up to $185 per month for value of employer-provided qualified parking in 2002.
Pension Plans	Providing guaranteed retirement benefits to employees based upon a nondiscriminatory formula or formulas. Typically, such formulas utilize either a defined benefit or a defined contribution approach (e.g., either a specific dollar benefit to the employee at retirement, or a specific dollar contribution each year by the employer).	Employer contributions not included in income until payments received. If the plan contains insurance, each employee reports the value of coverage using Table 2001 rates as set forth on page 496.
Per Diem	Paid to employees as a fixed reimbursement for subsistence items such as meals, lodging, laundry, tips, etc., while on business trips.	Rate authorized to be paid by the federal government for the area in which the travel is authorized may be excluded from income, as well as an additional amount per mile for transportation expenses.
Professional Dues and Publications	Paid by an employer for the benefit of key employees.	Usually taxable as additional compensation, but deductible by the employee as a miscellaneous itemized deduction (subject to 2% floor).
Profit Sharing Plans	Providing retirement benefits based upon a nondiscriminatory formula for allocating contributions among participants. There is no requirement to have a predetermined formula for calculating contributions (permissible maximum employer deduction after 2001 is 25% of total compensation of plan participants).	Employer contributions not included in income until payments received, and payments are then subject to favorable tax treatment.
Retired Lives Reserves (RLR)	See discussion on page 452.	Contributions not currently taxed; after retirement, cost of coverage is taxable in year provided.
Sabbaticals	Allowing key executives to undertake independent work and study for periods of 3 to	Wages paid during sabbaticals are considered income.

Benefit	Description	Taxation of Employee
Sabbaticals (continued)	12 months. The expected benefits are expanded horizons, life-goal reassessments, and renewed commitment to job performance.	
Salary Allotment Plans	See chart on page 215.	Employee allotments come from after-tax income.
Salary Deferral SEP (SARSEP)	New plans may not be established after 1996. These plans were established by employers with 25 or fewer employees (at least 50% of employees must participate). Contributions to existing plans are made on a cash or deferred basis. In 2002 the maximum annual employee elective deferral is $11,000.	Employee elective deferrals are not included in income. Employer nonelective and matching contributions are also not included in the employee's income. Distributions are subject to the same rules as IRAs. Nondiscrimination rules apply. See discussion on page 467.
Sick Leave	Paid to employees while absent from work due to sickness or accident.	Amounts paid are included in income. A tax credit is available if the employee is permanently and totally disabled (page 372).
Simple IRA	A simplified tax-favored retirement plan for small employers providing for elective contributions by employees. Within limits, employer can match employee contributions.	Both employee and employer contributions are not included in income until payments are received. See discussion on page 466.
Simplified Employee Pension (SEP)	Providing for employer contributions to the employee's IRA on a nondiscriminatory basis and under a written allocation formula. See discussion on page 467.	Employee may exclude up to lesser of 25% of compensation or $40,000 in 2002.
Social Security	Contributions to the Old-Age, Survivors, and Disability Insurance programs (FICA taxes). Refer to pages 304-305.	Employer contributions not included in income. However, retirement and disability payments may be partially or fully taxed (see page 468).
Split-Dollar Insurance	See chart on page 227.	Value of employer-provided coverage is taxable as additional compensation (footnote 3, page 229, and page 381).
Split-Dollar Rollout	See discussion on page 470.	Included in income to extent of policy's interpolated terminal reserve, roughly equivalent to the cash values (assuming employer owns all cash values).

Benefit	Description	Taxation of Employee
Stock Options –Incentive	Granted to key executives under a plan specifying the number of shares to be offered and the employees to be included. Certain requirements must be met, but stockholder-employees can be issued options (if more than 10% of stock is owned, additional limitations are imposed).	When option is exercised, no tax is paid, even on bargain element (i.e., the difference between the exercise price and the stock's value at time of exercise) if holding period and employment requirements are met. Sale of stock by the employee results in capital gain.
Stock Options –Nonqualified	May be granted to key executives, including stockholder-employees, with virtually no IRS imposed restrictions regarding time within which they must be exercised, exercise price, or period stock must be held before sale (also known as "nonstatutory stock options").	When option is granted, no tax is paid provided option does not have an ascertainable fair market value (closely held stock). When option is exercised, the spread between the option price and market value, at the time of exercise, is taxed as ordinary income (at same time company gets deduction).
Stock Options –Phantom	Providing selected employees a form of deferred compensation by awarding "units of participation." Each unit is equivalent to a share of stock. As the stock appreciates, so do the participation units. On retirement, the employee receives appreciation that occurred in the comparable stock, plus previously credited dividend equivalents. Also known as phantom stock plans (see discussion on page 433).	Not included in income until payments actually received for participation units and dividend equivalents, at which time all payments would be taxed as ordinary income, not as capital gains. Employee must have no rights in units. Could be used by S corporation without creating a second class of stock.
Stock Ownership Plan (ESOP)	Established on a nondiscriminatory basis, covering a wide range of employees. Stock is currently contributed to a trust to be eventually distributed to retiring employees. Not practical unless corporate payroll is at least $500,000 and the owner has a real desire to eventually transfer ownership to employees.	Not included in income at time the stock is contributed to trust. Taxable as ordinary income when the stock, or cash payment for stock, is transferred to the employee upon retirement. However, taxation may be deferred if the distribution is an "eligible rollover distribution."
Stock Purchase Plan	Providing employees the opportunity to purchase limited amounts of stock at a discount from fair market value. Purchases cannot be made by employees owning 5% or more of the voting control or value of all classes of stock.	Purchase is made with after-tax dollars. Subsequent appreciation will qualify as capital gain on sale if certain holding period and employment requirements are met.

Benefit	Description	Taxation of Employee
Supper Money	Paid to employees who voluntarily stay overtime, when furnished for the employer's convenience.	Not included in income.
Survivor Income Benefit Plan	See chart on page 239.	Pre-death "informal" funding of plan by employer is not included in employee's income. Benefits received by surviving family are taxable income.
Thrift Plans	Permit employees to make contributions to a pension, profit sharing, or stock bonus plan. The employer's contributions are usually geared to the amount or rate of the employee's contributions. Both employer and employee contributions are limited by nondiscrimination requirements.	Employee contributions are made with after-tax dollars. Employer contributions are not included in income until withdrawn from the plan. All accruals are tax-deferred.
Transportation	Provided to an employee in the form of transit passes or vanpooling in a "commuter highway vehicle."	May exclude from gross income a maximum of $100 per month in value of employer-provided qualified transportation in 2002.
Travel Accident Life Insurance	Provided to employees and covering accidental death while traveling on company business. Other variations can provide 24 hour accident coverage on and off the job.	Not included in income.
Unemployment Compensation	Benefits paid to unemployed workers who were previously employed by contributors to the system.	Included in income (also subject to substantial downward adjustments depending upon other income).
Vacation Travel	Combined with a trip made "primarily" for business purposes.	Business expenses including travel to and from business meetings are not taxable. Expenses associated with vacation would be taxable.
Vacations	Providing a paid rest from work and usually based upon years of service.	Wages paid during vacations are included in income.
Worker's Compensation	Providing both medical expense and direct payments to workers injured on the job, as well as survivors of workers who are killed on the job.	Premiums paid by employer and benefits received are not included in income.

EMPLOYEE BENEFIT STATISTICS

Total Employee Benefits
As Percent of Payroll   37.2%
As Dollars Per Payroll Hour $7.10
As Dollars Per Year Per Employee $14,655

	Benefit as Percent of Payroll	Annual Dollars Per Employee
Legally-Required	8.4	$3,220
Old-Age, Survivors, Disability, and Health Insurance (OASDHI)	6.9	$2,621
Unemployment Compensation	0.5	202
Worker's Compensation Insurance	0.9	371
State Sickness Benefits Insurance and Other	0.1	26
Retirement and Savings	8.7	3,244
Defined Benefit Pension Plan	3.3	1,299
401(k) and similar	1.9	715
Profit-Sharing	1.4	539
Stock Bonus/ESOP	0.1	114
Pension Plan Premiums	0.1	28
Administration Costs	0.2	89
Other	1.7	460
Life Insurance and Death Benefits	0.3	129
Medical	8.5	3,539
Medical Insurance Premiums	5.5	2,232
Short-Term Disability, Sickness or Accident Insurance	0.2	89
Long-Term Disability or Wage Continuation	0.2	79
Retiree Medical Insurance Premiums	0.9	464
Dental Insurance Premiums	0.5	219
Vision Care and Prescription Drugs	0.3	174
Other	0.9	283
Time Not Worked	10.6	4,220
Paid Breaks, Etc.	1.7	620
Payments for Vacations	4.6	1,857
Payments for Holidays	2.9	1,134
Sick Leave Pay	1.1	467
Maternity and Paternity Leave Pay and Other	0.3	142
Miscellaneous Benefit Pay	0.6	302
Severance Pay	0.3	165
Employee Education Expenditures	0.2	91
Other	0.1	46

Source: U.S. Chamber of Commerce, *Employee Benefits - 1999 Edition*, page 7, and Table 1, page 10.

COMPARISON
SPLIT-DOLLAR & EXECUTIVE EQUITY

	Split-Dollar	**Executive Equity**
Premium Payments	Shared between employer and employee under various arrangements.	Employer pays full premium and employee includes amount of premium in income.
Death Benefits	Usually shared between employer and employee, with employer death benefit equal to its cumulative premium payments.	All paid to employee's beneficiary.
Cash Values	Usually shared between employer and employee, but employer typically owns all cash values in early years (but see table on page 228, and discussion on page 381).	All owned by employee.
Contract Ownership	*Collateral assignment method*: contract is owned by employee with limited assignment to employer. *Endorsement method*: split ownership between employer and employee (but see table on page 228, and discussion on page 381).	Owned by employee.

Note: See charts on pages 219 and 227. A private split-dollar arrangement between individuals or between an individual and a trust is described in the chart on page 65.

COMPARISON
SPLIT-DOLLAR & DEFERRED COMPENSATION

	Split-Dollar	**Deferred Compensation**
Premium Payments	Shared between employer and employee under various arrangements. If bonus plan, then employer entitled to deduct a portion of payments as employee compensation (see page 226 and footnote 5, page 229). Employee cannot deduct premium.	All premiums are paid by employer and are not deductible (see footnote 6, page 245).
Death Benefits	Paid tax-free and shared between employer and employee, with employer death benefit equal to its cumulative premium payments.	Usually paid tax-free to employer. However, if employer is a C corporation, then could be subject to the alternative minimum tax (see pages 342-344). Proceeds can be used to make survivor income payments to employee's beneficiaries or offset costs of plan.
Cash Values	Usually shared between employer and employee, but employer typically owns all cash values in early years (but see table on page 228, and discussion on page 381).	Owned by employer and considered part of the employer's general assets, which are subject to the claims of the employer's creditors. Cash values are often used to informally fund retirement payments to employee.
Contract Ownership	*Collateral assignment method*: contract is owned by employee with limited assignment to employer. *Endorsement method*: split ownership between employer and employee (but see table on page 228, and discussion on page 381).	Entirely owned by employer. Employee has no interest in the contract.

Note: See charts on pages 227 and 243. A private split-dollar arrangement between individuals or between an individual and a trust is described in the chart on page 65.

QUALIFIED PLANS CHECKLIST

Element	Limitation

Maximum limits on benefits.

Defined Benefit Plan: for plan years ending after 12/31/01, benefits are limited to the lesser of 100% of pay, or $160,000.

Defined Contribution Plan: for 2002, the annual additions limit is the lesser of 100% of salary, or $40,000 (in a profit-sharing plan the total annual employer deduction is increased to 25% of total compensation of plan participants).

401(k) Plans: during calendar year 2002, the allowable employee deferral is $11,000 (during 2002 participants who are age 50 or over may be permitted to make additional catch-up contributions of $1,000).

These dollar amounts are indexed to the CPI and new limits are announced by the IRS in October of each year.

Eligibility to participate.

Exclusions are permitted for age and years of service (maximum of age 21 and 1 year service).

Integration with Social Security.

A plan integrated with Social Security will often permit significantly higher benefits for higher paid employees within certain limits.

Defined *contribution* plans may provide additional contributions of up to 5.7% of pay in excess of current Social Security wage base ($84,900 in 2002).

Defined *benefit* plans may provide additional monthl benefits of up to the lesser of .75% of earnings, or the base benefit percentage for the plan year.

In either type of plan the percentage of total contributions/benefits for those above the "integration level" may not be more than two times the percentage of contributions/benefits below that level. In addition, the disparity between the two percentages must be uniform with respect to all participants. If additional requirements are met, the "integration level" may be lower than the Social Security wage base.

Employee vesting.

Employer contributions need not become immediatel and irrevocably vested, but may be contingent upon continued employment. Thus, costs to the employer may be reduced or benefits increased for employees who continue their employment. "Top-heavy" plans, and certain employer match contributions, are subject to special rapid vesting rules.

Element	Limitation
Definition of a "top heavy" plan.	A plan is top heavy if for "key employees" the present value of accrued benefits in a defined benefit plan or account balances in a defined contribution plan exceeds 60% of accrued benefits or account balances for all employees. Key employees include: (1) officers earning more than $130,000 (indexed after 2002), (2) any 5% owner of the employer, and (3) any 1% owner who earns more than $150,000 per year.
For top-heavy plan purposes, definition of the term "officers".	The term "officer" has a very special meaning. Officers of any employer include no more than either: (1) 50 employees; or, if less, (2) the greater of 3 employees or 10% of the employee group. In other words, the maximum number of employees considered officers is 10% of the employee group, up to 50.
Fund investment flexibility.	Trustee may direct the investments into nearly any type of investment media. Strict fiduciary standards apply.
Distributions.	Generally, distributions to a non-5%-owner must be started by April 1 of the year following the year the individual attains age 70½ or retires, whichever is later. Distributions to a 5%-owner cannot be delayed until retirement.
Premature distributions.	Distributions prior to age 59½ will be subject to a 10% penalty tax (25% during first two years with SIMPLE IRA) unless distribution is due to death, disability, separation from service after age 55, or in the event of certain specified hardships. The penalty tax is also waived if the distribution is annuitized or to the extent needed to pay family medical expenses in excess of 7½% of adjusted gross income.
Federal estate tax status of death benefits.	Fully included in estate.
Availability of $3,000 IRA Deduction (in 2002).	*Not* available if covered by pension, profit sharing or stock bonus plan, a 403(b) plan, a SIMPLE IRA, a SEP, or a government plan and adjusted gross income in 2002 exceeds: (1) $44,000 - individual return (2) $64,000 - joint return *Partially* deductible if covered by plan (listed above) and adjusted gross income ranges from: (1) $34,000-44,000 - individual return (2) $54,000-64,000 - joint return *Fully* available if not covered by listed plan. See discussions on page 403 and page 456.

EMPLOYEE BENEFIT LIMITS[1]

Type of Limit	Year					
	2002	2003	2004	2005	2006	2007
Defined Benefit Section 415	160,000[2]	160,000[2]	160,000[2]	160,000[2]	160,000[2]	160,000[2]
Defined Contribution Section 415	40,000[3] or 100% of salary	40,000[3] or 100% of salary	40,000[3] or 100% of salary	40,000[3] or 100% of salary	40,000[3] or 100% of salary	40,000[3] or 100% of salary
Elective Deferral for 401(k) Plans, 403(b) Plans (TDAs), & SEPs	11,000	12,000	13,000	14,000	15,000	15,000[4]
Catch-Up for 401(k) Plans (age 50 and over)[5]	1,000	2,000	3,000	4,000	5,000	5,000[4]
Catch-Up for 403(b) Plans (TDAs)[5]						
age 50 and over	1,000	2,000	3,000	4,000	5,000	5,000[4]
15 years of service	3,000	3,000	3,000	3,000	3,000	3,000
Elective Deferral Limit for Section 457	11,000	12,000	13,000	14,000	15,000	15,000[4]
Catch-Up for Section 457 Plans - age 50 and over[5]						
other than last 3 years before retirement[6]	1,000	2,000	3,000	4,000	5,000	5,000[4]
during last 3 years before retirement	11,000	12,000	13,000	14,000	15,000	15,000[4]
Elective Deferral Limit for SIMPLE IRAs and SIMPLE 401(k) Plans	7,000	8,000	9,000	10,000	10,000[7]	10,000[7]
Catch-Up for SIMPLEs[5]	500	1,000	1,500	2,000	2,500[7]	2,500[7]
Highly Compensated Employee Definitional Limit	85,000[2]	85,000[2]	85,000[2]	85,000[2]	85,000[2]	85,000[2]
Maximum Compensation for Qualified Plans, SEPs, TSAs, & VEBAs	200,000	200,000[8]	200,000[8]	200,000[8]	200,000[8]	200,000[8]

[1] See Appendix E, *Tax Facts 1 (2002)* for detailed citations in support of this table, including cross references to specific questions and materials.
[2] Indexed in $5,000 increments.
[3] Indexed in $1,000 increments.
[4] Indexed in $500 increments beginning in 2007.
[5] Catch-up amounts are in addition to the elective deferral limit.
[6] Use the participant's compensation, reduced by any other elective deferrals made that year, if less then the applicable dollar amount shown in the table.
[7] Indexed in $500 increments beginning in 2006.
[8] Indexed in $5,000 increments beginning in 2003.

THE IRA SPECTRUM

Type	Eligibility For Plan	Limits On Contributions[1]	Deductible	Tax Advantages	Withdrawals/Distributions
Roth (page 456)	Individual: AGI[2] less than $110,000 (phase-out $95,000 - $110,000) Married filing jointly: AGI[2] less than $160,000 (phase-out $150,000 - $160,000)	Individual: $3,000. Married filing jointly: $6,000. Contributions allowed after age 70½. Catch-up for individuals who have reached age 50 is $500.	No	Tax-free earnings. Early withdrawals of contributions tax-free and penalty-free.	Tax-free if after 5 years, after age 59½, for first home, disability, or upon death. Distribution *not* required at age 70½.
Traditional - deductible (page 403)	Not active participant in employer-sponsored retirement plan, or Individual: In 2002 AGI[2] less than $44,000 (phase-out $34,000-$44,000). Married filing jointly: In 2002 AGI[2] less than $64,000 (phase-out $54,000-$64,000).	Individual: $3,000. Married filing jointly: $6,000. Contributions *not* allowed after age 70½. Catch-up for individuals who have reached age 50 is $500.	Yes	Tax-deferred earnings, but taxable upon withdrawal.	Penalty-free if after age 59½, for first home, higher education, or upon death. Distribution required at age 70½.
SIMPLE (page 466)	Self-employed or employed by company with 100 employees or less.	Employer: 3% matching or 2% non-elective. Employee: $7,000. Catch-up for individuals who have reached age 50 is $500.	Contributions are before taxes.	Tax-deferred earnings, but withdrawals taxable.	Required at later of age 70½ or retirement.
SEP (page 467)	Self-employed or employed by company with 25 employees or less.	Up to 25% of employees salary or $40,000 maximum. Catch-up for individuals who have reached age 50 is $1,000.	Contributions are before taxes.	Tax-deferred earnings, but withdrawals taxable.	Required at later of age 70½ or retirement.

[1] Combined annual contributions to both Roth IRA and Traditional IRA are limited to $3,000 or $6,000.
[2] AGI stands for adjusted gross income.

WHICH IRA — ROTH OR TRADITIONAL?

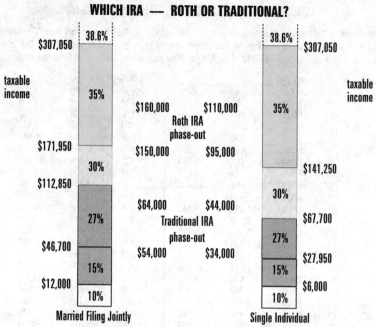

Married Filing Jointly   **Single Individual**

A Roth IRA offers the following potential advantages: (1) if used for higher education expenses, withdrawals can be made prior to age 59½ without penalty; (2) distributions are not required at age 70½; (3) contributions may continue after reaching age 70½; (4) phaseout limits are higher than those for deductible contributions to a Traditional IRA; and (5) tax-free retirement distributions will not push modified adjusted gross income above the threshold that triggers taxation of Social Security benefits (see page 468). This analysis focuses on after-tax accumulations and requires assumptions regarding tax rates prior to and after retirement (the above chart may help).

Assuming the **same** tax rate prior to and after retirement: (1) there is no difference between the after-tax distributions from a Roth IRA and a Traditional IRA if all funds can be deposited in a Traditional IRA, or other tax deductible fund (see Table A, page 302); (2) the Roth IRA offers the advantage of larger after-tax distributions if before-tax funds exceed the $3,000 limit that can be deposited in a Traditional IRA and the excess must be placed in a nondeductible side fund (see Table B, page 302). Further, the Roth IRA advantage increases if the side fund earnings are currently taxed.

Assuming a **lower** tax rate after retirement the Traditional IRA generally provides larger after-tax distributions (i.e., 27 percent prior to retirement and 15 percent after retirement). For active participants, no comparison need be made assuming a tax rate higher than 27 percent since deductible contributions to a Traditional IRA are phased out before reaching the 30 percent tax rate (i.e., no deduction is allowed in 2002 for "married filing jointly" once modified adjusted gross income exceeds $64,000 and for a "single individual" once modified adjusted gross income exceeds $44,000). Note that marginal tax rates in the above chart vary according to *taxable income*, whereas IRA contributions are phased out according to *modified adjusted gross income* (see pages 298, 300, 403, 456 and 492). Taxable income is equal to adjusted gross income less deductions and personal exemptions.

Assuming a **higher** tax rate after retirement, the Roth IRA provides larger after-tax distributions (e.g., 27 percent prior to retirement and 30 percent after retirement).

WHICH IRA — ROTH OR TRADITIONAL? (continued)

Table A – This table assumes an 8 percent interest rate and 27 percent tax rate. The nondeductible Roth IRA deposit requires $1,370 before taxes ($1,000/(1 - .27) = $1,370). This is the same as making a deductible deposit of $1,370 to a Traditional IRA. There is no Roth IRA advantage.

	Roth IRA			Traditional IRA		
Year	Deposit	Plus Interest	Value	Deposit	Plus Interest	Value
1	1,000	80	1,080	1,370	110	1,479
2	1,000	166	2,246	1,370	228	3,077
3	1,000	260	3,506	1,370	356	4,803
4	1,000	360	4,867	1,370	494	6,667
5	1,000	469	6,336	1,370	643	8,679
6	1,000	587	7,923	1,370	804	10,853
7	1,000	714	9,637	1,370	978	13,201
8	1,000	851	11,488	1,370	1,166	15,736
9	1,000	999	13,487	1,370	1,368	18,475
10	1,000	1,159	15,645	1,370	1,588	21,432
11	1,000	1,332	17,977	1,370	1,824	24,626
12	1,000	1,518	20,495	1,370	2,080	28,076
13	1,000	1,720	23,215	1,370	2,356	31,801
14	1,000	1,937	26,152	1,370	2,654	35,825
15	1,000	2,172	29,324	1,370	2,976	40,170
16	1,000	2,426	32,750	1,370	3,323	44,863
17	1,000	2,700	36,450	1,370	3,699	49,932
18	1,000	2,996	40,446	1,370	4,104	55,406
19	1,000	3,316	44,762	1,370	4,542	61,318
20	1,000	3,661	49,423	1,370	5,015	67,703
Less Taxes			0			18,280
Net Distribution			49,423			49,423

Table B – This table assumes an 8 percent interest rate and 27 percent tax rate. The nondeductible Roth IRA deposit requires $4,110 before taxes ($3,000/(1 - .27) = $4,110). This is the same as making a deductible deposit of $3,000 to a Traditional IRA *plus* a nondeductible deposit of $810 to a Side Fund ($3,000 + $810/(1 - .27) = $4,110). The Roth IRA advantage is $9,034 when compared to a currently taxed side fund ($148,269 - $108,236 - $30,999 = $9,034) and $6,435 when compared to a tax deferred side fund ($148,269 - $108,236 - $33,598 = $6,435).

	Roth IRA		Traditional IRA		Side Fund		
Year	Deposit	Value	Deposit	Value	Deposit	Currently Taxed	Tax Deferred
1	3,000	3,240	3,000	3,240	810	857	875
2	3,000	6,739	3,000	6,739	810	1,765	1,820
3	3,000	10,518	3,000	10,518	810	2,725	2,840
4	3,000	14,600	3,000	14,600	810	3,741	3,942
5	3,000	19,008	3,000	19,008	810	4,817	5,132
6	3,000	23,768	3,000	23,768	810	5,956	6,417
7	3,000	28,910	3,000	28,910	810	7,161	7,806
8	3,000	34,463	3,000	34,463	810	8,437	9,305
9	3,000	40,460	3,000	40,460	810	9,787	10,924
10	3,000	46,936	3,000	46,936	810	11,215	12,673
11	3,000	53,931	3,000	53,931	810	12,728	14,561
12	3,000	61,486	3,000	61,486	810	14,328	16,601
13	3,000	69,645	3,000	69,645	810	16,022	18,804
14	3,000	78,456	3,000	78,456	810	17,815	21,183
15	3,000	87,973	3,000	87,973	810	19,713	23,753
16	3,000	98,251	3,000	98,251	810	21,722	26,528
17	3,000	109,351	3,000	109,351	810	23,847	29,525
18	3,000	121,339	3,000	121,339	810	26,097	32,761
19	3,000	134,286	3,000	134,286	810	28,479	36,257
20	3,000	148,269	3,000	148,269	810	30,999	40,333
Less Taxes		0		40,033		0	6,435
Net Distribution		148,269		108,236		30,999	33,598

EDUCATIONAL TAX INCENTIVES
Contributions, Benefits & Offsets

Incentive	Limit	Tax Nature	Covers	AGI Phaseout[1]	Offsets
Hope Scholarship Credit (§25A)	1,500	Credit against taxes.	First two years of post-secondary education.	S: 41,000-51,000 J: 82,000-102,000	A B C D
Lifetime Learning Credit (§25A)	1,000[2]	Credit against taxes.	Unlimited number of years.		
Trade or Business Expense (§162)	None.	Below-line deduction (must itemize).	Employee expenses in maintaining or improving skills.	S: 68,650 J: 137,300	n/a
Education Expenses (§222)	3,000	Above-line deduction (need not itemize).	Qualified educational expenses.	S: 65,000 J: 130,000	A
Employer Tuition Reimbursement (§127)	5,250	Not included in income.	Covers both undergraduate and graduate programs.	None.	B
Coverdell Education Savings Account (§530)	2,000	Contributions not deductible; but earnings are tax-free.	Qualified education expenses.[3]	S: 95,000-110,000 J: 190,000-220,000	C
Student Loans (§221)	2,500	Above-line deduction for interest (need not itemize).	Student loan interest.	S: 50,000-65,000 J: 100,000-130,000	n/a
Section 529 Plans	Varies.	Contributions not deductible; but distributions are tax-free.[4]	Tuition, fees, special-needs services, room, board, books, supplies and equipment.	None.	D
Educational Savings Bonds (§135)	Varies.	Interest tax-free.	Qualified educational expenses.	S: 57,600-72,600 J: 86,400-116,400	n/a

A – Hope Scholarship and Lifetime Learning Credits are not available if Education Expense (§222) deduction is taken.

B – Hope Scholarship and Lifetime Learning Credits are not available for the same expense excluded as an Employer Tuition Reimbursement.

C – Earnings on Coverdell Education Savings Account are not tax-free if used for same expenses as Hope Scholarship and Lifetime Learning Credits.

D – Section 529 qualifying expenses are reduced to the extent they are used in determining Hope Scholarship and Lifetime Learning Credits.

[1] S – single taxpayer; J – married filing joint return.
[2] Increases to $2,000 beginning in 2003.
[3] Includes elementary and secondary education (K-12) at private, public, or religious institutions, and post secondary education at accredited public, nonprofit, and proprietary institutions (college and graduate programs).
[4] Applies to state-sponsored programs. Earnings portion of distributions from private prepaid educational arrangements will be taxable until 2004.

HISTORICAL INCREASES OF SOCIAL SECURITY TAXES

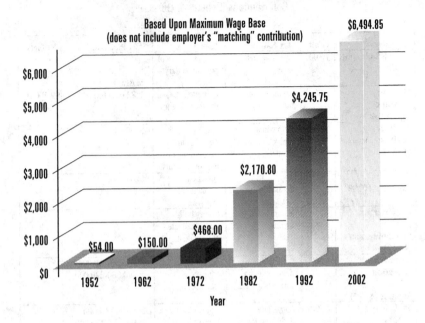

Based Upon Maximum Wage Base
(does not include employer's "matching" contribution)

Social Security Tax

The Social Security Tax (FICA) is paid by both the employer and the employee. For example, in 2002 an employer who pays an employee wages of $84,900 per year will pay an additional $6,494.85 (7.65 percent of $84,900) in Social Security Taxes. The employee must also pay $6,494.85. In 2002, $84,900 is the maximum amount of wages on which the 6.20% OASDI tax is paid by both the employer and the employee. However, there is no maximum amount for the 1.45% hospital insurance tax; all wages are subject to that tax.

Federal Unemployment Tax

In addition to these Social Security Taxes, Unemployment Taxes may have to be paid. In 2002, the Federal Unemployment Tax (FUTA) is 6.2 percent of the first $7,000 of wages paid to each employee, or $434 (credit is given to employers for contributions to state unemployment funds).

Self-Employment Tax

An individual who is self-employed must pay a Self-Employment Tax on net earnings from self-employment when these earnings are $400 or more. The tax is equal to the combined employer-employee Social Security tax and is 12.40% OASDI tax on the first $84,900 of self-employment income in 2002, or a maximum tax of $10,527.60, plus 2.90% hospital insurance tax on all self-employment income in 2002. Self-employed individuals may deduct one-half of their self-employment taxes for income tax purposes as a trade or business expense. This is the "Social Security Tax" for people who work for themselves.

SOCIAL SECURITY PAYROLL TAXES
Taxes in Future Years Subject to Change, Generally Upward!

Year	Maximum Tax Rate	Maximum Taxable Earnings	Tax
1959	2.5	4,800	120.00
1960-61	3.0	4,800	144.00
1962	3.125	4,800	150.00
1963-65	3.625	4,800	174.00
1966	4.2	6,600	277.20
1967	4.4	6,600	290.40
1968	4.4	7,800	343.20
1969-70	4.8	7,800	374.40
1971	5.2	7,800	405.60
1972	5.2	9,000	468.00
1973	5.85	10,800	631.80
1974	5.85	13,200	772.20
1975	5.85	14,100	824.85
1976	5.85	15,300	895.05
1977	5.85	16,500	965.25
1978	6.05	17,700	1,070.85
1979	6.13	22,900	1,403.77
1980	6.13	25,900	1,587.67
1981	6.65	29,700	1,975.05
1982	6.7	32,400	2,170.80
1983	6.7	35,700	2,391.90
1984	7.0	37,800	2,532.60
1985	7.05	39,600	2,791.80
1986	7.15	42,000	3,003.00
1987	7.15	43,800	3,131.70
1988	7.51	45,000	3,379.50
1989	7.51	48,000	3,604.80
1990	7.65	51,300	3,924.45
1991	7.65	53,400	4,085.10
1992	7.65	55,500	4,245.75
1993	7.65	57,600	4,406.40
1994	7.65	60,600	4,635.90
1995	7.65	61,200	4,681.80
1996	7.65	62,700	4,796.55
1997	7.65	65,400	5,003.10
1998	7.65	68,400	5,232.60
1999	7.65	72,600	5,553.90
2000	7.65	76,200	5,829.30
2001	7.65	80,400	6,150.60
2002	7.65	84,900	6,494.85

Note: All earnings above $84,900 are subject to an additional 1.45% hospital insurance tax (see page 304). The first tax was imposed in 1937. The rate was 1.0% on maximum taxable earnings of $3,000, producing a tax of $30.00.

SOCIAL SECURITY RETIREMENT BENEFITS
When To Take

Social Security retirement benefits are based upon the worker's primary insurance amount (PIA). The PIA is the monthly amount that would be paid to a worker who receives benefits at normal retirement age. The normal retirement age differs, depending upon the worker's year of birth.

Year of birth	Normal Retirement Age	Year of birth	Normal Retirement Age
Before 1938	65 years	1955	66 years, 2 months
1939	65 years, 2 months	1956	66 years, 4 months
1940	65 years, 6 months	1957	66 years, 6 months
1941	65 years, 8 months	1958	66 years, 8 months
1942	65 years, 10 months	1959	66 years, 10 months
1943-1954	66 years	1960 and after	67 years

A worker can take retirement benefits as early as age 62, but the amount received is calculated by reducing the PIA by 5/9 of 1 percent per month for the first 36 months, plus 5/12 of 1 percent for any additional months. For example, a worker taking payments three years prior to normal retirement age will receive only 80 percent of his PIA (i.e., 100 - (5/9 x 36) = 80). In addition, a worker who no longer pays social security taxes fails to increase his PIA.

Many authorities agree that, for the average worker, it is best to wait until normal retirement age to order to take full (unreduced) retirement benefits. Despite this, Social Security records indicate that well over 50 percent of retiring workers take early (reduced) benefits. Clearly, if life expectancy is less than average, then taking an early benefit is indicated. However, if an individual is in good health, and does not require the money to provide for retirement, the following table may assist in making the decision:

Cross Over Point Based Upon Life Expectancy*			
Discount Rate	When Reached	Discount Rate	When Reached
0%	14 yr, 0 mo	6%	17 yr, 10 mo
2%	15 yr, 3 mo	8%	19 yr, 3 mo
4%	16 yr, 6 mo	10%	20 yr, 8 mo

* Assumes payments begin 36 months prior to normal retirement age, and Social Security benefit increases of 2.6 percent per year (the average increase during the 10-year period 1993-2002).

This table compares the present values of the income streams produced by reduced (early) and unreduced (normal) retirement benefits. For example, using a discount rate of 4%, at 16 years and 6 months the present values of both reduced and unreduced retirement payments are approximately equal; assuming retirement three years prior to normal retirement age, and 2.6 percent annual increases in retirement benefits (i.e., after this cross over point, the present value of the unreduced benefits will exceed the present value of the reduced benefits). Absent other considerations, a person who views the time value of money at 4% should consider early retirement if he expects to live *less than* 16 years and 6 months. On the other hand, if he expects to live *more than* 16 years and 6 months, he should wait until normal retirement. See also, Compound Discount & Present Value of Money, page 504.

CONSUMER PRICE INDEX

(annual average)

Year	Yearly Increase	Cumulative Increase	Purchasing Power of the Dollar
1981	10.3	90.9	1.10
1982	6.2	96.5	1.04
1983	3.2	99.6	1.00
1984	4.3	103.9	.96
1985	3.6	107.6	.93
1986	1.9	109.6	.91
1987	3.6	113.6	.88
1988	4.1	118.3	.85
1989	4.8	124.0	.81
1990	5.4	130.7	.77
1991	4.2	136.2	.73
1992	3.0	140.3	.71
1993	3.0	144.5	.69
1994	2.6	148.2	.68
1995	2.8	152.4	.66
1996	3.0	156.9	.64
1997	2.3	160.5	.62
1998	1.6	163.0	.61
1999	2.2	166.6	.60
2000	3.4	172.2	.58
2001	2.8	177.1	.56

Source: Bureau of Labor Statistics, Washington, D.C., and Statistical Abstract of the United States, 2001, Table 691 on page 451 and Table 692 on page 453. The Consumer Price Index (CPI) is a measure of the average change in prices over time in a fixed "market basket" of goods and services purchased by urban consumers. The items include food, clothing, shelter, fuels, transportation, fares, charges for doctors' and dental services, drugs, etc. purchased for day-to-living. The reference base year is the 1982-84 period (i.e., 1982-84 = 100).

DECLINING VALUE OF A DOLLAR

The Ever-Increasing Costs Of The Things We Buy
What Will They Cost 20 Years From Now?

1934

- Franklin Roosevelt was President
- Greyhound cuts business fares in half to $8 between NY and Chicago
- 4.7 million families are on relief
- Los Angeles Farmers Market opens, booths cost 50¢ a day

Population	126,485,000
Single Family House	$5,972
Per Capita Income	$427
Ford Deluxe Coupe	$590
Bread, per loaf	8¢
Milk, one-half gallon	22¢
Steak (sirloin), 1 pound	32¢
New York Times	2¢
First-Class Postage	2¢

1954

- Dwight Eisenhower was President
- RCA introduces first color television set
- First nuclear-powered submarine, *Nautilus*, launched
- New York subway fare is 15 cents

Population	163,026,000
Single Family House	$10,625
Per Capita Income	$1,787
Ford Sedan, 4-door	$2,163
Bread, per pound	17¢
Milk, one-half gallon	46¢
Steak (round), 1 pound	91¢
New York Times	5¢
First-Class Postage	3¢

1974

- Richard Nixon was President
- 3M develops Post-it to stick paper to paper
- Pocket calculator marketed
- Highway speed lowered to 55 mph
- Richard Nixon resigns Presidency

Population	213,854,000
Single Family House	$35,900
Per Capita Income	$5,637
Ford LTD	$3,999
Bread, per pound	34¢
Milk, one-half gallon	78¢
Steak (round), 1 pound	$1.80
New York Times	15¢
First-Class Postage	10¢

1994

- Bill Clinton was President
- Shuttle crew repairs Hubble space telescope
- Jury awards 2.9 million dollars to woman for burns from hot coffee
- World Series cancelled by strike

Population	260,651,000
Single Family House	$130,000
Per Capita Income	$21,846
Ford Taurus GL	$15,699
Bread, per pound	75¢
Milk, one-half gallon	$1.44
Steak (round), 1 pound	$3.24
New York Times	50¢
First-Class Postage	29¢

Without Adequate Planning, Inflation Can Threaten Your Long-Term Financial Security

Sources: Events in 1934, 1954 and 1974, *The Value Of A Dollar*, Detroit, Gale Research, 1994, pages 229, 348 and 465. Population of the United States, *Statistical Abstracts of the United States (Statistical Abstracts)*, 1958, Table 2 on page 5, and *Statistical Abstracts*, 1995, Table 2 on page 8. Cost of single family house in 1934, *Historical Statistics of the United States, Colonial Times to 1970 (Historical Statistics)*, Series N 259-261 on page 647. Cost of single family house in 1954, 1974 and 1994, *Statistical Abstracts*, 1958, Table 998 on page 759, and *Statistical Abstracts*, 1995, Table 1216 on page 730. Per capita income, *Historical Statistics*, Series F 17-30 on page 225, and *Statistical Abstracts*, 1995, Table 706 on page 456. Prices of Ford automobiles, Ford Archives, Detroit, Michigan, and *The Atlanta Constitution*, January 2, 1974, page 21B, and *The Atlanta Constitution*, January 7, 1994, page 27S. Cost of bread, milk and steak (rounded to nearest penny), *Statistical Abstracts*, 1937, Table 352 on page 309, *Statistical Abstracts*, 1958, Table 424 on page 336, *Statistical Abstracts*, 1978, Table 801 on page 497, and *Statistical Abstracts*, 1995, Table 777 on page 507.

PROJECTED EARNINGS

5% Annual Increase In Earnings

Present	Yearly Earnings In				Total Earnings Over Next	
Earnings	5 Years	10 Years	15 Years	20 Years	10 Years	20 Years
10,000	12,763	16,289	20,789	26,533	125,779	330,660
12,000	15,315	19,547	24,947	31,840	150,935	396,791
14,000	17,868	22,805	29,105	37,146	176,090	462,923
16,000	20,421	26,062	33,263	42,453	201,246	529,055
18,000	22,973	29,320	37,421	47,759	226,402	595,187
20,000	25,526	32,578	41,579	53,066	251,558	661,319
25,000	31,907	40,722	51,973	66,332	314,447	826,649
30,000	38,288	48,867	62,368	79,599	377,337	991,979
35,000	44,670	57,011	72,762	92,865	440,226	1,157,308
40,000	51,051	65,156	83,157	106,132	503,116	1,322,638
45,000	57,433	73,300	93,552	119,398	566,005	1,487,968
50,000	63,814	81,445	103,946	132,665	628,895	1,653,298
60,000	76,577	97,734	124,736	159,198	754,674	1,983,957
70,000	89,340	114,023	145,525	185,731	880,452	2,314,617
80,000	102,103	130,312	166,314	212,264	1,006,231	2,645,276
90,000	114,865	146,601	187,104	238,797	1,132,010	2,975,936
100,000	127,628	162,889	207,893	265,330	1,257,789	3,306,595

8% Annual Increase In Earnings

Present	Yearly Earnings In				Total Earnings Over Next	
Earnings	5 Years	10 Years	15 Years	20 Years	10 Years	20 Years
10,000	14,693	21,589	31,722	46,610	144,866	457,620
12,000	17,632	25,907	38,066	55,931	173,839	549,144
14,000	20,571	30,225	44,410	65,253	202,812	640,667
16,000	23,509	34,543	50,755	74,575	231,785	732,191
18,000	26,448	38,861	57,099	83,897	260,758	823,715
20,000	29,387	43,178	63,443	93,219	289,731	915,239
25,000	36,733	53,973	79,304	116,524	362,164	1,144,049
30,000	44,080	64,768	95,165	139,829	434,597	1,372,859
35,000	51,426	75,562	111,026	163,133	507,030	1,601,669
40,000	58,773	86,357	126,887	186,438	579,462	1,830,479
45,000	66,120	97,152	142,748	209,743	651,895	2,059,288
50,000	73,466	107,946	158,608	233,048	724,328	2,288,098
60,000	88,160	129,535	190,330	279,657	869,194	2,745,718
70,000	102,853	151,125	222,052	326,267	1,014,059	3,203,337
80,000	117,546	172,714	253,774	372,877	1,158,925	3,660,957
90,000	132,240	194,303	285,495	419,486	1,303,791	4,118,577
100,000	146,933	215,892	317,217	466,096	1,448,656	4,576,196

Explanation of Tables. These tables assume that earnings increase at an annual rate of either 5 or 8 percent. For example, at annual increases of 5 percent an individual earning $50,000 today would be earning $81,445 in 10 Years, and total earnings over 10 Years would be $628,895. Projected earnings are also considered in the discussion of Human Life Value on page 14.

PENALTY OF WAITING

What It Takes To Save $100,000 By Age 65
Assuming 6% Interest

Current Age	Monthly Deposit	Total Deposits	Penalty Of Waiting 1 Year	Penalty Of Waiting 5 Years
21	40.42	21,342	877	4,707
22	43.06	22,219	905	4,867
23	45.88	23,124	945	5,043
24	48.92	24,069	973	5,208
25	52.17	25,042	1,007	5,387
26	55.66	26,049	1,037	5,567
27	59.40	27,086	1,081	5,758
28	63.44	28,167	1,110	5,944
29	67.77	29,277	1,152	6,137
30	72.45	30,429	1,187	6,334
31	77.49	31,616	1,228	6,535
32	82.94	32,844	1,267	6,740
33	88.83	34,111	1,303	6,950
34	95.20	35,414	1,349	7,168
35	102.12	36,763	1,388	7,382
36	109.63	38,151	1,433	7,604
37	117.81	39,584	1,477	7,830
38	126.73	41,061	1,521	8,059
39	136.48	42,582	1,563	8,289
40	147.15	44,145	1,610	8,528
41	158.87	45,755	1,659	8,769
42	171.79	47,414	1,706	9,010
43	186.06	49,120	1,751	9,257
44	201.87	50,871	1,802	9,507
45	219.47	52,673	1,851	9,760
46	239.14	54,524	1,900	10,017
47	261.22	56,424	1,953	10,277
48	286.16	58,377	2,001	10,536
49	314.47	60,378	2,055	10,800
50	346.85	62,433	2,108	11,067
51	384.17	64,541	2,160	11,338
52	427.57	66,701	2,212	11,610
53	478.56	68,913	2,265	11,878
54	539.23	71,178	2,322	12,160
55	612.50	73,500	2,379	12,433
56	702.58	75,879	2,432	12,697
57	815.74	78,311	2,480	12,971
58	961.80	80,791	2,547	13,268
59	1,157.47	83,338	2,595	13,542
60	1,432.21	85,933	2,643	14,067

Explanation of Table: This table shows the amount of money which must be deposited at the beginning of each month in order to accumulate $100,000 by age 65. Interest is credited at a 6 percent net annual rate and is compounded monthly (i.e., it is credited at the end of each month assuming a 6 percent annual after tax or untaxed growth). The Penalty Of Waiting 1 Year is calculated by subtracting total deposits at the current age from total deposits one year later (e.g., at age 45 the penalty of waiting one year is $54,524 - $52,673, or $1,851). The Penalty Of Waiting 5 Years is calculated by subtracting total deposits at the current age from total deposits five years later (e.g., at age 45 the penalty of waiting five years is $62,433 - $52,673, or $9,760).

EARLY SAVER vs. LATE SAVER

The Advantage Of Saving Early For Retirement
Assuming 8% Interest

Age	Early Saver	Late Saver	Age	Early Saver	Late Saver	Age	Early Saver	Late Saver
30	$2,000	0						
31	2,000	0						
32	2,000	0						
33	2,000	0						
34	2,000	0						
35	2,000	0						
36	2,000	0						
37	2,000	0						
38	2,000	0						
39	2,000	0						
40	0	$2,000	40	$2,000	0			
41	0	2,000	41	2,000	0			
42	0	2,000	42	2,000	0			
43	0	2,000	43	2,000	0			
44	0	2,000	44	2,000	0			
45	0	2,000	45	2,000	0			
46	0	2,000	46	2,000	0			
47	0	2,000	47	2,000	0			
48	0	2,000	48	0	$2,000			
49	0	2,000	49	0	2,000	50	$2,000	0
50	0	2,000	50	0	2,000	51	2,000	0
51	0	2,000	51	0	2,000	52	2,000	0
52	0	2,000	52	0	2,000	53	2,000	0
53	0	2,000	53	0	2,000	54	2,000	0
54	0	2,000	54	0	2,000	55	2,000	0
55	0	2,000	55	0	2,000	56	0	$2,000
56	0	2,000	56	0	2,000	57	0	2,000
57	0	2,000	57	0	2,000	58	0	2,000
58	0	2,000	58	0	2,000	59	0	2,000
59	0	2,000	59	0	2,000	60	0	2,000
60	0	2,000	60	0	2,000	61	0	2,000
61	0	2,000	61	0	2,000	62	0	2,000
62	0	2,000	62	0	2,000	63	0	2,000
63	0	2,000	63	0	2,000	64	0	2,000
64	0	2,000	64	0	2,000			
Total Invested	$20,000	$50,000		$16,000	$34,000		$12,000	$18,000
Amount At Age 65	$214,296	$157,909		$85,008	$72,900		$31,676	$26,973

Explanation of Table: This table demonstrates the advantage of beginning to save early for retirement. For example, a 40-year old Early Saver who saves $2,000 per year for eight years, and earns 8 percent per year on his savings, will accumulate $85,008 by age 65. In comparison, a 48-year old Late Saver who saves $2,000 per year until age 65, will accumulate only $72,900. Whereas the Late Saver has invested $18,000 more than the Early Saver, he has accumulated $12,108 less than the Early Saver ($34,000 - $16,000 = $18,000; $85,008 - $72,900 = $12,108). If savings had been placed in a tax deferred investment, then the Amount At Age 65 will likely be reduced by income taxes.

DOLLAR COST AVERAGING

Investing A Fixed Sum At Regular Intervals
means that
More Shares Are Bought At Low Prices Than High Prices
and
Average Cost Is Lower Than Average Share Price

Market Price Fluctuations

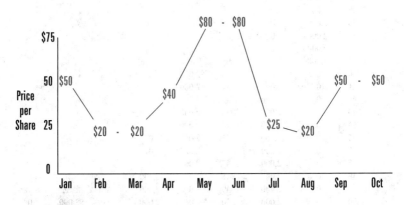

INVESTING FIXED SUM - DOLLAR COST AVERAGING

	Jan	Feb	Mar	Apr	May	Jun	Jul	Aug	Sep	Oct	Totals
Cost	$100	$100	$100	$100	$100	$100	$100	$100	$100	$100	$1,000
Shares	2	5	5	2.5	1.25	1.25	4	5	2	2	30

Average Cost Per Share $33.33

end up
with same
number of
shares

BUYING FIXED NUMBER OF SHARES

	Jan	Feb	Mar	Apr	May	Jun	Jul	Aug	Sep	Oct	Totals
Shares	3	3	3	3	3	3	3	3	3	3	30
Cost	$150	$60	$60	$120	$240	$240	$75	$60	$150	$150	$1,305

Average Cost Per Share $43.50

HOW MONEY GROWS

How Much Monthly Savings Will Accumulate To

Accumulated At 5%

Save Per Month	5 Years	10 Years	20 Years
50	3,414	7,796	20,637
100	6,829	15,593	41,275
250	17,072	38,982	103,187
500	34,145	77,965	206,373
1,000	68,289	155,929	412,746

Accumulated At 8%

Save Per Month	5 Years	10 Years	20 Years
50	3,698	9,208	29,647
100	7,397	18,417	59,295
250	18,492	46,041	148,237
500	36,983	92,083	296,474
1,000	73,967	184,166	592,947

Accumulated At 10%

Save Per Month	5 Years	10 Years	20 Years
50	3,904	10,328	38,285
100	7,808	20,655	76,570
250	19,521	51,638	191,424
500	39,041	103,276	382,848
1,000	78,082	206,552	765,697

Explanation of Table. All accumulations assume monthly contributions are made on the first day of the month with interest compounded monthly. All results are rounded to the nearest whole dollar. Accumulated amounts assume the funds are invested at a rate of 5, 8 or 10 percent *before taxes* (i.e., during the accumulation phase appreciation is not subject to current income taxation). For example, if an individual invested $100 per month and earned 8 percent compounded monthly, at the end of 10 years the funds would accumulate to $18,417. Referring to the table How Money Goes on page 314, if this $18,417 were invested at 5 percent per year compounded monthly, it would provide $195 per month for 10 years or $121 per month for 20 years. Withdrawing interest only without invading principal would provide $77 per month. All withdrawal amounts are before taxes.

HOW MONEY GOES

How Much Can Be Withdrawn Monthly From A Given Accumulation

Amount Accumulated	At 5% Interest			At 8% Interest		
	10 Years	20 Years	Forever	10 Years	20 Years	Forever
3,414	36	22	14	41	28	23
3,698	39	24	15	45	31	25
3,904	41	26	16	47	32	26
6,829	72	45	28	82	57	46
7,397	78	49	31	89	61	49
7,796	82	51	32	94	65	52
7,808	82	51	33	94	65	52
9,208	97	61	38	111	77	61
10,328	109	68	43	124	86	69
15,593	165	102	65	188	130	104
17,072	180	112	71	206	142	114
18,417	195	121	77	222	153	123
18,492	195	122	77	223	154	123
19,521	206	128	81	235	162	130
20,637	218	136	86	249	171	138
20,655	218	136	86	249	172	138
29,647	313	195	124	357	246	198
34,145	361	224	142	412	284	228
36,983	391	243	154	446	307	247
38,285	404	252	160	461	318	255
38,982	412	256	162	470	324	260
39,041	412	257	163	471	324	260
41,275	436	271	172	497	343	275
46,041	486	303	192	555	383	307
51,638	545	339	215	622	429	344
59,295	626	390	247	715	493	395
68,289	721	449	285	823	567	455
73,967	781	486	308	891	615	493
76,570	809	503	319	923	636	510
77,965	824	512	325	940	648	520
78,082	825	513	325	941	649	521
92,083	973	605	384	1,110	765	614
103,187	1,090	678	430	1,244	857	688
103,276	1,091	679	430	1,245	858	689
148,237	1,566	974	618	1,787	1,232	988
155,929	1,647	1,025	650	1,879	1,296	1,040
184,166	1,945	1,210	767	2,220	1,530	1,228
191,424	2,022	1,258	798	2,307	1,591	1,276
206,373	2,180	1,356	860	2,487	1,715	1,376
206,552	2,182	1,357	861	2,489	1,716	1,377
296,474	3,132	1,948	1,235	3,573	2,463	1,976
382,848	4,044	2,516	1,595	4,614	3,181	2,552
412,746	4,360	2,713	1,720	4,975	3,430	2,752
592,947	6,263	3,897	2,471	7,146	4,927	3,953
765,697	8,088	5,032	3,190	9,228	6,362	5,105

Explanation of Table. Withdrawals are assumed to be made at the beginning of each month with interest compounded monthly on the remaining funds invested at either 5 or 8 percent interest. Results are rounded to the nearest whole dollar. All calculations and amounts are before taxes. It is intended that this table be used with the table How Money Grows on page 313 (i.e., first obtain the amount accumulated from How Money Grows then enter this table). See explanation at the bottom of page 313.

HISTORICAL RATES OF RETURN

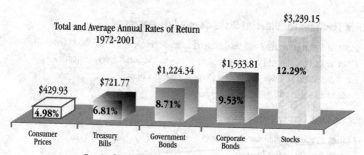

Total and Average Annual Rates of Return
1972-2001

Past Performance is no guarantee of future results.

Year	Consumer Prices	Treasury Bills	Government Bonds	Corporate Bonds	Stocks
1971	100.00	100.00	100.00	100.00	100.00
1972	104.98	106.81	108.71	109.53	112.29
1973	110.21	114.08	118.18	119.96	126.09
1974	115.70	121.85	128.47	131.39	141.59
1975	121.47	130.15	139.65	143.91	159.00
1976	127.52	139.02	151.82	157.63	178.54
1977	133.87	148.48	165.04	172.65	200.49
1978	140.54	158.60	179.41	189.09	225.13
1979	147.54	169.40	195.03	207.11	252.80
1980	154.89	180.93	212.02	226.85	283.88
1981	162.60	193.26	230.48	248.46	318.77
1982	170.70	206.42	250.55	272.13	357.95
1983	179.21	220.48	272.37	298.06	401.95
1984	188.14	235.49	296.09	326.46	451.36
1985	197.51	251.53	321.87	357.57	506.84
1986	207.35	268.66	349.91	391.64	569.14
1987	217.68	286.95	380.38	428.95	639.09
1988	228.52	306.50	413.50	469.83	717.65
1989	239.90	327.37	449.51	514.59	805.86
1990	251.85	349.67	488.66	563.62	904.91
1991	264.40	373.48	531.21	617.32	1,016.14
1992	277.57	398.91	577.47	676.14	1,141.04
1993	291.40	426.08	627.76	740.57	1,281.30
1994	305.92	455.10	682.43	811.13	1,438.79
1995	321.16	486.09	741.86	888.42	1,615.64
1996	337.16	519.20	806.46	973.06	1,814.23
1997	353.95	554.56	876.69	1,065.78	2,037.23
1998	371.58	592.32	953.04	1,167.33	2,287.64
1999	390.09	632.66	1,036.03	1,278.55	2,568.83
2000	409.53	675.75	1,126.26	1,400.38	2,884.58
2001	429.93	721.77	1,224.34	1,533.81	3,239.15

Source: Global Financial Data, Los Angeles, CA, "Total Returns on Bonds and Bills and Inflation in the United States, 1871-2002;" www.globalfindata.com (accessed: March 7, 2002). The base for all calculations is December 31, 1971 = 100. Consumer Prices are based upon the Bureau of Labor's Consumer Price Index. Returns on Treasury Bills uses the yield on 3-month Treasury Bills as found in Board of Governors of the Federal Reserve System, *Federal Reserve Bulletin* (1935-). Returns on Government Bonds uses the Federal Reserve Board's 10-year Treasury Bond index. Returns on Corporate Bonds uses data from Moody's index of yields on AAA Corporate Bonds. The source for returns on Stocks is Standard and Poor's, *Security Price Index Record*, New York (S&P 500 composite).

DISABILITY STATISTICS

Odds This Year For Different Risks Covered By Insurance

1 out of 5 that your auto will be damaged in an accident (National Safety Council).

1 out of 21 that you will have a disabling accident (National Safety Council).

1 out of 96 that you will have a fire (National Safety Council).

1 out of 114 that you will die (World Almanac).

Income Lost Through Disability Is

2 times as great as auto accident losses.

3 times as great as fire losses.

Risk of Disability Is Substantially Greater Than Risk Of Death (Male)

At age 30, long-term disability is 4.1 times more likely than death.

At age 40, long-term disability is 2.9 times more likely than death.

At age 50, long-term disability is 2.2 times more likely than death.

Risk Of Disability Within Groups Of People

The following chart indicates the odds of at least one long-term (90-day) disability occurring before age 65 to any one person out of one, two, or three persons.

Chances out of 1,000 of Disability Occurring Prior to Age 65

Age of Each Person	To Any One Person	To Any One Person out of Any Two People	To Any One Person out of Any Three People
30	467	716	849
35	451	699	835
40	430	675	815
45	401	641	785
50	360	590	738

From the chart we can conclude, for example, that 43 percent of all people age 40 will have a long-term disability prior to age 65.

Long-Term Disabilities

If a long-term (90-day) disability has lasted two years, it will probably continue longer – even for life.

Age When Disabled For 90 Days	Percentage Of People Still Disabled At End Of 2 Years And 90 Days	Percentage Of People Still Disabled At End Of 5 Years And 90 Days
25	63.5%	44.2%
35	69.7	52.6
45	73.6	58.0
55	77.6	59.6

Note: Figures based upon Commissioners Disability Table and Commissioners 1980 Standard Ordinary Mortality Table.

DISABILITY INCOME - TAX CONSIDERATIONS

	PREMIUM PAYMENTS Income Tax Effects As To		PROCEEDS Income Tax Effects As To	
	Employer	Insured	Employer	Insured
NONCONTRIBUTORY PLANS				
Employer pays premium	deductible IRC §162(a)		no effect	
Insured owns policy receives benefit		not taxable IRC §106(a)		taxable
Employer pays premium owns policy receives benefit	not deductible IRC §265		proceeds subject to AMT (see pages 342-344) but deductible when paid to employee	
Insured receives salary		not taxable IRC §106(a)		taxable when received from employer
CONTRIBUTORY PLAN (split-dollar)				
Employer pays part of each premium	deductible IRC §162(a)		no effect	
Insured owns policy pays balance of premium receives benefit		not taxable on employer's contribution		taxable on amount attributable to employer contribution but not taxable on amount attributable to own contribution
NO PLAN NECESSARY				
Employer pays bonus to insured	deductible IRC §162(a)		no effect	
Insured pays premium owns policy receives benefit		taxable as salary IRC §61		not taxable IRC§104(a)(3)

Note: Insured is assumed to be an employee (not partner or sole proprietor).

FACTS ABOUT . . .

Facts About Long-Term Care

An individual who turns age 65 has a 43 percent chance of spending some time in a nursing home. Once in a nursing home, 21 percent will stay for at least five years.

Two-thirds of single people and one-third of married people exhaust their funds after just 13 weeks in a nursing home. Within two years 90 percent will bankrupt themselves.

From East to West, in 2000, nursing home costs ranged from $286.00 per day ($104,390 per year) in Stamford, Connecticut, to $98.00 per day ($35,770 per year) in Garry, Indiana, to $169.00 per day ($61,685 per year) in San Francisco, California.

Facts About Retirement

In the world today, there are as many people alive over age 65 as in all previous history put together. The most rapidly growing segment of our population is the centenarians.

In 1900, 67 percent of individuals over age 65 worked; in 1950 this had fallen to half; and today just one sixth work after age 65. Despite this, the average sum of money Americans have at retirement is approximately $11,000.

According to the Social Security Adminstration, the ratio of "covered workers" (those paying into the system) to each beneficiary will drop from 3.2 in 1995 to 2.0 in 2030. This means that: (1) payroll taxes will have to be increased about 60 percent, or; (2) cash benefits will have to be decreased by about 37.5 percent, or; (3) some combination of (1) and (2).

To maintain his standard of living, a married wage earner (age 65, with spouse age 62) earning $50,000 annually prior to retirement will have to replace 35 percent of preretirement income (if earnings are $90,000, this increases to 57 percent). A single wage earner earning $50,000 will have to replace 42 percent of preretirement income (if earnings are $90,000, this increases to 65 percent).

Source of Facts About Long Term Care: Jeff Sadler, *The Long Term Care Handbook*, 2nd ed., Cincinnati: The National Underwriter Company, 1998; and Jeff Sadler, How To Sell Long-Term Care Insurance, 1st ed., Cincinnati: The National Underwriter Company, 2001.

Sources of Facts About Retirement: Walter M. Bortz II, M.D., *Dare To Be 100*, New York: Simon & Shuster, 1996, pages 23, 36 and 189; Craig S. Karpel, *The Retirement Myth*, New York: HarperCollins, 1995, page 11; Bruce A. Palmer, "Retirement Income Replacement Ratios: An Update," *Benefits Quarterly*, Second Quarter, 1994, page 68.

TABLE OF CONTENTS

MEDIA REFERENCES

Motivational

"A man's success is measured by the amount he can borrow. When he dies, his measure of success is now the amount his widow is able to repay."

> Judge Michael A. Telesca, "Estate Planning: A View From The Bench," *National Underwriter*, July 10, 1976, page2017.

"Two weeks of solid work on his estate may be worth more to an executive than his financial gains of the past ten to fifteen years."

> Joseph D. Coughlan, "Executive Blindspot," *Price Waterhouse Review*, Autumn 1966, pages 38-39.

"The legal right of a taxpayer to decrease the amount of what otherwise would be his taxes, or altogether avoid them, by means which the law permits, cannot be doubted."

> Mr. Justice Sutherland in the United States Supreme Court case of *Gregory v. Helvering*, 293 U.S. 465 (1935), page 469.

"As a teacher, advisor and consultant to many closely held businesses, I am convinced that the privately held company is an endangered species. The threat lies not so much from competition, regulatory legislation, consumer movement or other outside forces. The real threat to the private business lies primarily within the business practices and policies of its owners."

> Léon A. Danco, Beyond Survival – A Business Owner's Guide For Success. Cleveland: The University Press, 1975, pages 4-5.

"It may seem flattering when a friend or relative asks you to be the executor of his or her estate, but the task involves heavy responsibilities. To minimize complications, sit down with this person as soon as possible and ask: Where is the will? Two thirds of all Americans die without one."

> "News You Can Use – Acting As Executor: Be Ready," *U.S. News & World Report*, November 3, 1986, page 80.

Motivational

"The Robbie family likely must sell part of the Miami Dolphins to pay hefty estate taxes due this summer, a lawyer for two of Joe Robbie's children told a judge Thursday. . . . '[T]he biggest issue facing the Robbie children is not who gets what. . . . The fundamental problem here is taxes, and not enough money to pay them. . . . Selling part of the Dolphins is a likely probability unless we can find some money.' . . . [N]ow that both parents are dead, the Robbie children now must divide the estate and pay federal estate taxes. Estate taxes can be as high as 55 percent."

> David Satterfield, "Robbie Tax Bill May Force Sale Of Dolphin Stake,"
> *The Miami Herald*, January 10, 1992, page 1C.

"Kentucky could lose a multi-million-dollar collection of John Audubon's artwork if the state can't find a way to buy it from the famed naturalist's heirs. Audubon's four great-great-great-granddaughters face crushing inheritance taxes and plan to sell the rare paintings, which their family has leased to the state's Audubon Park Museum in Henderson, Ky., for decades. The possible dispersal of the treasures has auction houses drooling and state officials scrambling for money in the middle of a severe budget crunch. Losing the art would be devastating to the Henderson museum, which is finishing a $2.2 million renovation project aimed at protecting and preserving Audubon's works."

> Eric Gregory, "Tax Bill Imperils Art Collection," *The Atlanta Constitution*, February 10, 1993, page A3.

"Tryggvi McDonald, the 22-year-old son of the late 7th District Congressman Larry McDonald, did not return to the University of Georgia this semester for two reasons, he said in a telephone interview Tuesday. 'I can't afford to go to school,' young McDonald said, 'They've closed all my father's accounts, and they say there is no will.' . . . Congress voted this month to grant [Congressman McDonald's wife] a year's salary – $69,800 – but aides say she will get no pension because Congressman McDonald had not signed up for the available congressional pension plan."

> "Tryggvi McDonald Tries To Carry On," *The East Cobb Neighbor*, November 10, 1983, page 6B.

Motivational

"When there is an income tax, the just man will pay more and the unjust less on the same amount of income." – Plato, circa 390 B.C.

"The art of taxation consists in so plucking the goose as to obtain the largest possible amount of feathers with the smallest possible amount of hissing." – Jean Baptiste Colbert, attributed, circa 1665.

"If Patrick Henry thought that taxation without representation was bad, he should see how bad it is with representation." – The Old Farmer's Almanac.

"I'm proud to be paying taxes in the United States. The only thing is – I could be just as proud for half the money." – Arthur Godfrey, 1951.

"In this world nothing is certain but death and taxes." – Benjamin Franklin, 1789.

> The above quotations were obtained from: Al Cole, "Presidents and tax reform," *Modern Maturity,* April-May, 1993, page 11.

"The survival rate for family firms for a first- to second-generation transfer runs about 30%. For firms that stay in the family from the second to third generation, that number drops to 4%. For the fourth-generation transfer that put the company in my hands, it's a fraction of 1%. . . . According to a recent Gallup Poll, one-third of all small-business owners will have to sell outright or liquidate a part of their firm to pay estate taxes. Of those who have to liquidate to pay the Internal Revenue Service, half expect they'll have to eliminate 30 or more jobs. Another 20% of those firms put the number of employees they'll have to let go as high as 100 or more."

> David Pankonin, "Will Uncle Sam Inherit the Family Business?," *The Wall Street Journal,* November 28, 1995, page A15.

"[Having just won $770,000 in a double or nothing payoff at a craps table of the Horseshoe Club in Las Vegas, the gambler was heard to say:] 'You know . . . . this damned inflation was just eroding this money. I figured I might as well double it or lose it.' Having protected himself against the ravages of inflation, he drove off into the night."

> "Double or Nothing – $770,000 Rides on a Roll of the Dice," *The Washington Post,* September 26, 1980, page A1.

Motivational

"Keep in mind, Social Security benefits are not intended to meet all your financial needs. For example, when you retire, you'll probably need other income, such as savings or a pension."

> Shirley S. Chater, Commissioner of Social Security, in a letter addressed to individuals who are (or soon will be) age 60, November 27, 1996.

"Certainly, emphatically nothing should be left for the government to come in and plunder. . . . the idea that some clown in Washington will lay claim to the product of my life's energies, just because I wasn't smart or careful enough to divest myself of my property (to my family and chosen charities), fills me with horror. . . . I feel no debt of gratitude to the IRS for their gentle shepherding through life, and I choose passionately to leave nothing for them to pick over."

> Walter M. Bortz II, M.D., *Dare To Be 100*, New York: Simon & Schuster, 1996, pages 192 and 263.

"How large a role a 'bequest motive' plays for the compulsory accumulators who make our economy go round has been debated by economists. The contortions the wealthy go through to avoid the federal estate tax suggest it must be important. . . . The federal estate tax is torture to these people. It hovers over their heads and their lifelong exertions like the angel of death and redistribution. What somebody spent a lifetime creating can be, and often is, sucked up and splattered way in 12 seconds of federal pork barrel."

> Holman W. Jenkins, Jr., *Tax the Rich, Nuke the Poor*, The Wall Street Journal, May 27, 1997, page A19.

"'Would you tell me, please, which way I ought to go from here?' 'That depends a good deal on where you want to get to,' said the Cat. 'I don't much care where –' said Alice. 'Then it doesn't matter which way you go,' said the Cat."

> Lewis Carroll, *Alice's Adventures in Wonderland*, 1865.

"If you get up early, work late, and pay your taxes, you will get ahead – if you strike oil."

> J. Paul Getty, oil billionaire reputed to be the richest man in the world at the time of his death in 1976.

Motivational – Responses To EGTRRA 2001

"[EGTRRA 2001 is] the strangest, most reckless, most — well — hilarious estate tax law ever. Laughter is the only rational response."

> Jane Bryant Quinn, "The Estate Tax That Won't Stand Still," *The Washington Post*, June 24, 2001, page H2.

"It is hard to recall any other legislation that has been so widely regarded as flawed from its inception as the estate and GST tax repeal provisions of the 2001 Act."

> Ronald D. Aucutt, "Still Debating the Prospects for Estate Tax Repeal," *Estate Planning*, August 2001, page 388.

"[Regarding the drafting of legal documents] I think one has to be crazy to have opinions this quickly, because it takes years of debate to sort these things out (we had over 50 years to smooth out marital deduction planning.) But obviously discussion has to start somewhere. . . ."

> Jeffey Dennis-Strathmeyer, "Re: Drafting under HR 1836," ABA-PTL archives, June 2, 2001 (in replay to message from jweiler@BFCA.COM).

"As noted attorney Jonathan Blattmachr has said, 'Life insurance is the *only* asset that is certain to work in a time of great uncertainty.'"

> Stephan R. Leimberg and Albert E. Gibbons, "Dealing With EGTRRA's Impact on an Insurance Professional's Practice," *Estate Planning*, August 2001, page 404.

Motivational – Did They Really Say That?

"Profiles in noncourage: 'Everything is off the record,' a government official said at a recent conference on estate and gift taxes. 'So if I said anything quotable, it was a mistake or you heard it wrong.'"

> Tom Herman, "Tax Report," *The Wall Street Journal*, May 24, 2000, page 1.

Motivational – Did They Really Say That?

"Every good citizen . . . should be willing to devote a brief time during some one day in the year, when necessary, to the making up of a listing of his income for taxes . . . to contribute to his government, not the scriptural tithe, but a small percentage of his net profits."

> Cordell Hull, addressing the U.S. House of Representatives, April 26, 1913 (appointed secretary of state by President Franklin D. Roosevelt and served in that position 1933-1944).

"Read my lips – no new taxes."

> George Bush on August 18, 1988, at the Republican National Convention (41st president of the United States, 1989-1993).

"We don't pay taxes. Only the little people pay taxes."

> Leona Helmsley, (her tax evasion convictions were affirmed by the Second Circuit Court of Appeals on July 30, 1991).

"An accountant in the Washington, D.C., area called the IRS about an estate-tax issue. He says the IRS representative asked him: 'Are you the decedent?'. . ."

> Tom Herman, "Tax Report," *The Wall Street Journal*, March 6, 1996, page A1.

Motivational – The Very Short Will Of A Supreme Court Justice

"LAST WILL AND TESTAMENT OF WARREN E. BURGER.

I hereby make and declare the following to be my last will and testament. 1. My executors will first pay all claims against my estate; 2. The remainder of my estate will be distributed as follows: one-third to my daughter, Margaret Elizabeth Burger Rose and two-thirds to my son, Wade A. Burger; 3. I designate and appoint as executors of this will, Wade A. Burger and J. Michael Luttig.

IN WITNESS WHEREOF, I have hereunto set my hand to this my Last Will and Testament this 9th day of June, 1994."

> Warren E. Burger, served as 15th chief justice of the United States, 1969-1986.
> source: www.courttv.com/legaldocs/newsmakers/wills/

Motivational – The Public Will Of A Private Man!

"Care to know what Magness's will said about the disposition of [his TCI and Liberty Media stock]? Go fish. Right now the will is 'under security' in an Englewood, Colorado, court, which means it is locked away from public eyes. This may be a first, since wills are by definition public documents. Asked in early December about the Magness situation, one prominent trust and estate lawyer in New York said that in his decades-long career he had literally never before heard of a will being made 'private.'"

> "Dead Men Tell No Tales: The Secret Will Of TCI's Founder," *Fortune,*
> January 13, 1997, page 72.

"The will of Tele-Communications Inc. founder and chairman Bob Magness, with million-dollar bequests scrawled in its margins, was unsealed Thursday after seven months of mystery, raising as many questions as it answers. . . . The Denver Post, seeking clues about TCI's ownership control, went to court to open it."

> Stephen Keating, "Magness' Will Unsealed But Yields Few Surprises,"
> *The Denver Post,* June 13, 1997, page A-01.

"In courtrooms, judges' chambers, Denver's high-society party circuit and other rarefied venues, his widow, his two grown sons and a rich supporting cast of lawyers and business heavyweights are fighting for control of the biggest estate in Colorado history. At stake in this ugly personal dispute is more than $1 billion generated by a man dead from cancer barely a year. It's happening because, in the end, Bob Magness, a beloved Colorado tycoon and philanthropist, didn't take care of business. The three antagonists in the fight are widow Sharon Magness on one side and brothers Gary and Kim Magness on the other. . . . It's a situation that folksy patriarch Bob Magness would have abhorred. . . . In an era of aggressive tax planning, Magness appeared to have had a momentous lapse in judgment. He had made surprisingly little use of charitable trusts, family partnerships and other tax-sheltered gifts to transfer wealth to heirs. Executors somberly informed Kim and Gary that most of their father's TCI stock would probably have to be sold to pay an estimated $400 million-to-$500 million tax bill. . . . People who knew him . . . said Magness, even with rapidly progressing cancer, might have put off detailed estate planning because he believed there would be a better time later."

> "Fighting Over A Fortune - Second Wife Vs. The Sons," *Scripps Howard
> News Service,* December 16, 1997.

Motivational – In Just Two Short Months!

"Make no mistake, Forbes Inc. Chairman and chief shareholder Malcolm S. Forbes is rich. Experts value his company's flagship business magazine as high as $600 million, while its American Heritage magazine, suburban newspaper, real estate and art holdings almost certainly add $100 million or more to the Forbes family fortune. . . . On [his] death, Steve Forbes [his son] will inherit 51% voting control of the Forbes empire – along with a potential tax nightmare, because state and federal taxes on big estates are levied at approximately 55% . . . . According to Malcolm, much of his company's income is being used to purchase 'enormous sums of life insurance,' a device that can legally transfer millions of dollars in cash to his beneficiaries without an estate tax assessment."

Michael Cieply, "The Wary Capitalist," *Los Angeles Times,* December 31, 1989, page D1.

"The change of command at Forbes Inc. with the death on Saturday of Malcolm S. Forbes comes at a time when the Forbes publishing empire . . . has been flourishing and bent on diversification. . . . Steve Forbes was entrusted with control to fulfill his father's desire that the company remain a family business. [Steve Forbes said that his father] 'saw what happened at other family businesses where one person didn't have control, and would lose control and sometimes ultimately lose the company . . .' He [also] said that while the transfer of assets would require payment of substantial inheritance taxes, considerable estate planning had been done using several possibilities. He added that he believed there was enough cash available to pay the taxes without having to sell any assets or causing any disruption in business."

N. R. Kleinfield, "At Forbes, the Family Still Reigns," *The New York Times,* February 27, 1990, page D1.

"A line in the obituaries of Malcolm Forbes, the owner of Forbes Magazine who died last weekend, may have started many Americans thinking about their own family finances. Forbes' sons will inherit the family's business magazine, the article said, but also a potential tax liability of 55% of the firm's value. . . . [T]houghts of estate taxes . . . might occur these days to surprisingly large numbers [of people]. . . . What do they do about it? Do what Malcolm Forbes did, say financial planners. Buy life insurance."

James Flanigan, "Malcolm Forbes' Lesson on Estate Taxes," *Los Angeles Times*, March 4, 1990, page D1.

Motivational

"It's bad enough when a loved one dies, and it will get even worse if the person died without a will. Dying intestate leaves heirs with a bundle of legal, administrative and tax headaches. And even if you get an inheritance, there might be little you can do about crushing tax consequences. Beyond these practical problems, if husband and wife die together without wills, the decision of who will raise minor children is left to the court – not as you might have wished. These nightmares notwithstanding, more than half of American adults die without a will."

> Adrienne Sanders, "Willful Omission," *Forbes Magazine,* December 27, 1999.

"Bum advice and basic mistakes by banks, brokers and mutual funds are wrecking havoc with many people's individual retirement accounts. The result: Their heirs may end up loosing a bundle."

> Lynn Asinof, "Opps...How a Variety of Basic Foul-Ups Are Bedeviling the Beneficiaries of IRAs," *The Wall Street Journal,* March 29, 1999.

Annuity

"A dozen of the lawyers contesting the estate of the ice cream magnate Thomas Carvel have gathered before Judge Albert J. Emanuelli . . . . 'I came here in 1991, and this case is still being litigated,' the judge told the assembled attorneys. 'Seven years of litigation. I think it's tragic.' . . . Carvel died childless at the age of 84 in October 1990. He left behind most of the $80 million proceeds from selling his namesake ice cream chain . . . . [Today] the Thomas and Agnes Carvel Foundation has but $12 million, and has managed to distribute less than $6 million . . . . The widow isn't doing particularly well, either. Although she was supposed to receive income from her husband's fortune, she hasn't seen a penny from this part of the estate . . . . Carvel's probate case involves six entities that we know of . . . . He didn't need to be so complicated. His needs were simple: Set aside enough for his widow to live comfortably and leave the rest to charity. He could have accomplished all this very cleanly by purchasing an annuity for Agnes from an insurance company and leaving the whole estate to charity."

> Thomas Easton, "Meltdown Of An Ice Cream Fortune," *Forbes Magazine,* June 15, 1998.

Life Insurance

"Will Rogers once said, 'If a man doesn't believe in life insurance, let him die once without it. That will teach him a lesson.' Such a lesson could be expensive to the survivors."

> J. W. Looney, *Estate Planning For Business Owners*, Reston: Reston Publishing Company, 1979, page 100.

"[I]nsurance, which appears to be just another form of gambling, has actually exactly the opposite effects. For the same reasons that gambling is bad, insurance is economically advantageous. Whereas gambling creates risk, insurance helps to lessen and spread risks."

> Paul A. Samuelson, *Economics*, New York: McGraw-Hill Book Company, 1980, pages 424-25.

"Life insurance continues to be useful in providing the funds necessary to purchase the stock or interest of a deceased shareholder or partner upon his death. . . . [Section 303] partial redemptions will no doubt become more prevalent, as will the use of life insurance to fund such redemptions. Life insurance also remains an excellent device for funding cross-purchase plans."

> "Maximizing The Advantages Of Life Insurance As A Funding Device And As An Investment," *Estate Planning*, January/February 1986, page 4.

"When [a buy/sell] agreement is used, the cash necessary to buy the deceased's interest is often assured in advance by insurance on the life of each associate . . . . Without funding of some sort, it is doubtful that in the ordinary case the individual partners or shareholders would have sufficient cash or liquid assets on hand to finance completely a purchase of the decedent's interest . . . . If installment payments are unacceptable, or if there is some doubt as to the ability of the prospective purchaser to finance the agreed price, insurance may be the only answer."

> "The Use of Life Insurance to Fund Agreements Providing for Disposition of a Business Interest At Death," 71 *Harvard Law Review* (1958), page 688.

Life Insurance

"Life insurance is not very sophisticated. You do not talk about making a killing on your life insurance, or selling your policy short. Life insurance is a necessity and a responsibility, not a conversation piece. Perhaps you can make more money in the market. Some people do, some people do not. But, we are not talking about your making money in the stock market – we are concerned with a family spending money in the supermarket. Money is not an investment. It is the measure of an investment. Life insurance is not an investment. It is the measure of a person."

> John J. O'Connell, LL.M., J.D., CLU, "More Thoughts On Life And Life Insurance," *Techniques*, January 1979, Hartford: Aetna Life Insurance Company.

"In a capitalistic society, where credit is the life blood of that system, debt signals a need for life insurance."

> Judge Michael A. Telesca, "Estate Planning: A View From The Bench," *National Underwriter*, July 10, 1976, page 17.

"The most common purchase of life insurance is to cushion a family financially if the primary wage earner dies prematurely. In short, life insurance is a security blanket – something to replace your paycheck and to wrap around your dependents when you die. The funds from an insurance death benefit payable to a specified beneficiary are immediately and automatically available, while other funds may be held up in probate. . . . Life insurance benefits can be tailored to virtually any of your requirements or those of your beneficiaries."

> Leonard Sloane, *The New York Times Book Of Personal Finance*, New York: Times Books, 1985, page 96.

"It is possible to pass along millions of dollars' worth of insurance to your children or other heirs tax-free . . . . The device for doing so is the irrevocable life insurance trust. . . . 'Anyone potentially subject to federal estate taxes is a good candidate for a life-insurance trust. It's probably one of the last, best estate-planning opportunities available.'"

> "Irrevocable Life Insurance Trust Passes On Money To Heirs Tax-Free," *The Atlanta Constitution*, March 20, 1989, page 4C.

Life Insurance

"A partner's death can leave a gaping hole in a small business. And beyond the loss of a key player, the surviving partner or partners have to figure out how to deal fairly with the widow or widower, who has likely inherited a share of the business. If all parties agree in advance that the surviving partners should buy out the spouse, life insurance can provide the means. And a first-to-die policy can do the job more cheaply than individual policies on each partner."

"A Businesslike Solution," *U.S. News & World Report*, September 14, 1992, page 82.

"Life insurance is a wonderful thing. There is no substitute for it until a sufficiently large estate has been acquired to protect those dependent upon you. It can provide you with a way to guarantee that your dependents will have the financial means to continue to maintain your targeted standard of living in the event that you should die prematurely. It can be an economic extension of yourself. You should attempt to provide this protection for your dependents before you begin an investment program."

Venita VanCaspel, *Money Dynamics For The 1990's*. New York: Simon & Schuster, 1988, page 346.

"When's the last time you checked your life insurance? Most people buy policies soon after they start working, file them away and forget them. That can be a big mistake. The insurance that met your needs as a 25 year-old may be entirely inadequate later, when you may have a spouse, children or an elderly parent to look after. The average family has $65,000 in coverage, but your insurance needs can be much higher."

"Updating Your Life Insurance," *U.S. News & World Report*, September 7, 1987, page 65.

"There is probably no type of property more appealing as the subject of a gift than life insurance. The gift, made currently, involves only perhaps a premium or two or, perhaps, some small amount of cash. But the value removed from the insured's estate is the full face proceeds. And, of course, the fundamental combination of maximum death tax reduction with minimum current gift cost is almost irresistible."

Lawrence G. Knecht, "The Human Equation In Estate Planning," *Trusts & Estates*, December 1975, page 855.

Life Insurance

"Most couples with estates in the $2 million to $3 million range should look at the economics of using life insurance to pay estate taxes. . . . Using a life insurance policy allows you to leverage this money by using the annual gifts or chunks of the $600,000 to pay the premium. When you die, life insurance proceeds are not subject to income tax. If the policy is owned by someone else, such as a child or an irrevocable trust, it will not be part of your estate and will not be subject to estate taxes either."

Mary Rowland, "Using Life Insurance To Pay Estate Taxes," *The New York Times*, November 28, 1992, page 31.

"How much life insurance do you need? . . . James Hunt, a director of the National Insurance Consumer Organization, or NICO, has a rule of thumb. A four-person family, with one wage earner and two young children, should buy five times the wage earner's annual income. If you're making $40,000 a year, for example, you need $200,000 worth of coverage. This assumes the wage earner also has coverage through his or her company, equal to two or three year's salary, Hunt says. If not, you should buy a policy equal to seven to eight times income."

Jane Bryant Quinn, "Insurance Rule Of Thumb Signals How Much To Buy," *The Richmond Times-Dispatch*, April 13, 1992, page 16.

"Life insurance is extraordinary in the breadth and effectiveness of its estate and business planning applications. Used either as a funding device for a business buy-out or as a means of indemnifying the corporation for the loss of a key stockholder-employee, life insurance can help effectuate the close corporation stockholder's plans for retention or sale of his business interest. Life insurance policies can also frequently serve the purpose of furthering stockholder harmony by balancing the often divergent monetary needs of stockholder-employees and non-employees stockholder-heirs."

Life Insurance: Estate Planning Tool For Closely Held Corporations. Chicago: Commerce Clearing House, 1980, page 31.

Long-Term Care Insurance

"Given a choice, most people prefer to receive care in their own homes – another option seldom covered by medicaid. Purchasing long-term care insurance with the right benefits means you can decide where you will receive care while protecting your life savings."

> Mary Beth Franklin, "Insuring Against Life's Frailties," *Kiplinger's Personal Finance Magazine*, July, 1999.

Business Valuation

"[Fair market] value is a fact, the determination of which is, at least, generally difficult. The result is rarely satisfactory."

> United States Board of Tax Appeals in the case of *Estate of Leonard B. McKitterick*, 42 B.T.A. 130, page 136.

"The valuation of stock, like many questions of fact, cannot be completely rationalized."

> United States Tax Court in the case of *Estate of Paul M. Vandenhoeck*, 4 T.C. 125, page 138.

"The determination of the fair market value of stock in a closely held corporation absent previous sales of the stock at arm's length is an arduous task. It is an uncertain art at best . . . ."

> Judge Fay in the United States Tax Court case of *Dale F. Miller*, 77,039 P-H Memo TC, page 172.

Partial Stock Redemption

"Utilizing Code Sec. 303 redemptions to pay death taxes presents an opportunity for a decedent-shareholder's estate to withdraw earnings and profits from the closely held corporation on an income tax preferred basis."

> *Life Insurance: Estate Planning Tool For Closely Held Corporations*. Chicago: Commerce Clearing House, 1980, page 22.

Key Person Insurance

"What corporate purpose could be considered more essential than key man insurance? The business that insures its buildings and machinery and automobiles from every possible hazard can hardly be expected to exercise less care in protecting itself against the loss of two of its most vital assets – managerial skill and experience."

> From an opinion by Circuit Judge Staley in the 3rd Circuit of the U.S. Court of Appeals, Emeloid Co., Inc. v. Commissioner of Internal Revenue, 189 F.2d 230, page 233.

"In a capitalistic society, where credit is the life blood of that system, debt signals a need for life insurance . . . . The corporate or partnership debt, personally guaranteed by the deceased, makes the widow and his family absolutely vulnerable to the forced sale of assets. Everybody knows that 'a sale to settle an estate' means bargain prices."

> Judge Michael A. Telesca, "Estate Planning: A View From The Bench," *National Underwriter*, July 10, 1976, page 17.

"Take away my factories, my plants; take away my railroads, my ships, my transportation; take away my money; strip me of all these, but leave me my men, and in two or three years I will have them all again."

> Andrew Carnegie, Industrialist, as quoted in: Edward A. Stoeber, *How To Use Life and Health Insurance In Business And Estate Planning*, Cincinnati: The National Underwriter Company, 1980, page 57.

"Losses of key personnel are among the most serious setbacks a firm can have – particularly when the major asset of a firm, especially a small one, is the skills and training of its managers."

> Mark R. Greene, *Insurance and Risk Management for Small Business*. Washington: U.S. Small Business Administration, Third Edition, page 69.

Buy/Sell Agreements

"When the amount of a decedent's gross estate is substantial, but a major part of his estate is represented by stock holdings in a closely held corporation, the executor often has difficulty obtaining sufficient liquid assets to pay both the administrative expenses of the estate and the death taxes imposed by federal and state governments. A buy-out plan can ensure that the decedent's stock will be convertible into liquid assets when that is most necessary . . . That assurance of liquidity may be important to the shareholders in their personal estate planning."

> Professor Douglas A. Kahn, "Mandatory Buy-Out Agreements For Stock Of Closely Held Corporations," 68 *Michigan Law Review* (1969), page 3.

"Q: 'Is there anything I can do to help the sale of my business after I die so that my daughters are not penalized by estate taxes?'

A. 'Yes. Buy life insurance to provide the liquidity your business will need while it is being sold as well as for its tax advantage. More and more small business people are taking this step these days for precisely your reasons . . . . A widely preferred arrangement is the stock retirement agreement, under which your business itself buys your interest, pays the insurance premiums, and carries the insurance on its books as an asset. Buy-sell agreements guarantee your business will be sold at a fair price and that your estate will have sufficient assets to pay taxes and other expenses."

> Sylvia Porter, "Spending Your Money," *Ladies' Home Journal*, July 1979, page 39.

"The contract established a market value for the stock and at the same time fixed its value to testator's estate for tax purposes as well as for all other purposes. Resort to methods of estimating and computing the value of closely held stock is wholly unnecessary and improper when its actual value has been fixed and determined by a bona fide contract entered into by the testator."

> From an opinion of the Surrogate's Court Monroe County, New York, in the case of: *Matter of Miller*, 191 N.Y. Misc. 784, page 786.

Split-Dollar Insurance

"A split-dollar life insurance plan is used by companies to selectively reward and retain their key employees. It can be used to save taxes, solve estate planning problems and transfer major business interests to family members or valued employees."

"Split-Dollar Is Gaining Popularity As Planning Tack, Says Industry Exec," *Financial Services Week*, April 20, 1992, page 8.

"One of the most effective and economical ways to show an employee how valuable he is to your firm is to increase his financial security through the use of the split-dollar plan of life insurance."

Mark R. Greene, Insurance and Risk Management For Small Business. Washington: U.S. Small Business Administration, Third Edition, page 68.

"You can also use life insurance to ensure continuation of your business, whether you sell it or not, by providing key employees with incentives that tie them to the firm. Split-dollar insurance, for instance, enables your business and a major employee to split the cost of the insurance premiums. Deferred compensation plans combined with life insurance guarantee that your company will be able to meet its commitment to your employees after they retire."

Sylvia Porter, "Spending Your Money," *Ladies Home Journal*, July 1979, page 39.

Survivor Income

"The median age for 'new' widows is 52; almost six million widows are middle-aged or younger; further one out of four widows is under 45. More mind-boggling is the fact that one out of six women over 21 is a widow. You can talk and think about merry widows, too, but in reality, the average widow lives on little more than $6,000 a year – which doesn't make for too much merriment."

Rae Lindsay, *Alone And Surviving*. New York: Walker and Company, 1977, page 2.

Deferred Compensation

"Companies large and small have been signing up executives and other top employees for a generous tax break not available to other Americans. . . . The deal is simple: Rather than take all their pay, and pay taxes on it, executives let the company hold on to some. The company invests the money, and the executives do not pay taxes on any of it until they take the money years later. . . . This executive privilege is known as deferred compensation. Once rarely used, it has soared in popularity in recent years. . . ."

> Christopher Drew and David Cay Johnson, "Earn Lots Now, Pay Taxes
> Later," *The Atlanta Constitution*, October 13, 1996, page 34.

"While salary continuation agreements (SCAs) have long been used by employers, they recently have become much more important and appealing. This is due in part to enactment of further restrictions on qualified plans by the Tax Reform Act of 1986 and the Revenue Act of 1987 . . . . Nonqualified SCAs provide greater flexibility and permit the employer and employee to avoid much of the complexity of qualified plans."

> Robert G. Buydens and J. Thomas MacFarlane, "Salary Continuation
> Agreements Provide A Valuable Alternative To Qualified Plans," *Estate
> Planning*, November/December 1988, page 330.

"The Executive Retired Life Insurance Plan ('ERLIP') provides eligible executives of GTE and certain of its affiliated companies a post-retirement life insurance benefit on a graduated scale from one to three times final base salary. Participants in ERLIP are insured through the purchase of life insurance contracts that will allow GTE to recover the premiums and any supplementary retirement benefits paid through excess cash surrender values, death benefits or dividends under the life insurance contracts. Upon retirement, a participant can elect to continue life insurance coverage or convert the coverage to an annuity or lump-sum supplemental retirement benefit using actuarial equivalents."

> From proxy statement issued by GTE Corporation, Stamford,
> Connecticut, March 4, 1992, page 12.

ACCELERATED DEATH BENEFIT

An accelerated death benefit (ADB) is a portion of a life insurance death benefit that is paid to the insured after he has been diagnosed as either chronically or terminally ill. Provided certain conditions are met, payments received may be excluded from federal taxable income.

A person is considered *terminally* ill if certified by a physician to have an illness or physical condition that is reasonably expected to result in death within 24 months. A person is considered *chronically* ill if certified by a health care professional as unable to perform for a period of at least 90 days, without substantial assistance, at least two activities of daily living (i.e., eating, toileting, transferring, bathing, dressing and continence) or requires substantial supervision to protect himself from threats to health and safety due to severe cognitive impairment (i.e., a deterioration or loss of intellectual capacity that places the individual in jeopardy of harming self or others). These standards for the chronically ill also apply to long-term care benefits (see chart, page 259).

There is no limitation on the amount or use of payments made to a *terminally* ill person. However, payments made to a *chronically* ill individual must be for the actual costs incurred that have not been compensated for by insurance or otherwise. Amounts received from a qualified long-term care contract in 2002 are generally not includable in income up to the greater of $210 per day or actual costs incurred. The terms of the contract must comply with certain provisions of the Internal Revenue Code, standards adopted by the National Association of Insurance Commissioners (NAIC) and standards adopted by the state in which the policyowner resides. These are the same limits and requirements that apply to payments for long-term care (see chart, page 259).

As an exception to these rules, payments are included in income if made to someone other than the insured and the payee has an insurable interest in the insured's life because the insured is a director, officer or employee of the payee, or because the insured is financially interested in any trade or business carried on by the payee (i.e., business insurance).

In contrast to an accelerated death benefit *received* under a life insurance policy, when a chronically or terminally ill insured *sells* his death benefit at a discount to a third party it is known as a viatical settlement (see discussion, pages 485-486).

ACCOUNTING FOR BUSINESS LIFE INSURANCE

Premium Payments. With cash value insurance the excess of net premiums paid (i.e., the premiums paid less dividends declared, if any) over the increase in cash surrender values is considered an insurance expense. Because premium payments are generally *not* deductible as a business expense, they are usually considered an "Extraordinary Item" and placed on the profit and loss statement before "Net Income Before Taxes," as at **B** on page 340. Alternatively, the insurance expense could be shown on the balance sheet as a direct charge to capital, with no entry being made on the profit and loss statement (note that this method highlights the non-tax-deductible nature of the expense).

Cash Values. The general rule is that cash values are carried on the balance sheet under "Noncurrent Assets," as at **A** on page 340 ("noncurrent assets" are also referred to as "other assets"). It has been suggested that with universal life containing surrender charges the full cash values should be carried as an asset. However, this is not consistent with the position taken by the Financial Accounting Standards Board in FASB Technical Bulletin No. 85-4, entitled "Accounting for Purchases of Life Insurance." When responding to the question of how to account for an investment in life insurance, the bulletin states: *"The amount that could be realized* under the insurance contract *as of the date of the statement* of financial position should be reported as an asset. . . . the current capacity to realize contract benefits is limited to settlement amounts specified in the contract" [emphasis added]. When it is intended to surrender a universal life policy value during the normal operating cycle, the *surrender* values might be carried on the balance sheet as a "Current Asset," as opposed to a "Noncurrent Asset."

Policy Loans. Usually there is no intention of repaying the policy loan within the current year, in which case the loan should be reflected on the balance sheet as a deduction from the cash surrender value (i.e., net cash surrender values should be shown). If there is an intention to repay within the current year, the loan should be carried as a current liability and the full cash surrender value shown as an asset.

Death Benefits. The amount of the death benefit in excess of the cash surrender values is considered a gain to corporate surplus. The entry can be made as a negative expense under Extraordinary Items on the profit and loss statement (**B** on page 340). Assuming cash surrender values of $36,000 and a death benefit of $250,000, the actual entry would read, "Plus: proceeds of officers life insurance in excess of cash surrender value . . . 214,000."

(continued on next page)

ACCOUNTING FOR BUSINESS LIFE INSURANCE (continued)

BALANCE SHEET

ASSETS
CURRENT ASSETS:
Cash	$450,000
Notes and accounts receivable	850,000

FIXED ASSETS:
Land	300,000
Buildings	550,000
Machinery and equipment	220,000

NONCURRENT ASSETS:
Prepaid insurance, taxes, etc.	18,500	
Life insurance cash surrender values	<u>36,000</u> **A**	
Total Assets		<u>$2,424,500</u>

LIABILITIES AND STOCKHOLDER EQUITY
CURRENT LIABILITIES:
Notes and loans payable ?banks	$145,000	
Accounts payable	85,000	
Liability for income taxes	42,500	

LONG-TERM LIABILITIES:
Mortgages	<u>735,000</u>	
Total Liabilities		$1,007,500

STOCKHOLDER EQUITY:
Common stock authorized and issued	$900,000	
Retained earnings	<u>517,000</u>	
Total Stockholder Equity		<u>1,417,000</u>
Total Liabilities and Stockholder Equity		<u>$2,424,500</u>

PROFIT AND LOSS STATEMENT

Net Sales		$ 869,000
Less: Cost of Sales and Operating Expenses		
Cost of goods sold	$260,000	
Depreciation	95,000	
Selling and administrating expenses	<u>184,000</u>	
		(539,000)
Operating Profit		$ 330,000
Other Income		
Interest and dividends		<u>5,000</u>
Total Income		$ 335,000
Extraordinary Item		
Less: life insurance expense		(7,000) **B**
Net Income Before Taxes		$ 328,000
Provision for Income Tax		(113,900)
Net Profit for Year		$ 214,100

ACCUMULATED EARNINGS TAX

Accumulating corporate earnings and profits in excess of the reasonable needs of the business and for the purpose of avoiding income tax can result in a surtax of 38.6 percent of accumulated taxable income. This surtax is imposed on the current year's earnings, and once taxed, accumulated earnings are not again taxed in subsequent years during which the accumulation is retained.

However, a corporation is allowed to accumulate at least $250,000 without being subject to this surtax. This figure is reduced to $150,000 for personal service corporations, whose principal business consists of the performance of services in the fields of health, law, engineering, architecture, accounting, actuarial science, performing arts, or consulting.

Reasonable needs of the business can include: (1) providing for plant expansion; (2) acquiring another business through purchase of either stock or assets; (3) retiring indebtedness; and (4) making loans to suppliers or customers in order to maintain the business of the corporation. Insurance carried as *key person insurance*, or to help meet an employer's obligation under a *deferred compensation plan* or *entity purchase agreement (§302)*, is generally considered as carried for reasonable business needs. However, under Section 303 (partial stock redemption) only accruals in the year of death or thereafter are considered as carried for reasonable needs of the business.

For example, if a corporation in its first year of existence in 2002 has $425,000 of retained earnings for which no reasonable need exists, it would be subject to a penalty tax of $67,550. It is calculated as follows:

first $250,000   is exempt from tax
excess   175,000   is subject in 2002 to a tax of 38.6 percent, or $67,550

The penalty tax is imposed *in addition to* the regular corporate income tax.

ALTERNATIVE MINIMUM TAX

The alternative minimum tax (AMT) is designed to assure that the taxpayer with substantial economic income will not be able to avoid taxes merely by using available tax exclusions, deductions, and credits.

A corporation qualifying as a "small corporation" is not subject to the alternative minimum tax. A small corporation is a corporation that for its first tax year beginning after 1996 has average annual gross receipts not exceeding $5,000,000 for the preceding three-year period (if the corporation was in existence less than three years, then the test will be applied to whatever period it was in existence). Annualization of receipts is required for any short taxable year. Once a corporation qualifies as a small corporation, it will continue to be treated as a small corporation as long as its average gross receipts for the three-year period preceding the taxable year do not exceed $7,500,000.

Gross receipts include total sales (net of returns and allowances) and all amounts received for services. In addition, gross receipts include any income from investments, and from incidental or outside sources. For example, gross receipts include interest, dividends, rents, royalties, and annuities, regardless of whether such amounts are derived in the ordinary course of the taxpayer's trade or business. Gross receipts are generally not reduced by the cost of goods or property sold.

The following discussion applies only to those corporations that do not qualify as a "small corporation" and therefore are subject to the alternative minimum tax.

As it applies to corporations, the AMT requires that the corporate tax base be determined with certain adjustments and increased by specific tax preferences. Two of the more common tax preference items are accelerated depreciation and certain tax-exempt interest. In the process of determining the alternative minimum taxable income (AMTI) of a C corporation, 75 percent of the amount by which adjusted current earnings (ACE) exceed the tentative AMTI is added to the tentative AMTI. The resulting amount is then reduced by an exemption of $40,000 less 25 percent of the excess of AMTI over $150,000. The resulting tax base is multiplied by 20 percent to determine the tentative minimum tax. The corporation then pays a tax equal, in effect, to the greater of this amount or its regular tax.

Although ACE is not equivalent to current earnings and profits (E&P), some of the adjustments used in computing ACE rely on E&P concepts. For example, life insurance will *increase* ACE, since under generally accepted accounting principles E&P are increased by: (1) yearly cash value increases in excess of annual premiums; and (2) death proceeds (including outstanding loans) in excess of basis increased for cash value increases previously included in AMTI. Proceeds from

(continued on next page)

ALTERNATIVE MINIMUM TAX (continued)

disability income and buy-out policies payable to the corporation are also included in ACE.

Conversely, if premiums are paid for term insurance, or the cash value increase is less than the annual premium, there is a *decrease* of ACE that reduces exposure to the AMT. However, redemption of the deceased or disabled owner's stock in the same year as the proceeds are received will not avoid an increase in ACE.

The existence of the AMT does not mean that all, or even most, life insurance cash values or death proceeds will be subject to the tax. Much depends upon the corporation's taxable income, tax preference items, and other factors (e.g., S corporations are not subject to the ACE adjustment). Only a portion of cash value increases and death proceeds will be potentially exposed to this tax, since cash value increases will be partially offset by premiums; and death proceeds will be offset by cash values. Even when there is exposure, generally **the maximum rate is 15 percent** (i.e., a 20 percent tax on 75 percent of ACE). With many corporations payment of the tax will be an *acceleration of* rather than an *increase of* tax liability, since it then becomes a credit available to offset a portion of the corporation's tax liability in future years (unlimited carry forward). However, this credit may be useless to the closely held or professional corporation that will have little, if any, taxable income.

(continued on next page)

ALTERNATIVE MINIMUM TAX (continued)

Impact Of Alternative Minimum Tax
On Life Insurance Death Benefits
Payable To C Corporation

Taxable Income	Death Benefit				
	100,000	250,000	1,000,000	2,500,000	5,000,000
0	**7,000**	**31,375**	**150,000**	**375,000**	**750,000**
	7,000	31,375	150,000	375,000	750,000
25,000	**12,000**	**37,625**	**155,000**	**380,000**	**755,000**
	8,250	33,875	151,250	376,250	751,250
50,000	**17,000**	**43,875**	**160,000**	**385,000**	**760,000**
	9,500	36,375	152,500	377,500	752,500
100,000	**28,250**	**56,375**	**170,000**	**395,000**	**770,000**
	6,000	34,125	147,750	372,750	747,750
250,000	80,750	**87,500**	**200,000**	**425,000**	**800,000**
		6,750	119,250	344,250	719,250
500,000	170,000	170,000	**250,000**	**475,000**	**850,000**
			80,000	305,000	680,000
1,000,000	340,000	340,000	**350,000**	**575,000**	**950,000**
			10,000	235,000	610,000
2,000,000	680,000	680,000	680,000	**775,000**	**1,150,000**
				95,000	470,000

Note: This chart assumes the C corporation is not exempt from the alternative minimum tax (AMT) as a "small corporation." Small figure represents that portion of the income tax that is attributable to the death benefit (i.e., additional tax imposed under the AMT calculations). The corporation is assumed to have no tax preference items. No adjustments are made for cumulative premiums paid and for possible annual cash value increases in excess of premiums paid (i.e., "basis for ACE"). As an example of how to use this chart, assume a corporation has $500,000 of taxable income in a given year and also receives a death benefit payment of $1,000,000. The corporation will owe federal income taxes of $250,000 of which $80,000 is attributable to the effect of the AMT and the receipt of the life insurance death benefit. If this corporation received the same $1,000,000 death benefit but had $2,000,000 of taxable income, the corporation would owe $680,000 in taxes, none of which would be attributable to the death benefit and the AMT. This chart also indicates that a corporation with taxable income of $1,000,000 could consider increasing its key person life insurance on a key employee from $100,000 to $250,000 without additional exposure to the AMT (i.e., the income taxes remain at $340,000).

ASSET PROTECTION

The term "asset protection" has traditionally been used in referring to techniques that offer protection from the claims of personal and business creditors. However, today the term is used to describe a wide array of planning techniques, including those intended to reduce or eliminate income and estate taxes.

These techniques can range from the fairly simple to the very complicated. For example, in some states much, if not all, of a personal residence is protected from creditors. Many states exempt annuity values, substantial life insurance cash values and all death benefits. The assets of most retirement plans covered by ERISA are also protected (but not from tax deficiency claims or divorce disputes). Gifts can be made to family members or charitable organizations, provided they are not made with intent to defraud specific creditors (see charts on pages 49, 53 and 61). Gifts may also be made to an irrevocable trust or custodial account (see chart page 57, and discussions on pages 481-482). However, making substantial gifts to a spouse may no longer isolate assets from creditors and could eventually increase estate taxes (see chart, page 29).

More sophisticated techniques include limited liability companies and family limited partnerships (see chart page 169, and discussion on page 415 and pages 427-428). Trusts can be established with "spendthrift" provisions to prevent the creditors of trust beneficiaries from reaching trust assets. But this technique is not effective for the individual who desires to establish a trust as protection from his own creditors.

The most sophisticated of all asset protection techniques is probably the offshore or asset protection trust (APT). It is thought that using an APT to remove assets to a foreign jurisdiction will lead to more favorable terms in disputes with creditors. Just as some states have laws that are more favorable to asset protection, certain countries have gained similar reputations. Jurisdictions considered most favorable as a situs for APTs do not recognize foreign judgments (thereby forcing a retrial of claims), have weakened or no fraudulent conveyance laws, and permit a trust settlor to retain trust powers and benefits without subjecting the trust to the claims of creditors. APTs are not intended to avoid income taxes.

In our litigious society it is understandable why monied individuals and high-risk professionals have long been interested in adopting asset protection techniques. However, a few words of caution: not only will the concealment of assets from a known creditor be set aside by the courts, but assisting a debtor will likely subject both the debtor and his advisor to ethical, civil and criminal liability (e.g., Code section 7206, see page 430). Therefore, asset protection techniques must be implemented long *before* there is a need. Also, state laws vary widely in the protection they offer and should be specifically consulted.

BANK OWNED LIFE INSURANCE (BOLI)

In many respects, Bank Owned Life Insurance (BOLI) is similar to Corporate Owned Life Insurance (COLI), in that BOLI enables banks to recover, or to informally fund, the costs of nonqualified benefit plans (see page 364). However, there are important differences.

Banks are considered highly "balance sheet sensitive." From a bank investment perspective, the life insurance contract has been described as "a perpetual municipal with a yield that resets to the market." From a bank accounting perspective, the purchase of life insurance has been described as a "repositioning" of assets on the balance sheet, "from the securities portfolio to the BOLI portfolio," that generates "incremental income." Unlike traditional taxable investments, the cash value increases of BOLI are reflected on the balance sheet as "other non-interest income," without any reduction for income taxes (accounting for BOLI policies is subject to FASB Technical Bulletin 85-5, see page 339). When compared to currently taxed investments, BOLI can produce improved after-tax yields and a positive impact on earnings per share.

Unlike COLI, the purchase of BOLI by national banks is very tightly regulated by the Office of Comptroller of the Currency (OCC) (FDIC regulated state-chartered banks are typically subject to similar regulation). When purchasing BOLI, OCC Bulletin 2000-23 requires an informed decision "consistent with safe and sound banking practices." To that end, the bank must perform a *pre-purchase analysis* that includes determination of need, quantification of amount, vendor and carrier selection, review of insurance product characteristics, determination of reasonableness of compensation, analysis of benefits and risks, and alternatives. The purchase of BOLI, " . . . must address a legitimate need of the bank for life insurance. Life insurance may not be purchased to generate funds for the bank's normal operating expenses [or for] speculation . . ." However, the purchase of "key-person insurance, insurance on borrowers, insurance purchased in connection with employee compensation and benefit plans, and insurance taken as security for loans," are all found to fall within the "incidental powers [that are] necessary to carry on the business of banking."

BOLI policies are typically issued as either annual or single premium contracts. If purchased with a single premium, a BOLI policy is classified as a modified endowment contract (MEC), with the resulting LIFO taxation of policy withdrawals, loans and surrenders; and application of a 10 percent penalty tax on amounts includable in gross income (see Life Insurance Premium Limitations, page 413). However, provided the contract is held until the insured's death, the policy proceeds are received income tax-free (assuming no prior "transfer-for-value," see page 479). Banks may purchase variable life insurance, provided it is for the purpose of "hedging their obligations under employee compensation and benefit plans." In selecting the employees to be insured, a bank must be mindful of the state "insurable interest" requirements (see discussion, page 405).

BOOK VALUE

Many approaches to valuation require a consideration of book value. Simply stated, book value is assets less liabilities, or the net worth of the business. However, because assets are often carried at substantially *below* their fair market value, care must be taken to assure that book value is adjusted upward to reflect accurately the value of these underlying assets. This adjustment in book value results in an *adjusted book value*.

For example, land purchased many years ago is likely to have appreciated in value, yet it is often carried on the books at the original purchase price. Machinery and equipment may be depreciated for income tax purposes, yet be worth substantially more than is shown on the books (when carried at its depreciated value). If the LIFO (last in, first out) method of inventory valuation is used, the value of inventory will likely be carried at below market value. This can be seen in the following example:

1000 units purchased at $1.00 on June 1	$1,000
1000 units purchased at $1.50 on July 1	1,500
1000 units purchased at $2.00 on August 1	2,000
Total cost of inventory	$4,500
Less 1000 units sold on August 2 (charged to inventory at $2.00 per unit)	(2,000)
Remaining 2000 units carried at	$2,500
But to replace these units it would cost	$4,000
Inventory is undervalued by	$1,500

BUSINESS OVERHEAD EXPENSE INSURANCE

Business overhead expense insurance is designed to provide funds to cover overhead expenses during a business owner's disability. Business overhead expense insurance is intended to help maintain the business; it is not intended to replace disability income insurance (see chart, page 251) or disability buy-out insurance (see discussion, page 371).

Covered expenses include those that are tax deductible to the business. Typically these expenses include employee salaries, utilities, professional fees, rent, mortgage payments, lease payments for furniture and equipment, premiums for health, property and liability insurance, laundry services, janitorial services, and maintenance services. Not included are the insured's salary, salaries of co-workers who perform the same duties as the insured, salaries of family members, and depreciation.

Monthly benefits are paid upon the insured's total and continuous disability, and are limited to a maximum amount. Partial disability benefits are also available. During disability a "carry-forward" provision allows unused benefits to be carried forward from month to month. Extension of the benefit period allows unused benefits to be received beyond the original benefit period.

Waiting periods are typically either 30, 60, or 90 days. The cash flow requirements of the business are considered when selecting an appropriate waiting period.

Benefit periods are typically limited to 12, 18, or 24 months. Limited benefit periods assume that the insured will dispose of the business interest if disability lasts longer then the benefit period (see disability buy-out insurance, page 371).

Optional coverages are often similar to individual disability income policies (e.g., partial disability riders, guaranteed insurability riders, and lump-sum survivor benefits). Other optional coverages are unique to business overhead expense insurance (e.g., a professional replacement rider covering the cost of hiring someone to perform the insured's duties).

Eligible businesses include regular corporations, S corporations, limited liability companies, partnerships, and sole proprietorships. The business must have been in operation for a minimum period of time (e.g., 3 years). The business cannot have more than a specific number of owners (e.g., 5 professionals working in the business). This requirement recognizes that a substantial loss of revenue is less likely if the business has a large number of owner-employees. There are specific issue ages and medical underwriting requirements; and the insured must be actively at work full time (e.g., a minimum of 30 hours per week).

Premiums are deductible as a business expense. Although the *proceeds* are taxable, they are used for tax-deductible business expenses (i.e., taxable proceeds are offset by deductible business expenses).

CAFETERIA PLANS

Cafeteria plans, also described as "flexible benefit" plans or Section 125 plans, allow participating employees to choose between a number of non-taxable qualified benefits or taxable cash. Plans typically offer participants a "cafeteria menu" of items, including group term life insurance, medical expense insurance, dependent group term life insurance, child care, and dental expense coverage.

Among the advantages to an *employer* that establishes such a plan are reductions in FICA (Federal Insurance Contributions Act) and FUTA (Federal Unemployment Tax Act) taxes, expansion of employee benefits, and enhanced employee appreciation of the benefit package.

Employee advantages include the opportunity to select benefits most suited to individual needs, to pay for these benefits with before-tax, rather than after-tax, dollars to obtain benefits that may not be available for individual purchase, and to pay less FICA taxes by reducing taxable income.

The design of cafeteria plans can range from simple "premium only" plans to full-blown flexible benefit plans including flexible spending accounts. Premium-only plans, which are also referred to as "premium-conversion" plans, merely allow employees to use their before-tax, rather than after-tax, dollars for plan contributions. In contrast, flexible spending accounts allow employees to defer before-tax dollars to pay for dependent care expenses and unreimbursed medical expenses (such as deductibles and coinsurance payments, glasses, and eye exams).

The election to defer dollars must be made in advance of the plan year and can be changed only under limited circumstances. With flexible spending accounts, employees forfeit fund balances that are not used up by the end of the plan year, although typically an additional period is allowed after the close of the plan year for submission of claims incurred during the plan year. Forfeitures may be used to offset the employer's cost of administering the plan, reallocated proportionately to other employees, or given to charity.

Former employees may participate, but self-employed individuals may not. All plans are subject to special nondiscrimination rules. Proper administration of cafeteria plans requires preparing plan documents, conducting annual enrollments, tracking claims and benefit payments, and filing yearly 5500 reports.

CAPITAL GAINS

If property is classified as a "capital asset," then, upon its sale, any gain generally is considered a capital gain. Gain is the excess of the amount realized upon the sale over the basis (adjusted downward for depreciation or upward for additions to the property). The excess of net long-term capital gain over net short-term capital loss (if any) is net capital gain. "Adjusted net capital gain" is generally net capital gain determined without regard to: (1) collectibles gain; (2) unrecaptured Section 1250 gain; and (3) Section 1202 gain (see page 446).

For sales occurring after December 31, 1997, adjusted net capital gain on property held for more than 12 months is taxed at a maximum rate of 20 percent (the rate is 10 percent for taxpayers in the 15 percent marginal income tax bracket).

Gain on the sale or exchange of collectibles (e.g., rare coins, stamps, gems, and art) is subject to a maximum 28 percent rate if held for more than one year. Long-term capital gain that represents unrecaptured depreciation on Section 1250 property is generally subject to a maximum capital gains rate of 25 percent provided the property has been held for more than 12 months.

Includable gain on Section 1202 stock (i.e., qualified small business stock) is subject to a rate of 28 percent.

Beginning after December 31, 2000, if certain capital gain property has been *held for more than 5 years* the 20 percent rate may be reduced to 18 percent and the 10 percent rate may be reduced to 8 percent. However, this reduction is not applicable to gain on the sale of collectibles, gain that represents unrecaptured depreciation on Section 1250 property or certain gain on Section 1202 stock.

The lower 18 percent rate applies only to property held for more than 5 years *and* acquired after December 31, 2000 (i.e., the 18 percent rate will not be available until at least the year 2006); however, the lower 8 percent rate applies to assets held for more than 5 years, regardless of when the holding period began.

CHARITABLE GIFT ANNUITY

A charitable gift annuity is received pursuant to a contractual obligation by a charity to make annuity payments to a donor in exchange for the transfer of property to the charity. In comparison to charitable trusts they are less costly and relatively simple to adopt, typically requiring only an application and a one or two page agreement. The donor's tax-deductible gift is measured by the difference between the market value of the gift and the value of the retained life annuity. The annuity can be immediate or deferred and for a single life or the joint lives of two annuitants.

The actual rates used to calculate the annuity payout are typically based upon those published by the American Council of Gift Annuities. The council meets periodically in order to review interest rates and mortality assumptions and update the annuity rates. Although these rates are published in an attempt to avoid "rate bidding wars" between charities, the council has no enforcement authority. However, charities using the rates need not retain their own actuaries and have the assurance that the underlying actuarial assumptions will likely produce an ultimate charitable benefit.

The annuity receives favorable tax treatment. A portion of each payment is received tax-free as a return of principal (but excludable only until the investment has been recovered, thereafter taxed as ordinary income). The remaining portion is taxed as ordinary income. However, if the donor has transferred appreciated property to the charity, he has a gain (either capital gain or ordinary income depending on the property) to the extent the fair market value exceeds his adjusted basis. His basis in the property must then be allocated between the charitable gift and his investment in the annuity contract. As a result the return of principal element of each annuity payment is divided into two parts, one representing a return of gain (taxed as capital or ordinary gain) and the other representing a return of basis (excluded from income).

The contractual obligation to the annuitant is solely the charity's and the annuity payments are dependent upon the continuing financial stability of the charity. If desired, the charity can reinsure its obligation to the donor by purchasing a commercial annuity. This relieves the charity of the burden of investing the proceeds to assure that all payments will be made to the annuitant. To the extent that the cost of a commercial annuity is less than the amount realized from the gift the excess funds become immediately available to the charity.

CHARITABLE GIFTS OF LIFE INSURANCE

Gifts of life insurance policies and premiums have become a popular way of providing substantial gifts to a donor's favored charity. When properly implemented, the donor should receive charitable deductions for the value of the insurance contract and for all future premium payments.

In order to obtain the anticipated income, gift and estate tax deductions, the donor must make a gift of his *entire* interest in the policy. The donor will not qualify for these deductions if he retains the right to name or change the beneficiary, or gives less than his entire interest (e.g., assignment of death benefit but retention of cash values).

However, even when the donor appears to have given his entire interest in the policy to a charity, or where the charity originally applies for the insurance, a 1991 private letter ruling (withdrawn when state law changed) provided that the charity's lack of an insurable interest under state law would be a basis for denying the income, gift and estate tax deductions, since state law would also allow the insured's executor to sue for the proceeds (i.e., there would be a transfer of less than the donor's entire interest in the policy and premiums, since the threat of a suit by the executor renders the gifts incomplete). Even if the proceeds were actually received and retained by the charity, the Service would likely deny an estate tax deduction, because the charitable contribution would be deemed a result of the executor's action or inaction, rather than a transfer by the decedent-insured.

This could jeopardize a donor's income, gift and estate tax deductions (i.e., charity did not have an insurable interest, and executor could sue to recover life insurance proceeds paid to one not having an insurable interest). Following this ruling virtually all states have passed legislation that specifically provides that charities have an insurable interest in the lives of their donors. See *ASRS*, Sec. 12, ¶20.24.

The variety of state laws and likely changes to these laws make it imperative that specific state statutes be consulted prior to making gifts of life insurance and premiums, or having a charitable organization apply for life insurance (for an expanded discussion of insurable interest, see page 405).

CHARITABLE SPLIT-DOLLAR

Charitable split-dollar, also known as "charitable reverse split-dollar," was a highly aggressive planning technique that is no longer viable due to legislation passed in December of 1999.

Under the legislation, after February 8, 1999, no deduction is allowed for a transfer to a charitable organization if, in connection with the transfer, the organization pays a premium on a personal benefit contract with respect to the donor. A "personal benefit contract" is defined as a life insurance, annuity, or endowment contact where the donor, a member of the donor's family, or any other person named by the donor is a beneficiary under the contract. Also imposed is an excise tax on the charitable organization equal to the amount of premiums paid. Exceptions are provided for some contracts held by charitable remainder trusts and for certain charitable gift annuity agreements (see chart on page 61, and discussion on page 351). This legislation followed an earlier notice issued by the Internal Revenue Service regarding charitable split-dollar that stated both the donor and the charitable organization risked adverse tax consequences.

Prior to this legislation, a typical charitable split-dollar plan was implemented by first having the donor establish a trust for the benefit of the donor's children or other family members. The trust would then obtain a permanent life insurance policy, usually on the life of the donor, and concurrently enter into a split-dollar agreement with a charitable organization. The agreement would usually: (1) allocate a predetermined death benefit to the charity for a given period of time; (2) require that the charity pay a portion of the premiums (based upon the P.S. 58 rates); (3) provide that any charity premium advances be held in a "premium reserve account"; and (4) restrict policy loans and withdrawals by the trust. Thereafter, the donor made "unrestricted" cash gifts to the charity and the gifts were used to meet the charity's premium obligations.

Even before the 1999 legislation and the IRS notice, charitable split-dollar was surrounded by controversy. Some suggested that the arrangement provided the donor with an improper financial benefit in exchange for his charitable contributions (i.e., charitable donations shift large cash values to the family trust). Others pointed out that the partial interest rule of Code section 170(f)(3) requires that a deductible contribution must consist of an undivided portion of a donor's entire interest in property. In addition, charitable split-dollar appeared to raise other substantive tax issues, including the step transaction doctrine, donative intent, private inurement, self-dealing, quid pro quo, insurable interest, and substance-over-form.

CHARITABLE TRUSTS

Charitable trusts can be established for both individual and charitable beneficiaries. The requirements for charitable remainder trusts are specific and detailed in order to assure that an accurate determination can be made of the benefit the charity will eventually receive. Such trusts can offer both income and estate tax benefits, and include:

1. **Charitable remainder annuity trusts** are trusts under which a *fixed amount* of at least 5 percent, and for transfers after June 18, 1997 no more than 50 percent, of the initial fair market value of trust assets is paid annually to a noncharitable beneficiary. Payments to the noncharitable beneficiary may be for a set term not exceeding 20 years or for the life of the beneficiary. The amount of the grantor's tax deduction is measured by the present value of the charity's remainder interest at the time property is given to the trust. For transfers in trust after July 28, 1997, the value of the remainder interest generally must be at least 10 percent of the initial fair market value of all property placed in the trust. If the trust income is insufficient to make the required payments to the noncharitable beneficiary, then capital gains or trust principal must be used. If the trust income is more than required to make the payments the excess is reinvested in the trust. See page 61.

2. **Charitable remainder unitrusts** are trusts under which a *fixed percentage* of the net fair market value of the trust (valued annually) is paid at least annually to a noncharitable beneficiary. This percentage cannot be less than 5 percent and, for transfers after June 18, 1997, no more than 50 percent. Payments to the noncharitable beneficiary may be for a term not exceeding 20 years or for life. The amount of the grantor's tax deduction is the present value of the charity's remainder interest. For transfers in trust after July 28, 1997, the value of the remainder interest generally must be at least 10 percent of the net fair market value of each contribution as of the date the property is contributed to the trust. Payments to a survivor would further reduce the donor's charitable deduction. See page 61.

3. **Pooled income funds** are trusts created by public charities rather than private donors. The donors, or other income beneficiaries, receive from the commingled funds in the trust an income for life that is based upon the earnings of the trust. The amount of the grantor's tax deduction is the present value of the charity's remainder interest.

4. **Charitable lead trusts** allow a grantor to place funds in trust with an annuity or unitrust interest going to a charitable beneficiary and the remainder interest returning to the grantor or some other noncharitable beneficiaries. Although the grantor continues to be taxed on trust income under the grantor trust rules, he is entitled to an income tax deduction at the time of the gift equal to the present value of the charity's annuity or unitrust interest.

CHILDREN'S LIFE INSURANCE

Children's insurance, also referred to as "juvenile insurance," offers many advantages. The death proceeds can be used to pay medical bills and funeral expenses, provide a financial cushion for a grieving family or establish a lasting memorial (e.g., a scholarship fund in the child's name). Loans or withdrawals from policy cash values can be used for educational expenses, as a down payment on the purchase of a home, to start a business, or for emergency expenses. Adding a guaranteed purchase option will assure that in future years the child can purchase additional death benefits without evidence of insurability (see discussion, page 400).

Despite these advantages, placing insurance on a child's life is not without controversy. Opponents maintain that the lack of an underlying economic risk makes the purchase inappropriate and, further, that the wrong person is being insured. Clearly, if family resources are limited they should first be used to obtain adequate amounts of insurance on a child's parents (upon whom the child is economically dependent). Opponents also contend that if cash accumulations are desired it is better to save outside of a life insurance contract, thereby avoiding charges for the death benefit. Obviously, insuring a child can raise different issues than those encountered when insuring a spouse, parent, estate owner, employee or stockholder.

Since a minor cannot directly own a policy on his own life, it is important that the individual applying for the insurance have an insurable interest in the child's life (see discussion, page 405). Initially the contract will typically be owned by a parent, grandparent, trust, or obtained as a custodial gift under the Uniform Transfers to Minors Act or Uniform Gifts to Minors Act (see discussion, page 425).

A grandparent's purchase of insurance on the life of a grandchild can provide a meaningful gift to the grandchild while taking advantage of the gift tax laws (see chart, page 49). Virtually any form of permanent life insurance policy can be used. Single premium or limited payment plans are often used, or additional funds can be placed in a prepaid premium account (also referred to as a "premium deposit fund").

The amount of death benefit that can be purchased may be limited by state law and will be limited by insurance company underwriting standards. Purchase of a low death benefit with higher premiums will produce larger cash values. However, in making premium payments it is important to avoid classification as a modified endowment contract, since loans or surrenders of cash values could be subject to less favorable income taxation (see discussion, pages 413-414). It should also be recognized that a lower initial death benefit means that smaller amounts of additional insurance can be purchased under the guaranteed purchase option.

COLLEGE EDUCATION FUNDING

1. **Financial Aid.** In order to determine who qualifies for financial aid, a formula provided by the federal government subtracts the expected family contribution from the cost of attendance. Among other factors, this formula takes into consideration the assets and income of the parents and child. Because the formula gives substantially greater weight to the child's income and assets, large gifts should not be made to a child if financial aid is likely to be sought.

2. **Life Insurance And Annuities.** One advantage of life insurance cash values and annuities is that they are not included in the formula used by the government in determining eligibility for financial aid. Tax-deferred cash value accumulations, favorable loan provisions and a preferred status under the financial aid laws make permanent life insurance attractive for funding a college education. But there should be a real need for the insurance; otherwise, funds might better be invested where there would be no charges for a death benefit. And since a parent is most likely to be paying for college, it makes sense that a parent be the insured (with parent or trust the owner). Provided the parents are adequately insured, life insurance on the child might also be considered. However, a minor child should not be the owner of an annuity or life insurance contract (see page 425). Note also, that when the owner of an annuity is under age 59½ there is a 10 percent penalty tax upon surrender.

3. **Gifts.** Gifts can be made to a minor under either the Uniform Transfers to Minors Act or in trust (see page 482). However, the actual payment of college costs falls within a parent's obligation to support a child; therefore, such payments are not subject to gift taxation. Grandparents can take advantage of the annual exclusion to make gifts to the parents or grandchildren (see chart, page 49). Tuition costs paid directly to a university are free of gift and estate taxes.

4. **Section 529 Plans.** Also known as Qualified Tuition Programs, initial contributions to these plans must come from after-tax income. Contributions are not taxable gifts, but the account value would be included in the estate of the contributor should death occur prior to the funds being disbursed. See the table of Educational Tax Incentives on page 303, and the discussion of Section 529 Plans on page 463.

5. **Hope Scholarship Credit.** The Hope Scholarship credit provides an income tax credit of up to $1,500 per year, calculated as 100 percent of the first $1,000 of qualifying expenses and 50 percent of the next $1,000, for each of the first two years of college (the credit will be indexed for inflation). The student must be enrolled at least half-time in a qualifying educational institution. The student may be the taxpayer, his spouse or any educational institution.

(continued on next page)

COLLEGE EDUCATION FUNDING (continued)

The student may be the taxpayer, his spouse or any dependent. However, the credit may not be taken by an individual who is eligible to be claimed as a dependent on another taxpayer's return. The credit may not be taken if the student has ever been convicted of a state or federal charge of felony drug possession or distribution. There is no limit in any given year as to the number of Hope Scholarship credits a taxpayer may claim as to his dependents (i.e., limit is on a per-student basis). The credit is phased out ratably between modified adjusted gross income of $41,000 to $51,000 for unmarried taxpayers and $82,000 to $102,000 for married taxpayers filing joint returns.

6. **Lifetime Learning Credit.** The Lifetime Learning credit is 20 percent of the first $5,000 of qualifying education expenses (i.e., a maximum of $1,000 per year, but is scheduled to increase to $2,000 beginning in 2003). The Lifetime Learning credit limit is on a per-return basis, meaning that only $5,000 of educational expenses qualifies per year. The credit is phased out ratably between modified adjusted gross income of $41,000 to $51,000 for unmarried taxpayers and $82,000 to $102,000 for married taxpayers filing joint returns. The credit is available for expenses paid, and education furnished, after June 30, 1998. Unlike the Hope Scholarship credit, the Lifetime Learning credit can be taken for any year of postsecondary education (except a year in which the Hope Scholarship credit is claimed for the same student), does not require at least half-time enrollment, and study may be intended to improve the student's job skills and need not lead to a degree.

7. **Deducting Interest On Education Loans.** The deduction is phased out ratably between modified adjusted gross income of $50,000 to $65,000 for unmarried taxpayers, and $100,000 to $130,000 for married taxpayers filing joint returns. It is an "above the line" deduction, meaning that the taxpayer does not have to itemize in order to claim the deduction.

8. **Coverdell Education Savings Account.** In 2002 annual non-deductible contributions of $2,000 per beneficiary can be made. Funds distributed to pay qualified education expenses are income tax-free (see page 365). These accounts had previously been known as "Education IRAs."

9. **Penalty-Free Withdrawals From Regular IRAs.** Withdrawals from an IRA for qualified higher education expenses of the taxpayer are not subject to the 10 percent penalty tax for premature distributions (but are subject to regular income taxes).

10. **Series EE Bonds.** The purchase of series EE bonds can provide tax-free interest if the proceeds are used for the tuition and fees of a dependent. However, there is a phase-out of this exclusion once modified adjusted gross income exceeds a designated amount (for joint tax return filers in 2002 the phase-out is between $86,400 and $116,400).

COMMON DISASTER CLAUSE

The term "common disaster clause" has been loosely used to describe a variety of clauses dealing with presumptions as to the order of death of the insured and the beneficiary. The basic intent of these clauses is to prevent the death benefit from passing to a named beneficiary if that person dies at the same time or shortly after the insured. Thus, it is an attempt by the deceased to better control the disposition of property after death. Although this discussion refers to an insured and the death benefit paid from a life insurance contract, the same concepts apply to a testator and the transfer of property under a will.

Under a "true" common disaster clause when the beneficiary and the insured die as a result of a common disaster there is a *conclusive* presumption that the insured was the last to die, despite the fact that the beneficiary might survive the insured by days, or even months. Under the Uniform Simultaneous Death Act, enacted in almost all states, there is a *nonconclusive* presumption that the insured survived the beneficiary. However, if it can be shown that the beneficiary survived the insured, even for a moment, then the beneficiary receives the death proceeds. A "reverse common disaster clause" is used to assure that the marital deduction will be available. This clause assumes that a beneficiary-spouse survives the insured and therefore the death benefit passes to the estate of the beneficiary-spouse.

A "time clause" (or "short term survivorship clause"), on the other hand, refers not to the cause of death, but to the length of time the beneficiary must survive the insured. The time period is typically 30 days, but may be as long as six months. Periods longer than six months should be avoided if a surviving spouse is the beneficiary and the insured desires to take advantage of the marital deduction (see page 419). This is because property that does not vest in the surviving spouse within six months does not qualify for the marital deduction. For example, assume a time clause requires the spouse to survive for nine months after the insured's death. Once the spouse has survived the required nine months the death benefit is paid, but since it did not vest within six months, it does not qualify for the marital deduction, and will likely be subject to estate taxes.

Because of the difficulty of determining what time period to specify, it is often better to name contingent beneficiaries and have the insurance proceeds paid under a settlement option (other than a life income option that would terminate upon the beneficiary's death). Under such an arrangement the primary beneficiary might receive a few payments, but the bulk of the death benefits would pass to the contingent beneficiaries upon the death of the primary beneficiary (which occurs after the death of the insured). Providing the primary beneficiary with an unlimited right of withdrawal under the settlement option would qualify the death proceeds for the marital deduction.

COMMUNITY PROPERTY

Community property is a specialized form of property ownership that exists only between a husband and wife who are considered to have an undivided one-half interest in such property during marriage. In most community property states both spouses have an equal right and duty to manage community property, but neither spouse has the right to convert to his separate use or give away any substantial amount of community property without the other's consent (the gift can be voided by the nondonor spouse). In case of divorce each spouse becomes a tenant in common of his share of the former community property (see footnote 1, page 13). Upon death each may dispose of his own share of community property however he wishes. Without a will community property passes by state law (often to the surviving spouse), with the deceased spouse's separate property passing according to the state's intestacy statute.

The ten states that have adopted some form of community property law are: Alaska, Arizona, California, Idaho, Louisiana, Nevada, New Mexico, Texas, Washington and Wisconsin (Wisconsin uses the term "marital property"). However, community property laws are not exactly the same in each of these states. A married couple living in a community property state does not have the option of being governed by the state's community property law (except Alaska, where they may opt into the community property system). However, all community property states have provisions allowing for the partition of existing community property into separate property by gift from one spouse to the other, but this must be evidenced by a clear intention (retitling of assets will not suffice). During marriage merely placing newly acquired property in the name of either spouse is not enough to assure that it will be treated as separate property. Prenuptial and postnuptial agreements can be used to fix the property rights of existing or after-acquired property (but are considered invalid in some states).

Community property generally consists of: (1) property purchased during the marriage; (2) earned income during marriage; (3) fringe benefits derived from employment; (4) dividends, interest and capital gains earned on community property; and (5) dividends and interest earned on separate property during the marriage (Texas, Louisiana and Idaho). In addition, property that is otherwise separate property can become community property if it becomes so commingled with community property that it cannot be identified.

Separate property consists of: (1) property owned by either spouse before marriage; (2) earned income from work before marriage; (3) gifts and inheritances received before or during marriage; (4) capital gains on separate property; and (5) dividends and interest earned on separate property during the marriage (Arizona, California, Nevada, New Mexico and Washington).

(continued on next page)

COMMUNITY PROPERTY (continued)

A particular asset can be a mixture of both community property and separate property (e.g., purchase of home using funds earned before marriage and subsequent mortgage payments with community funds). Many community property states provide for other forms of co-ownership, such as joint tenancy and tenancy in common. For example, owning a home in joint tenancy rather than as community property avoids probate (but must be titled using explicit language). On the other hand, community property enjoys the specific advantage of getting a full step-up in income tax basis upon the death of one of the spouses (not available in common law states). There are also advantages to maintaining separate property, since it is generally not subject to pre-marriage debt or debt connected with the other spouse's separate property (but separate property could be subject to claims arising from "community debt").

Problems can occur when married couples move between community property and common law states. Common law property rights have been addressed by California's "quasi-community property" laws, whereas community property interests in common law states have been addressed by the Uniform Disposition of Community Property Rights at Death Act (adopted in a number of common law states).

When a life insurance policy is considered community property generally one-half of the proceeds will be included in the insured's estate. But unique problems can arise when life insurance is community property. If the *insured spouse* dies first and the beneficiary is someone other than the surviving spouse then one-half of the proceeds received by the beneficiary will be deemed a gift by the surviving spouse to the beneficiary, and subject to gift taxes on the surviving spouse's community share of the proceeds. If the *noninsured spouse* dies first the deceased's one-half interest in the policy is included in his probate estate.

Merely naming the noninsured spouse owner of a newly issued policy will likely not avoid the policy becoming community property. The ownership designation should read: "John Doe as his sole and separate property and for his sole use and benefit," or words to that effect. With an existing policy, a transfer can be made to the noninsured spouse using a formal release of the community property interest (see *ASRS*, Sec. 47, ¶100.4). Thereafter, all premiums should be paid from the noninsured spouse's separate funds. If premiums are paid with both separate and community funds, one of two approaches will be used to determine the amount included in the insured's estate, either the "premium tracing" rule or the "inception of title" doctrine (see **Q 520**, *Tax Facts 1 (2002)*).

Buy-sell agreements involving community property business interests should contain the written consent of both spouses to be bound by the agreement. They should also include provisions limiting the disposition of stock or partnership interests upon death or divorce.

CONSTRUCTIVE RECEIPT

A general rule of taxation is that income becomes taxable when it is "made available" to the taxpayer. The constructive receipt doctrine is used to currently tax cash basis taxpayers on income that is available to them, but which they have not actually received. The purpose of the rule is to prevent taxpayers from turning their backs on available income and thereby avoiding current taxation on that income.

However, even though the taxpayer could, under some circumstances, currently receive the money, he will not be taxed provided his control of its receipt is subject to substantial limitations or restrictions. For example, a substantial limitation or restriction might be a forfeiture of the right to continued participation in the plan, a suspension of plan participation for a period of time, or a reduction in plan benefits.

If an employee's rights to deferred compensation are *forfeitable*, there is no constructive receipt. Even where the employee's rights are *nonforfeitable*, there will be no constructive receipt, provided (1) the agreement to defer compensation is entered into before the services are performed, and (2) the employer's promise to pay is not secured in any way.

Employers will often informally fund a deferred compensation plan through the purchase of a life insurance contract. This can be done without adverse tax consequences to the employee provided the employee has no interest in the contract and it remains the unrestricted asset of the employer and, as such, subject to the employer's general creditors. The employer should be the applicant, owner, and beneficiary of the contract. If the employee has any interest in the contract, he may be subject to current taxation.

CONTINGENT OWNERSHIP

In planning their estates, clients are sometimes reluctant to give up control of policy values and death benefits. In these situations, "contingent" ownership of a survivorship life policy insuring both husband and wife can be used to provide some measure of flexibility. However, with this technique there is ongoing estate tax exposure that could be avoided by using a third party as the original policy owner (see chart, page 57). Flexibility is achieved by maintaining individual ownership of the life insurance policy and designating an irrevocable trust as contingent owner of the policy (which could subsequently be changed to a new irrevocable trust with different provisions and beneficiaries).

Assume that husband and wife need life insurance to cover estate taxes and other estate settlement costs. They apply for a survivorship life insurance contract paying a death benefit at the death of the second spouse to die (see page 475). The policy owner should be that person who is most likely to die first. Since the husband is older than his wife he is named policy owner (see table, page 498). An irrevocable life insurance trust is designated as both beneficiary and "contingent" owner (e.g., by endorsement to the contract specifying the trust as owner upon the husband's death). One of three scenarios is likely to occur:

1. **Husband dies first.** The trust becomes policy owner and the value of the policy at the time of death is its interpolated terminal reserve (approximately the cash values). This is the value of the policy to be included in the husband's gross estate (because many survivorship policies provide for a large cash value increase upon the first death this amount could be substantial). Since the wife never owned the policy, upon her subsequent death the policy proceeds paid to the trust are not included in her estate.

2. **Wife dies first.** If the husband continues to own the policy, the death proceeds will be included in his estate upon his subsequent death. However, the husband could gift the policy to the irrevocable trust (or to any third party), in which case the proceeds will be excluded from his estate *provided* he lives for more than three years after the gift (see pages 388-389). Although this exposure to estate taxation is aptly described as "estate planning roulette," with some clients it may be an acceptable risk if they are unwilling to give up control from the inception of the policy.

3. **Husband and wife die in a common disaster.** A "reverse common disaster" clause might be used to establish a conclusive presumption that the wife survives her husband (i.e., husband dies first). See discussion on page 358.

It is strongly recommended that this technique only be resorted to when a client is unwilling to have the insurance policy owned by an irrevocable life insurance trust. Such a trust can *assure* that both cash values and death proceeds are not subject to estate taxation (see chart, page 57).

CONTROLLING STOCKHOLDER

The concept of a controlling stockholder, also referred to as a "majority stockholder," is important with respect to split-dollar plans in which the death benefit is shared between the corporation and the insured's personal beneficiary. As with any key person insurance, that part of the *death benefit received by the corporation* on a policy insuring a controlling stockholder is included with other assets in valuing the corporation, and thus in determining the value of stock in the controlling stockholder's estate. But that part of the *death benefit received outside of the corporation* by the personal beneficiary will also be included in the insured's estate where the insured was a controlling stockholder, since any incidents of ownership held by the corporation are attributed to the insured through his stock ownership as a controlling stockholder. A person is considered a controlling stockholder when, at the time of his death, he owns more than 50 percent of the voting stock of a corporation.

Assume a split-dollar plan is funded by a $500,000 policy paying $100,000 to the corporation and $400,000 to the employee's beneficiary. Because corporate ownership is attributed to the controlling stockholder, the $400,000 death benefit paid to the personal beneficiary is included in the estate. The concept can be illustrated as follows:

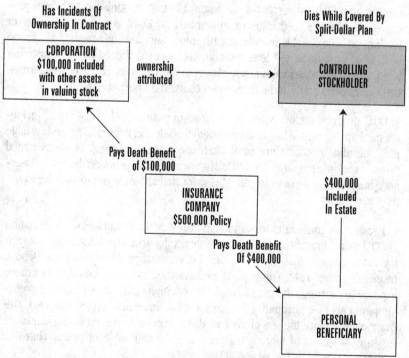

Note: See chart on page 73, discussions on pages 388 and 470, and **Q 515**, *Tax Facts 1 (2002)*.

CORPORATE OWNED LIFE INSURANCE (COLI)

Corporate owned life insurance (COLI) products have been developed and marketed to enable corporations to recover, or to informally fund, the costs of nonqualified benefit plans. Corporations, both large and small, use such nonqualified plans to provide additional income and benefits to key executives and other highly-compensated employees beyond those that can be provided through qualified plans.

COLI products are purchased by corporations on the lives of key employees to fund survivor income plans (chart, page 239), deferred compensation plans (chart, page 243), post-retirement medical benefits, and supplemental executive retirement plans (SERPS). SERPS include various types of nonqualified retirement income plans that are designed to supplement qualified retirement benefits. For example, assuming monthly pay of $12,000, an overall retirement objective of seventy percent of pre-retirement income would result in a monthly retirement objective of $8,400 (.70 x $12,000 = $8,400). If this objective were offset by assumed qualified plan payments of $5,000, the balance of $3,400 would be provided by a SERP ($8,400 - $5,000 = $3,400).

Key features of COLI products and plans include: (1) high early cash values ranging from 50 to 90 percent of premiums; (2) underwriting considerations providing either guaranteed issue or guaranteed standard issue; (3) flexibility in funding variable benefits from both cash values and death proceeds; (4) change of insured provisions; (5) levelized commissions; (6) limited pay or vanish features; and (7) contract guarantees relating to mortality charges, expense charges, credited interest rates, and interest rates charged on borrowed funds.

COLI products include virtually all forms of permanent life insurance, including participating whole life, interest sensitive whole life, universal life, and variable life. Individual products are most often used, although group products issued through multiple employer trusts (MET) are also used, provided the group insurance laws of the state in which the MET is located allow the employer to be a contract beneficiary.

Because tax considerations can weigh heavily in the design and implementation of COLI plans, limitations on the corporate tax deduction for interest paid on policy loans require that existing plans be reevaluated (see Minimum Deposit Insurance, page 424). Other plans are designed to keep corporate insurance expense low through the use of contracts with high cash values relative to premium payments (see Accounting For Business Life Insurance, pages 339-340). Still other plans feature the use of tax-free death benefits to recapture the insurance expense, any costs of funding the plan, and the time value of money (but see, Alternative Minimum Tax, pages 342-344).

COVERDELL EDUCATION SAVINGS ACCOUNT

A Coverdell Education Savings Account, originally called an "Education IRA," may be created for the purpose of paying the qualified education expenses of a designated beneficiary. Annual contributions are limited to $2,000 per beneficiary per year, and the beneficiary must be under age 18 (except in the case of a special needs beneficiary). This $2,000 annual contribution limit is phased out ratably for individual taxpayers with modified AGI between $95,000 and $110,000, and for married taxpayers filing jointly with modified AGI between $190,000 and $220,000. Contributors with modified AGI above this phase-out range are not allowed to make contributions to an Education Savings Account. This contribution limit is per beneficiary, meaning that multiple contributors cannot exceed the $2,000 per beneficiary per year limit (e.g., if grandfather contributes $1,800 for grandson then grandmother is limited to contributing an additional $200 for grandson).

Contributions to an Education Savings Account are not tax deductible, but will be treated as completed present interest gifts from the contributor to the beneficiary at the time of the contribution. A taxpayer may claim a Hope Scholarship Credit or Lifetime Learning Credit for the same taxable year there are distributions from an Education Savings Account, provided the distributions are used to pay for different education costs.

When the funds are distributed to pay the beneficiary's qualified education expenses, neither the principal nor the earnings will be included in the beneficiary's income. Qualified education expenses include elementary and secondary school tuition, expenses of special needs beneficiaries, post-secondary tuition, fees, books, supplies, uniforms, equipment, and certain room and board expenses. Distributions that are not used to pay for qualified education expenses are taxed to the beneficiary.

Any balance remaining in an Education Savings Account at the time a beneficiary becomes 30-years old (except in the case of a special needs beneficiary) or dies, if earlier, must be distributed. The earnings portion of such a distribution will be includable in gross income of the beneficiary and subject to an additional 10-percent penalty tax because the distribution was not for educational purposes. However, it is possible to avoid taxation by rolling the account balance over to another Education Savings Account benefiting a different beneficiary, who is a member of the family of the original beneficiary and who has not attained age 30 as of such date (except in the case of a special needs beneficiary).

CRITICAL ILLNESS INSURANCE

Major advances in medical sciences in recent years have resulted in substantial increases in the number of people surviving a critical illness. Survival periods have also been increasing. For example, in 1993, the American Heart Association reported that two-thirds of those individuals suffering a heart attack would be alive a year later. In 1994, the American Cancer Society estimated that 40 percent of those persons diagnosed with cancer would be alive five years later. Critical illness insurance is designed to provide for those suffering from, and surviving, such illnesses.

Critical illness insurance typically pays a benefit upon the *diagnosis* of the first occurrence of a named critical illness or condition. Some products provide for payments for a limited number of conditions, such as heart attack, stroke or cancer. Other products pay upon such wide ranging conditions as Alzheimer's Disease, multiple sclerosis, major organ transplant, kidney failure, loss of sight, loss of use of two or more limbs, any terminal illness, or death.

Although often resembling the more common "dreaded disease" products, critical illness insurance typically offers substantially greater coverages and benefits. For example, proceeds might be used to provide for home health care needs, replace lost wages of the insured or a care-giver, provide for housekeeping or child care services, pay for "experimental" treatment or drugs, pay medical copayments and deductibles, or make modifications to automobiles and homes for a disabled survivor. Benefits can vary widely. The amount can be either a fixed sum or a percentage of a life insurance death benefit. Payments can be made as a lump sum or over a number of years.

While critical illness insurance has apparently gained wide acceptance in the United Kingdom, Australia, and Japan, it has only recently been available in the United States. The product is likely to have wide application, not just to the married couple or business owner but also to the single person, who, after suffering a critical illness becomes his or her own dependent (traditionally a difficult market for life insurance).

It is currently offered in the form of a stand-alone product, as a rider to a life insurance policy, as group insurance, or as part of a health, term life, or universal life policy. However, payment of critical illness benefits from a life insurance policy could reduce death benefits and reduce or eliminate accumulated cash values.

There is debate as to whether critical illness insurance can give the purchaser a false sense of security (i.e., the product covers only specific illnesses when there is a need for comprehensive health insurance). Critical illness insurance is not available in many states.

CRUMMEY POWERS

By using the gift tax annual exclusion, in 2002 up to $11,000, as adjusted for inflation, can be given tax free each year to as many people (donees) as desired. However, this exclusion is available only when the donee has a right to the immediate use, possession or enjoyment of the property that is the subject of the gift (i.e., a "present interest" in the property as opposed to a "future interest").

Although outright gifts present no difficulty with this requirement, gifts made to trusts are often subject to substantial restrictions on the beneficiaries' (donees') rights to the trust property. Under these circumstances, in order to assure the availability of the annual exclusion it is important for the beneficiaries to be given powers to withdraw gifts placed in a trust. These powers are often referred to as "Crummey powers." The term is derived from the case of *D. Clifford Crummey v. Commissioner*, 397 F.2d 82 (9th Cir. 1968). A trust containing such powers is often referred to as a Crummey Trust.

Typically these withdrawal rights, or "Crummey powers," are exercisable only during a specific period of time (e.g., for 30 days after receiving notice of the gift to the trust). For the power to be effective, the beneficiary must receive timely notice of the gifts, but the withdrawal rights are noncumulative and will lapse after the designated period of time.

For example, an irrevocable life insurance trust might provide for each beneficiary to have "the right to demand up to $5,000, not to exceed the amount placed in the trust during the calendar year." Note that the power is usually limited to $5,000, rather than the full $11,000 allowed as the annual exclusion or the $22,000 allowed as a split-gift (the $11,000 annual exclusion is subject to indexing for inflation). Such a limitation avoids creating adverse gift and estate tax consequences for the *beneficiaries* of the trust (for a further explanation see page 48). A "hanging" Crummey power used to avoid a lapse of a power of withdrawal in excess of the greater of $5,000 or 5 percent of the trust corpus should be drafted by reference to such "5-or-5" limitation and not as a tax savings clause (see footnote 4, page 59).

An alternative to the Crummey power is the cumulative power, which is a vested withdrawal right that does not lapse. Use of a cumulative power enables the trust grantor to make annual gifts of $11,000 (subject to indexing) per beneficiary without causing problems with lapsing powers of withdrawal. However, these nonlapsing withdrawal powers are always subject to being exercised in case of bankruptcy or divorce, and would be included in the beneficiary's estate.

DEATH BENEFIT ONLY PLAN

Under the usual survivor income plan the present value of the survivor income payments is considered to be a part of the employee's taxable estate. With a larger estate the "death benefit only plan" (DBO plan) offers a particular type of survivor income plan that can be designed to keep these benefits out of the employee's taxable estate and thereby avoid federal estate taxes. However, because of the unlimited marital deduction there is no exposure to federal estate taxes unless benefits are payable to someone other than the surviving spouse (e.g., children or other heirs).

In order to establish a death benefit only plan, it is essential that the employee have no right to any post-retirement or disability benefits from his employer, other than those which would be made available under a qualified pension or profit sharing plan. Nor can the employee have any right to alter, amend, revoke, or terminate the survivor income agreement or change the beneficiary, either alone or with the consent of any other person.

Typically, the employer and employee enter into a legally binding agreement under which the employer agrees to provide a specified payment, or payments, to a named beneficiary of the employee. In the agreement it is the employer, not the employee, who names the beneficiary, and the employee cannot thereafter change the beneficiary. The actual payments are usually either a fixed amount or based upon some multiple of salary.

If life insurance is used to provide the employer with funds to meet his obligation under the agreement, the policy should be carried as key person insurance and the agreement itself should contain no specific mention of the insurance funding. Although, as with all key person insurance, the premiums paid by the employer come from after-tax dollars, none of the premiums are included in the employee's income. Should the employee die, the payments to his beneficiary are received as ordinary income and are deductible by the employer, provided they are considered as "reasonable compensation" for the employee's services (see page 483).

There may be some question as to whether a DBO plan would be successful in removing the death benefit from the estate of a controlling stockholder, since his voting control of the corporation gives him the right to alter, amend, or terminate the agreement.

DEFERRAL OF ESTATE TAX

The federal estate tax is normally due and payable *in cash* within nine months after death. However, special deferral provisions are available for a "closely held" business, provided: (1) the business interest exceeds 35 percent of the adjusted gross estate; and (2) the decedent was a sole proprietor, a partner in a partnership with 45 or fewer partners (or owning 20 percent or more of the partnership capital interest), or a stockholder in a corporation with 45 or fewer stockholders (or owning 20 percent or more of the voting stock in a corporation). Under EGTRRA 2001, the number of permitted partners or stockholders was increased from 15 to 45.

If an estate meets these requirements, then the estate taxes attributable to the business interest may be deferred for 4 years during which *interest only* is payable. Thereafter, there is a maximum period of 10 years during which annual installments of *principal and interest* must be paid (Code section 6166).

The interest rate is only 2 percent on the tax attributable to the first $1,100,000 in business value (as indexed in 2002 for inflation) in excess of the "applicable exclusion amount." Under prior law the applicable exclusion amount was known as the "exemption equivalent." In 2002 the applicable exclusion amount is $1,000,000 and the unified credit is $345,800; therefore, the maximum amount of tax deferrable at the 2 percent rate equals $484,000 ($829,800, the amount of tax on $2,100,000, reduced by $345,800). Any estate tax that is attributable to the business interest, in excess of $484,000, is deferrable at 45 percent of the rate applicable to underpayment of tax (6 percent in the first quarter of 2002). In 2002 thru 2009, increases in the exemption equivalent and reduction in the estate tax rates under EGTRRA 2001, will indirectly increase the amount of estate tax than can be deferred at 2 percent interest.

For example, assume that in 2002 the estate tax value of a closely held business interest is $3,000,000 and the adjusted gross estate (AGE) equals $5,000,000. Also assume other deductions of $1,000,000 produce a taxable estate of $4,000,000 and a tentative tax of $1,775,800. From this amount is subtracted the unified credit of $345,800 and the state death tax credit of $210,300 (the state death tax owed to a state cannot be deferred under Section 6166, see page 495). The estate tax payable is $1,219,700 ($1,775,800 tentative tax - $345,800 unified credit - $210,300 state death tax credit). The portion of the estate tax deferrable is $731,820 ($1,219,700 estate tax payable x ($3,000,000 business interest ÷ $5,000,000 AGE)). The portion deferrable at 2 percent interest is limited to $484,000, and the balance of $247,820 ($731,820 - $484,000) is deferrable at 45 percent of the rate applicable to underpayment of tax. See page 85 for the steps involved in calculation of the federal estate tax.

(continued on next page)

DEFERRAL OF ESTATE TAX (continued)

Before relying on the Section 6166 deferral provisions as an alternative to life insurance, a business owner should give serious consideration to **the following qualifications and restrictions**:

1. **The business interest must meet strict qualification standards and percentages** in order for the deferred payment provision to be available.

2. **Not all settlement costs can be deferred.** For example, federal estate taxes on non-business assets, state death taxes, income taxes, debts and administrative expenses must normally be paid in cash when due.

3. **The interest payments are not deductible.**

4. **Only a limited amount of tax** can qualify for the 2 percent interest rate (in 2002 the amount is limited to $484,000).

5. **All remaining payments may be accelerated** if either installment or interest payments are not made within 6 months of the due date, in addition to the payment of a 5 percent per month penalty. The remaining payments can also be accelerated if a significant portion (50 percent or more) of the business is disposed of by sale or liquidation before the estate tax is paid in full.

6. **The executor is personally liable** for payment of the tax and must post a bond of up to twice the amount of the deferred tax. In order to be relieved of personal liability and the bond requirement, the executor must make an election to accept a special IRS tax lien on the assets of the estate. All parties who have any interest in these assets must consent to the lien.

7. **Extensive delays** in the final disposition of the estate will often occur when there is a deferral of the estate tax.

8. **The tax must be paid.** The deferral provisions only allow the business to continue with another creditor (the IRS) making demands on cash flow. The fact that this creditor takes priority over all other creditors often makes it difficult to obtain needed additional credit from banks and suppliers.

9. **After-tax dollars must be used to pay the tax.** For example, an individual in a 35 percent bracket would require $1.54 of before-tax income in order to pay $1.00 of estate taxes ($1.54 - ($1.54 x .35) = $1.00).

There is no deferral allowed on the tax attributable to *estate assets other than the closely held business* unless: (1) under Section 6159 the Secretary determines that installment payments will facilitate payment of the estate tax; or (2) under Section 6161 the District Director finds that there is "reasonable cause" to grant an extension of up to 10 years. Although "reasonable cause" is not expressly defined, the regulations provide specific examples, such as estates with liquid assets outside of the control of the executor, or estates comprised in substantial part of rights to receive payments in the future. These deferral provisions are a matter of discretion and, if granted, interest would be paid at 3 percentage points over the short-term federal rate, not the reduced 2 percent rate or 45 percent of the regular underpayment rate as provided for in Section 6166. Prudent planning should not rely on qualifying for an extension that is granted at the discretion of the IRS.

DISABILITY BUY-OUT INSURANCE

Disability buy-out insurance is designed to provide funds for the purchase of a disabled owner's interest in a corporation or partnership after an extended period of *permanent and total* disability. The benefits of such insurance include: (1) providing funds for the purchase, which funds are not tied to the continued success of the business; and (2) assuring that the disabled owner will no longer be a drain on business income and assets. In contrast, see the discussion of business overhead expense insurance on page 348.

A business is usually not eligible for coverage until it has been in existence for two years, although exceptions can be found (e.g., professional corporations). Maximum amounts of coverage typically range from $300,000 to $1,000,000, with specific amounts limited to a percentage of the owner's interest (e.g., 80 percent of fair market value). As with disability income insurance, definitions of disability vary widely, from inability to engage in one's "own occupation," to inability to perform the duties of "any other occupation" for which one is reasonably suited. It is *absolutely essential* that the provisions of the purchase agreement be consistent with the definitions and terms of the disability buy-out policy.

Because a disabled individual's chances of recovery are highest in the early months of his disability, the waiting period is extended and typically lasts from 12 months to three years (see disability statistics, page 316). This attempts to avoid the forced sale of a business interest while the disabled owner might reasonably expect to return to work. Benefits are paid to the "loss payee," who is that individual or business entity having the contractual obligation to purchase the disabled owner's interest (i.e., entity purchase or cross purchase, see charts on pages 129 and 133). Payment of proceeds can vary from lump sum to installment, with lump sum having the advantage of simplicity, but losing the tax advantage of spreading gain over a number of years.

Successive disabilities can cause a problem when the insured returns to work after being disabled for less than the waiting period, and thereafter suffers a second period of disability. Some policies require satisfaction of a new waiting period, while others consider both disabilities to be "continuous," provided the gap between them does not exceed a certain period. If the insured recovers after the end of the waiting period, but prior to the last indemnity payment, some policies will stop all future payments, while others disregard the recovery and make payments as originally scheduled (i.e., a form of "presumptive" disability).

Although the premiums are not tax deductible, the benefits are received tax-free by the loss payee. As with any other lifetime sale of a business interest, the disabled owner is subject to capital gains taxation of any gain on the sale of his business interest.

DISABILITY INCOME TAXATION

The general rule is that disability income payments under an employer's plan are included in gross income and fully taxable to the disabled employee, including both pre-retirement and post-retirement payments. However, if the payments have been received under a plan to which the employee has contributed part of the premium, that portion of the benefit attributable to the employee's contributions will be received free of income taxes. The tax treatment is the same, whether such payments are characterized as disability payments, salary continuation, wage continuation, or sick pay. See page 468 for an explanation of the taxation of Social Security disability payments.

Under some circumstances, there is a tax *credit* available to individuals who are: (1) age 65 or older; or (2) under age 65 and retired on permanent and total disability. The credit is equal to 15 percent of the taxpayer's "Section 22" amount of income for the year: $5,000 for single taxpayers or married taxpayers filing jointly when only one spouse qualifies for the credit (i.e., $750 credit), and $7,500 for married taxpayers when both qualify for the credit (i.e., $1,125 credit). If the taxpayer is under age 65, the base amount is limited to the amount of taxable disability income.

The base amount used to figure the credit must also be reduced: (1) for nontaxable pension or disability benefits received under social security, railroad retirement and certain other nontax laws; and (2) by one-half of the amount by which adjusted gross income exceeds $7,500 for single taxpayers, and $10,000 for married taxpayers filing jointly. The impact of these rules means that *no credit is available* if a taxpayer receives more than the following amounts of income:

	Nontaxable Social Security, pension, or disability benefits	or	Adjusted gross income
Single	$ 5,000		$ 17,500
Married filing jointly with one spouse qualified*	5,000		20,000
Married filing jointly with both spouses qualified*	7,500		25,000

* A qualified individual is one who is either age 65 or older, or under age 65 and retired on permanent and total disability.

DISABILITY UNDER SOCIAL SECURITY

In order to qualify for Social Security disability benefits an applicant must meet *all* nine of the following tests:

1. He is fully insured by: (1) accumulating 40 quarters of coverage (a total of ten years of covered work); or (2) accumulating at least six quarters of coverage provided he has acquired at least as many quarters of coverage as there are years elapsing after 1950 (or, if later, after the year in which he reaches age 21) and before the year in which he becomes disabled.

2. He has worked under Social Security for at least five of the 10 years (20 out of 40 quarters) just before becoming disabled, or if disability begins before age 31 but after age 23, for at least one-half of the quarters after reaching age 21 and before becoming disabled (but not less than six).

3. He is unable to engage in "any substantial gainful work that exists in the national economy," whether or not such work exists in the area, a specific vacancy exists, or the applicant would be hired if he or she applied for the work (however, consideration is given to age, education, and work experience).

4. Such inability results from "a medically determinable physical or mental impairment" which is expected to result in death, or which has lasted (or can be expected to last) for a continuous period of not less than 12 months. A special definition of the term "disability" is provided for individuals age 55 or over who are blind.

5. He is under 65 years of age.

6. He has filed an application.

7. He has furnished the required proof of disability.

8. He has fulfilled a five-month waiting period.

9. He accepts state vocational rehabilitation services or has good cause for refusal.

DISCLAIMER

The use of disclaimers in estate planning can often result in obtaining greater flexibility by providing the opportunity for post mortem decisions when more facts are likely to be available regarding assets, taxes and beneficiaries.

Disclaimers can be employed with respect to gifts, wills, or life insurance proceeds. To be effective, disclaimers must comply with state as well as federal tax law, must be made in writing prior to acceptance of the property or any of its benefits, contain an irrevocable and unqualified refusal to accept an interest in the property, and must be given to the holder of legal title to the property within nine months after the date that the transfer was made which created the interest (i.e., after death or date of gift). Because of their inherent flexibility, disclaimers will be increasingly used to deal with the uncertainty brought about by EGTRRA 2001 (e.g., to allow a surviving spouse the opportunity to make post death adjustments to the amount placed in the family or non-marital trust under the Exemption Trust Will, see chart on page 29).

For example, the chart on page 29 shows an example of an **exemption trust will** under which the testator directs that the applicable exclusion amount ($1,000,000 in 2002) be placed in the family trust ("B" Trust). Similar results could be obtained by passing all property to the surviving spouse, but with provision for a "disclaimer trust." The **disclaimer trust** would come into being only if the surviving spouse disclaimed, or refused to accept, a portion of the estate under the will. When funded as a result of such a disclaimer, the trust would function in exactly the same way as the family trust illustrated in the chart, except that the surviving spouse would decide exactly how much property, if any, was to go into the trust. Disclaimers can also provide the opportunity for estate equalization by permitting the surviving spouse to disclaim some or all of the property in *excess* of the decedent's applicable exclusion amount. Although this will require payment of an estate tax upon the first death, it can avoid future appreciation of the property in the surviving spouse's estate and take immediate advantage of the graduated estate tax rates.

The following charts compare the exemption trust will on page 29 with a disclaimer of $1,375,000, which in 2002 would produce an estate tax of $156,250 (to be paid from disclaimer trust assets or by the beneficiaries).

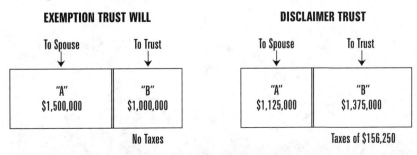

EXEMPTION TRUST WILL		DISCLAIMER TRUST	
To Spouse ↓	To Trust ↓	To Spouse ↓	To Trust ↓
"A" $1,500,000	"B" $1,000,000	"A" $1,125,000	"B" $1,375,000
	No Taxes		Taxes of $156,250

DIVORCE AND LIFE INSURANCE

Transfer of an existing policy incident to a divorce can generally be made without recognition of gain to the husband (this discussion assumes that property or income is being transferred from husband to wife, but the same principles apply if the transfer is from wife to husband). Because the wife is treated as having acquired the property by gift, the husband's cost basis is carried over to the wife, and since the transfer is within an exception to the transfer for value rule, the death proceeds can be received by the wife (or former wife) free of income taxes. A transfer is "incident to a divorce" if it is made within one year after the marriage is terminated or is made within six years after the divorce and pursuant to a divorce or separation instrument.

Payment of premiums pursuant to a divorce or separation agreement that qualify as alimony payments are deductible to the husband and taxable to the wife, provided the wife is owner of the policy. To qualify as "alimony": (1) the payment must be made in cash; (2) the divorce or separation instrument must not stipulate that the payments are not alimony; (3) there must be no liability to make payments after the death of the payee (wife); and (4) the parties must not be members of the same household.

Payment of death benefits to the divorced wife would be taxable as income if the policy had been owned and maintained by the husband pursuant to a divorce decree or agreement as security for post-death payments. However, if the policy had been owned by and payable to the divorced wife, the death benefits would be received free of income taxes.

DOMICILE

Domicile is the place that an individual has freely chosen as the center of his domestic and legal relations. It is the place he intends to remain indefinitely. However, residence without this intention to remain indefinitely does not constitute domicile. A person can have a number of residences, but only one domicile. Once acquired, a domicile is presumed to continue until it is shown to have been changed.

The impact of establishing domicile is far reaching. It determines a persons liability for state and local income taxes; liability for gift and estate taxes (some states still impose an amount in excess of the federal credit); potential limitations on the right to choose fiduciaries such as executors or trustees; rights of surviving spouses to take against a will; community property rights between spouses; divorce and child custody issues; availability of homestead exemptions or similar laws that reduce real estate taxes on a primary residence; where wills must be probated; how property is passed if there is no will; liability for intangible personal property tax on stocks, bonds and savings accounts; and the ability to vote in state and local elections.

To demonstrate the intent to establish a new domicile, the following actions should be taken: (1) register to vote in state and local elections; (2) obtain a new driver's license; (3) change automobile and boat registrations; (4) file for a homestead exemption on the new residence; (5) file a declaration of domicile, if the procedure is available in the new state; (6) remain physically present in the state for over one-half of the year; (7) file federal income tax with the Internal Revenue Service Center servicing the state and include new address on returns; (8) file state and local income tax returns for the new location; (9) file state and local intangible personal property tax returns, if imposed; (10) use the new address on all legal documents (e.g., contracts, wills, bills of sale and deeds); (11) adopt new wills and trusts; (12) provide notice of the new address to banks, credit card companies, professional associations, insurance companies, publishers, friends, relatives and others; (13) establish new relationships with doctors and dentists and have medical records transferred to them; (14) establish new relationships with professional advisers; (15) move stock brokerage accounts to local offices; (16) open checking and savings accounts at a local bank; (17) obtain a safe deposit box and place valuables and legal documents in it; (18) apply for a passport using the new address; and (19) become active in local social, civic and religious organizations.

See also the discussion of noncitizen estate planning on page 426.

DURABLE POWER OF ATTORNEY

A power of attorney is a written document executed by one individual, the "principal," authorizing another person, the "attorney-in-fact," to act on his behalf. Under a *general* power of attorney the powers are very broad and authorize the attorney-in-fact to enter into and discharge virtually all legal obligations on behalf of his principal. Under a *special* power of attorney the powers are very limited and authorize the attorney-in-fact to perform only specific functions on behalf of the principal. Typically, either power of attorney is limited to acts being performed at a time when the principal himself has legal capacity (e.g., is not disabled, mentally incompetent or under some other incapacity).

A *durable* power of attorney authorizes the attorney-in-fact to act even if the principal is incapacitated. This is particularly useful in estate planning situations where it may be desired to make gifts, file tax returns, or provide for the lifetime management of assets. The durable power of attorney has been recognized in some form in all states. Such powers of attorney may be either *immediate*, giving the attorney-in-fact power to act prior to an incapacity, or *contingent*, giving the attorney-in-fact power to act only when the principal has become incapacitated.

DYNASTY TRUST

The term "dynasty" trust is often used to describe a trust created for the benefit of multiple generations. Such trusts are also referred to as "generation-skipping," "legacy," "mega" or "super" trusts. They are often similar to the typical irrevocable life insurance trust, but adapted to take advantage of the generation-skipping transfer tax (GSTT) exemption.

The federal transfer tax system is designed to tax property each time it is passed from one generation to the next. To assist in accomplishing this objective the GSTT applies an additional tax to the normal gift or estate tax whenever property is transferred to persons two or more generations younger than the transferor, or whenever there are taxable distributions or terminations from a trust (see chart, page 39). However, a GSTT exemption is available which allows aggregate transfers of $1,100,000, as indexed in 2002 for inflation, to be exempt from this tax ($2,200,000 total for both husband and wife). These increases of the GSTT exemption under EGTRRA 2001, together with an increase of the gift tax unified credit equivalent, will make it even more attractive for individuals to establish dynasty trusts (see table Phase-In and Sunset Provisions of EGTRRA 2001, on pages 88-89).

A dynasty trust can be created during lifetime or upon death. In order to avoid the GSTT, the donor will typically allocate a portion of his GSTT exemption each time there is a transfer to the trust. Purchase of life insurance upon the life of the grantor, or upon the lives of trust beneficiaries, can result in a leveraging of trust assets through life insurance. Once assets are placed in the trust, and shielded from the GSTT, a properly drafted trust document would avoid subjecting the trust corpus to estate and gift taxes applicable to the trust beneficiaries (e.g., the trust beneficiaries would have no powers over trust assets such as would cause inclusion in their estates). However, a disinterested trustee could be given authority to make discretionary distributions of both trust income and corpus. Trust assets could be made available for use by trust beneficiaries and spendthrift provisions could protect trust assets from a beneficiary's estranged spouse and creditors. Special powers of appointments held by trust beneficiaries could also provide added flexibility (see page 434).

In its purest form a dynasty trust would forever avoid application of the federal estate tax by providing that trust beneficiaries in each generation never have anything more than an income interest in trust property. However, this is generally prevented by the rule against perpetuities, which requires that trust assets must vest in the trust beneficiaries after a certain period of time (see page 457). Apparently even this limitation can be avoided by establishing a trust in those few states where the rule has been eliminated by state statute.

The complexity of both the GSTT and state statutes effecting property interests make it extremely important to seek the advice of knowledgeable legal counsel when considering a dynasty trust.

EMPLOYEE STOCK OWNERSHIP PLAN (ESOP)

The benefits provided by an employee stock ownership plan are similar to those provided by a profit sharing plan, but they are distributable in stock of the employer, and contributions are not dependent upon employer profits.

An employee stock ownership plan (ESOP) must meet specific requirements pertaining to coverage, nondiscrimination in contributions, limits on contributions, diversification of investments, and nonforfeiture of rights upon termination of employment. If these requirements are met, then the plan can be useful in:

1. Motivating employees toward increased productivity (the value of corporate stock held by the trust is dependent upon the corporate profitability).

2. Providing retirement income as a supplement to Social Security and other retirement benefits.

3. Generating liquidity for principal stockholders through the sale of stock to the ESOP during lifetime or after death.

4. Securing funds for corporate growth and expansion with untaxed dollars.

5. Avoiding taxation of accumulated earnings.

6. Securing income tax deductions for an employer with little or no cash outlay.

7. Paying for life insurance on key employees with before-tax dollars.

To secure funds for corporate growth, the ESOP is used as a device for indirect corporate borrowing by having the trustee borrow funds from a lending institution (which loan might be guaranteed by the corporation). The trustee then uses the borrowed funds to purchase stock from either the corporation or the stockholders. Thereafter, the corporation makes tax-deductible contributions to the ESOP to enable the trustee to pay loan interest and principal.

To establish and administer such plans requires a fair degree of sophistication, and therefore they are probably not appropriate for the average small closely held corporation. However, under the appropriate circumstances they represent very effective planning devices for all concerned – the corporation, its employees and stockholders.

APPENDIX | 2002 Field Guide

ENHANCED DOLLARS

If a particular expenditure will not qualify as a tax-deductible business or personal expense, then it makes sense to use the lowest bracket taxpayer to make the payment. Understanding the concept of enhanced dollars will help in weighing the relative merits of executive equity or split-dollar, and cross purchase or stock redemption agreements (i.e., a corporate entity purchase agreement).

Enhanced after-tax dollars would be utilized when a corporation making less than $50,000 annually, and, therefore, in a 15 percent tax bracket, purchases and pays for insurance to fund a stock redemption agreement (chart, page 129). Although premium payments must be made with after-tax dollars, they will be made with enhanced 85 cent dollars, since the corporation gets to keep 85 cents of each dollar of taxable profit. This can be compared to a cross purchase agreement, under which the stockholders might have to pay premiums with their own after-tax dollars. In 2002, a married stockholder filing a joint tax return with taxable income over $112,850, and less than $171,951, is in a 30 percent marginal tax bracket, thus having 70 cent dollars available to pay premiums. Most clients would prefer to use 85 cent dollars rather than 70 cent dollars.

On the other hand, if the corporation was in a 34 percent tax bracket, only 66 cents of each corporate before-tax dollar is available to pay insurance premiums, as compared to the stockholder's 70 cent dollars. Under such circumstances a cross purchase agreement might be favored (chart, page 133).

See also, the tax rates set forth on page 492, and the Cost of Borrowed Dollars figures that appear on pages 189 and 190.

EQUITY SPLIT-DOLLAR

The term "equity split-dollar" is derived from the employee's interest (i.e., an "equity" interest) in policy cash values under a split-dollar plan. Should the arrangement be terminated during the employee's lifetime, the employer's interest in the policy is limited to its cumulative premium payments, and the employee receives the remaining cash values. Upon the employee's death, the employer is typically reimbursed only for its cumulative premium contributions, with the remaining death benefit paid to the employee's beneficiary. These plans have generally been established using the collateral assignment method (see footnote 2, page 167).

There has been a great deal of uncertainty surrounding the treatment of equity split-dollar. TAM 9604001 and Notice 2001-10 only added to the confusion. However, Notice 2002-8 appears to provide workable transition rules, safe harbors, and limited grandfathering of existing plans. In Notice 2002-8 the IRS has set forth its intention to publish proposed regulations that will dramatically alter the tax treatment of split-dollar plans. See table, Treatment Of Split-Dollar Plans Under Notice 2002-8, on page 228.

In split-dollar plans **entered into before January 28, 2002**, and *terminated before* January 1, 2004, the employee's equity will not be taxed. In split-dollar plans entered into before January 28, 2002, and *terminated on or after* January 1, 2004, the employee's equity will not be taxed, provided the plan is converted to a loan from the employer to the employee (if not converted to a loan, the employee will be taxed on all equity when the plan is eventually terminated).

In split-dollar plans **entered into on or after January 28, 2002**, if the plan is established by the *endorsement* method, and the plan is terminated and the policy transferred to the employee, the employee will be taxed on all equity (i.e., transfer to employee of contract owned by employer will cause taxation of employee). The employee's economic benefit will be determined using either the insurer's published premium rates or the Table 2001 rates. If the plan is established by the *collateral assignment* method, and the plan is terminated, the employee will not be taxed on equity (i.e., release of assignment to employer of contract owned by employee will not cause taxation of employee). All employer premium payments will be treated as loans to the employee.

The "no inference" language of Notice 2002-8 could be interpreted as allowing "business as usual" with new split-dollar plans established prior to final regulations. However, it is unlikely that new plans will accumulate substantial employee equity; assuming final regulations are issued prior to January 1, 2004. Clearly, the safer course is to follow the guidance set forth in Notice 2002-8. Until the issues surrounding equity split-dollar are resolved, the advice of competent tax counsel should be sought regarding both existing and contemplated equity split-dollar agreements. See also the discussion of the Split-Dollar Rollout technique on page 470.

EQUITY-INDEXED ANNUITY

This is an annuity that guarantees minimum interest earnings but links excess earnings to increases in an identified equity index. Because of the guarantees, it is generally not considered a security and therefore can be sold by agents who are not equity licensed (see footnote 6, page 79). However, the workings of an equity-indexed annuity (EIA) can be quite complicated and it is important for the agent to fully understand the product. Market conduct and disclosure are important issues with respect to EIAs. Because they can have so many "moving parts," the following discussion provides, at best, only a general outline of EIAs. Individual contracts can vary greatly. Second generation products are being introduced with new features and new complexities.

The EIA is particularly attractive to individuals who are concerned about the safety of principal but who want the opportunity to experience market related gains. Ideally, they should have available an easily understood product that provides the benefits of market appreciation without the risk of losing principal. In reality, they are likely to be faced with an array of products that are not easy to understand.

The minimum purchase amount is typically $5,000, but this can vary widely and is less for products sold in qualified markets. Both single premium and flexible premium contracts have been introduced. There are usually no sales charges (front-end loads), management fees or mortality costs. However, there are often large penalties for early withdrawals. Both level and declining surrender charges are used.

Contracts are linked to the growth of an index over a period that can range from one to ten years, although four to seven years appear most popular. This is referred to as the "term" of the contract or the policy period. While growth can be linked to the performance of virtually any equity index, the large majority of EIAs use Standard & Poor's 500 stock index (the S&P 500 Index). Virtually all EIAs that use the S&P 500 Index refer to the price-level version that excludes dividends. The other is the total-return version and it is determined using dividend reinvestment.

Central to the indexed annuity is a guarantee of principal at the end of the term. This is done by taking a set percentage of the purchase amount and accruing interest at a given percent for the contract term (e.g., 90 percent of a $100,000 deposit plus 3 percent over seven years provides a $111,000 end-of-term guarantee; .90 x $100,000 = $90,000; .03 x $100,000 = $3,000 x 7 = $21,000; $90,000 + $21,000 = $111,000). The reason that most contracts use 90 percent of deposit and 3 percent for earnings is due to state law minimum guarantee requirements for fixed annuities.

(continued on next page)

EQUITY-INDEXED ANNUITY (continued)

Most contracts use one of three different methods to determine gain in the contract. For example, assume that upon issue of a contract with a six-year term the S&P Index was 700. Thereafter the index stood as follows:

End Of Year	1	2	3	4	5	6
S&P Index	781	834	823	871	904	880
Point-To-Point	-	-	-	-	-	25.71%
High-Water Mark	-	-	-	-	29.14%	-
Ratchet (27.98%)	11.57%	6.79%	0%	5.83%	3.79%	0%

Using the point-to-point method the gain is calculated using the beginning point of 700 and ending point of 880 (880 - 700 = 180 ÷ 700 = .2571). In contrast, the high-water mark method, also known as the discrete look-back method, uses the highest point of 904 (904 - 700 = 204 ÷ 700 = .2914). The ratchet method, also known as the annual reset method, calculates gain by adding up the sum of annual gains (11.57 + 6.79 + 5.83 + 3.79 = 27.98). A drop in the index is counted as zero. Unlike the other methods, this has the effect of locking in gains and annually resetting the starting point of the index. Earnings are typically not credited until the end of the term, thus there is no compounding of interest earned. Averaging can be done daily, monthly or annually. The usual effect of averaging is to increase the rate in a decreasing market and reduce the rate in a rising market (e.g., averaging the monthly gains the first year would likely result in less than 11.57% gain).

A cap (maximum rate) may be set on annual gains in the contract. The participation rate is the percentage of the index movement that will be credited (this can vary widely from 60 to over 100 percent). Some contracts guarantee the participation rate for the term of the contract, while other contracts reserve the right to change the participation rate or even lower the cap.

Liquidity features can include nursing home/hospitalization/terminal illness waivers, partial surrenders and penalty-free withdrawals (e.g., 10 percent per year). However, loans are not usually allowed. At the end of the contract term the owner can: (1) renew for another term; (2) make a tax-free exchange for another fixed or variable annuity; (3) surrender the contract without penalty; or (4) annuitize the contract.

Insurance companies fund indexed products by investing in high grade bonds in order to cover the end-of-term guarantee of principal, pay commissions and make a profit. The remaining funds are used to purchase S&P 500 Index call options (i.e., the right to purchase stock at a fixed price at some future time). If the market goes up selling the call options provides funds for meeting the contract obligations.

ERISA

The purpose of the Employee Retirement Income Security Act of 1974 (ERISA) is to protect the interests of workers and their beneficiaries who depend on benefits from employee pension and welfare plans. Among other things, the law requires disclosure of plan provisions and financial information, establishes standards of conduct for trustees and administrators, and sets up funding, participation, and vesting requirements for pension plans.

ERISA covers employee pension and welfare plans that are established or maintained: (1) by any employer engaged in commerce or in any industry or activity affecting commerce; or (2) by an employee organization or organizations representing employees of such employers.

A **pension plan** includes any plan that provides *retirement income* to employees or results in a *deferral of income* by employees to the termination of employment or beyond.

A **welfare plan** includes any plan that provides medical, surgical or hospital care, or benefits in the event of sickness, accident, *disability*, *death* or unemployment (other miscellaneous benefits are also covered).

Title I, Subtitle B, of ERISA contains requirements relating to the following:

Part 1 - Reporting and Disclosure
Part 2 - Participation and Vesting
Part 3 - Funding
Part 4 - Fiduciary Responsibility
Part 5 - Administration and Enforcement

Deferred Compensation Plans

Unfunded deferred compensation plans for a select group of management or highly compensated employees are generally considered pension plans and are subject to the following requirements:

Part 1 - Reporting and Disclosure. Can comply with by: (1) providing a letter to the Secretary of Labor giving the employer's name and address, IRS identification number, a statement that the employer maintains a plan or plans primarily for the purpose of providing deferred benefits for a select group of management or highly compensated employees, and the number of plans and number of employees in each plan; and (2) providing plan documents to the Secretary of Labor upon request.

Part 2 - Participation and Vesting. Not applicable.

(continued on next page)

ERISA (continued)

Part 3 - Funding. Not applicable.

Part 4 - Fiduciary Responsibility. Not applicable, unless considered a welfare benefit plan because death or disability benefits are provided. Can then comply by naming the employer, through one of its officers, as the plan's fiduciary. These requirements may be met in a properly drafted deferred compensation agreement.

Part 5 - Administration and Enforcement. Can comply by providing a definite procedure for handling claims, including providing a written explanation of any denial of benefits. These requirements may be met in a properly drafted deferred compensation agreement.

Split-Dollar Plans

Plans providing split-dollar insurance are generally considered welfare benefit plans under ERISA and are subject to the following requirements:

Part 1 - Reporting and Disclosure. Compliance is generally dependent upon the type of split-dollar plan, for example:

1. A noncontributory split-dollar plan (e.g., an employer-pay-all plan) for a select group of management or highly-compensated employees is exempt from these requirements, except for the requirement that plan documents be provided to the Secretary of Labor upon request.

2. A contributory split-dollar plan (e.g., a single or double bonus plan) having less than 100 participants is also exempt from these requirements, except for the requirement that plan documents be provided to the Secretary of Labor upon request and the need to provide the employee with a summary plan description. Generally, the summary plan description requirement can be satisfied by providing the employee with a copy of the split-dollar agreement and any policy ledgers prepared as part of the proposal.

Part 2 - Participation and Vesting. Not applicable.

Part 3 - Funding. Not applicable.

Part 4 - Fiduciary Responsibility. Can comply by naming the employer, through one of its officers, as the plan's fiduciary. Additionally, the plan documents must set forth procedures for funding the plan, allocating operational responsibilities, amending the plan, and making payments from the plan. These requirements may be met in a properly drafted split-dollar agreement.

Part 5 - Administration and Enforcement. Can comply by providing a definite procedure for handling claims, including providing a written explanation of any denial of benefits. These requirements may be met in a properly drafted split-dollar agreement.

ESTATE FREEZES

Code sections 2701-2704, together referred to as "Chapter 14," contain special valuation rules that maximize the gift tax value of many intra-family transfers by assigning zero value to specific retained interests (unless the retained interest is entitled to "qualified payments").

With Chapter 14 it is possible for a stockholder to freeze the value of a retained corporate interest (the preferred stock) and have a minimal gift tax value assigned to the common stock given to family members (see chart on page 173). However, recapture rules insure that the stockholder actually receives the anticipated dividends that are claimed to increase the value of the retained preferred stock (similar rules apply to partnership interests).

These valuation rules affect three categories of retained rights:

1. A *cumulative* distribution right with a preference upon liquidation is generally valued as the present right to future "qualified payments."

2. A *noncumulative* distribution right, or one that lacks preference upon liquidation, is valued at zero unless a "qualified payment" election is made.

3. A retained liquidation, put, call, or conversion right is valued at zero, unless the right must be exercised at a specific time and amount, or the right contains certain provisions which insure that its holder can share in appreciation.

For example, assume that pursuant to a recapitalization a stockholder transfers common stock to a family member and retains *noncumulative* preferred stock (a noncumulative distribution right under #2 above). Since the preferred stock (the retained interest) does not encompass a "qualified payment" (cumulative rights) it is valued at zero, meaning that the common stock represents the entire value of the corporation and is subject to gift taxes on that amount (to avoid this result the transferor could elect into "qualified payment" treatment, with dividends to be paid in the amounts and at the times specified in the election). Alternatively, assume that after the transfer of common stock to a family member the transferor retains *cumulative* preferred stock with a liquidation preference (a cumulative distribution right under #1 above). In this instance the transferor has retained a right to a "qualified payment" (i.e., to a dividend payable on a periodic basis and at a fixed rate or at a variable rate with a fixed relationship to market value). The value of the gift of common stock is then determined by subtracting the value of the qualified payment/preferred stock interests from the total value of the corporation (meaning that the common stock will have substantially less gift

(continued on next page)

ESTATE FREEZES (continued)

tax value). However, this reduction in the value of the common stock is limited by an additional provision requiring that all common stock (termed the "junior equity" interest) be given a value of at least 10 percent of the total value of the corporation (which, for this purpose, includes a gross-up equal to the total amount of corporate indebtedness to the transferor and family members).

For the statute to apply: (1) the transfer must be to the transferor's spouse, lineal descendants of the transferor or the transferor's spouse and the spouses of such descendants; and (2) the transferor and applicable family members immediately before the transfer must "control" the entity by owning, by vote or value, 50 percent of the stock. For purposes of "control" a person is treated as holding any interest held by his ancestor or his spouse's ancestor, or a spouse of such ancestor, or a lineal descendant of his parent or his spouse's parent (see Degrees Of Kindred chart, page 103).

The valuation rules assume that payments on the cumulative preferred will be made as scheduled. If payments are not made in accordance with a statutorily provided grace period, the rules provide for additional *gift* tax to be paid at the time of a subsequent lifetime transfer, or for additional *estate* tax at the death of the transferor (i.e., recapture). The increase in the taxable gift or taxable estate is the compounded value of the unpaid dividends using the same discount rate employed in determining the preferred stock's value.

Excluded from the scope of these valuation rules are interests in publicly traded stock, interests of the same class as the transferred interest, and interests that are proportionately the same (without regard to differences relating to nonlapsing voting power).

Affected by Chapter 14 are Buy/Sell Agreements (discussion in footnote 3, page 127), Family Holding Companies (discussion on page 391), Family Limited Partnerships (chart, page 169, and discussion on pages 427-428), Grantor Retained Income Trusts (discussion on page 398), Personal Holding Companies (discussion on page 432), Recapitalizations (chart, page 173), and Remainder Interest Transactions (discussion on page 451).

Not affected are Deferred Compensation (chart, page 243), Installment Sales (chart, page 45), Life Insurance Trusts (chart page 57), and Private Annuities (chart, page 45). For a further discussion of the impact of Chapter 14 on specific techniques, see **Q 812-816**, *Tax Facts 1 (2002)*.

ESTATE TAXATION OF LIFE INSURANCE

Section 2042 Proceeds of Life Insurance.

Incidents of ownership – Any incidents of ownership in a policy held by decedent at the time of death will cause the proceeds to be included in his estate. The regulations under Section 2042 state that the term "incidents of ownership" is not limited in its meaning to ownership of the policy in the technical legal sense. These rights include the power to: (1) the economic benefit of the policy, including the power to change the beneficiary; (2) surrender or cancel the policy; (3) assign the policy; (4) revoke an assignment; (5) pledge the policy for a loan; or (6) obtain a policy loan. However, direct or indirect payment of premiums is not an incident of ownership.

Proceeds payable to estate – When proceeds are payable to or for the benefit of the deceased's estate they are subject to taxation in the insured's estate (e.g., when a trustee or third party is required to use the proceeds to pay estate taxes or other estate obligations).

Controlling stockholder – If the insured is a controlling stockholder and the corporation has any incidents of ownership in the policy, then proceeds paid to someone other than the corporation will be included in the estate of the insured. Under a split-dollar plan, an incident of ownership includes the right to borrow cash values (see expanded discussion and chart on page 363).

Fiduciary capacity – Under the regulations an individual is considered to have an "incident of ownership" in an insurance policy on his life which is held in trust if he (either alone or in conjunction with another person or persons) has the power (as trustee or otherwise) to change the beneficial ownership of the policy or its proceeds, or the time or manner of enjoyment of the policy or its proceeds, even if he has no beneficial interest in the trust. It has been held that a co-trustee who has the right to elect a settlement option has a power to effect the time and manner of enjoyment of the policy proceeds insuring himself (i.e., he has an economic benefit). The courts are not consistent in their interpretation of the regulations (see **Q 532** *Tax Facts 1 (2002)*).

Section 2035 Transfers of Life Insurance.

Transfer of a policy by an insured within three years of his death will cause the proceeds to be included in his gross estate. It is not necessary that the insured have outright ownership of the policy, since transfer within three years of death of any of the above "incidents of ownership" is sufficient to cause the policy proceeds to be included in his estate.

(continued on next page)

ESTATE TAXATION OF LIFE INSURANCE (continued)

Under the pre-1982 versions of Code section 2035, using a "beamed transfer" theory the courts found constructive transfers of life insurance policies by insureds within three years of death where: (1) the policy was purchased on the initiative of the insured; (2) the insured supplied the funds used to purchase the insurance; and (3) the insured died within three years of the purchase. However, after the change to Code section 2035 in 1981, the courts have refused to extend this beamed transfer theory to insureds dying after 1981 (*Estate of Leder*, 10th Cir. 1989, *Estate of Headrick*, 6th Cir. 1990, and *Estate of Perry*, 5th Cir. 1991).

In July of 1991 the IRS issued an action on decision in which the Service announced that it would no longer litigate the issue of whether life insurance proceeds are includable in the insured's estate where the life insurance policy is procured by a third party at the instance of the insured, the insured pays the premiums, and the insured dies within three years of procurement of the policy by the third person (i.e., the "beamed transfer" theory). This means that the incidents of ownership in a policy on the decedent's life that is issued to a trustee of an irrevocable life insurance trust will not be imputed to the decedent by reason of the fact that the decedent initiated the procurement of the policy, paid the premiums, or filled out the application for the policy in his capacity as the prospective *insured* (as distinguished from the prospective *owner* of the policy).

Recommended method of purchase and ownership. Despite the Service's favorable decision, it is recommended that whenever possible: (1) a third party be the original applicant, owner, and premium payer; (2) premiums come from an account held in the name of someone other than the insured, i.e., a trustee or adult child; (3) gifts should not be in the same amount as the premiums; (4) the gifts should be made at times other than premium due dates; (5) the insured not be named trustee of an irrevocable trust which owns a policy on his life; and (6) split-dollar plans involving controlling stockholders should avoid giving the corporation any incidents of policy ownership (see page 363). See also, table of ownership and beneficiary arrangements, page 96.

Section 2036 Retained Life Estate.
Section 2037 Reversionary Interests.
Section 2038 Revocable Transfers.

Property given away is still included in the decedent's estate if he: (1) retained the income from, use or enjoyment of, or the right to designate who will ultimately receive the property or its income; or (2) had a reversionary interest worth more than 5 percent of the value of the property at his death, and the person to whom the gift was made could obtain possession or enjoyment only by surviving the

FAIR MARKET VALUE

Property included in a decedent's gross estate is valued at its fair market value on the date of the decedent's death or, if the executor elects, its fair market value 6 months after death (i.e., the "alternate valuation date"). Fair market value is defined in Treasury Regulations as the price at which an item of property, or a business interest, would change hands between a willing buyer and a willing seller, neither of whom is under any compulsion to buy or sell, and both of whom have a reasonable knowledge of all the relevant facts.

When it comes to valuing an interest in a closely held business, the above definition of fair market value is often of little practical assistance. In Revenue Ruling 59-60, the Internal Revenue Service set forth the following eight factors that are considered essential in valuing a closely held corporation:

1. The nature of the business and the history of the enterprise from its inception.

2. The economic outlook in general and the condition and outlook of the specific industry in particular.

3. The book value of the stock and the financial condition of the business.

4. The earning capacity of the company.

5. The dividend-paying capacity.

6. Whether the enterprise has goodwill or other intangible value.

7. Sales of stock and the size of the block to be valued.

8. The market price of stocks of corporations engaged in the same or a similar line of business having their stocks actively traded in a free and open market, either on an exchange or over the counter.

It is interesting to note that factor number 6 is goodwill, and that four of the other factors play a part in the capitalization of earnings formula demonstrated in the chart on page 125.

In determining fair market value, discounts are allowed for minority interests and lack of marketability. For publicly traded stock, it is also possible to obtain discounts using the "blockage" theory, which recognizes that placing a large block of stock on the market would likely have a depressing effect on its price. However, a "control premium" might increase the stock value of a person owning more than 50 percent of the business.

FAMILY HOLDING COMPANY

The *family* holding company, or asset holding company, which is a method of recapitalization, should not be confused with the *personal* holding company. When a new family holding company is formed, it is authorized to issue both voting preferred stock and non-voting common stock. The business owner then transfers his common stock in the original operating corporation to the family holding company in exchange for the voting preferred stock and the non-voting common stock.

Traditionally, the intention is to "freeze" the interest of the business owner in the operating corporation by subsequent gifts of the non-voting common stock of the family holding company. Although gifts of family holding company stock would be subject to the impact of Chapter 14, the techniques used to reduce or avoid the effect of these valuation rules will also work with a family holding company (see pages 386-387, and **Q 812-813**, *Tax Facts 1 (2002)*).

The problems with Section 306 stock do not exist with respect to the formation of the family holding company. A family holding company *could* become a personal holding company if it generates personal holding company income (i.e., passive income such as dividends, rents, and royalties). If there were personal holding company income, a distribution could avoid the personal holding company tax of 38.6 percent in 2002.

As with a recapitalization, there is a definite need to establish an accurate fair market value of the operating corporation prior to a transfer of its common stock to the family holding company.

FINANCIAL UNDERWRITING

Underwriting is the process of risk selection. In addition to *medical* underwriting it is also important to consider *financial* underwriting, where the objective is to issue an amount of insurance that indemnifies but does not enrich the beneficiary.

The key to good financial underwriting is good communication and information. The more information that can be supplied the more likely that a case will be fairly and efficiently underwritten. Typically, the following kinds of information will be required: (1) sales proposals establishing reasons for the life insurance; (2) W-2 forms or latest income tax returns; (3) certified personal financial statements; (4) audited reports of assets, liabilities and operating income of the business; (5) business purchase agreements; and (6) letters of transmittal setting forth reasons for the insurance, details of the agent's knowledge of the applicant and other pertinent information about the case.

When applying for life insurance it is important to be familiar with the insurance company's specific financial underwriting guidelines. Although different carriers may have similar guidelines, carriers will often differ in their published standards and the application of these standards.

Personal life insurance is intended to provide ongoing income to a surviving family by replacing human life value (see chart, page 15). The maximum amount is typically based upon the insured's age and annual *earned* income (but not including *unearned* income such as interest, dividends, rents and royalties). For example, between ages 50 and 54 the amount might be 8 times income, whereas between ages 20 and 30 the amount might be increased to 15 times income. These guidelines are sometimes exceeded when the proposed insured has a potential for substantially increased future income (e.g., the young medical intern).

Key person life insurance is intended to protect a business from the loss of technical and business talent and the resulting loss of profits (see chart, page 157). The amount of insurance is typically limited to some multiple of the insured's compensation (e.g., from three to ten times annual compensation). For a discussion of these formulas, see page 188.

Estate liquidity life insurance provides for final expenses, debts and estate taxes (see charts, pages 19, 27 and 29). Projections of liquidity needs at reasonable rates of estate growth for 5 to 10 years are often allowed (e.g., 8 percent growth over 10 years, see chart, page 23).

Buy/sell life insurance is issued to fund the purchase of a business interest. Determining the amount of insurance requires a consideration of the reasonableness of the value placed upon the business under the agreement. Insurance will likely be required on all owners, but not necessarily with the same carrier (see charts, pages 129, 133, 137 and 141).

FIRST-TO-DIE LIFE INSURANCE

First-to-die life insurance, also known as "joint life insurance," insures two or more lives, and pays a benefit upon the *first* death. Generally, the premium required for a permanent product is substantially less than those for individual policies on each insured.

Uses for first-to-die life insurance include: (1) income replacement in two wage-earner families (e.g., to pay off mortgage); (2) social security replacement for retirees; (3) estate tax payment to facilitate early transfer of appreciating assets to heirs; (4) key person insurance (chart, page 157); (5) funding split-dollar rollout of survivorship life insurance (page 470); and (6) funding both entity purchase and cross purchase agreements (charts, pages 129 and 133).

When funding a cross purchase agreement it is appropriate to have joint *ownership* of the contract. With equal ownership interests an appropriate *beneficiary* designation would be: "surviving insureds, equally." With unequal interests an appropriate designation would be: "surviving insureds as their interests may appear in the cross purchase agreement dated _____."

First-to-die life insurance is very effective in reducing the number of policies required to fund multiple-owner cross purchase agreements. For example, funding of a four stockholder cross purchase agreement requires twelve individual policies, but only four first-to-die policies (Options 1 and 2 below). A trusteed cross purchase agreement using an escrow agent requires four individual policies, but only one first-to-die policy (Option 3 below). If available, a survivor purchase option provides an effective means of acquiring ongoing insurance for surviving stockholders. Exercising this option appears to resolve the "transfer for value" problem caused by a transfer of policy interests following the death of a stockholder under a trusteed cross purchase agreement funded with individual policies (see footnote 7 on page 139, and pages 479-480).

OPTION 1 — Owner → A B C D
12 individual policies insuring: B C D | A C D | A B D | A B C

OPTION 2 — Owner → A B C D
4 first-to-die policies insuring: B C D | A C D | A B D | A B C

OPTION 3 — Owner → ESCROW AGENT
1 first-to-die policy insuring: A B C D

FUNERAL TRUSTS

A funeral trust is an arrangement under which an individual during his lifetime purchases funeral services or merchandise from the provider of funeral and burial services. Pursuant to a contract between the individual and the provider the individual selects the services and merchandise to be provided at death and agrees to make payments during lifetime into a trust.

A "qualified funeral trust" is a trust arising out of a contract with a person in the business of providing funeral or burial services, the sole purpose of which is to hold, invest and reinvest funds in the trust and to use such funds to make payments for the funeral or burial services of beneficiaries under the trust. Contributions to the trust can only be made for the benefit of beneficiaries and cannot exceed in total $7,700 (as indexed in 2002 for inflation) for any one beneficiary. Contributions to the trust are not deductible for income tax purposes. However, the trustee of the trust can elect to have the trust earnings taxed to the trust and payable by the trustee (i.e., elect exemption from the grantor trust rules that would cause trust income to be taxed to the grantor). Each beneficiary's interest is treated as a separate trust for this purpose. However, a qualified funeral trust is not allowed a personal exemption.

GIFT TAX vs. ESTATE TAX

The unified credit of $345,800 allows an individual to give away $1,000,000 of property in 2002, without paying a gift tax. In larger estates this can result in substantial savings by removing future appreciation on the gift from the estate. For example, assuming 8 percent appreciation, a $5,000,000 estate will grow to $6,802,445 in 2006, resulting in estate taxes of $2,209,125, and leaving $4,593,320 for the heirs. In contrast, a gift of $1,000,000 reduces the estate to $4,000,000. This reduced estate will grow to $5,441,956 in 2006, resulting in estate taxes of $2,043,300 and $4,759,145 for the heirs ($3,398,656 estate after taxes + $1,360,489 appreciated gift).

		Value At 8% Appreciation			
	Year 2002	Year 2006	Year 2009	Year 2010	Year 2011
NO GIFT					
Estate Size	5,000,000	6,802,445	8,569,121	9,254,651	9,995,023
Less: Estate Tax	1,930,000	2,209,125	2,281,104	0	4,792,263
Total To Heirs	3,070,000	4,593,320	6,288,017	9,254,651	5,202,760
GIFT OF $1,000,000					
Original Estate Size	5,000,000				
Less: Gift	1,000,000				
Remaining Estate	4,000,000	5,441,956	6,855,297	7,403,721	7,996,019
Less: Estate Tax		2,043,300	1,959,884	0	4,242,810
Estate To Heirs		3,398,656	4,895,413	7,403,721	3,753,208
Plus: Value Of Gift	1,000,000	1,360,489	1,713,824	1,850,930	1,999,005
Total To Heirs		**4,759,145**	6,609,237	9,254,651	5,752,213
Advantage Over NO GIFT		165,825	321,220	0	549,453
GIFT OF $1,500,000					
Original Estate Size	5,000,000				
Less: Gift	1,500,000				
Less: Gift Tax	210,000				
Remaining Estate	3,290,000	4,476,009	5,638,482	6,089,560	6,576,725
Less: Estate Tax		1,618,964	1,427,317	0	3,527,199
Estate To Heirs		2,857,045	4,211,165	6,089,560	3,049,526
Plus: Value Of Gift	1,500,000	2,040,733	2,570,736	2,776,395	2,998,507
Total To Heirs		**4,897,778**	6,781,901	8,865,955	6,048,033
Advantage Over NO GIFT		304,458	493,884	-388,696	845,273

Increasing the gift to $1,500,000 requires payment of a gift tax, but the heirs receive an additional $138,633 ($4,897,778 - $4,759,145). Provided the donor lives for more than three years after making the gift, the following will be removed from the estate: (1) appreciation of the gift; (2) the gift tax; and (3) appreciation of the gift tax. Because EGTRRA 2001 repeals the estate tax in 2010, if death occurs in that year there would be a loss of $388,696 (the future value of the $210,000 gift tax). Before making a gift substantial enough to require payment of a gift tax, the following variables should be carefully evaluated: (1) the value of the estate; (2) the size of the gift; (3) the rate of projected growth; (4) the assumed year of death; and (5) the likelihood and nature of congressional changes to the estate tax laws.

GOLDEN PARACHUTE RULES

Under these rules, a corporation is barred from taking an income tax deduction for an "excess parachute payment" made to an officer, shareholder or highly compensated individual when the payment is contingent upon a change in ownership or control of the corporation. In addition, a nondeductible 20 percent excise tax is imposed on the employee's excess payment.

Parachute payments are generally defined as any payments in the nature of compensation, that are contingent upon a change of ownership or effective control of the corporation when the present value of such payments equals or exceeds three times the individual's average annual compensation in the five taxable years ending before the date of the change. If the individual has been employed by the corporation for fewer than five years, then average annual compensation is determined by using the years actually employed.

These rules can adversely impact a *supplemental* deferred compensation plan if the plan calls for an acceleration of vesting or payment of benefits due to a change in control. However, these rules do not impact a pure *deferral* plan under which the executive has made an election to actually defer income previously earned. There are also limited exceptions for payments made by closely held corporations.

The golden parachute rules should not be confused with the $1,000,000 compensation deduction limitation placed upon publicly-held corporations (i.e., those that issue stock required to be registered under the Securities Exchange Act of 1934). Under this limitation, such corporations may not deduct compensation in excess of $1,000,000 paid to the chief executive officer and the four highest paid officers of the corporation. In effect, this limitation declares such excess compensation to be unreasonable per se, and therefore not deductible. Both split-dollar and executive bonus plans for this group of executives could be impacted. However, excluded from the limitation are: (1) amounts paid by reason of worker's compensation, medical or hospitalization expenses, or payments made to any qualified plan or SEP; (2) commission payments; (3) performance-based compensation meeting strict qualifications and standards; and (4) stock options and stock appreciation rights.

GRANTOR TRUST RULES

Under the grantor trust rules a grantor who retains interests in a trust created by the grantor may be treated as the owner of all or part of the trust and thus taxed on all or a portion of the trust income. Retention of the following powers or interests can cause a trust to be considered a grantor trust: (1) reversionary interests in the income or principal of any portion of a trust that exceed five percent of the value of the trust; (2) the power to control the beneficial enjoyment of any portion of the trust that can be exercised without the approval of an adverse party (excepted is the power to limit distributions of principal to a beneficiary using a "reasonable definite standard"); (3) administrative powers, including the power to deal with trust funds for less than full and adequate consideration and to borrow without adequate interest or security; (4) power to revoke the trust; and (5) income of the trust is *or may be* distributed to or held for the future use of the grantor or the grantor's spouse, used to discharge a legal obligation of the grantor, or used to purchase life insurance on the life of the grantor or the grantor's spouse.

Thus, transfer of income-producing property to a trust and the subsequent use of that income to pay life insurance premiums will result in the income being tax to the grantor. The results are less clear when a trust merely authorizes the payment of premiums from trust income but does not use trust income for this purpose. In order to avoid grantor trust status most authorities recommend that the trust language specifically prohibit the use of trust income to pay life insurance premiums on the life of the grantor or the grantor's spouse.

A "defective" trust is an *irrevocable* trust that intentionally violates one or more or the grantor trust rules (see chart, page 69). With a defective trust, application of the grantor trust rules can work to the taxpayer's advantage: (1) *To take an income tax deduction for interest paid on a life insurance policy loan.* An irrevocable life insurance trust considered a grantor trust enables the grantor to take an income tax deduction (if available) for loans on policies held by the trust, with no estate tax inclusion. (2) *To transfer additional amounts to trust beneficiaries without gift tax consequences.* Income taxes paid by the grantor on trust income distributed to beneficiaries may not be included in the value of gifts made by the grantor. (3) *To avoid the transfer for value rules.* A grantor trust that is taxed as if owned by the grantor/insured can purchase or obtain existing policies on the grantor's life without adverse tax consequences (i.e., the transaction falls within the "transfer to the insured" exception, see page 479). (4) *To avoid disqualification of the S corporation election.* An irrevocable grantor trust can be a stockholder, but limited to 2 years after the grantor's death.

It is important that any powers or interests retained by the grantor not cause the trust to be included in the grantor's taxable estate. Clearly, application of the grantor trust rules can be very complicated and the advice of competent tax counsel should always be sought.

GRITs, GRATs, AND GRUTs

Prior to the changes brought about by the special valuation rules of Chapter 14, a grantor retained income trust (GRIT) was an effective technique for transferring property between generations. For example, a GRIT was created by having a grantor establish an irrevocable trust from which he retained the right to trust income for a specified period. At the end of this period the succeeding trust beneficiaries (or remaindermen) received the trust principal. Because of the reserved income interest, the gift tax value of the transferred remainder interest was usually substantially less than the current value of the property.

However, except for a personal residence, Chapter 14 effectively eliminated the GRIT as a viable estate planning tool, since the grantor's right to trust income is deemed to have no value, meaning that the gift tax value of the remainder interest is equal to the *entire* value of the trust property (see pages 386-387). The gift tax cost is exactly the same as if the grantor had made a direct gift of the property to the remaindermen.

In place of a GRIT, the grantor retained annuity trust (GRAT) and grantor retained unitrust (GRUT) are available to leverage gifts between generations. The GRAT is an irrevocable trust in which the grantor retains the right to receive *fixed payments* payable at least annually for life or for a term of years. The GRUT is an irrevocable trust in which the grantor retains the right to receive a *fixed percentage* of the trust's assets payable at least annually for life or for a term of years (and which must be revalued annually).

The GRAT is actuarially similar to the charitable remainder annuity trust, whereas the GRUT is actuarially similar to the charitable remainder unitrust (see page 60). With both the GRAT and the GRUT, the value of the transferred remainder interest is equal to the value of the entire property reduced by the value of the retained interest.

In contrast to the GRIT, the GRAT *must pay* a fixed annual payment to the grantor, regardless of the income earned (whereas the GRIT often experienced substantial appreciation while yielding only a modest income). However, in contrast to the GRAT, the GRUT will provide increasing payments to the grantor if the value of the trust increases (or decreasing payments if the value of the trust decreases). If the grantor is seeking to reduce his estate, additional smaller gifts that qualify for the annual exclusion can be made with the funds provided by trust payments.

GROUP CARVE OUT

The term "group carve out" is often used to describe the *replacement* of group term insurance for a selected class of executives with individual permanent insurance policies. Increased popularity of this concept has been due to the prohibition against individual selection in providing amounts of coverage to key employees.

Although a variety of plans are used to fund a group carve out, the more popular include Executive Equity (chart, page 219) and Split-Dollar Insurance (chart, page 227). The advantages of group carve outs include: (1) the provision of permanent post retirement insurance for the executive; (2) lower long term cost for the employer; (3) elimination of the increasing long term cost after retirement to both the executive and the employer; (4) flexible structure with no ERISA or nondiscrimination requirements; (5) cost recovery options for the employer; and (6) portability of the policy for the executive.

The design of individual illustrations will differ widely depending upon the circumstances of the existing group program and the proposed method of funding the group carve out. However, it is essential to compare annual costs to both the employer and executive, both before and after the carve out. This includes estimates of the current and projected group premiums for the executive's coverage under the group plan, together with the after-tax costs of bonuses, if any, given the executive to cover his tax cost of amounts of coverage in excess of $50,000. These same employer after-tax dollars are then placed in an Executive Equity or Split-Dollar program. Should the group carve out plan require additional executive costs (i.e., either direct premium payments or increased tax costs), then it is important to make a direct year-by-year comparison of this cost to the executive's ownership of policy cash values.

GUARANTEED PURCHASE OPTION

At the time a life insurance policy is issued it is often possible to purchase an option that provides the policyowner with the right to purchase, without evidence of insurability, additional amounts of permanent insurance at stated intervals or upon stated events. This option is usually issued as a rider to the basic policy and terminates at a specified policy anniversary. Some options provide an overall limit on the amount of additional insurance that may be purchased. Premiums for the option are based upon the insured's attained age and are payable until the rider terminates. Guaranteed purchase options are also referred to as "insurability options." Use of a guaranteed purchase option is particularly attractive when insurance is issued on the life of a child (see the discussion of children's life insurance on page 355).

When the option is exercised the insurance purchased does not have to be the same plan as the basic policy. Premiums for the additional insurance are at standard rates. For example, a typical rider might provide for the option to purchase $20,000 of additional insurance every 3 years until the policy anniversary nearest the insured's age 40. Additional option dates might also include the insured's marriage and the birth of each of the insured's children.

Other forms of guaranteed purchase options offer guaranteed insurance under cost-of-living adjustments that are tied to increases in an economic inflation indicator, such as the Consumer Price Index. Another variation, known as a "beneficiary purchase option," allows the beneficiary, upon the death of the insured, to elect to use part or all of the proceeds to purchase insurance without evidence of insurability. However, at the time the underlying policy is issued the beneficiary must prove insurability. This option is used as a substitute for survivorship life insurance and may offer greater flexibility (i.e., the surviving spouse uses some of the proceeds to pay estate taxes at the first death and the remaining proceeds to exercise the "last to die" option). Still another variation, known as a "surviving spouse option," is used with survivorship insurance (see the discussion of survivorship life insurance on page 475). This option allows the policyowner to purchase an additional amount of insurance on the primary insured following the death of his or her spouse.

INCENTIVE TRUST

The dilemma faced by many wealthy individuals is how to pass down the family fortune without taking away their children's ambition, drive and willingness to lead productive lives. Recent creation of substantial wealth in the stock market and the large inheritances being passed to today's "baby boomers" has only added to the number of families facing the challenge of "financial parenting." The incentive trust is a response to these concerns.

In contrast to the traditional trust with its set distribution times and amounts, the incentive trust goes beyond the age-linked distribution formulas by attaching conditions to distributions. For example, the incentive trust might contain provisions that tie the timing and size of distributions to the achievement of certain goals by the beneficiaries, such as receipt of good grades, graduation from college, obtaining a graduate degree, a first job or rewarding the attainment of specific levels of income. More controlling provisions might reward certain conduct or community service, such as staying at home to take care of children, serving as a missionary, or remaining alcohol or drug free (i.e., "tough love" when there has been a prior history of abuse).

The potentially restrictive and controlling nature of such trusts is a matter of some debate. To some, incentive trusts might be seen as nothing more than an attempt to unduly "control from the grave." Yet it seems most laudable when parents desire to teach their children to be good stewards of family wealth. Establishing such a values-oriented trust will likely require a great deal more thought and effort then is required of the typical tax-savings and distribution trust (see charts on pages 29 and 57).

When creating an incentive trust, a "one size fits all" approach is not appropriate. Ideally, the trust will accomplish the grantor's objectives without unduly restricting the trustee's ability to respond to changing circumstances, such as a beneficiary's marriage, medical emergency, or behavior. A good trust must be carefully drafted. While encouraging positive social goals and distributing income, the trust should also act as an economic safety net for children and other heirs.

Use of an institutional trustee together with an individual co-trustee who is either a family member or friend will avoid the undue pressure that can be placed on an individual trustee by beneficiaries demanding distributions that are inconsistent with trust objectives. It also seems quite reasonable to include provisions for the replacement of an unsatisfactory trustee by the beneficiaries.

In addition to the incentive trust, private foundations and family limited partnerships are also used as a means of involving children and other heirs in the responsible charitable distribution of a family's wealth.

INCOME IN RESPECT OF A DECEDENT

The term "income in respect of a decedent" (IRD) refers to those amounts which a decedent was entitled to as gross income, but which were not includable in his taxable income for the year of his death. For example, the following are considered IRD: (1) payments to a surviving spouse under an individual deferred compensation agreement; (2) compensation for services rendered before death; (3) renewal commissions of a life insurance agent; (4) dividends declared but unpaid to a stockholder prior to his death; (5) interest owed the decedent at the time of his death; (6) the decedent's distributive share of partnership income; (7) amounts paid for unrealized receivables upon the sale or liquidation of a partnership interest; (8) distributions from a 403(b) tax deferred annuity; (9) distributions from a decedent's individual retirement account; and (10) proceeds from sales on the installment method.

It is important to recognize that, unlike other property included in an estate, the recipient of IRD does not receive a stepped-up basis for the purpose of computing gain or loss (see the discussion of stepped-up basis on page 473). Thus, the estate or beneficiary who receives IRD will pay tax on that income in the same manner as the decedent. If the income would have been ordinary income to the decedent, then it is ordinary income to the estate or beneficiary. Likewise, if the income would have been treated as capital gains to the decedent, then it is treated as capital gains to the estate or beneficiary.

However, an income tax deduction is available which somewhat alleviates this "double" taxation (i.e., subjecting the IRD to both estate taxation and income taxation). The recipient of IRD generally may take an income tax deduction for any estate taxes paid by the estate on the IRD. The amount of the deduction is determined by comparing the actual estate tax paid with the amount of estate tax that would have been paid had the IRD not been included in the estate (i.e., the deduction is determined at the highest estate tax rates to which the estate was subject). The deduction can also be taken for generation-skipping taxes paid on the IRD. This is a *deduction* to be used in determining the income taxes of the estate or beneficiary receiving the IRD, it is not a *credit* against the income tax due.

INDIVIDUAL RETIREMENT ARRANGEMENTS (IRAs)

There are two types of regular individual retirement arrangements, individual retirement accounts and individual retirement annuities. Each is often referred to as an "IRA" (see also pages 301-302 and 456). Generally an individual retirement *account* is set up as a trust or custodial account with a bank, a federally insured credit union, or a savings and loan association, whereas an individual retirement *annuity* is established by purchasing an annuity contract from a life insurance company. Life insurance may not be purchased by the IRA.

Contributions may be made up to the time when the individual's tax return is due (excluding extensions). In order to deduct contributions an individual must: (1) have compensation (including earned income as an employee or self-employed person, or alimony); and (2) not have attained age 70½ during the taxable year for which the contribution is made.

In 2002 a deduction may be taken for amounts contributed up to the lesser of $3,000 or 100 percent of compensation includable in gross income. An additional "catch-up" contribution of $500 is allowed for individuals who attain age 50 before the close of the taxable year. Deductions may be reduced or eliminated if the individual is an "active participant" in a qualified plan. The phase-out range for a *married couple filing jointly* is between $150,000 and $160,000 for a spouse who is not an active participant, and between $54,000 and $64,000 for a spouse who is an active participant. The phase-out range for a *single individual* who is an active participant is between $34,000 and $44,000. Similar deductions may be taken for contributions to the IRA of a lesser-compensated spouse.

Generally, funds accumulated in a plan are not taxable until they are actually distributed. However, amounts distributed prior to age 59½ are considered premature distributions and are subject to a 10 percent penalty tax. Exceptions to the penalty tax include distributions: (1) made on or after death; (2) attributable to disability; (3) which are part of a series of substantially equal periodic payments made (at least annually) for the life or life expectancy of the individual or the joint lives or joint life expectancy of the individual and a designated beneficiary (e.g., an annuity payout); (4) for medical expenses in excess of 7.5 percent of adjusted gross income; (5) for health insurance premiums for those receiving unemployment compensation; (6) to pay for a first home; or (7) to pay for qualified higher education expenses. Distributions from a plan must usually begin by April 1 of the year after the year in which the individual reaches age 70½.

In order to prevent current taxation IRAs are frequently used for "rollovers" of distributions from qualified plans, 403(b) plans, or eligible 457 government plans. An IRA that meets certain requirements may accept an expanded rate of contribution as a simplified employee pension (SEP). SEPs are discussed on page 467.

INSTALLMENT SALE

An installment sale provides a method by which the gain on the sale of property, and the income tax on that gain, can be spread over a period of time. No payment is required in the year of sale; the only requirement is that at least one payment be made in a taxable year after the year of the sale. Payments can be tailored to fit both the seller's income and tax requirements, since gain and the payment of tax on that gain is prorated according to the amount received each year.

When there is a sale between related parties (spouses, children, etc.), any resale by the buyer within 2 years accelerates the gain to the seller unless such resale occurs after the death of either of the related parties. The seller's gain will also be accelerated if the seller cancels the buyer's obligation (this may also include a cancellation by bequest or by the seller's executor). However, it appears that this technique of making gifts is available with an installment sale, provided there is a forgiving of each installment payment as it comes due. See the expanded discussion of self-cancelling installment notes, page 465.

If the amount of debt does not exceed $4,217,500 (as adjusted in 2002 for inflation) and the installment sale does not provide for a *minimum* interest rate equal to the "applicable federal rate," the IRS will generally impute an interest rate at the lower of the applicable federal rate or 9 percent, compounded semiannually. However, with intra-family aggregate sales of land of not more than $500,000 during a calendar year, the imputed interest rate would be the lower of the applicable federal rate or 6 percent. Applicable federal rates are determined by the Secretary of the Treasury on a monthly basis (for this purpose it is the lowest rate in effect during the 3-month period ending with the month in which there is a written contract).

Unless it can be shown that avoidance of income tax was not a principal purpose, the sale of *depreciable property* to a controlled entity may not be reported on the installment basis. Accrual method taxpayers generally may once again use the installment method for sales or other dispositions retroactive to December 17, 1999 (except in the case of property used in the trade or business of farming, timeshares, and residential lots).

INSURABLE INTEREST

The issuance of an insurance contract to someone who does not have an insurable interest in the life of the insured is void as a matter of public policy. Generally stated, an insurable interest arises from the relation of the party obtaining the insurance to the insured, provided there is a reasonable expectation of advantage or benefit from the continuance of the insured's life. An insurable interest is based upon relationships which involve: (1) pecuniary or economic advantage through the continued life of the insured or loss by reason of his death; or (2) love and affection in case of individuals closely related by blood or marriage.

The following are generally considered to have insurable interests: (1) a person on his own life; (2) a wife in her husband's life and a husband in his wife's life (see *ASRS*, Sec. 13, ¶200, regarding the rights of a divorced spouse named as beneficiary); (3) a fiancée in her fiancé's life and a fiancée in his fiancée's life; (4) a parent on a minor child's life (but not necessarily on an adult child's life); (5) a creditor in the life of his debtor; (6) an employer in the life of a key employee (but not a rank and file employee); (7) each of the partners, and the partnership itself, in the life of a partner whose death would result in a substantial loss; (8) each of the partners to a buy/sell agreement in the life of another partner, provided the beneficiaries do not stand to gain upon the death of the insured; and (9) among stockholders in a closely held corporation to the extent, and on the same basis, that an insurable interest exists among partners. See page 352 regarding charities having an insurable interest in the lives of donors.

Provided the insurable interest requirements are satisfied at the *inception* of the contract, in most states a policy remains valid thereafter even if at the insured's death the policyowner-beneficiary no longer has an insurable interest (but Texas requires that the beneficiary have an insurable interest at the time of death).

In most states there can be a valid *subsequent assignment* of a policy even if the assignee does not have an insurable interest in the life of the insured (but in Kentucky and Kansas, the assignment to one having no insurable interest in the life of the insured, other than charitable, benevolent, educational or religious institutions that are irrevocable beneficiaries, is void as contrary to public policy; for a special rule in Texas, see *ASRS*, Sec. 12, ¶20.14(b)).

If the applicant has no insurable interest at the time a policy is taken out, the proceeds will be taxed as gain from a wagering contract. If a policy is found to be void for lack of an insurable interest, the insurance company is generally required to refund premiums paid plus interest. Since the existence of an insurable interest is governed by the case and statutory law of each state, it is essential to refer to these specific state laws for answers to questions regarding an insurable interest (see *ASRS*, Sec. 12, ¶ 20.22).

INTEREST ADJUSTED NET COST

Net Cost Method. Prior to introduction of the interest adjusted net cost method, the cost of life insurance was frequently determined by the "net cost" method, which consisted of simply adding up the net premiums (premiums less dividends), subtracting out any cash values, dividing by the number of years, and then dividing by the number of thousands of insurance. For example, assume a $150,000 nonparticipating contract with premiums of $900 per year yields $6,000 of cash values in the 10th year:

Premiums per year	900
Number of years	x 10
Total premiums paid	9,000
Less cash values	(6,000)
	3,000
Number of years	÷ 10
Cost per year	300
Number of thousands	÷ 150
Cost per year per thousand	2.00

Interest Adjusted Net Cost Method. But the above calculation fails to account for the time value of money. The *interest adjusted* net cost (IANC) method has been adopted by most states in order to provide some index for comparing one life insurance contract with another, and is particularly useful where there is a difference in amount and timing of premiums, availability of dividends and amounts of cash values. The IANC method assumes that the purchaser would be helped by comparing the results of his purchase to those that he could obtain by investing his money in a 5 percent savings account, with interest compounded annually. The basic question involves determining what amount of annual deposit would be required to end up with the same cash accumulation. Assuming the same $150,000 nonparticipating contract:

Life Insurance Contract		
Premiums per year		900.00
Cash values in 10 years	6,000	
5% Savings Account		
Cash value objective	6,000	
Interest factor (table, page 500)	÷ 13.207	
Annual deposit required		(454.30)
Cost per year for insurance		445.70
Number of thousands of coverage		÷ 150
Cost per year per thousand		2.97

INTEREST DEDUCTION

The deductibility of interest depends on its classification. For example, investment interest is generally deductible only to the extent of investment income, *qualified residence interest* is generally deductible in full, trade or business interest is generally deductible as a business expense, and personal interest is not deductible at all (except student loan interest; see page 357).

Personal interest includes interest on personal loans and interest on personal life insurance policy loans used to pay premiums on the policy. Investment interest may be deducted to the extent of net investment income. There are no limitations on deductibility of interest on amounts borrowed for ordinary and necessary business purposes.

For policies that are minimum deposited (i.e., carried with loans from the cash values) the inability to deduct the interest paid on these loans means that it will cost the individual policy owner more to maintain the policy. If this cost is unacceptable, then the following alternatives might be considered:

1. Borrow from a home equity mortgage and use the proceeds to pay off the life insurance loan (assuming that payments on the home equity mortgage would be deductible).

2. For those who are officers or 20 percent stockholders of a corporation, if there is a need for key person insurance, transfer the policy to the corporation and allow the corporation to take the interest deduction on debt up to $50,000 (but subject to strict limits, see Minimum Deposit Insurance, page 424). There would be no taxable gain to the transferor provided the loan does not exceed his basis in the contract. The interest payments must be a reasonable business expense (e.g., the corporation must have a need for key person insurance) and the contract must be "tax qualified" (again, see page 424). Such a transfer would be an exception to the transfer for value rules (see page 479).

INTEREST-FREE LOANS

At one time the use of interest-free, or below market, loans between parent and child, or employer and employee, was generally considered an effective means of transferring income that offered many tax advantages. The Supreme Court decision in *Dickman* (1984), the introduction by the Deficit Reduction Act of 1984 of the concept of "forgone interest" and the phasing out of the deduction for personal interest by the 1986 Tax Reform Act limited these tax advantages. Nevertheless, there may still be circumstances in which such loans would be appropriate to accomplishing nontax objectives (parent loans to child to buy life insurance, or corporation loans to nonstockholder-employee as a form of "golden handcuffs").

Gift Loans. When a below market or term loan is treated as a "gift loan" the lender is deemed to have transferred to the borrower, and the borrower is deemed to have retransferred to the lender, an amount equal to the forgone interest. The effect of this treatment is that the forgone interest is included in the gross income of the lender, and the borrower is considered as having paid the interest (for individuals, there is no deduction for personal interest, as discussed on page 407).

Compensation-Related Loans. The same transfer and retransfer of forgone interest is deemed to have occurred with loans between employers and employees, or corporations and stockholders, as with gift-loans. The employer will be deemed to have interest income in the amount of the forgone interest, which would be offset by a corresponding deduction for compensation paid (if reasonable). The employee is considered as having paid the interest. However, with stockholder-employees, the forgone interest will be treated as a nondeductible dividend payment.

Exceptions. There is a $10,000 de minimis exception for compensation-related or corporation-stockholder loans that do not have tax avoidance as a principal purpose. Another exception is available when the total loans between individuals (husband and wife are considered one individual) do not exceed $10,000 unless the gift loans are directly attributable to the purchase or carrying of income-producing assets. These exceptions may protect low interest loans used to purchase life insurance, unless the life insurance is considered an income-producing asset in the case of a gift loan, or there is a tax avoidance purpose in the case of a corporation-employee or corporation-stockholder loan.

IRA DISTRIBUTION PLANNING

New rules for IRA required minimum distributions were proposed in 2001, replacing earlier regulations proposed in 1987. IRA distributions required *for* 2001 could be calculated under either set of rules (regardless of whether the individual began distributions in an earlier year). The new rules are simpler and generally result in lower distribution amounts. IRA distributions for years after 2001 must be calculated under the new rules.

For most individuals, the calculation of required minimum distributions during life is very simple under the 2001 rules: the account balance as of December 31 of the preceding year is divided by a single life expectancy based on the account owner's age in that year, using the table on page 495. This method is used regardless of the age of the beneficiary, except that if the beneficiary is a spouse more than 10 years younger than the owner, a different table is used (Table VI, as provided in the 1987 regulations).

Designated beneficiary (DB) - the individual (or certain trusts) designated to receive the IRA proceeds, either by the terms of the IRA document or by an affirmative election by the IRA owner, or surviving spouse. Generally under the 2001 rules, the designated beneficiary will be determined as of the last day of the calendar year following the calendar year of the owner's death.

Required beginning date (RBD) - April 1st of the year following the owner's attaining age 70½.

Required minimum distribution (RMD) - the minimum required payments from an IRA (a penalty tax of 50 percent is imposed on any RMD not made).

Stretch IRA - uses a combination of beneficiary designations and life expectancy elections to delay receipt of distributions (also referred to as "multi-generation IRAs"). Typically assumes IRA owner and spouse will not need the funds for retirement or for estate taxes. Use of disclaimers may allow post-mortem planning (see discussion on page 374).

If an individual owns more than one IRA, the required minimum distribution must be calculated separately for each IRA, but the total RMD may then be taken from any one or more of the IRAs. Failure to take a minimum distribution will result in a penalty tax of 50 percent.

If an IRA owner dies before his required beginning date, distributions must be made under one of two methods: (1) five year rule: the entire interest must be distributed within five years after the death of the IRA owner (regardless of who or what entity receives the distribution); or (2) life expectancy rule: if any portion of the interest is payable to a designated beneficiary, that portion must be distributed over the life (or life expectancy) of the beneficiary, beginning within one year of the owner's death.

(continued on next page)

IRA DISTRIBUTION PLANNING (continued)

If the IRA owner dies on or after his required beginning date, but before his entire interest in the IRA has been distributed, the entire remaining balance must generally be distributed at least as rapidly as under the method of distribution in effect as of the owner's date of death.

Estate taxes on the IRA will be due at the death of the owner or his spouse, depending upon the beneficiary designation. Incorrectly changing the name on an inherited IRA account can result in the IRA becoming subject to income taxes within a year. When dealing with an inherited IRA the following should be determined: (1) have distributions started; (2) has the required beginning date (RBD) been reached; (3) has a beneficiary been named; and (4) who is the beneficiary. The answers will determine which of the following options are available:

IRA inherited by spouse before RBD: a surviving spouse beneficiary may (1) withdraw the assets within five years; or (2) elect to treat the IRA as her own (or transfer assets to her own IRA), name a new beneficiary, and take distributions over her lifetime (beginning either at end of the year following husband's death or by end of the year he would have turned age 70½). Option (2) allows for naming a new designated beneficiary and deferral of distributions until spouse's age 70½, but is available only when the spouse is the sole primary beneficiary.

IRA inherited by spouse after RBD: a surviving spouse beneficiary may (1) continue receiving distributions under the method in effect before her husband's death; (2) take distributions over her lifetime, beginning no later than the end of the year following her husband's death; or (3) transfer assets into her own IRA (unless they have been annuitized). In order to treat the IRA as her own she must be the sole primary beneficiary.

IRA inherited by non-spouse before RBD: a non-spouse beneficiary may (1) withdraw the assets within five years; or (2) take distributions over his or her lifetime, beginning no later than the end of the year following the owner's death (if multiple non-spouse beneficiaries must use life expectancy of oldest beneficiary).

IRA inherited by non-spouse after RBD: a designated beneficiary must withdraw assets over his or her life (or life expectancy), beginning no later than the end of the year following the owner's death.

No "designated beneficiary": under the 2001 regulations, if the owner does not have a designated beneficiary as of the date on which the designated beneficiary is determined (i.e., December 31 of the year after death), proceeds are distributed over his remaining life expectancy, using the age of the owner in the calendar year of his death, reduced by one for each calendar year that elapses thereafter.

LEGAL EXPENSE BENEFIT

Given our litigious society, it is hardly surprising that the legal expense benefit has grown in popularity as an employee benefit. Intended to provide affordable access to legal services, these benefits are referred to as "legal service plans," "prepaid legal services," and "discount legal plans." Plans providing legal expense benefits are offered in a variety of forms, including legal referral networks, prepayment plans, and indemnity plans.

Prepayment plans are similar in concept to HMOs, and provide for services from specific groups of lawyers employed by or under contract to the plan, specific lists of attorneys, or attorneys of choice. Less common are indemnity plans that provide benefits by reimbursing employees for specific legal services, with reimbursements limited to flat amounts, hourly rates, and maximum annual benefits.

Benefits are provided on either a comprehensive or scheduled basis. Plans providing comprehensive benefits typically provide full legal services, with specific services excluded. More common are plans providing only scheduled services. Typical of all plans is their emphasis on preventative law.

A variety of services are available. Most plans offer telephone consultations, document review, phone calls on the client's behalf, letter writing, and contract review. While many services are available without limit, limits are likely to be placed on some services (e.g., contract review limited to 10 pages; trial preparation and representation limited to 75 hours of attorney time). Excess time is typically charged at reduced rates.

Covered are family law matters such as divorce, adoption, child custody, will services and estate planning; property rights such as real estate and probate matters; IRS audit representation; and trial defense on civil matters. Criminal defense work is excluded except, for moving vehicle violations and work-related criminal charges. Generally no coverage is provided for plaintiff actions, and virtually all nonunion plans specifically exclude actions against the sponsoring employer.

In evaluating a plan, it is important to determine the availability of attorneys, as well as the specific services offered (e.g., attorneys may not be available for face-to-face consultations, or appointments may be difficult to get).

Most plans are enrolled by payroll deduction, with the individual employee paying for his share of plan costs. These costs are not deductible, but the benefits are tax-free. If the plan is paid for by the employer, the costs are deductible by the employer, provided the employee's total compensation is reasonable. Although the employee must include in income his prorata share of these costs, any benefits received are tax-free.

LEVERAGED BENEFIT

The "best" type of fringe benefit is one that is not taxable to the employee, or at least not currently taxable, yet currently deductible by the employer. Because of this favorable tax treatment, it can be considered a leveraged benefit.

For example, assume that in 2002 an *employee* in a 27 percent marginal tax bracket is in need of $30,000 of additional life insurance protection and is presently receiving only $20,000 of group term coverage. If insurance were individually purchased by the employee for $200, the employer could pay for the benefit by giving the employee a salary of $274 ($200 ÷ .73 = $274). The tax cost of the additional salary of $274 is $74, leaving the employee with $200 to pay the insurance premium. Assuming an *employer* in a 34 percent marginal tax bracket, the after-tax cost to the employer of the salary increase is $181 ($274 x .66).

To provide a leveraged benefit, the employer could increase the group term coverage by $30,000, which would be tax-free to the employee. Assuming this would cost the employer $200, the after-tax cost of providing the same benefit to the employee is now only $132 ($200 x .66). The employee gets the needed $30,000 of additional life insurance protection, but the employer has saved $49 by using a leveraged benefit.

Other leveraged benefits include physical examinations, increased mileage allowances, medical expense reimbursement, and employer paid premiums for disability income insurance.

LIFE INSURANCE PREMIUM LIMITATIONS

TAMRA limitations. Under the Technical and Miscellaneous Revenue Act of 1988 (TAMRA) a life insurance contract issued on or after June 21, 1988, is subject to being classified as a modified endowment contract (MEC) if cumulative premiums paid during the first seven contract years exceed the sum of "net level premiums" (the seven-pay test). Net level premiums are determined by each carrier and reflect the premiums required to pay up the contract during the first seven years using guaranteed mortality costs and interest rates. Distributions from a MEC are subject to "gain first" taxation to the extent there is gain in the contract (i.e., cash values exceed investment in the contract). Such distributions include withdrawals, loans, and use of the policy as collateral for a loan. Generally, the investment in the contract is the sum of premiums paid, less dividends received, plus prior taxable loans (but not prior taxable withdrawals).

Additionally, a 10 percent penalty tax is imposed on amounts includable in gross income if the distribution is made prior to the contract owner's attaining age 59½, unless the owner is disabled or receives the cash values under a life annuity settlement option. However, the penalty tax is always applicable if the contract owner is a "non-natural person" (e.g., a corporation or trust).

For example, assume that the "net level premium" for a particular contract is $2,500 and the following payment plans is being considered:

Year	Cumulative Net Level Premium	Plan A Annual	Plan A Cumulative	Plan B Annual	Plan B Cumulative
1	2,500	2,000	2,000	2,500	2,500
2	5,000	1,000	3,000	2,500	5,000
3	**7,500**	1,500	4,500	3,000	**8,000**
4	10,000	5,500	10,000	2,000	10,000

Plan A is not a MEC, since at no time did the cumulative amount paid exceed the cumulative net level premiums. However, Plan B became a MEC in year 3, since the cumulative amount paid ($8,000) exceeded the allowable cumulative net level premium ($7,500). In summary, a policyowner can "catch up" after falling behind, but he cannot "get ahead" by paying premiums in advance.

Now assume premiums are paid according to Plan B, and at the end of year 4 the cash values are $11,000. A withdrawal of $2,500 would result in a taxable gain of $1,000, since there is gain of $1,000 in the contract (cash values of $11,000 less cumulative premiums of $10,000).

(continued on next page)

LIFE INSURANCE PREMIUM LIMITATIONS (continued)

Once a contract becomes a MEC, it forever stays a MEC (except for limited opportunity given insurance company to correct procedural errors). In addition, even though a contract is "grandfathered" because it was issued prior to June 21, 1988, it can become a MEC if a "material change" occurs with respect to its benefits or terms. Since it is very broadly defined, virtually any alteration in benefits is likely to be treated as a material change, except for death benefit increases of up to $150,000 (or cost of living increases tied to a broad-based index). Potential material changes can occur when: (1) exchanging an old contract for a new contract; (2) converting term insurance to permanent cash value insurance; (3) adding a new insured to the contract; and (4) increasing the death benefit voluntarily. Contracts issued after June 21, 1988 are also subject to the material change rules.

While it is important to be aware of the potential adverse tax implications of TAMRA, this law will have no adverse effects if: (1) the contract was issued prior to June 21, 1988; (2) the death proceeds are the only payments received under the contract; (3) the premium payments do not exceed the seven-pay limits; or (4) the only payment received is pursuant to a complete surrender of the contract after age 59½.

DEFRA limitations. In contrast to TAMRA, it is *absolutely essential* to comply with the guideline premium and corridor test or meet the cash value accumulation test of the Deficit Reduction Act of 1984 (DEFRA). A failure to abide by the DEFRA limitations will produce disastrous tax results since the contract will immediately lose its status as life insurance, all cash value increases will be subject to current income taxation, and the death benefit will be taxed as ordinary income (to the extent it exceeds cumulative net premiums paid).

For example, assume Plan A is being tested for DEFRA compliance:

	TAMRA	DEFRA		Plan A	
	Cumulative	Guideline	Cumulative		
Year	Net Level	Single	Annual	Annual	Cumulative
1	2,500	9,000	1,000	2,000	2,000
2	5,000		2,000	1,000	3,000
3	7,500		3,000	1,500	4,500
4	10,000		4,000	5,500	10,000

In year 4, Plan A violates both DEFRA guideline premium tests. Under this test the cumulative annual premiums cannot exceed either the greater of: (1) the guideline single premium ($9,000); or (2) the guideline cumulative annual premiums ($1,000 per year). Although the cumulative annual premiums were exceeded beginning year 1, Plan A cumulative premiums fell within the guideline single premium ($9,000) until year 4.

LIMITED LIABILITY COMPANY

The increasingly popular limited liability company (LLC) offers owners the limited liability of C corporations together with the tax and management advantages of partnerships, without the restrictions and complexities of S corporations. All states have enacted statutes providing for LLCs. An LLC is created by filing articles of organization and complying with the relevant state law. The participants are called "members" and the rules governing the operation of an LLC are usually set forth in an "operating agreement."

The primary *advantages* of the LLC include: (1) no liability of owners for business debts (enjoyed by corporations and S corporations but not by general partnerships); (2) flow through of income and expenses to the individual owners (enjoyed by S corporations and partnerships but not by corporations); (3) the ability to allocate income and losses among members and include business liabilities in cost basis (enjoyed by partnerships but not by corporations and S corporations); and (4) freedom from the stringent requirements and restrictions of S corporations in the formation, operation and disposition of the business. For further discussions of partnerships and S corporations see the chart on page 169, pages 427-429 and pages 458-460. It has also been suggested that the LLC could serve as a viable alternative to the irrevocable life insurance trust, by affording the insured greater control and flexibility, in much the same way as the limited partnership (see discussion, page 428).

The main *disadvantage* of the LLC is the fact that it is a relatively new technique involving some uncertainty. There is often a lack of uniformity among existing state statutes. The current lack of uniformity means that the LLC is most attractive to the smaller business operating within just one or two states.

An LLC formed *after* December 31, 1996, will generally be taxed as a partnership if it has more than two owners, or as a sole proprietorship if it has only one owner, unless it elects to be taxed as a corporation. This election can be made under the "check the box" regulations by filing Form 8832 (Entity Classification Election). An LLC formed *before* January 1, 1997, will generally be treated as it was prior to January 1, 1997, unless it elects otherwise.

LIVING TRUST

A living trust is established during lifetime and may generally be revoked or amended at any time prior to death. Provided the trust includes provisions similar to the exemption trust will, it can offer the same *estate* tax benefits (see chart, page 29). However, because it is revocable, the trust does not remove assets from the estate, and since the grantor is considered the owner of the trust corpus, there are no *income* tax advantages (i.e., all trust income is taxed to the grantor).

Among the primary advantages offered by a revocable living trust are: (1) lifetime management of assets; (2) avoidance of probate costs; (3) lessening of chances for a successful election against, or challenge of, the will; (4) prompt transfer of assets to beneficiaries; (5) maintenance of confidentiality by not having to file a will; and (6) avoidance of ancillary administration of assets located in another state.

In recent years, many proponents of the revocable living trust have presented this technique as one that offers a multitude of advantages for virtually everyone. While it is certainly true that the living trust can offer many advantages, it is just as true that it is not a panacea, and the merits of this type of trust should be carefully evaluated in light of the circumstances and needs of each individual.

It is also wise to evaluate the actual costs being avoided, since establishing and maintaining a living trust involves both time and expense. In most states and locations, attorneys' fees and probate costs are quite reasonable. Although executor's fees can be avoided with a living trust, most estates never actually pay these fees, since the typical will provides for a waiver of fees and commissions if a family member is appointed to act as executor.

Use of a revocable living trust appears most appropriate during the later years of life when an individual may wish to reposition assets in order to provide for management of assets during periods of incompetency. At that time, deciding between an individual or institutional trustee can be, at best, a difficult decision. On balance, most individuals will probably be better served by the administrative, investment, legal, and tax expertise offered by a competent institutional trustee, provided the individual has the ability to pay and the fees charged are reasonable in light of the assets to be managed.

LIVING WILL

The living will is a legal document that allows an individual to state in advance his unwillingness to be subjected to life-sustaining medical measures once there is no chance of recovery. Such a document relieves others of the legal and emotional burden of making such decisions.

For example, it can ease a doctor's fears of civil or criminal liability, since he is abiding by his patient's wishes in withholding or withdrawing life-prolonging treatment. It can ease the stress and emotional pain for the family, which might otherwise be faced with having to make a most difficult decision as to what their loved one would have wanted. Further, it offers some hope of avoiding the legal battles that have occurred when a medical facility is unsure of its responsibility to the patient, and thus provides the family some protection from the financial devastation that a protracted death can cause.

Almost all of the states have some form of legislation governing living wills. Generally such a document must be in writing, dated, and witnessed by two persons who are not family members or possible heirs. The document must usually be notarized if a durable power of attorney is included giving another person the power to make medical treatment decisions. In addition, language can be included providing for organ donation.

Copies of the living will should be given to close relatives, the family doctor and the family attorney. Both the living will and the durable power of attorney can be revoked at any time by either destroying all copies or by executing a signed and notarized statement revoking the prior document.

MANAGED CARE

Managed care is a comprehensive approach to health care with the intent of lowering costs by arranging for care at predetermined or discounted rates, specifying which doctors and hospitals the patient can use and overseeing physicians' treatments and referrals. The basic variations of managed care plans include:

1. **Health Maintenance Organization (HMO):** A health plan that combines coverages of health-care costs and delivery of health care for a prepaid premium. Members receive services from individuals employed by or under contract to the HMO. HMOs generally require patients to select a primary-care physician (PCP) who coordinates the patient's care. Patients usually need referrals from the PCP before going to a specialist or a hospital. The PCP is often referred to as a "gatekeeper". In return for accepting these restrictions, patients are relieved of deductible or coinsurance payments and copayments are typically only $5 to $10 per visit to the doctor. This is in contrast to the traditional major medical plan or fee-for-service plan under which patients can choose both their doctors and hospitals, but must pay 20 percent of the costs (subject to caps).

2. **Point-Of-Service (POS):** A managed-care option that allows members to seek care outside the HMO network, but at a higher cost (usually in the form of higher premiums, co-payments and deductibles).

3. **Preferred Provider Organization (PPO):** A network of independent physicians, hospitals, and other healthcare providers who contract with insurance companies to provide care at discounted rates. Members are given incentives to use the PPO physicians but for a higher cost are allowed to use doctors and hospitals outside the network. This is also referred to as a "managed indemnity" plan.

Managed care has recently been the target of much public criticism. In HMOs the direct relationship between the financing and delivery of health care has generated criticism of: (1) the existence of "gag rules" that prohibit physicians from discussing all possible treatment options with patients; (2) the denial of access to specialists; (3) the denial of reimbursements for emergency room charges in hospitals outside the plan; (4) limits placed on hospital stays for certain procedures; and (5) treatment decisions designed to save money and adverse to the patient's health. A number of states have passed consumer rights bills and it is likely that the U.S. Congress will pass some form of federal legislation in the near future. The challenge faced by legislators will be to address these issues of choice and access, yet avoid substantial increases in health care costs or forcing health care providers out of the marketplace.

MARITAL DEDUCTION

By taking advantage of the marital deduction unlimited amounts of property can be passed between spouses, during lifetime or at death, and free of gift taxes and estate taxes. However, the marital deduction is generally not allowed if the property represents a terminable interest (i.e., an ownership right that will come to an end after a period of time or upon the occurrence of some specified event in the future).

Generally, in order to qualify for the marital deduction, property must pass in a manner that would cause it to be included in the surviving spouse's estate. In theory, this affords a delay in estate taxation, but not an escape from estate taxation, because property passed to the surviving spouse in excess of the unified credit equivalent ($1,000,000 in 2002) will be eventually subject to estate taxes (at least to the extent that it is not consumed by the surviving spouse). See footnote 6, page 21, regarding future increases in the unified credit equivalent.

The marital deduction can be obtained through the use of any of the following techniques:

1. **Outright transfer** – passes property directly to the surviving spouse. This can be accomplished in a variety of ways, to include: joint ownership with rights of survivorship; beneficiary designation; bequest or devise; inheritance; and dower or curtesy (or under state intestate succession laws).

2. **Power of appointment trust** – gives the surviving spouse a right to all income for life and general power of appointment over the trust assets (i.e., the unlimited right to withdraw property during lifetime or appoint property at death). In the chart on page 29 the "A" trust represents a power of appointment trust, which is also referred to as a "marital deduction trust." An expanded discussion of "general power of appointment" is contained on page 434.

3. **QTIP trust** – gives the surviving spouse a right to all income for life, with principal to children, or others, upon death of the surviving spouse (the executor or executrix must make this election, it cannot be mandated in will). Property placed in a QTIP trust is subject to being taxed in the surviving spouse's estate. See the discussion and chart on pages 34-35.

4. **Estate trust** – can accumulate income without payments to the surviving spouse, but must be paid to the estate of the surviving spouse (i.e., surviving spouse determines who eventually receives property placed in this trust, plus any accumulated income).

5. **Qualified domestic trust** – assures collection of the federal estate tax when the surviving spouse is a non-citizen. An expanded discussion is contained on page 442.

MEDICAL INFORMATION BUREAU

The Medical Information Bureau (MIB) is a nonprofit trade association of over 700 life insurance companies that was first organized in 1902 to conduct a confidential interchange of underwriting information among its members as an alert against fraud. This interchange enables MIB member companies to protect the interests of both insurance consumers and life and health insurance providers. MIB's basic purpose is to detect and deter fraud and misrepresentation in connection with the underwriting of life and health insurance and claims.

Upon receipt of an application accompanied by a suitable authorization, member companies conduct a search of MIB records as part of their usual underwriting procedure. Members are also required to report relevant results of their underwriting evaluation to the MIB; that is, of conditions that are significant to health or longevity. Both favorable and unfavorable medical information is reported. Certain nonmedical information of a very restricted nature regarding insurability is also reported (e.g., confirmed adverse driving record, hazardous sports activity and aviation activity). In order to help preserve confidentiality the information is reported and maintained in code symbols. Members may not report codes based on claim information.

MIB information is used only to alert member companies to the possible need for further information. It *may not* be used as a basis for establishing eligibility for insurance. An MIB report does not indicate either the underwriting action of the reporting company or how much coverage was applied for.

Only member companies have access to MIB information and then only after receiving written authorization from the proposed insured in the course of the application process. The proposed insured's spouse cannot give this authorization. MIB information is not released to nonmember companies, credit or consumer reporting agencies, or governmental agencies, except pursuant to court order or authorization from the consumer.

The consumer who applies for life, health or disability insurance receives a brief written notice which describes MIB and its function. In addition, this notice tells how the consumer can access and correct his MIB record when needed. To obtain a copy of their MIB record, if one exists, or to seek correction of the MIB record, consumers can contact the MIB at: P.O. Box 105, Essex Station, Boston, MA 02112 (phone 617-426-3660). Their web site is located at http://www.mib.com.

MEDICAL SAVINGS ACCOUNTS

A medical savings account, renamed Archer medical savings account (Archer MSA), may be established, in conjunction with a "high deductible health plan," by self-employed individuals or "small employers" (generally those employing 50 or fewer employees). This is a pilot program, ending in 2003, that limits participation to a maximum of 750,000 individuals over a period of up to four years.

In 2002, a high deductible health plan is one that has an annual deductible for individuals of $1,650 to $2,500 and for families of $3,300 to $4,950. Further, annual out-of-pocket expenses (other than premiums) required to be paid must not exceed $3,300 for individual coverage and $6,050 for family coverage. Maximum annual contributions to an Archer MSA are 65 percent of the annual deductible amount under the high deductible plan for single coverage and 75 percent of the annual deductible amount for family coverage (i.e., if Mr. Smith had a $4,000 annual deductible for his family coverage under a high deductible health plan, then that year he could contribute up to $3,000 to his Archer MSA).

Either the employer or the account holder can make contributions, but not both in the same year. Employee contributions to an Archer MSA are fully deductible from income. Employer contributions are excludable from the employee's income and are not subject to Social Security taxes. Employer contributions must be "comparable" (i.e., same dollar amount or percentage of the annual deductible limit). Earnings within the Archer MSA are exempt from income tax.

Distributions from an Archer MSA for qualified medical expenses are not taxable to the individual, provided the expenses are not covered by insurance. The payment of health insurance premiums is not considered a qualified medical expense, with limited exceptions. Any distributions that are included in income are subject to an additional 15 percent penalty tax, except for distributions received after the Archer MSA holder becomes disabled, dies, or reaches the age of Medicare eligibility.

Unlike flexible spending accounts, funds unused at the end of each year are not forfeited by the account holder, meaning that very substantial amounts might be accumulated over the years. Generally, transfers of an Archer MSA to a spouse pursuant to a divorce are not taxable. If a spouse is named beneficiary of the account, then, upon the account holder's death, the Archer MSA becomes the surviving spouse's Archer MSA without taxation. With a beneficiary other than the spouse, the value of the account is included in the beneficiary's gross income.

Beginning in 1999, another type of MSA, a Medicare+ Choice Account, became available to a limited number of individuals entitled to benefits under Part A of Medicare and enrolled under Part B.

MEDICARE AND MEDICAID

Social Security and Medicare social insurance programs are divided into four distinct parts: (1) Old-Age and Survivors Insurance (OASI) pays monthly cash benefits after a worker retires or dies; (2) Disability Insurance (DI) pays monthly cash benefits after a worker becomes disabled (OASI and DI together are referred to as OASDI); (3) Hospital Insurance (Medicare Part A) pays for hospital care of the long-term disabled and those aged 65 and over; (4) Supplementary Medical Insurance (Medicare Part B) pays for doctor bills and other medical expenses for the long-term disabled and those aged 65 and over.

Medicare is primarily intended to provide for acute care, to include hospitalization, visits to a doctor's office, medical tests, and a limited amount of skilled nursing care for recuperation from an acute illness. (See chart on next page for Medicare hospital and medical benefits available in 2002.)

Although Medicare does provide a limited benefit for home health care, it is the Medicaid system that is intended to provide for nursing home care. In contrast to the Medicare system, which is funded and administered by the federal government, the Medicaid system is funded by both federal and state contributions, and the states have a great deal of discretion in setting up and administering their specific programs. Despite federal minimum requirements and standards, Medicaid planning can be made difficult by frequent changes in these rules, administrative inconsistencies between the states, and enforcement of income, resource and transfer limitations, which are intended to carry out the original objective of limiting Medicaid to the "indigent" individual in need of long-term custodial care.

Basic to qualifying for Medicaid assistance is the requirement that the applicant not have sufficient *income* to provide for his own care. Most states permit an individual with excess income to qualify for Medicaid provided he "spends down" this income by incurring medical expenses (but some "income cap" states deny benefits whenever there is excess income). Medicaid qualification also requires that the applicant have very limited amounts of personal *resources* (spousal impoverishment rules allow a non-institutionalized spouse to maintain separate property).

In attempting to preserve family assets, individuals in the past have transferred assets outright to children, or to an irrevocable trust, often called a "Medicaid trust." However, the effectiveness of these techniques has been reduced by major changes in the rules governing transfers of assets, the periods of ineligibility, Medicaid trusts, and the state's rights of recovery.

For example, to discourage institutionalized applicants from making transfers for inadequate consideration, transfers during the 36 months before application

(continued on next page)

MEDICARE AND MEDICAID (continued)

for Medicaid benefits (the "look-back" period) can delay eligibility for a period equal to the amount of the transfers divided by the average cost to a private patient of nursing facilities in the state (e.g., a delay of 100 months assuming transfer of a $250,000 home and an average cost of $2,500 per month for nursing home care). The look-back period for certain transfers involving trusts is 60 months. These changes have substantially reduced the effectiveness of newly established or funded Medicaid trusts.

	Benefit	Individual Pays	Medicare Pays
HOSPITAL (Part A)			
Hospitalization	first 60 days	$812	balance
	61st to 90th day	$203 a day	balance
	91st to 150th day	$406 a day	balance
	beyond 150 days	all costs	nothing
Skilled Nursing	first 20 days	nothing	all (as approved)
Facility Care	next 80 days	$101.50 a day	balance
	beyond 100 days	all	nothing
Home Health Care	first 100 days in spell of illness	nothing for services 20% for durable medical equipment	all balance
Hospice Care	unlimited (doctor must certify)	outpatient drugs and inpatient respite care	balance
MEDICAL (Part B)			
Medical Expenses	unlimited	$100 deductible plus 20% of remaining	balance
Clinical Laboratory Services	unlimited	nothing	all
Home Health Care	unlimited (but covers only what is not covered under Part A)	nothing for services 20% for equipment	all balance
Outpatient Hospital Treatment	unlimited	$100 deductible plus 20% of remaining	balance

Benefits must be medically necessary. Under Part A hospitalization benefits from 91st to 150th day are the 60 "reserve" days that may be used only once in a lifetime. This is an abbreviated chart, for a more complete description of services and conditions of payment see *ASRS*, Sec. 15, ¶ 100.

MINIMUM DEPOSIT INSURANCE

This term is used to describe the payment of premiums for a life insurance contract with borrowed cash values from the policy. It is not a particular type of life insurance contract.

Because consumer interest is not deductible, minimum deposit insurance is unattractive for most individual policy owners (see page 407). Nevertheless, within strict limits a business (including a corporation, partnership, or sole proprietorship) can deduct interest payments that are reasonable business expenses on a policy that is "tax qualified." This deduction is limited to loan interest paid on policies insuring a "key person" for up to $50,000 of indebtedness. A key person is an officer or a 20 percent owner of the business. The number of individuals who may be treated as key persons is limited to the greater of: (1) five persons; or (2) the lesser of five percent of the total officers and employees or 20 individuals (i.e., no more than 20 persons can be treated as key persons).

In addition, interest in excess of an "applicable rate" cannot be deducted (referred to as an interest rate "cap"). The applicable rate is that rate described in Moody's Corporate Bond Yield Average - Monthly Average Corporates, as published by Moody's Investors Service.

Except for application of a modified interest rate cap, contracts issued prior to June 21, 1986, are "grandfathered" (e.g., they are not subject to the key person provisions described above). Loans taken on nongrandfathered policies before 1996 are subject to a phase-in of the disallowance of the interest deduction. No deduction is allowed for the part of the taxpayer's interest expense which is "allocable to unborrowed policy cash values," which are defined as the excess of the cash surrender values (determined without regard to surrender charges) over the amount of any policy loans. However, there is an exception which applies to policies and contracts owned by entities if the policy covers only one individual who, at the time first covered by the policy, is: (1) a 20-percent owner of the entity; or (2) an individual who is an officer, director or employee of the trade or business. See **Q 406**, *Tax Facts 1 (2002)* for a more complete explanation of the above limits on policy loan interest.

Most plans of minimum deposit insurance can be best explained as follows: (1) cash values are borrowed at a relatively low rate of interest; (2) borrowed cash values are used to pay premiums; (3) if any 4 out of the first 7 years' premiums are paid from unborrowed funds and borrowing in the other 3 years does not exceed the annual premiums, the policy is considered "tax qualified" and the interest paid on the borrowed cash values is deductible within the limits established under IRS regulations; (4) if the interest is deductible, after-tax cost is reduced; (5) if desired, beginning in the 8th year, both the premium and the after-tax cost of interest payments can be borrowed.

MINORS AND LIFE INSURANCE

Insurance companies will not knowingly accept a minor as the direct owner or beneficiary of a life insurance contract (for minor as insured, see page 355). Although trusts provide the most flexible way of managing policies and proceeds, establishing and administering them involves both time and expense. Ownership and beneficiary arrangements involving minors are governed by either the Uniform Transfers to Minors Act (UTMA) or the Uniform Gifts to Minors Act (UGMA) (see page 482). At the beginning of 2002, 48 states had statutes based upon the UTMA. The older and more restrictive UGMA was still in effect in the states of South Carolina and Vermont. It is important to consult individual state laws, since states typically alter the text of the uniform versions.

If the beneficiary designation includes a custodial nomination, the proceeds can be transferred to a custodian without appointing a guardian. Any trust company or adult other than the insured can be nominated custodian (an adult under state UTMAs is usually age 21). A designation paying a death benefit to a child of the insured might read: "to [name of child], child of the insured; provided that if any proceeds become payable when [name of child] is a minor as defined in the [state] Uniform Transfers to Minors Act, such proceeds shall be paid to [name of adult] as custodian for [name of child] under the [state] Uniform Transfers to Minors Act." Note that this language covers the possibility that the child might become an adult by the time a death benefit is paid. A substitute custodian should be named in case the primary custodian cannot serve.

Without a custodial nomination, it is likely that the insurance company will require appointment of a guardian of the minor's property prior to making payment of death proceeds. The only exception allows for payment of small amounts, usually $10,000, to either a trust company or an adult member of the minor's family (a no-nomination transfer).

To give an *existing* policy to a minor, the owner merely signs a change of ownership form. To give a *new* policy, the custodian is designated as owner on the application. In either situation the ownership designation might read: "to [name of adult] as custodian for [name of child] under the [state] Uniform Transfers to Minors Act." In contrast, the purchase of a policy using custodial funds is a reinvestment of funds. If the minor is the insured then the minor's estate should be named beneficiary. If someone else is the insured then the beneficiary must be the minor, the minor's estate, or a custodian, and the designation must be irrevocable so long as the custodianship remains in effect. In this situation the beneficiary designation might read: "to [name of child], child of the insured, if living, otherwise to the estate of [name of child]; provided that the proceeds shall be paid to [name of adult] as custodian for [name of child] under the [state] Uniform Transfers to Minors Act if the proceeds become payable while such custodianship remains in effect; without the right to change while such custodianship remains in effect."

NONCITIZEN ESTATE PLANNING

For the purpose of estate and gift tax planning it is helpful to recognize three categories of individuals: (1) U.S. citizens; (2) resident aliens (i.e., non-citizens who are resident in the United States); and (3) nonresident aliens (i.e., non-citizens who are resident in another country).

Resident aliens. The property of a resident alien is subject to United States estate and gift tax laws, no matter where it is located. For estate and gift tax purposes residency means that the person is actually "domiciled" in the United States. Generally, a person acquires a domicile by living in a place, even for a brief period of time, with no definite present intention of leaving and living elsewhere. This is a rather subjective determination that is influenced by where the individual's time is spent, as well as the location of other family members, business interests, social activities, driver's license, financial and tax relationships. It is important to recognize that although a person can have more than one "residence," they can have only one domicile (i.e., do not confuse the terms "residence" and "residency"). See the expanded discussion of domicile on page 376.

Although a resident alien is generally subject to the same estate and gift taxes rules and rates as a U.S. citizen, the unlimited marital deduction is unavailable if the *surviving* spouse is not a U.S. citizen (see page 442). Because of the unified gift and estate tax system, gifts made prior to becoming a resident may also be included in the resident alien's estate. However, resident aliens can take advantage of the full unified tax credit (page 19), annual exclusion gifts (pages 49 and 53), split-gifts with spouses (page 49) and irrevocable life insurance trusts (page 57).

Nonresident aliens. Property located within the United States is subject to both gift and estate taxes (i.e., it has a "situs" within the U.S. and is therefore taxed). Only the first $60,000 of property is free of transfer taxes and the unlimited marital deduction is not available unless the surviving spouse is a U.S. citizen. Gifts of *tangible* property and *real estate* are subject to gift taxes (but gifts of *intangible* property are generally free of gift taxes). However, bank deposits and life insurance are specifically excluded from both gift and estate taxation (i.e., they are deemed not to have a "situs" within the U.S.). Thus, the proceeds of a life insurance policy on the life of a nonresident alien are not subject to estate taxes, even though the beneficiary is a resident or citizen of the U.S.

A foreign death tax credit is available for *estate* taxes actually paid to a foreign country, or U.S. possession, in which the property is located (but there is no credit for foreign *gift* taxes). Foreign death and gift tax treaties can also offer relief from the double taxation often imposed upon both resident and nonresident aliens. However, such planning can be very complicated, and the advice of competent tax counsel should be sought.

PARTNERSHIPS

Family Limited Partnership

A chart describing the family limited partnership (FLP) is on page 169. The following advantages, disadvantages and requirements will help in better understanding this important planning technique.

The principal *advantages* of the FLP include:

1. **Retention of control** by the general partner, who has property which he is willing to transfer to family members but is reluctant to lose control over the property. A general partner operating under a well drafted partnership agreement can maintain indirect control without adverse income and estate tax consequences.

2. **Shifting of income** within certain family partnership limits. The general partner often has the power to retain current profits for investment and reasonable business needs.

3. **Protection of partnership assets** from the creditors of limited partners by restricting the limited partners ability to dispose of their limited partnership interests. Because the general partner has the ability to retain profits, the flow through nature of partnership income taxation gives him the ability to create a tax liability without making cash distributions for tax payments (i.e., an "ugly" asset).

4. **Reduction of value** through minority discounts and lack of marketability. The typical limited partnership gift represents a minority interest. Lack of marketability can be established by prohibitions against terminating the partnership without the concurrence of all partners (this prohibition is usually limited to 40 years or less). Valuation discounts can range from 30 to 70 percent.

5. **Facilitating gifts** of assets which otherwise are not easily divisible (e.g., the family farm). Often the ultimate goal is for the parent to eventually own only modest partnership interests, with the bulk of the FLP being held by other family members.

Some *disadvantages* of the FLP include:

1. The traditional partnership freeze is subject to the impact of the Chapter 14 valuation rules (see pages 386-387). However, most of the techniques used to reduce the effect of, or to avoid, these rules with respect to recapitalizations will also work with partnerships.

2. Much of the ability to reduce taxes by shifting income from parent to younger children has been curtailed by the "kiddie tax" (see discussion on page 482).

(continued on next page)

PARTNERSHIPS (continued)

3. There are additional expenses associated with establishing and accounting for an FLP (e.g., an information tax return must be filed).

4. Gifts do not receive a step-up in income tax basis.

5. Retained partnership interests continue to appreciate in the parent's estate until they are transferred during lifetime or at death.

The principal *requirements* for an FLP are:

1. Capital must be a material income-producing factor. A personal service business where income consists primarily of fees or commissions would not qualify for operation as a family partnership (i.e., lawyer, doctor, photographer, plumber, etc.).

2. If the partnership has been created by gift, the donor (parent) must be given a reasonable salary for services rendered to the partnership before profits can be allocated among the partners (the concept of "gift" also includes intra-family sales).

3. Profits of the partnership must be allocated, or divided, in proportion to each partner's capital investment.

4. All partners must actually own a "capital interest" (i.e., an interest in partnership assets which is distributable to the partner upon his withdrawal from the partnership or upon partnership liquidation).

Partnership Used As Alternative To Irrevocable Life Insurance Trust

Partnerships are increasingly being used as a substitute for the irrevocable life insurance trust. When contrasted to the irrevocable life insurance trust the primary advantages of a partnership are the *control* that a general partner can exercise over the partnership, which is not available with a trust since the grantor cannot be a trustee, and the *flexibility* a partnership offers to adjust to changing circumstances, which is not available with the irrevocable life insurance trust. Implementation of the technique involves creation of either a general or limited partnership of which the insured is the managing or general partner. Limited partnership interests are obtained by family members either by having the insured make cash gifts to them, after which the funds are contributed to the partnership in return for partnership interests, or by having the insured contribute cash to the partnership in return for partnership interests which are then given to family members. Assuming the insured holds no incidents of ownership, and the death proceeds are paid to the partnership, only his proportionate partnership share, including the insurance proceeds, will be in his estate.

(continued on next page)

PARTNERSHIPS (continued)

Partnership Created To Avoid
Transfer For Value Problem

Insurance death benefits paid to a C corporation to fund a stock redemption agreement may be subject to the corporate alternative minimum tax (see pages 342-344). Although the AMT can be avoided by converting to a cross purchase agreement, transferring existing corporate owned policies to co-stockholders of the insured can run afoul of the transfer for value rules, meaning that the death benefits would be subject to ordinary income taxes (see pages 479-480). Transfers to a partnership of which the insured is a partner are exempt from the transfer for value rules. In a private letter ruling the IRS has approved the creation of a partnership for the purpose of receiving corporate-owned policies. Although a partnership must be for a valid business purpose, and not just for avoiding taxes, this ruling appears to approve a partnership whose *sole purpose* is to "engage in the purchase and acquisition of life insurance policies on the lives of the partners." However, use of this technique might cause the proceeds received by the partnership to be taxed in the insured's estate, since the proceeds are not being retained by the partnership, but rather distributed to the surviving partners to fund a cross purchase agreement (i.e., as a partner the insured possesses an incident of ownership in the policy on his own life and there may be no double taxation issue since the value of the proceeds are not included in valuing the insured's partnership interest). It is probably advisable to avoid using such a "sole purpose" partnership until this estate taxation issue is resolved.

APPENDIX | 2002 Field Guide
Terms & Concepts

PENALTIES – ESTATE AND GIFT TAXES

Failure to file return. A 5 percent penalty if the failure is for not more than 1 month, with an additional 5 percent for each additional month, not to exceed a total of 25 percent; unless it is shown that the failure was due to reasonable cause and not due to willful neglect. If the failure to file is fraudulent then the monthly penalty is increased from 5 percent to 15 percent, and the total penalty from 25 percent to 75 percent. *Section 6651.*

Failure to pay tax. A 0.5 percent penalty if the failure is for not more than 1 month, with an additional 0.5 percent for each additional month, not to exceed a total of 25 percent; unless it is shown that the failure was due to reasonable cause and not due to willful neglect. *Section 6651.*

Fraud penalty. Penalty is 75 percent of the underpayment attributable to fraud. If the IRS establishes that any portion of an underpayment is attributable to fraud, the entire underpayment will be treated as such. The taxpayer must establish the part not attributable to fraud. *Section 6663.*

Accuracy related penalty. A 20 percent penalty is imposed on any underpayment attributable to a substantial valuation understatement, which exists if the value of property on the return is 50 percent or less of the amount determined to be the correct amount (penalty is 40 percent if property on return is 25 percent or less of correct amount). No penalty is imposed if the underpayment is $5,000 or less, or if the taxpayer acts with reasonable cause and good faith. *Sections 6662 and 6664.*

Statute of limitations on assessment. Generally, 3 years after return filed. If the taxpayer omits items that exceed 25 percent of total amounts stated on return, statute of limitations is 6 years after date of return. There is no statute of limitations if no return is filed, or if return was false or fraudulent and filed with intent to evade tax. *Section 6501.*

False statement as crime. Any person who under the penalties of perjury willfully makes and subscribes a return, statement, or other document, and who does not believe it to be true and correct, is guilty of a felony, and will be fined not more than $100,000 or imprisoned not more than 3 years, or both, together with the costs of prosecution. *Section 7206.*

Removal or concealment as crime. Any person who removes or conceals any goods with intent to evade or defeat the assessment or collection of taxes, is guilty of a felony, and will be fined not more than $100,000 or imprisoned not more than 3 years, or both, together with the costs of prosecution. *Section 7206.*

Statute of limitations on criminal prosecutions. If the taxpayer willfully attempts to evade any payment or willfully fails to make a return or pay a tax, the statute of limitations is 6 years. *Section 6531.*

PER STIRPES - PER CAPITA

These terms are used in making beneficiary designations in life insurance policies, wills and trusts.

The term **per stirpes** is used when it is desired that the share of a deceased beneficiary go to the beneficiary's children (in Latin it means "by the trunk," "by right of representation" or "by roots or stocks"). For example, assume John Smith desires to name his wife primary beneficiary of his life insurance policy with his children as contingent beneficiaries. However, should one of his children predecease him, John wants the children of that child (i.e., his grandchildren) to share equally their deceased parents share. The following beneficiary wording might be used: "Sally Smith, wife of the insured, if she survives the insured, otherwise in equal shares to the surviving children of the insured, and to the surviving children of any deceased children of the insured, per stirpes." If Sally died before John and upon his subsequent death John had two children who were alive (A and B) and one child who had previously died leaving two children (deceased child C who left John's grandchildren D and E), then A and B would each take one-third of the proceeds and D and E would each take one-sixth of the proceeds (i.e., they would share their deceased parents one-third). In some jurisdictions the term "by representation" is used in lieu of "per stirpes."

The term **per capita** is used when it is desired that the children of a deceased beneficiary share equally with the surviving members of the original group of beneficiaries (in Latin it means "by the head," "according to the number of individuals," or "share and share alike"). Again, assume that John Smith desires to name his wife primary beneficiary of his life insurance policy with his children as contingent beneficiaries. However, should one of his children predecease him John wants the children of that child (i.e., his grandchildren) to share equally with all other beneficiaries. The following beneficiary wording might be used: "Sally Smith, wife of the insured, if she survives the insured, otherwise in equal shares to the surviving children of the insured, and to the surviving children of any deceased children of the insured, per capita." Again, if Sally died before John and upon his subsequent death John had two children who were alive (A and B) and one child who had previously died leaving two children (deceased child C who left John's grandchildren D and E), then A, B, D and E would each take one-fourth of the proceeds (i.e., all beneficiaries would share equally).

For an expended discussion of beneficiary designations involving minors, see page 425.

PERSONAL HOLDING COMPANY

A personal holding company exists when more than 50 percent of a corporation's outstanding stock is owned by 5 or fewer individuals, directly or indirectly, and 60 percent of the corporation's adjusted ordinary gross income is personal holding company income. Personal holding company income is essentially passive income such as dividends, rents and royalties. If this income is not distributed during the year it will be subject to a 38.6 percent penalty tax in 2002.

Because of the limited marketability of personal holding company stock, courts have often allowed substantial valuation discounts (i.e., the stock of the personal holding company is held to be worth less than the value of its underlying assets). Because of this, under some circumstances personal holding companies can function as a particularly effective means of transferring future appreciation to other family members.

For example, an individual with a large estate containing a portfolio of stock that is expected to appreciate substantially would form a corporation with both voting and nonvoting common stock. His portfolio of stock is transferred to the personal holding company in return for the voting and nonvoting common stock. Thereafter, the nonvoting common is transferred by gift, or by sale, to other family members, and all future appreciation of this stock is shifted outside the stockholder's estate. By retaining ownership of the voting common the stockholder maintains control of the personal holding company (and of the investment decisions).

In addition to the penalty tax on undistributed income, a personal holding company can result in double taxation if appreciated assets are sold and the proceeds distributed to stockholders. Also, it is important to avoid running afoul of the special valuation provisions of Chapter 14 (see discussion on pages 386-387).

The penalty tax can be avoided with regard to a personal service contract by having the corporation reserve to itself the right to designate the professional who is to render services rather than giving the client the right to make the choice. In that case the income from such a personal service contract is not treated as personal holding company income.

PHANTOM STOCK PLAN

Phantom stock plans are a form of nonqualified deferred compensation made available to select employees. They are also referred to as "shadow stock plans" or "as if" deferred compensation (i.e., the amount deferred is treated as if invested in the employer's stock).

The advantage to the employee is that his efforts and loyalty are rewarded by having an economic interest or stake in the business similar to that of the owners. The advantage to the owners of a small and closely held family business is that they are able to retain a valued employee without diminishing their percentage of ownership. Phantom stock plans are used in both regular and S corporations, limited liability companies, partnerships, and sole proprietorships.

To implement a phantom stock plan, a bookkeeping account in the name of the employee is established. This account is then credited with hypothetical shares of stock (when used with a noncorporate employer, the business equity credited to the employee is referred to as a "participation unit"). Periodically, the account can be credited with additional stock, as well as with dividends and stock splits. The deferral period is usually set at a specific number of years or upon the employee's retirement. At the end of the deferral period, the employee is entitled to receive cash payments equal to the excess of the market value of the stock on that date over its value on the date awarded. If appropriate, a vesting schedule can be used that provides for nonforfeitable appreciation rights prior to the end of the deferral period.

The terms "stock appreciation right" and SAR have been used to describe a benefit under which the employee receives only the appreciation of the stock, but not the stock value itself. For example, assume that ten shares of stock are awarded to an employee, with a current value of $150 each. If, at the end of the deferral period, the stock has increased in value to $275 per share, the employee is entitled to a payment of $1,250 ($275 - $150 = $125 appreciation per share; $125 x 10 shares = $1,250). Alternatively, in addition to any appreciation, the plan could provide for the employee to receive the underlying value of the stock. Assuming such a design, the employee would be entitled to a payment of $2,750 ($1,500 initial stock value plus $1,250 appreciation).

As with other nonqualified deferred compensation plans, the employer's obligation to the employee is unsecured. Income is not recognized by the employee until the benefits are actually paid or made available. The employer then deducts the payment made to the employee (assuming compensation is reasonable, see page 483). Phantom stock plans are often informally funded with cash value life insurance. Life insurance also allows the employer to provide a preretirement death benefit payable to the employee's family (see chart entitled Deferred Compensation on page 243, and footnotes 5 and 6 on page 245).

POWER OF APPOINTMENT

A power of appointment is the delegation of authority from one individual (the donor) to another individual (the donee) to direct the transfer, use, benefit or enjoyment of property, both real and personal. A power exercisable in favor of the power-holder, his estate, his creditors, or the creditors of his estate is a *general* power of appointment. Any other power of appointment is a *special* power of appointment.

Whether a power of appointment is general or special is important, since a general power of appointment will cause the assets subject to the power to be included in the power-holder's estate, whereas a special power of appointment is generally excluded for estate tax purposes. The existence, release or lapse of a general power of appointment all have the potential of causing the property subject to such power to be included in the estate of the power-holder.

With the exemption trust will, as shown in the chart on page 29, property placed in the marital trust ("A" trust) will qualify for the marital deduction only if the surviving spouse has a general power of appointment over the property (an exception to this statement would be a trust that qualified as a QTIP trust). This assures that even though the property was not taxed at the first death it will eventually be subject to estate taxes upon the subsequent death of the surviving spouse.

If the power to consume, invade, or appropriate property from a trust is limited to *ascertainable standards*, it will not be considered to be a general power of appointment (e.g., for "health, education, maintenance, or support," but not for "comfort, welfare, or happiness"). Again referring to the chart on page 29, a surviving spouse can be given the right to invade the family or nonmarital trust ("B" trust) without causing the trust property to be included in her estate, provided the power is limited to such ascertainable standards, and therefore not treated as a general power of appointment.

Even though it might be considered a general power of appointment, a noncumulative power of appointment that does not exceed the greater of $5,000 or 5 percent of the corpus of a trust will not cause the lapse of such a power to be treated as a gift or included in the power-holder's estate. However, such a power held at death would be included in the power-holder's estate. See also, the expanded discussion of the Marital Deduction on page 419.

PRIVATE ANNUITY

The private annuity has been most effectively used in family situations where it is desired to make a transfer of a business interest, or other asset, from one generation to the next free of estate taxes (see chart, page 45). Under a typical private annuity transaction, a parent will sell part or all of the business interest, or other asset, to his child or children. In return, the children would promise to pay the parent an income for life (called a "straight life" annuity). While the annuity obligation cannot be secured, it does represent a contractual obligation that is legally enforceable. Since payments terminate at the parent's death, the annuity has generally been considered to have no value and to escape taxation in the parent's estate.

The amount of the annual payment is determined by use of annuity valuation factors. The payments are made up of gain, interest income, and a nontaxable recovery of basis. If it is desired to provide an ongoing income to *both* surviving parents, a reduced income can be paid for as long as either parent is alive (called a "joint and survivor" annuity). Although the value of the survivorship benefit is includable in the estate of the first parent to die, it should escape taxation because of the unlimited marital deduction. At the time the annuity is established, the child receives a "temporary basis" equal to the value used in calculating the annuity. After the parent's death, this temporary basis is adjusted to reflect the amount actually paid.

It would be best to avoid stipulating lower annual payments than those calculated under the annuity tables. Such annuity payments result in a gift from the parent to the child (i.e., the child is not paying full value from his separate funds). If there is a gift element, then its value is the difference between the fair market value of the asset and the present value of the annuity payments.

Furthermore, if the child does not pay full value, the property transferred for the private annuity could be included in the parent's estate as a gift with a retained life estate.

PRIVATE FOUNDATION

A private foundation is a not-for-profit organization established by an individual charitable donor that operates as either a trust or a corporation. The foundation is controlled by the foundation's board or trustees, who may be selected by the founder. Private foundations are particularly suited to those individuals who wish to make substantial donations while providing a lasting legacy in the family name. Unlike outright gifts to public charities, the founder and his family are able to maintain control over assets given to the foundation and retain the flexibility to redirect charitable gifts with changing community needs. Active involvement of the founder's children and other family members as board members has the ancillary benefit of teaching others how to share the family wealth consistent with the founder's values and vision.

To assure that private foundations adequately serve a public purpose there are very strict rules and regulations governing their operation. In particular, a prohibition against "self-dealing" prevents any transactions, with certain exceptions, between the foundation and "disqualified persons." Such disqualified persons include the founder, the founder's spouse and lineal descendants, as well as the foundation managers and others involved in business relationships with a substantial contributor to the foundation. Compliance with these rules is essential and penalties for self-dealing are substantial. One exception to these rules allows disqualified persons to be paid by the foundation for reasonable and necessary work performed for the foundation, provided the compensation is reasonable.

Although the earnings on investments held by private foundations are not subject to income taxes, they are subject to an excise tax of 2 percent on investment income. Income on investments must be distributed to qualified charities each year. Regardless of income, approximately 5 percent of its "average net assets" are required to be distributed within 12 months of the close of the fiscal year. Specific steps must be taken to verify the tax-exempt status of grant recipients. Added to these requirements are annual information tax returns, corporate filings, documentation of gifts received and requirements for public inspection and disclosure.

The maximum amount a donor may deduct in one year for gifts to a private foundation is 30 percent of his contribution base, generally equal to adjusted gross income. This is reduced to 20 percent for appreciated capital gain property (see footnote 4, page 63). Private foundations cannot receive gifts of interests in a closely held or family-owned business stock under the rules governing "excess business holdings."

PRIVATE PENSION

Several years ago, the use of the term "private pension" was popular in describing life insurance products that offer investment elements in addition to death benefits. For the following reasons it is recommended that agents and their companies avoid using the term in the marketing and sales of individual life insurance policies.

It is suggested that to the average consumer the term "pension" implies a plan that is sponsored by an employer and qualified under the tax code as to the deductibility of employer contributions, without current taxation to the employee. *Webster's New Dictionary* defines a "pension" as "a stated allowance to a person for past services; an allowance to one who has retired or has been disabled or reached old age, or has been widowed, orphaned, etc." The term "private pension plan" can be found in section 2(c) of the Findings And Declaration Section of ERISA, which states: "It is hereby further declared to be the policy of this Act to protect . . . the interests of participants in *private pension plans* and their beneficiaries by improving the equitable character and the soundness of such plans . . . [emphasis added]." Clearly, the individual life insurance policy does not fall within either of these definitions or usages of the term "pension."

An illustration which fails to inform a prospect that life insurance is being offered is considered a misrepresentation and false advertising of life insurance in violation of the National Association Of Insurance Commissioners (NAIC) Model Laws entitled Unfair Trade Practices Act and Rules Governing The Advertising Of Life Insurance, which have been adopted in many states. Determining what constitutes a "failure to inform" can be difficult. For example, it may not be sufficient to include a short reference to life insurance at the bottom of page seven of an eight page "Private Pension Plan" proposal. While this may be subject to some debate, a more important concern should be how regulators will view such sales illustrations in light of industry difficulties concerning the marketing of life insurance as a retirement plan without adequate disclosure.

The unique benefit of life insurance is its ability to provide food and clothing for a surviving family, keep them secure in their home and educate the children. Business life insurance enables a business to continue after the death of an owner and can provide funds for purchase of the deceased's business interest by the surviving owners. These noble objectives have more than justified the current tax deferred nature of the internal cash value buildup of the permanent life insurance contract. This tax deferred status should not be threatened by placing an unwarranted emphasis on its tax benefits.

PROBATE

Although the term is now used in referring to the entire estate settlement process, "probate" originally referred to the act of proving a will before a court or other authorized person. Courts having jurisdiction over probate matters are called probate courts, surrogates courts or orphans courts. The first step in settling an estate is to offer the will for probate. If the will is not likely to be contested, informal proceedings, usually called probate in *common form*, establish that the document offered is the valid last will of the decedent. However, if there is any doubt regarding validity, formal probate proceedings, usually known as probate in *solemn form*, are required.

After admission of the will to probate, the court appoints an executor (male) or executrix (female) and provides them with letters testamentary as evidence of their appointment. If there is no will the court appoints an administrator (male) or adminstratrix (female) and provides them with letters of administration. The personal representative (a term including an executor, executrix, administrator and adminstratrix) is then qualified to carry out his duties. Typically the personal representative will hire an attorney to advise and assist in settling the estate.

The personal representative then collects, safeguards and manages estate assets, has assets appraised, prepares lists of assets, converts personal property into cash, distributes assets as directed by the decedent (pursuant to specific bequests in the will), disposes of business interests, publishes notices giving creditors of the estate an opportunity to file their claims, and pays death taxes, income taxes, property taxes, court costs, appraisal fees, and fees and reimbursement expenses of the personal representative and the attorney. After a court accounting (called a judicial settlement of the account) is made and accepted by the court, the personal representative makes a distribution of the net estate to the heirs as required by either the will or the statute of intestate succession (see pages 105-111).

In recent years much has been written about the benefits of "avoiding probate." The advantages cited include avoiding fees associated with the probate process, maintaining confidentiality, better control of assets, reduction in delays and avoiding ancillary probate of property located in another state. However, there are some distinct advantages to having an estate go through probate. For example, protection is provided beneficiaries by having a court oversee the collection and distribution of assets. By giving creditors notice and the opportunity to make claims against the estate, beneficiaries are provided with clear title to estate assets. In addition, the Uniform Probate Code, as enacted by many states, simplifies and streamlines the probate process by providing for self-proved wills, proof of a will by affidavit of witnesses, waiver of bond and unsupervised administration.

PROFESSIONAL CORPORATION

Professional corporations are closely held corporations formed by doctors, dentists, optometrists, lawyers, and others. They may be established by an individual or by a group of professionals and are organized primarily to take advantage of the tax deductible benefits available to employees of corporations but not to sole proprietors or partners. Typically they are organized under state professional corporation and professional association acts.

A professional in a high personal tax bracket incorporates, becomes an employee of the corporation (as well as an owner-stockholder) and receives a salary from the corporation. The usual business deductions are allowed, including salaries for stockholder-employees, as well as special corporation deductions.

Professional corporations are taxed under the same rules as other corporations. However, professional corporations in which substantially all of the activities involve the performance of services in the fields of health, law, engineering, architecture, accounting, actuarial science, performing arts, or consulting are considered qualified personal service corporations and corporate income is taxed at a flax rate of 35 percent.

A wide variety of employee benefits are available to the stockholder-employees of a professional corporation, including accident and health plans, group term life insurance (chart page 211), salary allotment (chart page 215), executive equity (chart page 219), split-dollar insurance (chart page 227), survivor income (chart page 239), deferred compensation (chart page 243), disability income plans (chart page 251), medical expense reimbursement plans (chart page 255) and qualified pension and profit-sharing plans (chart page 263).

State laws generally restrict ownership of stock in professional corporations to qualified professionals (as a condition of continued authorization to provide professional services). Therefore, with professional corporations it is most important to implement buy-sell agreements that prevent the transfer of stock to anyone who is a nonprofessional. In addition to providing for the sale of stock upon death, such agreements should also contain provisions for sale in the event of retirement, permanent disability, termination of employment or professional disqualification.

While the typical choice involves either an entity purchase agreement (chart page 129) or a cross purchase agreement (chart page 133), hybrid arrangements involving "wait and see" buy/sell agreements (chart page 141) and partial stock redemptions (chart page 149) are also used. Whichever method is chosen, adequate funding with life insurance will provide funds to meet the underlying obligations.

PRUDENT INVESTOR RULE

Under the Uniform Prudent Investor Act of 1994 the prudent *investor* rule replaced the prudent *person* rule (the prudent person rule is also known as the prudent *man* rule). A majority of states have now enacted some form of the prudent investor rule.

With its focus on minimizing risk, the prudent person rule forces trustees to adopt conservative fixed-income approaches to investing trust assets. Such a conservative approach may well be appropriate for the small to mid-size trust whose primary function is to provide support for the current beneficiary, (e.g., a marital deduction trust for the support of a surviving spouse, as in the chart on page 29). However, with larger trusts, application of the rule often results in underperforming investments and dissatisfied life and remainder beneficiaries (amusingly referred to as the trustee's duty to "disappoint equally").

State Principal and Income Acts further compounded the problem. These statutes defined "income" to include dividends, interest and rents, but not capital gains. As a result, investment decisions were often driven by the character of the return, rather then the rate of return (e.g., trustees could distribute to income beneficiaries interest from low-yield certificates of deposit, but were prohibited from using capital gain from highly appreciated stock). The Uniform Principal and Income Act of 1997 gives trustees the authority to allocate principal to income, but it has not been adopted in many states.

Under the prudent investor rule a trustee is required to develop an overall investment strategy having risk and return objectives reasonably suited to the trust and its beneficiaries. The trustee is to be judged by considering the performance of the portfolio as a whole rather than individual investments. Although the trustee may delegate investment functions, there remains a duty to review and monitor overall performance. Consistent with modern portfolio analysis, the trustee may invest for capital appreciation in a diversified portfolio of equity and growth stocks. A reduction in the risk of loss is achieved by a reasonable diversification of investments. Because the trustee has a positive duty to reduce investment costs, passive investment strategies are permitted (e.g., the purchase of indexed mutual funds). It is appropriate for the trustee to seek to maintain the beneficiaries' purchasing power, and the tax implications of trust investments and distributions may be considered. Clearly, the flexibility provided by the prudent investor rule enables a trustee to better serve all beneficiaries and sizes of trusts.

Some planners have suggested that a total return unitrust can take maximum advantage of this flexibility. As with the charitable remainder unitrust, the total return unitrust requires the trustee to pay a fixed percentage of the trust principal to the life beneficiary each year. See the discussion of the total return unitrust on page 478.

QUALIFIED CONSERVATION EASEMENT

The executor of a decedent dying after 1997 may elect on the estate tax return to exclude from the decedent's taxable estate up to 40 percent of the value of any land subject to a "qualified conservation easement." In addition to meeting the requirements of a "qualified conservation contribution" the land must be located within the United States or its possessions and must have been owned by the decedent or a member of his family for 3 years. The exclusion is generally not available when the property is debt-financed or the donor has retained development rights (i.e., the donor cannot retain the right to develop property for general recreational use by the public, such as a ski resort). The granting of the easement can be made by the decedent before death or by the decedent's executor.

The exclusion amount is limited to $500,000 in 2002 and thereafter. The 40 percent exclusion percentage is reduced by 2 percent for each percentage point by which the value of the qualified conservation is less than 30 percent of the value of the land. For example, assume that property with a basis of $500,000 has a value of $1,000,000 before an easement is granted and the easement reduces the value of the property to $750,000, a reduction of 25 percent. This is 5 percent less than the minimum 30 percent threshold. Therefore, the 40 percent exclusion must be reduced by 10 percent to 30 percent (40 - (5 x 2)). The property is included in the estate at a reduced value of $525,000 ($750,000 x .30 = $225,000 reduction; $750,000 - $225,000 = $525,000 reduced value). The value of the property excluded from the decedent's estate under this provision does not receive a step-up in basis. This means the new basis is $675,000 ($525,000 stepped-up basis plus $150,000 carryover basis attributable to fact that 30 percent of the property was excluded from the gross estate; $500,000 x .30 = $150,000).

A "qualified conservation contribution" requires that the donor convey a qualified real property interest to a qualified organization exclusively for conservation purposes. A taxpayer who makes such a contribution may take a charitable income tax deduction equal to the difference in the value of the land immediately before and after the easement is placed on the property (i.e., the loss of value due to the placement of the easement). A portion of the income tax savings might be used to fund a wealth replacement trust for family members (as in the chart on page 61).

Granting a conservation easement during lifetime can provide the property owner with an income tax deduction plus a potential estate tax savings attributable to both the easement's depressing the value of the property and to the partial exclusion of that reduced value from the gross estate. However, because the exclusion reduces the adjusted gross estate it could affect qualification for a partial stock redemption (page 148), estate tax deferral (page 369), special use valuation (page 448) and the qualified family-owned business deduction (page 443).

QUALIFIED DOMESTIC TRUST

The federal estate tax is imposed on the taxable estate of every resident of the United States, wherever the property is located, and whether the decedent is a citizen or a noncitizen. In order to prevent a noncitizen surviving spouse from leaving and removing property from the United States, the unlimited marital deduction is not available, unless: (1) the noncitizen surviving spouse becomes a citizen prior to the time for filing the deceased spouse's federal estate tax return; or (2) the property is passed to a qualified domestic trust (QDOT). In short, no federal estate tax marital deduction is available when the surviving spouse is a noncitizen, unless use is made of a QDOT.

Both probate and nonprobate property will qualify for QDOT treatment if transferred directly from the decedent to the QDOT, or irrevocably assigned to the QDOT prior to the time that the federal estate tax return is filed. However, it is not necessary that property be placed in the QDOT in any particular fashion or by any particular person.

The requirements for a QDOT are: (1) there must be an irrevocable election for QDOT treatment; (2) the trust must require that at least one trustee be a U.S. citizen and that no distribution can be made unless such trustee has the right to withhold any estate tax which may become due; (3) the transfer must otherwise qualify as one which would be eligible for the marital deduction; and (4) specific additional procedural requirements must be met in order to ensure collection of the estate tax.

Events that trigger an estate tax on assets placed in a QDOT include: (1) failure of the QDOT to meet any of the above requirements; (2) the surviving spouse's death; or (3) any payment to the surviving spouse other than income or a "hardship" distribution. The surviving spouse cannot be given a power to invade the trust unless the U.S. trustee can withhold any estate tax from the distribution (compare chart on page 29).

When property previously placed in a QDOT becomes subject to estate taxes, it is taxed using the marginal estate tax rate of the deceased citizen spouse. This means that although the unified credit is available to the surviving noncitizen spouse, it cannot be used unless the surviving spouse dies in possession of a separate estate.

There is available a gift tax exclusion which allows for annual tax-free transfers of up to $110,000 (as indexed in 2002 for inflation) to a noncitizen spouse. Taking advantage of this annual exclusion will create a separate estate for the noncitizen spouse, part of which could be used to purchase life insurance on the citizen spouse. Provided the noncitizen spouse was both policy owner and beneficiary, the life insurance proceeds would not be included in the estate of the insured citizen spouse. This would diminish the need to fund a QDOT in order to provide support for the surviving noncitizen spouse.

QUALIFIED FAMILY-OWNED BUSINESS

Provided strict requirements are met, up to $675,000 of a "qualified" family-owned business interest may be deducted from the gross estate. If the deduction is taken, the unified credit equivalent is changed to equal the lesser of: (1) the regular unified credit equivalent; or (2) $1,300,000 minus the amount of the qualified family-owned business deduction (see footnote 6, page 21, for an explanation of the unified credit equivalent). The effect of this limitation is to exclude, at most, $1,300,000 from the estate tax. Although EGTRRA 2001 repeals the qualified family-owned business deduction after 2003, the loss of the deduction is more than offset by increases in the unified credit equivalent.

A qualified family-owned business interest is defined as any interest in a trade or business (regardless of the form in which it is held) with a principal place of business in the U. S. if ownership of the business is held at least 50 percent by the decedent's family; or 70 percent by two families, or 90 percent by three families, as long as the decedent's family owns at least 30 percent. However, an interest in a business does not qualify if the stock was publicly-traded at any time within three years of the decedent's death. An interest in a business also does not qualify if more than 35 percent of the adjusted ordinary gross income of the business for the year of the decedent's death was personal holding company income.

A decedent's estate qualifies for the special treatment only if the decedent was a U.S. citizen or resident at the time of death, and the value of the decedent's business interests that are passed to "qualified heirs" exceeds 50 percent of the decedent's adjusted gross estate. The application of this complicated 50-percent liquidity test involves very specific rules with respect to business assets and estate values (e.g., gifts to family members which are held until the decedent's death). For this purpose, qualified heirs include any individual who has been actively employed by the business for at least 10 years prior to the date of the decedent's death, and members of the decedent's family.

The benefit of the exclusion for qualified family-owned business interests is subject to a recapture tax if, within 10 years of the decedent's death and before the qualified heir's death, one of the following occurs: (1) the qualified heir ceases to materially participate in the business for at least five years of any eight-year period; (2) the qualified heir disposes of any portion of his interest, other than by a disposition to a member of the qualified heir's family or through a charitable conservation easement; (3) the principal place of business ceases to be located in the U.S.; or (4) the qualified heir loses U.S. citizenship. The percent of reduction that is recaptured varies depending upon how long the heir materially participated in the business. Also, the heir is personally liable for the recapture tax.

The complexity and risks associated with this law are such that many individuals may be discouraged from taking advantage of its benefits. Under such circumstances it may be wise to utilize other techniques for either reducing or paying estate taxes.

QUALIFIED LONG-TERM CARE INSURANCE

A "qualified" long-term care insurance contract: (1) must provide only coverage for "qualified long-term care services"; (2) cannot pay or reimburse for services covered under Medicare; (3) must be guaranteed renewable; (4) cannot provide a cash surrender value; (5) must apply premium refunds or dividends to either reduce future premiums or increase future benefits; and (6) must satisfy consumer protection provisions, disclosure and nonforfeitability requirements as set forth by the National Association of Insurance Commissioners (NAIC).

Qualified long-term care services are defined as necessary diagnostic, preventive, therapeutic, curing, treating, mitigating, and rehabilitative services, and maintenance or personal care services, which are required by a chronically ill individual and are provided under a plan of care set forth by a licensed health care practitioner. A person is considered "chronically ill" if certified by a health care professional as unable to perform for a period of at least 90 days, without substantial assistance, at least two activities of daily living (i.e., eating, toileting, transferring, bathing, dressing and continence) or requires substantial supervision to protect himself from threats to health and safety due to a "severe cognitive impairment" (i.e., a deterioration or loss of intellectual capacity that places the individual in jeopardy of harming self or others).

Beneficial tax treatment is afforded to a qualified long-term care insurance contract. However, there is uncertainty regarding the tax treatment of nonqualified long-term care contracts issued after the enactment of the Health Insurance Portability and Accountability Act of 1996.

Premiums paid by an employer are deductible by the employer and are not includable in the employee's income. Self-employed individuals can also deduct premiums within the following limits: 70 percent in 2002; and 100 percent in 2003 and later years. Individuals can deduct premiums as medical expenses, but the deduction is limited to expenses in excess of 7.5 percent of adjusted gross income. This deduction for premiums paid is further limited in 2002 according to the insured's age: $240 if age 40 or less; $450 if age 41 through 50; $900 if age 51 through 60; $2,390 if age 61 through 70; and $2,990 if age 71 and over. These limitations are indexed for inflation.

Amounts received from a qualified long-term care contract in 2002 are generally not included in income up to the greater of $210 per day or the actual costs incurred. It is not necessary to prove a need for medical care in order to deduct unreimbursed long-term care expenses for nursing homes, assisted-living facilities, adult homes and home care. This is very much to the taxpayer's advantage.

QUALIFIED PERSONAL RESIDENCE TRUST

A qualified personal residence trust, also referred to as a "residence GRIT," is created by transferring a residence, or a second home, into a split interest trust for a specific period of time, typically between 10 and 20 years. The principal advantages of such a trust include transfer of the property at a low gift tax value and shifting of future appreciation out of the grantor's estate, provided he lives to the end of the trust term.

At the time of the transfer the value of the gift is determined by the value of the remainder interest in the residence calculated using actuarial tables (i.e., the value of the property is discounted for the fact that it will not be available to the remainderman for many years). The grantor can also transfer limited amounts of cash to the trust in order to service debt and maintain the residence. The grantor can serve as trustee. Although a taxable gift is made when establishing a qualified personal residence trust, the value of the gift is minimized by the remainder interest calculations, and the grantor can avoid actually paying gift taxes by utilizing unused unified credit. However, because the gift is of a future interest, the annual exclusion is not available (see page 48).

Unlike other transfers with a retained interest, the grantor can continue to use the residence throughout the term of years established by the trust, yet the property will be removed from his estate provided he lives to the end of the term (the same as a GRIT, see page 398). Although death prior to the termination of the trust would cause the full date of death value to be brought back into the grantor's estate, purchase of life insurance on the grantor's life could provide for payment of any estate taxes. A desire to lengthen the trust term in order to lower gift tax exposure upon establishing the trust must be balanced against the loss of all estate tax benefits if the grantor dies before the end of the trust term.

The trust can also give the grantor a contingent reversionary interest, which will cause the residence to revert back into his estate in case of death before the end of the term. With such a provision the grantor could utilize the marital deduction by passing the residence to a surviving spouse, thereby postponing estate taxes, while at the same time causing the trust to be classified a "grantor trust," which would allow the grantor to deduct property taxes and mortgage interest on his own tax return during the term of the trust. The existence of such a reversionary interest would also cause a further reduction in the value of the gift, measured by the probability that the grantor would not survive the term of the trust.

Upon the termination of the trust the grantor may wish to continue living in the residence. To accomplish this he can either rent the residence from the remainderman, or purchase the residence prior to the expiration of the trust term (for a fair rental rate or a fair market value). However, regulations prohibit a sale of the residence to the grantor or the grantor's spouse during the original term or while a grantor trust.

QUALIFIED SMALL BUSINESS STOCK

In order to help small businesses raise capital, the 1993 Revenue Reconciliation Act designated certain stock as "qualified small business stock." Provided all statutory requirements are met, noncorporate investors may exclude 50 percent of their gain from the sale of such stock. Gain that may be excluded from a single issuer of stock is limited to the greater of 10 times the stockholder's adjusted basis in the stock or $10 million (but reduced to $5 million for married couples filing separately). Since the capital gains tax generally would otherwise be limited to a top rate of 20 percent (see discussion on page 350), the savings on the amount excluded is equal to 10 percent of the stock's appreciation; however, the includable gain is subject to a rate of 28 percent. The benefits of the small business stock exclusion can be passed by gift or inheritance.

In order to be eligible for this favorable tax treatment, the following qualifications must be met:

1. The stock must have been issued by a domestic C corporation after August 10, 1993.
2. The stock must be acquired at its original issue and held for more than five years.
3. The issuing corporation must be engaged in a "qualified trade or business," which is defined to be any trade or business other than those involved in:
   a. the performance of services in the fields of health, law, engineering, architecture, accounting, actuarial science, performing arts, consulting, athletics, financial services, brokerage services, or any trade or business where the principal asset is the reputation or skill of one or more of its employees;
   b. banking, insurance, financing, leasing, investing or similar business;
   c. farming (including the business of raising or harvesting trees);
   d. the production or extraction of products for which a percentage depletion deduction is allowed; or
   e. operating a hotel, motel, restaurant, or similar business.

If all requirements are met the corporation need not be a newly formed business. But stock is not eligible if the corporation, within certain periods of time, purchases stock from the stockholder, or persons related to the stockholder.

There is an active business requirement, meaning that the corporation must use at least 80 percent by value of its assets in the active conduct of one or more qualified trades or businesses. Also, there is a gross asset test requiring that, both before and immediately after the stock's issue date, the corporation's gross assets cannot exceed $50 million. The corporation must also agree to submit periodic reports documenting its status as a qualified small business.

RABBI TRUST

The term "rabbi" trust comes from an early IRS ruling on the subject, which involved a trust established by a religious organization for its rabbi. A rabbi trust is used to accumulate assets to support deferred compensation arrangements and to provide the employee with some measure of assurance that he will actually receive the promised future payments. Because the funds placed in such a trust continue to be subject to claims of the employer's creditors, the security is in large measure "psychological."

However, because the trust is generally made *irrevocable*, it does protect the employee from being denied payment of the funds by a change of management, as might occur under the conditions of a hostile takeover.

The rabbi trust is currently one of the more popular devices for informally funding deferred compensation. In fact, this popularity has caused the Internal Revenue Service to publish a model trust instrument in Revenue Procedure 92-64. The model trust serves as a safe harbor for employers adopting rabbi trusts; used properly, the model trust will not cause current taxation of employees under either the constructive receipt or the economic benefit doctrines.

REDUCED VALUATION

An executor of an estate may elect special methods for valuing real property used in a farm, trade, or business. When available, these methods allow the real property to be valued on the basis of current use, rather than on its fair market value.

To qualify, the following requirements must be met:

1. As of the decedent's death, the real property must have been involved in a "qualified use"; i.e., used as a farm for farming purposes, or in a trade or business.

2. The adjusted value of all business or farm property, both real and personal, must be at least 50 percent of the adjusted gross estate.

3. The adjusted value of the business or farm real property must be at least 25 percent of the adjusted gross estate.

4. The decedent, or a member of his family, must have owned and been a "material participant" in the operation of the business or farm for at least 5 of the last 8 years preceding the earliest of the decedent's death, disability, or retirement (rental property does not qualify).

5. The business or farm must pass to a "qualified heir," including, among others, his spouse and immediate family.

In determining current use value the following factors apply:

1. The capitalization of the fair rental value of the land for farmland or closely held business purposes.

2. The capitalization of income that the land can be expected to yield for farming or closely held business purposes.

3. Actual assessed land values if the state provides a use value assessment law for such land.

4. Comparable sales of other farm or closely held business land located in an area where nonagricultural use is not a significant factor in determining the sales price.

5. Any other factors that could be fairly used to determine the farm or closely held business value of the land.

(continued on next page)

REDUCED VALUATION (continued)

Alternatively, when farm land is to be valued, the executor can elect a formula utilizing the average annual Gross Cash Rental for comparable land, less the average annual State and Local Real Estate Taxes for comparable land, divided by the average annual effective Interest Rate For Federal Land Bank Loans in the farm credit bank district in which the property is located (from 7.98 percent to 9.90 percent in 2001). The formula reads:

$$\frac{\text{Gross Cash Rental - State and Local Real Estate Taxes}}{\text{Interest Rate For Federal Land Bank Loans}}$$

Before relying on the reduced valuation provisions, a business owner should give serious consideration to the following qualifications and restrictions that are imposed:

1. The special methods for valuation cannot decrease the estate by more than $820,000 (as adjusted in 2002 for inflation, rounded down to the next lowest multiple of $10,000).

2. The business or farm must be continuously operated by a qualified heir for 10 years after the decedent's death (a 2-year grace period immediately following death is available, but it extends the recapture date). It is permissible to make a cash lease to a member of the lineal descendant's family, who then continues to operate the business or farm.

3. If within 10 years the property is sold or the use is discontinued, the taxes must be recomputed based upon the original fair market value (a sale to another qualified heir does not trigger recapture).

4. The qualified heir who receives the property must sign an agreement to be personally liable for the additional tax. It is due and payable within 6 months after the date of sale, or cessation of the use.

REINSURANCE

In its simplest form, reinsurance is the sharing of a risk by a number of insurance companies so that the mortality and profits of any one company are not greatly impacted by its claims experience. A reinsurance agreement between companies is often referred to as a reinsurance "treaty." The three main elements involved in reinsurance are retention limits, automatic reinsurance and facultative reinsurance.

"Retention" is the face amount of coverage on one life that a company retains. The amount retained is influenced by numerous considerations, including capital, surplus, insurance in force, and average policy size.

Under an **automatic** agreement the primary or ceding company (i.e., the company sending the risk out for reinsurance) must offer – and the reinsurer must accept – all risks that fall within the terms of the reinsurance agreement. The primary company does not provide the reinsurer with underwriting information. For example, the automatic agreement might provide that the reinsurer will accept the lesser of $3,000,000 or four times the primary company's retention limit, provided the total amount of insurance in force and applied for in all companies is $12,000,000 or less. If the total amount of insurance exceeds these limits then the automatic agreement is not effective and the companies resort to facultative reinsurance.

Under a **facultative** agreement the primary carrier submits the application and underwriting information to the reinsurer for review. The reinsurer then makes an independent underwriting decision and communicates its offer to the primary carrier. With larger or special risks the reinsurer may itself have special reinsurance arrangements.

"Best offer" underwriting is often used in substandard cases and typically involves sending the case to a number of reinsurance companies for underwriting. The primary company then issues the case utilizing the best offer obtained.

Reinsurers may refuse to consider a case if they receive notice that multiple applications have been submitted to a number of primary insurance companies. Because of this it is most important not to submit applications on the same insured to multiple companies unless they are fully informed of the submissions.

See also the discussion of financial underwriting on page 392.

REMAINDER INTEREST TRANSACTION (RIT)

Considered an aggressive estate planning technique, the RIT has been used as a means of shifting the future appreciation of an asset from one individual to another. As with GRITs, the RIT falls squarely within the scope of the Chapter 14 special valuation rules (see Estate Freezes, pages 386-387, and **Q 814**, *Tax Facts 1 (2002)*). However, a special rule allows for market valuation of RITs involving tangible property with respect to which the non-exercise of rights under the term interest would not have a substantial effect on the valuation of the remainder interest (e.g., non-income producing property such as a painting or undeveloped real estate).

Remainder interest transactions have taken advantage of the fact that property interests can be divided between *life estates* (i.e., the right to the use of property for life) and *remainder interests* (i.e., the right to ownership of property once the life estate of another has terminated). To the extent they are still viable, a RIT for a *term of years* rather than a life estate would exclude the property from an estate provided death occurs after the end of the term of years.

Where still viable, it is important that the sales contract for a RIT involving the retention of a life estate require that the purchaser (the remainderman) pay full and adequate consideration for the remainder interest (there is a split in the courts regarding whether adequate consideration should be measured by the remainder interest or by the value of the entire property). Without payment of full and adequate consideration the IRS may treat the whole transaction as a gift with a retained life estate, with the result that the full date-of-death value of the property is included in the seller's estate.

RETIRED LIVES RESERVES (RLR)

Retired lives reserves are funds that can be established to continue group term life insurance for retired employees. Contributions to the fund are generally tax deductible to the employer, yet not taxable income to the employee. Upon either retirement or permanent disability, the employee can continue to receive limited amounts of tax-free coverage. In regard to the exclusion of the first $50,000 of coverage, see the discussion on page 210.

If the illustrated interest rate assumptions are not achieved, or if the employees live beyond actuarial life expectancy, the employer must make additional payments to the fund in order to provide the anticipated death benefits for the retired employees.

Much of the attractiveness of RLR rested upon the tax deductibility of corporate contributions to fund large amounts of insurance for key employees. Because of this, the RLR concept lost favor with passage of the Deficit Reduction Act of 1984, which imposed the following restrictions on RLR plans:

1. Generally, no deduction can be taken for RLR funding for insurance in excess of $50,000.

2. A separate account must be established for each covered key employee and benefits paid only from that separate account.

3. The group term rate for excess coverage after retirement must be reported in income (i.e., coverage over $50,000).

4. In a discriminatory plan the higher of the Table I or the actual term cost of the coverage (including the first $50,000) is taxable to retired key employees.

5. There is a 100 percent excise tax on funds returned to the employer to the extent they are attributable to deductible contributions.

Because of these severe restrictions, it may be advisable to consider other alternatives for funding personal insurance for key employees. Executive Equity (chart, page 219), Restrictive Bonus Plan (chart, page 223) and Split-Dollar Insurance (chart, page 227) offer viable alternatives to RLR.

REVERSE MORTGAGE

A reverse mortgage is a loan against a home that requires no repayment so long as the homeowner lives in the house. With a traditional mortgage, payments *made by* the homeowner increase home equity (rising equity, falling debt); whereas, with a reverse mortgage, payments *received by* the homeowner reduce home equity (falling equity, rising debt).

The qualifications to obtain a reverse mortgage generally include: (1) all of the homeowners must be at least 62 years old; (2) the home cannot be subject to a mortgage (or the mortgage must either be paid off prior to the loan or paid from loan proceeds); and (3) the home must be the homeowner's principal residence (single family house, 2-4 housing unit, federally-approved condominium or planned unit development). Note that there are no income qualifications.

In addition to the costs found with the typical mortgage (e.g., interest charges, origination fees and closing costs), the reverse mortgage can include an "equity sharing" or "shared appreciation" fee.

The mortgage is a "nonrecourse" loan, meaning that the amount owed can never be more than the net proceeds received from the eventual sale of the home. For example, assume that upon a homeowner's death the amount owed under the reverse mortgage is $76,000, but the amount realized from the home's sale is only $70,000. The estate is not liable for the $6,000 difference. On the other hand, if the net proceeds from the sale were $100,000, the estate would be entitled to the excess $24,000.

The most widely available reverse mortgage programs are the "Home Equity Conversion Mortgage" (HECM) and Fannie Mae's "Home Keeper" mortgage, both of which are federally-insured. The amount obtained from a reverse mortgage *can vary substantially* depending upon the program selected, the interest rate, the homeowner's age and the home's location and value. Funds can be paid as an immediate cash advance, a creditline account, a monthly cash advance (payable either for a specific number of years, as long as the homeowner lives in the home, or for life by purchasing a commercial annuity), or any combination of these methods. Creditline accounts can be either flat or increasing each year by a specified rate (available from HECM but not from Fannie Mae). A commercial annuity offers the advantage of ongoing income for life whether or not the home is sold, but the disadvantage of a high loan balance in case of early death (i.e., cash advance purchases annuity).

The National Center for Home Equity Conversion, an independent not-for-profit organization, is an excellent source for more information (see www.reverse.org).

REVERSE QTIP ELECTION

In order to take full advantage of the GSTT exemption, the first spouse to die must pass $1,100,000 (as indexed in 2002 for inflation) net of estate tax to the grandchildren; at least $100,000 more than is sheltered from estate taxes by the $345,800 credit in 2002. Without the reverse QTIP election, estate taxes must be paid on the excess $100,000, or the first-to-die must reduce to $1,000,000 the amount passed to grandchildren.

The reverse QTIP election enables the executor of the first to die to divide the QTIP into two portions, with the second portion treated for GSTT purposes as if the QTIP election had not been made. Because both portions of the divided QTIP will qualify for the marital deduction, the first spouse to die can take full advantage of the $1,100,000 GSTT exemption, yet postpone any estate taxes until the surviving spouse's death. The following example assumes a desire to take maximum advantage of the GSTT exemption and both deaths occur in 2002 (compare with charts on pages 35 and 39).

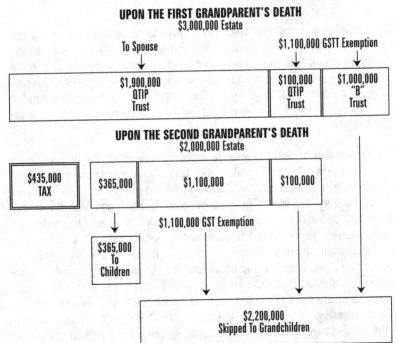

UPON THE FIRST GRANDPARENT'S DEATH
$3,000,000 Estate

To Spouse	$1,100,000 GSTT Exemption	
$1,900,000 QTIP Trust	$100,000 QTIP Trust	$1,000,000 "B" Trust

UPON THE SECOND GRANDPARENT'S DEATH
$2,000,000 Estate

$435,000 TAX	$365,000	$1,100,000	$100,000

$1,100,000 GST Exemption

$365,000 To Children

$2,200,000 Skipped To Grandchildren

Under EGTRRA 2001, both the unified credit equivalent and the generation-skipping exemption will equal $1,500,000 in 2004. This means that, beginning in 2004, the first-to-die can take advantage of the entire generation-skipping exemption by placing $1,500,000 into the "B" trust, without using a QTIP trust. See also, Phase-In and Sunset Provisions of EGTRRA 2001, pages 88-89.

RISKS - TYPES OF

There are many categories and types of risks, from physical risks to social risks, and ethical risks to monetary risks. The following risks are associated with risk management in financial and retirement planning.

1. **Market Risk** - the risk that unrelated factors will decrease the value of an investment (i.e., world events or legislation). Market risk can be lessened by diversification of investments and dollar cost averaging (see chart, page 312, and table, page 315).

2. **Interest Rate Risk** - the risk that interest rates will rise, decreasing the value of bonds or other fixed interest rate investments (see table of interest rates, page 191).

3. **Concentration Risk** - the risk that concentration of investments in a particular stock, bond, or market segment could result in a large loss of portfolio value (e.g., investing 50 percent of a portfolio in a particular stock). This risk can be reduced by acquiring a combination of fixed and equity investments, including mutual funds.

4. **Economic Risk** - the risk that the economic environment will decrease the value of an investment or other source of income. For example, the increasing costs of the Social Security system might require a change in the amount or timing of benefits (see footnote 2, page 265).

5. **Political Risk** - the risk that the political climate will result in changes in regulations and laws that impact the economy, tax laws and Social Security benefits.

6. **Tax Risk** - the risk that changes in the tax laws will result in greater taxes. For example, prior to 1984 Social Security benefits were free of income taxes, but under present law 50 percent of Social Security benefits are subject to income taxes (see discussion, page 468).

7. **Inflation Risk** - the risk that goods and services will cost more in future years and that inflation will erode the purchasing power of fixed income or investments (see inflation adjuster, page 95, consumer price index, page 307, and declining value of a dollar, page 308).

8. **Longevity Risk** - the risk that a person's longevity will result in outliving his income or suffering a loss of purchasing power (see mortality table, page 498). This risk can be reduced through the purchase of life annuities and equity investments.

9. **Security Risk** - the risk that there could be a failure of a financial institution (e.g., bank or insurance company).

10. **Currency Risk** - the risk that a decrease in the underlying value of a nation's currency will reduce the purchasing power of income or investments paid in that currency.

ROTH IRA

In 2002, the Roth IRA permits individuals to make *nondeductible* contributions to an IRA of up to the lesser of 100 percent of compensation or $3,000 per year. An additional "catch-up" contribution of $500 is allowed for individuals who attain age 50 before the close of the taxable year. Unlike traditional IRAs contributions may be made after age 70½ and husband and wife may contribute amounts without regard to whether either of them is a participant in another qualified plan as long as there is sufficient compensation.

The annual contribution limit is reduced (dollar-for-dollar) by all contributions to a traditional IRA. Also, the maximum yearly contribution is subject to a pro rata phaseout for *taxpayers filing jointly* with modified adjusted gross incomes between $150,000 and $160,000 (for *single taxpayers* with modified adjusted gross incomes between $95,000 and $110,000). In contrast, with a traditional IRA if the participant is an active participant in a qualified plan the deductible phaseout limits in 2002 are $54,000 to $64,000 for taxpayers filing jointly and $34,000 to $44,000 for single taxpayers (see pages 300-302, and page 403).

As with the traditional IRA, the Roth IRA accumulates tax-deferred. Provided the account has been held for at least five years *distributions are not subject to income taxes* if: (1) the owner is at least age 59½; or (2) the distribution is made after the owner's death; or (3) the distribution is attributable to the owner being disabled; or (4) the distribution is for qualified first-time home buyer expenses (limited to $10,000 for both the owner and specified family members). A 10 percent penalty tax applies to the taxable portion of withdrawals that are not qualified (but even if withdrawals are not qualified the owner can withdraw his original nondeductible plan contributions free of both income taxes and the 10 percent penalty tax, only the earnings are subject to these taxes). Unlike traditional IRAs there are no requirements that distributions be started or completed by any particular date, unless the owner dies.

Provided modified adjusted gross income does not exceed $100,000, a Roth IRA may generally accept a conversion from a traditional IRA. However, distributions in excess of basis from the traditional IRA are included in gross income (but not for purposes of determining modified adjusted gross income).

The following factors might be considered when determining whether for a particular taxpayer the Roth IRA is better than a traditional IRA, or whether to make a taxable rollover to a Roth IRA: (1) the current age of the taxpayer; (2) the taxpayer's current and anticipated future marginal income tax brackets; (3) the taxpayer's need for a current income tax deduction; (4) the availability of other funds to pay the taxes on Roth IRA contributions or rollovers; and (5) anticipated reduction of taxes on Social Security income caused by receiving untaxed IRA income.

RULE AGAINST PERPETUITIES

This is a common law principle that no interest in property is good unless it must vest, if at all, not later than 21 years after some life or lives in being at the time of creation of the interest. The reason for this rule is to prevent an individual from unreasonably attempting to control from the grave the disposition of his estate by creating property interests in succeeding unborn generations. In some states a wait-and-see rule would permit the trust to function until it became clear the rule was violated, as opposed to an immediate termination of all interests.

EXAMPLE A

Testator leaves Blackacre to "my wife, W, for her lifetime, then to my son, S, for his lifetime, then to S's children who survive him for their lifetimes, and then in equal shares to such of my great grandchildren as are alive when the last of my son S's children dies."

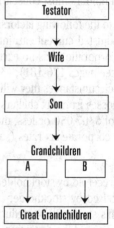
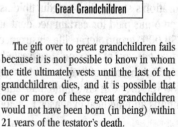

The gift over to great grandchildren fails because it is not possible to know in whom the title ultimately vests until the last of the grandchildren dies, and it is possible that one or more of these great grandchildren would not have been born (in being) within 21 years of the testator's death.

EXAMPLE B

Testator leaves Blackacre to "my wife, W, for her lifetime, then to my son, S, for his lifetime, then in equal shares to such of my grandchildren as are alive when S dies."

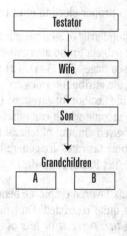

This devise is good, since there are no circumstances under which the interest would fail to vest within the required period. The gift over to the grandchildren is good since it is limited to grandchildren who are alive when son dies, son being either a life in being at testator's death or the gift to the grandchildren will vest immediately.

S CORPORATION

This is a corporation that elects to have its income taxed to its stockholders, rather than to the corporation. The manner of taxation is very similar to a partnership, in that it avoids the double taxation that can occur when dividends are paid by a regular corporation (C corporation). The following conditions must exist for subchapter S status to be effective:

1. It must be a domestic corporation.

2. It must not have more than 75 stockholders, none of whom is a non-resident alien (a husband and wife are considered one stockholder).

3. Only individuals, certain trusts and estates, and certain charitable organizations and qualified retirement plans (but not corporations or partnerships) may own stock.

4. It can have only one class of stock outstanding (but there may be variations in voting rights).

5. A proper election must be made (all stockholders must consent).

The popularity of S corporations can be traced to the following factors: (1) they are not subject to the alternative minimum tax adjusted current earnings adjustment (see pages 342-344); (2) provided the S corporation has no earnings and profits, the attribution rules are not a problem (see pages 176-181); (3) there is no double taxation of earnings; (4) under some circumstances they will generate passive income which can offset passive activity losses from tax shelters; and (5) for any given amount of federal taxable income of $307,050 or less, the individual income tax rates are generally lower than the corporate tax rates (see Federal Income Tax Rates, page 492).

The tax-favored employee benefits that can be received by stockholder-employees are quite restricted. Only those benefits received by stockholder-employees owning *two percent or less* of the S corporation's stock will be deductible as a business expense by the corporation (e.g., amounts paid for certain accident and health plans, and the cost of up to $50,000 group term life insurance). Stockholder-employees owning *more than two percent* of the stock are treated in the same manner as partners in a partnership and the cost of their benefits is generally not deductible to the corporation. However, they can take limited advantage of the rules covering health insurance premiums and medical expenses (see footnote 1, page 257).

Tracking of basis is very important with S corporations, since a stockholder's basis in his stock shields him from taxation when he receives distributions of income

(continued on next page)

S CORPORATION (continued)

(or sells his stock). The higher the basis the higher the untaxed distribution that can be received. A *stockholder's basis increases* when the corporation has income, either taxable or tax exempt. A *stockholder's basis decreases:* (1) when income is distributed; (2) when there is a loss; (3) when there is a nonde-ductible expenditure (e.g., a life insurance expense); and (4) when there is a capital distribution.

Example 1: How basis works - tax-free distribution of death benefit

A and B form S corporation, with A contributing $14,000 and B contributing $6,000. The corpora-tion purchases a $500,000 term life insurance policy on key employee C. Ignore the Accumulated Adjustments Account (it is explained in Example 3).

Year 1: Corporate income of $35,000 and a $4,700 premium is paid for the $500,000 term insur-ance policy. Basis is increased for $35,000 of income taxed to stockholders, and reduced for the nondeductible $4,700 life insurance expense.

Year 2: Corporate income of $44,000 and a $5,100 premium is paid. Basis is increased for $44,000 of income taxed to stockholders and reduced for the nondeductible $5,100 life insurance expense.

Year 3: C dies and $500,000 death benefit is paid to corporation. Basis is increased for $37,000 of income taxed to stockholders and the $500,000 death benefit, which is tax-exempt income. Basis is decreased $500,000 for distributions to stockholders.

			Stock Basis		Accumulated
			A	B	Adjustments
		Total	70% Owner	30% Owner	Account (AAA)
Year 1:	Opening Basis	20,000	14,000	6,000	0
	Taxable Income	35,000	24,500	10,500	35,000
	Premium Expense	(4,700)	(3,290)	(1,410)	n/a
	Ending Basis	50,300	35,210	15,090	35,000
Year 2:	Opening Basis	50,300	35,210	15,090	35,000
	Taxable Income	44,000	30,800	13,200	44,000
	Premium Expense	(5,100)	(3,570)	(1,530)	n/a
	Ending Basis	89,200	62,440	26,760	79,000
Year 3:	Opening Basis	89,200	62,440	26,760	79,000
	Taxable Income	37,000	25,900	11,100	37,000
	Tax Exempt Income	500,000	350,000	150,000	n/a
	Total	626,200	438,340	187,860	116,000
	Distributions	(500,000)	(350,000)	(150,000)	
	Ending Basis	126,200	88,340	37,860	

Example 2: A reason to purchase permanent cash value insurance

Stockholder basis is not reduced for any expense "properly chargeable to capital account." The term "capital account" includes policy cash values. Therefore, with permanent insurance the basis reduc-tion should be limited to the amount of the premium less the cash value increase (or cumulative pre-miums in excess of cumulative cash values). For example, if the $5,100 premium in year 2 of Example 1 was for permanent insurance, a cash value increase of $2,000 in that year would result in basis being reduced by only $3,100. A higher basis allows stockholders to receive increased tax-free distributions from the corporation.

(continued on next page)

S CORPORATION (continued)

Example 3: Dealing with prior earnings and profits

If an S corporation has earnings and profits (E&P) it maintains an Accumulated Adjustments Account (AAA) in order to prevent double taxation of stockholders, while at the same time assuring that distributed E&P will be taxed as a dividend. This account increases when the corporation earns taxable income and decreases when the income is distributed to stockholders. Referring to Example 1, a distribution of the $500,000 death benefit with prior E&P of $100,000 would be taxed as follows (steps 1 and 3 reduce basis, whereas step 2 does not reduce basis):

	Total	A 70% Owner	B 30% Owner
Basis At End Of Year 3	626,200	438,340	187,860
1. Tax-free (up to AAA)	116,000	81,200	34,800
2. Taxable (up to E&P)	100,000	70,000	30,000
3. Tax-free (up to basis)	284,000	198,800	85,200
Total Distribution	500,000	350,000	150,000

Example 4: Avoiding a wasted increase of basis

Now assume that stockholder B was insured by the $500,000 term life policy for the purpose of funding a purchase of B's stock by the corporation. B dies on May 10th of Year 3 and the death proceeds are received by the corporation prior to the sale of B's stock to the corporation on June 11th. Allocating the $500,000 of tax exempt insurance proceeds and the $37,000 of taxable income using the normal "per share, per day" method recognizes that B owns 30 percent of the stock for only 161 days out of 365 days, or 44.11 percent of the year. Therefore, multiplying this 44.11 percent by his 30 percent of ownership results in allocating 13.23 percent of all income to his stock's basis, or a total of $71,045 (.1323 x 37,000 = 4,895; .1323 x 500,000 = 66,150; 4,895 + 66,150 = 71,045). However, allocating the full $71,045 to B's stock is considered a "wasting" of the allocation, because his stock already received a full step-up in basis as a result of his death (page 473).

		Total	A 70% Owner	B 30% Owner
Year 3:	Opening Basis	89,200	62,440	26,760
	Taxable Income	37,000	32,105	4,895
	Tax Exempt Income	500,000	433,850	66,150
	Ending Basis	626,200	528,395	97,805

If the S corporation is a cash basis taxpayer, then an election can be made by *all* stockholders in their stock purchase agreement to terminate the taxable year whenever any stockholder terminates his interest in the corporation (e.g., by sale of all stock after death). This division of the taxable year into two short years is known as a "books and records" election. However, the redemption of stock must take place *prior* to the receipt of the insurance proceeds. Payment for B's stock could be made with a corporate note, which would be paid upon subsequent receipt of the death proceeds. This election would provide A with a basis increase equal to the full $500,000, which could be used to absorb subsequent tax-free distributions to A. The following assumes $20,000 of taxable income *before* the sale of B's stock and $17,000 of taxable income *after* the sale of B's stock:

		Total	A 70% Owner	B 30% Owner
Year 3:	Opening Basis	89,200	62,440	26,760
	Taxable Income	37,000	31,000	6,000
	Tax Exempt Income	500,000	500,000	0
	Ending Basis	626,200	593,440	32,760

SECTION 303 AND THE UNLIMITED MARITAL DEDUCTION

Under Section 303, the partial redemption, or sale, of stock may be made between the corporation and only that party having liability for the federal and state death taxes, funeral, and administrative expenses (see discussion, page 148). Because of this restriction, the utility of a Section 303 redemption to a surviving spouse is limited since no federal estate taxes will be paid if the marital deduction is fully used. For this reason, there may be some *advantage* to incurring a federal estate tax by passing more than the unified credit equivalent in stock to a surviving child, trust, or beneficiary other than the surviving spouse. This would not only allow full advantage to be taken of a redemption under Section 303, but would also avoid subsequent appreciation of the stock in the surviving spouse's estate. For an explanation of the unlimited marital deduction, see the chart entitled, Exemption Trust Will, on page 29.

In contrast to the chart on page 29, a Marital Plan Will (also referred to as the "Old Marital") divides the estate into two shares, with each share being equal to one-half of the adjusted gross estate. When more than $1,000,000 is placed in the family (or non-marital) trust in 2002 an estate tax is due at the first death, which can often be paid using the provisions of Section 303. Upon the first death, a Marital Plan Will would function as follows:

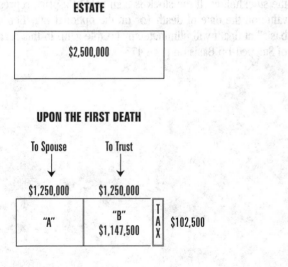

ESTATE

$2,500,000

UPON THE FIRST DEATH

To Spouse   To Trust

$1,250,000 $1,250,000

"A"   "B"   T A X $102,500
                   $1,147,500

SECTION 306 STOCK

In a recapitalization, preferred stock issued as a dividend on outstanding common stock is generally considered Section 306 stock, to the extent that the issuing corporation has undistributed "earnings and profits." For this purpose, the term "earnings and profits" has a special meaning. Section 306 stock is said to be "tainted," in that a subsequent sale of the stock will produce ordinary income, not capital gain.

Upon the subsequent sale of Section 306 stock such ordinary income treatment can cause adverse tax consequences beyond the loss of favorable capital gains treatment (see discussion, page 350). If the sale is a capital transaction, the seller can subtract his basis in calculating any gain subject to taxation. If the sale is of Section 306 stock, the amount realized is first treated as a withdrawal of earnings and profits and the seller could be taxed on the full amount received.

Even in a "true" recapitalization (i.e., an exchange of *all* of a stockholder's stock for a different class of stock), the problem of tainted Section 306 stock cannot be avoided if, at the time of the recapitalization, other family members are, and continue to be, stockholders. The family attribution rules (as set forth on pages 177-181) have been extended to apply to such "true" recapitalizations. However, this whole problem can be avoided if the stock is not sold until *after* the death of the stockholder. If the stock is then sold at a price representing the fair market value on the date of death (or on the optional valuation date), the "stepped-up basis" at death will eliminate any taxable gain. In this regard, see the discussion of Stepped-Up Basis on page 473.

SECTION 529 PLANS

Section 529 plans, also called qualified tuition programs (QTPs), are state-sponsored programs, authorized by federal law, that allow a taxpayer to: (1) purchase tuition credits or certificates on behalf of a designated beneficiary under a prepaid educational arrangement (PEA); or (2) make contributions to an educational savings account (ESA) established to fund the "qualified higher education expenses" (QHEEs) of a designated beneficiary. QHEEs include tuition, fees, special-needs services, room and board, and the costs of books, supplies, and equipment, required by a designated beneficiary at an eligible educational institution (post secondary education to include graduate school). There is a large difference among individual programs, many of which are more restrictive than required by Section 529. Before selecting a plan, the investor would be well advised to carefully review the individual account agreement. Beginning in 2002, private colleges and universities may establish PEAs, but not ESAs.

Federal law does not place any limits on who may participate as an account owner, contributor, or designated beneficiary (except that the beneficiary must be an individual). In order to avoid excess contributions, they are typically limited to the amount necessary to provide five years of education at more expensive schools (e.g., some programs allow for contributions of up to $250,000). Contributions must be in cash, are not tax deductible, and are treated as completed gifts eligible for the gift tax annual exclusion ($11,000 in 2002). This gift tax treatment is unusual, given the owner's power to withdraw funds from the account – subject to penalties and taxes – or to designate a new beneficiary. Gifts in excess of the annual exclusion may be "front-loaded," meaning that a donor may avoid using available unified credit by treating the gift as made over a period of 5-years (for a maximum of $55,000 per spouse, or $110,000 per couple, to each designated beneficiary).

State-sponsored ESAs may permit the owner to choose among different investment strategies offered by the plan: (1) when the account is opened, (2) once every 12 months, and (3) whenever the beneficiary designation is changed. Certain age-based plans automatically move to more conservative investments as the beneficiary ages. Separate accounting must be maintained for each designated beneficiary, with no pledging of the account assets by either the owner or the beneficiary. However, the account can be attached by the creditors of the owner, but not by the creditors of the beneficiary. In contrast, the value of the account is included in estate of the designated beneficiary.

All account earnings are tax deferred. Beginning in 2002, distributions from state-sponsored QTPs used to pay QHEEs are excluded from gross income (prior to 2002 the earnings portions of distributions was taxable to the beneficiary). Beginning in 2004, this exclusion will be extended to "private" PEAs. Distributions not used for QHEEs are subject to a 10-percent penalty tax on the taxable portion of the distribution.

SECULAR TRUST

The "secular" trust (as distinguished from a "rabbi" trust) is used to formally fund and secure nonqualified deferred compensation. Funds placed in a secular trust are not subject to the claims of the employer's creditors. So, unlike the rabbi trust (see page 447), the secular trust can protect employees from both an employer's future *unwillingness* to pay promised benefits and an employer's future *inability* to pay promised benefits due to bankruptcy or other financial difficulties.

However, the security offered by the secular trust comes at a price to the executive, because he is generally subject to current taxation. To offset the executive's current tax liability, the employer will sometimes pay a bonus to the executive. Current taxation of the executive is attractive to the employer because it provides the employer with a current tax deduction. Of course, as with any deferred compensation arrangement, all deferrals and bonuses must be reasonable compensation (see page 483).

There are two principal types of secular trusts: the employer-funded trust and the employee-funded trust. Because of its negative tax treatment, the employer-funded trust is losing popularity.

In an *employer*-funded secular trust, it is the Service's position that highly compensated employees will generally be taxed each year, not just on vested contributions to the trust, but also on any vested earnings of the trust. And because the Service further believes that employer-funded trusts cannot be employer-grantor trusts, the trust itself would also be taxed on this same income! Funding the secular trust with life insurance might avoid this double taxation by eliminating trust taxation: the cash value increases should be tax-deferred to the trust. Unfortunately, life insurance funding might not relieve the executive from taxation on trust earnings, because the Service appears to believe that these cash value increases would be currently taxed to highly compensated executives. It has generally been thought that distributions from employer-funded secular trusts will be taxed under the rules relating to annuities. But the Service has questioned the applicability of those rules to distributions to highly compensated employees from most employer-funded secular trusts.

In an *employee*-funded secular trust, either the employee contributes cash to the trust *or* the employer contributes cash to the trust after giving the employee a choice between receiving cash (or some cash equivalent) or a trust contribution. The employee is currently taxed on either the cash he actually receives and contributes to the trust, or on the employer contributions to the trust (he is considered to have constructively received the money). The employee-funded trust is generally considered an employee-grantor trust and its income is taxed to the employee only. Because the employee is fully taxed on both trust contributions and income, distributions from the trust should be free of income taxes.

SELF-CANCELLING INSTALLMENT NOTES (SCINs)

A self-cancelling installment note (SCIN) is an installment debt obligation that by its terms is extinguished at the death of the seller-creditor. SCINs are also referred to as "death-terminating installment sales." Although a hybrid of the installment sale and private annuity, SCINs retain most of the tax advantages of the installment sale. For example, unlike a private annuity, SCINs may be secured without jeopardizing their installment sale status (see chart, page 45).

Under the typical installment sale deferred gain is eventually recognized by either the seller or the seller's heirs. If the balance of the note is unpaid at death, the present value of future payments is includable in the seller's estate. Cancellation of the installment sale note at death does not avoid inclusion of the fair market value of the note in the seller's estate. When the seller and buyer are related the fair market of the note is considered to be no less than its full face value (i.e., the unpaid principal of the note).

With a SCIN nothing will be included in the seller's gross estate (similar to a private annuity). Generally having gain reported in the *decedent's* tax return offers far more advantages than requiring the *estate* to report the gain, because the income taxes may then be claimed as a deduction for estate tax purposes. However, in 1993 the Eighth Circuit held that gain was to be recognized and reported by the seller's estate (*Est. of Frane v. Commissioner*, which overruled the Tax Court).

To properly establish a SCIN, the installments should be for a term shorter than the seller's life expectancy (this avoids characterization of the arrangement as a private annuity). In addition, the purchaser must pay a "risk premium" to the seller as consideration for the cancellation of the note at the seller's death. There is no specific statutory or regulatory guidance as to how this risk premium should be calculated. Apparently the premium can be reflected as an increase in the sales price, referred to as a SCIN-PRIN, or as an increase in the interest rate, referred to as a SCIN-INT. Despite these and other unresolved tax issues, the SCIN provides substantial flexibility in allocating income and deductions between seller and purchaser, while freezing the value of an asset through purchase by children or other family members. Under the right circumstances the SCIN can be an attractive estate and income tax planning tool.

In contrast to a SCIN, a private annuity for a term of years (PATY) is a private annuity for a (fixed) term of years or until the seller's death, whichever comes first. One advantage of a PATY over a SCIN, is that no deferred gain will be recognized upon the seller-annuitant's death. However, the SCIN can be secured and typically offers greater income tax benefits to the seller.

SIMPLE IRA PLANS

SIMPLE IRA plans ("SIMPLE" stands for Savings Incentive Match Plan for Employees) are easier to install and administer than a qualified plan. The SIMPLE IRA is considered a replacement for the SARSEP and must be established by an employer for employees using either Form 5304-SIMPLE or Form 5305-SIMPLE.

In order to set up a SIMPLE IRA plan the employer must not maintain another employer-sponsored retirement plan (including qualified plans, tax-sheltered annuities and SEPs) and in the preceding year must have employed 100 or fewer employees earning at least $5,000. The plan must cover any employee who has earned at least $5,000 in any 2 preceding years and is reasonably expected to earn at least $5,000 in the current year. However, the employer may establish less restrictive eligibility requirements. Self-employed individuals may establish and participate in a SIMPLE IRA plan.

The employee is allowed to contribute up to $7,000 per year (in 2002). Although the deferral amount is expressed as a percentage of compensation there is no limit on this percentage (e.g., in order to defer the maximum $7,000 per year, an employee earning $10,000 could elect to defer 70 percent of compensation). The $3,000 limit for traditional IRAs does not apply to a SIMPLE IRA. In addition, if the plan so provides, an individual age 50 or over may make catch-up contributions of up to $500 in 2002.

The employer is required to either contribute 2 percent of the entire payroll (under a *nonelective contributions* formula) or match contributions of up to 3 percent of each employee's salary (under a *matching* formula). However, a special rule permits the employer to elect a lower percentage under the matching formula, but not less than 1 percent, and it cannot be used for more than 2 out of any 5 years.

A SIMPLE IRA plan is not subject to nondiscrimination testing or top-heavy rules, and the reporting requirements are simplified. All contributions are excludable from the employee's income and must be fully vested. The penalty for early withdrawal prior to age 59½ is 25 percent during the first two years of participation and 10 percent thereafter (unless one of the exceptions applies).

A SIMPLE 401(k) plan is a 401(k) plan that satisfies the non-discrimination requirement by adopting certain SIMPLE 401(k) provisions that are similar to the above requirements. Such a plan is not subject to nondiscrimination tests and the top-heavy rules, but it will be subject to other qualified plan requirements. For details, see **Q 340**, *Tax Facts 1 (2002)*.

SIMPLIFIED EMPLOYEE PENSION (SEP)

A simplified employee pension (SEP) is an employee's individual retirement account that may accept an expanded rate of contribution from his employer. Because payments are made into an IRA established for each employee they are also referred to as SEP-IRAs. SEPs can be established with sole proprietorships, partnerships or corporations, and are particularly attractive for the self-employed who has no employees or the individual who has additional income from outside employment. Generally, all employees must be included in a SEP except for: (1) employees who have not worked for the employer three out of the last five years; (2) employees who earn less than $450 (as indexed in 2002 for inflation); (3) employees who have not reached age 21; (4) employees covered by a collective bargaining agreement; and (5) non-resident aliens. They are generally easy to set up and require little administration.

SEPs can be established and funded as late as the due date (plus extensions) of the employer's (or self-employed's) tax return. Pre-tax contributions are limited to the lesser of 25 percent of the first $200,000 (in 2002) of net earned income or $40,000 (with sole proprietorships and partnerships the owners are effectively limited to 20 percent). No minimum funding standards are imposed. Contributions are not subject to income tax withholding, FICA or FUTA. Typically these plans are self-directed, in that the individual participant decides how funds will be invested. All earnings within the plan accumulate on a tax-deferred basis. The employer may not prohibit withdrawals from the plan, although they are subject to a penalty tax if made before age 59½. Essentially, there are four types of SEP plans with varying degrees of complexity:

5305-SEP is very easy to implement, requiring only the completion of five questions on IRS Form 5305-SEP. However, this may not be used by employers who maintain other qualified retirement plans, use leased employees or have had a defined benefit plan.

SEP prototype plans are provided by financial institutions (with or without a fee). Prototype plans are particularly useful if the employer wants to integrate the SEP contributions with Social Security (i.e., provide increased contributions for highly paid employees).

Individually designed plans are typically drafted by an attorney. They tend to be more expensive and complicated, therefore less often used.

SARSEP plans are salary reduction SEPs that allow employees to make pretax contributions to their IRAs. The provisions permitting the establishment of these plans were terminated at the end of 1996. SARSEPs already in existence prior to 1997 may continue to operate under preexisting law, receive contributions, and add new employees, but new SARSEPs may not be established. In their place individuals may wish to consider the SIMPLE IRA (see discussion on page 466).

SOCIAL SECURITY - TAXATION OF BENEFITS

Under a two-tier system, up to 85 percent of Social Security benefits may be subject to income taxation. Under the **first tier**, if modified adjusted gross income (adjusted gross income plus tax-exempt income, or MAGI) plus one-half of Social Security income exceeds a base amount, an individual must include in gross income the *lesser* of: (1) one-half the benefit; or (2) one-half of such excess over the base amount ($32,000 for married couples filing joint returns, zero for married couples filing separately who lived together during any portion of the year, and $25,000 for all other taxpayers). Under the **second tier**, if a taxpayer's MAGI plus one-half his Social Security benefit exceeds an "adjusted" base amount, he must include the *lesser* of: (1) 85 percent of the Social Security benefit, or (2) the sum of (a) 85 percent of such excess over the adjusted base amount, plus (b) the smaller of the amount includable under the first tier of taxation (see above), or $4,500 (single taxpayers) or $6,000 (married taxpayers filing jointly). The "adjusted" base amount is $44,000 for married couples filing joint returns, zero for married couples filing separately that lived together during any portion of the year, and $34,000 for all other taxpayers.

For example, the taxable benefit would equal $8,550 for a married couple filing jointly who had Social Security benefits of $14,000, adjusted gross income of $37,000 and tax-exempt interest of $3,000:

		The Lesser Of
85% of Social Security benefit (85% x $14,000)		$11,900
		or
Modified adjusted gross income	$40,000	
One-half the Social Security benefit	+ 7,000	
Total	47,000	
Adjusted base amount	(44,000)	
The excess multiplied by 85%	2,550	
Lesser of amount includable under first tier ($7,000) or $6,000	+ 6,000	
Sum of 85% of excess plus smaller of amount includable under first tier, or $6,000		$8,550

Effective for tax years after 1999 there is no longer any reduction in benefits once an individual reaches normal retirement age. However, there can still be a reduction of benefits in the year the individual reaches normal retirement age. In 2002 earnings earned during the calendar year before the month the individual reaches normal retirement age will reduce benefits in 2002 by $1.00 for each $3.00 of earnings over $30,000. Earnings earned during and after the month the individual reaches normal retirement age will not reduce benefits.

SPECIAL NEEDS PLANNING

Special needs planning involves providing for a physically or mentally disabled member of the family. Most often the disabled individual is a minor or adult child, but special needs planning also involves planning for dependent parents or other relatives. With a disabled adult child such planning should provide for him once his parents (the caregivers) become disabled or die. The ability of the disabled child to function will determine the required level and cost of care. Although caring for a person with a mental illness is generally considered more difficult and complicated than caring for a person with a developmental or physical disability, each situation is unique and must be planned for on an individual basis.

Even when other members of the family, such as siblings, are willing to assume the duties of caregiver, it is still important to provide for the management of assets. Either a testamentary or living trust can be used for these purposes (see discussion, page 416). Such a trust, sometimes called a "special needs trust," should: (1) appoint someone to take care of the child's property and money; (2) select a guardian for the child; (3) set out instructions on how the child is to be cared for; (4) ensure, to the extent possible, that the child will not lose payments or benefits from government agencies; and (5) integrate the trust with the remainder of the parent's estate plan (e.g., achieve equity among family members). Survivorship life insurance on both parents would provide a cost-efficient means of funding this trust upon the deaths of both parents (see discussion, page 475). Disability income insurance on a working parent should also be considered.

At one time or another during his lifetime a disabled person could receive benefits from Social Security Disability Income (SSDI), Supplemental Security Income (SSI), Medicare and Medicaid. With a special needs trust the objective is to have the child's inheritance supplement, not replace, these government programs.

Eligibility for government assistance can be negatively affected by the *disabled child's assets* (e.g., for purposes of the SSI benefit a single disabled person cannot own more than $2,000 in cash and liquid assets). Even when a trust consists of *third party assets*, if the discretionary powers of the trustee are not carefully limited, state laws may cause trust assets to be "available" to the beneficiary. However, under the federal Medicaid statute a trust established with the assets of a third party, such as a parent, is not considered "available" to the trust beneficiary.

Special needs planning may also affect other estate planning techniques. For example, under federal law a Medicaid recipient cannot refuse a gift. This means that a disabled child should not be given Crummey withdrawal powers, since his failure to make a withdrawal could jeopardize his Medicaid eligibility (see discussion, page 367).

SPLIT-DOLLAR ROLLOUT

This term refers to the termination of a split-dollar agreement (i.e., cash values are "rolled out" to pay off the employer). The rollout can be at any time, but is usually timed to occur once the employee reaches normal retirement age. At the time of the rollout the employer is reimbursed for all cumulative premiums paid under the split-dollar agreement (but not for those portions of the premiums paid by the employee). There had been disagreement as to the tax consequences of a rollout, when the employee had an equity interest in the cash values of a life insurance policy under a collateral assignment split-dollar plan (see footnote 2, page 167). However, IRS Notice 2002-8 provides specific guidelines on how the IRS will treat a rollout involving collateral assignment split-dollar. Under IRS Notice 2002-8 the IRS sets forth "two mutually exclusive regimes" for the taxation of split-dollar plans. See table entitled Treatment Of Split-Dollar Plans Under Notice 2002-8, on page 228, and note under Table 2001 Rates, on page 496. See also, the discussion of Equity Split-Dollar, on page 381.

If the plan is established in the **collateral assignment** form, the employee owns the contract, and the employee-owned *cash values are not subject to taxation* (both during the life of the split-dollar plan and when the employer releases the assignment). However, employer-paid premiums are treated as a series of loans to the employee and are subject to taxation under Code §7872 (below market loan deemed interest that produces deemed compensation) and possibly Code §§1271-1275 (original issue discount). If the employee is not obligated to repay the employer, then employer-paid premiums are treated as taxable compensation.

If the plan is established in the **endorsement** form, the employer owns the contract and, under Code §83, the employee is *taxed on all cash values* if the contract is subsequently transferred to the employee (i.e., the employee can acquire a currently untaxed right to a portion of the cash values, but will be taxed when the policy is transferred or "rolled out"). Presumably, the employee will not acquire an income tax basis for premium contributions toward the value of the life insurance protection. For example, assume that under an endorsement form of split-dollar, cumulative premiums totaled $23,000, with the employer paying $15,000, and the employee paying $8,000 ($8,000 is equal to the value of the employee's death benefit). Under the split-dollar agreement, the employer's "interest" in the cash values is limited to its cumulative premium payments, with any excess cash values "payable" to the employee. Also, assume that policy cash values total $25,000, meaning that there are additional cash values of $10,000, over and above the employer's $15,000. Upon termination of the agreement and transfer of the policy to the employee, under Code §83 the employee must include in income both the employer's $15,000 interest in the cash values, *and* the additional $10,000 "payable" to the employee. In effect, as to the cash values, the arrangement will be treated as a form of nonqualified deferred compensation.

"SPRINGING" TRUST

Virtually every buy/sell agreement has a built-in bias in favor of the surviving owner or owners. For example, assume that two stockholders, A and B, each own one-half of the stock in a corporation valued at $1,000,000. Under the traditional approach to designing buy/sell agreements, either cross purchase or stock redemption, the owners would obligate themselves and their heirs to sell their stock interests for $500,000. If A dies and his stock interest is sold to B pursuant to a cross purchase agreement, or to the corporation pursuant to a redemption agreement, A's family gets $500,000 cash and B gets a business worth $1,000,000 (providing the business value is not depressed by A's death).

Now assume B dies shortly thereafter and leaves the business to his family. Under these circumstances, because A died first his family gets only $500,000, whereas B's family gets a $1,000,000 business. Use of a "springing" trust provides a technique that can compensate for this built-in bias favoring the surviving owner or owners. And it is not necessary to disturb the existing buy/sell agreement, which can be left in place together with current life insurance funding.

In order to implement the springing trust, as co-grantors A and B establish a single irrevocable life insurance trust (i.e., they both sign the trust document as grantor). Funding the trust with a $500,000 first-to-die policy insuring both A and B provides a death benefit upon the prior death of either one of them. Although individual policies could be used, the first-to-die policy appears to more efficiently provide the funds required at the prior death of either A or B (see page 393). The trust is made irrevocable in order to assure that the proceeds are excluded from the decedent's taxable estate.

The beneficiaries named in the trust are contingent, in that they are the spouse and children of the first to die of either A or B. The contingent nature of the beneficiary designation is what gives the "springing" trust its name (i.e., the beneficiaries of the insurance "spring" forward once the policy pays a death benefit). The trust document is drafted similar to the typical irrevocable life insurance trust, except for having co-grantors and the provisions for contingent beneficiaries.

With the springing trust it is important to determine the amount of gifts required from each owner for trust premium payments. If the trust were funded with individual policies each owner would typically gift to the trust an amount equal to the premium on his or her life. However, when the trust is funded with a single first-to-die policy it becomes necessary to allocate the first-to-die premium among the insured owners, taking into consideration differences in age, sex, smoker or non-smoker classification, and the amount of insurance coverage (i.e., in those circumstances where the first-to-die policy provides unequal amounts of insurance).

STEP TRANSACTION DOCTRINE

In construing tax statutes the step transaction doctrine requires that interrelated steps of an integrated transaction be taken as a whole rather then treated separately. The doctrine is used by both the IRS and the courts to link several pre-arranged steps or contemplated steps, even though there is no contractual obligation or financial compulsion to follow through. The following are examples of circumstances that could attract application of the doctrine:

(1) Transfer by the insured of a life insurance policy on his life will cause the death proceeds to be included in the insured's estate if he dies within three years (see pages 388-389). In an attempt to avoid application of this three-year rule, a partner in a limited partnership contributes dollars to the partnership and these funds are subsequently used to purchase the policy from the partnership (a "sale" for adequate consideration is not considered a transfer for estate tax purposes, and is also an exception to the transfer for value rules, see pages 479-480). The step transaction doctrine might be applied to collapse the contribution-to-partnership and sale-to-partnership into one "nonsale" transfer of the insurance contract to the partnership.

(2) Parent gives money to a child who then purchases an annuity naming the parent as the annuitant, and the child as both owner and beneficiary. If the child subsequently and consistently gives the annuity proceeds to the parent, the step transaction doctrine might be applied to collapse the parent-to-child and child-to-parent gifts.

(3) Borrower places a second mortgage on his house and uses the funds to purchase a single premium annuity. Normally, interest paid on a second mortgage is deductible (within limitations). But no deduction is allowed for loans taken to purchase a single premium annuity. The step transaction doctrine could be applied to collapse the borrowing-on-mortgage and purchase-of-annuity transactions.

In attempting to understand the step transaction doctrine, it is important to recognize that the following overlapping, and sometimes indistinguishable, doctrines can also be applied to any given set of facts: (1) the tax avoidance doctrine (transaction primarily intended to reduce taxes rather than to achieve nontax business or personal objectives); (2) the substance-over-form doctrine (transaction has minimal, if any, nontax consequences); and (3) the business purpose doctrine (transaction has no business purpose). It is suggested that one way of recognizing when a proposed transaction might run afoul of one or more of these doctrines, is to apply the "if it is too good to be true, it probably is" test.

STEPPED-UP BASIS

In Years 2001-2009, 2011 And Later

At death, the income tax basis of appreciated property in an estate is increased, or "stepped-up," to its fair market value as of the date of death. For this reason, when property is subsequently sold there is no taxable gain if the sales price, or amount realized, is the same as the value on the date of death. However, when property has decreased in value the basis will be "stepped-down" under the same rules as govern the determination of a step-up in basis.

The step-up in basis applies only to property that is included in the decedent's estate for federal estate tax purposes. This value can sometimes be influenced by the personal representative of the estate by filing an election to have the gross estate, including stock in a closely held corporation, valued on an alternate valuation date, usually six months after death. If this is done, the stepped-up basis equals the fair market value as of the alternate valuation date. Note, however, that use of the alternate valuation date is permitted only if its use would result in a reduction in the value of the gross estate and a reduction in the sum of the estate tax and generation-skipping transfer tax payable.

With property owned jointly between husband and wife, the stepped-up basis applies to only one-half of the property, since only one-half the value of such property is included in the estate of the first to die.

Special rules apply in order to prevent the transfer of property in anticipation of the donee's death. Therefore, there is no step-up in basis when property is acquired by a decedent (the donee) within one year of death and this same property is then at death passed back to the original donor or the donor's spouse.

In Year 2010

Under EGTRRA 2001, in 2010 the step-up in basis is replaced by a modified carryover basis. This is essentially a carryover basis, but modified to allow: (1) an aggregate step-up of $1,300, 000; plus (2) a spousal step-up of $3,000,000 for assets passed to a surviving spouse; plus (3) the decedent's unused losses. The $1.3 million and $3 million are indexed for inflation after 2010 (assuming that the sunset provision of EGTRRA 2001 does not take affect). To be entitled to the $3 million spousal step-up, the property must be "qualified spousal property" (i.e., the interest cannot be a terminable interest). See footnote 1, page 37. Not eligible for a step-up in basis will be items considered to be income in respect of a decedent (IRD) and property received by the decedent within three years of death (except for certain gifts from the decedent's spouse). See page 402. In order to comply with this modified carryover basis system, detailed and onerous record keeping will have to be maintained for virtually all assets.

STRUCTURED SETTLEMENT

Structured settlements are used to provide long-term financial security in physical injury cases, by providing the injured party with periodic payments tailored to meet medical expenses and the needs of basic living. Whereas lump sum payments often result in the proceeds being poorly invested or squandered, structured settlements provide a stream of tax-free income from a reliable financial institution.

Situations appropriate for structured settlements involve: (1) wrongful death where a surviving spouse and/or children require ongoing income; (2) worker's compensation; (3) guardianship involving minors or incompetents; and (4) disabled or severely injured individuals.

To initiate a structured settlement, an agreement is reached between the plaintiff and the defendant regarding the benefits due to the injured party. This agreement can be reached before, during, or after a lawsuit. It may be agreed to privately, or it may be by order of the court (e.g., in situations involving the support of a minor child). Calculations on the costs of providing for the injured party's long-term needs are made by a structured settlement specialist, or structured settlement broker. There is great flexibility in designing the terms of a structured settlement. For example, periodic payments can be provided for a specific number of years, or made for the lifetime of the injured party with a guaranteed minimum number of years.

Once a settlement has been reached, the defendant, or its insurer, generally transfers the obligation to a financially secure and experienced life insurance company. This assignment relieves the defendant of any further obligation to make payments to the injured party. The life insurance company will typically use an immediate annuity to make the required payments. To assure that payments are received free of federal income taxes, the injured party, or annuitant, does not own the annuity contract; it is owned by the defendant, or its insurer.

Under Federal law the benefits under a structured settlement may not be assigned as collateral for a loan. However, in recent years there is a growing market involved in the purchase of existing structured settlements. In response, some states have enacted consumer protection statutes strictly regulating these transactions.

SURVIVORSHIP LIFE INSURANCE

Survivorship life insurance, also known as last-to-die insurance or second-to-die insurance, insures two lives, and pays a death benefit after the death of both insureds. Generally, the premium required is less than that for comparable insurance on either individual life, since the odds of two individuals dying during any given year are substantially less than of one individual dying.

While the many potential uses of survivorship life include charitable gifts (chart, page 61, and discussion, page 352), family income for surviving children (chart, page 15), key person insurance (chart, page 157), and funding installment sales within a family (chart, page 45); survivorship life is most often used to fund the payment of estate taxes, when the marital deduction defers taxes until the death of both spouses (chart, page 29). Survivorship life offers the advantage of simplicity by paying a death benefit exactly when taxes are due – upon the second death. With a rated or uninsurable client, coverage can usually be obtained, provided the spouse is insurable at standard rates.

There are some disadvantages to relying solely upon survivorship life insurance to fund the payment of estate taxes. For example, when the marital deduction is used to defer all estate taxes until the second death, appreciation of assets in the surviving spouse's estate can substantially increase total estate taxes. The flexibility provided by the use of disclaimers may be severely limited when there are no funds for payment of estate taxes at the first spouse's death (see discussion, page 374). After divorce the unlimited marital deduction is no longer available, unless the bulk of the estate is left to a new spouse.

Split-dollar is often used to pay the premiums for a survivorship policy funding a life insurance trust (chart, page 235). Since the trust's share of premiums is also the measure of the donor's gift to the trust, the trustee's premiums have been kept very low by using the Table 38 rates set forth on page 497. This has allowed substantial coverage to be purchased within the $5,000 per year per beneficiary limit (footnote 4, page 59). However, the death of either insured would increase the value of the annual gift, since these rates apply only to two insureds.

Although Table 38 is actuarially consistent with the P.S. 58 rates, the only authority for using Table 38 is an unofficial letter from the General Actuarial Branch of the IRS. In Notice 2002-8 the IRS announced that the P.S. 58 rates may no longer be used for split-dollar plans entered into on or after January 28, 2002. Until further guidance is received, an argument could be made for using the Table 38 rates for survivorship policies in split-dollar plans entered into before January 28, 2002. As to plans entered on or after January 28, 2002, it is clear from Notice 2002-8 that the rates used should reflect "appropriate adjustments" to the Table 2001 rates set forth on page 496. Actuarial guidance should be requested from the issuing life insurance company.

TAX-FREE EXCHANGE

Tax-free exchanges recognize that when property is exchanged by a taxpayer for "like kind" property, gain or loss need not be recognized and the transaction should not be subject to current taxation, since the taxpayer is in essentially the same position after the transaction as he was before the transaction. Real estate transactions are frequently structured as tax-free exchanges.

Life insurance and annuity contracts can also benefit from the provisions for tax-free exchanges, which are often referred to as "Section 1035 exchanges" (after the governing Code provision). In an exchange situation, life insurance policies are the most flexible, since they may be exchanged for another life insurance policy, an endowment contract or an annuity. Although an endowment contract cannot be exchanged for a life insurance policy, it can be exchanged for either an annuity or another endowment contract (provided the maturity date of the new contract is not later than the maturity date of the original contract). An annuity contract is the least flexible contract as it can be exchanged only for another annuity contract.

For purposes of a Section 1035 exchange, an endowment contract is considered a contract "which depends in part on the life expectancy of the insured, but which may be payable in full in a single payment during his life." The exchange of an endowment contract must be made *prior* to its maturity date.

In an exchange involving life policies, the policies must be on the life of the *same* insured and the new policy must be issued to the same person owning the old policy. Term insurance appears inappropriate for a tax-free exchange.

Tax-free exchanges can be particularly useful when it is desired to avoid taxation of cash values in excess of the policy owner's basis in the contract (net premiums paid, or generally total premiums paid less dividends, if any), or when it is desired to preserve the old contract's basis (substantial premiums have been paid in excess of available cash values). The old policy need not have been issued by the same company issuing the new policy. Some companies will accept assignment of policies containing an outstanding loan.

If there is a loan against the policy given in exchange, and no loan (or a lower loan) against the policy received in the exchange, the difference is treated as cash received. The lesser of this amount or any gain in the policy given is taxable income. There is gain if total cash values, including loans, exceed total premiums paid, less dividends, if any. If there is no gain, then there is no tax (the amount simply reduces basis).

TAX LAW – SOURCES

Because many sources are cited as tax authority, it is important to understand the differences in the weight given them by the courts and their reliability as precedent. The citation at the end of each paragraph provides an example of how each source is cited.

Legislative and Administrative Sources

Internal Revenue Code. Congressional legislation that is the primary source of our federal tax law. [*IRC Sec. 417(a)(6)*]

Treasury Regulations. Amplify, supplement and interpret the Code. Given substantial weight by the courts and may generally be relied upon by taxpayers. Proposed regulations usually are not considered binding. [*Reg. §1.401(a)-20*]

Revenue Rulings. Issued by the National Office of the IRS. Although not as authoritative as regulations, they are given varying weight by the courts. Can generally be relied upon by taxpayers. Although revenue rulings can be revoked by the IRS, revocation is rarely retroactive. [*Rev. Rul. 72-25*]

Revenue Procedures. Reflect the internal management and state procedures the IRS will follow in specific situations. [*Rev. Proc. 95-3*]

Private Letter Rulings. Issued to a particular taxpayer by the National Office of the IRS. Although letter rulings are only uncertain indications of one line of reasoning by the Service and are not binding precedents, courts have considered them in reaching decisions. [*Let. Rul. 9212024*]

Technical Advice Memoranda. Issued to IRS personnel by the National Office of the IRS to assist with application of the Code, regulations and other precedents. Generally have the same effect as private letter rulings. [*TAM 9050006*]

Field Service Advice. Non-binding opinion written by IRS attorneys for internal use. Provides some insight into the thinking of the IRS at the time written. [*FSA 1998-252*]

Judicial Sources

Supreme Court. All courts follow Supreme Court decisions. The few tax cases it hears are accepted as a matter of discretion (certiorari). [*Gregory v. Helvering*, 293 U.S. 465 (1935)]

U.S. Courts of Appeals. Organized in thirteen circuits. Decisions of a court of appeals bind those lower courts within its appellate jurisdiction. [*Crummey v. Comm.*, 397 F.2d 82 (9th Cir. 1968)]

Tax Court. The majority of tax cases are litigated in this court (it was formerly the Board of Tax Appeals). Taxes need not be paid before initiating a suit and there is no jury. Decisions reviewed by the entire Tax Court take precedence over unreviewed decisions (either regular or memorandum); unreviewed "regular" decisions take precedence over unreviewed "memorandum" decisions. The Tax Court has said that unreviewed memorandum decisions are not precedents, but this policy may be changing. Appeals (where available) are made to the appropriate U.S. court of appeals. Other federal courts and the Service are not bound by Tax Court decisions in future cases. [*Estate of Vandenhoeck*, 4 T.C. 125 (1944)]

Federal District Courts. Taxes must be paid before initiating suit, but a jury may be requested (jury decides facts, judge decides law). A district court is expected to follow its decisions, but its decisions do not bind other federal courts or the Service in future cases. Appeals are made to the appropriate U.S. court of appeals. [*Silberman v. U.S.*, 333 F. Supp. 1120 (W.D. Pa. 1971)]

U.S. Court of Federal Claims. Taxes must be paid before initiating suit and there is no jury. The court (previously, the U.S. Claims Court) is expected to follow its decisions, but does not bind other federal courts or the Service in future cases. Appeals are made to the Court of Appeals for the Federal Circuit. [*Arkla, Inc. v. U.S.*, 27 Fed. Cl. 226 (1992)]

TOTAL RETURN UNITRUST

The traditional "income and principal" trust directs that the trustee pay all trust income to the income beneficiary, with corpus distributed to the remainder beneficiaries upon the death of the income beneficiary (e.g., "income to my wife for life, then payment of the corpus in equal shares to my children"). Under traditional state law, the concept of "income" included interest and dividends, but excluded capital appreciation of the trust assets.

Typically, trust assets were invested in fixed *income* investments (bonds) in order to provide for the income beneficiary. In view of the strong stock market performance of recent years, it is easy to understand how this can lead to **disgruntled remainder beneficiaries** (e.g., the children). To remedy this situation, a majority of states have enacted some form of the prudent investor rule (see discussion, page 440). Under this rule, trustees can utilize modern portfolio theory and invest for capital *appreciation* in a diversified portfolio of equity and growth stocks. However, foregoing trust income in order to attain greater trust appreciation can lead to a **disgruntled income beneficiary** (e.g., a surviving spouse).

Caught in the middle is the trustee – who has a duty of fairness to both the income and remainder beneficiaries. The "total return unitrust" is an attempt to balance the competing interests of the income and remainder beneficiaries while obtaining greater trust appreciation.

Rather than focusing on income producing investments, under the "total return" approach a trustee, governed by the prudent investor rules, can invest in equities in order to obtain greater long-term growth of trust assets. With a "total return unitrust" the trustee is required to pay out a fixed percentage of the fair market value of the trust assets each year; thereby *enabling the income beneficiary to enjoy the benefits of trust appreciation.* A "smoothing" formula is used to cushion rapid year-to-year changes in trust value (e.g., using a 3-year rolling average to determine fair market value).

The IRS has issued proposed new regulations intended to accommodate state law changes to the concepts of income and principal. Under the regulations, allocations between income and principal will be respected by the Service if state law provides for a "reasonable apportionment" between the income and remainder beneficiaries of the total return of the trust, to include ordinary income, capital gains, and unrealized appreciation (e.g., a unitrust amount of three to five percent would be considered reasonable).

Transfers in trust avoid current gift and estate taxes provided a spouse, as income beneficiary, is entitled to all trust income for life (i.e., the trust qualifies for the unlimited marital deduction, as in the "A" trust on page 29). Under the proposed regulations, this "all income to spouse" requirement is met – and the marital deduction is preserved – when a unitrust makes such a "reasonable apportionment" of the total return of the trust.

TRANSFER FOR VALUE

The transfer for value of a life insurance contract jeopardizes the income tax-free payment of its proceeds. Under the transfer for value rule, if a policy is transferred for a valuable consideration, the death proceeds will be taxable as ordinary income, except to the extent of the consideration, the net premiums and certain other amounts paid by the transferee.

The transfer for value rules extend far beyond outright sales of policies (see **Q 64**, *Tax Facts 1 (2002)*). The naming of a beneficiary in exchange for any kind of valuable consideration would constitute a transfer for value. Consideration does not have to be in money, but could be an exchange of policies or a promise to perform some act or service. However, the mere pledging or assignment of a policy as collateral security is not a transfer for value.

Specific *exceptions* to this rule allow a transfer for consideration to be made to the following, without jeopardizing the income tax-free nature of the death benefit:

1. Transfers to the insured.
2. Transfers to a partner of the insured.
3. Transfers to a partnership in which the insured is a partner.
4. Transfers to a corporation in which the insured is a stockholder or officer.
5. Transfers between corporations in a tax-free reorganization if certain conditions exist.

A *bona fide gift* is not considered to be a transfer for value and subsequent payment of the proceeds to the grantee (donee) will be income tax-free.

The transfer for value problem does not exist with a partnership, because a transfer to a partner of the insured is one of the exceptions to the rule. Thus, it is possible to convert from an entity purchase agreement to a cross purchase agreement and use the same policies to fund the new agreement.

With respect to a corporation, once a stock redemption agreement (i.e., entity purchase agreement) has been funded with life insurance, it is *not* possible to change to a cross purchase agreement and use the *same* policies to fund the new agreement. Transfer by the corporation of an existing policy on the life of one stockholder to another stockholder would be a violation of the transfer for value rule (but transfer to a partner or a bona fide partnership of which the stockholder was a partner would fall within exceptions to the transfer for value rule). However, this problem does not exist in changing from a cross purchase agreement to a stock redemption agreement: the transfer to a corporation in which the insured is a stockholder is an exception to the rule (see 4 above).

(continued on next page)

TRANSFER FOR VALUE (continued)

Some planners have suggested the use of a trusteed cross purchase agreement to avoid a problem of multiple policies when there are more than just 2 or 3 stockholders. Under this arrangement, a trustee would be both owner and beneficiary of just one policy on each of the stockholders. However, it is likely that there is a prohibited transfer for value when one of the stockholders dies and the surviving stockholders then receive a greater proportional interest in the outstanding policies that continue to insure the survivors.

For example, assume A, B, C and D are equal stockholders in a corporation with a funded trusteed cross purchase agreement. Under the arrangement each stockholder is the beneficial owner of a one-third interest in the policies insuring the other three stockholders. Now assume D dies. A prohibited transfer for value could occur if D's proportional interests in the outstanding policies insuring A, B and C pass to the surviving stockholders upon D's death. However, the problem can be avoided by having the corporation purchase D's interests in the policies insuring A, B and C, with the intention of funding a combined cross purchase and entity purchase agreement (see chart entitled, "Wait And See" Buy/Sell Agreement, on page 141). Alternatively, the problem could also be avoided by simply using a stock redemption agreement, as shown in Entity Purchase Agreement chart on page 129. See page 136, for an expanded discussion of the Trusteed Cross Purchase Agreement.

Transfer for value problems can occur in rather unexpected circumstances. For example, the transfer of existing life insurance policies insuring stockholders to the trustee of a trusteed cross purchase agreement does not fall within one of the exceptions to the transfer for value rule. To avoid this initial ownership problem the trustee should be the original applicant, owner and beneficiary of the policies.

A prohibited transfer for value can also occur when a split-dollar agreement involving a trustee is terminated pursuant to a "rollout" (see page 470). When the agreement is between the employer and the trustee of an irrevocable trust, using endorsement split-dollar would require a transfer of the policy to a trustee who does not fall within any of the exceptions to the transfer for value rules. However, using collateral assignment split-dollar will avoid this "transfer for value" problem. See footnote 2, page 167, for a discussion of endorsement and collateral assignment split-dollar.

TRUSTS FOR MINORS

In order for a gift to qualify for the annual exclusion the donee must have the right to immediate use and enjoyment of the property (chart, page 49). As a matter of principle, many donors will object to placing title to property in the name of a minor, and it can create problems in dealing with the property. Fortunately, for those who intend to make substantial gifts over a number of years, the Code authorizes two types of trusts that can be used to obtain the annual exclusion:

Section 2503(c) Trust. Under this trust both income and principal may be expended by or on behalf of the beneficiary prior to age 21, and the unexpended income and principal *must* be paid to the beneficiary upon attaining age 21 or sooner. If the minor beneficiary dies before age 21, the trust corpus passes to the minor's estate or is subject to a general power of appointment by the minor. It is permissible for the trustee to purchase life insurance on the minor's life and pay premiums from trust income (if the trust authorizes purchase of insurance on the grantor's life, or on the life of the grantor's spouse, there will be a violation of the grantor trust rules, and all income will be taxable to the grantor). Distributed income is taxable to the minor, and accumulated income is taxable to the trust. The donor should not be named trustee, as that will cause the trust assets to be included in his estate if he dies prior to the minor's reaching age 21.

Section 2503(b) Trust. This trust should be considered by the donor who does not want trust corpus and unexpended income to be distributed at age 21 or sooner. The principal can be paid to the beneficiary at whatever dates or times are established by the donor, and need not ever be paid to the beneficiary, but rather paid to another person specified by the donor or the trust beneficiary. However, such a trust must provide for a *mandatory distribution of income* to the beneficiary, at least annually, or more frequently (but could be deposited to a custodial account). Making the gift requires a calculation that involves dividing the gift into an income portion (that which qualifies for the annual exclusion) and a principal or remainder portion (that which is considered a gift of a future interest).

Because establishment of both types of trusts can be expensive and time consuming, many donors may find it more convenient to make gifts under the Uniform Transfers to Minors Act or the Uniform Gifts to Minors Act (page 482).

UNIFORM TRANSFERS/UNIFORM GIFTS TO MINORS ACTS

Gifts can be made to a minor by transferring property to a custodian under the Uniform Transfers to Minors Act (UTMA) or the Uniform Gifts to Minors Act (UGMA). Because the UGMA places restrictions on the types of property that can be the subject of a custodial gift, most states have now adopted the UTMA. It appears that life insurance policies may be the subject of a gift in all states. However, in most states there are restrictions on who may be named insured; there may also be restrictions on who may be named beneficiary (see discussion of Minors and Life Insurance, page 425).

Gifts made under either act can qualify for the annual exclusion (see chart, page 49). All income from the gift will be taxable to the minor (unless it is used to discharge the legal obligation of another person, in which case the income would be taxable to that person). Unlike a minor's trust, the custodian does not file a separate tax return and all income is reported by the minor on his own tax return. The minor has the right to receive possession of the property upon attaining the age specified in the relevant state's statute (age varies from state to state, and may depend upon instructions of donor or nature of the transaction that created the custodianship).

If the donor appoints himself as custodian, the property will be included in his taxable estate if he dies while serving as custodian. There can be only one beneficiary per custodial account, and therefore separate accounts must be established for multiple beneficiaries. Likewise, each account can only have one custodian and successor custodians are usually the minor's guardians.

Generally, for 2002, children under age 14 with unearned income of more than $750 or total gross income in excess of the standard deduction (the greater of (a) $750, or (b) earned income plus $250, but not exceeding $4,550) must file a tax return. The amount of unearned income of a child under age 14 that exceeds $1,500 generally is taxed to the child at the *parent's* maximum rate (known as the "kiddie tax"). Once the child has reached age 14, the unearned income is taxed at the child's rate. A parent can elect to claim the unearned income of a child under age 14 on the parent's return if: (1) the child's income is solely from interest and dividends; (2) the income is more than $750 but less than $7,500; and (3) there has been no backup withholding or estimated tax payments under the child's taxpayer identification number. If the election is made, the parent includes as income taxable at the parent's rate any gross income of the child in excess of $1,500. With respect to the first $1,500 for each child to whom the election applies, there is a tax of 10 percent of the lesser of $750 or the excess of the gross income of the child over $750.

UNREASONABLE COMPENSATION

The payment by a corporation of an "excessive" amount to an employee for services rendered is considered to be unreasonable compensation. Whether compensation is excessive, and therefore unreasonable, is often determined by reference to payments by similar corporations to employees performing like services. The problem is most often encountered with regard to employee-stockholders, where a *salary* would be a deductible business expense to the corporation, but a *dividend* would be nondeductible.

Underlying any discussion of employee benefits is the assumption that, if challenged by the Internal Revenue Service, the increased compensation could be shown to be reasonable. Compensation includes not only money, but also payments "in kind." For example, the personal use of an automobile, lodging for the employee's family while on vacation, premiums for group term insurance, medical expense reimbursements, or premiums for such coverages, and premiums paid under an executive equity or the Table 2001 cost of insurance under a split-dollar plan, are all considered to be compensation. It should be noted that no deduction is allowed for compensation that is paid to certain highly compensated officers of publicly-held corporations in excess of $1,000,000 (see discussion on page 396).

However, it appears to be the experience of many accountants and tax advisors that the threat of a successful challenge by the Service is more imagined than real. This may often be due to a belated recognition by the courts, as well as the Service, that the business owner spent many years being underpaid while the business grew, and now has the "right" to compensation for those earlier services. After all, it was the owner who made the small closely-held business a success, and sooner or later he should be paid for his efforts. However, the determination depends on the circumstances of each situation.

VARIABLE ANNUITIES

With a variable annuity the annuity owner has the opportunity to allocate his premiums among a number of subaccounts. In return for the opportunity to benefit from any appreciation in underlying investments, the owner assumes the risk that his investments may decrease in value, thereby resulting in lower accumulation values or a lower monthly income. The variable annuity is considered a "security" under federal law and anyone selling a variable annuity must have the required securities licenses and the purchaser must be given a prospectus (see footnote 3, page 285). The purchase can be made with either a single premium or a series of premiums.

In addition to a fixed or general account, the typical variable annuity might offer the following investment options: (1) growth or common stock fund; (2) balanced fund; (3) index fund; (4) global fund; (5) bond fund; (6) government securities fund; and (7) money market fund. Asset management or investment fees will vary depending upon the type of fund. In addition to an annual administration fee, an annual mortality charge is made for a guaranteed "death benefit" (e.g., provided the owner dies prior to age 80 his beneficiary is guaranteed to receive the greater of his original investment or the policy's value at the time of death, less withdrawals). Some contracts offer "stepped up" death benefits that lock in investment gains at a given point in time.

During the *accumulation* phase premium payments are applied toward the purchase of accumulation units. The value of an accumulation unit is determined by dividing the market value of the underlying investments by the total number of units outstanding. Dividends and capital appreciation or depreciation are reflected in the value of the accumulation units. The owner also has the option to transfer funds between investment subaccounts, subject to certain dollar amounts and timing limitations. Unlike mutual funds, all accumulations are tax deferred and transfers of assets between accounts are free of current income taxes. A decreasing surrender charge is generally applied if the annuity is surrendered within a given period (see chart, page 283).

During the *distribution* phase the annuity owner can cash in the contract, take periodic withdrawals, or annuitize the contract. All gains are taxed as ordinary income when distributed. Annuity payments can be received on a fixed or variable basis, or a combination of both, and can be paid as a single life annuity or joint and survivor annuity. If variable benefits are to be received the accumulation units are first exchanged for annuity units. Unlike accumulation units, the number of annuity units then remains constant. Variable benefit payments will differ from month to month, or from year to year, depending upon the value of the annuity units. A new living benefit feature currently being developed offers a guaranteed minimum account value, or minimum payout amount, regardless of the actual performance of the subaccounts.

VIATICAL SETTLEMENTS

The sale of a life insurance policy to an investor is called a viatical settlement. The term "viatical" has its roots in the Latin word viaticum, a term used to describe the provisions that ancient Roman families provided to soldiers going off to war. A "viator" is the owner of a life insurance policy who enters into a contract to sell the policy to a third party, usually a viatical settlement provider. The owner of the policy does not have to be the insured (e.g., policy owned by one spouse on the life of the other spouse). A viatical settlement is not the same as payment of an accelerated death benefit by a life insurance company (see discussion, page 338). Most policies can be viaticated, including term, whole life and universal life. The AIDS epidemic brought increased attention and much controversy to these settlements, particularly in regard to the fees charged and the discounts used in determining the purchase price.

Provided certain conditions are met proceeds from the sale of a policy may be excluded from income. These conditions, including a "business insurance" exception, are the same as those that apply to receipt of an accelerated death benefit (see discussion, page 338). To obtain this favorable income tax treatment the viatical provider must be licensed in the state in which the insured resides. If the insured resides in a state not requiring such licensing, then there must be compliance with certain provisions of the Viatical Settlements Model Act and requirements of the National Association Of Insurance Commissioners relating to standards for evaluating the reasonableness of payments. To protect the viator the Model Act sets forth minimum percentages of the policy face that must be paid (ranging from 80 percent when the insured's life expectancy is less than six months, to 50 percent when the insured's life expectancy is 24 months or more).

The National Viatical Association, a trade group representing viatical companies, has published a disclosure list that members distribute when an application for a viatical settlement is taken. Included are warnings that: proceeds may be subject to taxes; insured could lose other rights and benefits contained within the policy; proceeds may adversely affect eligibility for Medicaid; and policy might qualify for a tax-favored viatical settlement if life expectancy is 24 months or less.

Viatical proceeds will be subject to income taxation if a viatical settlement fails to meet the conditions to be excluded from income (e.g., the insured is not expected to die within 24 months). Previously it had generally been accepted that any gain would be taxed as ordinary income. However, commentators have recently suggested that the viator should pay ordinary income taxes on the difference between his tax basis and the cash values, and *capital gains* on the difference between the cash values and the proceeds received from the sale. Since there is

(continued on next page)

VIATICAL SETTLEMENTS (continued)

limited authority for this position the prudent viator will seek guidance from competent tax counsel.

Although there appears to be no industry agreement regarding precise classifications, viaticating generally involves individuals who either: (1) have less than two years to live; (2) have a shortened life expectation that is longer than two years; (3) are healthy and insured by a policy with a relatively large death benefit (over $250,000); or (4) purchase policies with the intention of selling them shortly thereafter. Categories (2) and (3) are variously referred to as "senior settlements," "high net worth settlements," or "high net worth transactions." Category (4) has been described as a "contestable viatical settlement" or "wet ink" transaction wherein a policy is purchased with the express intention of selling it shortly thereafter (within the two-year contestability period). When this happens the insurer may attempt to void the insurance contract by having the sale characterized as a wagering contract or by alleging the insured made an invalid assignment of his insurable interest (see discussion, page 405). The term "life settlement" has been used to describe virtually all viatical settlements.

The following are examples of the changing circumstances which can lead to viatical settlements: (1) business is sold and policies purchased to fund buy/sell agreement are no longer needed; (2) executive leaves business or retires and there is no need for policy intended for key person insurance; (3) premiums are no longer affordable (due to change in financial condition or failure of policy to perform as originally projected); (4) large policy loans make it very expensive to maintain policy; (5) changing family circumstances reduce or eliminate need for insurance coverage (e.g., death of spouse, divorce or newly acquired wealth); (6) desire to replace individual policy with last-to-die policy; and (7) decrease in size of estate or increase in tax credits or exemptions result in lowered estate taxes.

The consumer who invests in viatical settlements is attempting to identify a greater mortality risk than was originally identified when the policy was issued (i.e., the insured's health has changed for the worse or the issuing company made a pricing or underwriting mistake). In some states viatical settlements are considered securities and the sale of viaticals is formally regulated and subject to registration. In these states agents must be licensed to sell viaticals. In view of the recent and ongoing changes in the state regulation of viaticals, the agent should contact the appropriate state insurance or securities departments before engaging in the solicitation or sale of viaticals.

WELFARE BENEFIT TRUST

The welfare benefit trust (WBT) is a fund into which employer(s) make deposits to provide specific benefits to their employees. Typical benefits include severance pay and preretirement death benefits. Contributions can be deductible when made, within special limitations. Those limitations do not apply to contributions made to a "10 or more employer plan" that does not maintain experience ratings with respect to individual employers. A "10 or more employer plan" is a plan: (1) to which more than one employer contributes; and (2) to which no individual employer normally contributes more than 10 percent of the total contributions. In 1997 the *Booth* case denied this exception to a plan that maintained individual employer experience ratings.

While not clear, it would seem that benefits provided are included in, or excluded from, income under general tax rules. For example, fully insured group term life insurance proceeds payable by reason of the death of the employee would be excludable from income. The death benefit can be free of estate taxes, provided the employee makes an irrevocable beneficiary designation more than three years prior to death. Further, medical expense reimbursements would be excludable from income.

The WBT is not a qualified plan, nor is it a plan of deferred compensation (which would result in the employer losing his current tax deduction). To avoid classification as deferred compensation, plans are designed to: (1) include a broad group of employees; (2) cover businesses with more than one employee; (3) base funding on actuarial determinations; and (4) avoid any reversion of assets to employers. Plans cannot provide medical and life insurance benefits exclusively for retirees.

All funds received by a multi-employer trust (MET) are pooled to pay benefits to employees as they become eligible. Because of such pooling it is possible that any excess contributions of a particular employer, beyond what would be needed to pay promised benefits to his employees, might go toward providing benefits for the employees of another employer.

An employer funded voluntary employees' beneficiary association (VEBA) is a special kind of WBT. A VEBA is exempt from regular federal income tax; such exemption is generally conditioned upon, among other things, limiting annual compensation taken into account to determine benefits to $200,000 (as indexed in 2002 for inflation).

Although use of a WBT to prefund employee benefits appears to offer an attractive supplemental employee benefit, it would be prudent to seek guidance from qualified counsel on plan design and any unresolved tax questions.

Forms

FORM 706 – ESTATE TAX RETURN

Form **706**
(Rev. November 2001)

Department of the Treasury
Internal Revenue Service

United States Estate (and Generation-Skipping Transfer) Tax Return

Estate of a citizen or resident of the United States (see separate instructions).
To be filed for decedents dying after December 31, 2000, and before January 1, 2002.
For Paperwork Reduction Act Notice, see page 25 of the separate instructions.

OMB No. 1545-0015

Part 1.—Decedent and Executor

1a Decedent's first name and middle initial (and maiden name, if any)	1b Decedent's last name		2 Decedent's Social Security No.
3a Legal residence (domicile) at time of death (county, state, and ZIP code, or foreign country)	3b Year domicile established	4 Date of birth	5 Date of death
6a Name of executor (see page 4 of the instructions)	6b Executor's address (number and street including apartment or suite no. or rural route; city, town, or post office; state; and ZIP code)		
6c Executor's social security number (see page 4 of the instructions)			
7a Name and location of court where will was probated or estate administered			7b Case number

8 If decedent died testate, check here ▶ ☐ and attach a certified copy of the will. | 9 If Form 4768 is attached, check here ▶ ☐

10 If Schedule R-1 is attached, check here ▶ ☐

Part 2.—Tax Computation

1	Total gross estate less exclusion (from Part 5, Recapitulation, page 3, item 12)	1
2	Total allowable deductions (from Part 5, Recapitulation, page 3, item 23) . .	2
3	Taxable estate (subtract line 2 from line 1)	3
4	Adjusted taxable gifts (total taxable gifts (within the meaning of section 2503) made by the decedent after December 31, 1976, other than gifts that are includible in decedent's gross estate (section 2001(b)))	4
5	Add lines 3 and 4	5
6	Tentative tax on the amount on line 5 from Table A on page 12 of the instructions	6
7a	If line 5 exceeds $10,000,000, enter the lesser of line 5 or $17,184,000. If line 5 is $10,000,000 or less, skip lines 7a and 7b and enter -0- on line 7c . **7a**	
b	Subtract $10,000,000 from line 7a **7b**	
c	Enter 5% (.05) of line 7b	7c
8	Total tentative tax (add lines 6 and 7c)	8
9	Total gift tax payable with respect to gifts made by the decedent after December 31, 1976. Include gift taxes by the decedent's spouse for such spouse's share of split gifts (section 2513) only if the decedent was the donor of these gifts and they are includible in the decedent's gross estate (see instructions)	9
10	Gross estate tax (subtract line 9 from line 8)	10
11	Maximum unified credit (applicable credit amount) against estate tax . **11**	
12	Adjustment to unified credit (applicable credit amount). (This adjustment may not exceed $6,000. See page 4 of the instructions.) **12**	
13	Allowable unified credit (applicable credit amount) (subtract line 12 from line 11) .	13
14	Subtract line 13 from line 10 (but do not enter less than zero)	14
15	Credit for state death taxes. Do not enter more than line 14. Figure the credit by using the amount on line 3 less $60,000. See Table B in the instructions and **attach credit evidence** (see instructions) .	15
16	Subtract line 15 from line 14	16
17	Credit for Federal gift taxes on pre-1977 gifts (section 2012) (attach computation) **17**	
18	Credit for foreign death taxes (from Schedule(s) P). (Attach Form(s) 706-CE.) **18**	
19	Credit for tax on prior transfers (from Schedule Q) **19**	
20	Total (add lines 17, 18, and 19)	20
21	Net estate tax (subtract line 20 from line 16)	21
22	Generation-skipping transfer taxes (from Schedule R, Part 2, line 10)	22
23	Total transfer taxes (add lines 21 and 22)	23
24	Prior payments. Explain in an attached statement **24**	
25	United States Treasury bonds redeemed in payment of estate tax . **25**	
26	Total (add lines 24 and 25)	26
27	Balance due (or overpayment) (subtract line 26 from line 23)	27

Under penalties of perjury, I declare that I have examined this return, including accompanying schedules and statements, and to the best of my knowledge and belief, it is true, correct, and complete. Declaration of preparer other than the executor is based on all information of which preparer has any knowledge.

Signature(s) of executor(s)   Date

Signature of preparer other than executor   Cat. No. 20548R   Address (and ZIP code)   Date

Note: The executor of the estate must sign this form "under penalties of perjury." This is the first page of a form which is 44 pages in length (a complete copy can be obtained from the Internal Revenue Service). See page 85 for the estate tax calculation steps. (Use of form has been extended beyond expiration date.)

INSTRUCTIONS FOR FORM 706

Instructions for Form 706
(Rev. November 2001)

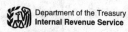
Department of the Treasury
Internal Revenue Service

United States Estate (and Generation-Skipping Transfer) Tax Return

(For decedents dying after December 31, 2000, and before January 1, 2002.)
Section references are to the Internal Revenue Code unless otherwise noted.

Prior Revisions of Form 706

*For Schedules A, A-1, C, D, E, F, J, and M, see instructions in the Form 706 itself.

General Instructions

Changes To Note

▸ Use this revision of Form 706 only for the estates of decedents dying in calendar year 2001.

▸ Except for the returns of nonresident U.S. citizens, all estate tax returns should be filed at the Cincinnati Service Center. See **Where To File** on page 2.

▸ Various dollar amounts and limitations relevant to Form 706 are indexed for inflation. For decedents dying in 2001, the following amounts have increased:

  ▸ the ceiling on special use valuation is $800,000;

  ▸ the generation-skipping transfer tax exemption is $1,060,000; and

  ▸ the amount used in computing the 2% portion of estate tax payable in installments is $1,060,000.

The IRS will publish amounts for future years in an annual revenue procedure.

▸ To expedite closing the estate, a copy of the **Estate Tax Closing Document** is included in the back of the form package. See the instructions on the reverse side of the Closing Document.

▸ The Victims of Terrorism Tax Relief Act of 2001 provides special treatment for the estates of decedents who died as the result of certain terrorist acts. See the instructions for **Lines 6–9** on page 5 for more information.

▸ The qualified conservation easement exclusion has been expanded to include all land in the United States and its possessions, and the amount of the exclusion for the estates of decedents dying in 2001 is $400,000.

A. Purpose of Form

The executor of a decedent's estate uses Form 706 to figure the estate tax imposed by Chapter 11 of the Internal Revenue Code. This tax is levied on the entire taxable estate, not just on the share received by a particular beneficiary. Form 706 is also used to compute the generation-skipping transfer (GST) tax imposed by Chapter 13 on direct skips (transfers to skip persons of interests in property included in the decedent's gross estate).

B. Which Estates Must File

For decedents dying in 2001, Form 706 must be filed by the executor for the estate of every U.S. citizen or resident whose gross estate, plus adjusted taxable gifts and specific exemption, is more than $675,000.

To determine whether you must file a return for the estate, add:

1. The adjusted taxable gifts (under section 2001(b)) made by the decedent after December 31, 1976;

2. The total specific exemption allowed under section 2521 (as in effect before its repeal by the Tax Reform Act of 1976) for gifts made by the decedent after September 8, 1976; and

3. The decedent's gross estate **valued at the date of death.**

Gross Estate

The gross estate includes all property in which the decedent had an interest (including real property outside the United States). It also includes:

▸ Certain transfers made during the decedent's life without an adequate and full consideration in money or money's worth;

▸ Annuities;

▸ The includible portion of joint estates with right of survivorship (see the instructions on the back of Schedule E);

▸ The includible portion of tenancies by the entirety (see the instructions on the back of Schedule E);

▸ Certain life insurance proceeds (even though payable to beneficiaries other than the estate) (see the instructions on the back of Schedule D);

▸ Property over which the decedent possessed a general power of appointment;

▸ Dower or curtesy (or statutory estate) of the surviving spouse;

▸ Community property to the extent of the decedent's interest as defined by applicable law.

For more specific information, see the instructions for Schedules A through I.

U. S. Citizens or Residents; Nonresident Noncitizens

File Form 706 for the estates of decedents who were either U.S. citizens or U.S. residents at the time of death. For estate tax purposes, a resident is someone who had a domicile in the United States at the time of death. A person

Cat. No. 16779E

Note: This is the first page of instructions which are 28 pages in length (a complete copy can be obtained from the Internal Revenue Service).

FORM 709 — GIFT TAX RETURN

Form **709**	United States Gift (and Generation-Skipping Transfer) Tax Return	OMB No. 1545-0020
	(Section 6019 of the Internal Revenue Code) (For gifts made during calendar year 2001)	2001
Department of the Treasury Internal Revenue Service	▶ **See separate instructions.**	

1 Donor's first name and middle initial	Donor's last name	3 Donor's social security number
4 Address (number, street, and apartment number)		5 Legal residence (domicile) (county and state)
6 City, state, and ZIP code		7 Citizenship

Part 1—General Information

		Yes	No
8	If the donor died during the year, check here ▶ ☐ and enter date of death.............. , ...		
9	If you received an extension of time to file this Form 709, check here ▶ ☐ and attach the Form 4868, 2688, 2350, or extension letter .		
10	Enter the total number of separate donees listed on Schedule A—count each person only once. ▶		
11a	Have you (the donor) previously filed a Form 709 (or 709-A) for any other year? If the answer is "No," do not complete line 11b .		
11b	If the answer to line 11a is "Yes," has your address changed since you last filed Form 709 (or 709-A)?		
12	Gifts by husband or wife to third parties.—Do you consent to have the gifts (including generation-skipping transfers) made by you and by your spouse to third parties during the calendar year considered as made one-half by each of you? (See instructions.) (If the answer is "Yes," the following information must be furnished and your spouse must sign the consent shown below. **If the answer is "No," skip lines 13–18 and go to Schedule A.)**		
13	Name of consenting spouse	14 SSN	
15	Were you married to one another during the entire calendar year? (see instructions)		
16	If the answer to 15 is "No," check whether ☐ married ☐ divorced or ☐ widowed, and give date (see instructions) ▶		
17	Will a gift tax return for this calendar year be filed by your spouse?		
18	**Consent of Spouse**—I consent to have the gifts (and generation-skipping transfers) made by me and by my spouse to third parties during the calendar year considered as made one-half by each of us. We are both aware of the joint and several liability for tax created by the execution of this consent.		

Consenting spouse's signature ▶   Date ▶

Part 2—Tax Computation

1	Enter the amount from Schedule A, Part 3, line 15	1		
2	Enter the amount from Schedule B, line 3	2		
3	Total taxable gifts (add lines 1 and 2)	3		
4	Tax computed on amount on line 3 (see Table for Computing Tax in separate instructions). . .	4		
5	Tax computed on amount on line 2 (see Table for Computing Tax in separate instructions). . .	5		
6	Balance (subtract line 5 from line 4)	6		
7	Maximum unified credit (nonresident aliens, see instructions)	7	220,550	00
8	Enter the unified credit against tax allowable for all prior periods (from Sch. B, line 1, col. C) .	8		
9	Balance (subtract line 8 from line 7)	9		
10	Enter 20% (.20) of the amount allowed as a specific exemption for gifts made after September 8, 1976, and before January 1, 1977 (see instructions)	10		
11	Balance (subtract line 10 from line 9)	11		
12	Unified credit (enter the smaller of line 6 or line 11)	12		
13	Credit for foreign gift taxes (see instructions)	13		
14	Total credits (add lines 12 and 13)	14		
15	Balance (subtract line 14 from line 6) (do not enter less than zero)	15		
16	Generation-skipping transfer taxes (from Schedule C, Part 3, col. H, Total)	16		
17	Total tax (add lines 15 and 16)	17		
18	Gift and generation-skipping transfer taxes prepaid with extension of time to file	18		
19	If line 18 is less than line 17, enter **balance due** (see instructions)	19		
20	If line 18 is greater than line 17, enter **amount to be refunded**	20		

Attach check or money order here.

Sign Here

Under penalties of perjury, I declare that I have examined this return, including any accompanying schedules and statements, and to the best of my knowledge and belief, it is true, correct, and complete. Declaration of preparer (other than donor) is based on all information of which preparer has any knowledge.

Signature of donor	Date

Paid Preparer's Use Only

Preparer's signature ▶	Date	Check if self-employed ▶ ☐
Firm's name (or yours if self-employed), address, and ZIP code ▶		Phone no. ▶ ( )

For Disclosure, Privacy Act, and Paperwork Reduction Act Notice, see page 12 of the separate instructions for this form.   Cat. No. 16783M   Form **709** (2001)

Note: The donor must sign this form "under penalties of perjury." This is the first page of a form which is 4 pages in length (a complete copy can be obtained from the Internal Revenue Service). See page 85 for the gift tax calculation steps.

Forms

INSTRUCTIONS FOR FORM 709

20**01**

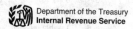

Department of the Treasury
Internal Revenue Service

Instructions for Form 709

United States Gift (and Generation-Skipping Transfer) Tax Return

(For gifts made during calendar year 2001.)
For Disclosure, Privacy Act, and Paperwork Reduction Act Notice, see page 12 of the instructions.
Section references are to the Internal Revenue Code unless otherwise noted.

If you are filing this form solely to elect gift-splitting for gifts of not more than $20,000 per donee, you may be able to use **Form 709-A,** United States Short Form Gift Tax Return, instead of this form. See **Who Must File** on page 3 and **When the Consenting Spouse Must Also File a Gift Tax Return** on page 5.

For Gifts Made After	and	Before	Use Revision of Form 709 Dated
– – –		January 1, 1982	November 1981
December 31, 1981		January 1, 1987	January 1987
December 31, 1986		January 1, 1989	December 1988
December 31, 1988		January 1, 1990	December 1989
December 31, 1989		October 9, 1990	October 1990
October 8, 1990		January 1, 1992	November 1991
December 31, 1992		January 1, 1998	December 1996

Changes To Note

▶ For 2001, mail this form to Internal Revenue Service Center, Cincinnati, Ohio, 45999. See **Where To File** on page 4.
▶ For gifts made to spouses who are not U.S. citizens, the annual exclusion has increased to $106,000. See page 3.
▶ The generation-skipping transfer (GST) lifetime exemption has increased to $1,060,000. See page 10.
▶ Act section 561 of the Economic Growth and Tax Relief Reconciliation Act of 2001 (code section 2632) made several changes to the special rules for allocation of GST exemption. One of the changes creates an automatic allocation of GST exemption to "indirect skips." Other changes create special elections including an election out of the automatic

allocation. See the instructions for **Line 5** on page 11.

Photographs of Missing Children

The IRS is a proud partner with the National Center for Missing and Exploited Children. Photographs of missing children selected by the Center may appear in instructions on pages that would otherwise be blank. You can help bring these children home by looking at the photographs and calling **1-800-THE-LOST** (1-800-843-5678) if you recognize a child.

General Instructions

Note: *If you meet all of the following requirements, you are **not** required to file Form 709:*

1. You made no gifts during the year to your spouse;
2. You gave no more than $10,000 during the year to any one donee; and
3. All of the gifts you made were of present interests.

For additional information, see **Transfers Not Subject to the Gift Tax** *below and* **Who Must File** *on page 3.*

Purpose of Form

Use Form 709 to report the following:
▶ Transfers subject to the Federal gift and certain generation-skipping transfer (GST) taxes and to figure the tax, if any, due on those transfers, and
▶ Allocation of the lifetime GST exemption to property transferred during the transferor's lifetime. (For more details, see the instructions for **Part 2—GST Exemption Reconciliation** on page 10, and Regulations section 26.2632-1.)

All gift and GST taxes are computed and filed on a calendar year basis regardless of your income tax accounting period.

Transfers Subject to the Gift Tax

Generally, the Federal gift tax applies to any transfer by gift of real or personal

property, whether tangible or intangible, that you made directly or indirectly, in trust, or by any other means to a donee.

The gift tax applies not only to the gratuitous transfer of any kind of property, but also to sales or exchanges, not made in the ordinary course of business, where money or money's worth is exchanged but the value of the money (or property) or money's worth received is less than the value of what is sold or exchanged. The gift tax is in addition to any other tax, such as Federal income tax, paid or due on the transfer.

The exercise or release of a general power of appointment may be a gift by the individual possessing the power. General powers of appointment are those in which the holders of the power can appoint property subject to the power to themselves, their creditors, their estates, or the creditors of their estates. To qualify as a power of appointment, it must be created by someone other than the holder of the power.

The gift tax may also apply to the forgiveness of a debt, to interest-free or below market interest rate loans, to the assignment of the benefits of an insurance policy, to certain property settlements in divorce cases, and to the giving up of some amount of annuity in exchange for the creation of a survivor annuity.

Bonds that are exempt from Federal income taxes are not exempt from Federal gift taxes.

Code sections 2701 and 2702 provide rules for determining whether certain transfers to a family member of interests in corporations, partnerships, and trusts are gifts. The rules of section 2704 determine whether the lapse of any voting or liquidation right is a gift.

Transfers Not Subject to the Gift Tax

Three types of transfers are not subject to the gift tax. These are transfers to political organizations and payments that qualify for the educational and medical exclusions. These transfers are not "gifts" as that term is used on Form 709 and its

Cat. No. 16784X

Note: This is the first page of instructions which are 8 pages in length (a complete copy can be obtained from the Internal Revenue Service.)

FEDERAL INCOME TAX RATES

(Tax Years Beginning in 2002)

MARRIED FILING JOINTLY

Taxable Income Over	To	Tax Equals	Plus %	Of Excess Over
0	12,000	0	10	0
12,000	46,700	1,200.00	15	12,000
46,700	112,850	6,405.00	27	46,700
112,850	171,950	24,265.50	30	112,850
171,950	307,050	41,995.50	35	171,950
307,050		89,280.50	38.6	307,050

The amount allowable as a deduction for personal exemptions is reduced by 2% for each $2,500 (or fraction of that amount) by which the taxpayer's adjusted gross income exceeds $206,000.

SINGLE

Taxable Income Over	To	Tax Equals	Plus %	Of Excess Over
0	6,000	0	10	0
6,000	27,950	600.00	15	6,000
27,950	67,700	3,892.50	27	27,950
67,700	141,250	14,625.00	30	67,700
141,250	307,050	36,690.00	35	141,250
307,050		94,720.00	38.6	307,050

The amount allowable as a deduction for personal exemptions is reduced by 2% for each $2,500 (or fraction of that amount) by which the taxpayer's adjusted gross income exceeds $137,300.

ESTATES AND TRUSTS

Taxable Income Over	To	Tax Equals	Plus %	Of Excess Over
0	1,850	0	15	0
1,850	4,400	277.50	27	1,850
4,400	6,750	966.00	30	4,400
6,750	9,200	1,671.00	35	6,750
9,200		2,528.50	38.6	9,200

CORPORATIONS

Taxable Income Over	To	Tax Equals	Plus %	Of Excess Over
0	50,000	0	15	0
50,000	75,000	7,500	25	50,000
75,000	100,000	13,750	34	75,000
100,000	335,000	22,250	39	100,000
335,000	10,000,000	113,900	34	335,000
10,000,000	15,000,000	3,400,000	35	10,000,000
15,000,000	18,333,333	5,150,000	38	15,000,000
18,333,333		6,416,667	35	18,333,333

Note: **Personal service corporations** are subject to a flat rate of 35 percent; and include corporations in which substantially all of the activities involve the performance of services in the fields of health, law, engineering, architecture, accounting, actuarial science, performing arts, or consulting, and substantially all of the stock of which is held by employees, retired employees, or their estates. Appendix B, *Tax Facts 1 (2002)* contains tables for Heads Of Households and Married Persons Filing Separately.

FEDERAL ESTATE & GIFT TAX RATES

(Unified Rate Schedule)

TAXABLE ESTATE/GIFT OVER	TO	TAX EQUALS*	PLUS %	OF EXCESS OVER
0	10,000	0	18	0
10,000	20,000	1,800	20	10,000
20,000	40,000	3,800	22	20,000
40,000	60,000	8,200	24	40,000
60,000	80,000	13,000	26	60,000
80,000	100,000	18,200	28	80,000
100,000	150,000	23,800	30	100,000
150,000	250,000	38,800	32	150,000
250,000	500,000	70,800	34	250,000
500,000	750,000	155,800	37	500,000
750,000	1,000,000	248,300	39	750,000
1,000,000	1,250,000	345,800	41	1,000,000
1,250,000	1,500,000	448,300	43	1,250,000

Upper Brackets: 2001, 2011 and later

1,500,000	2,000,000	555,800	45	1,500,000
2,000,000	2,500,000	780,800	49	2,000,000
2,500,000	3,000,000	1,025,800	53	2,500,000
3,000,000	10,000,000	1,290,800	55	3,000,000
10,000,000	17,184,000	5,140,800	60	10,000,000
17,184,000		9,451,200	55	17,184,000

Upper Brackets: 2002

1,500,000	2,000,000	555,800	45	1,500,000
2,000,000	2,500,000	780,800	49	2,000,000
2,500,000		1,025,800	50	2,500,000

Upper Brackets: 2003

1,500,000	2,000,000	555,800	45	1,500,000
2,000,000		780,800	49	2,000,000

* Less unified credit of $354,800 in 2002-2003. Under EGTRRA 2001, the estate tax unified credit is scheduled to increase during the years 2004 to 2009. These increases are: $555,800 in 2004 and 2005, $780,800 in 2006 thru 2008, and $1,455,800 in 2009. In 2010 the estate tax is repealed, but will return in 2011 under the sunset provisions of EGTRRA 2001. In 2011 and thereafter, the estate tax unified credit is $345,800. The gift tax unified credit remains level at $345,800, except for 2010 when it decreases to $330,800. If any part of the prior $30,000 gift tax exemption was used for gifts made after 9/8/76, the unified credit must be reduced by 20 percent of the amount of the exemption used. Included in the table for the years 2001, 2011 and later is a 5 percent "add on" tax on amounts between $10,000,000 and $17,184,000.

(continued on next page)

FEDERAL ESTATE & GIFT TAX RATES (continued)

TAXABLE ESTATE/GIFT				OF EXCESS
OVER	TO	TAX EQUALS*	PLUS %	OVER

Upper Brackets: 2004

1,500,000	2,000,000	555,800	45	1,500,000
2,000,000		780,800	48	2,000,000

Upper Brackets: 2005

1,500,000	2,000,000	555,800	45	1,500,000
2,000,000		780,800	47	2,000,000

Upper Brackets: 2006

1,500,000	2,000,000	555,800	45	1,500,000
2,000,000		780,800	46	2,000,000

Upper Brackets: 2007-2009

1,500,000		555,800	45	1,500,000

Gift Tax: 2010

TAXABLE GIFT				OF EXCESS
OVER	TO	TAX EQUALS**	PLUS %	OVER
0	10,000	0	18	0
10,000	20,000	1,800	20	10,000
20,000	40,000	3,800	22	20,000
40,000	60,000	8,200	24	40,000
60,000	80,000	13,000	26	60,000
80,000	100,000	18,200	28	80,000
100,000	150,000	23,800	30	100,000
150,000	250,000	38,800	32	150,000
250,000	500,000	70,800	34	250,000
500,000		155,800	35	500,000

* Less unified credit of $354,800 in 2002-2003. Under EGTRRA 2001, the estate tax unified credit is scheduled to increase during the years 2004 to 2009. These increases are: $555,800 in 2004 and 2005, $780,800 in 2006 thru 2008, and $1,455,800 in 2009. In 2010 the estate tax is repealed, but will return in 2011 under the sunset provisions of EGTRRA 2001. In 2011 and thereafter, the estate tax unified credit is $345,800. The gift tax unified credit remains level at $345,800, except for 2010 when it decreases to $330,800. If any part of the prior $30,000 gift tax exemption was used for gifts made after 9/8/76, the unified credit must be reduced by 20 percent of the amount of the exemption used. Included in the table for the years 2001, 2011 and later is a 5 percent "add on" tax on amounts between $10,000,000 and $17,184,000.

**Less credit of $330,800 in 2010.

See page 85 for calculation steps.

STATE DEATH TAX CREDIT

(For the year 2002 - as changed by EGTRRA 2001)

ADJUSTED TAXABLE ESTATE		CREDIT		OF EXCESS
OVER	TO	EQUALS*	PLUS %	OVER
0	90,000	0 ...... see below		40,000
90,000	140,000	300	1.2	90,000
140,000	240,000	900	1.8	140,000
240,000	440,000	2,700	2.4	240,000
440,000	640,000	7,500	3.0	440,000
640,000	840,000	13,500	3.6	640,000
840,000	1,040,000	20,700	4.2	840,000
1,040,000	1,540,000	29,100	4.8	1,040,000
1,540,000	2,040,000	53,100	5.4	1,540,000
2,040,000	2,540,000	80,100	6.0	2,040,000
2,540,000	3,040,000	110,100	6.6	2,540,000
3,040,000	3,540,000	143,100	7.2	3,040,000
3,540,000	4,040,000	179,100	7.8	3,540,000
4,040,000	5,040,000	218,100	8.4	4,040,000
5,040,000	6,040,000	302,100	9.0	5,040,000
6,040,000	7,040,000	392,100	9.6	6,040,000
7,040,000	8,040,000	488,100	10.2	7,040,000
8,040,000	9,040,000	590,100	10.8	8,040,000
9,040,000	10,040,000	698,100	11.4	9,040,000
10,040,000		812,100	12.0	10,040,000

For purpose of calculating the state death tax credit, the term "adjusted taxable estate" means the taxable estate reduced by $60,000. Tax rate on the first $90,000 is 6/10ths of 1 percent of the amount by which the adjusted gross estate exceeds $40,000. Under EGTRRA 2001, this table includes a reduction of 25 percent from 2001 rates. Further reductions from 2001 rates are scheduled as follows: (1) 50 percent in 2003; and (2) 75 percent in 2004. In 2005 the credit is scheduled to be replaced by a deduction for state taxes actually paid.

REQUIRED MINIMUM DISTRIBUTIONS

Age	Distribution Period	Age	Distribution Period	Age	Distribution Period	Age	Distribution Period	Age	Distribution Period
70	26.2	80	17.6	90	10.5	100	5.7	110	2.8
71	25.3	81	16.8	91	9.9	101	5.3	111	2.6
72	24.4	82	16.0	92	9.4	102	5.0	112	2.4
73	23.5	83	15.3	93	8.8	103	4.7	113	2.2
74	22.7	84	14.5	94	8.3	104	4.4	114	2.0
75	21.8	85	13.8	95	7.8	105	4.1	115 &	
76	20.9	86	13.1	96	7.3	106	3.8	Over	1.8
77	20.1	87	12.4	97	6.9	107	3.6		
78	19.2	88	11.8	98	6.5	108	3.3		
79	18.4	89	11.1	99	6.1	109	3.1		

Application: Used in calculating required minimum distributions from IRAs, qualified plans, and TSAs. For example, assume an individual turned age 74 in 2002, and on December 31, 2002, his account balance was $325,000. Using this table, his life expectancy is 22.7 years. He must receive a distribution of $14,317 ($325,000÷22.7 = $14,317) for the 2002 year, no later than December 31, 2003. Use of this table is required for 2002 and later. See the discussion on pages 409-410.

Source: Prop. Reg. §1.40(a)(9)-5, A-4(a)(2)

TABLE 2001 RATES
&
P.S. No. 58 RATES

One Year Term Premiums For $1,000 Of Life Insurance Protection

Age	Table 2001	P.S. 58	Age	Table 2001	P.S. 58	Age	Table 2001	P.S. 58	Age	Table 2001	P.S. 58
15	.38	1.27	32	.93	2.70	49	2.13	8.53	66	13.51	34.28
16	.52	1.38	33	.96	2.86	50	2.30	9.22	67	15.20	37.31
17	.57	1.48	34	.98	3.02	51	2.52	9.97	68	16.92	40.59
18	.59	1.52	35	.99	3.21	52	2.81	10.79	69	18.70	44.17
19	.61	1.56	36	1.01	3.41	53	3.20	11.69	70	20.62	48.06
20	.62	1.61	37	1.04	3.63	54	3.65	12.67	71	22.72	52.29
21	.62	1.67	38	1.06	3.87	55	4.15	13.74	72	25.07	56.89
22	.64	1.73	39	1.07	4.14	56	4.68	14.91	73	27.57	61.89
23	.66	1.79	40	1.10	4.42	57	5.20	16.18	74	30.18	67.33
24	.68	1.86	41	1.13	4.73	58	5.66	17.56	75	33.05	73.23
25	.71	1.93	42	1.20	5.07	59	6.06	19.08	76	36.33	79.63
26	.73	2.02	43	1.29	5.44	60	6.51	20.73	77	40.17	86.57
27	.76	2.11	44	1.40	5.85	61	7.11	22.53	78	44.33	94.09
28	.80	2.20	45	1.53	6.30	62	7.96	24.50	79	49.23	102.23
29	.83	2.31	46	1.67	6.78	63	9.08	26.63	80	54.56	111.04
30	.87	2.43	47	1.83	7.32	64	10.41	28.98	81	60.51	120.57
31	.90	2.57	48	1.98	7.89	65	11.90	31.51			

Application: As a measure of the value of insurance protection provided under; (1) split-dollar plans, (2) qualified pension and profit sharing plans, and (3) tax sheltered annuities.

Source: Notice 2002-8, 2002-4 IRB 1; Revenue Ruling 55-747, 1955-2 CB 228; and Revenue Ruling 66-110, 1966-1 CB 12. Notice 2002-8 provides Table 2001 rates for below age 15 and above age 81 (Appendix C, Tax Facts 1 (2002) contains the full table).

NOTE: For split-dollar plans entered into before January 28, 2002, either Table 2001 rates or P.S. 58 rates (if specified by the split-dollar agreement) can generally be used. For plans entered into on or after January 28, 2002, only Table 2001 rates may generally be used. Notice 2002-8 also sets forth additional limitations on using an insurer's published premium rates as an alternative to the above rates. For plans entered into before January 28, 2002, the insurer's published premium rates may generally be used. For plans entered into on or after January 28, 2002, until further IRS guidance is received, the insurer's published premium rates may be used with the qualification that for periods after December 31, 2003, the insurer must actual make known and sell term insurance at these rates.

TABLE I RATES

Value Per $1,000 Of Life Insurance Protection For One Year

Ages	Value	Ages	Value	Ages	Value
Under 25	.60	40 to 44	1.20	60 to 64	7.92
25 to 29	.72	45 to 49	1.80	65 to 69	15.24
30 to 34	.96	50 to 54	2.76	70 & Over	24.72
35 to 39	1.08	55 to 59	5.16		

Application: As a measure of the value of excess group term insurance.

Source: Reg. §1.79-3(d)(2) – the rates as set forth in the regulation are given in costs per $1,000 of protection for 1-month periods (i.e., the cost at age 42 is 10 cents per $1,000 per month).

TABLE 38

Probability Of Dying In Each Year Of Age

Age	Probability (q)	Age	Probability (q)	Age	Probability (q)
20	.00165	49	.00874	78	.09644
21	.00171	50	.00945	79	.10479
22	.00177	51	.01022	80	.11382
23	.00183	52	.01106	81	.12358
24	.00191	53	.01198	82	.13413
25	.00198	54	.01299	83	.14550
26	.00207	55	.01408	84	.15776
27	.00216	56	.01528	85	.17094
28	.00226	57	.01658	86	.18511
29	.00237	58	.01800	87	.20032
30	.00249	59	.01956	88	.21661
31	.00263	60	.02125	89	.23402
32	.00277	61	.02309	90	.25261
33	.00293	62	.02511	91	.27239
34	.00310	63	.02730	92	.29341
35	.00329	64	.02970	93	.31568
36	.00350	65	.03230	94	.33921
37	.00372	66	.03514	95	.36399
38	.00397	67	.03824	96	.39001
39	.00424	68	.04160	97	.41721
40	.00453	69	.04527	98	.44555
41	.00485	70	.04926	99	.47493
42	.00520	71	.05360	100	.50525
43	.00558	72	.05831	101	.53638
44	.00600	73	.06344	102	.56816
45	.00646	74	.06901	103	.60039
46	.00695	75	.07506	104	.63286
47	.00750	76	.08162	105	1.00000
48	.00809	77	.08873		

Explanation of Table. Table 38 has been used as a measure of the value to the employee of insurance protection provided under split-dollar plans involving survivorship life policies. Although based on the underlying actuarial assumptions of the P.S. 58 rates, the only authority for use of the Table 38 rates is an unofficial letter from the General Actuarial Branch of the IRS. In this letter it was suggested that: "it is acceptable to apply the formula for the one year term rate on an insurance of two lives, payable on the second death, as expressed by the symbols v q^x q^y where v is 1/1.025 and q^x q^y are the annual mortality rates for ages x and y computed from values in U.S. Life Table 38." The probability of two individuals dying in the same year can be calculated by multiplying their individual probabilities. For example, the probability of two individuals ages 65 and 70 dying in any one year is .0015911 (.03230 x .04926 = .0015911). The value per year per thousand of death benefit is $1.55 (1/1.025 x .03230 x .04926 x 1,000 = 1.55).

Limitations on Application: In Notice 2002-8 the IRS announced that the P.S. 58 rates can no longer be used for split-dollar plans entered into on or after January 28, 2002. Until further guidance is received, an argument could be made for using Table 38 rates in split-dollar plans entered into before January 28, 2002. As to plans entered on or after January 28, 2002, it is clear from Notice 2002-8 that the rates used should reflect "appropriate adjustments" to the Table 2001 rates set forth on page 496. Actuarial guidance should be requested from the issuing life insurance company. See also, Treatment Of Split-Dollar Plans Under Notice 2002-8, on page 228, and the discussion of survivorship life insurance, on page 475.

COMMISSIONERS
1980 STANDARD ORDINARY MORTALITY TABLE

Age	Male deaths per 1,000	Male average future lifetime	Female deaths per 1,000	Female average future lifetime	Age	Male deaths per 1,000	Male average future lifetime	Female deaths per 1,000	Female average future lifetime
0	4.18	70.83	2.89	75.83	50	6.71	25.36	4.96	29.53
1	1.07	70.13	.87	75.04	51	7.30	24.52	5.31	28.67
2	.99	69.20	.81	74.11	52	7.96	23.70	5.70	27.82
3	.98	68.27	.79	73.17	53	8.71	22.89	6.15	26.98
4	.95	67.34	.77	72.23	54	9.56	22.08	6.61	26.14
5	.90	66.40	.76	71.28	55	10.47	21.29	7.09	25.31
6	.85	65.46	.73	70.34	56	11.46	20.51	7.57	24.49
7	.80	64.52	.72	69.39	57	12.49	19.74	8.03	23.67
8	.76	63.57	.70	68.44	58	13.59	18.99	8.47	22.86
9	.74	62.62	.69	67.48	59	14.77	18.24	8.94	22.05
10	.73	61.66	.68	66.53	60	16.08	17.51	9.47	21.25
11	.77	60.71	.69	65.58	61	17.54	16.79	10.13	20.44
12	.85	59.75	.72	64.62	62	19.19	16.08	10.96	19.65
13	.99	58.80	.75	63.67	63	21.06	15.38	12.02	18.86
14	1.15	57.86	.80	62.71	64	23.14	14.70	13.25	18.08
15	1.33	56.93	.85	61.76	65	25.42	14.04	14.59	17.32
16	1.51	56.00	.90	60.82	66	27.85	13.39	16.00	16.57
17	1.67	55.09	.95	59.87	67	30.44	12.76	17.43	15.83
18	1.78	54.18	.98	58.93	68	33.19	12.14	18.84	15.10
19	1.86	53.27	1.02	57.98	69	36.17	11.54	20.36	14.38
20	1.90	52.37	1.05	57.04	70	39.51	10.96	22.11	13.67
21	1.91	51.47	1.07	56.10	71	43.30	10.39	24.23	12.97
22	1.89	50.57	1.09	55.16	72	47.65	9.84	26.87	12.28
23	1.86	49.66	1.11	54.22	73	52.64	9.30	30.11	11.60
24	1.82	48.75	1.14	53.28	74	58.19	8.79	33.93	10.95
25	1.77	47.84	1.16	52.34	75	64.19	8.31	38.24	10.32
26	1.73	46.93	1.19	51.40	76	70.53	7.84	42.97	9.71
27	1.71	46.01	1.22	50.46	77	77.12	7.40	48.04	9.12
28	1.70	45.09	1.26	49.52	78	83.90	6.97	53.45	8.55
29	1.71	44.16	1.30	48.59	79	91.05	6.57	59.35	8.01
30	1.73	43.24	1.35	47.65	80	98.84	6.18	65.99	7.48
31	1.78	42.31	1.40	46.71	81	107.48	5.80	73.60	6.98
32	1.83	41.38	1.45	45.78	82	117.25	5.44	82.40	6.49
33	1.91	40.46	1.50	44.84	83	128.26	5.09	92.53	6.03
34	2.00	39.54	1.58	43.91	84	140.25	4.77	103.81	5.59
35	2.11	38.61	1.65	42.98	85	152.95	4.46	116.10	5.18
36	2.24	37.69	1.76	42.05	86	166.09	4.18	129.29	4.80
37	2.40	36.78	1.89	41.12	87	179.55	3.91	143.32	4.43
38	2.58	35.87	2.04	40.20	88	193.27	3.66	158.18	4.09
39	2.79	34.96	2.22	39.28	89	207.29	3.41	173.94	3.77
40	3.02	34.05	2.42	38.36	90	221.77	3.18	190.75	3.45
41	3.29	33.16	2.64	37.46	91	236.98	2.94	208.87	3.15
42	3.56	32.26	2.87	36.55	92	253.45	2.70	228.81	2.85
43	3.87	31.38	3.09	35.66	93	272.11	2.44	251.51	2.55
44	4.19	30.50	3.32	34.77	94	295.90	2.17	279.31	2.24
45	4.55	29.62	3.56	33.88	95	329.96	1.87	317.32	1.91
46	4.92	28.76	3.80	33.00	96	384.55	1.54	375.74	1.56
47	5.32	27.90	4.05	32.12	97	480.20	1.20	474.97	1.21
48	5.74	27.04	4.33	31.25	98	657.98	.84	655.85	.84
49	6.21	26.20	4.63	30.39	99	1000.00	.50	1000.00	.50

Source: Selected figures from published table. Age is given as nearest birthday.

COMPOUND INTEREST TABLE

The Sum To Which One Dollar Principal Will Increase

					Rate				
Years	5%	6%	7%	8%	9%	10%	12%	15%	18%
1	1.050	1.060	1.070	1.080	1.090	1.100	1.120	1.150	1.180
2	1.102	1.124	1.145	1.166	1.188	1.210	1.254	1.323	1.392
3	1.158	1.191	1.225	1.260	1.295	1.331	1.405	1.521	1.643
4	1.216	1.262	1.311	1.360	1.412	1.464	1.574	1.749	1.939
5	1.276	1.338	1.403	1.469	1.539	1.611	1.762	2.011	2.288
6	1.340	1.419	1.501	1.587	1.677	1.772	1.974	2.313	2.700
7	1.407	1.504	1.606	1.714	1.828	1.949	2.211	2.660	3.185
8	1.477	1.594	1.718	1.851	1.993	2.144	2.476	3.059	3.759
9	1.551	1.689	1.838	1.999	2.172	2.358	2.773	3.518	4.435
10	1.629	1.791	1.967	2.159	2.367	2.594	3.106	4.046	5.234
11	1.710	1.898	2.105	2.332	2.580	2.853	3.479	4.652	6.176
12	1.796	2.012	2.252	2.518	2.813	3.138	3.896	5.350	7.288
13	1.886	2.133	2.410	2.720	3.066	3.452	4.363	6.153	8.599
14	1.980	2.261	2.579	2.937	3.342	3.797	4.887	7.076	10.147
15	2.079	2.397	2.759	3.172	3.642	4.177	5.474	8.137	11.974
16	2.183	2.540	2.952	3.426	3.970	4.595	6.130	9.358	14.129
17	2.292	2.693	3.159	3.700	4.328	5.054	6.866	10.761	16.672
18	2.407	2.854	3.380	3.996	4.717	5.560	7.690	12.375	19.673
19	2.527	3.026	3.617	4.316	5.142	6.116	8.613	14.232	23.214
20	2.653	3.207	3.870	4.661	5.604	6.727	9.646	16.367	27.393
21	2.786	3.400	4.141	5.034	6.109	7.400	10.804	18.822	32.324
22	2.925	3.604	4.430	5.437	6.659	8.140	12.100	21.645	38.142
23	3.072	3.820	4.741	5.871	7.258	8.954	13.552	24.891	45.008
24	3.225	4.049	5.072	6.341	7.911	9.850	15.179	28.625	53.109
25	3.386	4.292	5.427	6.848	8.623	10.835	17.000	32.919	62.669
26	3.556	4.549	5.807	7.396	9.399	11.918	19.040	37.857	73.949
27	3.733	4.822	6.214	7.988	10.245	13.110	21.325	43.535	87.260
28	3.920	5.112	6.649	8.627	11.167	14.421	23.884	50.066	102.967
29	4.116	5.418	7.114	9.317	12.172	15.863	26.750	57.575	121.501
30	4.322	5.743	7.612	10.063	13.268	17.449	29.960	66.212	143.371
31	4.538	6.088	8.145	10.868	14.462	19.194	33.555	76.144	169.177
32	4.765	6.453	8.715	11.737	15.763	21.114	37.582	87.565	199.629
33	5.003	6.841	9.325	12.676	17.182	23.225	42.092	100.700	235.563
34	5.253	7.251	9.978	13.690	18.728	25.548	47.143	115.805	277.964
35	5.516	7.686	10.677	14.785	20.414	28.102	52.800	133.176	327.997
36	5.792	8.147	11.424	15.968	22.251	30.913	59.136	153.152	387.037
37	6.081	8.636	12.224	17.246	24.254	34.004	66.232	176.125	456.703
38	6.385	9.154	13.079	18.625	26.437	37.404	74.180	202.543	538.910
39	6.705	9.704	13.995	20.115	28.816	41.145	83.081	232.925	635.914
40	7.040	10.286	14.974	21.725	31.409	45.259	93.051	267.864	750.378

COMPOUND INTEREST TABLE

The Sum To Which One Dollar Per Annum,
Paid At The Beginning Of Each Year, Will Increase

				Rate				
	5%	6%	7%	8%	9%	10%	12%	15%
Years								
1	1.050	1.060	1.070	1.080	1.090	1.100	1.120	1.150
2	2.152	2.184	2.215	2.246	2.278	2.310	2.374	2.472
3	3.310	3.375	3.440	3.506	3.573	3.641	3.779	3.993
4	4.526	4.637	4.751	4.867	4.985	5.105	5.353	5.742
5	5.802	5.975	6.153	6.336	6.523	6.716	7.115	7.754
6	7.142	7.394	7.654	7.923	8.200	8.487	9.089	10.067
7	8.549	8.897	9.260	9.637	10.028	10.436	11.300	12.727
8	10.027	10.491	10.978	11.488	12.021	12.579	13.776	15.786
9	11.578	12.181	12.816	13.487	14.193	14.937	16.549	19.304
10	13.207	13.972	14.784	15.645	16.560	17.531	19.655	23.349
11	14.917	15.870	16.888	17.977	19.141	20.384	23.133	28.002
12	16.713	17.882	19.141	20.495	21.953	23.523	27.029	33.352
13	18.599	20.015	22.550	23.215	25.019	26.975	31.393	39.505
14	20.579	22.276	24.129	26.152	28.361	30.772	36.280	46.580
15	22.657	24.673	26.888	29.324	32.003	34.950	41.753	54.717
16	24.840	27.213	29.840	32.750	35.974	39.545	47.884	64.075
17	27.132	29.906	32.999	36.450	40.301	44.599	54.750	74.836
18	29.539	32.760	36.379	40.446	45.018	50.159	62.440	87.212
19	32.066	35.786	39.995	44.762	50.160	56.275	71.052	101.444
20	34.719	38.993	43.865	49.423	55.765	63.002	80.699	117.810
21	37.505	42.392	48.006	54.457	61.873	70.403	91.503	136.632
22	40.430	45.996	52.436	59.893	68.532	78.543	103.603	158.276
23	43.502	49.816	57.177	65.765	75.790	87.497	117.155	183.168
24	46.727	53.865	62.249	72.106	83.701	97.347	132.334	211.793
25	50.113	58.156	67.676	78.954	92.324	108.182	149.334	244.712
26	53.669	62.706	73.484	86.351	101.723	120.100	168.374	282.569
27	57.403	67.528	79.698	94.339	111.968	133.210	189.699	326.104
28	61.323	72.640	86.347	102.966	123.135	147.631	213.583	376.170
29	65.439	78.058	93.461	112.283	135.308	163.494	240.333	433.745
30	69.761	83.802	101.073	122.346	148.575	180.943	270.293	499.957
31	74.299	89.890	109.218	133.214	163.037	200.138	303.848	576.100
32	79.064	96.343	117.933	144.951	178.800	221.252	341.429	663.666
33	84.067	103.184	127.259	157.627	195.982	244.477	383.521	764.365
34	89.320	110.435	137.237	171.317	214.711	270.024	430.663	880.170
35	94.836	118.121	147.913	186.102	235.125	298.127	483.463	1013.346
36	100.628	126.268	159.337	202.070	257.376	329.039	542.599	1166.498
37	106.710	134.904	171.561	219.316	281.630	363.043	608.831	1342.622
38	113.095	144.058	184.640	237.941	308.066	400.448	683.010	1545.165
39	119.800	153.762	198.635	258.057	336.882	441.593	766.091	1778.090
40	126.840	164.048	213.610	279.781	368.292	486.852	859.142	2045.954

COMPOUND INTEREST & FUTURE VALUE OF MONEY

Given the choice of being paid $1.00 today,
or $1.00 four years from now,
you would choose to be paid $1.00 today.

AND

Given the choice of being paid $1.00 today,
or $16.00 four years from now,
you would choose to be paid $16.00 four years from now.

HOWEVER

Given the choice of being paid $1.00 today,
or $1.50 four years from now,
your decision would require you to carefully consider the

FUTURE VALUE OF MONEY

The future value of money is a very important concept in estate and business planning and can be best understood by referring to the Compound Interest Table on page 499. If you took the $1.00 today and could invest it at 8 percent, you would have $1.36 in four years (read down the 8 percent rate column until year 4). By waiting four years, you could receive $1.50, which is 14 cents more than you would get by taking the money and investing it at 8 percent.

However, if you believed that you could invest your funds at 18 percent, you would expect to have $1.94 in four years ($1.00 x 1.939 = $1.939). In this case you would probably take the $1.00 today rather than the $1.50 in four years.

But what if your choice was as follows:

Being paid $1.00 each year for the next 4 years,
or being paid $5.50 4 years from now.

The Compound Interest Table on page 500, will help you make the decision, since it shows the sum to which one dollar per year will grow if placed in accounts at varying rates of interest. If you took the $1.00 each year and were able to invest it at 8 percent, you would have $4.87 in four years ($1.00 x 4.867 = $4.867). By waiting four years, you could receive $5.50, which is 63 cents more than you would have by taking the money and investing it at 8 percent.

However, if you believed that you could invest your funds at 15 percent, you would expect to have $5.74 in four years ($1.00 x 5.742 = $5.74). In this case you would probably take the $1.00 each year for the next four years.

COMPOUND DISCOUNT TABLE

The Worth Today of One Dollar Due In The Future

	5%	6%	7%	8%	Rate 9%	10%	12%	15%	18%
Years									
1	.9524	.9434	.9346	.9259	.9174	.9091	.8929	.8696	.8475
2	.9070	.8900	.8734	.8573	.8417	.8264	.7972	.7561	.7182
3	.8638	.8396	.8163	.7938	.7722	.7513	.7118	.6575	.6086
4	.8227	.7921	.7629	.7350	.7084	.6830	.6355	.5718	.5158
5	.7835	.7473	.7130	.6806	.6499	.6209	.5674	.4972	.4371
6	.7462	.7050	.6663	.6302	.5963	.5645	.5066	.4323	.3704
7	.7107	.6651	.6227	.5835	.5470	.5132	.4523	.3759	.3139
8	.6768	.6274	.5820	.5403	.5019	.4665	.4039	.3269	.2660
9	.6446	.5919	.5439	.5002	.4604	.4241	.3606	.2843	.2255
10	.6139	.5584	.5083	.4632	.4224	.3855	.3220	.2472	.1911
11	.5847	.5268	.4751	.4289	.3875	.3505	.2875	.2149	.1619
12	.5568	.4970	.4440	.3971	.3555	.3186	.2567	.1869	.1372
13	.5303	.4688	.4150	.3677	.3262	.2897	.2292	.1625	.1163
14	.5051	.4423	.3878	.3405	.2992	.2633	.2046	.1413	.0985
15	.4810	.4173	.3624	.3152	.2745	.2394	.1827	.1229	.0835
16	.4581	.3936	.3387	.2919	.2519	.2176	.1631	.1069	.0708
17	.4363	.3714	.3166	.2703	.2311	.1978	.1456	.0929	.0600
18	.4155	.3503	.2959	.2502	.2120	.1799	.1300	.0808	.0508
19	.3957	.3305	.2765	.2317	.1945	.1635	.1161	.0703	.0431
20	.3769	.3118	.2584	.2145	.1784	.1486	.1037	.0611	.0365
21	.3589	.2942	.2415	.1987	.1637	.1351	.0926	.0531	.0309
22	.3419	.2775	.2257	.1839	.1502	.1228	.0826	.0462	.0262
23	.3256	.2618	.2109	.1703	.1378	.1117	.0738	.0402	.0222
24	.3101	.2470	.1971	.1577	.1264	.1015	.0659	.0349	.0188
25	.2953	.2330	.1842	.1460	.1160	.0923	.0588	.0304	.0160
26	.2812	.2198	.1722	.1352	.1064	.0839	.0525	.0264	.0135
27	.2678	.2074	.1609	.1252	.0976	.0763	.0469	.0230	.0115
28	.2551	.1956	.1504	.1159	.0895	.0693	.0419	.0200	.0097
29	.2429	.1846	.1406	.1073	.0822	.0630	.0374	.0174	.0082
30	.2314	.1741	.1314	.0994	.0754	.0573	.0334	.0151	.0070
31	.2204	.1643	.1228	.0920	.0691	.0521	.0298	.0131	.0059
32	.2099	.1550	.1147	.0852	.0634	.0474	.0266	.0114	.0050
33	.1999	.1462	.1072	.0789	.0582	.0431	.0238	.0099	.0042
34	.1904	.1379	.1002	.0730	.0534	.0391	.0212	.0086	.0036
35	.1813	.1301	.0937	.0676	.0490	.0356	.0189	.0075	.0030
36	.1727	.1227	.0875	.0626	.0449	.0323	.0169	.0065	.0026
37	.1644	.1158	.0818	.0580	.0412	.0294	.0151	.0057	.0022
38	.1566	.1092	.0765	.0537	.0378	.0267	.0135	.0049	.0019
39	.1491	.1031	.0715	.0497	.0347	.0243	.0120	.0043	.0016
40	.1420	.0972	.0668	.0460	.0318	.0221	.0107	.0037	.0013

COMPOUND DISCOUNT TABLE

The Worth Today of One Dollar Per Annum
Paid At The End of Each Year

Years	5%	6%	7%	8%	9%	10%	12%	15%	18%
1	.952	.943	.935	.926	.917	.909	.893	.870	.847
2	1.859	1.833	1.808	1.783	1.759	1.736	1.690	1.626	1.566
3	2.723	2.673	2.624	2.577	2.531	2.487	2.402	2.283	2.174
4	3.546	3.465	3.387	3.312	3.240	3.170	3.037	2.855	2.690
5	4.329	4.212	4.100	3.993	3.890	3.791	3.605	3.352	3.127
6	5.076	4.917	4.767	4.623	4.486	4.355	4.111	3.784	3.498
7	5.786	5.582	5.389	5.206	5.033	4.868	4.564	4.160	3.812
8	6.463	6.210	5.971	5.747	5.535	5.335	4.968	4.487	4.078
9	7.108	6.802	6.515	6.247	5.995	5.759	5.328	4.772	4.303
10	7.722	7.360	7.024	6.710	6.418	6.145	5.650	5.019	4.494
11	8.306	7.887	7.499	7.139	6.805	6.495	5.938	5.234	4.656
12	8.863	8.384	7.943	7.536	7.161	6.814	6.194	5.421	4.793
13	9.394	8.853	8.358	7.904	7.487	7.103	6.424	5.583	4.910
14	9.899	9.295	8.745	8.244	7.786	7.367	6.628	5.724	5.008
15	10.380	9.712	9.108	8.559	8.061	7.606	6.811	5.847	5.092
16	10.838	10.106	9.447	8.851	8.313	7.824	6.974	5.954	5.162
17	11.274	10.477	9.763	9.122	8.544	8.022	7.120	6.047	5.222
18	11.690	10.828	10.059	9.372	8.756	8.201	7.250	6.128	5.273
19	12.085	11.158	10.336	9.604	8.950	8.365	7.366	6.198	5.316
20	12.462	11.470	10.594	9.818	9.129	8.514	7.469	6.259	5.353
21	12.821	11.764	10.836	10.017	9.292	8.649	7.562	6.312	5.384
22	13.163	12.042	11.061	10.201	9.442	8.772	7.645	6.359	5.410
23	13.489	12.303	11.272	10.371	9.580	8.883	7.718	6.399	5.432
24	13.799	12.550	11.469	10.529	9.707	8.985	7.784	6.434	5.451
25	14.094	12.783	11.654	10.675	9.823	9.077	7.843	6.464	5.467
26	14.375	13.003	11.826	10.810	9.929	9.161	7.896	6.491	5.480
27	14.643	13.211	11.987	10.935	10.027	9.237	7.943	6.514	5.492
28	14.898	13.406	12.137	11.051	10.116	9.307	7.984	6.534	5.502
29	15.141	13.591	12.278	11.158	10.198	9.370	8.022	6.551	5.510
30	15.372	13.765	12.409	11.258	10.274	9.427	8.055	6.566	5.517
31	15.593	13.929	12.532	11.350	10.343	9.479	8.085	6.579	5.523
32	15.803	14.084	12.647	11.435	10.406	9.526	8.112	6.591	5.528
33	16.003	14.230	12.754	11.514	10.464	9.569	8.135	6.600	5.532
34	16.193	14.368	12.854	11.587	10.518	9.609	8.157	6.609	5.536
35	16.374	14.498	12.948	11.655	10.567	9.644	8.176	6.617	5.539
36	16.547	14.621	13.035	11.717	10.612	9.677	8.192	6.623	5.541
37	16.711	14.737	13.117	11.775	10.653	9.706	8.208	6.629	5.543
38	16.868	14.846	13.193	11.829	10.691	9.733	8.221	6.634	5.545
39	17.017	14.949	13.265	11.879	10.726	9.757	8.233	6.638	5.547
40	17.159	15.046	13.332	11.925	10.757	9.779	8.244	6.642	5.548

COMPOUND DISCOUNT & PRESENT VALUE OF MONEY

Given the choice of being paid $1.00 three years from now,
or $1.00 four years from now,
you would choose to be paid $1.00 three years from now.

AND

Given the choice of being paid $1.00 three years from now,
or $2.00 four years from now,
you would choose to be paid $2.00 four years from now.

HOWEVER

Given the choice of being paid $1.00 three years from now,
or $1.15 four years from now,
your decision would require you to carefully consider the

PRESENT VALUE OF MONEY

The present value of money can be calculated by referring to the Compound Discount Table on page 502. If you viewed money as having a time value of 8 percent, the present value of that $1.00 payment due in three years from now is 79 cents ($1.00 x .7938 = $.7938). The present value of a $1.15 payment four years from now is 84 cents ($1.15 x .7350 = $.84525). You would accept payment of $1.15 four years from now.

However, if you viewed money as having a time value of 18 percent, the present value of that $1.00 payment due in three years from now is 61 cents ($1.00 x .6086 = $.6086). The present value of a $1.15 payment four years from now is only 59 cents ($1.15 x .5158 = $.59317). You would not accept the offer to pay $1.15 four years from now, but would rather demand payment of $1.00 three years from now.

But what if your choice was as follows:

Being paid $1.25 at the end of each year for the next 3 years,
or being paid $1.00 at the end of each year for the next 4 years.

The Compound Discount Table on page 503, will help you make the decision. If you viewed money as having a time value of 8 percent, the present value of that $1.25 payment at the end of each year for the next three years is $3.22 ($1.25 x 2.577 = $3.22125). The present value of a $1.00 payment each year for four years is $3.31 ($1.00 x 3.312 = $3.312). You would accept payment of $1.00 per year for the next four years.

However, if you viewed money as having a time value of 18 percent, the present value of that $1.25 payment at the end of each year for the next three years is $2.72 ($1.25 x 2.174 = $2.7175). The present value of a $1.00 payment each year for four years is $2.69 ($1.00 x 2.690 = $2.690). You would not accept payment of $1.00 per year for four years, but would rather demand payment of $1.25 per year for the next three years.

AMORTZATION TABLE

Annual Payment Necessary To Amortize A Loan Of $1,000

				Rate				
	5%	6%	7%	8%	9%	10%	12%	15%
Years								
2	537.80	545.44	553.10	560.77	568.47	576.20	591.70	615.12
3	367.21	374.11	381.06	388.04	395.06	402.12	416.35	437.98
4	282.01	288.60	295.23	301.93	308.67	315.48	329.24	350.27
5	230.97	237.40	243.90	250.46	257.10	263.80	277.41	298.32
6	197.02	203.37	209.80	216.32	222.92	229.61	243.23	264.24
7	172.82	179.14	185.56	192.08	198.70	205.41	219.12	240.37
8	154.72	161.04	167.47	174.02	180.68	187.45	201.31	222.86
9	140.69	147.03	153.49	160.08	166.80	173.65	187.68	209.58
10	129.50	135.87	142.38	149.03	155.83	162.75	176.99	199.26
11	120.39	126.80	133.36	140.08	146.95	153.97	168.42	191.07
12	112.83	119.28	125.91	132.70	139.66	146.77	161.44	184.49
13	106.46	112.97	119.66	126.53	133.57	140.78	155.68	179.12
14	101.02	107.59	114.35	121.30	128.44	135.75	150.88	174.69
15	96.34	102.97	109.80	116.83	124.06	131.48	146.83	171.02
16	92.27	98.96	105.86	112.98	120.30	127.82	143.40	167.95
17	88.70	95.45	102.43	109.63	117.05	124.67	140.46	165.37
18	85.55	92.36	99.42	106.71	114.22	121.94	137.94	163.19
19	82.75	89.63	96.76	104.13	111.74	119.55	135.77	161.34
20	80.24	87.19	94.40	101.86	109.55	117.46	133.88	159.77
21	78.00	85.01	92.29	99.84	107.62	115.63	132.25	158.42
22	75.97	83.05	90.41	98.04	105.91	114.01	130.82	157.27
23	74.14	81.28	88.72	96.43	104.39	112.58	129.56	156.28
24	72.47	79.68	87.19	94.98	103.03	111.30	128.47	155.43
25	70.95	78.23	85.82	93.68	101.81	110.17	127.50	154.70
26	69.56	76.91	84.57	92.51	100.72	109.16	126.66	154.07
27	68.29	75.70	83.43	91.45	99.74	108.26	125.91	153.53
28	67.12	74.60	82.40	90.49	98.86	107.46	125.25	153.06
29	66.05	73.58	81.45	89.62	98.06	106.73	124.67	152.66
30	65.05	72.65	80.59	88.83	97.34	106.08	124.15	152.31
35	61.07	68.98	77.24	85.81	94.64	103.69	122.32	151.14
40	58.28	66.47	75.01	83.87	92.96	102.26	121.31	150.57

INSURANCE COMPANY RATINGS

Rating Categories[1]	A.M. Best[2]	S&P[3]	Moody's[4]	Weiss[5]	Fitch[6]
Superior	A++ A+	AAA	Aaa		AAA
Excellent	A A-	AA+ AA AA-	Aa1 Aa2 Aa3	A+ A A-	AA A
Good	B++ B+	A+ A A-	A1 A2 A3	B+ B B-	BBB
Fair (Adequate)	B B-	BBB+ BBB BBB-	Baa1 Baa2 Baa3	C+ C C-	BB
Marginal	C++ C+	BB+ BB BB-	Ba1 Ba2 Ba3	D+ D D-	
Weak	C C-	B+ B B-	B1 B2 B3	E+ E E-	B
Poor (Below Standards)	D E[7], F[8]	CCC CC R[7]	Caa Ca C	 F	CCC CC, C DDD[7] DD[7], D[7]

[1] The comparative distribution of rating categories is approximate. Therefore, the ratings definitions of each agency should be consulted. The basic mission of all of these independent agencies is to assess an insurer's financial strength in terms of its ability to meet policyholder and other contractual obligations, and to communicate those findings to the financial and investment communities. Due diligence requires not just a determination of the assigned rating, but an understanding of how each rating agency determines its published ratings.

[2] A.M. Best Company publishes Best's Ratings of Life and Health Companies (has rated insurers since 1899).

[3] Standard & Poor's (S&P) publishes Insurer Claims-Paying Ability Ratings (has rated debt issues for over 50 years and insurers for approximately 20 years).

[4] Moody's Investor's Service publishes Life Insurance Credit Report, which includes the *Life Insurance Handbook* (has rated bond issues since 1904 and insurers since the 1970s).

[5] Weiss Research, Inc. publishes Insurance Company Safety Ratings (has rated insurers since 1989).

[6] Fitch, Inc. publishes Insurer Financial Strength (Fitch was formed by the merger of Fitch IBCA and Duff & Phelps; Duff & Phelps had rated insurers since 1986). Ratings below AAA and above CC may be appended with a "+" or "−" to indicate relative position within the rating category.

[7] Under regulatory supervision.

[8] In liquidation.

INDUSTRY ASSOCIATIONS

Conference Dates

Association for Advanced Life Underwriting
2901 Telestar Court
Falls Church, VA 22042
703-641-9400 (www.aalu.org)

AALU Annual Meeting
2002 - Wash., D.C., Apr. 14-17
2003 - Wash., D.C., May 4-7

College For Financial Planning
6161 South Syracuse Way
Greenwood Village, CO 80111-4707
303-220-1200 (www.fp.edu)

National Conference
2002 - none
2003 - not available as of Mar. 11, 2002

Financial Planning Association
5775 Glenridge Drive NE, Suite B300
Atlanta, GA 30328-5364
404-845-0011 (www.fpanet.org)

Success Forum
2002 - New Orleans, Sep. 28-Oct. 1
2003 - not available as of Mar. 11, 2002

GAMA International
2901 Telestar Court
Falls Church, VA 22042
800-345-2687 (www.gamaweb.com)

LAMP Annual Meeting
2002 - Orlando, Mar. 17-20
2003 - San Antonio, Mar. 16-19

LIMRA International
300 Day Hill Road
Windsor, CT 06095-4761
860-688-3358 (www.limra.com)

LIMRA Annual Meeting
2002 - Boston, Oct. 27-29
2003 - Chicago, Oct. 26-28

Million Dollar Round Table
325 West Touhy Avenue
Park Ridge, IL 60068-4265
847-692-6378 (www.mdrt.org)

MDRT Annual Meeting
2002 - Nashville, Jun. 23-27
2003 - Las Vegas, Jun. 22-26

Top of the Table Annual Meeting
2002 - Orlando, Oct. 9-12
2003 - not available as of Mar. 11, 2002

National Association of Health Underwriters
2000 North 14th Street, Suite 450
Arlington, VA, 22201
703-276-0220 (www.nahu.org)

Annual Convention & Exhibition
2002 - Dallas, Jun. 23-26
2003 - San Diego, Jun. 29-Jul. 2

National Association of Independent
Life Brokerage Agencies
8201 Greensboro Dr., Suite 300
McLean, VA 22102
703-610-9020 (www.nailba.org)

Annual Convention
2002 - Boca Raton, Nov. 21-23
2003 - Scottsdale, Nov. 6-8

National Association of Insurance
and Financial Advisors
2901 Telestar Court
Falls Church, VA 22042
703-770-8100 (www.naifa.org)

NAIFA Annual Convention
& Career Conference
2002 - Charlotte, Sep. 21-25
2003 - Las Vegas, Sep. 11-15

Society of Financial Service Professionals
270 South Bryn Mawr Avenue
Bryn Mawr, PA 19010-2195
610-526-2500 (www.financialpro.org)

Financial Service Forum
2002 - Seattle, Mar. 2-6
2003 - Honolulu, Oct. 26-29

COOL WEB SITES

www.access.gpo.gov/nara/cfr/cfr-table-search.html
Contains the text of public regulations issued by Federal government agencies. Search by code section, title, or by words or phrases.

www.aicpa.org
American Institute Of Certified Public Accountants. Current issues of the monthly *Journal of Accountancy* are posted online. Also, contains the table of contents for each monthly issue starting with January 1996.

www.benefitslink.com
Internet link to information and services for benefit plans. Check out Q&A Columns, Search Engine, and Source Documents. A lot of "good stuff."

www.ca-probate.com
Has not been maintained, but still contains interesting material, particularly the collection of links to the wills of celebrities and ordinary people. Unfortunately, some links don't.

www.el.com/elinks/taxes
Loaded with links to tax-related sites. There is so much here the site should be added to your favorites.

www.estateplanninglinks.com
A great collection of links to other sites, containing a wide variety of subjects (Advanced Planning, Calculations, Valuation and lots more).

www.fidelity.com
A well designed and easy to navigate site, containing concise and helpful information. Check out the Planning & Retirement tab, it has something for everyone, surviving spouses, inheritors and executors. Lots of helpful calculators everywhere.

www.fsonline.com
Offers an array of both industry tidbits and solid articles by financial planning professionals. Includes cost-free access to the Financial Services Journal Online.

www.life-line.org
The Life and Health Insurance Foundation for Education (LIFE). Offers a wide range of well-developed insurance topics. Recommend for both advisors and their clients.

www.nuco.com
This industry resource center contains news archives, a career kiosk, meetings & events, and industry links. Check out Online Communities. Here Tax Facts[fx] offers articles, useful calculations, tables, an e-Newsletter, and a message board. It just keeps getting better!

www.pgdc.net
Contains sales, marketing and technical resource materials for 401(k) and retirement planning. Takes some effort to subscribe, but it is free and worth the effort.

www.smartmoney.com
A very enriched web site. Click on the Tools tab or the Personal Finance tab for easy-to-understand explanations of income tax and retirement planning concepts. Many screens contain quickie "what if" calculators.

www.tax.org
Tax Analysts is a nonprofit organization. Visit the Tax History Project, explore the Tax History Museum, the Image Gallery, and the Presidential Tax Return Gallery. For fun and profit this remains a "very cool" site.

Note: These sites were last accessed on March 11, 2002. Have you discovered a web site that should be included in the next edition of *Field Guide To Estate Planning, Business Planning, & Employee Benefits?* If so, please e-mail your nominations to cady@efieldguide.com.

CODE CRIB SHEET

A Listing Of Selected Code Provisions

Code Section	Description	Field Guide Page	2002 Tax Facts 1 Question
22	Credits for the permanently disabled.	372	732
25A	Hope and lifetime learning credit.	303 356-357	734
55	Alternative minimum tax - Section 56 provides for ACE adjustment.	342	727, 737
61	Gross income defined.	218, 317	51, 227
72	Annuities; living proceeds of endowment and life insurance contracts - income tax treatment.	76, 282	1-11, 29, 31, 105, 126, 405
79	Group-term life insurance purchased for employees.	210	174, 177
83	Taxation of property transferred in connection with performance of services - "substantial risk of forfeiture."	242, 274, 447, 464, 470	77, 135, 141, 427
101	Certain death benefits - exclusion of life insurance death benefits from income (includes "transfer for value" rules).	72, 96, 338, 413, 479	62-65, 67-71, 81, 88, 94, 122-123, 126, 130, 132, 266, 170
102	Gifts and inheritances - exclusion from income.	26, 28 48, 52	702
104	Compensation for injuries or sickness.	250, 254, 317, 371	155-157, 227
105	Amounts received under accident and health plans.	250, 254, 372	215-218
106	Contributions by employer to accident and health plans.	250, 254, 317	213, 219
125	Cafeteria plans.	349	96-98
127	Educational assistance programs.	303	702
129	Dependent care assistance programs.	286	152
135	Income from United States bonds used to pay higher education tuition and fees.	303	702
162	Trade or business expenses - deductibility.	218, 303, 317, 483	45, 47, 51, 60

Note: This table contains selected citations. A complete listing of citations to IRC Sections is contained on pages 981-1000 of *Tax Facts 1 (2002)*.

Code Section	Description	Field Guide Page	2002 Tax Facts 1 Question
163	Interest - deductibility.	407	406, 720, 722
170	Charitable contributions and gifts - deductibility.	60, 352, 353, 354	107-110, 723-724
220	Medical savings accounts.	421	281-292
221	Interest on education loans.	303, 357	722
222	Qualified tuition and related expenses.	303	712
264	Business life insurance - premiums not deductible but policy loan interest deductible within strict limits.	424	45, 47, 56-57, 60, 114-115, 406-407
265	Expenses and interest relating to tax-exempt income.	317, 371	225, 227
302	Distributions in redemption of stock.	128, 140, 151	82-83
303	Distributions in redemption of stock to pay death taxes - partial stock redemptions.	148, 152, 461	85, 89
306	Dispositions of certain stock - tax treatment of stock received as a dividend pursuant to a recapitalization.	172, 462	85
318	Constructive ownership of stock - "attribution."	128, 176,	82, 85
368	Definitions relating to corporate reorganizations - "recapitalizations."	172, 386	72
401	Qualified pension, profit sharing and stock bonus plans - including "Section 401(k)" plans.	262, 266, 278, 379	295, 299, 303-320, 329-332, 334-335, 337-349, 360, 362, 376, 390, 399
402(b)	Taxability of beneficiary of nonexempt trust.	464	133-134, 137
403(b)	Taxation of annuities purchased by Section 501(c)(3) organizations and public schools.	270, 273	417, 430, 432-437, 441-442, 445, 453, 457-458
408	Individual retirement accounts and annuities.	262, 298, 300, 301, 403, 409, 466, 467	228, 233, 240-242, 246, 252, 254-259

Note: This table contains selected citations. A complete listing of citations to IRC Sections is contained on pages 981-1000 of *Tax Facts 1 (2002)*.

Code Section	Description	Field Guide Page	2002 Tax Facts 1 Question
408A	Roth IRAs	300, 301, 456	230-236, 243, 246
410-412	Minimum participation, vesting, and funding standards - qualified plans.	262, 297	305-306, 307, 311, 333, 337, 346-347, 362-364
415	Limitations on benefits and contributions under qualified plans.	262, 297	233, 313, 333, 360, 362, 434
419	Treatment of funded welfare benefit plans.	487	457-458
453	Installment method of reporting income.	44, 404, 465	706
457	Deferred compensation plans of State and local governments and tax-exempt organizations.	274	148-151
483	Interest on certain deferred payments.	404	706, 803
501	Exemption from tax on corporations, certain trusts, etc. - includes religious, charitable, scientific and educational organizations.	270, 273	133, 148, 431
529	Qualified tuition programs.	303, 356 463	-
530	Cloverdell Education Savings Accounts.	303, 365	710
531	Accumulated earnings tax.	341	737
541	Personal holding company tax.	432	737
664	Charitable remainder trusts.	60, 354	724
671-677	Grantor trust rules.	397	743
691	Income in respect of decedents.	21, 402	396-398, 726
701-761	Partnerships.	168, 427	92, 509, 511-513, 740-741, 813
1001	Determination of amount and recognition of gain or loss.	350, 476	34, 227
1014	Basis of property acquired from a decedent (stepped-up).	473	86, 715
1015	Basis of property acquired by gifts and transfers in trust.	48, 52	715

Note: This table contains selected citations. A complete listing of citations to IRC Sections is contained on pages 981-1000 of *Tax Facts 1 (2002)*.

Code Section	Description	Field Guide Page	2002 Tax Facts 1 Question
1035	Certain exchanges of insurance policies - "tax-free exchange" of life insurance and annuity contracts.	476	34
1041	Transfer of property incident to divorce.	375	132, 165-166
1202	Gain from small business stock.	350, 446	702, 714
1361	S corporation defined.	458	738
2001	Imposition and rate of estate tax.	18, 22, 493	752, 760, 767
2002	Executor's liability for payment of estate tax.	370	517
2010	Unified credit against estate tax.	18, 493	767
2014	Foreign death tax credit	426	766
2031	Definition of gross estate.	10, 18, 441	761, 762
2032	Alternate valuation - six months after death.	390, 473	513, 762
2032A	Valuation of certain farms and other real property.	448	513, 762
2033	Property in which the decedent had an interest - transfers at death.	18	500, 753
2035	Adjustments for gifts made within 3 years of decedent's death - transfers of life insurance.	56, 72, 388	526, 542-543, 618, 760
2036	Transfers with retained life estate - power to designate possession or enjoyment of property.	389, 434	555, 753, 760
2037	Transfers taking effect at death.	389	543, 753
2038	Revocable transfers - retention of power to revoke interest in property includes value in the estate.	102, 389	550, 753
2039	Annuities - taxation of surviving beneficiary's interest.	282	502, 504, 548, 572-575, 584-586
2040	Joint interests - including co-tenancies with right of survivorship.	10	753-754
2041	Powers of appointment - "general power of appointment."	419, 434	553, 577, 580-582, 753
2042	Proceeds of life insurance - payable to estate or in which decedent had "incidents of ownership."	72, 96, 388	509-512, 515, 526-527, 530-534, 542-544, 545, 753

Note: This table contains selected citations. A complete listing of citations to IRC Sections is contained on pages 981-1000 of *Tax Facts 1 (2002)*.

Code Section	Description	Field Guide Page	2002 Tax Facts 1 Question
2044	Certain property for which marital deduction was previously allowed - "qualified terminable interest."	34, 419	553, 578, 764
2046	Disclaimers.	374	-
2053	Expenses, indebtedness, and taxes - allowable deductions for claims against the estate.	10, 18, 85, 167	751, 763
2054	Losses - those deductible from taxable estate.	85	517, 751
2055	Transfers for public, charitable, and religious uses - estate tax charitable deduction.	60, 352, 354	516, 763
2056	Bequests to surviving spouse - estate tax marital deduction.	26, 28, 419, 454	563-564, 763-764
2056A	Qualified domestic trust.	442	764
2057	Family-owned business exclusion.	443	761
2206	Recovery by executor of estate taxes on life insurance proceeds.	21	536
2207A	Recovery by decedent's estate of estate taxes on certain marital deduction property.	21	-
2503	Present interest gifts - including gifts in trust for minors.	48, 52, 102, 367, 481	616, 625, 803, 817-818
2505	Unified credit against gift tax.	52, 395	822
2514	Powers of appointment (including lapse of "Crummey" power).	59, 434	627, 803
2522	Charitable and similar gifts.	60, 352, 354	607, 821
2523	Gift tax marital deduction.	419	603, 803, 820
2601	Generation-skipping transfers.	38	-
2701-2704 2701	*Also known as Chapter 14.* Special valuation rules in case of transfers of certain interests in corporations or partnerships.	124, 172 386	813-814, 816
2702	Special valuation rules in case of transfers of interest in trusts.	386, 398, 445, 451,	814
2703	Special valuation rules (e.g., with regard to buy/sell agreements certain rights and restrictions disregarded).	386	513, 815-816
2704	Treatment of certain lapsing rights and restrictions.	386	753, 816

Note: This table contains selected citations. A complete listing of citations to IRC Sections is contained on pages 981-1000 of *Tax Facts 1 (2002)*.

Code Section	Description	Field Guide Page	2002 Tax Facts 1 Question
6018	Estate tax returns - generally must be filed if gross estate exceeds applicable exclusion amount.	18	751
6075	Time for filing estate and gift tax returns.	18	751, 801
6159	Installment payment of tax when it will. facilitate payment	370	751
6161	"Reasonable cause" extension of time for paying estate tax (maximum 10 years).	370	751
6166	Extension of time for payment of estate tax where estate consists largely of interest in closely held business (14 2/3 years).	369	751
6324	Special liens for estate and gift taxes.	18, 370	517, 608
6531	Statute of limitations on criminal prosecutions.	430	-
6651	Failure to file return or pay tax.	430	-
6663	Penalty for fraud.	430	-
7206	Concealment of goods to evade taxes,. including false statement, is a felony	345, 430	-
7702	Life insurance contract defined - guideline premium requirements.	414	6, 7, 122, 125, 266
7702A	Modified endowment contract defined.	413	6, 7, 125, 404
7702B	Long-term care.	258, 444	267-276
7872	Treatment of loans with below-market interest rates.	408	705, 803

Note: This table contains selected citations. A complete listing of citations to IRC Sections is contained on pages 981-1000 of *Tax Facts 1 (2002)*.

INDEX

(References in parentheses are to footnotes – All other references are to page numbers)

(References in parentheses are to footnotes – All other references are to page numbers)

(References in parentheses are to footnotes – All other references are to page numbers)

(References in parentheses are to footnotes – All other references are to page numbers)

(References in parentheses are to footnotes – All other references are to page numbers)

(References in parentheses are to footnotes – All other references are to page numbers)

(References in parentheses are to footnotes – All other references are to page numbers)

(References in parentheses are to footnotes – All other references are to page numbers)

(References in parentheses are to footnotes – All other references are to page numbers)

(References in parentheses are to footnotes – All other references are to page numbers)

(References in parentheses are to footnotes – All other references are to page numbers)

(References in parentheses are to footnotes – All other references are to page numbers)

(References in parentheses are to footnotes – All other references are to page numbers)

(References in parentheses are to footnotes – All other references are to page numbers)

(References in parentheses are to footnotes — All other references are to page numbers)

(References in parentheses are to footnotes – All other references are to page numbers)

(References in parentheses are to footnotes – All other references are to page numbers)

(References in parentheses are to footnotes – All other references are to page numbers)

(References in parentheses are to footnotes – All other references are to page numbers)

(References in parentheses are to footnotes – All other references are to page numbers)

(References in parentheses are to footnotes – All other references are to page numbers)

(References in parentheses are to footnotes – All other references are to page numbers)

Need Additional Copies?

Call **1-800-543-0874** to order and ask for operator BB or fax your order to **1-800-874-1916**. Order on the web at www.nationalunderwriter.com. Ask about our complete line of products.

Payment Information

Add shipping & handling charges to all orders as indicated. If your order exceeds total amount listed in chart, call 1-800-543-0874 for shipping & handling charge. Unconditional 30 day guarantee. Prices subject to change.

SHIPPING & HANDLING *(Additional)*

Order Total	Shipping & handling
$20.00 to $39.99	$6.00
40.00 to 59.99	7.00
60.00 to 79.99	9.00
80.00 to 109.99	10.00
110.00 to 149.99	12.00
150.00 to 199.99	13.00
200.00 to 249.99	15.50

Shipping and handling rates for the continental U.S. only. Call 1-800-543-0874 for overseas rates. Any order of $250.00 and over, call 1-800-543-0874 for shipping & handling charges.

SALES TAX
(Additional)

Sales tax is required for residents of the following states:

CA, DC, FL, GA, IL, KY, NJ, NY, OH, PA, WA.

The
NATIONAL UNDERWRITER Company
PROFESSIONAL PUBLISHING GROUP

Orders Department
P.O. Box 14448 · Cincinnati, OH 45250-9798

2-BB

_____ Copies of *2002 Field Guide To Estate Planning, Business Planning, & Employee Benefits* (#1790002) $29.99
_____ 12-Month Internet Supscription to *Field Guide Online* (#1799101) $70.00
_____ Copies of *Tax Facts 1* (Print#2920002) $29.99 (CD-ROM#2929002) $70.00 (Internet#2929101) $70.00
_____ Copies of *Tax Facts 2* (print#2930002) $29.99 (CD-ROM#2939002) $70.00 (Internet#2939101) $70.00

❏ Check enclosed* ❏ Charge my VISA/MC/AmEx (circle one) ❏ Bill me
*Make check payable to The National Underwriter Company. Please include the appropriate shipping & handling charges and any applicable sales tax.

Card # _____ Exp. Date _____
Signature _____
Name _____ Title _____
Company _____
Street Address _____
City _____ State _____ Zip _____
Business Phone (_____) _____ Fax (_____) _____
May we e-mail you? ❏ e-mail _____

The
NATIONAL UNDERWRITER Company
PROFESSIONAL PUBLISHING GROUP

Orders Department
P.O. Box 14448 · Cincinnati, OH 45250-9798

2-BB

_____ Copies of *2002 Field Guide To Estate Planning, Business Planning, & Employee Benefits* (#1790002) $29.99
_____ 12-Month Internet Supscription to *Field Guide Online* (#1799101) $70.00
_____ Copies of *Tax Facts 1* (Print#2920002) $29.99 (CD-ROM#2929002) $70.00 (Internet#2929101) $70.00
_____ Copies of *Tax Facts 2* (print#2930002) $29.99 (CD-ROM#2939002) $70.00 (Internet#2939101) $70.00

❏ Check enclosed* ❏ Charge my VISA/MC/AmEx (circle one) ❏ Bill me
*Make check payable to The National Underwriter Company. Please include the appropriate shipping & handling charges and any applicable sales tax.

Card # _____ Exp. Date _____
Signature _____
Name _____ Title _____
Company _____
Street Address _____
City _____ State _____ Zip _____
Business Phone (_____) _____ Fax (_____) _____
May we e-mail you? ❏ e-mail _____

NO POSTAGE
NECESSARY
IF MAILED
IN THE
UNITED STATES

BUSINESS REPLY MAIL
FIRST-CLASS MAIL   PERMIT NO 68   CINCINNATI   OH

POSTAGE WILL BE PAID BY ADDRESSEE

ORDERS DEPARTMENT
THE NATIONAL UNDERWRITER COMPANY
PO BOX 14448
CINCINNATI OH   45250-9798